D0934222

BYLINES

BYLINES

BY
Bernard Weinraub

DOUBLEDAY & COMPANY, INC., GARDEN CITY, NEW YORK
1983

Grateful acknowledgment is made to authors and publishers for permission to reprint the following copyrighted material:

Excerpt from "Alexander's Ragtime Band" by Irving Berlin, copyright © 1911 by Irving Berlin. Copyright © renewed 1938 by Irving Berlin. Reprinted by permission of Irving Berlin Music Corporation.

Excerpt from "Bye Bye Blackbird" by Mort Dixon and Ray Henderson, copyright © 1926. Copyright renewed by Warner Bros., Inc. All rights reserved. Used by permission.

Excerpt from "You Mustn't Kick It Around" by Rodgers & Hart Copyright © 1940 by Chappell & Co., Inc.
Copyright Renewed
International Copyright Secured
ALL RIGHTS RESERVED
Used by permission

Library of Congress Cataloging in Publication Data
Weinraub, Bernard.
    Bylines.
    I. Title.
PS3573.E3964B9   1983   813'.54
ISBN: 0-385-17000-9
Library of Congress Catalog Card Number 80-3000

For Judy

Acknowledgments

Tony Marro and Carl Feldbaum were always there to answer my questions, and I am deeply indebted to them.

Jack Fuller read the manuscript, offering invaluable guidance. Beyond this, he was a constant source of support.

At the Pentagon, Major Arnie S. Warshawsky, Harry Zubkoff and Ronald H. Stivers provided generous assistance.

I am also grateful to Dr. Daniel G. Haller, Ed Gunther, John Morton, Jerome Hyman, Emily Friedrich, Gretchen Doss, Faye Drummond, Jacques Leslie, Jonathan Kandell, Michael Pillsbury, Peter Darrow and Lynda Zengerle.

Numerous colleagues in New York and Washington helped. Thank you.

My agent, Lynn Nesbit, has been there from the very start, always encouraging.

And Kate Medina was a wise, patient and enthusiastic editor. Her assistant, June Petrie, deserves special thanks for her skill and humor during some difficult moments.

This book could not have been written without the love of my wife, Judy, and our children, Claire and Jesse.

BYLINES

Tuesday

CHAPTER 1

At the moment when Evan Claiborne jumped out the window of his apartment on Fifth Avenue, his wife, Lucy, was in the living room on the phone to her mother.

"Evan's sleeping, Frieda." Lucy spoke quietly, having just left Evan naked on the bed when the phone rang. His eyes had been closed; he was snoring.

"How is he feeling?" Frieda Steiner asked.

"Bad. He's feeling bad."

"Is he still taking the pills?"

"Of course he's taking the pills."

"Darling, I'm just *asking*."

Lucy shut her eyes.

"What does Wasserman say?" Frieda asked.

"I haven't seen Wasserman in weeks."

"He's the best in the business, isn't he?"

"One of the best."

Lucy heard a window open. It was an April day, chilly and gray. "Mother, I think he's up, I hear him in the bedroom."

"What?"

"He's up." Lucy rubbed her thumb into the palm of her hand, still moist with the lubricant.

"I'm having lunch with Skipper tomorrow," said Frieda. "Why don't you join us?"

Lucy waited a beat. "Tomorrow." Her voice went blank. She wanted to end the call and take a shower and call Dave Fitzgerald. Avoid a confrontation with her mother.

"I better go in and see how he is, he's up," said Lucy. Her

mother began speaking, but Lucy interrupted. "I've got to *go,* Mother."

Lucy abruptly placed the phone on the receiver. It was too quick, too rude, but these afternoon sessions with Frieda left her shaking with anger.

She sat for a moment on the wing chair and stared down the hallway. Evan was silent behind the closed door. It was five minutes after two, and she knew that Evan wanted to be in the office by three. The window. Maybe it hadn't been Evan at all. The building was filled with cleaning women on Monday afternoon; she saw them in the lobby and the elevator, hefty, sullen women carrying shopping bags, staring vacantly at the floor.

Gripping the collar of her bathrobe, Lucy walked barefoot down the corridor and paused outside the bedroom door. Silence. She knocked, then gently opened it.

Cold air struck Lucy as she stared at the empty bed. Strangely, Evan had neatly tucked in the sheets and straightened the bed cover, puffed up the pillows; it looked as if he had never thrashed in the bed moments earlier in his failed attempt to make love. "Evan?" Lucy stepped in, almost angry, eyes darting around the room. "Evan!" The bathroom door was open. She blinked twice, and walked hesitantly across the bedroom into the bathroom.

The window overlooking the courtyard was lifted high, and the curtains fluttered in a tangle. Lucy saw snowflakes, heard street noises, a car horn that echoed.

Calmly, instinctively, she stood on the toilet seat, just as Evan had stood on it. She pushed aside the curtains and stared out the window into the courtyard, ten stories below.

Later, she told David Fitzgerald that she wore her dark glasses when the ambulance and the police arrived. "I didn't want them to see that I wasn't crying," she said.

CHAPTER 2

To the reporters and editors on the New York *Star,* the fifth-floor newsroom seemed to mirror, almost too harshly, the paper's own financial decline. If wealthy papers such as the Washington *Post,*

the New York *Times,* the Chicago *Tribune* and the Los Angeles
Times had remodeled their newsrooms in recent years with soft
lights and carpeting and private cubicles for reporters, and furniture in warm, earth hues, the *Star*'s management had too many
other priorities to spend money on redecoration.

Despite stark, fluorescent bulbs, the newsroom seemed dimly
lit, even at midday. The tile floor was stained and piled chaotically
with newspapers set beside desks scarred with age. Chairs creaked
and fell apart. A yearly paint job each summer failed to keep the
walls from peeling the following spring, with tiny clumps of plaster continually dropping off the ceiling onto a head, or into a
coffee container, causing an outburst of curses and laughter. Recently, mice and roaches had become a serious problem, so that a
platoon of night cleaning women now left the newsroom smoth-
ered in a bracing scent of disinfectant, leaving a faint hospital
smell in the cramped room.

As a family-owned daily, the *Star* retained some traditions that
seemed unusual, if not unique, in the newspaper business. One of
these traditions involved the role of the publisher. Although the
publishers of other major American newspapers gave their editors
complete control of news coverage and assignments, although the
other major publishers carefully distanced themselves from the
"news side" and concentrated almost entirely on the "business
side" of the running of the paper, the publisher of the smaller New
York *Star* played the central role in *both* areas. He oversaw what
appeared on the front page as well as profits and losses.

Befitting his position, the current publisher, Mark Steiner,
known as "Skipper," would settle in his chair at 3 P.M. at the head
of a brass-based rectangular table made of three-inch-thick granite
from Italy. Facing him, and seated in swivel armchairs, would be
Evan Claiborne, the managing editor, and his deputy, Maury
Kramer. Between them sat a half-dozen editors.

To this daily conference each editor carried a sheaf of papers—
summaries of stories filed earlier in the day by reporters out in the
field or in New York. The editors badgered their reporters constantly to provide 100-word summaries in advance of the pivotal
three o'clock conference with the publisher. Skipper would decide
then, with Evan and Maury, which stories needed questions answered, which stories could be held off and published later in the
week or Sunday (the *Star*'s diminishing sales and advertising pages

meant, of course, fewer stories) and, most significant, which stories were to be placed on the front page.

To Sally Sims, the national editor and the first woman to rise to a senior editor's job, the afternoon conference often seemed a bit self-congratulatory, given the paper's financial difficulties. But the publisher, Skipper Steiner, whose affair with Sally was one of the worst-kept secrets in the newsroom, was said to dismiss such criticism with a tight grin and a curt, "You don't understand, dear. We brag *because* we're the underdogs."

In fact, Skipper was neither boastful nor self-congratulatory. He was, most people said, a decent man—for a publisher. Besides, Skipper was not the figure who set the tone at each conference. The man who did, who virtually overpowered the editors and sometimes even treated the publisher disdainfully, was the managing editor, Evan Claiborne, Jr.

It was Evan who often launched the meeting (after Skipper asked for a review of the day's stories) with an insult aimed at the *Star*'s competition. "Ladies and gentlemen, I have one question this afternoon," he once said somberly. "Why couldn't *we* get Dolly Parton to pose for our front page that way?" Everyone had laughed. They always laughed at Evan's jokes. They had to.

Or else Evan would criticize the *Times* for publishing the text of a presidential news conference, using up a valuable page that could otherwise have been used for advertising. Or he found some reason to ridicule other newspapers, comparing them unfavorably to the *Star*. "That was one hell of a good welfare piece," he would say to Barry Cohen, the city editor whose brash investigations had revived the *Star*'s prestige and led to a string of newspaper awards. Or he would turn to Ward Parsons, the foreign editor, to comment on a sensitive piece from Moscow on the wife of a Russian dissident.

Ward, who still retained the boyish Ivy League looks that most of his friends outside the *Star* envied, would crinkle his lips into a smile and feel the spasm of ulcer pain suddenly disappear in the pit of his belly—an ulcer that struck him with clockwork precision on every weekday afternoon at two fifty-eight, just as he settled into a chair in Skipper's office.

"Amazing," Ward would say later. "One kind word from old Evan works like magic on my bruised gut."

Although implicitly in charge, even Skipper seemed to shrink under the sheer strength of his managing editor, who, in Evan's final, troubled years, plainly terrified most of his editors. Like children craving gifts, they became desperately eager to please him. And a casual comment by Evan—"Wasn't that piece on South Africa a bit long?"—sent ripples across the paper:

Ward Parsons would probably write a private letter to all foreign correspondents, saying, "Our venerable leader, Chairman Evan, has suggested that stories are running too long. Please, children, adhere to his admonition, or said another way, my ass will be in a sling if you don't keep every goddamn story to six hundred words."

On the other hand, Barry Cohen, the city editor, who was as abrasive as he was successful in overhauling the once-sluggish local staff, would call reporters together to a private meeting in a lounge beside the cafeteria. Loosening his tie, his light blue eyes darting over the crowd, Barry would say, frowning, "If you want to write long, you write the great American novel. We're a newspaper! Everyone understand that? A *struggling* paper. We need bright, terse stories, boys and girls. Stories that make folks read the paper. Six-hundred-word stories. Any questions?"

And Sally Sims, the national editor, would send a memo to the staff of the Washington bureau, and the paper's three domestic correspondents, in Chicago, Atlanta, and Los Angeles. (The three were scheduled to return to New York in the next six months—their offices were to be closed as a cost-saving measure.)

Sally's memo would be typically straightforward, to the point. "Stories are getting intolerably long. From everyone's point of view, I would suggest that it would be far more satisfactory if you trim your stories yourself, instead of leaving the job to us and complaining later. Thanks."

Evan would simply laugh. He knew that his power and control over editors and reporters made them overreact. He promoted and crippled, he punished and forgave, he weeded out incompetents and, like the four previous managing editors who had soared through the ranks of the *Star* and inherited the mantle of ultimate command, Evan blunted the powers of those who were too independent, too feisty. The managing editor controlled the salaries, careers, even marriages of his staff—the new generation of working wives annoyed Evan, and he made it plain that he wanted his correspondents to marry pliant types who followed meekly behind their husbands, like veiled Moslem women in purdah.

More important, the managing editor made the decisions that shaped every major story. Who writes it? Where is the story played? What does it *say?* Several months before his death, Evan told Skipper Steiner, as they stepped into the afternoon conference, that a newspaper mirrored its managing editor's tastes and interests and intelligence and flaws. And one had to assess the future choice for the job with extraordinary care—a comment that surprised Skipper and made him aware that Evan's intimidating tempers and moods at the 3 P.M. conference were calculated, a ritual designed to keep the editors off-balance, intensify the competition, watch them.

The daily conference, after all, was not only created to work out a front page and discuss the best stories of the day. It was also a traditional way of sizing up an editor—seeing who had managerial potential (one of Evan's favorite phrases). Did Sally Sims strike the right note of confidence and toughness, even though she was a woman? Was Barry Cohen *too* abrasive, street-smart but without the sophistication and restraint absolutely critical for the job? Was Maury Kramer, the deputy managing editor, imaginative and daring, a leader? Or was Maury a permanent deputy, like many on the *Star,* locked into a number-two job? And Ward Parsons. The right breed and class. But did he have an ounce of Barry's toughness, or Maury's experience, or Sally's patience and skill in working with reporters?

"You need toughness and humanity to sit in the managing editor's chair," Evan told Skipper at the last office Christmas party. "And you've *got* to be a heartless son of a bitch too."

*

Thirty minutes before the 3 P.M. conference, on what had been a slow day, Nick Simons, the city desk clerk, got a call from Sgt. Frank Rosales of the 19th Precinct, at 153 East Sixty-seventh Street. The city desk, set in the center of the newsroom, was cluttered with an array of phones, a portable television set, a low, gray police radio that was flicked on loud during fires, riots, and demonstrations. Beside a spike that held wire service copy rested two fat Rolodexes. One held the names and phone numbers of

Star employees; the other one was crammed with the public and private numbers of politicians, officials, cops, lawyers, theatrical producers, clergymen, activists of every ilk, union leaders, VIPs. On a corner of the desk, clamped between two metal book marks, were telephone directories, cross directories that listed house and apartment addresses and the phone numbers of the occupants, as well as a set of crumbling books with detailed maps of the five boroughs.

"Nick, I got some interesting news for you," Frank said. Frank had been the subject of a profile six months before in the *Star* (written by Nick in his spare time) detailing the policeman's undercover work with a splinter group of Puerto Rican nationalists. Following that newspaper story, Frank had earned a letter of commendation from the mayor, a promotion, and a phone call from two show-business agents who said his story would make a terrific vehicle for Al Pacino. (The agent later told Frank Rosales that Pacino was tired of police parts, but Robert DeNiro was mildly intrigued with the story.)

Frank's voice dropped. "You ever hear of the late Evan Claiborne?"

Nick sucked in his breath. "Holy shit."

"What?"

"I said, 'Holy shit.' "

"DOA. Lenox Hill. Jumped out the window."

"Where did he jump from?" Nick gasped, starting to write quickly.

"His apartment at 1140 Fifth," said Frank Rosales. "Wearing a bathrobe. The missus was upstairs too."

"Holy shit," said Nick.

"Your boss," said Frank.

"What time?"

"Reported to us by a Dr. Marvin Wasserman, of 120 East Eighty-fourth Street, at two-twenty. He was the first one that the missus called. He called emergency immediately thereafter."

"Who's Wasserman?"

"Your friendly shrink."

"Oh, shit," said Nick. He stopped writing. "What about the missus?"

"The missus is under sedation by Wasserman," said Frank Rosales. "The missus, by the way, has a juicy ass."

"The missus does not play with cops," said Nick. "Especially
uncircumcised Puerto Ricans."

"Who does the missus play with?"

"How the fuck do I know?" said Nick. "Anyone else in the
apartment?"

"Only her," said Frank. "Evan was taking a nap, she says. She
was in the living room. She heard the window open."

"Any notes?"

"So far, no."

"What's the missus say, what's the reason?"

"Evan was depressed, quote unquote," said Frank. "The missus
said Evan was under sedation. Spent two weeks at Payne Whitney
last month. Evan was—how did she put it—going through profound
depressions."

"The doctor?"

"We're talking to him now."

Nick released his breath. "It's a good story," he said.

"Huh?"

"It's a very good story."

"Well, I thought you'd be interested," said Frank dryly.

"The *News,* the *Post,* maybe even the *Times* is gonna enjoy this
one. You gonna call the *News* right after us?"

"Gotta play ball with everyone," said Frank. "No favorites with
the press. Don't fuck with the free press."

"Frank?"

"Yeah."

"You know the first thing my boss is gonna say?"

"What's that?"

" 'Is there anything we can do?' "

Frank's voice mimicked. " 'Is there anything we can do?' We
got a jumper on Fifth Avenue, not a spade on 116th Street. Right?
There were three police cars and a Lenox Hill ambulance on the
scene. Two neighbors—at *least* two neighbors—saw Superman
flying through the air. Every fucking maid in the building was
looking at that courtyard when we got there. What can we say it
was, a heart attack?" Frank let out a slow whistle. "Come on,
Nickie boy. I called you first as a favor. Now, you go tell your

boss, and he'll say what terrific contacts little Nickie has with the
cops. Terrific sources you got, Nickie. Terrific reporter you'll
make. Thinking of your *career*."

Nick said, "You're sweet, Frank."

"What a nice ass she has."

"Thanks for the tip."

"Thinking of your career, Nickie." Frank hung up.

*

Ward Parsons, the foreign editor, was just returning from lunch
with Mark Kaiserman, a correspondent who had recently completed a tour of duty in Johannesburg, one of the overseas bureaus
that the paper had closed down in recent weeks. Parsons placed
his worn tweed jacket on an empty chair beside his desk, sat
down, and opened the top drawer to remove a bottle of Maalox.
His eyes lifted to the bulletin board behind the desk, on which
names of at least twenty-five countries were tacked up in alpha-
betical order. Below each name were the correct spellings of government and opposition leaders. Flanking the board, a set of a
dozen movable cardboard planks held maps.

Ward closed his eyes. He was tall, a little under six feet, and
carried his bulk easily, wearing mostly turtleneck sweaters in the
newsroom, a slight affectation that puzzled Barry Cohen, who favored expensive striped shirts with white collars in the style of
Evan Claiborne. Ward knew he wasn't handsome like Barry, but
his glittering black eyes, his gaunt, bony cheeks and strong mouth,
and even his coarse, curly hair that was rapidly thinning gave the
foreign editor an "interesting" face in his forties that had seemed
bland and predictable twenty years before.

Ward's flaw, he sensed, was the faint merriment with which he
looked at the world—and the *Star;* a merriment that (he knew)
cast doubts about the intensity of his ambitions, yet made him a
highly popular and effective foreign editor. If Ward was not quite
as buoyant as he appeared—if he suffered, in fact, the bleakest of
moods and moments of terrible anguish since his last posting in
India—he managed to convey to his colleagues a kind of engaging
charm that masked (for himself, for others) the wretchedness he
had felt for the past year.

Even before his assignment to New Delhi, Ward's marriage had
begun to crack apart. But then events struck with numbing sud-

denness: the death of his youngest daughter in a drowning accident in Delhi; his promotion to foreign editor; the inexplicable decision by his wife, Karen, to remain behind in India with their two
other daughters; the harrowing grief—and guilt—that drove him to
heavy drinking and led to vicious ulcer pains; the loneliness that
finally propelled him into the arms (and apartment) of Florence,
his secretary. She cooked for Ward, watched him cut down his
drinking, ordered him on a physical regimen that eventually included a five-mile daily jog around Central Park. Even if he
wasn't in love with her, Ward needed her.

Florence leaned over and said softly, "Milk?"

"I must look like I feel," Ward said, opening his eyes. The
medicine tasted gritty, blurring the pain in his stomach. Milk
would obliterate the ache.

"You look like you had three martinis."

"Two. Not three. And a bottle of wine. I skipped the cognac."

"How's Mark?" Florence asked, lifting a message off her desk,
which faced Parsons' desk at a perpendicular angle.

"Mark is a . . . how shall I put it?"

"Asshole."

"You said it."

"Is that why you got drunk?"

"That's why I got drunk." Ward stared at the message between
Florence's fingers. "You're about to tell me something. Make it
happy."

"Happy it's not. From our London bureau chief."

"Larry Lake. Married to a British aristocrat. They're into antiques, old furniture. Name-dropping. Prize asshole."

"That's the one."

"Once a decent reporter. Won the Pulitzer. Isn't he related to
Frieda Steiner?"

"A nephew, darling." Florence smiled, and read from the
message. " 'Sorriest but unable to go to Belfast. Have unbreakable
commitment tonight . . .' "

Ward shut his eyes again. "Meaning they have a party."

". . . and will arrive in Belfast tomorrow." Florence looked
up.

"Get me Lake on the phone," said Ward.

"Direct lines to London are out. Had to book. It'll be three, three-fifteen." She leaned forward. "I'll get the milk."

Tony Lazzarutti, the foreign desk clerk, had arrived fifteen minutes late (as usual) and was busily sorting out incoming copy and messages. Instead of asking him to do the errand, Florence pushed her chair back and walked toward the coffee wagon. Ward caught a whiff of her perfume as she stepped past, a bracing, musky scent that stirred him.

Ray Silver, Ward's deputy foreign editor, brushed past Florence, gripping a sheaf of papers.

"The Chinese have broken off border talks!" It was Ray Silver's habit to blink his black eyes according to a story's importance. He was blinking now like a firefly.

Ward looked up at Ray's high-domed head, shiny with sweat.

"Both sides attacking one another," Ray was saying. "*Very* strong language in *Pravda*. Ernie Richards is filing. Says heavy fighting has broken out on the border, along the Amur River. A-M-U-R."

"Evan and Maury are going to ask the same question," said Ward. "Like, 'How significant is this?'"

"According to Ernie, *very* significant." Silver stared at his scribbled notes, and Ward wondered why he had never noticed before that his deputy's fleshy face held traces of unusual delicacy, especially the slender, slightly downturned mouth.

"Ernie's Western sources say—"

"The German Ambassador," said Ward dryly.

"The German Ambassador's *wife*," said Florence, returning.

Ward and Florence laughed. It was common knowledge on the foreign desk that Ernie Richards, after four lonely years in Moscow, had reluctantly settled into an affair with the two-hundred-pound wife of the German Ambassador, who was providing a sizable share of his exclusives.

Ray spoke impatiently. "Ernie's Western sources say talks between the Russians and Chinese are severed. Hasn't happened since the mid-sixties. Chinese insist they have a legitimate claim to a huge territory—"

"Russians said *nyet*," said Ward. "All right, tell Ernie to get that high up in the story, not later than the fourth graf." He frowned at Ray Silver. "You saw Maury's memo." Ray nodded.

Maury Kramer, Evan's deputy managing editor, had sent Ward a memo saying that the stories on the Russian-Chinese dispute were gobbledygook. That for such stories, please think of our readers as middle-aged, middle-class, fairly intelligent, and extremely busy people. Would *they* understand what Ernie was writing about?

Silver said, "You look tired, Ward."

"Christ, you're the second one to tell me," Parsons said. "I had lunch with Kaiserman."

"That'll do it," said Silver. "Bet Kaiserman's happy to be back in New York."

"Delighted," said Ward. "Blames it on his wife." He studied a story summary on his desk. "Silly bitch feels unfulfilled."

"Wives!"

"She wanted to work." Ward turned at the perfume scent to watch Florence place the milk container before him. Why did liquor make him so horny?

Ray was saying: "Women's Lib. It's *killing* us. In ten years every foreign correspondent will be a bachelor or a fag."

"Or a woman," said Florence, sitting down.

"A fag foreign staff!" Ray Silver started laughing. " 'The Pope was wearing an absolutely *stunning* cloak over his shoulders, but—' "

Florence picked up on it. "But his shoes were *incredibly* tacky."

Suddenly Ward said, "Kaiserman wants to go to Washington."

"Hughie won't have him," Ray said somberly.

"I know. I told Kaiserman he'll have to stay in New York."

"Poor bastard," said Florence.

Tony Lazzarutti, the foreign desk clerk, suddenly interrupted. "Bulletin on AP from Washington. The President's called an emergency meeting of the National Security Council." He placed a copy of the wire service lead on Silver's desk.

"Kaiserman's been a foreign correspondent for twelve years," Ward went on. "That's what he kept saying. Vietnam. Beirut. Warsaw. South Africa. Interviewed kings and prime ministers. Covered *continents*. He says he can't just come home and chase fires in the Bronx."

"I've heard that one before," Silver said.

"'Evan Claiborne's your rabbi,' I told Kaiserman. 'You won't chase fires in the Bronx.'"

Ward and Ray began reviewing the summaries of stories filed by other correspondents in the field, in advance of the three o'clock conference. They set aside the five or six stories that seemed front-page possibilities: the breakdown in border talks between China and the Soviet Union; from Washington, the President's reaction to the crisis, written by White House correspondent Barney Fischer; a Bonn spy story; a Belfast story, if Larry Lake flew up there, about an Irish Republican Army explosion in downtown Belfast that had left a priest and four others dead; a story from Jerusalem, by the *Star*'s correspondent in Israel, on divisions in the Cabinet over further peace talks with Jordan; a "farewell" story by the Tokyo correspondent, who was taking a year's leave to write a spy novel. (The Tokyo job, like the one in South Africa, was being left vacant because of the *Star*'s ailing finances.)

"That's a good story from Tokyo," said Silver, "but we either trim it or hold it. It's nearly two columns." Space for stories was an ongoing problem on the paper, whose advertising department was in constant battle with the news side over how many columns were to be set aside for news.

"It's holdable," said Ward, watching Florence's breast as she lifted the ringing phone.

It was the call to Lake in London. Larry had been the London bureau chief for two years, a laurel bestowed after he had won the Pulitzer Prize for his series on Henry Kissinger. To Ward, there was no question that Larry had been a first-rate journalist. But his analytical skills, his ability to quickly shape complex issues and events into a readable, accurate story—the mark of a superior reporter—were overshadowed now by a snob British wife and a personality made abrasive partly by the fact that he was Frieda Steiner's nephew. Another untouchable.

The phone line crackled, and Ward could barely hear Lake's voice. "Larry, about Belfast," Ward said.

"Yes. Well, look, Ward, it's impossible tonight. Impossible. We have a long-standing dinner, impossible to get out of."

"What?"

"We are giving a *dinner* party, Ward."

Not only is he a prick, Ward thought, but he's a condescending prick.

"We have cabinet ministers and ex-cabinet ministers coming. We have Dennis Healey and Shirley Williams. Tony Benn. Heath is probably coming. How the hell can I *not* show up? Serena will murder me."

Ward lit a cigarette and blew one circle, then two. It was unthinkable, at least when Ward had been a foreign correspondent, for someone in the field to reject an assignment simply because he had a dinner party. To reject an assignment for *any* reason. Being a foreign correspondent for the *Star* meant that your personal life was dwarfed by the paper's needs. The wife of one correspondent had given birth in a Saigon hospital while the Viet Cong were assaulting the neighborhood, and while her husband was filing a story in Danang; the Beirut bureau chief had spent so much time away from home in covering the Middle East that his wife had fallen in love with a Greek dentist and wound up asking for a divorce. The Cairo correspondent once told Ward that over the past twelve years in the Middle East he had missed every anniversary, every family birthday, and the high school graduations of his two children. It was known on the foreign staff that anyone passing through Cairo should phone up the correspondent's wife for dinner at the Nile Hilton and a blow job afterward; her husband was never in town.

Larry said: "I've booked myself on the eight o'clock flight tomorrow morning."

"That's too late," said Ward, his voice clenched. "Too *late*. We want someone up there tonight." Florence and Ray were staring at him.

Larry began speaking, but Ward cut him off. "Five people killed, including a Catholic priest. We've got a lousy stringer there. Larry, we . . ."

"So what do you suggest?" Larry said mildly.

"I suggest you get your ass up there tonight. File a story for the first edition and then an over-all piece tomorrow. By then we'll get Sam back from Stockholm and he'll take over and you can get back to London."

"I can't do it."

"What?"

"I can't do it." Lake articulated the words slowly. His voice had developed an English inflection that deepened Ward's rage. Larry said: "Look. We'll win the Pulitzer anyway. Sam's coverage has been superb." Sam Roth was the second man in the London bureau.

Ward accepted defeat with a deep sigh. The seed of ulcer pain took root, flourishing into his ribs. Ward murmured good-bye, gently placing the phone down. "Scumbag," he said, staring at the phone.

"Lady Serena's having a dinner party," said Florence.

"La-de-da," said Ray. "Claiborne's gonna be pissed."

"No, he won't," said Ward tensely. *"He* picked Larry. So did Skipper. If they want to pull him out of London, fine. He's *their* boy." Ward looked up at Ray. "Let's use AP, and let's get the city desk to do a six-hundred-word wrap-up on Ireland. Make it eight hundred words, a good background piece explaining the place, the 1921 War, British policy, etcetera. Pegged to the bombing. Call Sam in Stockholm and tell him to get to Belfast tomorrow. Keep Larry in London."

Suddenly Ward heard shouts from Barry Cohen's desk; a crowd was swarming around the city editor, who was on the phone. Barry's deputy, Pat Donlon, and his clerk, Nick Simons, were listening in on extensions. Ward pushed his chair back and walked over to Linda Fentress, an investigative reporter who stood on the fringe of the crowd.

"What's up?"

"Evan Claiborne jumped out of a window," Linda said in a single breath.

Ward heard Florence behind him gasp.

"He's dead," Linda Fentress said, as Ward pushed through the crowd to reach Cohen, who was still on the phone.

Ward turned around quickly, almost instinctively, to face Claiborne's office, a private suite in a corner of the newsroom. Outside the office sat the managing editor's confidential secretary, Mary Phelps. Mary was staring at the newsroom, her large, almost expressionless eyes unblinking, her face looking stunned and pale.

*

Even reporters who detested Barry Cohen conceded that the city editor had successfully (and ruthlessly) purged incompetents and burned-out writers from the staff, and shaped a vigorous investigation team that would soon win a Pulitzer Prize. The *Star*'s last prizewinner was, in fact, Barry, for his eyewitness account of the storming of the American Embassy by panicky Vietnamese during the collapse of Saigon.

As city editor, Barry set aside each Tuesday lunch for Howie Bishop, the *Star*'s chief investigative reporter. Cohen had discovered Bishop in real estate news, the paper's graveyard, and had plucked him out of that job and set him loose as an investigator. What had intrigued Cohen was Bishop's obsession with work, his zeal in covering a story, and his brash confidence that seemed a throwback to the "Front Page" era.

Bishop had just completed a two-part series on prostitution in New York, and the network of pimps, hotel operators, narcotics dealers and lenient judges who abetted the problem. Predictably, the mayor cited the series in announcing yet another cleanup of Forty-second Street—by now, an annual event, guaranteed to make the front page, like the St. Patrick's Day Parade.

"What now?" Cohen had asked that day at lunch. They were sitting in Fritzi's, the newspaper's hangout, whose rear tables were crammed with reporters and editors eating lunch. The bar stools up front, on the other hand, were favored by drivers, printers, and linotypists. The twain rarely met; there was a tacit hostility between the sides.

Howie Bishop had given Barry an upward glance. "Payoffs. Senator Davey Fitzgerald."

Barry chewed his lip. "I *like* that one."

"Could be a biggie. Rumor's been floating for a while."

"What do we have?"

"Whispers, gossip. . . ."

"It could be good."

"Or it could be shit," said Bishop, suddenly frowning.

"Would Jerry Paley help?"

"No."

"Why?"

"Jerry may be involved."

Jerry Paley was a former political reporter on the *Star*, who had left the paper to work in Washington as administrative assistant to New York Democratic Senator Fitzgerald.

Bishop pushed his chair forward as a waitress, balancing a tray of food, stepped past the table.

"We got a problem if we go after the story," said Bishop, eyeing Barry. There was a slight quiver in Howie's lower lip. "Fitzgerald's banging Lucy Claiborne."

They sat in silence as a waitress removed their plates.

Howie's tinted glasses cast a vaguely sinister glow to his narrow, sharp-nosed face, pitted with black eyes that narrowed when he spoke. He kept his thinning hair neatly parted, and his cheeks were absolutely pallid, as if drained of blood. A narrow scar curled beneath the center of his jaw. He lit a cigarette.

"You're sure?" Barry asked.

"Sure of what?"

"Lucy and Fitzgerald."

"Positive."

Barry winced. "Let's get the story on Fitzgerald anyway."

"What about Jerry Paley?"

"What *about* Jerry Paley? Fuck him. So he used to work for us. If he's involved, he's *involved.*

"Don't worry," said Cohen, who heard the phone ring in the booth beside the kitchen's swinging doors and stiffened when one of the waitresses shouted his name. He left the table, aware that the noise at the tables had suddenly ebbed. Reporters looked up at him.

Phone calls in the middle of lunch usually meant . . . *crisis.* An assassination. A plane crash. Unexpected announcement from City Hall, the governor's office, the White House. A major story. Barry felt a spark of tension. His heart hammered.

It was his city desk clerk, Nick Simons.

"Barry. Evan Claiborne. He's jumped out of a window and killed himself."

Instinctively Cohen reached into his suit pocket for a ball-point pen. "I'm listening." Barry felt sweat start to break out on his face.

"A good source, a cop. Just called me."

Barry's fingers tightened on the phone and he thought, incongruously, This kid, Nick, will make the staff soon. Nick was brash, smart, burning with ambition.

Now Barry heard Nick's voice flutter. "He jumped from his apartment. Two-twenty."

Cohen sat down, grabbing a sheet of paper from his breast pocket and writing "2:20" on it.

Nick spoke quickly. He said the managing editor had been dead on arrival at Lenox Hill and that Mrs. Claiborne, who was in the apartment at the time, was under sedation. Evan had been naked. There were no notes. A psychiatrist named Wasserman was in the apartment now.

"Does Skipper know? Anyone else know?" asked Barry.

"I called you first," Nick said quickly.

Cohen said, "Can we act fast? Talk to the cops and the hospital?"

"About . . ."

"About not making it a suicide."

"Barry, I . . ."

"A heart attack. An accident."

"Barry, I tried. Christ! Believe me, I have tried. There is no way. The *doorman* knows."

"We can buy him."

"Barry. Our friends in the precinct will not do it."

"Why?" Barry Cohen's lips tightened.

"It's a big building, that's why. There were ambulances and police cars out there. People saw what happened. How can we say it was a coronary? There were cops in back cleaning up. What about the fucking hospital? Is Lenox Hill gonna do *us* a favor?"

Sweat dampened Barry's spine. "Did the wires get it yet?"

"They will. In about fifteen minutes. They'll scream. The *Daily News,* the *Times,* and Christ knows the *Post*'ll scream because it wasn't on the ticker immediately. They'll know what happened."

"Fuck them. Check with your source again. Make sure Evan left no notes. I'll call Skipper. Christ. The *Daily News* is going to love the naked business."

Nick lowered his voice. "Who's gonna take over?"

"What?"

"Who's gonna be managing editor? Maury?"

"Could be Maury," said Barry. "Could be anyone."

"How about you?"

Barry winced, tasting the salt on his lips. "What a sweet idea,
Nickie boy."

After hanging up the phone, Barry shut his eyes. His mouth was
very dry, his throat clenched with nausea. He rooted in his pocket
for some coins, and dialed the publisher's direct line with trembling fingers.

*

It was drizzling and chilly when the taxi pulled up to the *Star*
building on West Fifty-first Street. Sally Sims, wearing a mink-
lined raincoat and dark glasses, shivered as she walked quickly
through the revolving doors of the lobby crowded with employees
returning from lunch. The newspaper building was nearly eighty
years old, the lobby narrow and brightly lit.

At midday a receptionist sat behind a circular desk sheathed in
Plexiglas in the center of the lobby, responding to questions from
visitors, waving to employees, nodding to the swarms of school-
children and tourists who visited the *Star* daily. Plants and potted flowers—leathery-leaved evergreen shrubs margined with red
sword fern, scarlet poinsettias, honey-scented hybrids—filled the
enclosure at the insistence of Frieda Steiner, who sought at least a
semblance of serenity in the corridors leading up to the newspaper.

To the right of the indoor entrance a large newsstand—carrying
New York and out-of-town dailies, magazines, intellectual quar-
terlies, show-business weeklies and a smattering of pornography—
served the *Star*'s employees and, for that matter, the neighborhood. The newsstand itself was flanked by two alcoves that
seemed carved out of the gray marble wall.

One of these cubicles, open eight to six daily, employed two
women who not only accepted classified ads in person, but retained copies of the New York *Star* dating back three years. The
second cubicle held a uniformed guard who kept a careful,
if vaguely hostile, watch over those who entered and left the
building.

In this surge of activity—in the flow of reporters, editors, secretaries, printers, linotypers, deliverers, executives, clerks and visitors—two oil portraits on the left-hand wall seemed quite uninten-
tionally ignored.

The portraits were of Frederic Steiner, founder of the *Star,* and Jonathan Steiner, his son.

The elder Steiner had posed for the portrait at the age of seventy-one, four years before his death. A hefty, powerful man, Frederic gazed sternly over the lobby, his wide, dark eyes peering through rimless glasses. His lips were pursed; his round, bland face seemed muscular, commanding. He wore a formal blue suit with a vest and key chain over a high-collared white shirt and black silk tie pierced by a diamond stickpin.

The face of his son was gentler. Jonathan Steiner, who died of a heart attack in 1968 at the age of fifty-four, smiled eagerly, his high forehead, wide dark eyes and square face mirroring his father's. There was a soft, almost playful quality about the younger man. He wore a wide-collared white shirt, a shimmering blue silk tie flecked with red dots, and a double-breasted navy-blue suit with a white handkerchief tucked neatly into his breast pocket. His left hand rested on a walnut table—obviously the same table, painted in a softer, russet shade, that his father had posed beside. The backdrop of both pictures was the same: the family library on the tenth floor, the library that Skipper now used for conferences and small receptions.

Sally rode the elevator to the fifth floor, glancing at her watch—it was 2:50 P.M.—annoyed that her lunch with Dorothy Faye had taken so long. Dorothy was an old friend who had worked on the *Star*'s city staff before going to Saigon in the late 1960s. After returning home from twenty months in Vietnam, Dorothy had quit the paper to write a book, which was fairly well received except, ironically, by the *Star*'s chief book critic, who had called it "morally ambiguous" and "deceitful" because it sympathized with the Viet Cong's killing of Americans. The review severed Dorothy's links to virtually everyone on the *Star* except Sally.

Midway through lunch at an Italian restaurant on West Twelfth Street, Dorothy had announced there would be a party the following week for Mark Kaiserman and Marty Kaplan. Kaiserman had just returned from South Africa; Marty was arriving from Buenos Aires for home leave.

"I heard from Mark that morale is rock bottom on the city staff," Dorothy said.

"Dodo. Morale is always at rock bottom on the city staff."

"Barry is such a prick."

Sally sipped her glass of white wine.

Dorothy leaned forward. "In Saigon the bureau fell apart under Barry. He is *not* a nice man. There was one month, *one entire month,* when Barry, me and Marty were not talking to one another. Barry hogged stories, undercut us. An insecure schmuck."

Sally had heard the Saigon stories about Cohen before. Dorothy sensed her mood and changed the subject to ask about Sally's husband.

"How's Charles?"

"Charles is in Key West. Interviewing Tennessee Williams for a Canadian magazine."

Sally avoided Dorothy's glance, the waiter brought salads and they watched in silence as he ground pepper over each plate.

Dorothy finally said: "I liked the series you did on abortion."

"No, you didn't. It was weak, timid. We shouldn't have printed it."

"Who wrote it?"

"I basically *rewrote* it. Skipper rewrote *me.* And Mama did a final number on it."

"Uh-oh."

"Mama is squeamish about abortion. And she doesn't think much of school busing, or of the President either."

"She does seem to think much of Senator David Fitzgerald."

Sally stared at her.

"The piece the other day," said Dorothy.

"Saturday?"

"Came on strong."

"I had nothing to do with that."

"I didn't think so."

"Orders from the tenth floor."

"Skipper?"

"*Mama!*"

"Fitzgerald wants to be President," Dorothy said.

"What Davey wants, Davey gets." Sally examined her right hand.

"Like Lucy, for instance."

"What?"

"Lucy Steiner Claiborne. He wants."

Sally sucked in her breath. "I've heard."

"Fitzgerald needs the *Star*."

Sally looked at Dorothy. "Doesn't have the *News*. Doesn't have the *Times*."

"If he's serious about running for President . . ."

"*If* he's serious!" Sally said scornfully.

"If he's serious, then he needs his wife, as well as the *Star*. The good wife."

"Celia is against his running."

"Celia is crazy to put up with the bastard," Dorothy said.

"Celia is crazy, remember?"

"She drinks. A problem."

"You remember her father?" Sally lit a cigarette. "Late great majority leader. Merton Keefer. Drunk on the Senate floor. Once *peed* on the Senate floor. Drank himself to death. Fitzgerald's father-in-law."

"She had a brother, too," said Dorothy.

Sally's left hand reached up, her fingers outstretched, as if trying to catch the name. "*Joey*. Joey Keefer."

"Yes!"

"A tinhorn Joe McCarthy."

"That's it," said Dorothy. "Had the movie industry terrified for about nine and a half minutes. State investigation committee. What ever happened to Joey Keefer?"

"Dead," said Sally, crushing her cigarette in the ashtray. "Died in Mexico City."

In the taxi back to the office, Sally lit a cigarette with a shaky hand. Saturday's story about Fitzgerald had been shoddy—the paper's flattering him a humiliation. Months before, Sally had flared at Skipper about his mother's relentless interference; Skipper's response was an uncharacteristic silence, his lips pursed in irritation; a look of strain wrenched his face.

Turning away from Skipper, Sally had felt her cheeks burn with embarrassment. She had obviously stumbled over a boundary, and hated herself for doing so. It was just too painful, too personal for Skipper to take a stand against his mother.

When Sally walked into the newsroom, Rose, her secretary, handed her three phone messages and said Charles had just called from Key West to say he would be arriving at LaGuardia at about nine-fifteen tomorrow night and hoped to be home by ten.

Sally examined the messages.

The office of the Secretary of Defense had called to request that some Pentagon people fly to New York to brief Sally and Fosdick on a proposed new mobile missile system—a weapon that the *Star* had termed wasteful. Sally scrawled, "Okay. Mon. or Tues. AM," and set it in her out-box.

Hugh Finch, the *Star*'s Washington bureau chief, had called to place a news analysis on the schedule for Sunday's paper, dealing with the restiveness in the Democratic Party toward the President. Why, thought Sally, *why* after all these years was Hugh, who was the first black to head a major newspaper bureau in Washington, still driven to prove himself, still obsessed by the need to compete with colleagues as well as competitors, to publish a story daily, to get his byline in print *every single day* . . .

Sally turned to the final message.

The editor of *The Atlantic* wanted to have lunch with her the following Thursday or Friday. Sally wrote: "Friday." In the past six months Sally had written pieces for *The Atlantic* and *The New Yorker* and had suddenly realized how much she missed reporting and how the prestigious national editor's job had weighed her down. The bickering and one-upmanship and intense competition, the *Star*'s financial pressures that limited travel and had reduced the national staff, Frieda's nagging interference on stories, the remorseless tensions of constantly proving that, as the highest-ranking woman editor on the paper, she was not merely an affirmative-action hand-me-down but tough and aggressive as well.

Suddenly swinging her eyes to Peter Fosdick's empty chair, Sally felt the blood rush to her face and winced at her fury that he was *not* there, that her deputy was late again, playing his goddamn squash game at the New York Athletic Club with his goddamn Princeton pals.

Horse's ass, Sally thought. "Where's my missing goddamn *deputy?*"

Rose looked up.

"I've got to get rid of that son of a bitch," Sally said tensely.

"What's wrong?" Rose's voice was gentle.

Sally stared at her. There was an unspoken bond between the

two women that Sally found comforting. She trusted Rose as she trusted few people, and was fully aware that Rose had a sensitivity to her moods almost eerie in its accuracy.

"Just tired," said Sally, examining a story from Washington that Hugh Finch had filed in the morning. Decline in President Bergen's polls, unrest within the Senate and House about Bergen's leadership.

What was wrong with her?

Skipper. *Charlie!* Stumbling into an affair with Skipper that seemed sometimes as pointless as it was absolutely necessary.

She tried to concentrate on Hugh's story. *Some Democratic strategists said the decline in President Bergen's polls were inevitable, given his high ratings shortly after the election. Others said, however, that the President's unexpected low-keyed style had disappointed even some ranking cabinet . . .*

Sally shut her eyes. It was so easy to misplace her anger onto Frieda Steiner. The old woman's personally typed memos were *tangible,* blunt words that intimidated even Skipper—the publisher, Frieda's son—and left Sally mired in her own helplessness.

Sally could almost hear Frieda's high-pitched voice as she typed her memos.

"Skipper, aren't we hitting President Bergen too hard? Aren't we asking too much too soon? Should we print this critical news analysis now?"

Sally had fought Frieda too many times—even, once, on the annual saccharine national roundup involving the first day of spring. ("Isn't it too early for this?" Frieda had asked in a handwritten note to Skipper. "My garden is bare. The crocuses lifeless. Won't we look silly if it snows next week?")

Frieda had been right. An Arctic snowstorm had abruptly and unexpectedly veered into the city three days later, dumping nine inches of snow in Manhattan, twelve inches in the suburbs, crippling New York for two days.

Perhaps Frieda was right more often than wrong. Perhaps Frieda knew the *Star* and its readers better than Sally did, better than *anyone.* Perhaps the instincts of this sharp-witted woman were precisely attuned to the demands and boundaries of the newspaper founded by her husband's father. Perhaps Frieda mirrored the *Star*'s views with unconscious—and startling—accuracy.

Suddenly Sally felt faint and chilled. What was bothering her was more than Frieda, goddamn it. Of *course* it was more than Frieda. Frieda was actually irrelevant. It was Skipper. And . . . Charlie. It was the *Star,* the spiral for power that dazed and alarmed her.

A buzz from the green phone on her desk, which connected directly to the publisher, startled Sally. She reached for it.

"Sally, I have some dreadful news," Skipper said. His voice choked. "Darling," he said, "Evan has killed himself."

CHAPTER 3

Eight minutes later, Maury Kramer, Evan Claiborne's deputy, heard news of the managing editor's death in a phone call from Skipper. Kramer, seated behind his desk facing the newsroom, reacted in a way that, he confessed later, puzzled him. He was suddenly furious.

Maury was furious first at Evan, his mentor and old friend, for killing himself without talking first to him. He was furious at Barry Cohen for his one-upmanship: for calling Skipper to convey the news and making it plain that he was on top of everything when, in fact, Cohen sure as hell knew that he should have informed the deputy managing editor *first.* It was *Kramer's* job to call Skipper. It was a typical end run by Cohen to impress the publisher—the son of a bitch was always making points.

And Maury was furious at himself for failing to sense that, in all their drinking bouts together, despite Evan's depressions and temper, despite his bursts of exuberance followed by those eerie, paralyzing silences, Evan was, indeed, suicidal. It was somehow weirdly inappropriate for Evan Claiborne to die this way.

Maury told Evan's secretary, Mary Phelps, to get the editors into the managing editor's office in five minutes. With the clock ticking toward deadline, they would map out the front page *now,* placing Evan's picture and the story of his death and obituary conspicuously on top of the fold. Or should they put the story beneath it? It was a family decision, of course, but the editors would offer their proposal at the three o'clock meeting in Skipper's office.

Maury's mind raced. Having started as a copy boy on the *Star* twenty-eight years ago, he knew instinctively how the paper should react to the death of its managing editor—an embarrassing death.

There would be a fourteen-hundred-word story by Mickey Wagner, the most respected rewrite man on the city staff, recounting the career of Evan Claiborne. A straight story, the lead saying that he had jumped to his death and the police were listing it as a suicide. The second paragraph quoting the police saying that no notes had been found. It was up to the family to decide whether or not the paragraph should close with a sentence saying that in recent months Mr. Claiborne had been under a psychiatrist's care for depression.

The third paragraph listing survivors: Mrs. Claiborne, who was in the apartment at the time of his death. Again, it was up to the Steiner family to decide whether or not they wanted it high up in the story, or buried in it, that Mrs. Claiborne was the sister of the *Star*'s publisher and the granddaughter of the paper's founder. The other immediate survivor: a daughter, Johanna Claiborne, a student at Harvard.

The bulk of the story would encompass Claiborne's career.

A solid story. Factual. No bullshit.

There would be a separate unbylined story inside the paper detailing tributes from the governor, the mayor, the two senators from New York, the head of the Archdiocese, the chief rabbi of the Park Avenue Synagogue, as well as from the League of New York Theaters, the Urban League, the American Society of Newspaper Editors, the Yale alumni fund, the director of the Metropolitan Museum of Art, the National Association for the Advancement of Colored People, the American Bar Association.

Maury saw the editors start to move toward the managing editor's office. He picked up his phone and dialed an internal line to the Washington bureau, to tell Hugh Finch so he could inform the bureau. Finch was at the State Department, but Sam Hunter, his deputy, said he would try to reach him immediately and would post a notice on the bulletin board announcing Evan's death. Maury, perspiring now and breathing heavily, hung up the phone and put on his blue blazer; he always wore a sport jacket over a plain shirt and suspenders. As he stood, Maury grabbed a stick of gum off his desk and tore apart the wrapper—he chewed gum frenziedly in the hours approaching deadline, working out his anxiety in slow, rhythmical jaw movements. Then Maury walked into Evan's office to start the meeting.

*

In fact, Hugh Finch was not at the State Department. The first black to be appointed Washington bureau chief was in an apartment on Cathedral Avenue with his secretary, Francine Miles, who was pounding him on the back with her fists and heaving her buttocks high as Hugh, swearing and moaning, thrust into her. Francine's eyes were shut. She threw both hands around his neck, pushing Hugh's face onto hers, her mane of blond hair cascading around his head.

He drove his penis deep, pushing her mouth open with his tongue. He licked her neck, she groaned. He gripped her breasts, his thumbs pressing, rubbing, as his tongue traveled. He smelled her perfume and sweat, and heard her whispers. "Hughie." He began to laugh now, thrusting into her, tensing his body and holding his breath, moaning, "no, no, no," seconds before the phone began to ring.

Thursday

CHAPTER 4

Frieda Steiner's nine-room apartment on Park Avenue and Eighty-first Street had, in recent years, served the needs of the entire family. It was splendid, an heirloom Frieda had inherited, covered in thickly carpeted Persian and Chinese rugs, discreetly sprinkled with eighteenth- and nineteenth-century oak and walnut and Philippine mahogany sideboards and tables.

Antiques were a family tradition that dated back to Frederic Steiner. The *Star*'s founder had been born poor in Vienna, and had come to New York at the age of eleven. With the same gusto and business acumen that had marked his years as publisher, enabling him to turn a small, impoverished newspaper into a formidable and wealthy journal, Steiner had abruptly turned his energies to furniture and paintings. While in his sixties, he had traveled to Paris and London each year with a series of mistresses, tracking down Louis XVI armchairs and cylinder-top desks made for Marie Antoinette, eighteenth-century bookcases veneered in rosewood, Chippendale mahogany commodes and secretaries.

Initially the dealers in Mayfair and Belgravia had viewed Steiner with scorn: a rich American with an open checkbook; a New York Jew whose blond girlfriends giggled and expressed boredom at these elegant objects; a businessman without taste who bargained mercilessly over some pieces, and spent a fortune without a word on others.

In fact, Frederic Steiner always knew precisely what he wanted. He pored over books and journals on eighteenth- and nineteenth-century English and French furniture. He spent hours with young art curators at the Wallace Collection in London or the Victoria and Albert Museum, paying them privately to teach him the wonder of elegant art. With typical bluntness, he told them that he had little taste in paintings and furniture and wanted to make some acquisitions. He told them to teach him the mysteries of beauty.

At first the young men, born of wealth and breeding, responded with derision, puzzled by this unusual figure who hounded them with questions, who told them with disarming candor that he wanted to acquire taste. By Steiner's final years, however, as he began amassing a sizable European collection, the same young men were discreetly phoning Frederic on his private line at the *Star* to whisper that a Sheraton gilt-wood settee and several Chippendale mahogany standing cabinets could be purchased privately from the widow of a stockbroker who was moving from her Gramercy Park townhouse; or a painting by Monet of the seaside near Le Havre, a lush work by Degas of women bathing, could be bought cheap from a businessman in Grosse Point who was in need of quick cash to pay off gambling debts. Frederic paid these young men handsomely.

Steiner's family—his wife Dora, and their two sons, Arnold and Jonathan—had moved from Riverside Drive to the big apartment on Park Avenue in 1926. Although the onset of the Depression had forced the *Star* to drop, temporarily, building plans in New Jersey and an extension of the Manhattan office, the Wall Street collapse actually had little impact on the family's personal wealth, which was tied up then in the newspaper and in building property on Madison Avenue that Frederic had purchased in 1923. Coupled with the rockbed security of his paintings and antiques, Frederic's ownership of the office building and the newspaper provided a steady, if diminished, income for the family through the worst of the Depression.

Shrewdly, Frederic sensed that it was a perfect opportunity to buy—and not rent—the Park Avenue apartment, an enclave that could provide the space for his acquisitiveness and serve as a symbol of his success. He was at the peak of his career. He bought it for Dora and the boys and his grandchildren.

His mistress, the last one, an actress named Helena Standish, was nestled in an apartment on Seventy-eighth Street near Second Avenue. Dora was ailing, complaining of migraines, dissolving into tears in the midst of breakfast, and visiting a German psychiatrist on East Eighty-seventh Street four times a week. Dora, poor Dora, a shy, frail girl who had never grown into a woman.

And the boys. *His* boys. Arnold and Jonathan. Jonathan and Arnold. They were young men, prized young men. Two years apart, yet so . . . different; the same seed but so different.

Arnold, the older boy, clever, mischievous, even wild, a resourceful and handsome boy who, from the time he was twelve or thirteen, one assumed would take over the *Star*. A strong, clever lad, the relatives said.

Jonathan was the second child. Sickly from the day he was born. He almost killed poor Dora during eighteen hours of labor in the delivery room of Mt. Sinai. Dora had never been the same.

As Arnold grew like a sturdy tree, Jonathan seemed to shrivel. Scarlet fever at four. A bout of TB at nine. A dreamy boy who write poetry at Fieldston and opted to go to Dartmouth instead of Princeton or Columbia, which were Frederic's choices. A distant child, a mama's boy. Aloof, like Dora. He had no interest in the *Star,* except for book reviews and theatrical news, a boy who wanted to teach college English, a boy who showed no interest in girls except one, Frieda Schiffer. He had met the Schiffer girl at a Christmas dance at the St. Regis Hotel in 1932; she was the daughter of a German-Jewish stockbroker who scorned the gruff, often crude, Frederic Steiner. Schiffer had warned his daughter he disapproved of this nouveau-riche family that gave "Our People" the worst kind of name.

Frieda was one year older than Jonathan, and one of the few Jewish girls to attend The Brearley School. She spent summers at the family home in Oyster Bay. Since young women did not generally go to college—and since Frieda's father refused to allow her a European tour like her friends—Frieda was left with little to do but to write letters and read in her family's apartment on Madison Avenue and Seventy-second Street. She did volunteer work three afternoons a week at the Henry Street Settlement House. The Schiffer family's task, of course, was to find Frieda a suitable husband.

A restless young woman with lively black eyes and a sharp, pointed face that failed to attract the right young men, Frieda, by the age of twenty, had virtually given up hope of marrying. Her nose was too long—in Brearley some cruel girls had called her

"Horseface." Her bosom was too big, making her look topheavy. She knew that she was smarter than most of her friends, and more willful—but she was not prettier. If she wasn't married by the time she was twenty-one, she vowed, she would flee to Paris, teach English, have a love affair—in general, break out of the Park Avenue prison that her stern father had created to protect her.

Being a willful young woman, Frieda Schiffer *would* have gone to Paris in 1933—and her life would have taken a totally different course. But a fortuitous flu had afflicted her younger sister, Sarah, during Christmas vacation of 1932. The family had already purchased a ticket for Sarah to go to the annual charity ball for war widows at the St. Regis. More important, Mrs. Mildred Schiffer had looked forward for weeks to attending the dance, as her daughter's chaperone: she planned to wear her new spangled twenty-eight-dollar Hattie Carnegie dress. And so Mrs. Schiffer demanded that Frieda take Sarah's place at the dance. Every eligible boy in town is in from college, she said. One never knows. Grudgingly, Frieda went with her mother in the family's Dodge coupe, secure in the knowledge that this would be her last Christmas dance at the St. Regis. Next year, Paris.

Frieda had heard, of course, about the Steiners, largely because the world of wealthy Jewish families in New York was a rather select one, an inbred world that often intermarried, went to the same clubs and schools and hospitals and shops and restaurants. Arnold Steiner, the handsome one, was reputedly wild, a boy in his twenties who went with older girls to parties in Greenwich Village, played poker in Harlem, was seen in a Third Avenue bar with a married woman and was—according to Sarah—trouble with a capital T. (Frieda knew that her sister Sarah, who was only seventeen, had a secret crush on Arnold Steiner.)

The younger Steiner boy, Jonathan, was said to be a funny-looking intellectual, and when he shyly asked Frieda to dance at the St. Regis that night she thought yes, he is, indeed, odd-looking. His tuxedo seemed to sag on his body and, as the band began to play, she felt the trembling in his icy hands.

> *Come on and hear*
> *Come on and hear*
> *Alexander's Ragtime Band.*

Come on and hear
Come on and hear
It's the best band in the land.

You dance very well, she said.
Thanks, so do you, he said.
You're Jonathan Steiner.
Yes, I am. What's your name?
Frieda Schiffer. We live on Madison and Seventy-second. Do you go to school?
Yes, he said. I'm getting out of Dartmouth. I'm going to teach English. Have you ever heard of Ezra Pound?
Yes, of course, she said.
Have you heard of Gertrude Stein?
Yes.
Have you read "The Waste Land"?
No, she said, my father watches what I read.
A boy in a striped jacket onstage was singing softly:

No one here can love and understand me.
Oh what hard luck stories they all hand me.
Make my bed and light the light.
I'll arrive late tonight.
Blackbird bye bye.

Can I see you again?
She laughed. I guess so, she said.
Three months later, on a cold and golden Sunday afternoon, Frieda Schiffer walked into her father's study as he sat reading the financial page of the New York *Times*. She told him with as much certainty as she could muster that Jonathan Steiner had asked her to marry him and that she had accepted. And that if her father objected, or refused to go to the wedding, or made the slightest scene, the young couple would elope and she would never see him again. Ever!
The couple were married at Temple Emanu-El on Fifth Avenue, March 1, 1934.
Nine months later Frieda gave birth to Mark Steiner, who was eventually nicknamed "Skipper" by his Irish nurse because he never seemed to walk, but always to skip. The following year

Frieda gave birth to a daughter, Lucy, whose high forehead and slender mouth eerily resembled the infant's delighted grandfather, Frederic. Their father, Jonathan, had just begun teaching at New York University.

To Frederic, the wedding and its aftermath stirred uneasy feelings, the sense that life was drifting by, that he was aging. He was a fifty-one-year-old man and it was all . . . fleeting. The women who pampered themselves for him, performed for him, provided the comfort and sex that he needed daily, even in his fifties and sixties—Frederic impatiently thrust them away and picked up new women, younger women, cheaper women, until he met Helena Standish, a dark-eyed widow who did precisely what she wanted to do in bed, who demanded her own satisfaction too, and taught Frederic for the first time how the needs of a woman, this woman, were satisfied with his tongue and mouth and hands.

The children—so different. Jonathan, the intellectual, so remote, so nervous and guarded. Married now to Frieda Schiffer, a plain and bossy girl, a spoiled girl with a head on her shoulders. Why does a young man marry a woman like this? Why does any man marry any woman? Not love. Was it convenience? Sex? Did she help him that way? Was he able to do things with her?

Frederic sensed that Jonathan's marriage went beyond certain rational reasons or desires. Was it Jonathan's desire, above all, to flee from the apartment on Park Avenue. To thrust himself loose from Frederic and the *Star?* To liberate himself with the help of a powerful woman, older yet.

And what about her? Was it love, whatever that means? Or was it a grasp at freedom? A last grasp at marriage, a convenient marriage with a dreamy, pliant man, a younger and less powerful man.

His brother Arnold was, after all, the *prize,* the heir who began visiting the *Star* each Saturday morning at the age of fourteen, who plunged into the newspaper business with a fervor that took Frederic's breath away.

These workers, Frederic told his son at sixteen, make the *Star.* The printers, linotypists, compositors, editors, deliverers, reporters, typists, telephone operators—they are all *family.* Treat them as family, as your own blood relatives, because without them

the Steiners are nothing. It is their commitment to the *Star,* these
employees, that make the newspaper great.

As Arnold grew into manhood, he went beyond the advice of
his father. He preferred the friendship of reporters and *Star* employees to the rich young men who went to Fieldston and Princeton with him. He drank with them at Bleeck's and went whoring
with them in Newark and made speeches at their farewell parties. He made it a point to send notes and bottles of perfume
to wives who were in the hospital. And if Arnold ignored his
studies at Princeton—and took young women to the Stork Club
and demanded his rights after one date—Frederic was left with little option but to reprimand his older son, sternly lecturing that a
college degree was the most important piece of paper for a young
man to possess in America, that playing around with women, the
wrong women, would land Arnold in trouble and embarrass the
entire Steiner family.

Frederic, of course, adored his son, with the unrestrained passion that made his eyes fill with tears when he watched the boy,
and then the young man, drift off to sleep or knot a four-in-hand
tie or walk forcefully through the corridors of the *Star,* stopping
off to greet the elevator operators and the cleaning women and the
printers and the reporters by their first names. That boy, Frederic
said, has peasant blood. He came from the old Steiner stock; the
shrewd peddlers, tailors, even petty gangsters who were forced
into thievery to feed families during the vicious antisemitic po-
groms in Russia and Austria at the turn of the century.

By the time Arnold enlisted in the Army in 1943, the paper had
enough prestige—and Frederic knew two cabinet officers in the
Roosevelt administration and even had a passing acquaintance
with both the President and the First Lady—so that they believed
the family's eldest son could settle into a job at the Office of War
Information in Washington. It would seem perfectly natural: Dora
begged Frederic to take the train quietly to Washington and speak
to his friends about the boy.

Instead, Frederic took the train to Fort Polk, Louisiana, where
Arnold was taking basic training. Frederic told his son that he
could serve the nation just as profitably, perhaps even more so, by
accepting a job in Washington. Arnold stared at his father for a
long moment and then told Frederic icily that if he were assigned

to the home front he would enlist in the Marines or the Coast Guard or the Navy until he finally went overseas. He said he would sever his ties to his father, permanently, if Frederic pulled strings to keep him on the home front.

For the first time in Frederic's adult life he began attending synagogue on Friday nights and Saturday mornings, and even weekday mornings. He went to Temple Emanu-El, praying silently in Hebrew and English, whispering with closed eyes, please God to make the boy come back, keep him healthy. On business trips to Boston and Philadelphia and Atlanta his secretary was ordered to find the name of a synagogue near his hotel, and he appeared, often in a limousine, to pray silently each morning, usually beside orthodox men in prayer shawls who reminded Frederic of his father and his uncles in Austria. Frederic would place five twenty-dollar bills in the contribution box of each synagogue, except the synagogues that had the musky smell of aged men, the synagogues whose walls were peeling and whose benches left splinters in the buttocks. In those he would place three hundred dollars in the box and then disappear into his waiting limousine, a mysterious benefactor. Once, after a visit to a synagogue in Durham, when Frederic's fears and loneliness overwhelmed him and he began weeping during the prayers for the dead, the kaddish, he sent a check to the synagogue for a thousand dollars, with a note to the rabbi that he wanted his gift to remain anonymous.

Arnold was killed in combat near LaForge, France, in September 1944. A telegram said that he had died assaulting an enemy stronghold, that his body would be returned to the United States within the next month, and that the family would be notified of the exact date of the body's delivery.

Within the week the family received a second telegram, signed by President Roosevelt, informing them that Arnold Steiner had been awarded the Congressional Medal of Honor.

For displaying supreme courage and heroic initiative beyond the call of duty.

As a rifle platoon leader, Sergeant Steiner had been assigned the mission of expelling an estimated enemy force of two hundred and fifty men from a heavily fortified position near LaForge. Advancing to within fifty yards of the German position, the platoon was caught in a torrent of heavy machine-gun and rifle fire which inflicted heavy casualties on Sergeant Steiner's troops. Leaping to his feet, leading his soldiers into the raking fire, shouting encouragement, Sergeant Steiner had jumped into the lead enemy position, knocked out the gunner with his rifle, dropped a grenade and jumped out before it exploded. Crawling from one machine-gun nest to another—supported by his battered troops who pinned down the enemy with machine-gun fire—Sergeant Steiner destroyed three German positions before a grenade hurled by one of the two remaining Germans inflicted grave wounds. Suffering and bleeding profusely and against immense odds, he continued to crawl, lobbing his last grenades into the two enemy positions. He died moments after his last grenade detonated.

It was Frederic who decided that his firstborn son would be buried, with other war heroes, in Arlington Cemetery in Virginia, and that he would have a military burial, with an army rabbi officiating. He would lie in the earth like other American boys; the son of an American family, not first-generation, or Jewish, but American. The family had shed its blood, its finest blood, for America, and Arnold's death was for Frederic the ultimate confirmation that the Steiners were not strangers in America anymore, but were fixed, embedded now, in the soil of the nation that had adopted them.

*

By all outward appearances, the relationship between Frederic and Dora hardly changed after the death of Arnold Steiner. Frederic seemed absorbed in his work and in the *Star*'s expansion in the nineteen-forties and early fifties. He opened the paper now to Jonathan Steiner, who had been rejected from the military as 4-F because of chronic asthma.

Nothing unusual was said to Jonathan after the death of his brother, but two days after Arnold's funeral, Jonathan appeared in Frederic's office. Gazing shyly at his father, he said he had quit his job at New York University and was prepared to go to work for the paper. Frederic looked at his younger son and nodded his head. "Thank you," he said.

Frederic struggled to teach Jonathan every nuance of the newspaper trade, every major and minor stratagem that Arnold had picked up so effortlessly: which loyalists to promote and how to dismiss incompetents and troublemakers; whom to bribe in the police department to ensure that delivery trucks blocking the street didn't get parking tickets; whom to call in Brooklyn, if absolutely necessary, to break a stubborn union leader's leg; whom to trust in the business community and how to massage the executives of Macy's, Gimbels, Bonwit and Altman; how to deal with competitors and loosen the *Daily News*'s grip on the Negro community, the *Times*'s and *Herald Tribune*'s hold over New York's middle-class and suburban readers, the *Post*'s reign over Jewish readers. How to make dents in the circulation and advertising of the *World-Telegram,* the *Daily Mirror,* the *Journal-American* . . .

Not even Frederic's closest aides sensed that the teaching process was isolating and painful for the publisher, and that from the moment Arnold died Frederic began dying too. Although he went on living, although the paper expanded in the postwar years under his aegis, Frederic Steiner was quietly yielding to despair and knew that he had stopped reacting and was merely waiting . . .

At odd moments in the day he would open the center drawer of his George III mahogany partners' desk to stare at a photograph of Arnold, in a soldier's uniform, smiling mischievously, Arnold's smile.

Frederic began drinking rather heavily at the Harmonie Club, and on some days he would sit in the limousine after lunch and stare out the window on Central Park West and lose his memory, unsure where he was going or where he had been. He gained weight. His hands and face broke out in yellowing spots, and his chest turned flabby, like an old woman's. His speech grew blurred.

It was, indeed, ironic, that although Frederic treated women either indifferently or contemptuously during most of his life, the only people who sensed that he had surrendered to death were three disparate women—his wife Dora, his mistress Helena Standish and his daughter-in-law Frieda.

Whatever relationship had existed between Dora and Frederic before Arnold's death was now gradually severed. It was as if the years of Dora's humiliation, the years of physical pain wrought by Jonathan's birth, the years of anguish had finally climaxed in terrible grief and overwhelmed them. They barely spoke. She had done her duty, had broken her body to produce two sons, two heirs: and the one who had been the favorite, the prize, was now, stupidly, dead.

After Frederic had returned from visiting Arnold at Fort Polk, he had merely told Dora: "The answer was no. Period." At the time, her panic over Arnold staying at the home front was partly selfish: if he died, even for his own country, she would lose the child whose wildness and free spirit affirmed her own life. He had emerged from her frail body, a boy with Dora's burning eyes and a mouth so delicate (like hers) that her eyes glittered with tears when he moved close to her. Her firstborn. A beautiful child that made her life meaningful. He had to *live*.

But Dora's own needs were soon twisted, she knew, by her rage at Frederic. She despised him for his hungers and now, finally, his weakness—he had failed to keep the boy home. And Dora used this failure as a weapon, and Frederic, enduring her hatred, accepting his own guilt, fell victim to her.

Helena Standish knew that she was Frederic's slender lifeline after the death of his son. If Helena didn't quite love him, she was deeply fond of him—unlike her attitude to the other wealthy men in her past—and she sensed his own fevered yearning for her. She knew it would destroy him if she rejected him now.

She watched him age. She cooked dinners for him. Frederic would listen to the radio, to Jack Benny or the Lux Radio Theatre or Town Meeting of the Air, until he fell asleep. Then she would ring up the chauffeur and he would come and take Frederic home. Eventually Frederic bought a television set, one of the early ones, and set it up in Helena's living room, and Helena would flick the dials with delight as they watched a Yankees or Giants game. She insisted, when he seemed especially lonely, that they dine at the Colony—her favorite—or see *Carousel,* or go to the company box at the Polo Grounds and watch a Giants–Dodgers night game.

If she didn't quite know that Frederic wanted to die, she sensed his pain and vulnerability. At times she fondled him like a child; other times she made him a man, and he wept after he came into her. He abruptly told her, one evening as he sipped coffee and watched the late news, that she was being taken care of, that she would be a comfortable woman for the rest of her life. It was the first time Frederic had indicated to her that he had thought about dying. She said, "Thank you." And when she wanted to say something further, he lifted his hand and said, "That's enough."

Frieda Schiffer Steiner was hardly the kind of young woman

that Frederic would have favored: she was not pretty, and since she had proved somewhat pushy, Frederic initially preferred to avoid her, daughter-in-law or not. He knew, moreover, that she came from old German-Jewish stock that viewed people like Frederic Steiner with contempt. If Frederic was barred from the Shinnecock Club in Southampton and from the New York Athletic Club because he was Jewish, he was also barred from an assortment of German-Jewish clubs in New York City and Westchester because he was not German-Jewish. It was all too demeaning and complicated, he told Frieda, and she agreed.

He knew that Frieda enacted the role of a traditional Park Avenue mother and housewife, a woman who cared about the children, dinner, vacations and making her home as pleasant as possible for her husband. But he knew, too, that Frieda had an instinctive grasp of the newspaper business. She was surprisingly street-smart and, although she initially reserved her judgments and opinions for Jonathan when he returned home from the *Star,* she began gradually to voice them loudly to Frederic. She even began typing memos to Frederic!

Shouldn't the Star's *women's page employ a cook who can write recipes?*

Shouldn't the staff write more about the problems of returning servicemen?

At a dinner party the other night, people were talking about Henry Wallace—perhaps the Washington bureau should see him.

Wouldn't it be interesting to have Margaret Truman talk about living in the White House?

I've heard (from our maid) that there's a slew of Negro jazz clubs in the East Fifties as well as in Harlem. Is that a story?

The circulation problem on Eighty-sixth and Lexington Avenue remains unsolved. Friends who get there at 10 A.M. can't find a copy of the Star. *Isn't that appalling? We still don't deliver enough papers to the newsstands . . .*

At first Frederic was amused, then annoyed, and then he began reading the memos from his daughter-in-law more carefully because he noticed that her only motive (since her husband was fated to be publisher) was to create a better newspaper. He began taking her to lunch and listening to this strong-willed, opinionated, not always tactful young woman whom his son had had the good sense to marry.

Although Frieda may have sensed her father-in-law's despair, she knew it was neither her business nor good manners to pry into a man's—especially an older man's—life. He listened to her attentively and patted her on the hand, and they spoke of young Skipper and little Lucy during dessert. It was only when she stopped talking and stared into his eyes—mournful, vacant, liquid eyes—that Frieda realized the depth of her father-in-law's suffering and pain.

*

After the death of Jonathan in 1968, Frieda, with her children grown and married, began extending her weekends at the Steiner family home in Purchase, arriving on Friday morning and returning to New York on Monday or Tuesday. Within a year she had moved up to Purchase, with Hector and Louisa, who had served the Steiners for years. Hector was driver and handyman; Louisa served as cook, maid and, to Frieda, companion.

Frieda spent hours each morning in the gardens surrounding the house, tilling the soil, seeding and pruning the leaves of thyme and mint that flourished each spring, spraying the tomatoes and eggplant and summer squash that were presented proudly to her children.

Late in the mornings, after Louisa had served a cup of freshly brewed coffee in the sun room, Frieda would light up a cigarette that she smoked through an art deco holder. Having read the *Star,* the *Times* and the *Daily News* at breakfast, she now scanned *The Wall Street Journal* and made her daily round of phone calls to friends in New York. Especially to Eli Faber, her financial adviser.

Eli briefed Frieda on any last-minute circulation or advertising problems on the *Star,* listened to her grumbles about a story in the *News* or the *Times* that beat the *Star,* heard her complaints about the way Sally Sims or Ward Parsons or Barry Cohen handled their respective staffs. Frieda seemed to focus on one editor every few days, targeting Sally, for example, for failing to get more colorful national pieces, or being "obsessed" with such issues as abortion or school prayer, publishing too many downbeat stories on poverty and racial issues.

Eli endured these telephone conversations because Frieda was lonely and cranky, and because he knew—as most of the staff knew—that this elderly woman still reigned firmly over the *Star* and assured his position as an executive on the board. Skipper only tolerated him, the way the publisher tolerated Frieda's other favorites. And Eli was aware, with equal measures of forbearance and bitterness, that the nearly forty years he had given to the *Star* —he had started out, after all, as a fifteen-year-old messenger in Frederic Steiner's office—would inevitably turn into ashes; that the publisher, who had grown up before Eli's eyes, would gracelessly shuffle him aside once Frieda departed.

The long telephone chat would end with a ritual review of early trading on the stock market, with what was happening to Frieda's substantial holdings in Xerox, RCA, DuPont, General Motors, and an assortment of small utilities and computer firms whose value had grown sharply since the early fifties. Frieda and Jonathan had quietly purchased these stocks at Faber's suggestion.

After she hung up the phone, Frieda would return to the garden and the array of tulips, lilies and irises flanking the stone driveway. Bougainvillea draped over the door of the house, a Mediterranean-style villa purchased by Frederic in 1943, nine years before he died.

It was a splendid home that isolated Frieda from New York and the *Star*. The Park Avenue apartment, with its works by Augustus John, Tintoretto and John Singer Sargent, with its Chinese wallpaper covering the bedroom and dining room, its mahogany-paneled library and Regency cut-glass chandeliers, bore the shadow of, the presence of, Frederic Steiner.

It had been Frederic's dream to turn Bella Verde into his own version of San Simeon—smaller and more tasteful, of course—but, nonetheless, a flamboyant showplace whose receptions and dinners would welcome the politicians of the day, the writers and artists, the thinkers, the economists and teachers. It was envisioned as a house to serve as Frederic's final monument. But Arnold's death shattered that dream. Frederic had stopped buying art sometime in 1944, and Bella Verde gradually was handed over, except in title, to Jonathan and his family for weekends and holidays. Frederic rarely visited the place after 1944, except for Thanksgiving dinners with Jonathan, Frieda, Lucy and Skipper.

At his death in Helena Standish's apartment in 1952, Frederic had visited the opulent home in Purchase fewer than half a dozen times.

When Jonathan Steiner appeared in Helena Standish's apartment after her anguished phone call, and saw his father sprawled on the bed in his beige silk shorts, he ordered Helena to stop crying and shut up, called the police commissioner, who sent an unmarked ambulance and removed Frederic to Bellevue Hospital, where the publisher was pronounced dead. The police commissioner, who had dined with Frederic once a month at the publisher's office and had managed to find an envelope containing five hundred dollars under his plate of overcooked roast beef at each luncheon, was only too pleased to accommodate the Steiner family. Officially, Frederic Steiner collapsed of a heart attack in his apartment on Park Avenue at about 8:30 P.M. while dining with his son Jonathan, who called a police ambulance. The driver of the ambulance and the medical attendant (two Navy veterans who had been wounded in the Pacific and honorably discharged in 1944) signed the official police certificate after separate chats with the commissioner. Coincidentally, the driver and the medical attendant were promoted to sergeant three days after the funeral.

Because Frederic had been unable to leave his powerful imprint on Bella Verde, the house was warm, eclectic, and relatively simple, its dining room and kitchen covered with dark-beamed ceilings, its tile and wood floors blanketed with matting and Mexican rugs. The decor somehow calmed Frieda, a jittery woman, who in Purchase walked barefoot through the house, humming and listening to the radio.

Once a week now, perhaps twice, depending on the time of year, Frieda came in to New York for lunch with Skipper or Lucy. For a matinee with her sister. Or a museum visit. Or for financial consultations with Eli Faber. Or, as Frieda knew, to escape the silence of Bella Verde. To stay in touch.

On these trips to the city, Frieda spent the night in the Park Avenue apartment. It seemed increasingly remote and eerie—as if she were a guest in the quarters of a wealthy stranger, or as if the apartment was not rightfully hers, as if the Steiner children had not been raised there. Skipper, since his divorce, had held large dinner parties there; the grandchildren used it on trips to New

York; the family held conferences in the living room, private conferences away from the newspaper.

It was unthinkable to sell the apartment because it represented Frederic and the past, it symbolized the family's tradition. And, of course, it was enormously useful.

And on the morning of Evan Claiborne's funeral, Frieda was, indeed, grateful that the family had an apartment where she could freshen up before the service, where Paul, of Kenneth, could slip in and shape her hair, and where the Steiners could properly receive guests after the funeral.

The 10 A.M. funeral service at St. Thomas's Episcopal Church on Fifth Avenue at Fifty-third Street was packed, the pews filled with the powerful in New York's interlocking community of financiers, businessmen, publishing executives, politicians and heads of foundations. In the first row, facing the ornate marble reredos, with its sculptured saints and angels and lambs drinking from rivers, sat the Steiner family: Lucy Steiner Claiborne in black crepe and veil, flanked by her daughter Johanna, and her brother Skipper.

Beside Skipper sat his son Larry, as well as his mother, Frieda, who had taken two Valiums and who stared throughout the service at the center of the reredos, behind the altar, with its cross of the vine rising from a shield containing a chalice circled by a crown of thorns. She read the words, "This do in Remembrance of Me." Frieda's hands, gripping the Bible, began trembling as the brief service began.

There was no option *except* a service at St. Thomas's. Evan had been a nominal Episcopalian who had endured two separate marriage ceremonies to Lucy, one at St. Thomas's, the other at the Park Avenue Synagogue. At his death, a church funeral was inevitable.

And yet the decision left Frieda in a dark mood. She hated walking up the steps of St. Thomas's—or, for that matter, into St. Bartholomew's on Park Avenue, or the Madison Avenue Presbyterian Church; she was uncomfortable with their smooth-faced ministers preaching love of mankind and forgiveness.

Too many memories. Antisemitic slights by the power brokers in New York who heard the word of God in these churches. She knew that Skipper and Lucy laughed at her touchiness, but what they failed to understand—*what they could never understand*—was that the incidents and attitudes of the 1920s and 1930s and even 1940s had made Frieda fiercely sensitive to overt and latent antisemitism. Petty hypocrisy had kept Jonathan out of the New York Athletic Club, and Skipper out of two Princeton eating clubs, the Jewish quotas at Brearley and Bryn Mawr, the first fight that Frederic touched off at the Shinnecock Golf Club when a Wall Street friend and member of the club was turned away after Frederic signed his name to the guest list; the nasty innuendos and comments that stung Frieda at dinner parties, leaving her aware that Jews were, indeed, vulnerable, and that even in New York there were powerful worlds in which Jews were scorned.

After the brief service, as she moved through the central door of the church, Frieda, leaning on Lucy's arm, whispered: "Norman was perfect." The *Star*'s European columnist, Norman Walker, Jr., who had attended Yale with Evan, had delivered a sermon.

"He always is."

"He caught Evan beautifully," Frieda said, ignoring the dry sarcasm in Lucy's voice.

Two photographers hurried down the steps, pointing their cameras at the two women. Larry Steiner, Skipper's son, moved beside Lucy and took her left arm. Frieda, in an ankle-length mink and low black shoes, held shakily onto Lucy.

"Aunt Lucy, I'm sorry," whispered Larry, kissing her on the cheek.

"Don't be," said Lucy in a hoarse whisper.

"Widowhood becomes you."

"I look dreadful," Lucy murmured.

Frieda, confused, overhearing Lucy, said firmly, "You look like a widow."

"Are those *ours?*" asked Lucy, glaring at the two photographers.

"The girl is from *People*," said Larry. "The boy, I think, is *Women's Wear*."

A crowd converged around them on the steps. Frieda extricated her fingers from Lucy's hand to embrace Eli Faber.

"I want to get out of here," said Lucy, elbowing Larry forward, pressing through the crush of churchgoers, leaving her mother behind and walking determinedly down the steps.

A row of black limousines, lined up in front of the church, stretched along Fifty-third Street. Reporters and photographers clustered at the bottom of the steps, plastic New York City police cards draped around their necks.

"A media event," Larry said.

"Just stay with me," said Lucy, gripping his slim, cold hand. She winced at Frieda's too loud voice behind her, bellowing orders like a battlefield commander.

"Lucy! You and Skipper get in the first car. I'll join you. Larry, you ride in the second car with Johanna."

Lucy saw Linda Fentress threading through the crowd, trailing blond hair. She was a striking girl whose tight jeans and clinging shirts in the newsroom had upset Frieda and led her to make a quiet complaint to Evan about what some of the younger staff women, specifically Ms. Fentress, wore to work. Instead of dealing with the problem seriously, however, Evan had leaned back on his swivel chair and laughed. His authority over the newsroom did not extend to telling sexy women what to wear, he said. And besides, wouldn't the confrontation with Linda lead to something like a dozen articles in *New York Magazine* and *The Village Voice,* to a ballet, an opera, an off-Broadway play, and a candlelight march to the *Star* building to protest the *Star*'s oppression of women? Evan had stopped laughing and turned serious. Fentress is tough, Frieda, she's smart . . .

Beyond Linda Fentress, Lucy noticed David Fitzgerald walking down the church steps. Confronted by photographers, Fitzgerald tilted his chin up and started to smile, then caught himself awkwardly—the occasion was too somber for even a perfunctory little grin.

Then Lucy saw Fitzgerald narrow his eyes on a point in the crowd beside the photographers. He stiffened; his lips curled in an odd grimace. Lucy followed his gaze: Barry Cohen and Howie Bishop were standing perfectly still at the base of the steps, staring at Fitzgerald. For a moment Lucy was transfixed, startled at the silent exchange. A look of anger (was it contempt?) passed across Fitzgerald's face.

"We should go to the cars, Aunt Lucy," Larry said quietly. "Frieda's ready."

Then he murmured, "You're playing the role very well. Like a Joan Crawford movie."

"Lana Turner," Lucy said.

"Bette Davis." He reached to open the door of the limousine. Lucy lifted her eyes and caught David Fitzgerald watching her.

*

Sally saw Ward Parsons escorting Florence through the crowd on the church steps, and waved, mouthing the word "Office?" and pointing toward Fifty-third Street. Florence nodded, and the three of them found a taxi. They rode then in silence, Sally staring vacantly out the window. Ward saw the same look of strain wrench her mouth and deep-set hazel eyes that he had seen over the past few months. He was about to ask her about her husband Charlie, but held back.

"Can Maury handle the job?" Florence suddenly said.

Ward waited a beat. "He'll be first-rate."

"Maury *deserves* it," said Sally.

"Maury's always been second man, though," said Ward, glancing at Sally. "Always a deputy. A good deputy, but always a deputy. Never been overseas either."

"He *deserves* it," said Sally, impatiently, stubbing out her second cigarette.

"He deserves it," said Ward, "but he may not *get* it."

Florence looked at Ward. "You want it, darling, don't you?"

Ward turned to face Florence and Sally. "I got calls yesterday. Evan not even dead twenty-four hours. From the press section of *Time, New York Magazine.* Asking who would get the job. Was I up for it."

"Of *course* you're up for it," said Florence quickly. "You and Maury and . . . Barry. City staff's gonna win a Pulitzer under Barry, wait and see." She stared at Ward. "Who else? Hugh Finch. Don't ignore Hughie. Wouldn't it give Skipper and Frieda *points* to name a black managing editor. And speaking of points . . . I wouldn't ignore the possibility of a *woman* managing editor."

Sally looked up at Ward. "They called me too."

"Honey, you'll be on the cover of *Ms.* magazine," Florence said.

Sally ignored the coldness in Florence's voice. "What I've always craved," she said lightly.

It was raining harder now, as the taxi glided to a halt in front of the *Star* building on West Fifty-first Street. The two women walked quickly into the building, and waited for Ward in the lobby as he paid the fare.

Stepping into an elevator, Ward turned to Florence as he pressed the seventh-floor button, and said that he was stopping at the cafeteria for coffee.

"Join me," he suddenly said to Sally. Florence's eyes darted from Ward to Sally and back again to Ward, and she smiled vaguely as the elevator door rumbled open on the fifth floor. Florence got out without a word.

Sally studied Ward's face, aware of an abrupt dryness on her tongue. His thin, gaunt, muscled look testified to the changes in his life, a life in ferment. The death of his child followed by his wife's decision to remain behind in India, Ward's drinking that stopped when he began to live with Florence, and his ulcers, his jogging and squash, had given his face a weathered, almost haunted look that Sally found intriguing for the first time. In the past, Ward's engaging charm had been just a little too boyish and bland. No more.

Sally eyed his charcoal pinstripe suit. "Quite elegant," she said, as they waited in line in the dank cafeteria. Because the elderly women behind the counter babbled and called to each other in German and Polish, the newsroom staff referred to the cafeteria as the Gulag.

"My one new suit. It *fits*. Two hundred and ninety-five bucks. Broke my budget." He carried their coffee on a tray to a corner table.

As Sally sat, looking up at Ward, she felt her hands run cold. "Must be difficult financially. Karen in India . . ." Sally flinched, regretting the words at once.

"Most of my money goes to Karen and the girls. The rest to Florence. I have about thirty cents spending money."

"Is that why you want the job?"

"I'd be *good,* Sally. Damn it, I *know* I'd be good." He drew back, surprised at the intensity of his voice. "We have *talent* on the paper. Wasted, burned-out reporters. People shunted aside years ago. Guys who gave up. The walking wounded in the newsroom."

"You'll bring them back to life, is that it?"

"The paper's in trouble, right? We're in a financial squeeze. Can't hire reporters. Morale's at rock bottom. Well, let's *ignite* the staff. Produce a paper that makes us proud. We've been so beaten down over the past few years we can do it, we can . . ."

"The job is Maury's," said Sally, looking right at him. "It *should* be Maury's."

"You want it too."

She kept her eyes fixed on his face. "Yes."

"It may be time for a woman."

"That's a dumb put-down."

"It wasn't meant to be."

"Ward, we need someone imaginative. *Creative.*"

"And if you're a woman, you're more . . ."

"Goddamn it, listen to me. We've got to get away from the tired, old, clichéd way of covering stories. Try some new approaches. Shake things up a bit. Be *daring.*" Suddenly Sally paused and looked down at her coffee. "I won't get it, Ward. I'm a woman, yes, and besides it's just too . . ."

"Complicated." Ward spoke with a gentleness that surprised her. She opened her mouth as if to speak, but held back.

"Yes," Sally whispered. "Complicated.

"There are five of us, Ward. Five contenders. You heard Florence."

"Maury's the front-runner."

"Good newspaperman. Honest. Hardworking." She stared at Ward. "It'll destroy Maury if he doesn't get the job."

Ward's gaze slid to the table. "Then there's you, Sally. You and me. And Barry . . ."

"Barry's the throat-cutter, the son of a bitch," interrupted Sally. "Watch out."

"And Hugh Finch," said Ward quietly.

"A little too brash," said Sally. "Hotheaded."

"Hugh's the guy to watch," said Ward, absently folding his

paper napkin. "The kind of surprise choice that Frieda and Skipper may just turn to. They're pushing black readership now. They say that's the untapped market in town, the market we've never exploited."

"And Hugh is black and la-de-da."

"So what do we have?" He looked at her, smiling. "Maury's in the lead. Hugh and me neck and neck behind him. Barry coming up fast. Sally Sims, starting slow, a long shot, but some last-minute heavy betting on the elegant filly with the good breeding."

"The elegant filly has very little chance against the studs. The elegant filly wants to win but is ambivalent, and feeling vulnerable." She tried to laugh.

"How's Charlie?" Ward abruptly asked.

"Charlie is . . . fine." She let it hang in the air, then said, "Heard from Karen?"

"Last week. Four-page letter."

"Still in Delhi?"

"Still in Delhi," Ward said. "Still screwing around with her dancing and her yoga. Still . . . screwing."

Sally watched the slant of sun on Ward's forehead.

"Is he nice?" Sally asked, biting her lip at the foolishness of the question.

"For an Indian pediatrician and widower he's nice. Very nice. Too fucking nice." Ward smiled. "Karen wants to stay through the kids' school year. She doesn't want to talk about divorce. She wants to talk about her dancing . . ."

"What's it called?"

"Bharatanatyam. It's the so-called 'true dance' of India. She takes lessons every morning. She swims or goes horseback riding each afternoon. She reads Jane Austen. She's found *peace.*"

"And the kids?"

"The kids are going to the American School at great expense. *My* great expense."

"It's cheaper than her having a breakdown in New York."

"She's so *angry!*"

Sally watched his hands crumple the paper napkin beside his coffee cup. He opened his fist, tearing the soft paper into scattered pieces with both hands.

"Look, I know she's pissed," said Ward. "I know she did not

want to move back after being in Delhi only fourteen months. We'd moved all over, enough. She's *had* it with moving. Sick of it. Tokyo. Moscow. That was a bitch for her. She was pregnant most of the time. Then Cairo. Tel Aviv. She's tired. She wanted something to hang onto, something for herself. She'd raised the kids alone, that's true. I played foreign correspondent and she played housewife. She wanted to stay in *one place* for a while. She wanted to get into something, do something with her *life*. She cried when we left Tel Aviv. She had just enrolled in school there. I understand, I know. It's a crummy life for a woman, dragging after a husband who's never there. I *understand*. And then Lacey died and everything just unraveled."

He spoke with such intensity that, for several seconds, Ward failed to notice the pudgy, frizzy-haired blond woman in a white cafeteria uniform standing beside him. She was the sandwich woman, the one that copy boys called Eva Braun.

"Mr. Parsons, excuse," she said in a heavy European accent. "Telephone call. Your desk. Foreign desk."

He stared at the woman, then nodded. "I'll be right back," he said.

It was Florence.

"Ward, Carl Ross is on the phone from Hong Kong. Says it's urgent. Wants to talk to you."

"Be down in a minute. Hold him on the phone."

Carl Ross.

Ward set the phone down.

Carl. A correspondent who had spent twenty-six years in Asia, spoke Mandarin, ran the Peking bureau now.

Carl and Ruth Ross.

Ward stepped quickly to the table and told Sally that he had an urgent call from Carl Ross in Hong Kong. Ward saw her smile and thought he caught the tremor on Sally's lips.

She knew. Of course she knew. Did anyone on the *Star* not know about his affair with Ruth Ross. Part of the newsroom's folklore: Ward banged Ruth Ross while poor, dumb Carl was off in the boondocks . . .

"See you soon, Foreign Editor," said Sally.

He turned on his heels and threaded through the cafeteria, feeling the sweat dampen his chest. *Ruth Ross*. There was the wife of

a Swedish diplomat in Moscow, the blond Israeli photographer
who said he reminded her of Montgomery Clift, the Radcliffe junior on an archaeological dig in Cairo, and . . . Ruth.

"I'm another Hong Kong widow," she had said, letting him
light her cigarette across the dinner table on the screened porch of
the Repulse Bay Hotel. It was 1969. Carl was in Saigon, Ward on
a week-long holiday in Hong Kong. His knee brushed against hers
for a moment, and Ruth let it linger when he shifted his feet beneath the table. Her children were visiting friends in Singapore,
she said, smiling.

In the Rosses' apartment, she began unbuttoning his shirt and,
with her left hand, running her fingers over his chest. Ward
pushed her down a little too hard on a leather sofa in the center of
the living room. He bit her on the ear, and then licked her neck as
his right hand pushed beneath the caftan. He felt her wetness, her
eagerness. He was trembling. He had spent weeks in Vietnam,
working and traveling and losing himself in the story. He needed a
woman.

His visits to Hong Kong were timed then to coincide with Carl's
trips to Saigon. When Ruth's children were home she spent the afternoons with Ward at the Mandarin, eating lunch in his room and
then making love and taking a shower together and finally leaving
at five or six. On some evenings he even accompanied her to dinner parties—there were always Vietnam reporters moving in and
out and mingling at the parties given by the Hong Kong wives,
who seemed either lonely and tortured or who reveled in the fruits
of colonial living, playing tennis and buying clothes and employ-
ing a Chinese cook and ayah.

He saw her persistently over the years, the last time in Delhi
when the Rosses visited them. Ruth feigned illness the first day as
Karen took Carl and the children to Agra and the Taj Mahal. Moments after they left, Ward stepped into her room at the Ashoka
Hotel, lifting her up in his arms in a fever, plunging into her again
and again and . . .

Four days later—while accompanying the Rosses to Bombay, he
didn't have to go, absolutely unnecessary it was except for one
more taste of Ruth—he got the hysterical call from Karen.

Lacey had woken from her bed in the middle of the afternoon
while everyone napped, the child had moved downstairs, man-

aged to unfasten the gate to the fence, and toddled over to the
pool . . .

Damn. *Damn!*

Ward was standing in the elevator now, clenching his fists, a
spasm of ulcer pain twisting like a knife in the pit of his stomach.
His eyes, shut tight, burned with tears as he listened to the creak
of the elevator drop slowly to the fifth-floor newsroom.

CHAPTER 5

On the church steps Maury had gripped Nancy Chang's hand and
begun moving, with the surging crowd, toward the street. Her
body was sheathed in a snug black leather coat with fur collar.
She shivered as the wind buffeted Fifth Avenue.

"You take a cab, luv, I'll walk," she had said.

"Going home?"

"Eventually," she said. "I just want to walk downtown for a
while. Get this out of my head."

Maury saw Ward, Florence and Sally climb into a cab. Senator
David Fitzgerald and his aide, Jerry Paley, were stepping into a
black limousine right behind them. He held onto Nancy.

"Stay with me," Maury said.

"Darling . . ."

"Stay with me for a couple of minutes."

"Not here."

"Why?"

"*Not* here."

He turned to her and sought to smile. At these moments, Maury
knew, Nancy was somehow unreachable, gripped by inner terrors
that seemed to engulf her. The crowd—the scene—terrified her.

He held tight onto her hand, ushered her through a cluster of
Newsweek and Washington *Post* people huddled together on the
steps. One of them, a *Newsweek* senior editor who had floundered
on the *Star* for a year and then quit, turned to stare at Nancy.

Her silky black hair was tousled, in disarray. Maury smelled
her perfume, the Givenchy that she used like water.

"Who was that?" she whispered as they reached the street.
"That guy staring . . ."

"Some *Newsweek* prick who didn't make it on the *Star*. He's
envious."

"Of what?"

"Of me," Maury said. "For having you."

"I'm walking downtown," she said.

"Supposed to rain. I want to kiss you."

"Here? In front of all . . ."

"Yeah."

"No. *No*. Later." She tightened her hand on his, and then extricated her fingers. "You're going to be managing editor, darling.
Managing editors don't kiss their live-in mates in front of the
troops."

*

Hugh Finch pushed through the crowd quickly, eyes darting,
aware of a surge of unexpected sorrow in his throat. Evan had
promoted him, named him Washington bureau chief, the first
black to hold the job. Plucked Hugh from the White House beat
and placed him at the top.

He saw Maury Kramer climb into a cab in front of 666 Fifth
Avenue, and started to cross the street to try and catch him, but
the light flicked to red and two cars lurched past him. He cursed
and glanced at his watch—eleven-fifteen—and dashed, instead,
across Fifth Avenue to hunt for a taxi on Madison.

Despite the bulk of his leather attaché case and his Aquascutum
trench coat, Hugh began trotting east. He *had* to catch the noon
shuttle from LaGuardia to Washington. He *had* to make that
plane.

His 1:30 P.M. appointment with the Secretary of Defense, Edward Belling, had been made that morning when Belling's military
assistant had called to ask Hugh if he could appear at the Defense
Secretary's office at nine-thirty. Hugh, who had sought a meeting
with Belling for weeks, had said he was flying to New York to attend the funeral of his managing editor and could they fix another
time. Was it possible for Hugh to show up at one-thirty? Hugh
had agreed, knowing it would be a close call to make the appointment on time, wondering why the hell Defense Secretary Belling
wanted to see him so urgently.

He found a cab on Madison and told the driver he had to catch the noon shuttle to Washington. The driver, a middle-aged black man who kept the *Daily News* and a thermos of coffee on the seat beside him, looked at his watch and turned.

"Don't worry, Ace," he said. Hugh grinned and settled back in the cab.

It had been a funeral service devoid of sentiment and passion, he thought, a rich white man's last honors that seemed cold, impassive. He hated funerals, dreaded them. His first one, at the age of six, had terrified him because his mother and grandmother and aunts had wailed and pounded their chests. And when the audience sang, "What a friend we have in Jesus," as Hugh's father's pallbearers carried the casket up the aisle of the Bebee Memorial Christian Methodist Church on Thirty-first Street in Oakland, Hugh dissolved into tears, shameless, uncontrollable tears that humiliated the little boy who had just been told by the Reverend Robinson from the pulpit that he was now the man in the family. The tears turned to fear—a fear of death that haunted him.

He was forty-two years old: his father was dead, killed by two white policemen after a foolhardy attempt to rob a liquor store near the Oakland Army Terminal; his mother was a cleaning woman who read the Bible twice a day and attended a Methodist church on North Capitol Street in Washington, D.C., all day Sunday.

He had an ex-wife at George Washington University Medical School whom he never saw, and two pampered children at Sidwell Friends who moved so effortlessly in the white world that it angered him. He had a white mistress who fondled his cock in the movies and, last week, had jerked him off at a Chinese restaurant on I Street.

He had had scholarships to Howard University and then the Columbia University School of Journalism (where he met such editors on the *Star* as Maury Kramer, who taught courses there). Shrewdness and an innate confidence enabled him to operate on a white man's newspaper, through a fiber of toughness that allowed him to distance himself from a past that could have crippled him. Hugh Finch was now one of the most prominent black journalists in the country.

He had begun as a reporter in New York covering the courts,

but was quickly transferred to the Washington bureau, which was in dire need of a black reporter under Arthur Weaver, the *Star*'s bureau chief. Years ago, Weaver had had the luck to win a Pulitzer Prize (for his coverage of a plane crash in Queens) and the wisdom to ingratiate himself with Frieda Steiner, who appointed him chief of the three-person Washington bureau in 1955. Before Hugh Finch took over, the bureau had grown to ten people under Weaver—ten carefully selected and perfectly groomed Californians who, like Weaver himself, were remarkably tall, remarkably thin and, by and large, shockingly incompetent (especially compared to their colleagues on the *Times* and *Daily News*).

It had been impossible for the *Star* to compete with other papers while Weaver was bureau chief. The *Star* had been hurt badly by the *Times*'s exclusive on the Pentagon Papers, the Washington *Post*'s Watergate coverage. Weaver was an untouchable; whenever he was threatened by such bullies (his phrase) as Evan and Maury, he phoned Frieda, and the editors were forced to back down.

Before his retirement at sixty-five, Weaver had groomed his successor, Barney Fischer, a Yalie and son of a diplomat with a reputation for nastiness. ("He backstabbed his way to the middle," Evan said.) Adamant that the line of succession had to be broken, Evan, Skipper and Maury met secretly, like plotters of a Middle East coup, to decide how to wrest Washington away from Arthur Weaver and his acolytes. The opportunity came during Frieda's vacation in London and Paris.

With startling abruptness Skipper announced late one Friday afternoon that he was saddened to report Arthur Weaver's retirement and the appointment of White House correspondent Hugh Finch to replace him as Washington bureau chief. The formal announcement had stunned Weaver and enraged Frieda, but by the time she had returned to New York—and received congratulatory messages from her friends and several interreligious and black groups praising the *Star* for its appointment of a black man to run its largest, most prestigious bureau—Frieda was mollified to the point of telling Skipper that the selection of Hugh Finch was, indeed, a credit to the liberalism of the *Star*. Ironically, Barney Fischer, who told his friends that he was a victim of affirmative action, wound up as a surprisingly able reporter covering the

White House, a man whose sudden midlife crisis resulted in two divorces, elaborate EST therapy, and a reputation for womanizing that would have amazed his former mentor, Arthur Weaver.

Hugh was told by the New York office to enliven the coverage from Washington, and he did so. He brought in New York reporters, hired some tough investigative types from the Detroit *News* and Philadelphia *Inquirer,* and stole away some women and blacks from *Newsday* and AP.

Hugh was aggressive—too aggressive, according to his own reporters. He wrested stories from his own staff and manipulated the bureau to his own needs—he wrote news analyses and front-page stories that should have been written by Fischer and the others; he accompanied the diplomatic correspondent on major trips undertaken by the Secretary of State and skimmed off the cream, wrote the stories; he set up interviews with the Secretary of Health and Human Services, and failed to inform the reporter who covered that agency.

As bureau chief, Hugh wasn't precisely running the staff of reporters—proud, insecure, independent reporters—he was competing with them, seeking to prove, somehow, that he was the best reporter in Washington, that his blackness was irrelevant, that his appointment was made on merit, and merit alone.

In the past six months, though, Hugh had eased off. It was naïve, he thought, naïve and counterproductive to ignore his color as one of the key motives for his promotion. Sam Hunter, his deputy, who had worked for Weaver and covered Congress for years, told him gently over numerous lunches at Mel Krupin's and The Class Reunion, that he was pressing too hard, undercutting morale, which, even in the best of times, was precarious in Washington.

Hugh slowed his pace and began to choose his stories selectively, focusing on exclusives and "think pieces" that were prominently displayed in the *Star.* Morale in the small bureau was gradually picking up. And Hugh, increasingly confident, began to move into the social whirl that he had ignored because it had intimidated him. He started attending parties at Polly Fritchey's and Pamela Harriman's salons; he *was* the *Star*'s Washington bureau, an articulate, good-looking black man, a perfect guest on the Washington circuit.

The taxi arrived at the Eastern shuttle terminal at eleven forty-five—fifteen minutes to spare—and Hugh thanked the driver, tipping him two dollars. He walked quickly into the terminal, scribbled his name on the boarding pass and stopped, suddenly, for a flickering moment. Why, *why* was Defense Secretary Belling so eager to see him?

*

He removed a yellow pad and a felt-tipped pen from his briefcase and began writing memos to members of the bureau, memos that his secretary would type up and place in the reporters' mail slots. The first memo was to his deputy Sam Hunter.

"Sam, let's get together with the staff to talk about the Administration's internal divisions. CIA versus Defense. CIA has the Vice President in its corner. Defense has Dave Fitzgerald. (What's at stake? Money? Power? Both of them circling each other in advance of next year's presidential election.)

As the front door of the plane closed, Hugh looked up and watched the last few passengers step through the aisle. His eyes locked on one of them, a man in his fifties. Curly gray hair and dark eyes that peered through square, rimless glasses. He carried a blue overcoat in his left hand, and a zippered, pale-brown leather overnight bag in his right. The man wore a fitted tweed jacket with two pens stuck in the lapel, a pale-blue shirt with striped tie, gray cuffless trousers and—Hugh noticed—black tasseled loafers. He brushed against Hugh's armrest and moved toward the rear of the plane. Hugh noticed that his fingernails were carefully manicured. He smelled of expensive cologne.

Hugh turned and watched him. The man was familiar. Was he someone Hugh had interviewed, or met, or seen on television? It was several years ago.

Who was he?

The man asked the stewardess to hang up his coat and then sat down in an aisle seat at the rear of the plane. Hugh turned forward, biting his lip.

He could be a college professor or an economist. A consultant. The clothes were just a bit too carefully chosen and expensive. Everything fit perfectly. The man went to a chic barber, his nails manicured, his overnight bag was Italian-made, thickly leathered.

The gleaming black tasseled loafers added a frivolous touch, jaunty.

A New Yorker en route to Washington. Dapper. Moneyed. Pens in his lapel. *Familiar.*

Hugh shook his head, then tried to concentrate on the yellow pad as the plane lumbered over the runway.

Following takeoff, when the stewardess announced that seat belts could be unlocked, Hugh turned to look at the man, who was hidden now behind the rows of seats. Restless, the image of the man gnawing at him, Hugh opened his briefcase, placed his yellow pad inside and rose.

He walked to the rear of the plane toward the toilets, staring at the man, who glanced up at Hugh and then returned to his newspaper. He was reading the *Star.*

Hugh stood at the rear of the plane, picking up old magazines in black cardboard covers that crowded two shelves.

It was someone who had attended a press conference. A press conference in Washington. At the White House. Two years ago, maybe three.

Hugh stared at the man intently—he caught his profile as the man read the *Star*'s editorial page. A woman gripping the hand of a three-year-old boy moved past Hugh toward the toilet. Hugh leaned forward, catching a view of the man's leather attaché case resting on the seat beside him. Above the lock on the case there were three initials: S.E.P.

The man was a New Yorker. Well-to-do. Not in government. A teacher . . . an economist . . . a doctor.

A doctor.

A doctor.

The man was one of the doctors who had treated the Speaker of the House for cancer. Spoke to reporters after Merton Keefer, Democrat of Florida, had his lung removed.

Hugh remembered covering the crowded, chaotic press conference on the steps of Walter Reed Army Hospital when the President had visited Keefer. The doctor had stood beside the President —it was snowing softly, shortly before Christmas—and answered questions about Keefer's condition.

It was the same man. Dr. . . . Pomerance. Seymour Pom-

erance. A prominent cancer specialist. Connected with New
York Hospital. Dr. Seymour E. Pomerance.

Hugh walked down the aisle and settled into his seat as the
stewardesses collected fares. He removed the air travel card from
his wallet and waited for the stewardess to reach him.

Seymour E. Pomerance. Doctor.

*

Ward reached for the phone on the foreign desk.

"Carl?"

"Can you hear me, Ward?"

"Speak louder."

"All right. We got a hell of a story here. The shit is flying on
the Russian-Chinese border. *Heavy* fighting. Damansky Island is
one place. Artillery, tanks, A.P.C.'s, the works. *Major* battle. Russians are calling it a quote somber and impudent provocation
unquote."

Ward said: "Damansky Is . . ."

". . . the same place the Chinese and Soviets fought in sixty-
nine," said Ross. "Both China and Russia claim it. One of hundreds of islands created by a river there, the Ussuri, a border
river. Peking radio said the incident is developing quote unquote."

"Look, Carl, get all that high up in the story. Explain all this
bullshit like . . . like you're talking to an average reader. Like A-
B-C. Like say where this area is."

"Like it's the eastern part of the Chinese-Soviet border."

"Explain it. *Explain* it."

Ray Silver jumped up, his eyes blinking. "Here it is," he cried.
"Reuters. AP bulletin." He tossed two sheets of paper on Ward's
desk.

"Okay," said Ward into the phone. "AP and Reuters are starting to file. What else do you have?"

"Unconfirmed report of at least three, maybe four explosions
on the Trans-Siberian Railroad."

"That's new."

"That's new and that's bound to inflame the Russians. *Outrage*
them. That railroad is a lifeline. Food to the military. Fuel. Supplies."

"Americans at the mission here and in the Embassy in Peking
are in a tizzy," Carl Ross went on. "About thirty minutes ago

Peking radio interrupted its news commentary with some very, *very* strong language on the Russians and then played twenty-five minutes, *unscheduled* minutes, of martial music. That, coupled with the border fighting and railroad explosions . . ."

"We'll get Soviet reaction," said Ward.

"I'll file in the next couple of hours."

"Early copy. Give me a story soon. How much space you need?"

"Column and a half."

"Okay. Get back to Peking soon as you can," said Ward. "Where are you staying?"

"The Repulse Bay."

Ward waited a beat. "How's Ruth?"

"She's bearing up in Peking. Misses Hong Kong. The good life."

Ward stared at Florence, typing his letters on her electric typewriter. Virtually all his letters were gentle rejections of applicants for jobs.

Ward mumbled, "Good-bye, keep in touch." He heard the click, and turned to Florence.

"Did you see Hugh Finch at the funeral?"

She switched off her typewriter, nodding. "He's probably en route back to Washington right now."

"Call Washington and leave a message for Hugh to call me as soon as he gets in. Let's get a piece on the President's foreign policy problems. Tensions in the Cabinet. Throw in a graf or two on how he hasn't had a press conference in four weeks."

"Five," said Florence, returning to her typewriter. "Poor man looks awful."

CHAPTER 6

At six-fifteen the morning of the funeral the phone had rung in Barry Cohen's apartment on West Ninth Street, jolting him out of a deep sleep. He grabbed for it.

"Barry, it's Howie Bishop."

Cohen shut his eyes. "Good morning," he'd said, struggling to sound alert. Barry's head pounded, and he wondered why his best investigative reporters, Howie Bishop and Linda Fentress, inevitably woke him up. Obsessed characters they were, stories absorbed them, didn't even apologize at six-fifteen.

Howie said: "Wanted to catch you before you left for the funeral. Got to see you."

Barry heard a groan behind him, and twisted his head around. The woman on the bed, whom Barry vaguely recognized, had opened her eyes and was peering at him.

Howie's voice strained with urgency. "I can come down to your place now."

Barry returned the woman's gaze. Her face was absolutely impassive, lips set in a frown. "No," said Barry into the phone.

"Let's meet outside, then," Howie insisted. "Seven o'clock. Okay?" Howie suggested that they rendezvous beneath the Washington Square arch—two blocks from Barry's apartment; they had held several meetings walking around Washington Square Park. Barry agreed, keeping his eyes fixed on the woman. She had brown hair that fell to her shoulders, narrow blue eyes, a delicate upturned nose. She was in her late twenties.

"Who are you?" Barry asked after setting the phone down. He was naked.

"You don't remember?" Her voice was hoarse.

"Mary."

"Try again."

"I give up."

"Margie."

"Margie who?"

"Margie, Margie."

He smiled, and saw the cleavage of her breasts beneath the white bedsheet. A woolen blanket, usually atop the sheet, was curled at the edge of the king-size bed.

"I had a bad night," Barry said.

She winced slowly.

"Was I drunk?"

"Yes. Very drunk," she said.

"Where did we meet? I began drinking at Fritzi's. Then some of us went to The Lion's Head. Then we went to . . . ."

"Elaine's."

"Yeah. Elaine's."

Barry's tongue ran over his dry lips.

"What do you do, Mary? I mean, Margie."

"What do you mean, 'What do I do?'"

"For a living."

"I'm a photographer."

He paused. "Who do you take pictures of?"

"What are you, a cop?"

"Just making small talk."

"I don't like small talk."

"Okay. You know my name?"

"Barry Cohen."

"In living color."

"You work for the *Star*. City editor."

He stared at her. "You like people who work on the *Star?*"

"Sometimes." She twisted herself toward him. "I like newspaper people."

She touched his thigh, rubbing her hand gently over the hair above his knee. He lifted the white sheet, dropping it to her stomach. He leaned down and kissed her hard.

"What do you like to do with newspaper people?"

"I like to fuck newspaper people."

"All newspaper people?"

"Some newspaper people."

Confidently, she placed the palm of her left hand on his neck while her right hand fondled his soft penis. He opened her mouth with his tongue, kissing her. His hand found her moist center.

"I fuck the *Star*," she whispered. "I *like* the *Star*. I don't fuck the *Daily News* or *Post*. Sometimes I make it with the *Times*."

"You fuck the *Star*," he said, kissing her navel, stroking her belly, rubbing the inside of her. His tongue licked the wet hairs. She groaned. "The *Star* is quite good."

"Would you do anything for the *Star?*" he murmured.

"Anything within reason."

"What's within reason?"

"Anything."

"Turn over."

She stared at him, unblinking, for a long moment, and turned onto her stomach. Barry stood up, grabbed the sheet and threw it off her body. He walked to a closet and opened it, aware that she was both humming and staring at him.

He twisted a brown pigskin belt off a hook and looped it. He was breathing heavily now as he approached her.

"We-ell," she said.

His first thrash over her buttocks was weak; the belt too loose in his hands. He tightened his right hand on the circled whip, spreading apart his legs and standing over her. He thrashed again, harder, and followed up quickly with another slap. Her eyes were shut; she groaned softly.

He smacked her back and forth, staring at the red welt that flared on her buttocks and legs after each strike. Beads of sweat—his sweat—fell on her back.

Barry's face was wet and pink, his jaw trembled. He was panting. Grasping the center of the belt, letting it fall loosely, Barry raised his arm and in a single fluid move smacked the buckle against her ass. Margie arched her back but remained oddly still. His entire body was shaking as he tightened his fingers over the belt and struck Margie again. Her body seemed to crumple as he struck her again, staring with widened eyes at the flecks of blood that stained the center of her buttocks.

"Stop," she said, coiling her body over and grabbing his hard penis. He told her to sit up.

Holding the belt tight with both hands, Barry draped it over her shoulders and pulled her toward him.

Her fingers cradled his balls. She moved closer, running her tongue over his penis, biting gently and kissing and licking the tip. The belt tightened over her shoulders, trapping her, thwarting her from moving, as she placed the penis in her mouth.

Barry moaned. He swayed against her, forcing her to gag for a moment. He dropped the belt from his left hand and, with his palm tightly beneath her chin, arched her jaw and felt the outline of his penis in her mouth. He was breathing heavily now, moving back and forth, gripping her jaw. Then he came into her mouth, finally, holding onto her face.

"Swallow it," he said, before he let her go.

She swallowed.

"Move over," Barry said hoarsely. He lay down on the bed, shutting his eyes. Barry tasted the salt on his lips.

"Good show," he whispered.

"Thanks."

"Can I see you again?"

"Maybe."

He turned to her.

"I'll be around," said Margie, staring at the ceiling.

"Got to shower and run," said Barry.

"Busy day," she said vaguely.

"Stay here," he said. "Stay here for a while."

The phone was ringing.

"I'll leave you a key," said Barry. "Drop it in the mailbox downstairs." He reached for the phone and heard a staccato voice.

"Barry, is that you?"

"Who's this?"

Margie had lifted herself onto her right elbow, kissing his stomach, darting her tongue into his navel.

The voice over the phone softened. "It's Dave Fitzgerald."

Barry flinched. "Who?"

"Dave Fitzgerald. Senator . . ."

Barry crooked his right foot, watching her kiss his chest, lick his nipples perfunctorily, a farewell gesture. He felt the tightness in the pit of his stomach.

"Perhaps we can meet this morning. Before the funeral. I was thinking about breakfast. I'm at the Carlyle. Eight-fifteen?"

Barry glanced at the electric clock beside the telephone. His mind raced. "Make it eight-thirty," he said.

Margie lay on her back, watching Barry as he replaced the phone. He stared blindly at her. "Got to meet one of my reporters in the park, and then I'm seeing a man for breakfast." He bent low and kissed her. "Going to a funeral this morning."

"I hate funerals," she murmured.

*

Barry saw Howie Bishop standing beneath the base of the Washington arch, hands thrust into his coat pockets. Howie wore tinted glasses and, as Barry approached, Bishop's shoulders stiffened.

"The senator is in deep shit," said Howie, without introduction.

The two men began walking south into the park. "The senator . . ."

"Let's call him Dave."

"Dave had a legislative assistant named Cheryl Thomas. Earned thirty-eight five. Worked on health stuff and some education. The problem is that Cheryl is not very smart—in fact, sort of flakey—and no legislative experience."

"From New York?"

"San Francisco. A former stewardess on Western Airlines. University of Nevada dropout."

"Give me a guess. What's she have?"

"Tits. Incredible tits. Flat tummy. A wonderful ass."

"How old?"

"Twenty-nine, thirty. So Cheryl meets Fitzgerald when he's flying from L.A. to San Francisco to make some bullshit talk at Berkeley. Dave, naturally, can't keep his pecker dry for more than two hours and invites Cheryl to his room at the Mark Hopkins for a chat about the Middle East. Cheryl is so interested that she spends the night, and the next morning we have a new Senate aide for New York's pride and joy."

"How long did she work for him?"

"Seven, maybe eight years. Receptionist, private secretary, aide."

"And?" Barry stared fixedly in front of him.

"And he managed, so far as I can tell, to bang her in a little private office he had in the Senate at least once a day, sometimes twice. In the meantime, Cheryl gets a reputation."

"Meaning?"

"Meaning if you're a lobbyist or a diplomat with money and power, she spreads her legs."

"What happened?"

"Dave meets Lucy Claiborne and it gets heavy."

"He drops Cheryl."

"He wants out. Cheryl is turning into an embarrassment. After all, Dave has certain national aspirations."

"So Cheryl's pissed."

"First he fucks her in her apartment. Then he takes her to a fancy French restaurant for lunch, orders champagne, and when the waiter brings the espresso he drops the bomb. Thanks and good-bye. Best this way for both of us. I'm exploiting you. I'm holding you back. In the meantime, he had to get that extra final fuck in."

Barry watched two glassy-eyed derelicts on a bench. Why had Fitzgerald just called him, Barry wondered.

"Cheryl doesn't know what hit her," said Howie Bishop. "First the stupid bitch agrees with him. He's doing this for *her* benefit. Right? Then she thinks about it, talks to a friend or two and realizes she's been fucked over badly by our friend. He says he'll help her get a job for another senator or congressman. He says she'll get a job with the Administration."

Howie's voice dropped. "She waits one week, two weeks. Zilch. Then he stops answering her phone calls." He sighed. "She is very, very pissed.

"In fact, she's more than pissed," said Howie. "She wants to get even."

The two men stopped. Their eyes locked.

"Dave used Cheryl for errands," said Bishop, removing a small notebook from his pocket and flipping it open. "Once, sometimes twice a week Cheryl would get a phone call from, say, an oil lobbyist—Dave is on the Energy Committee—or a real estate developer from Utica who wants Dave's support for the purchase of some government land, or a grain producer who wants Dave to push for high-priced grain supports, or a gentleman from the government of Nigeria who wants a friendly voice on the Foreign Relations Committee, especially with all those torture allegations."

"What happened?"

"The gentlemen invite Cheryl to lunch—sometimes Tiberio, or Lion D'Or, Cantina D'Italia. Fancy Washington restaurants."

"And then?"

"And then, after the waiter has brought the coffee and the cognac, the gentlemen take envelopes out of their pockets and hand them to Cheryl."

"Does Cheryl know what's in the envelopes?"

"Some of these gentlemen are quite impressed with Cheryl. So impressed that she starts picking up some extra cash. And bits and pieces of information. Not so much for her views on the tax bill but for a little extracurricular bang on the side. A Nigerian chargé d'affaires. A Saudi Arabian press counselor. A guy working for the gun lobby."

Barry stared at Howie Bishop.

"Who does she give the envelopes to?"

Bishop took a deep breath.

"Jerry Paley."

Barry sighed. "Why is Paley such a dumb son of a bitch?" He turned and started to walk. "Who's your source, Howie?" It was a delicate question, one editors rarely asked reporters.

Barry counted to nine before hearing Howie's slow release of breath.

"FBI guy," said Howie. "Friend of mine. This is all he knows. Cheryl came to them."

Barry bit his lip.

"FBI ain't exactly interested," said Howie. "Fitzgerald and the associate director, old friends . . ."

"Of course."

"Went to Fordham together. Asshole buddies. Fitzgerald got him the job." Howie Bishop nodded. "This friend of mine says we got a big fucking story here, *waiting* . . ."

"You call Cheryl?"

"Left three messages."

"Let's talk to Jerry."

"Paley comes back tomorrow from Panama. On a trip down there for the Foreign Relations Committee." Bishop walked in silence beside Barry. "You knew the son, Mike Paley, in Vietnam."

Barry nodded. Howie spoke distractedly. "Jesus, why did Jerry get involved with that cocksucker Fitzgerald?"

Why, why did Fitzgerald call him this morning? thought Barry. Why wasn't he telling Howie?

"There's a diary," Howie was saying. Barry stopped to stare at him. "That's all this FBI guy knows. Cheryl kept a diary, she told them."

They were standing on Thompson Street now, a raw wind whipping up flecks of dirt that stung Barry's eyes.

"I'll try to get to Cheryl. Get the diary." Bishop paused, looked at Barry. "So you're in the running," he said. There was a slight edge to his voice. "You. Parsons. Finch. Sally Sims. Maury."

"Maury last but not least. Maury's the *one*." Barry swallowed. "The family likes him."

"The family is *divided* over him."

Barry examined Howie's hawk face. "What do you hear?"

"They're waiting."

"Creative tension, right?"

"Survival of the fittest," said Howie Bishop. "You produce a winner in the next couple of days, your stock rises. Parsons shapes up, he's the one. Our black friend or Sally shows some moxie. . . ."

"It's Maury's to lose." Barry stared blindly at him.

Howie chewed his lip. "We're in trouble, Barry. Losing circulation. Losing ads. Losing a fortune."

"So?"

"We're standing on the edge. We're . . . dying." Howie stepped close to Barry. "You want someone young to take over. Decisive. Tough. *Not Maury.*"

Barry felt the skip in his heart.

Howie grinned. "You got balls, Barry."

"True."

"Chutzpah."

"True enough."

"You're a mean son of a bitch too."

"Thanks."

"All the qualifications."

"Except style." Barry spoke through stiff lips. *"That's* important. I'm not a smoothie, like Ward Parsons. Didn't go to Yale or Princeton, right? Old Dad didn't exactly finance my education. I didn't tiptoe through the Columbia Journalism School. No connections. Just busted my ass. Guys like me go so far, and that's it."

"To the top."

"Look at my suit. Look at the tie I wear. I try. But it doesn't work, Howie. Listen to my accent. I'm not executive material."

Barry swayed, aware of the intense flush on his face. His heart was pounding violently.

"It's yours to win," Howie Bishop said.

*

The Secretary of Defense, Edward Belling, bustled into his suite of offices in Room 3E880. His thirty-minute swim downstairs at the Pentagon Officers Athletic Club, which usually buoyed his mood, had barely eased the tension that had left him sleepless and short-tempered over the past forty-eight hours.

Nodding distractedly to his two secretaries, Belling passed through the open door held by his aide, Colonel Walker, who stood ramrod stiff, lips pursed, right hand outstretched with the morning file stamped EYES ONLY.

Belling scooped up the folder and stepped inside the large, high-ceilinged office. The door shut softly behind him.

"Sir!"

Belling whirled around and saw the colonel thrust his hand into his breast pocket to remove a single sheet of paper. The Defense Secretary took a step forward and caught sight of Walker's taut mouth.

Belling examined the papers.

"The doctor, Pomerance," said Belling, eyes fixed on the sheet.

"Arriving later today."

Belling frowned, lifted his eyes and started to speak, but dropped his gaze to the paper once more. "My appointment with that black fellow . . ."

"Hugh Finch. One-thirty."

Belling turned and walked to the window beside his desk.

His back toward Colonel Walker, the Defense Secretary jutted his chin and watched, through the filmy curtains, a Boeing 707, wheels lowered, surge toward National Airport. Colonel Walker waited.

"Did you see the Washington *Post* this morning, sir?"

"Only the front page."

"Story inside the paper. Says that some Democrats on the Hill are mentioning you as a possible candidate . . ."

"*Christ!*" He spun around. "Call Dave Fitzgerald and tell him not to pee in his pants over that one. Call him now."

Their eyes locked until Belling turned away. His face showed strain. Frowning, he plucked a document off the top of his desk, stared at it with distaste and murmured: "What the bloody hell are they up to now?"

"Inscrutable Chinese."

"Russians are alarmed," said the Defense Secretary, easing into his chair. He leafed through the documents on his desk without enthusiasm.

Colonel Walker stood perfectly still. "Shall I ask Kitty, sir?"

Kitty White was a Georgetown hostess with whom Belling had been having a none too discreet affair.

Belling gave the colonel a brief upward glance.

"Yes," murmured the Defense Secretary. Belling's mouth softened, and his lips stretched into a smile. "*Yes!*"

*

Barry walked down the seventh-floor corridor of the Carlyle at eight-fifteen, reaching the open door of Room 704 as a room-service waiter was leaving. He stepped inside.

"I've already ordered," said Senator Fitzgerald, stepping toward him and shaking his hand.

Fitzgerald was wearing black pinstripe trousers, a starched white shirt and blue silk tie flecked with red circles. His cordovans gleamed.

A former New York State attorney general, Dave Fitzgerald was the son of a Yankee left-fielder who, in his five seasons as a major-league ballplayer, earned enough money in the mid-forties to send his son to Fordham and then Columbia Law School. Fitzgerald had his father's muscular build—he was tall, over six feet two inches, with a broad chest and powerful hands and wrists that were hardened by years of working out with weights and swimming daily at his home in northwest Washington. His straight black hair was tinged with gray now—the only concession to age for a man who was one of the more controversial figures in the Democratic Party machine in New York.

"When was the last time we met, Barry?" he said, standing beside a silk damask sofa covered with the morning newspapers. Fitzgerald's sunken blue eyes, framed by thick, dark eyelashes, lent a mysterious, ominous dimension to a handsome, otherwise open face.

"Six, maybe eight months ago. Lunch in Skipper's office."

Fitzgerald's eyes narrowed. "You kept hounding me about my presidential ambitions."

Barry returned Fitzgerald's cold stare.

"Jerry Paley should be here," said Fitzgerald. "Don't like talking to reporters without Jerry beside me."

Barry caught the sneer in Fitzgerald's voice.

"Popular man, Jerry is," said Barry, setting his eyes on the breakfast table in the center of the room. "Popular man at the *Star*."

"Let's eat," said Fitzgerald, spinning around and walking toward the table whose pink cloth was covered with coffee cups, juice glasses, a basket of pastries and croissants. A single rose was stuck in a narrow vase in the center of the table.

Fitzgerald tasted the juice. "Jerry'd be here today but he's down in Panama. Committee business. Coming back tomorrow to take his boy out of the hospital."

"Mike."

"Sad business." Fitzgerald drained the glass. "Mike's been in the hospital a couple of weeks. In and out since he got home from Vietnam."

"I met Mike in Vietnam."

"*Nice* kid." Fitzgerald was pouring coffee. "Terrible what Vietnam did to him. Got sprayed with that shit . . ."

"Agent Orange."

". . . got sprayed and just about destroyed Mike's life. That little girl Mike's got. Jesus, that's tragic."

Barry watched Fitzgerald's hand shake as he lifted the cup. "Little girl's everything to Jerry. Proud grandfather." Barry tried to smile. "The sun rises and sets for Jerry on his granddaughter."

Barry saw the slightest flicker in Fitzgerald's lower eyelids.

"Jerry wanted to get here for Evan's funeral service," said Fitzgerald, tearing apart a croissant. "Still feels close to the *Star*." He concentrated on chewing. "I've lost a friend, Barry. Met Evan years ago when I was district attorney. Had your job, didn't he?"

"He was national editor once."

"You're city editor. Of course. Not national. Sally Sims is national."

Barry nodded.

"I get them confused."

"A lot of people do."

"What's the difference?"

"Different turf. My job is to cover the city and the suburbs. And anything from Washington involving New York."

"Like me, for instance."

"Like you."

Fitzgerald wiped the sides of his mouth with a linen napkin. His sturdy fingers were covered with curly tufts of hair, the nails polished, delicately manicured.

"Let's talk off the record."

Barry caught a tremor in Fitzgerald's voice.

"You're investigating my office."

Fitzgerald's eyes seemed to dim, soften.

"We're looking into some rumors," Barry said.

"What rumors?"

"Some rumors."

Fitzgerald's face was suddenly flushed—he seemed on the edge of exploding. But he spoke with icy authority.

"I hear your man has made some phone calls to my office."

Barry knew his voice was a little too confident. "I don't want to play games with you, Senator. We've just begun our investigation. If it turns up nothing, fine. If it turns up something, you'll hear from us."

"You're awfully smug."

"What?"

"You smug motherfucker. You guys play judge and jury these days. Anyone is grist for you. Anyone is up for grabs for your bullshit investigations."

Barry pushed back his chair and stood.

"Sit down!"

Cohen dug his nails into the table but remained standing, feeling sweat begin to break out on his spine. "We've begun an investigation," Barry said calmly. "We . . ."

"Your investigations are a *fucking joke,*" Fitzgerald yelled. "What's this guy's name—Bishop? One of your big stars. Investigate the Mafia. I used to read his stories when I was DA and laugh. We laughed our fucking heads off. I used to *leak* those stories."

"They were good stories."

"Good stories, bullshit. Nice, readable, self-serving, bullshit stories. Leaked to you schmucks because we couldn't get indictments. *Leaked.* All this bullshit you guys publish about organized crime, about who's running which Mafia family. A joke. We leak it, and you lap it up."

He took a long gulp of coffee. "Organized crime. You know what's organized? Chase Manhattan is organized. ITT is organized. Exxon is organized. You know what organized crime is? Geriatric Italians ordering cargo heists in the Bronx. Not this bullshit that you write about."

Fitzgerald stood up and walked to the Tuscan credenza beside a window. He bent forward to open the door and remove a bottle of scotch, then poured himself a quarter of a glass.

"Who's this cunt that works for you? Another investigative hotshot. The blonde with the ass. Linda something."

"Fentress."

"Linda Fentress." Fitzgerald returned to the table and sat down. "Won this award for finding Nazis in New York. *Nazis.* As if she was finding Adolf Eichmann. Well, who the fuck did she actually find? Who? Latvians and Lithuanians who were minor police functionaries. Crazy old ladies who gave blow jobs to Nazis in Estonia. All based on leaks, right? Leaks by the Immigration and Naturalization Service, whose counsel couldn't get indictments. So he leaks to her. And bangs her too. And suddenly we have stories about the *effectiveness* of the Immigration and Naturalization Service, which, believe me, spends most of its time worrying about the kitchen help in Chinese restaurants and doesn't know one Chink from another."

Fitzgerald laughed. "Your investigations are a crock of shit, Mr. Cohen."

Suddenly Fitzgerald sighed. "What do you want, Barry?"

The question startled him.

"For Chrissake, sit down," said Fitzgerald impatiently. "What do you want?" Fitzgerald repeated. "You want the job, right? Evan's job."

Barry felt his heart thud.

"Not going to be easy," said Fitzgerald. "You got competition. Hugh Finch. Aggressive son of a bitch. There's Maury Kramer. Sally. The foreign editor."

Barry returned his gaze. Fitzgerald whispered.

"Let's work together. I somehow think we can work together, you and me."

Barry watched in fascination as a nerve twitched in the center of Fitzgerald's forehead. Fitzgerald began to smile but decided against it. "Just can't drop this investigation by Howie Bishop, can you? Don't expect you to. News travels. It's all over town. Christ, you wouldn't believe how news travels. You can't drop this investigation unless you have a better story."

Outside the door, Barry heard the wheels of a chambermaid's cart. A door slammed.

"A much better story," said Fitzgerald.

"Jerry Paley," said Barry through stiffened lips.

"That's the story," sighed Fitzgerald, examining his drink.

"Jerry Paley." Barry repeated the words, wincing.

"We can help you, Barry. Assist your reporter." Fitzgerald nodded, smiling. "Gathering information right now, we are. It's *yours,* Barry." Fitzgerald took a deep gulp. "I can *help* you. Yes! Get the diary. Cheryl's diary. You've heard . . ."

"I've heard . . ."

"Names and dates. Figures. All went to Jerry. *Get it.*"

Fitzgerald's intensity made Barry fix his eyes on the table. Why, *why* did he detest Fitzgerald?

"I want the job," Barry said abruptly.

"It's yours," said Fitzgerald, not missing a beat.

Barry looked up, and there was something in Fitzgerald's cold certainty that restrained Barry from asking the obvious question. Bloody fucking sure, aren't you, I'll get the job. You're banging Lucy and you got Frieda under your thumb, but does that assure me the job?

Barry flinched when the phone rang, watched Fitzgerald push back his chair and walk to a table beside the sofa. As Fitzgerald lifted the phone, a ray of sun caught his face, giving an eerie white cast to his nose and lips. Fitzgerald asked the caller to wait.

"I'll expect to hear from your Woodward and Bernsteins," Fitzgerald said, putting the phone down.

Barry stood up.

"Who's your best investigative reporter, Barry? After Bishop, who is it? The blonde?"

Barry stared at him.

Fitzgerald wet his lips. "The *Daily News* is working on a story, Barry. So is the *Times.*" Fitzgerald started to smile. "Get her ass on to it." The two men stared at each other until Fitzgerald dropped his gaze.

Barry turned and walked to the door, swiveled back and caught Fitzgerald's stare. In the elevator perspiration seeped down his neck. This gray flannel suit is too heavy for such a mild day, he thought; he needed some air. He dug into his trousers, found two dimes, and headed for the telephone booths as soon as he stepped off the elevator.

He opened the Manhattan phone book, but Linda Fentress wasn't listed. He knew approximately where she lived—West Seventy-fourth or West Seventy-fifth Street, off Central Park West. Barry dialed the number of the city desk and Nick Simons, who came on at eight-thirty each morning, answered.

Barry told Nick to phone Linda Fentress at home and ask her to call him immediately at the phone booth number. If Linda was not there, Nick should call him back. Barry gave Nick the phone booth number and hung up.

The phone rang within a minute.

"Barry?" she said.

"Linda. What are you working on now?"

"Some Nazi stuff. A lady in Staten Island who was possibly a camp guard in . . ."

"Drop it," said Barry in a tight voice. "The *Times* and *Daily News* are working on something. Don't know what it is but I want to find out."

A pause. Linda said it sounded like a national desk story.

"No. It's *our* story," said Barry in a tight voice. "I'll tell the national desk when I want to. If it's good I want it." He loosened his tie. "Start this morning. Snoop around. Tell no one. I'll take care of the desk. Between you and me."

"Got it," said Linda uncertainly.

After hanging up, he opened the door of the booth, unfastened the top button of his shirt, and with his second dime dialed his home phone.

It rang six times before he hung up.

*

At that moment, David Fitzgerald was draining another whiskey with his left hand, and grasping the telephone with his right hand.

"We're going to make Barry managing editor, Eli," he said.

CHAPTER 7

At the request of Lucy Claiborne, the cemetery service at Wood-lawn in the Bronx was attended only by the immediate family and one *Star* photographer, who stood discreetly at a distance.

The family huddled under umbrellas. Reverend Taylor, a lanky, hollow-cheeked man in his fifties who spoke with a North Carolina drawl, spoke somberly: "Who shall ascend the hill of the Lord? And who shall stand in his holy place? He who has clean hands and a pure heart, who does not lift up his soul to what is false, and does not swear deceitfully."

Johanna Claiborne stood beside her uncle, biting her lip. As the minister intoned, "He will receive blessing from the Lord," Johanna gripped Skipper's hand and, as the coffin was lowered, she turned away and stared at her mother, whose eyes were shut. Frieda, standing beside Lucy, was dabbing at her eyes with an embroidered handkerchief.

"Grandmother seems so old and frail," Johanna whispered as they walked over the stone path to the limousine.

"Frail, like a two-ton truck," Skipper said. Johanna smiled.

Frieda had stopped for a moment to gaze at the high marble tombstones that adjoined Evan's burial site. At the base of the three ash-gray tablets—bearing the names of Jonathan Steiner, Frederic Steiner and Dora Steiner—lay neatly arranged fleurs-de-lis, white chrysanthemums, phlox and, at each grave, a dozen red roses. She continued on to the limousine.

"You're going to stay with us for a while, aren't you? Stay in New York?" Skipper said to Johanna.

"Going back tomorrow afternoon."

He turned to her. "Johanna, I want to talk to you."

Johanna stared at her uncle. "I'm catching a five-fifteen train to Boston tomorrow. Let's have lunch before I go. Take me to a restaurant. A fancy one."

"Twenty-one?"

"I'll even get dressed up. They'll think I'm your new mistress."

Skipper's cheeks flushed. "I'm not that lucky," he said.

"Come on. You *are* that lucky. I've . . ."

Frieda interrupted them. "Skipper, you'll ride with me. Lucy will ride with us too. Johanna, darling, you ride in the second car with Larry."

Two black chauffeurs held open the rear doors of the limousines. As Skipper helped Frieda into the first car, she turned and said: "We will all go to the apartment now."

Larry Steiner and Johanna climbed into the second car. It was raining heavily now.

"I don't want to face a day like this again, ever. *Ever*," said Frieda, as the limousine moved off. "And I don't think I will."

Skipper leaned forward, pressing a circular button beside the ashtray. A glass partition slid upward, separating the driver and the passengers in the rear seat, isolating them.

They sat in silence. Finally Lucy lifted her dark glasses, placing them atop her head.

"Are you all right?" Frieda asked.

"Yes."

"Johanna seems fine."

"She's taking it well."

"She's attractive."

"She has Evan's eyes, cheekbones."

"She'd be beautiful if she lost fifteen pounds."

"I don't think she cares."

"Why not?"

"I don't think she cares about that. She never did."

Skipper said, "Mother, is this an elaborate lunch at the house?"

"Not elaborate," said Frieda. "We'll have some nice salads. Turkey, chicken, tongue. French bread and brie. I have Hector and Louisa, two people in the kitchen, and two others serving, including the bartender."

Age masked Frieda's face. She was a thin woman whose cheeks were seamed with lines that seemed to deepen beneath lynx eyes. Her fragile hands, dotted with freckles, gripped her lap, but as Frieda spoke she began moving her fingers, then twisting the big oval-shaped diamond.

"How many people do we expect?" asked Lucy.

"I don't know. Seventy-five, a hundred. They'll come in and out. The governor's stopping by. He told me at the church. Dave Fitzgerald. Eli. Some people from the paper—the business side." She eyed Lucy, who slumped against the window.

"You can rest in the bedroom anytime you want to," said Frieda. "It's perfectly understandable. No one expects you to stay on your feet."

Lucy stared out as the limousine moved slowly through traffic eastward on Gun Hill Road. They sat in silence for several minutes until Skipper said: "Let's meet Monday to talk about Evan's replacement."

"I'm thinking about it already," said Frieda. "I'm confused."

"Confused about what?" said Lucy, still staring out the window.

"Confused about the kind of person, the *right* kind of person to be managing editor of the *Star* now."

"I thought Maury was the inevitable choice," said Lucy.

"No one is inevitable," interrupted Skipper. "No one at all."

"Exactly." Frieda spoke firmly. "This is not something to be done *quickly*. I'm a bit uncomfortable with Maury. The news staff needs a powerful hand. The paper is in turmoil."

Skipper turned to Frieda. She seemed lost in thought, her lips pursed.

Finally, she said, "Circulation's dropping, advertising's down. Gets worse and worse." Her voice shook. "I saw the figures, Skipper, the losses. We can't go on this way, can we?" She stared at him. *"Can* we?" Frieda breathed a sigh. "Costs are alarming. Newsprint! Personnel! We're about to spend a fortune on automation. Other papers are fully automated, and we're just starting."

"The wave of the future," said Skipper quietly.

"Of course," said Frieda, almost angrily. "Have to automate. It *is* the future. Computer terminals and video screens and lasers. My God! An *explosion* of new technology. How are we going to pay for it?"

"Cutbacks," Skipper said dully. "Ten percent reductions in the newsroom." Lucy glanced up as Frieda's eyes searched her son's face.

"I think that's wise," said Frieda quickly. "Eli has been suggesting . . ."

"We're *not* doing it because Eli Faber suggested it," Skipper said through tight lips.

"The Guild will scream," said Lucy. "Threaten . . ."

"I'd love to see that union leader's face. Mr. Frank Lazzarutti," said Frieda, her eyes flashing.

Skipper leaned forward, and Lucy watched her brother intently, suddenly aware that his face was gray. He looked stricken, fearful.

"It's a risk," Skipper said. "Lazzarutti will scream, but that's all he can do so long as nine other unions, especially the drivers, don't support him."

"Drivers are the key," said Frieda, staring blankly ahead. "Always the key. Without the trucks to deliver the papers, we can't . . ."

"We're taking care of the drivers," said Skipper. "It's a pivotal time for the *Star*. It's crucial! We've got to make tough decisions, up and down the line. Where are we heading? Whom are we competing with? Who are our readers? How do we break into the suburbs?"

He examined his fingernails. "We've *got* to pick the right person to be managing editor."

"We owe it to Maury," said Lucy.

"We owe it to no one," said Skipper. "Now, I like Maury. He's able and sensible. Good news judgment. But there are others. Ward Parsons. There's Barry Cohen."

Lucy said, "Sally."

Skipper's voice softened. "Yes, Sally. Maybe Hugh Finch."

"Hugh Finch," said Frieda. "I hadn't thought of Hugh Finch!"

"First black managing editor of a New York paper," Lucy said.

"He needs some seasoning. Never been overseas," Skipper put in.

"Very attractive, though," said Frieda. "Doesn't he have family problems?"

"Too attractive," said Lucy.

The limousine, on the New England Thruway now, glided smoothly downtown. Rain pelted the sides of the windows, and the windshield wipers moved back and forth noiselessly as the car eased through the Bronx into Manhattan.

Frieda nervously tapped the fingers on her left hand against the palm of her right hand.

"I'm not excluding Maury in any way," she said. "Maury is competent, he knows the paper, he knows us. He has taste."

"And he has the support of the staff," Skipper said.

"He would bring continuity, a sense of order," said Frieda, absently shaking her head. "Isn't he living with someone now? A Chinese girl?"

"She's a copy editor," said Skipper.

"What I am saying is . . ."

"Let's be careful," said Skipper.

"Precisely."

"It's a very delicate time, a special time," said Skipper. "I want the decision made soon, but not in a hasty way."

"Maury . . . Ward Parsons . . . Sally," said Frieda.

"Barry Cohen, Hugh Finch," said Skipper.

They rode in silence for ten minutes, the limousine finally climbing onto the East River Drive, moving south past the housing projects of East Harlem. Lucy opened the window two inches, and closed her eyes as cool, wet air breezed over her face. Frieda gripped Skipper's wrist and held it firmly.

"He had so much to live for," Frieda whispered. "He had *everything.*"

"He was sicker than we thought," Skipper said.

"He was so brilliant," said Frieda. "All those doctors and . . . nothing."

Lucy opened her eyes. "All those doctors couldn't do a damn thing, because Evan wanted to die."

"He never seemed . . ."

"Mother, stop it, for God's sake!" Lucy flared. "You didn't know him, you didn't live with him, *endure* him. Of course he was brilliant. He was also mean, ugly . . ."

"Lucy!" her brother snapped.

"Oh, my God. I just don't understand," said Frieda, and shut her eyes.

*

The noon Eastern Airlines shuttle landed at National Airport at one-ten, a delay caused by incoming traffic from Chicago and Miami.

Gripping his trench coat in his left hand and his attaché case in his right, Hugh was the fourth passenger off the plane. He bounded down the steps and moved quickly into the waiting room, stopping at a row of telephones. He had twenty minutes to make it to the Pentagon—plenty of time.

He dialed his direct line at the bureau.

"Where are you?" his secretary Francine Miles asked.

"National. Just got back. Any messages?"

"A couple. Senator Long can see you on Tuesday, five o'clock. Polly Fritchey has a buffet next Thursday before the Kennedy Center benefit. Invites you. You're also invited to a dinner at Joe Kraft's house for Kissinger, a week from this Monday. And tomorrow is your son's birthday. It's on my calendar. Don't forget."

"I did. How are you?"

"I am swell, Mr. Finch."

"Am I seeing you tonight?"

"It's on my social schedule."

"How much time have you booked for me?"

"Time? How much time do you want?"

"All night."

"Mr. Finch, you're exploiting me. Working me day and night."

"That's not exploitation. That's . . ."

"Fucking."

"You said it."

"I'll see you later in the afternoon."

Hugh walked to the newspaper and magazine stand near the baggage carousel. His habit, nurtured by years of traveling from Washington's National Airport into the city, was to buy the Washington *Post* to read in the taxi.

He glanced at his watch. One-fifteen. It would take less than ten minutes to reach the river entrance of the Pentagon.

He dug into his trouser pockets to find some coins, and glanced up, suddenly catching his breath. Alvin Simmons moved past, less than a dozen feet away, and now stepped quickly toward the incoming shuttle passengers.

Hugh opened his mouth to call to his friend but suddenly held back, aware of a faint skip in his heart. Who the hell was Alvin meeting at the shuttle?

Alvin Simmons was a black Secret Serviceman, hired during the

Gerald Ford years, and now deputy chief of the White House Secret Service. Hugh had met Simmons on the 1976 Jimmy Carter
campaign, and because they were two black men about the same
age they had struck up a casual relationship that had deepened
into friendship.

On a campaign flight from Portland to Kansas City, as they ate
hamburgers, Hugh had asked Alvin where he had grown up.
When Alvin replied Oakland, the friendship was cemented. Without acknowledging it to one another, the two men accepted the
fact that each of them—coming from poor black grandparents in
Louisiana who emigrated, like many black families, to Oakland so
the men could work in the shipyard—had, indeed, traveled a long
way.

They had reminisced about attending Lowell Junior High
School and McClymones High—where Alvin, who was five years
younger than Hugh, was second-string on the Warriors basketball
team. And about playing football and swimming in Infirmary Park
and going to the "Quarter Pound," where all the kids went after
high school, and growing up blocks away from each other—Alvin
in a housing project on Peralta and Eighth in West Oakland;
Hugh, for a time, in a wooden, white-painted house with green
trim on the corner of Twelfth Street.

By the end of the 1976 campaign the two men were the closest
of friends.

Simmons lived in Arlington with his second wife, Faye. His first
wife had been a Vietnamese girl whom he had met in the Dragon
Bar in Saigon in 1969, while he was assigned to Ton Son Nhut
airbase as a military policeman. Simmons had married her when
he was nineteen, despite the pleas of a chaplain and his commanding officer, a captain from Americus, Georgia, who had warned
Simmons that while some bar girls were as loyal as sheep dogs and
made damned good wives, Li Thi Hua was trouble.

The captain from Americus, Georgia, had been absolutely
right. Two months after returning home to Los Angeles, where
Alvin was working as a car salesman and making plans to attend
the University of Southern California on the GI bill, he abruptly
dropped by the apartment one afternoon at twelve-fifteen to pick
up a set of keys that he had left on a dresser beside the bed.

The two Montgomery Ward delivery men, one in jockey shorts, the other in baggy, pale-blue boxers, scrambled off the bed in a panic, lunging for their clothes on the floor. Li Thi Hua lay on the bed naked, staring open-mouthed at her husband.

Alvin grabbed one of the men in a hammer lock, smashing him in the stomach twice with the side of his clenched fist, then dropping the man to his feet and punching him one more time in the stomach. The man gagged, his tongue dangling, and crumpled to the floor.

He tackled the other man, a pudgy, redheaded youth in his twenties, from the waist and lifted him up squealing like a wounded animal, and spun him around. Overwhelmed by rage, Alvin stared at the youth's terrified eyes for one second and drove his fist into the victim's face. Alvin heard a crunch, a fearful crunch, and saw blood spurting over the youth's nose and mouth. The youth lifted his hands toward Alvin, weeping.

Alvin ran to the door, opened it and lifted the first man, dragging him across the living room and flinging him outside the door. The second man, who was gagging on his blood, was crawling out the door. Alvin walked into the bedroom, ignoring Li Thi Hua for a moment, picked up the clothing of the two men and flung it through the door.

Years later, recounting the story to Hugh on Air Force 1 as the President flew to London, Alvin confessed that he had been all set to kill Li Thi Hua.

She had cowered in the bedroom, clutching a robe, pleading in Vietnamese when he approached and slapped her so hard that she crumpled to the bed, burying her face in her hands. He moved over her. She began shrieking, and he placed his hand over her mouth to shut her up, his left hand on her slender neck.

He could have broken her neck in thirty seconds. His fingers tightened around her; he heard her gag and saw her eyes bulge, staring at the ceiling with final terror.

Whatever impulse kept him from killing her in those few seconds—and thereby destroying himself—was impossible for him to understand. He hated her with a passion that overwhelmed him.

But he lifted his hand from her mouth, and loosened the grip on her neck, still keeping his fingers beneath her jaw. Too frightened to speak, she merely stared at him with haunted eyes. She was trembling. He opened her robe, exposing her body, so thin and fragile, so delicate, the body that, like many Vietnamese women, left her embarrassed in open light. Her pale-brown pubic hair curled, in small tufts, around the V of her crotch. She had a child's navel.

He stood beside the bed, breathing heavily, staring at the terrified woman who had deceived and humiliated him. With his right arm, he gripped her right ankle and roughly thrust her leg to the edge of the bed, opening her to him. She began to whimper.

He removed his trousers and shorts, climbed on the bed, and she turned away. He grasped her face to stare at him. He was sweating now, breathing heavily, and when he thrust into her, she closed her eyes and pursed her lips, as if too frightened to utter a sound.

Pinning her shoulders down with the palms of his hands, Simmons plunged through her violently, as if to break her. She opened her mouth and gasped, and when he began to weep she thought he had gone insane. His tears fell on her startled face.

After Alvin came into her, he arose and stepped over the broken lamps and overturned table in the bedroom and walked into the kitchen where he kept three hundred dollars in a coffee mug. He took the money, mostly twenty-dollar bills, and returned to the bedroom. Her eyes were swollen with tears now, her body covered with a blue bedsheet. Simmons tossed the money on the bed and told her to get out by the time he returned home.

Then Alvin walked out of the apartment.

When Alvin recalled the story in a whisper that night on the darkened President's plane, the confession somehow deepened the bond between the two men, altering their casual friendship into a tie that seemed filial.

Alvin and Faye Simmons were virtually the only people Hugh instinctively trusted. As Hugh's marriage dissolved, as his life in Washington and at the bureau grew more intricate, Hugh turned increasingly to Alvin and Faye. Hugh would phone up abruptly and invite himself out to their house in Arlington for dinner. He brought bottles of red wine and beer, together with the ribs and chicken and candied yams from Scott's Barbecue on Mt. Pleasant and Irving, or Chinese food from the Szechwan. They all shared the food—Alvin, Faye, and their nine-year-old daughter and seven-year-old son.

After dinner, after they had kissed the children good night, Hugh would take off his shoes and they would watch the Bullets or the Redskins on television. Faye, who taught in elementary school in Fairfax, would wander off to grade papers, or read, and the two men would sit and drink beer and talk.

If the mood struck, Alvin would climb up to the attic where his bookcase included a leather-bound Bible that, when open, was an empty shell filled with envelopes of hashish and marijuana. (Alvin seized the Bible while making a casual check of the luggage of a black paratrooper who was returning to Vietnam from Bangkok. Alvin, standing at the customs table in his MP outfit, placed the Bible under his arm, called the frightened GI a stupid fuck and waved him through customs.)

Alvin would light up a pipe, and the two men would pass it between them, sipping beer. Often Hugh would doze off, and then borrow a pair of Alvin's pajamas to sleep over on the living-room sofa bed, returning to the District the following morning.

His relationship with Alvin and Faye was casual but powerful: they demanded nothing of him, yet when Hugh wanted to talk to them—separately or together—they were eager to listen and help. He once told Faye that she and Alvin, although his contemporaries, were family to him, family that he needed, family that he never quite had. He loved both of them.

*

For a moment Alvin was lost in the crowd of incoming passengers. Then Hugh, stepping away from the newsstand, saw the back of Alvin's head, saw him turn and talk and point toward the terminal entrance. Hugh craned his neck, unable to see the person whom Alvin was talking to.

Alvin was now walking back along the crowded corridor, speaking animatedly. He would move past Hugh within seconds. Hugh quickly moved to the baggage carousel, mingling with passengers waiting for their luggage. He leaned against a pale-green column, peering over his shoulder, feeling foolish spying on his closest friend.

One-twenty. Ten minutes to get to the Pentagon. He would

make it just in time. But Hugh was too curious. Alvin was stepping past him, less than a dozen feet away.

A screaming little boy and his mother, passengers on the shuttle from New York, moved in front of Hugh. He stepped aside.

Alvin was dressed in a crisply ironed blue suit, white shirt and blue-and-red striped tie. He wore sunglasses and a gold and pale-blue Secret Service pin clamped to his lapel. Hugh stared at him as he quickly moved toward the exit.

For a moment, Hugh failed to notice the man whom Alvin escorted through the crowd. A short man. Dapper. Hugh squinted his eyes and sucked in his breath.

Dr. Pomerance.

Hugh ran up the stairs after them, but Alvin and Pomerance were out the doors of the airline terminal and walking to a glistening, four-door brown Impala that was parked at the curb. The car had an aerial on its roof, like all White House cars.

Alvin opened the back door for Pomerance. As the driver started the engine, Alvin slammed the door and moved to the front of the car to sit in the passenger seat. Pomerance sat alone in the back.

Hugh watched the car glide away. He looked at his watch.

One twenty-five.

He ran to the taxi stand.

CHAPTER 8

When Hugh arrived at the river entrance of the Pentagon at one thirty-five, he showed his White House pass to the guard, then climbed up one flight, two steps at a time, and walked down the wide, glistening E corridor to Room 3E880. An Air Force colonel waited at the door; he introduced himself as Gerard Walker, military aide to Secretary of Defense Belling.

"Follow me," said Walker, turning on the balls of his feet and stepping from the reception room into a maze of inner offices. Hugh swallowed hard, walking behind the officer, suddenly puzzled at the colonel's strangely flat singsong voice. Two women

secretaries looked as Hugh walked past; one of them, a pert
blonde with a cigarillo, returned his gaze without flinching.

A door was flung open, and Hugh was shown into the cavernous office of the Secretary of Defense.

Belling glanced up, his tortoise-rimmed glasses clamped atop
his forehead, a pipe dangling loosely from his mouth. The pipe
was a trademark, picked up by Herblock and Oliphant in car-
toons. Belling was jacketless, wearing a button-down shirt and
plaid tie, charcoal-gray pinstripe trousers.

Although Hugh had interviewed Belling once before in the Pentagon, he remained dazzled at the sheer size of the Defense Secretary's office. It was dominated by a nine-foot walnut desk (once
used by General John J. Pershing). Looming behind the desk was
the vaguely ominous oil portrait of James V. Forrestal, the first
Secretary of Defense, and a reminder of defeat to every Secretary
of Defense. Forrestal had been a Wall Street broker who had
struggled to cement civilian control over the military services, had
worked seven days a week and withstood fierce pressures from the
White House and Congress and the military: but he broke under
the strain and was hospitalized, and appeared to be recovering
until one morning in May when he slipped out of his hospital
room at the National Naval Medical Center in Bethesda, Maryland, loosened a window screen and plunged thirteen stories to his
death.

Belling motioned to Hugh to sit in an armchair facing his desk.
Mozart's String Quartet in D played softly in the room. Two glis-
tening glass ashtrays and some matchbooks marked "Secretary of
Defense" decorated the low pine table beside Hugh.

Belling slumped in his chair. "Tragic about Evan," he said. "I
knew him when he was national editor."

Hugh nodded.

"Yale man, wasn't he?"

"Yes."

"Sad business."

Hugh placed his notebook on the table and removed the cap of
his felt-tipped pen. Behind the desk, a pink pushbutton telephone
panel glittered with flashing lights. Two telephones—one black, the
other red—were on the desk.

Hugh said lightly: "Just saw the Washington *Post*. Democrats on the Hill are talking about a possible compromise . . ."

Belling broke into an empty smile.

". . . candidate."

"You newspaper fellows amaze me," said Belling, his voice oddly low. "Last week I was supporting Dave Fitzgerald. This week *I'm* a dark-horse candidate. How many trees are cut down to print this garbage?"

As he spoke, Belling pushed forward and picked up his pipe off the center of the desk. Hugh felt his mouth turn dry.

The bastard was such a Washington type.

Someday he would write about the Edward Bellings of Washington, the clique of men who glide smoothly between well-paying jobs in academe, foundations and government; defense and foreign affairs specialists who straddle these worlds and manage, somehow, to avoid being tainted by the failed or reckless policies they helped shape and nurture. Institutional and journalistic memories are, after all, weak in Washington; administrations are swept into office, and then collapse, bringing on new administrations, new disorder at the top, but leaving a layer of specialists just beneath the top who either cling to their jobs in the State Department, the Pentagon, the National Security Council, the Central Intelligence Agency, or who move on to other posts, perhaps at the Brookings Institution or the Ford Foundation or the World Bank or any one of a number of East Coast and West Coast universities eager to hire ex-government officials. These worlds had blurred, especially in recent years, and there was, perhaps, no one in government more adept at exploiting the overlap between government, the foundations, and the universities than Edward Lewis Belling.

A man in his fifties who was an early adviser to John F. Kennedy and who was dutifully rewarded with a job under Robert S. McNamara at the Pentagon, Belling, like most of his colleagues, was deeply involved in the early planning of the war, the troop buildup, pacification of the countryside, the initial bombings of North Vietnam. He served as deputy Air Force Secretary, head of the International Security Agency at the Pentagon, and then, under Lyndon Johnson, was appointed a deputy director of the Central Intelligence Agency.

With several of his academic colleagues in government, Belling
managed, quite successfully, to leave few footprints, to deplore
privately what he was publicly carrying out, to convey the singular
impression (at Georgetown dinners, at Ethel Kennedy's lunches)
that what he was doing by day was not precisely what he believed
in, that he was locked in fierce battle with colleagues about Vietnam policy. Actually, it was a lie—Belling believed deeply in the
war effort. But his Ivy League academic credentials, his ties to the
Kennedys, his well-known liberalism, his trenchant Vietnam post-
mortems in *The Atlantic* and *Foreign Affairs* magazines, his
friendships with liberal columnists and editorial writers, left him
surprisingly unscarred by the war.

He emerged as one of the eminent defense and foreign policy
analysts in the Democratic Party, a member of the liberal wing's
"shadow government" who had served on the National Security
Council and, again, in the Pentagon during the years of the Carter
administration. Now, as Defense Secretary, Belling's publicized
turf battle with the CIA, his shrewd friendships with Senator
David Fitzgerald and others on Capitol Hill that enabled him to
exert political clout within the Administration, his private luncheons at the Metropolitan and Cosmos clubs at which he carefully doled out leaked information to select columnists and bureau
chiefs—all combined to make Belling one of the most influential
men in town. He was increasingly mentioned as a potential "dark
horse" candidate for President.

"This meeting never took place," Belling was saying.

Nodding, Hugh carefully opened his notebook.

"My aide and my secretaries of course know you're here," said
Belling. "My secretaries believe you're working on a magazine
piece about me. And Colonel Walker, whom you've met, can be
trusted."

Belling lit his pipe with a faint sucking sound, keeping his eyes
steady on Hugh. "We're off the record."

Hugh saw the slightest agitation in Belling's lower eyelids.

"We all agree China is playing hardball," said Belling, slowly
picking his words. "They ended the talks. Resumed border attacks. Cut the Trans-Siberian Railroad. *Why?* It's all extremely
provocative." Belling paused, seeming to concentrate on the whirr
of a helicopter outside. "Provocative and . . . puzzling."

Hugh stopped writing, looked up and caught Belling's glance.

Belling said: "Puzzling because the Administration has made certain assumptions about China's military capabilities, China's relatively backward capabilities. Question: why would China behave in such an aggressive way against the Soviets if their weaponry, if their defenses were as low-grade, as inferior, as our intelligence people say they are?"

"You mean the CIA," said Hugh.

"The CIA," replied Belling. "Yes, of course, the CIA." He removed his pipe and examined it with distaste. Belling shifted forward.

"Forty-eight hours ago the Chinese asked us, and the Russians, to clear all our ships from a one-hundred-mile area in the northern Pacific, an area called the Kamchatka Peninsula. The Chinese told us they planned to hold a missile test on Monday in this area, the same area where the Russians conduct *their* tests."

Belling's lips moved, then he spoke tensely. "The ostensible reason for asking us to clear our ships was that the Chinese didn't want to endanger the ships, they wanted them out of range of the test missile." Belling waited, watching Hugh.

"And the actual reason is that the Chinese wanted, in fact, to alert us," Belling said, frowning. "By telling us in advance to clear our ships, the Chinese guarantee that we and the Russians will be watching their test closely. They *want* us to watch."

"Why?"

"Ask me Monday," said Belling.

Hugh began to speak, but Belling lifted his hand. "The assumption in this building is that China has made some breakthrough, some key breakthrough in their ICBM force." He stared at Hugh. "Obviously, they're firing a long-range missile into Kamchatka, which is six thousand miles away from their test site. Obviously, in telling us and the Russians, the Chinese are showing extreme confidence in the success of their test."

"What can I write?"

"About the test—nothing."

"It'll leak."

"It will *not* leak. About fifteen people in the United States Government know about it." Belling waited. "After the test you'll be informed."

"Then, why the hell are you telling me all this now?"

"Because Dave Fitzgerald wanted me to." Belling returned Hugh's stare. Hugh was aware that in the last few minutes the lines around Belling's mouth seemed to have deepened. Belling spoke hoarsely.

"There's a story here, Hugh, there's a story that can be done. I wanted to give it to one of the big boys, the Washington *Post,* the *Times,* papers with *im*pact, but Dave Fitzgerald suggested *you.*"

Hugh swallowed. "Why?"

"Ask Fitzgerald."

Sweat tingled the nape of Hugh's spine. He stared at his notebook. "What's the story?"

Now he was writing in a fever, breathing hard, his mouth parched, the words from Belling an echo.

"You can say this now: as the current border crisis gets worse, as the poor quality of our intelligence—our lack of intelligence—becomes evident, I have made a proposal to the President that seeks to . . . to . . . *streamline* our intelligence branches into a single agency. An agency that combines the intelligence branches of the CIA, DIA, NSA, even the FBI under a single roof."

"You'll take over this agency."

There was the slightest hesitation in Belling's voice. "Well, *yes.* You can say that Belling has the support of a bipartisan group of influential senators. You can say that a growing number of government officials are deeply upset about the faulty intelligence we're getting, the Administration's fumbling, the Administration's strange inaction . . ."

Hugh took his breath in little gasps, feeling the same lighthearted exhilaration and tension that always filled his throat and belly and groin whenever a story, a front-page story, started to form.

"And the Chinese test on Monday . . ."

"If successful—and we assume it will be—the Chinese test will shock Congress, startle the American people. What are the Chinese up to? We don't know. And why? Because our intelligence has failed us. The public will have every right to ask why our intelligence . . . collapsed. Just like the Bay of Pigs. Only far more dangerous. Why were we caught off guard? Why didn't we *know* about China's nuclear advances? Why?"

Hugh was writing in a fever; his impulse was to laugh.

So . . . what.

So what if Belling was using him to float a classic trial balloon, to pressure the President, to build up congressional support in his turf skirmish with the CIA. The Monday test fits into Belling's hands like a perfect glove. The bastard wants to control intelligence and defense, super czar, and he's orchestrating his leaks.

"I'll deny I saw you, of course," Belling was saying.

So . . . *what*.

Old Washington ritual it is. Lie down and spread your legs and a "reliable source" pumps away and you love it. Jesus, you love it.

Front-page byline, top of the fold.

Hugh heard the door open and turned to see Colonel Walker step in, movements as lithe as a cat; he handed Belling a note. Hugh watched Belling frown while he scribbled an answer.

There were more questions to ask. What was the latest intelligence from the border? Could he see Belling again tomorrow, slip up here during the Pentagon news briefing?

Hugh looked at his notebook.

Why did Fitzgerald want the story leaked to *him,* leaked to the *Star?*

He felt a drumming in his ears, and suddenly thought of Pomerance. Dr. Seymour E. Pomerance.

Why . . . why was Alvin Simmons meeting Pomerance?

*

From the Claiborne funeral, Linda Fentress had rushed to the *Star* building, stopping first in the cafeteria for coffee. In the newsroom she unlocked the top drawer of her desk to remove a lined yellow pad and two razor-point black pens. She placed a Librium on her tongue and swallowed it with the coffee. Then she stared at the blank page.

How to start an investigation with no leads, no clues, no sources? No idea what the story was about. How to start from behind when the *Daily News,* the *Times* and God-knows-who-else is working on something. On *what?* Barry Cohen didn't know— he'd simply ordered her to find out.

Make a list. *NYT. Daily News.*

Write the names of their investigative reporters beneath each heading.

Make a separate list, writing the names of friends and sources at each paper.

Linda phoned Valerie French, a fashion reporter on the *Daily News,* with whom Linda had shared a summer house in Sag Harbor. Four men and four women had rented the cedar beach house —reporters and editors with the *Star,* the *Daily News, Newsday* and NBC—starting out that summer with a serene Memorial Day cheese and wine party that had begun at dusk and lasted until 2 A.M., when the police finally arrived by jeep. They broke up a fight between a drunk New York *Post* reporter and an ABC reporter over the *Post* reporter's comment that there was no such thing as a television reporter; they were all entertainers, performers, show-biz personalities.

It was the start of a summer that had rapidly plummeted into constant weekend verbal skirmishes and, at times, open warfare over refrigerator thefts of personally labeled individual necessities such as low-fat cottage cheese, ripe peaches, bagels, Fresca, nitrate-free bacon, and additive-free lettuce.

Valerie French was a plain, moody young woman constantly on a diet who once confessed to Linda that men with hairy legs turned her on.

Valerie listened now in silence to Linda's appeal and grumbled yes, yes, if she could find out anything she would, but please don't count on it. Valerie was pointedly cool, and Linda sensed that she had never quite been forgiven for consuming half a box of Valerie's fat blueberries one August night.

Damn, thought Linda, hanging up.

She dialed the number of Arnie Grayson, a sports reporter, who once picked her up at a *Star* party on Riverside Drive, and then pawed her in a taxi on the way home as if they were teen-agers. Poor Arnie. Little, short guy. Couldn't get it up. Seemed quite small down there too.

A desk clerk told her that Arnie was traveling with the Yankees, he had left that morning, and wouldn't be back for at least ten days, but phoned in for his messages. Did she want to leave her name?

No, thanks.

Merde. *Merde!*

Try another tactic at the *Daily News*. Find out if their investigative reporters are in New York.

Linda called the *Daily News* metro desk.

"Is Charlie Farrell there?" she asked.

"No," said the clerk, his voice raspy and impatient.

"Oh. Is he in town?"

"No."

"Is there a way of reaching him? It's a personal . . ."

"You can leave a message with me, honey. He calls in."

"But it's a personal . . ."

"We are not allowed to give out Mr. Farrell's whereabouts. I would be happy to . . ."

"Is Marty Pirota there?" She suddenly felt desperate.

"No, Marty Pirota is not here either." Dumbo sounded like he was losing patience, she thought.

"Is he with Mr. Farrell?"

"Who is this, please?"

It was a losing battle with this surly desk clerk, and she had to extricate herself gently, so the clerk wouldn't tell the two investigative reporters that a woman had been prying about where they were. Too easy to trace.

Linda lowered her voice.

"Well, can I leave a message for Mr. Farrell and Mr. Pirota?"

"Of course you can. That's what I've been saying all along."

"Tell them that I am a fan of theirs and I have a wonderful story."

"A *ha*." The clerk sounded wary. "Where can they reach you?"

"Well, frankly, they can't, I'm in the hospital."

"I *see*." The clerk was now convinced that she was the third fruitcake to call the metro desk that day.

Linda went on, "When the doctors find out that I have spoken to the New York *Daily News* they'll rape me."

"Rape?" She knew that he was probably marking wire-service copy and had tuned out.

"Rape, yes, rape. There's a black doctor who drugs and rapes the white patients and staff. I have seen him violate a nun. Sister Felicity Margaret. Perform unspeakable acts on her person."

"Well, thank you very much, ma'am."

"And thank *you* very much, young man, and God bless you

and your loved ones and please inform Mr. Farrell and Mr. Pirota . . ."

"Yeah."

"That naked black doctors have taken over Bellevue Hospital. Do you hear me?"

"I hear you, honey. Take care of yourself. Gotta go. Bye."

Linda lit a cigarette. She tapped the point of her pen on the yellow pad. Find out where Farrell and Pirota are.

Charlie Farrell. Fast-talking, dark glasses, sharkskin suit, fiftyish, looks and behaves like a cop. Very good sources at Police Headquarters, the Drug Enforcement Administration, and the FBI. Shared Pulitzer with Pirota on a series about waterfront crime.

Charles X. Farrell.

Linda found no listing for Charles X. Farrell in the Manhattan telephone book, but found three in Queens.

The first one was a fireman.

On the second call, at a Whitestone address, she found his wife.

"Hi, I'm looking for Charles Farrell of the *Daily News.*"

"Yes."

"Oh, Mrs. Farrell?"

"Yes, who is this?"

"I'm Mary Ellen Johnson of *Parade* magazine. The *Daily News* told me that your husband was out of town and I'm trying to reach him about a magazine assignment."

"I see." A long pause. "I'm not allowed to give out where he's staying, but if you leave me your phone number I'll pass it on to him and he'll get back to you."

"There's no way of talking to him now? It's urgent."

"Sorry, no. I'll reach him if you want . . ."

"Well, when is he due back?"

"I'm not sure, Miss . . ."

"Johnson."

"Miss Johnson. Can I get your phone number?"

Linda inhaled her cigarette deeply. Then she babbled. "I'd rather write to him direct. I'm going out of town, traveling in the Midwest, and I'll write to him at the *Daily News.*"

"If you . . ."

"Anyway, thank you very much. Bye."

Bitch!

Their wives were trained to shut up, yield no information about their husbands' whereabouts.

A final try. Marty Pirota.

Two years ago she met Marty at the Federal Courthouse on Foley Square covering the trial of a former city councilman from Staten Island accused of tax evasion. On the third day of the trial they had had dinner at Wo Ping's in Chinatown—Marty said the cracked crab was the best in the city—and then took a cab to her apartment, where they smoked a joint and danced to an Ella Fitzgerald record of Cole Porter songs.

By ten-thirty they were in bed, by ten thirty-eight Marty had come after perfunctorily kissing her and biting her nipples, and by eleven o'clock he was zipping up his trousers to leave and catch a train for Sayville, Long Island.

Good old Marty.

She phoned information for Pirota's phone number.

A child answered the phone. "Hello."

"Hi, who's this?" Linda said.

"This is Anthony Frank Pirota." He sounded about four.

She abhorred the sound of anyone under twelve answering a phone, forcing her to ask for their mommy or daddy, to make baby talk. Humiliating.

Linda began asking for his mommy, when the words tumbled out of her mouth.

"Anthony, where's your daddy?"

"My daddy's in Los Angeles, California."

She heard a woman's sharp cry, "Tony," the scuffle of hands wrestling the phone away from the boy, whispers that ended when the child's mother said, loudly, angrily, "Hello!"

Linda waited, but knew further questions were futile. It was enough. She hung up.

"Thanks, Tony," she said. Lifting her eyes, Linda saw Barry Cohen, who was speaking intently on the city desk phone.

*

"Listen, Howie," Barry was saying. "The story's Jerry. Jerry Paley. You got it? Forget the Fitzgerald angle. It's Jerry. Don't raise your voice to me, Howie. *Listen!* We're going to do a number on Jerry, okay? *That's* the story, you hear me? *Jerry!* Not

Fitzgerald. It's *Jerry*. And we're going to get some help on it, my friend, some *documents*. Some heavy leaks. Can't tell you, Howie, but that's the story, okay? Now the diary. Cheryl's diary. *Get it*. That's what you do. You get the diary, and you see Jerry and you leave all the rest to me. And you know what, Howie? You're gonna get a front-page byline on this one. It's gonna be a biggie, Howie. You work from your end, and I'll work from mine, and we're gonna do one hell of a job on Jerry Paley."

*

Slipping into the master bedroom, Lucy closed the door and rested her back against it. She was breathing heavily, rapid short breaths.

She moved across the bedroom, a setting of baroque splendor dominated by one of her father's final purchases, a bed from the Barberini Palace made for Pope Urban VIII. She lay down on the golden bedcover, placing the palm of her left hand across her eyes.

Lucy heard blurred voices from the living room, guests talking, the New York street sounds of car horns and, somewhere in the distance, fire engines. She placed her hands over her ears and twisted her head back and forth, the tension and panic and rage swelling to choke her, leaving her dizzy with sorrow. Her body was screaming.

She bit her hand, then rubbed her palms into her eyes. Struggling to breathe, Lucy heard the gasps, the groans engulfing the room before accepting that they were, yes, hers.

She began weeping high-pitched and fevered, rolling back across the bed. She heard the door open, a surge of noise from the living room, but she was beyond apologies or embarrassment. Lifting her knees to her stomach, her arms around her head, Lucy was trapped in a torrent of despair.

She felt a hand on her shoulder.

"Go away, please go away," she said, refusing to look up.

The hand, a gentle hand, remained. Someone kissed her hair. It was her nephew, Larry Steiner.

"Oh, Larry. My God."

"Don't."

"I couldn't . . ."

"Don't say a word."

She embraced him, tightening her fingers on his slender shoulders.

"The food was lousy anyway," he said, sitting up.

She struggled to laugh.

"I couldn't *take* it. Couldn't take my daughter's anger. I couldn't take your father—Skipper's mournful eyes. Couldn't take Frieda one more *second*. Couldn't take those people coming in and staring at me."

"Here," he said. "Valium."

"Give me two."

He rose from the bed and disappeared into the bathroom, returning a moment later with a glass of water.

"Saw you coming in here." he said. "I knew you were in trouble."

"You're sweet, Larry."

He shrugged. "Sweet Larry."

His tone made her wince.

"I remember when you were born, Larry. Christ, I feel old." Lucy stuck the Valium on her tongue and sipped the water.

"Skipper was so proud. A son. An *heir*. Your grandfather was beside himself. Frederic went down to Macy's and spent, I would say conservatively, five thousand dollars on toys, gifts and assorted junk. Mother was furious." Lucy smiled. "I think Frederic knew he was going to die." She sighed. "You were such a handsome little boy."

"I still am."

"Come on."

"Still a handsome little boy. Don't you want to grow up?"

"Are you echoing your shrink?"

"Who else?"

"How's the job?"

"The job." He opened the vial of Valium, took one, and swallowed it with the remaining water. "Work in the business department for eight months, news department six months, advertising for a year. I drift. Keeps me out of trouble. Keeps me *sane*."

Her smile faded.

"Now, don't you worry," he said quietly. "I'm not into self-destruction. I don't think *that* runs in the family, though every now and then I want to check back into old Chestnut Lodge but just to get *away,* play some tennis, ride, have some peace and quiet."

She watched him.

"This family's lousy at human contact," said Lucy.

"Mothers and daughters. Fathers and sons."

"Do you ever talk to your father?"

"Talk? To Skipper? Come on, Aunt Lucy. Skipper spends his day talking to the head of advertising, the managing editor, the financial editor, the labor people, the Macy's and Gimbels folks, maybe the mayor and probably a girlfriend. Not his little boy. Why the hell should he?"

"He loves you."

"Bullshit."

"He's not that bad."

"I'm not saying he's *bad.* I'm saying that the *Star* is his life. And besides . . ."

She watched his soft, pleasant face dissolve, the smooth skin at each side of his mouth turning white.

"He's embarrassed about me," Larry said.

Larry ran his fingers over his coarse black hair, cut short all over.

"The faggot son that he couldn't teach baseball. Not that he tried very hard. The son that dropped out of Princeton and N.Y.U. The son that wanted—if I wanted anything—to be a dancer. The son's that's a humiliation to Skipper, his major failure in life."

Lucy felt the dampness of his right hand, clasped between her fingers. "Margo looked terrific at the church," she said.

"Darling, Mother always looks terrific. If you spent five hours a day exercising at Manya Kahn's, or having your legs waxed at Elizabeth Arden, having your hair dyed at Kenneth's, eating bean sprouts and starving yourself to look like a *Vogue* model, then you'd look terrific too. I shouldn't say that—you look better."

She smiled wanly.

"The trouble is, that's all Margo cares about. That's *it.* I used to think she's vain but she's not. She's a walking mummy, intent on staying preserved."

"Afraid of getting old."

"Look, what I mind is the cruelty. I shouldn't care, should I?

I'm a big boy. But she still talks about her pregnancy, when she had me. How awful she looked. How it took her a whole fucking year to get her figure back. She's an empty, frightened woman."

"She was *very* beautiful," said Lucy.

"That's why he married her. Two weeks ago I accused her of hating me because I looked Jewish. She threw a shoe at me. A Charles Jourdan black pump. She wanted a golden-haired little WASP for a son, and when she looks at me she hates what she sees. A WASP I'm not. Neither is Dad. I should become a Hasidic rabbi to get even."

"Larry, I don't see you as . . ."

"The religious type. The long beard. Ringlets. Black coat. Rabbi Lawrence Steiner of Park and Seventy-seventh to see the duchess. Wouldn't that blow my mother's mind."

Lucy laughed, and suddenly her eyes were wet with tears.

"I'm relieved Evan's dead," she whispered. "At some point last month, Larry, I began wishing for his death. Humiliating me. Humiliating *us*. Calling us kikes. Screaming at me at parties."

"He was in pain, Lucy."

"Johanna despises me." The afternoon sun caught her stricken face. "While her father was in and out of Payne Whitney and Riggs, her mother was seeing David Fitzgerald. She despises me for that."

The door burst open, another flood of noise from the living room filled the bedroom.

"*There* you are," said Frieda, moving in, looking distracted, her eyes blinking nervously. "Lucy, darling. People are starting to leave."

Lucy stiffened. She held Larry's hand firmly, and climbed off the bed to walk toward the bathroom. "Must look beastly," she muttered.

Frieda didn't hear. "Larry, you come in too. There are people in there that you should know."

"I'll be in soon, Grandmother," he said.

Frieda shut the door, and Larry lay down on his right side, crooking his arm and placing his chin in his right hand. With his left hand he dug into his jacket pocket and removed the bottle of Valium, flipping off the top. He placed a tablet on his tongue and gulped it down without water. Then he lay back on the bed, still gripping the open bottle.

Lucy emerged from the bathroom, placing wraparound dark glasses over her eyes. "Don't tell me I look all right," she said. "I don't."

He climbed off the bed. "I'll be in there in a sec." He kissed her on the cheek and watched her leave.

He stepped to the mahogany table beside the bed and picked up the phone and dialed. It rang three times before a man's voice answered.

"Hi," said Larry.

"Where are you?"

"Still at the house. Everyone's leaving."

"Is it awful?"

"It's awful. How's the magazine piece?"

"Struggling."

"Can I see you? This afternoon?"

"Like when?"

"Like three-thirty, four. I'm horny."

"Oh, my." There was laughter. "Sure, four o'clock."

"My place?"

"Right."

After he hung up the phone, Larry began moving toward the living room. As he reached for the bedroom door, he realized that the plastic bottle of Valium was still in his hand. Quickly his fingers lifted out another tablet, dropped it on his tongue. Then he clamped on the cap and thrust the bottle in his jacket, wishing his heart would stop pounding.

*

As the foreign editor of the *Star,* Ward Parsons controlled a staff of eleven correspondents, a choice group of men and one woman. The selection—by Skipper, Evan, Maury and Ward—was based on age, talent and availability—bachelors were prime candidates—and although the newspaper editors and the owner spent weeks, sometimes months, writing confidential memos to one another and conferring privately about which young reporter should be sent to London or Moscow, to Jerusalem or Tokyo, the staff was a surprisingly uneven mixture of talents.

Some reporters could cover City Hall brilliantly, but when they

were sent to Cairo or New Delhi and left to themselves, without
guidance or pressure, without major competition, without a breaking news story, they floundered and failed to produce copy. And
when they did, the foreign desk would toss up its hands and groan
about this incoherent effort by a hapless fuck-up who actually
missed New York, whose wife had migraines, whose children had
dysentery, who felt victimized by editors who had never worked as
reporters and failed to grasp the fact that urgent man-in-the-street
reaction was unavailable at 2:30 A.M. in Salisbury. Or that filing
from god-awful places like Kampala meant counting the words
yourself, pasting the copy on a form and getting to the post office
by 4 P.M.; that flying from Buenos Aires to an earthquake in
Managua took sixteen uncomfortable hours (while it took less
than two hours from Miami); that living in places like Lagos was
punishing in a million ways. ("Lagos smells like Secaucus on a
hot, still August evening," said Homer Bigart, one of the great foreign correspondents.)

As the first foreign editor to have actually worked in the field,
Ward Parsons struggled to understand the needs and fears of the
younger correspondents. In this business, he knew, you were only
as good as your last story. You were frighteningly insecure about
your talent and had a compulsive need for a byline three days a
week, at least—as if to confirm the fact that you were a pro, on top
of the story, that they adored you in the home office and that you
weren't slipping. You hungered for space in the paper and exclusives and front-page stories, but what happens if you're stuck in
goddamned Lagos or Dacca or Rawalpindi or Kinshasa? Suppose
you hung around Belgrade for years, waiting for Tito to die? So
the historic day arrives. And there's no civil war, no riots, no Russian invasion. Nothing.

What happens when day after day your stories are overheld because of Middle East news, or a crisis in southern Africa, or an
election at home? And when your prized feature story finally runs,
it's buried without a picture, on page 24, next to the brassiere ads
in Sunday's paper, recklessly butchered by a copy editor with an
itchy pencil and a tin ear who cut out the poetry.

And what happens, worst of all, if the competition from
the news agencies and the other papers starts heating up and
the feared rockets pour in from New York . . . "AP REPORTS

PAKISTANI COUP STOP CAN YOU CONFIRM SOONEST QUERY . . . UR-
GENT AND IMMEDIATE NYTIMES AND WASHPOST HAVE STORIES
EARLY EDITIONS REPORTING IDI AMIN SIGHTED IN PARAGUAY STOP
PLEASE MATCH SOONEST STOP IS THERE MENGELE CONNECTION
QUERY REGARDS . . . OPPOSITION SAYS POPE ILL STOP ARE YOU
THERE QUERY HAVE UNHEARD FROM YOU FOR TEN DAYS STOP
AWAITING REPLY . . ."

Of course, once a reporter's confidence melted—once he turned
vulnerable—the insecurities that usually hovered just beneath the
surface took over and crippled him. Unsure of his own talent, nervous about the competition, confused about what to file in New
York, the reporter is soon labeled a loser by the desk. A self-
fulfilling prophecy.

"Jee-sus! They're like sharks here," Florence told Ward the
night before Evan's funeral as the foreign editor was struggling
with the fate of Mark Kaiserman, the *Star*'s hapless outgoing Johannesburg correspondent. "Once they sniff blood, they all move
in."

Some older correspondents abroad produced too much, six-
hundred-word stories churned out daily based on government
handouts, a rewrite of AP and a lazy phone call or two, stories
that seemed to drop like a weight within the *Star,* unreadable, forgotten.

Some correspondents were abroad too long (like Larry Lake in
London). They lost touch with the paper, adopting a country and
apologizing for it, turning native and, at the same time, turning
into a good-will ambassador sought after by the BBC in any capital to explain and translate the latest White House pronouncement
or congressional vote.

And some reporters, of course, wrote with sensitivity about the
texture of a country or a people, struggling to inform readers that
this is what Jakarta smells like, here is what people in Stockholm
are talking about, this is precisely what it's like in Kabul, *this is
what I am seeing.*

Ward was puzzled about the uneven caliber of his staff. Given
the fact that it cost at least one hundred and fifty thousand dollars
a year to keep a single American abroad, given the *Star*'s worsening finances that made overseas bureaus extremely vulnerable to
cutbacks (there were rumors that the offices in Bonn, New Delhi

and Bangkok were to close after Tokyo and Johannesburg), given the time spent nurturing potential correspondents, Ward was bitterly disappointed that the quality of his people abroad was simply not the best in the business.

"Damn it, damn it, *damn* it," he said, standing up at his desk shortly after returning from the funeral and flinging several pages of copy to Ray Silver. "Look at this garbage from Paris. Norman Walker. Marked exclusive."

He turned to Ray. "Send him a message." Ray dutifully picked up a sheet of paper and grabbed a sharpened pencil. Ward said:

"Norman, please run your mood of Europe story through the typewriter one more time. You say the mood of Europe is uneasy and, according to well-informed diplomatic observers, fearful over the border clashes. You say nations of the Atlantic Alliance are concerned about the Bergen administration's refusal to play an active role. Well, can you back that up with some solid reporting and quotes . . ."

"Instead of lifting up the phone, Norman," interrupted Florence.

"And calling some jerk at the American Embassy who gets *his* information from the International *Herald Trib*," said Ray.

"May I finish?" said Ward.

"Ward!" Florence's tone made Ward and Ray turn. "You got a call before from Moscow, Ernie Richards." Ward stared at her, puzzled. "Just to remind you. He starts his two-week vacation. Tuesday."

"*Vacation!*"

"You approved it in January, dear. Remember?"

Ward slumped in his chair. "Jesus! Isn't there a crisis somewhere? Has old Ernie . . ."

"Old Ernie has not seen his ten-year-old kid in over a year," said Florence patiently. "She's flying in from Denver. Spending Easter vacation with him in Paris. There's *always* a crisis."

"Poor bastard," said Ray. "Four years in Moscow."

Ward frowned at his coffee. He heard Ray's voice. "I won't show you Larry Lake's copy now. The Northern Ireland situation."

Ward closed his eyes. "Break it gently."

"Written from London, that's the first problem. He obviously didn't get his ass out into the streets to talk to a Catholic or Protestant, or to ordinary people."

"Lake doesn't talk to ordinary people," said Ward.

Ray lifted the sheet of copy. "He begins with an anecdote at the Reform Club. A British minister leaning back on his overstuffed leather chair, taking a sip of heavily sweetened tea and speaking gently."

Ward felt his cheeks turning hot. "If that bastard has one more lead starting with a British minister drinking tea, I will . . ."

"Do nothing," said Florence, smiling. "Larry Lake is untouchable, remember?"

"Frieda's favorite nephew," said Ray.

"Any Irish quotes?" asked Ward.

"One or two at the end. A priest and a Protestant dockworker. Unnamed. Mildly radical types."

"Our great radical," said Ward, folding his hands, pressing his thumbs against his lips. "Up the PLO. Up African guerrillas. Our great radical who treats ordinary people . . ."

"Like me," said Florence, thrusting the message from her typewriter.

"Like shit," said Ward.

Ward picked up Lake's copy, and told Ray that he would read it after the 3 P.M. conference in the publisher's office. He had twenty minutes before the meeting to read the summaries of stories that the foreign desk was offering for the next day's paper, stories dominated by the China-Soviet conflict. The foreign desk "package" was impressive.

There was Carl Ross's nine-hundred-word story from Hong Kong on the abrupt disruption of the Trans-Siberian Railroad by the Mongolian People's Liberation Movement, as well as outbreaks of violence in Sinkiang Province.

There was Hugh Finch's exclusive, also nine hundred words, on Defense Secretary Belling's dispute with the Administration over our China policy, on defense officials charging that the CIA's intelligence on China had been faulty, and that the agency was "mishandling" the Chinese border crisis. "There is, at this point, a sense of anxiety, even alarm, over the ominous situation on the Russian-Chinese border, as well as impatience over the Administration's 'strange inaction,' according to one ranking official," wrote Finch. (Ward phoned Hugh to ask if the sentence wasn't a bit strong, but Hugh insisted it wasn't. The two finally agreed to insert the phrase "by a handful of defense aides" after the word "alarm.")

There was a late story from Moscow by Ernie Richards, eight hundred words, quoting Western diplomats (obviously the German Ambassador via his wife, Ernie's bedmate), suggesting that a war with China would inevitably involve the use of nuclear weapons and "would not spare a single continent." Another front-pager.

And finally a nine-hundred-word exclusive by Barney Fischer, the paper's White House correspondent, a story on a private poll by the Democratic Party, coinciding with the Soviet-China crisis, that showed widespread unhappiness among leaders and delegates toward President Bergen, and support in next year's convention focused on Vice President Tom Nelson and New York Senator Dave Fitzgerald. At Ward's request, Barney also threw in a line from the morning's Washington *Post* that said Defense Secretary Edward Belling, who was known to be close to Fitzgerald, was also being mentioned as a possible dark-horse candidate.

(Barney's Washington exclusives were a staple on the paper; his corn-gold hair, flecked with gray, and ice-blue eyes, had devastated a White House secretary, a congresswoman from Michigan, the wife of a well-known conservative southern senator, a woman who worked as a key aide to the Secretary of State as well as a ranking Administration economist, each of whom provided him with front-page stories.)

Ward watched Maury step across the newsroom toward Evan's office, smiling at Mary Phelps as he stepped inside. It was a ritual among editors to gather in Evan's office before venturing upstairs to the publisher's office on the tenth floor.

Ward looked at his watch. Two-fifty. He stared for a moment at the pile of summaries facing him, but looked up again at Mary, who stood at a file cabinet, thrusting papers in folders.

Mary turned now and looked up coolly across the newsroom, as if to signal the editors that the story conference was about to begin. Cohen moved toward the managing editor's office, so did Sally Sims.

Mary Phelps then averted her eyes, sitting down in her swivel chair and rummaging through the top middle drawer of her desk. It was an elaborate ritual—Mary's staring at the watch, her signal to the editors that Evan was ready, her avoidance of eye contact with the men and women moving into her boss's office. An elaborate ritual now obsolete.

Ward picked up the pile of summaries, neatly folded on his desk. He glanced at Florence, earnestly typing letters; at Ray Silver; at Nick Simons, the city desk news clerk across the aisle, who was busily transcribing a late summary on his video terminal, a phone clamped against his ear.

A copy girl, who had graduated from Barnard and spoken to him six months ago about her yearning to go to Africa one day, walked past Ward with some morgue folders for the foreign copy desk.

It was changing, thought Ward, pushing his seat back and standing. *It was changing.* Even if Maury was appointed managing editor, Evan's generation was fading, shadows forming. A new generation of men and women in their late thirties and forties was taking over, a generation of reporters and editors that shared Vietnam and Watergate and the movements of the sixties and seventies that divided them from Maury's and Evan's generation.

The older men had witnessed the upheavals of the sixties and seventies, but failed to grasp its impact on the staff of the *Star.* Maury, a decent man, seemed incapable of understanding that many good reporters now would not travel overseas because the mystique was fading, because wives held jobs now and refused to tag along, because reporters held values now that reached beyond the needs of the paper.

Perhaps most important, the younger reporters felt little obligation to the *Star.* It was a job, not a way of life. Strikes and labor unrest had embittered too many reporters. Frederic Steiner's benevolence to the professionals on his staff had now been overtaken by the dollars-and-cents calculations of the accountants and businessmen under his grandson. Reporters were dispensable, like elevator operators. Reporters were easily replaced. Ten younger kids were waiting in the wings to shove aside the reporter who has covered coups in Iran and Afghanistan and seen the faces of Bengali children, their hair bleached by starvation, and hovered in a C-140 from Plciku littered with the body bags of American soldiers. At thirty-eight or thirty-nine, reporters got tired. No encores after forty.

Perhaps young reporters today have more common sense than I do, thought Ward. Perhaps they're more realistic, less romantic. He brushed a wisp of hair off his charcoal turtleneck, frowned at his scruffed black wing-tip shoes. He stepped toward the managing editor's office, feeling the slither of ulcer pain claw his stomach.

*

Two fifty-five. Skipper Steiner was finally in a cab, moving crosstown on Seventy-ninth Street toward Central Park and the drive downtown to the *Star*. He would be late, but he hoped to catch the final few minutes of the news conference; Maury would fill him in on the details.

He had spoken to Maury over the phone from Frieda's apartment. The Sino-Soviet story was a developing one, somewhat ominous, and would dominate the paper the next day. Maury said he was weighing the assignment of another reporter to fly to Asia on temporary assignment, given the potentially critical story there. Was this agreeable to Skipper? Meaning, of course, did the paper want to spend the money?

Skipper said yes, without hesitation. Let other newspapers skimp on traveling, or foreign coverage, on deploying all the staff necessary for a major story. The *Star*, struggling in the last few years to rival the *Times* and the Washington *Post*, would use its resources to cover this crisis, to cover *any* crisis in a style that would have made his father and, yes, his grandfather, proud.

He settled back in the seat, digging his hand inside the inner pocket of the navy-blue double-breasted suit that he had carefully selected for the funeral. He found his leather-bound datebook, opened it and removed the Laque fountain pen from his shirt pocket. Sally had given him the pen over Christmas, one of her many gifts.

Skipper began writing on the notebook's pale-blue paper.

Eli.

He would speak to Eli Faber about Lucy's finances, her stocks, her certificates of deposit, municipal bonds, mutual funds and trust. Set up a monthly package now for his sister out of the family's stock holdings.

Johanna.

Have his secretary reserve a quiet table at "21" for luncheon tomorrow with his niece.

Harry.

Reschedule his meeting with Harry Watson, the *Star*'s vice president in charge of labor relations. Draft the final memo on staff cutbacks, and have it prepared for distribution Tuesday morning.

Break Lazzarutti, Skipper recalled Eli saying. *Break the union son of a bitch.* That's what Eli said. *Break him and we're home free. All this new technology, Skipper, makes the unions obsolete. A bunch of anachronisms. They know it, for Chrissake, they're scared, the balance has turned. We can produce a paper with a bunch of executives and a half-dozen secretaries. We don't need the Frank Lazzaruttis telling us how to run the paper. Mr. Union tough guy. Ambitious bastard, dying for a strike. Well, let's surprise him. Give him one. Confront him. Start cutbacks . . .*

Cutbacks mean a strike, Eli. Scares the hell out of me.

Scares me too. A long strike could . . . cripple us. Break *us. But where are the options, Skipper? We have to automate. We need financing. We're swollen with expenses, unnecessary expenses. We got deadwood floating all over this building. Get rid of them. Cut to the bone! Let's crush Lazzarutti.*

Drivers are pivotal, Eli. If we get the drivers to cross the picket line we can get the paper out.

They'll cross the line, Skipper. We'll take care of them.

Pivotal! Can't afford a long strike, Eli.

We'll take care of them! They'll cross the line!

Skipper tapped his pen on the notebook, recalling his grandfather's advice to Jonathan, which was subsequently passed on to him: union leaders can be bought off with a nice meal and a Christmas present. If they're wise-ass, break their thumbs. Skipper smiled.

What would the old man do with the Newspaper Guild's Frank Lazzarutti? And how would Frederic have dealt with the revolution in printing technology?

After a decade-long struggle, Skipper had triumphed with other publishers in 1974 over the printers, New York Typographical Union No. 6, the leader of the newspaper unions. Linotype machines were placed on the scrap heap, traditional featherbedding rules were overturned, and the paper was now allowed to set type through the use of computers and lasers. Later, the number of pressmen were thinned in a bitter strike in 1978, a strike that pitted members of all the unions, including reporters, against management, a strike where all health and life insurance was suspended by publishers for members of the Guild and the craft unions who were not working.

Despite the anger that lingered months after the strike, Skipper felt it was not his task to soothe ruffled feelings in the newsroom. Those days had vanished. The *Star* was, first and foremost, a business enterprise run by accountants and lawyers and marketing experts. To survive, a newspaper needed flinty executives. Paternalism was out of the question. What, after all, was best for the staff, a profitable paper or a dying paper?

The facts were painfully evident. Newspapers were hardly a growth industry. There were barely as many newspapers in the country today as there were in World War II. Although population had grown 50 percent since 1946, daily newspaper circulation had risen only 20 percent.

Too many young people were simply not reading newspapers. Television was one key reason. And then there was the deterioration of the cities, resulting in a reduction of newspaper sales after dark, cuts in home deliveries. And increased labor, newsprint and mailing costs had led to higher newspaper prices. A rising standard of living meant boating, golfing and camping were taking up a larger portion of leisure time. And the growth of suburban shopping centers had curbed the need for people to buy newspapers for store ads, had slashed the amount of department store advertising in the inner cities.

And . . . and . . .

Advertising was down and production costs were climbing. The *Star* was running fewer pages, partly to conserve newsprint. Skipper had reluctantly agreed to a no-hiring freeze, and confidential memos were sent to Evan and senior editors ordering a cutback in budgets and, especially, in travel. Was it necessary to follow a football team to Los Angeles on every trip? Is it sensible to send a reporter from London to Oslo to cover a Norwegian election? Let's use the wires on the American Bar Association convention in New Orleans.

Goddamn it. Frederic could afford to serve as paternal godfa-

ther over the staff during an era when profits flowed in comfortably and the *Star,* like the *Daily News* and *Times* and *Post,* could
afford to be unconcerned about tomorrow.

The unions had been pliant then. The city was stable. There
was plenty of advertising to go around—it accounted for 70 percent of the *Star*'s revenue. Newsprint costs were ridiculously
cheap. And the news staff was *different,* a different quality, a
different type of reporter and editor.

The staff was crammed with poor boys who were the sons of
immigrant parents. Grateful to work overtime, willing to go anywhere, to serve the needs of a newspaper that was like family, a
newspaper that rewarded them with modest fame, decent wages, a
free ticket to exotic places, *a taste of power.* Was there any other
job like being a reporter?

Under Frederic, poor boys like Maury had begun as copy
boys and junior reporters. They climbed up in the hierarchy under
Jonathan Steiner, whose reign had straddled the old and the new,
the congenial paternalism of his father coupled with the early
efforts of the newer breed of executive to control costs, to open
the newspaper to new technology, to blunt the increasingly feisty
unions.

It was converging now under Skipper.

The younger staff bore little sense of gratitude toward the *Star.*
And the *Star* itself needed to take measures, sometimes ruthless
measures, to remain competitive and to survive.

Skipper returned to his notebook and began writing.

Acquisitions.

He blinked in recollection of the funeral service. The crush outside the church, catching Ernie Dunlap's eyes fixed on him.

Dunlap was a thug who yearned to buy the *Star* with his older
brother Charles. The Dunlap boys. Building developers who
wanted the *Star* with a passion that Skipper could not quite
fathom. Years ago he had heard Frieda's story of Frederic and old
man Dunlap, the details hazy. *They want revenge, Skipper, Skipper, that's what they want . . .*

Skipper felt a gentle tug in his chest. His lips mouthed a single
word: *Lucy.*

He shut his eyes and saw his sister's stricken face.

The Dunlap boys were the money men behind Fitzgerald, Dave

Fitzgerald, that's the rumor. The Dunlaps financed Fitzgerald's campaign, and now Lucy was Fitzgerald's lover, for Chrissake.

Sweat trickled down his side and, quite suddenly, Skipper felt heavy with fatigue. His mind wandered.

Ernie Dunlap.

Lucy on the church steps chatting with Larry.

Frieda. Yes, he would inform Frieda that a California conglomerate had shown some interest in the *Star*. A California conglomerate and the Dunlaps.

As if Frieda would ever sell.

Skipper stared out the window blankly; he recalled Maury outside the church, whispering to his Chinese girlfriend, moving close to kiss her.

Maury.

Shrewd. Able. Second man.

Was he creative enough, strong enough, loyal enough, *ruthless* enough to cut off someone's balls for the benefit of the *Star? Did he have it?*

Like Evan? Jesus, Evan could be ruthless. But was that what you need to run a newspaper?

Evan Claiborne did not take prisoners. Newsweek had once published the comment by a typically unnamed source—news magazines sometimes used unnamed sources as the convenient kicker to a story, or for its opening line, because in all likelihood the quote was made up by the writer in New York. Yet Evan roared with delight at the comment.

Skipper smiled now, recalling the sight of Evan waving the article at the daily story conference.

That's what you need to run a newspaper. Someone who's ruthless and smart. And loyal.

Was it Maury? Cohen? Hugh? Ward Parsons? What about Sally?

Skipper looked out the window at the browned and mellowed yellow-brick buildings on Central Park West. As the cab neared Seventy-third Street Skipper gazed up at the third floor of the Dakota—Sally and Charlie's apartment overlooking Central Park had chalk-white curtains. His eyes traveled higher to the gables and cupolas and pinnacled dormers of the splendid building.

The taxi driver cursed the driver of a car that weaved in front

of him, and the taxi lurched to a stop for a red light. Skipper saw
Charlie Sims, on the far corner of Seventy-second Street and Central Park West, hailing a taxi.

Charlie looked terrific, a deep tan on his face and neck, his
hair sun-bleached. He wore frayed Adidas sneakers, faded blue
jeans and a white cashmere turtleneck sweater beneath a tan
lambskin jacket. He looked like a goddamn movie actor, which he
probably should have been.

Skipper leaned back on the seat. Within moments, when the
taxi reached Seventy-first Street, Skipper turned to the rear window and watched Charlie climb into a cab.

Skipper bit his lip. He would call Sally first. He needed her. He
would call her as soon as the story conference ended.

*

L.A.

Linda Fentress wrote the letters on her lined yellow pad. First
find out what hotel Charlie Farrell and Marty Pirota were staying
at. Find out who they're seeing. Details.

She walked to the telephone answering desk where Bethel Trus-
cott kept a stack of out-of-town phone books and domestic and
international hotel listings. Linda found the hotel book and carried
it to her desk.

Her last visit to Los Angeles, two years earlier, had involved
an investigation of murky financial dealings in the movie industry,
an investigation sparked by one producer, Gregory Hamalian, who
blew the whistle to federal prosecutors about kickbacks and bribes
to studio executives from independent producers seeking to ob-
tain financing for their movies. Under the system outlined by Hamalian, independent producers offered to build tennis courts or
swimming pool extensions at the homes of executives so that one
scene of a film could be made at the court or pool. The producers
got their financing, the executives their payments. Scripts were
often mangled to ensure at least one scene with a pool, a tennis
court, perhaps a sable coat—all of which would eventually fall into
the hands of studio executives.

Although the practice of siphoning money, either in cash or luxury items, from a motion picture budget had been a virtual tradition in Hollywood, Gregory Hamalian had cited names, films and
studios to Linda. Her series on Hollywood film financing had won

a New York Newspaper Guild Award, a Silurians Prize, had been nominated for the Pulitzer Prize, and had earned Linda a sizable raise in pay.

In Hollywood the Internal Revenue Service had launched a publicized investigation that, after two months, quietly sputtered and died. And Gregory Hamalian, although officially lauded by the movie industry and Los Angeles civic officials as a courageous figure, found it increasingly difficult to find work and to finance his projects. Several agent friends told him privately that the word was out in the film industry: Hamalian was a troublemaker who deserved to be ignored.

The intricate web of floating money, complex deals, skimming money, and loose financial controls that characterized the industry remained untouched.

Working out of the federal courthouse on that trip, Linda had stayed at the Bonaventure.

Okay. If Pirota and Farrell were spending time at the court-house they would stay at the Bonaventure or the Hyatt Regency or the Biltmore.

But most reporters from New York wanted to stay in Beverly Hills, even if it meant a twenty-minute drive into downtown Los Angeles, even if the rooms cost $145 a night. Editors in New York and accountants didn't know a goddamn thing about L.A., and assumed, wrongly, that reporters were staying in hotels convenient for their stories. What the hell. Why not Beverly Hills? Pirota and Farrell were hardly the types to pass up a week in the vicinity of starlets eager to have their picture on page five of the New York *Daily News.*

She phoned the Bonaventure anyway. They weren't registered. Nothing at the Hyatt Regency or Biltmore. She phoned the Century Plaza. Then the Beverly Hills hotel.

Sorry.

All right. She would try four or five other hotels and, if she couldn't reach them, would change to another tactic. She would impersonate one of their mothers. Call the newspaper desk at nine-thirty in the morning, or 2 A.M., when a young and hopefully inexperienced clerk was working. Ask where my son Martin Pirota, perhaps you heard of him, is staying in Los Angeles be-

cause I have a, uh, slight emergency and I want to speak to my
boy. Can you assist me, please, young man? Thank you kindly.

The Beverly Wilshire.

"May I speak to Mr. Charles Farrell or Mr. Martin Pirota."

"One moment."

Linda was on hold.

"Mr. Charles Farrell of New York?" said the operator.

"Yes."

"Do you want to speak to him?"

"Uh. No. I'd prefer to speak to Mr. Pirota."

There was a two-second pause, followed by an annoyed
murmur.

"One moment."

The operator was businesslike. "I'll connect you now," she said.

Linda's nervousness strained her words. "Operator, can I have
the room number?"

"I'm sorry, we do not give room numbers."

Linda would hang up if Marty answered, but he wasn't there.

"Thank you very much, I'll call later," Linda said.

She hung up, took a deep breath and picked up the phone
again, dialing the Beverly Wilshire. Linda asked for the reception
desk.

The clerk who answered sounded harassed; Linda heard talking
in the background—people were checking in or checking out. A
telephone was ringing.

Linda's voice dropped. "This is Mrs. Martin Pirota. P-I-R-O-T-
A. I'm downtown at I. Magnin and I want a package delivered to
my room. I don't have the key. Would you mind telling me the
room number?"

She paused. "That's P-I-R-O-T-A."

She hoped the clerk would check the last name and not give her
trouble because a Mrs. Pirota was not listed. These mistakes happen anyway.

"Yes. Mrs. Pirota. Seven twenty-three."

"Thank you very much."

She wanted to wait but was zeroing in. Starting an investigation,
playing the phones, filling in the puzzle, cheating, lying, manipulating—massaging an ego here and there—left her mouth dry.

"Okay, one more time, one more time," she said to herself. She phoned the Beverly Wilshire and asked, once more, for the reception desk. The same clerk answered. Damn!

"I'm so sorry to bother you, this is Mrs. Pirota again. Do we have any telephone messages? That's seven twenty-three."

"Hold on." He was eager to help. Sweet boy.

"Yes. Let me see, Mrs. Pirota. There are two messages for your husband. Do you want them?"

"Would you mind?"

"The first one was Mr. Elliott Hanley. That was at ten-thirty. The second one was Mr. Marcus Lynn. Democratic National Committee until 4 P.M. After that at his office. Do you want the numbers?"

"Yes," said Linda, writing the phone numbers on her yellow pad. She thanked the clerk.

"Excuse me, would you kindly do me a favor? What's your name, please?"

"Len." He sounded uneasy.

"Len, I'm buying a surprise gift for my husband. Would you *not* tell him, please, that I phoned."

"Don't worry, Mrs. Pirota." He sounded relieved.

"Thank you, Len."

She put the phone down and studied her pad. Their names were vaguely familiar—Hanley was a movie director, or producer, or *something* in the film industry. Marcus Lynn was a wealthy Democratic Party official in California; she recalled reading a personality piece about him in *New West* magazine.

Linda yelled "Copy" and asked the copy girl who approached her desk for the clips on Elliott Hanley and Marcus Lynn.

She had one more phone call to make. Gregory Hamalian.

Hamalian lived in a small beach house in Malibu, crammed with African artifacts and dynastic Egyptian masks picked up in his travels abroad. He was now writing a book about his years in Hollywood, and looking for work on television.

He greeted her enthusiastically.

"Gregory," she said. "Talk to me about Elliott Hanley."

"Hanley. Hanley. Basically a second-rate director who's making a brief splash. Knocked around for years. Grade-B stuff. Some television. Then eighteen months ago or so he lucked out. Got a Neil Simon picture and was nominated for an Academy Award."

"Neil Simon?"

"A fluke. They wanted Jack Lemmon and Sally Ann Field. Both had four months free. But no director. Herb Ross, Mike Nichols, Alan Pakula were booked. Everyone else was off somewhere, so Hanley got to direct."

"Is he political?"

"He's your standard Hollywood queen director. I think he once signed an antiwar thing that appeared in the L.A. *Times*. I think— and I'll check—he was blacklisted for a couple of years. Blacklisted by this asshole Keefer, Joey Keefer, state senator for a while. Keefer died about five years ago."

Linda wrote the name Joe Keefer at the top of her yellow pad.

"Familiar name," she said.

"Father was some hotshot in Washington. Majority leader."

"Merton Keefer. From Florida. That's it."

Linda watched Nick Simons, the city desk clerk, step past, gripping a container of coffee. Why didn't she like that kid? she wondered.

"What do you know about Marcus Lynn?" she asked.

"Marcus Lynn. Big-time lawyer, a lot of movie clients. Years back defended a bunch of Keefer's victims, blacklisted actors. Used to be a big buddy of Nelson. Vice President Nelson."

"What happened?" Linda spoke distractedly. Staring at the name. Joe Keefer.

"Big falling out. Don't know what . . ."

"Isn't Keefer's sister somebody? Isn't she married . . ."

"Sure. She's married to your senator," said Gregory Hamalian. "David Fitzgerald. Keefer was the senator's brother-in-law."

Linda wrote Fitzgerald's name on her pad, wondering what to ask next.

"Odd business," Gregory was saying. "At the end of Keefer's life he was a drunk, a rummy."

"Runs in the family," murmured Linda. "So's his sister."

"The odd part was that he worked for Marcus at the end. Real low-level stuff. Messenger. Chauffeur when he wasn't drunk."

Linda examined her notebook. The pieces made no sense. "How's Rita?" she finally asked.

"Rita's terrific. Still going to U.C.L.A."

"Still baking?"

"Better than ever."

Linda Fentress was about to hang up.

"She baked a wonderful brunch the other Sunday. Baked some croissants. We thought of you. We had someone over here that you might know. A guy . . . hold on . . . I'm looking at the book . . . Martin Pirota of the New York *Daily News*."

Linda held her breath. "What did Pirota want?"

"Wanted to know everything I knew about the Vice President."

"The Vice President. Nelson. Nelson and Marcus Lynn."

"Well, who Nelson's friends are. His background. How he began. Family life. Kept asking how Nelson *began* in Hollywood. I didn't know. Gave him names of people who might help."

"Including Hanley?"

"Right. Hanley directed Nelson in an early picture. I gave Pirota some other names."

Linda watched Cohen walk into the newsroom with Howie Bishop. Her hands were trembling now.

Hamalian asked: "Will we see you soon?"

"Yes," she said. At the city desk, Nick Simons was laughing on the phone. *"Yes!"*

Linda stood up and walked over to Barry Cohen.

*

As Sally Sims unlocked the door of her apartment at the Dakota shortly before six forty-five, she heard sounds from the television in the study.

"Hi!" she called out, hanging her raincoat in the hallway closet and dropping her leather case on a chair.

"Hello!" Charlie Sims called back.

She glanced at the pile of mail on the mahogany side cabinet in the hall, then walked through the living room into the study. Charlie, seated on a wicker rocking chair, was sipping a can of Tab, a copy of *Esquire* resting on his lap.

She kissed him on the cheek.

"Busy day?" asked Charlie.

"Got one *hell* of a good piece by David Gelber." Gelber was the *Star*'s Washington-based legal correspondent. Sally said: "Going to run it on Sunday, God and Frieda willing. On all the recent court rulings that limit press freedoms. Good *strong* piece."

Charlie smiled at her enthusiasm. "Someone from *Time* called," he said.

Sally kicked off her shoes and sat down in the Eames chair facing the rocker. For a moment their eyes met and Sally noticed the red rims that underlined his lids. Charlie turned away.

"Named . . . one second . . . here it is . . ." He picked up a notepad from the floor. "Marilyn Cheever. Sounded about twelve years old, no relation to John, called and wanted to talk to you about the *Star*'s struggle to stay alive, the competitive atmosphere quote unquote at the *Star*."

"If *Time* is doing it . . ."

"*Newsweek* can't be far behind."

"I dread this."

"You love it."

"No, I *don't*." Sally's vehemence surprised her. "I don't love it. Not at all."

Charlie's smile held as Sally spoke.

"I don't love it, because competing is not my thing. Power is not my thing. It never was. But now when I lose out it's going to be humiliating. Publicly humiliating."

"Maybe you won't lose."

"I *will*."

"Do you want it?"

She gazed at him.

"You *do* want it, don't you?" said Charlie. He tasted his soda.

"I'm ambivalent. Confused."

"Bullshit."

"You're so sympathetic."

"Well, you want the job. That's no crime."

"Stop trying to pin me down." Sally stood up so suddenly she felt dizzy. Anger and fatigue choked her voice.

"You're worried, aren't you? Right? My oh-so-liberated husband."

"Temper."

"Worried that I'll get that goddamn job and you'll be . . ."

"Mr. Norman Maine," Charlie said.

"What?"

"James Mason. *A Star Is Born*."

She finally smiled. "I need a drink."

"I'll walk into the water at Bridgehampton. Disappear like Norman. Never return."

"Do you want a drink, Norman?"

"I'm sticking to the diet stuff. Sshh. Here's Brokaw."

Tom Brokaw began the news with a report about the Russians blaming Chinese-supported guerrilla forces for new cuts along the Trans-Siberian Railroad. There was a satellite report from the NBC correspondent in Moscow.

"We've got a good story tonight on this from Hughie Finch. Exclusive. Just saw it as I was leaving." Sally poured herself a vodka on ice.

Charlie, half-listening to the Moscow report and a follow-up from Peking, said: "Hughie was mentioned by Miss Cheever. I asked her, Who are the contendahs? Besides my sweet little lady? Besides Maury, who else?"

"And what did she say?"

"Finch. And Cohen. And your friend Ward Parsons."

She ignored the innuendo. "Any favorites?" Sally asked.

"I asked her. She said Maury, but . . ." Charlie said nothing further.

"What does that mean?"

"Means that Maury is the favorite, but there's got to be opposition to him. Opposition from Frieda, maybe Skipper."

She stared at Charlie. He was watching an automobile commercial, featuring a sleek young couple driving through the desert.

Sally sipped her drink. "What time do we have to get there tonight?" They were going to the mayor's official residence, Gracie Mansion.

"Eightish."

"I wish we didn't have to . . ."

"Tired?"

Sally nodded, keeping her eyes fixed on Charlie.

His handsomeness was effortless, flagrant. Early in their marriage, when they lived on West Tenth Street, she would gaze at him as he thrust his shirt into his trousers, as he knotted his tie and combed his hair. It was a bland handsomeness, she knew, unblemished, unmarred by paunch, by baldness, by age. He had salt-and-pepper hair, a high forehead, dark, guarded eyes and a slender, delicate nose. Even as Charlie reached forty he remained trim—in fact, muscular—through a regimen of dieting as well as daily workouts at the Y and jogging four miles daily around Central Park's footpaths.

It was the kind of handsomeness, she knew, that either deepened or abruptly turned inward upon itself, the kind of face that turned elegant or flaccid once youth disappeared.

"How did it go today?" she asked.

"With Tennessee? I'm halfway through. Good quotes. He was marvelous." Charlie turned to his wife. "What are you looking at?"

"You."

"Me? Why?"

"You're very handsome."

He smiled. Sally said, "You know that, of course." She watched his eyes flicker, the redness beneath his lids. On the television screen a correspondent standing in front of the Pentagon was citing intelligence of expanding Soviet air bases along the Chinese border.

Sally leaned over and grasped her husband's cold hand. "Charles, I . . ."

The phone rang. "Damn! I'll get it."

She rose from the chair and stepped to the phone. Sally said, "Hello." There was a two-second pause, and then the caller clicked off.

She stared at the phone, then put it down.

On the television set there was a filmed report from Los Angeles showing Vice President Tom Nelson at a Democratic Party fund-raising dinner the previous night at the Century Plaza.

"Who was it?" Charlie asked.

Sally shrugged, her eyes fixed on Charlie. "Wrong number. Keeps happening." Her lips parted. Sally wanted to raise a question, but drew back. Charlie smiled at her.

"You were going to say something before. As the phone rang."

She walked over to him and grasped his hand. "Yes." She kissed him on the forehead. "Charles, I . . . you're very sweet." They kissed briefly on the lips.

*

By eight forty-five on spring evenings, the drawing rooms of Georgetown were crammed with the capital's power brokers—the men and women who write newspaper columns, run editorial pages, head cabinet departments, dominate Congress, toil in the highest levels of the bureaucracy and work as partners in one of the dozen or so ranking law firms in Washington, D.C.

An interlocking group with a fixed cast of characters, these brokers welcome the newcomers to the city after each presidential election—the Texans, the Californians, the Georgians—and then, in most cases, drop them mercilessly as soon as they slip from power, nurturing the next group, then the one after that.

Outsiders would probably find dinner and conversation at Georgetown salons surprisingly boring—but, then again, it hardly matters what outsiders think about the latest appointments at the Department of Health and Human Services or which White House staff member is squabbling with the Secretary of Transportation or whether the Secretary of State is being undercut by the head of the National Security Council or why the Administration's newest peace effort in the Middle East seems doomed to failure.

For outsiders, after all, would not be invited to the half-dozen Georgetown salons run with meticulous care by hostesses like Kitty White, who spent an inordinate amount of time keeping close watch on the rise and fall (and sometimes rise again) of politicians and high-level bureaucrats and even journalists.

On this evening the guests in Kitty White's drawing room overlooking Q Street—a room that occupied the entire second-floor front of her polished red-brick, nineteenth-century home—were a striking cross-section of Washington's establishment, and it was not especially unusual or surprising to see the Secretary of Defense, Edward Belling, standing beside the Italian marble console, his back to the noisy guest room, locked in conversation with the junior senator from New York, David Fitzgerald, and his wife Celia.

"You look so *well*," said Celia.

"If the body goes first, the head follows," said Belling, smiling, a bit condescending.

"I remember Bob McNamara, Mel Laird, Harold Brown, these men seemed to me to *age,* the job was too . . . . much." She spoke in a quavering voice, blinking her eyes and abruptly placing the fingers of her right hand against her forehead as if to calm herself.

"He wants to keep his body in shape for all these women who want it," said Fitzgerald without smiling.

"David, please," Celia said. A rebuke.

"She thinks I'm a crude son of a bitch," said Fitzgerald. "After all these years she still thinks I'm some New York mick, unsophisticated, waiting to learn manners like a good southern gentleman." His lips curled into a smile.

"I couldn't teach you anything, David," said Celia.

She seemed weary. Her black satin-belted crepe dress, plainly expensive, hung loosely, too loosely, over her frail body. She toyed with the cameo at her throat.

Celia stared at the melting ice cubes in her glass. "I need another ginger ale—I've become a ginger ale junkie," she smiled. "Excuse me."

They watched her move into the crowd.

"Is she okay?" said Belling.

"Going to A.A. Wants to get off the sauce." Fitzgerald paused. "The old man had the same problem. The brother had the same problem."

"Joey Keefer," said Belling. "Poor Joey."

Fitzgerald stepped closer, examining his scotch and soda.

"Has Pomerance arrived?" he murmured.

"This afternoon."

"Anything?"

They were interrupted by Kitty White. "Business, business," she said in a throaty voice. She grasped Belling's hand.

"Edward, I'm so glad you came tonight. I thought with this China crisis you'd be working."

Fitzgerald interrupted: "He wouldn't miss your party if World War III were approaching."

She laughed. "Come on, dinner is served."

"You look beautiful," said Fitzgerald, kissing her on the cheek.

"David, you tell that to all the girls."

"When can I sleep over?"

"*David.*" She gripped his arm as they stepped away from the window. "We've *got* to keep that secret."

Kitty guided them through the open doors into the dining room. Guests wandered around the banquet table hunting for name cards, then sat on antique Sheraton chairs. Fitzgerald found his seat between two women, the wife of the British Ambassador and a *Time* magazine White House reporter.

Belling leaned forward, gripping Fitzgerald's arm, and whispered with a smile, "Nothing yet."

The Secretary of Defense spotted his name card. Across the table he saw Bobby Patton, a Yale classmate, now a partner at Covington and Burling. Christ, old Bobby had aged. His face was a mask of soft, pink flesh. Belling waved.

Two black waiters began pouring burgundy. Belling turned and started to walk to Lois Roberts, the wife of Roy Roberts, a Harvard dean who now ran policy and planning at the State Department and who worked in the Pentagon under Bob McNamara. Lois, dear Lois, was working with black children in northeast Washington and had written a charming article about her experiences for *The Atlantic* magazine. She told him that she was also on the Mayor's Committee for Public Education.

Belling asked Lois how her children were, and Lois said the two boys were at Sidwell and doing fine, just fine. Lois asked if Edward and Nan were going to the Vineyard for August, and Belling said he doubted that he could get away for more than one week but Nan would probably stay at the house for the entire summer. Lois took a bite of her pâté.

Belling smiled. Across the room he noticed Ben Lefkowitz, a professor of jurisprudence at Oxford who had the good luck to marry an heiress. Ben, on leave from Harvard, had just written an article for the *New York Review of Books* attacking the Supreme Court's recent decisions limiting the rights of criminal suspects. Ben also wrote for *Rolling Stone*.

Beside Ben sat Lydia Stewart, the wife of the Washington *Post* columnist Tony Stewart, a popular Georgetown figure who had adopted the cause of the PLO and other radical movements. Tony had just returned from Saudi Arabia and the Persian Gulf states. Belling studied Tony Stewart, noticing the high forehead and bobbing head that moved rapidly when the columnist spoke.

Belling knew that he should phone Tony and invite him over for lunch at the Pentagon to discuss the Middle East and the recent visit to Jidda and Riyadh. Tony was a first-rate intellect.

He took a bite of the moist, spiced pâté, and sipped the wine. A light, fruity taste. He let the wine linger in his mouth and then swallowed it. The waiters hovered beside the table.

It was good to be among friends.

*

Eight-fifty. Ward Parsons stared at his watch for a moment in the elevator of the apartment house on Riverside Drive and Eighty-eighth Street, and when the door creaked open he stepped quickly down the corridor. Unlocking the apartment door, he was engulfed by the heavy aroma of melted cheese, tomato sauce, mixed spices.

"Hi," Ward called out. "What smells so delicious?"

"Lasagna."

"Wonderful." He was already rifling through the envelopes in the hallway: a telephone bill, two catalogues, a Brooks Brothers ad, an overdue American Express bill. A letter from Karen.

He dropped his jacket on a chair, stuffing the letter from his wife into his rear pocket, and stepped into the kitchen and gently kissed her.

Her face, flushed with heat, was dotted with tiny freckles that arched over the bridge of her nose. Her hair was tied with a loose knot that left a tangle of wet strands resting over her ears. Her blue eyes shimmered.

"I'm starved," she said.

"One second." He gripped her shoulders, pressing his lips against hers. She was sweaty, and sweet with perfume, and pleasantly soft.

"Rough end of the day?" she asked.

"A pisser." He opened the refrigerator, removed an ice tray and placed two ice cubes into a glass.

"Anything happen after I left?"

"Maury and then even Skipper got into the act," he said, pouring a quarter of a glass of Bourbon and then dousing it with water. "Maury wanted Finch to flesh out the story, put a little more analysis into it. What the hell the Chinese are up to. As if anyone knows. Skipper said we should get reaction from the White House —what the President is doing, how serious he views it, etcetera. Hugh was inserting that when I left."

"How serious *is* it?" She was tearing apart lettuce leaves.

"Ross thinks the Chinese are up to . . . something. Nothing this *provocative* has happened before."

He watched her pour oil on the salad, then vinegar. In her jeans and sandals, without makeup, Florence seemed slighter, younger, touchingly vulnerable.

"You look terrific," he said quietly.

"Me?"

He nodded.

"My beauty emerges in the kitchen." She was smiling.

"I'm not saying that."

She took three steps toward Ward and kissed him.

"Dinner's ready."

"I'll wash up."

He walked into the bedroom and placed his jacket over a closet door, then stepped into the bathroom and turned on the hot and cold water taps, scrubbing his hands and face with soap.

Gazing into the bathroom mirror, Ward noticed his right eye was inflamed and, with a day's growth of beard, he looked tired, old, rumpled. But his sandy hair—always a strong point—curled over his ears in a sexy way, cut by a barber named Maxwell who charged twenty-five dollars. It was his one extravagance.

He walked into the bedroom. The smell of garlic and oregano and melted Parmesan cheese hung pleasantly in the air. Ward realized that he was hungry now that the tension of the day was starting to fade from his body, the tension that clutched his stomach and filled his chest virtually every morning when he confronted the incoming stories, the pressures from Maury and Skipper, the crises, the letters and messages from correspondents abroad—most of them vulnerable and tired. The requests, the pleas, the decisions and, beyond all that, the competition that seemed to ebb silently through the newsroom. Cover your ass and second-guess. Watch your assistant and keep an eye always on the competition from Barry and Sally. The long knives are out.

As Ward stepped toward the door, his hand brushed over his back pocket and he suddenly felt the soft-tissue airmail envelope. He reached into his pocket, pulled out the letter and opened it.

It was on paper-thin Indian stationery with Karen's unmistakable scrawl, long straight letters, elaborate curves, heavy dots that Ward linked to all those girls who went to fashionable private schools and then swept into Wellesley, Radcliffe or Smith.

He scanned the letter, knowing he would reread it slowly, and then read it one more time after that. And after curling the letter into a ball and flinging it away, the phrases would linger.

Ward sat down on the bed. The letter was dated ten days earlier. He read quickly:

Dear Ward. As you see, I'm in Kashmir, and I'll be here for three or four weeks. I'm at a Yoga study group—I've been reading about Yoga, doing some of my own (self-taught) at the house, when I heard about this place run by some interesting Americans and Indians. I jumped at the chance.

Ward felt the sweat start on his forehead, his mouth went dry. He read about children being on school vacation, Chris on a hiking trip to Simla and Mussoorie for eight days, Val staying in Delhi with a friend whose father was deputy chief of mission at the American Embassy.

Karen said she was still immersed in her bharatanatyam dance, which gave her a certain peace and discipline, the movements angular, relying mostly on mime. It was fascinating, she said, the control demanded over the body, the face, the hands. Like a turn-on.

As I've told you so many times, I want to control my life, not have the Star *control it, or anything or anyone else, and my bharatanatyam may be an extension of my feelings.*

Karen said the current trip to Kashmir was not some kookie ripoff, but a serious attempt at Yoga; waking up at 5 A.M., sipping tea made from rheem bush, spending most of the day on a houseboat in Dal Lake, doing breathing exercises, meditating, eating sparingly (meat forbidden) and immersing oneself in the scientific disciplines of Yoga, which is a union of the mind with God.

The setting is utterly spectacular, Karen wrote, *the apple trees are bursting. There are eight people on the boat—six Americans and a British girl who has been sick every day.*

What can I tell you about my Yoga? I suppose the central idea is that you are more than either a body or a mind. A daily practice of asanas, breathing, mantras, study and decent all-vegetarian nutrition—together with some kind of work—is the road to personal fulfillment. Concentration, meditation, inner freedom *are the keys. That is not crazy.*

I won't bore you any further. This whole experience is very exciting for me. By the way, I've stopped living with my friend for an assortment of complicated reasons, personal and otherwise. (The children were a major factor.) Suffice to say, he's a sweet, gentle, very patient man, but at this point I don't think I'm ready for a sweet, gentle, patient man. I think I want to be a little bit alone. Chris and Val have been wonderful, and very, very understanding. They miss you. And can you remember Chris's birthday is June 6. I hope you're well. I'm sure you're taking care of yourself. Best wishes. Karen.

He stared at her name.

Florence said quietly, "Dinner." She was standing at the bedroom door, and she smiled. "What does she say? . . . I saw the envelope."

Ward shook his head. His shoulders and back hurt.

"She's into Yoga." He paused. "She's still angry."

He placed the letter on the bed, stood up, and said, "Let's have dinner," even though he was not especially hungry.

Friday

CHAPTER 9

"The point is," said Barry Cohen evenly, "it's Linda's story. *She* dug it up."

He was seated in the managing editor's office early in the morning, facing Maury, who, as acting managing editor, sat behind Evan's desk, a splendid desk of satinwood veneer inlaid with ebony. The desk—like the suede-upholstered Le Corbusier armchair, the brown suede sofa and the bookcase crammed with art deco figurines and vases—was purchased and set up by Lucy shortly after the Steiners appointed Evan managing editor. The furnishings were now in the family collection, and would be moved out of the office once the Steiners had named the new managing editor.

"It's a national desk story. It's Sally's story," said Maury, an edge in his voice. "*Not* city desk."

"I thought . . ."

"Goddamn it. Since when is California, the movies, *and* the Vice President *your* turf? That's all *national* desk."

Barry spoke quietly.

"Linda flew to California this morning."

Maury sat perfectly still, his eyes fixed on Cohen.

"I told her to go," Barry said. "The *Daily News,* the *Times,* and Christ knows who else is working on the same story. It's *competitive.* Every day that goes by . . ."

"You got her out there before I had a chance to say no."

"For the good of the paper."

"For the good of Barry Cohen." Maury's voice was tight with rage.

Barry leaned forward. "What do you want to do? Spend three

days fiddle-fucking around here, deciding whose turf it is, who should go, is it national desk or city desk or maybe Washington. Is it a story at all, one we should chase?"

"You saying we've done a poor job?"

"I'm saying the man who sat in the desk before you was a disaster. Worshiped the fucking establishment. Kissed ass. All these tributes about the great newspaperman he was. Bullshit! You think Evan would publish the Pentagon Papers? You think he'd go after Watergate?"

Barry leaned forward.

"Every time we got something big against the establishment, Evan panicked. We futzed around and stood with our cocks in our hands, arguing proprieties, arguing whether we're going too far, while everyone beat the shit out of us."

Maury said quietly, "Evan cared about standards. An old-fashioned word. I sometimes think Watergate was the worst thing that happened to American journalism. It's the 'in' thing now—set loose a bunch of reporters who act like undercover cops—self-righteous undercover cops. Reporters think nothing of stealing grand jury minutes and printing them, never mind that someone hasn't been indicted. Print self-serving leaks from prosecutors who can't prove their cases in court; who destroy people with innuendo and gossip and piped quotes. The investigative journalist—spare me."

"So you think Evan was right?" Cohen said.

"Evan was careful. And honorable. And he didn't enjoy the kind of twenty-five-year-old schmucks who run around now, taking themselves so seriously, giving interviews to other journalists about the terrific job they're doing. Jesus, these guys should be hauled down to start writing obits again."

"Face reality, Maury."

"I am."

"No, you're not. You want the good old days. We *believed* police commissioners and governors and senators and presidents. And shit—look what happened. If we had moved our asses a little earlier, maybe we could have avoided some of that fucking war. Right? And I mean early on, the early sixties."

"Name of the game." Maury leaned back, examining his hands. "Investigative reporting. You're right. The road to stardom."

"And Pulitzers."

"You want another one bad."

"Me? No. For the city staff."

"Cut the bullshit." Maury mimicked him. "Not for me, for my staff."

"You made me . . ."

"What you are, my little Frankenstein. Smart-ass kid from the Bronx. You had potential, Barry. You were hungry."

The two men stared at one another, and Barry thought he saw Maury's eyes suddenly chill with fear.

"Barry, take a word of advice. You won't, but take it anyway. It's not worth the end runs. The shiv in the back, the finger in the eye. Whether it's a story, or a job, it ain't worth it."

"I want the job, Maury. So do you."

"We all get screwed," said Maury, ignoring him. "It's the nature of the business. Some people get elegantly screwed. Promotions. Fancy titles. Good pensions. Others just get fucked. Shafted. Discarded. Humiliated. Old whores are treated better."

Barry fingered his tie. "I shouldn't have sent Linda," he said. "I'm sorry, Maury."

"No, you're not."

Maury lifted the ringing phone. It was Hugh Finch.

Barry watched Maury, who seemed oddly out of place in the big office, the walls still covered with informal autographed photos of Evan with politicians and VIP's. Barry sensed Maury's discomfort.

Although Maury habitually dressed in the casual manner of a man who cared little about clothes—loose-fitting suits, plaid sport jackets, wide ties and suspenders—although he inevitably walked around the newsroom without a jacket, often in a short-sleeve shirt, stuffing sticks of gum into his mouth as deadlines neared, today he was wearing a blue suit with a vest, a starched, wide-collared white shirt and red-and-blue striped silk tie. A white handkerchief, barely visible, peeked out of his breast pocket. His hair, graying at the sideburns, was neatly parted and lacquered down.

As night national editor, Maury had noticed Barry Cohen shortly after the kid was hired as a copy boy. Barry was skinny, fast-stepping, aggressive—he bombarded the city and national desks with story ideas. His hunger to make it on the *Star* was so fierce, so powerful, that Maury was drawn to him, perhaps against his better judgment, and began quietly to guide and advise him. What bound Maury to the youth was a deep, almost filial affection —Maury was smart enough to sense that Barry could have been the son he never had. With his non-Ivy League background and brash style, Barry reminded Maury of *his* early days on the *Star,* somewhat out of place amidst the prep school boys.

As the months turned into years, Barry rose from rewrite man to police reporter to City Hall bureau chief to foreign correspondent, Maury grew aware that the younger man's aggression masked a certain vulnerability, and an intense solitude, evident only in his eyes. They seemed to strain and turn inward, the lashes flickering.

Cohen had few friends, he confided in no one, and except for one moment, on the night before Barry left for Vietnam, Maury realized that he knew very little about him.

It had been the close of a noisy farewell party at Fritzi's—even Skipper and Eli Faber had showed up—and Maury's wife Sarah had embraced Barry, who was by then drunk. Then Barry grasped Maury's hand, swallowed and confessed he was scared, scared out of his head, scared with the same panic that had engulfed him as a kid in the Bronx when his mother was first taken away to the hospital on Staten Island, the hospital whose screened porch overlooked the city's skyline.

Maury had felt the blush rise in his cheeks. He was aware that Barry was staring at him intently, his damp hand firm between Maury's fingers, and then Barry suddenly drew away.

In the first months that Barry was in Vietnam, filing stories from Saigon and Can Tho and Danang and Pleiku, Maury kept recalling the comment, as if Barry had inexplicably offered him a clue to his personality that was designed somehow to cement Barry's trust in the older man, to link them irrevocably. The memory faded, but nearly three years later, when Barry returned in triumph with his Pulitzer Prize and the job of city editor, Maury abruptly thought of it once more.

What did it mean?

Maury saw this complex side of Barry again in the grim months before the death of Sarah Kramer. As Maury's wife lay shrunken and tranquilized and, at times, in horrific pain at Mt. Sinai Hospital, Barry sat up for hours with him in the Kramers' apartment on Riverside Drive. Barry cooked for Maury, took him to Shea Stadium, watched television with him, gossiped with him about the *Star*.

Barry cared for him too, the numbing weeks that followed Sarah's death, the weeks when Maury began to drink through the nights and early mornings, as if his pent-up grief could only exorcise itself through whiskey, as if his sorrow was so private, so locked up, that only whiskey could unleash it as well as bury it.

It was Barry who gently told Maury that unless he planned on destroying himself, he had to go to Alcoholics Anonymous. It was Barry who took him by taxi to the A.A. office on East Eighty-sixth Street. And it was Barry, months later, when Maury was back at work and picking up the strands of his life without Sarah, who told the older man that his celibacy was unnatural and that, first off, he should phone Nancy Chang, a copy editor on the foreign desk. Start off with Nancy, he said, you'll like her. Chinese. Nice-looking. Easy to be with.

Nancy Chang. Barry said with a laugh that she had a great body —and that she had a thing about Jewish men. And who could be more Jewish than Maury?

And although Barry's impulse had been purely to help Maury breathe life after the year of watching his wife die, the relationship that developed between Maury and Nancy reached beyond Barry's wildest dreams. Maury and Nancy were now living together.

"He's sitting right in my office," Maury was saying to Hugh Finch over the phone.

Barry glanced up.

Maury grabbed a pen. "That's P-O-M-E-R-A-N-C-E. Seymour Pomerance."

"What's that about?" said Barry after Maury hung up.

Maury shrugged. "Running a check on a doctor named Pomerance, cancer specialist at Sloan-Kettering. Hugh saw him on the shuttle to Washington. Picked up by a Secret Serviceman at National Airport."

Maury paused and seemed to straighten his tie.

"Hughie may come up to New York to do some snooping. Wanted to inform you, Barry. Respecting your *turf*." Maury grinned, let the words linger. He moved on to Howie Bishop's investigation of David Fitzgerald.

"Is Jerry Paley involved?" Maury lit a cigarette.

"Jerry's involved."

"What do we have?" Maury asked.

"We have the lady saying that she handed payoffs over to Jerry. Kept a little black book of names and dates. Amounts."

Maury Kramer suddenly crushed out his cigarette in the ashtray on his desk. "Stupid bastard."

"Who?"

"Jerry."

"Howie's seeing him this afternoon."

"Better inform Hugh. Washington's *his* turf." Maury stared blankly past Barry Cohen's shoulder. "Stupid *bastard,*" he repeated. Maury seemed lost in thought for a moment, but then he stood up; Barry was being gently dismissed.

"You like this role," said Barry. It was a statement.

Maury's eyes narrowed. "So would you," he said.

*

Sally was dictating a letter asking Washington bureau chief Hugh Finch about ideas for political coverage in next year's presidential elections when the direct line from the publisher's office buzzed. It was ten fifty-five.

As Sally reached for the phone, her eyes met Peter Fosdick's across the desk.

"Skipper?" Sally's voice lowered and she thought she saw Peter's thin mouth curl. God, she hated him. Fosdick belonged at *Time* magazine or one of those Wall Street firms that specialized in dumb Yalies.

Old Peter was part of the deal, he was. You want to be national editor, Sally, you want to be cited in *Ms.* magazine, you want to appear on "Meet the Press" and "MacNeil/Lehrer," then you've got to accept Frieda's specially wrapped package. *Peter Fosdick will be a perfect deputy for you, Sally.*

Sally heard Skipper's low voice. "Frieda doesn't like the David Gelber piece on press freedom. Says it's too strong."

"That's precisely . . ."

"Let me finish, dear. She wants him to rewrite it. Her point,

Sally, is that we've got to stop assuming our powers are unlimited. We can't cry wolf each time the court makes a decision."

"We disagree," said Sally, her mouth tight with rage.

"In the name of freedom of the press all kinds of sins are committed. That's Frieda's point. Got to balance our responsibility to publish news with the rights of citizens to fair trial, to privacy . . ."

Sally watched Peter Fosdick push back his chair and whisper to Rose. The son of a bitch was going to an early squash game.

"I'll get a rewrite on it today." The tremor in her voice surprised Sally.

"What's wrong?"

What's wrong. Peter Fosdick's wrong. Frieda Steiner's wrong. Barry's seizing the California story is wrong.

Sally heard herself ask Skipper to meet her for lunch.

"Taking out my niece," he said softly. "What about later? After the party tonight?"

Sally watched Rose thrust a sheet of stationery in her electric typewriter.

Twisting in her swivel chair, Sally whispered, "Charlie's back from Key West, remember?" She closed her eyes.

"Tomorrow night?" he asked.

"Saturday, no. Let's make it Sunday. Afternoon. I'll phone you in the morning. Let's be alone," said Sally, her voice cracking. "Let's not go anywhere." Sally bent forward to fling open her pocketbook to find a tissue.

God*damn!*

Was it Evan's death? The sense of upheaval, disorder on the paper? Was it Frieda or that asshole Fosdick? Was it Barry's easy little triumph sending Linda to California?

Was it the phone call once again, this morning, just as she was leaving? Picking up the phone, saying, "Hello," and then the click.

Was it Charlie's shrug? Just another crazy, he said.

Was it Charlie?

Charlie . . .

*

"Why do you stay with her?"

"Why? I love her."

Charlie Sims and Larry Steiner were in bed in Larry's apart-

ment on a second-floor brownstone on East Seventy-sixth Street.
A blue sheet was wrapped around Larry's waist. Charlie, in jockey
shorts, leaned over and lit a cigarette.

"You're kidding," said Larry.

"No, I'm not," said Charlie, blowing a circle in the air.

"But you're . . ."

"Gay? So what? I'm not gay anyway. I'm bisexual."

"Come on. That is bullshit. Does she know?"

"Sally?" He shrugged. "I suppose so."

"She doesn't care?" said Larry.

"I think Sally's a complicated woman."

"Do you go to the bars, the baths?"

A vague smile played on Charlie's face.

"No," Larry said. "*You* can pick and choose. You're quite
beautiful."

Charlie walked toward the bathroom. "Nice you can take this
time off in the middle of the day," he said, leaving the door open.

Larry smiled. "If *I* can't, who can?" he called. "I come and go
as I please. I work on the business side six months, then show
business news. I just drift." Larry waited until the toilet flushed
and watched Charlie return.

"My father, my grandmother, want it that way," said Larry.
"I'm the bad seed, they're *ashamed*. My father once got angry at
me and yelled, 'To think I was Frederic Steiner's great-grand-
son.' " Larry grinned.

"What do you want to do?"

Larry's eyes settled on the billowing curtains.

"Go to dance school. Ballet. Join a company. That's my fantasy."

"Why not?"

He shook his head.

"Why should I? I've got a steady job. I come and go as I
please. Independent. Fuck the fantasy. That's what I say."

"What does your shrink say?"

"My shrink says I'm avoiding adulthood. Reality. Afraid of
breaking off from the Steiner tree because I may hurt myself, lose
their support. He's probably right."

"How old are you?"

"Twenty-one. How old are you?"

"Don't ask."

Charlie sat up, placing his cigarette in the glass ashtray on the floor. Larry leaned forward, kissing him.

"You still feel guilty," said Larry.

Charlie smiled, saying nothing.

Larry's fingers slid beneath the cover, touching Charlie's thigh.

"Not now," said Charlie. "I should go. I've got some work."

"You're beautiful," Larry whispered. "I'm repeating myself."

Charlie Sims twisted off the bed and walked to a chair beside the window, lifting his crumpled trousers. He zipped them up and pushed back the curtains to gaze at Seventy-sixth Street, damp with rain.

"What about tonight?" said Larry, eagerness yielding to embarrassment.

Charlie watched a taxi hurtle past. He closed his eyes in the wet breeze. "Difficult," he said.

"You going to the party?"

Charlie nodded.

"Frieda's big number," said Larry, moving off the bed and stepping toward the kitchen.

Charlie silently buttoned up his wrinkled, blue button-down shirt, stuffing the tail and front portion into his faded jeans.

Suddenly he sat down and pressed his trembling fingers against his forehead, shutting his eyes tight.

"Something wrong?" Larry said. He held a soda in his right hand.

"Migraine. I get them."

"You want anything? An aspirin? Valium?"

Charlie said no. Slowly he put his sneakers on, his eyes revealing pain.

"Must be awful."

Larry watched the flush rise in Charlie's cheeks. Pushing himself up, Charlie walked toward the door. A soft rain brushed the window.

"Will I see you again?" asked Larry. He swallowed hard, regretting the question at once, knowing that Charlie would come back to him.

*

Within the Washington press hierarchy there were pointed distinctions between reporters who covered the White House, the State Department and the Pentagon, distinctions marked by the caste differences placed unwittingly on those reporters by editors in New York or Los Angeles or Chicago.

The White House press generally viewed themselves as elite largely because the outside world—their editors—deluded themselves into believing that serving in the White House pressroom places a journalist at the pinnacle of his profession. Isn't the White House the awesome dead center of power, the pivot of decision-making, the primal root that nurtures the capital?

Actually, many reporters found it a boring, empty job. They sat most of the day in the dank pressroom in the White House west wing, stumbling over television wires and television technicians who hogged the sofas and stared, with sullen eyes and lobotomized expressions, at quiz shows and soap operas on the tube. Reporters spent most of the day keeping an eye on other reporters ("Who is that bastard whispering to on the phone?"), waiting hungrily for briefings, making conversation with a scowling, often hostile, twenty-three-year-old pressroom secretary who found it painful to pick up the phone and find out what the President's wife had for lunch with the wife of the President of France, and what both women wore. The questions may be dumb, but the folks out there *cared*.

The State Department was another ball game. Thinkers. Analysts. Ponderous foreign-policy specialists. Rich-timbred television correspondents who pontificated on the air that "Administration sources told me . . ." Actually, the source was the State Department's press secretary, who didn't want his name used, or an aide to the Secretary of State, who was delighted to leak some self-serving gossip, or a middle-level official who knew less than he appeared to but was flattered that NBC had indeed called him.

Unless there was a war or military conflict, the Pentagon was no-man's-land to most journalists. Its briefings were generally cluttered with a handful of people from the wire services, military trade journals and big newspapers who accepted the fact that, although no one quite understands what the Pentagon is doing, one should, in fact, make an attempt to cover it, since a sizable, perhaps excessive, amount of tax dollars were flowing into the building.

Given Hugh Finch's story in this morning's *Star,* the eleven-thirty Pentagon briefing was unusually crowded. As soon as Tom Shaw, the Pentagon spokesman, walked into the briefing room on the second floor, klieg lights engulfed the platform, and television cameras from the three major networks began to roll.

"I have nothing to report today," said Shaw.

"Well, Tom, how serious *is* the Chinese-Soviet border fighting?" It was the CBS man who spoke up.

"How serious? I would say it's somewhat serious."

"Is the Administration concerned about it?" (this from *The Wall Street Journal*)

"You'll have to ask the White House."

"Is there division in the Administration about what to do?" (the New York *Times*)

"That's not for me to answer."

"Well, the *Star* story said . . ."

"If there is division in the Administration, the White House will have to comment. Next question, please."

"Tom, the *Star* reported today that Mr. Belling wants control of the entire intelligence community, CIA, FBI . . ." (the AP)

"No comment."

"Well, what is Belling proposing to the President?"

"That's not for me to say, that's private between the Secretary of Defense and the President."

"Tom, you said before that the situation was somewhat serious. What do you base that on?" (the Chicago *Sun-Times*)

Shaw finally opened a briefing book on the lectern. He paused, weighing his words. "It's based on the fact that when you have two major powers, two major *nuclear* powers, at arm's length of one another and in a hostile stance toward one another, it's a cause of concern. I would say it's somewhat serious."

"What are your latest reports from the border?" (*Newsday*)

Shaw turned the pages of his briefing book.

"The latest reports are of an escalation of border activities on both sides," said Shaw.

The television cameras continued to whirr, reporters wrote rapidly on notebook pads.

The spokesman looked up, then glanced at his briefing book. "We have reports—sketchy reports, I might add—of railroad cuts in Mongolia near the border. Also in Siberia."

"Where in Mongolia?" someone called out.

"Just south of Ulan Bator. Also in the East near Khalkin-gol." He spelled the names.

"Who did it?" (*The Wall Street Journal*)

"We don't know."

"Was it the Mongolian People's Liberation Front?" (Washington *Post*)

"We do not know."

"Why these areas?" (CBS)

"These are the areas of, uh, major Soviet troop concentrations. We assume this is the reason."

"When you say 'cuts,' what does that mean?" (UPI)

"Explosions."

"With what? What kind?" (Baltimore *Sun*)

"I'd rather not go into that."

"What about Siberia?" (ABC)

Shaw turned the pages of his briefing book. "Our latest reports, and this is as of early this morning, is that there has been a cut in the Trans-Siberian Railroad at the junction in Skovorodino . . ."

"Please spell." (AP)

"S-K-O-V-O-R-O-D-I-N-O. No further details. And a series of explosions on the new railroad the Russians are building."

"What new railroad? Where?" (a chorus of voices)

"One at a time, please."

"Tom, this new railroad. Is this the one that's supposed to parallel the Trans-Siberian Railroad?" (Baltimore *Sun*)

"Yes. I think the Russians have called it 'the construction project of the century.' Railroad's called the Baikal-Amur Mainline."

"How big is this railroad?" (AP)

He turned the pages of the briefing book. "Two thousand or so miles. Across Siberia to the Pacific."

"Designed to do what?" (Washington *Post*)

"What?"

"What's the purpose of the railroad?"

"The railroad is designed to serve as a key transportation and supply route. It's designed to ship oil and minerals produced in western Siberia to Pacific ports."

"Is this the first time that the new line has been hit, the Mainline?" (Los Angeles *Times*)

Shaw wet his lips. "So far as we know, yes."

"Have the Russians reacted?" (Reuters)

"To the cuts?"

"Yes."

"They have not said, or done, anything yet."

"Do we expect them to?" (*Time*)

"Why don't you ask them?"

"*Oh fuck.*"

The television cameras clicked off.

"Can we proceed, please?" said Tom Shaw, perspiring.

Several reporters were yelling out questions at once. Brooke Webb, the ABC correspondent, who had just completed combing her blond, shoulder-length hair in a mirror that was held up for her by an aide, shouted firmly, as the camera beside her swayed onto her face:

"Why are the Chinese doing this?"

Shaw said evenly: "We're not saying the Chinese are doing it."

"Well, the Russians are saying so."

"Let the Russians say so. We're not."

"Well, who *is* doing it?" (the New York *Star*)

"According to published reports, the Mongolian People's Liberation Front. Various insurgent groups, various nationalist groups, possibly some dissidents in the Soviet Army."

"Who's backing these groups?" (Washington *Post*)

"I would be giving you hearsay and conjecture. I'd rather not."

"What impact are these railroad cuts, the explosions, having on the Soviets' ability to move supplies?" (the New York *Times*)

Shaw stared at the reporter. "We can only speculate. The cuts on the Baikal-Amur Mainline are obviously designed to keep coal, oil, resources from moving through Siberia to Pacific ports. This has been a huge undertaking by the Russians, and having the lines cut in this way is an obvious setback. That's as far as I can go."

"Tom, Tom, where were the cuts? Can you specify?" (ABC)

*

One floor above, Edward Belling twisted the intercom; the voices at the news conference lowered to an inaudible hum. Belling looked up and frowned at Hugh Finch.

"Perfect press secretary," he said. "Knows precisely what *not* to say."

Hugh watched him lift a pipe off the rack on his desk and, with his thumb and forefinger, thrust tobacco into the holder.

"For attribution to Administration sources," said Belling. Hugh saw him clamp the pipe between his teeth, sucking the stem as he circled a lit match over the tobacco.

"Two hours ago the Cabinet urged the President to begin talks with both sides, the Russians *and* the Chinese. The President agreed . . . reluctantly." He leaned forward. "It was your story, Hugh, that did it . . ." The door opened. "Nice front-page play. Upset the White House. Upset the *CIA*."

Colonel Walker moved noiselessly toward them and placed a folder, conspicuously stamped *Top Secret,* in Belling's outstretched hand.

As Belling read the first page in silence, Hugh looked up and saw Walker's slightly protuberant eyes widen on the Defense Secretary. Belling turned the page, murmuring.

" 'Heavy troop movements reported in Mongolia now, estimates of Soviet forces range as high as 1.8 to 2 million men eastward from Irkutsk.'

"Mongolia," Belling said, gazing at Walker. "Mongolia!"

"Hinge of the earth."

"What?"

"Hinge of the earth. That's what Genghis Khan termed Mongolia—hinge of the earth. Both need Mongolia."

"Sit down, Jerry," said Belling, almost irritated. "Stop standing at attention."

Belling turned to Hugh. "What would I do without him? One of the brightest officers in the Army. China expert. Served two tours in Peking. Speaks Mandarin." Belling's smile froze.

Colonel Walker, unmoved by the compliment, stared fixedly at Belling. Strange bird, thought Hugh, as Walker sat self-consciously in a chair facing the desk. Suddenly Walker was speaking in a flat monotone; Hugh began writing in his notebook.

It was China's intention to incite the growing non-Russian ethnic minorities which have been suppressed for decades. Turn the Russian countryside into a landscape of guerrilla wars. In the Ukraine, Latvia and Lithuania. In Georgia and Central Asia. In southern Siberia and especially in Mongolia.

Hugh spoke up. "China says Mongolia is *theirs*."

Walker's smile startled Hugh. "Mongolia awaits exploitation," said the colonel. "Vast resources there, oil and minerals. Farmland. Food. In twenty years one out of three people in the world will be Chinese. They need *land*."

"You think China can win a war?" asked Hugh, suddenly embarrassed at his childlike tone.

"Win?" said Walker, derisively. "Who wins, and who loses? Perhaps Vice Premier Phung is willing to provoke a war, a nuclear war, that would certainly leave three hundred million, perhaps three hundred and fifty million, Chinese dead."

"To what end?" asked Belling, sucking his pipe.

"There would be five hundred million Chinese survivors." Walker paused. "Is that callous? Is that insane? Is that immoral? I think China is playing a deliberately provocative game."

The telephone panel behind Belling's desk glowed with a half-dozen lit buttons. Hugh and Belling sat silent under the weight of Colonel Walker's intensity.

"Kamchatka, a Chinese nuclear test there, alarms me," said Walker. He slowly arose.

Belling lifted the document off his lap, flipping to the first page. His eyes fixed on the words: "The Russians just placed all aircraft, ground troops and tactical missiles in the Far East on twenty-four-hour alert," Belling said.

Walker's tight face whitened. He gazed at Belling, then turned on the balls of his feet and left the office.

In the tense silence, Hugh listened to the hum of voices over the intercom; the news conference was grinding to a close. Belling leaned forward to raise the volume.

"Brilliant officer," he said distractedly, suddenly turning to Hugh. "Kept in a North Vietnamese prison five years. Solitary for at least three. Tortured, but didn't break. He had an ethnic Chinese guard who smuggled him books—the Chinese alphabet, works of Mao, selected Chinese history. That's how he began."

As Belling lifted the volume, Hugh recognized the rasping voice of ABC's Brooke Webb. "Tom, would you call this a major crisis?"

There were groans in the audience.

"No, I would not call it a major crisis."

Brooke Webb said angrily, "Well, Tom, what's the Administration *doing* about it?"

"We're watching with keen interest," Tom Shaw said.

*

Seven miles away a gray heron alighted from a birch, splaying its wings and seeming to glide lazily past the seventh-floor window; a pair of binoculars were fastened against the glass pane.

"Damn!"

Alex Vikas, whose official title was CIA Deputy Chief, Operations, placed his binoculars on the sill and reluctantly turned in his swivel chair to rewind the tape recorder on his desk. Over his shoulder he watched the heron and listened to the voice of Defense Secretary Belling, the telephone wiretap making a slight echo.

"Any word about Pomerance?"

"Still at Walter Reed, sir."

Alex Vikas smiled in recognition of Colonel Walker's voice.

With his right index finger, Vikas pressed the lever that replayed the exchange. He listened, then flipped the "off" button. Vikas shouted, "Mai." Over his shoulder, once more he saw the heron flapping gently and disappearing into the forest, silvery-green and damp. He heard the door open, and turned with a deep sigh to stare at the face of his Vietnamese secretary, Mai Ling. Pink, moist lipstick against mocha skin and slender, almond eyes.

Bloody gorgeous, she was.

"Darling, get me Ward Parsons at the *Star* in New York," Alex Vikas said.

*

"Grandmother told me if I lost the fifteen pounds by June first she'd give me a thousand dollars," said Johanna Claiborne.

"Subtle Frieda." Skipper tasted his martini.

"It used to be a dollar if I didn't have ice cream."

"What'd you say?"

"No, thanks." Johanna smiled. "Said she expected me to reject her." Resting her head against the banquette, Johanna glanced across the restaurant. "Thanks for taking me here. I'm used to the Wurst House on Harvard Square."

Skipper lit a cigarette. "Where are you living now?"

"Small apartment on Everett Street."

As Johanna grew older, her face was settling into the Steiner mold except for her liquid brown eyes—Evan's eyes—that seemed shrunken and heavy-lidded. She had the same broad mouth as Frederic, the same jutting chin and wide, flat nose, giving a strength to her features that had once embarrassed her.

As a teen-ager, Johanna had yearned for a slender, finely chiseled face, but gradually she had accepted the fact that the heavy features inherited from the Steiners had stamped her face with intelligence, not beauty, and that, in the end, this simplified her life because she only appealed to select men, secure men.

Her speech, her bearing, her personality eerily resembled her father's. Like Evan, Johanna spoke slowly, tilting her head ever so slightly to the right, staring firmly at her listener, restlessly hunting the eyes for a signal, a hint of response.

Often Johanna had the same remoteness as Evan, the same tension masked by a smile. Her moods shifted, as did her weight. With Evan one never quite knew what precisely was on his mind, what his words meant, what lay behind the shell of privacy. Cruel one moment, extraordinarily generous and sympathetic the next. A fierce temper—yet somehow calculated, controlled.

Johanna was not quite so mercurial in the same ways, but she had inherited Evan's distance. A shadow of suspicion dominated her every move, every conversation.

Skipper smiled at her.

"Still living with . . ."

"Tony. Yes. He finishes school next year."

"And then?"

"He'll probably teach in some college. Hopefully. He's taking his doctorate in English Lit."

"Will you go with him?" The waiter brought their menus.

She shrugged. "I have two more years at the Fogg. After that . . . I wouldn't mind getting a job in some medium-size museum. Working in Cleveland or Dallas or Minneapolis."

"Not New York?"

"No, not New York." She sipped her drink. "Too close."

"To the family?"

"Skipper, I want some space in my life."

He placed a breadstick on his plate and broke off a chunk. "I'm sure we can arrange some job at the Museum of Modern Art or even the Met . . ." He buttered the breadstick and took a bite.

"I don't *want* that kind of arrangement." Johanna drew back, forcing a smile.

"What courses are you taking?" Skipper asked, deciding to move into neutral ground.

"My specialty is Renaissance. Michelangelo. Renaissance City. Renaissance Painting. The fifteenth- and sixteenth-century Italians. Leonardo. Titian. Giorgione." Johanna's eyes met Skipper's. "Why did you want to see me?"

"Do you have any questions about your father?"

"No, no questions."

"Have you spoken to your mother?"

"She's upset. And *I'm* upset." Her thumb fingered the rim of her glass, brushing off an imaginary speck. "And when we're both this way we upset one another even more. Even if we try not to. Don't get along with Mother even in the best of times. These are not the best of times." She tasted her white wine. "Different values. Different needs." Johanna's cheeks flushed. "She's her mother's daughter. She wouldn't like to hear that, but she is. Maybe, as I get to be older, I'll get to be my mother's daughter. Probably will."

She laughed, a brief, angry laugh. "I find this business of her affair with Fitzgerald appalling."

"Fitzgerald's smart."

"And mean."

"He wants to be President."

"He's using her, isn't he?"

A waiter approached, but Skipper waved him away.

"I want you to think about coming to New York, Johanna. I want you to work on the *Star*."

He studied her face, but her expression betrayed nothing. She waited for him to go on.

Skipper said quietly, "It's changing now, the entire business. I've hired a new breed of department head. Smart, tough, aggressive. We're plunging into computer technology—we've had to, we've all had to, Christ knows. Newspaper production, not just ours but practically everyone's, was archaic. The unions are fighting like hell. Lazzarutti, Frank Lazzarutti, head of the Newspaper Guild. The bastard's fighting us tooth and nail. But we're going to *win*, Johanna."

Skipper watched her as he spoke, hunting for a hint of reaction. Her face remained impassive. He lowered his voice and leaned forward.

"We're heading for a confrontation with the Guild. We're going to start cutbacks in personnel. It's going to be bloody. We're not a rich paper, Johanna."

"I know."

"Not the *Times* or the Washington *Post*. Not the L.A. *Times*.

"We've got to take risks or else we . . . or else we *die*. Other papers diversify, other papers have resources, but all we have is the *Star*. We have to cut to the bone."

Eli's words. He shocked himself—he was using Eli's words.

Skipper reached for the martini with a trembling hand.

"We're in a period of flux," he said, glancing past her. "Costs are up and profits are, well, profits are a thing of the past. We're losing money. We're *sliding,* Johanna."

Skipper's face had thinned, she thought; his eyes looked stricken with tension.

"Contracts are up in September, but we're heading for another confrontation with the unions *before* then. Lazzarutti's pushing for a fight." The fingers of Skipper's left hand lay taut and outstretched on the table. "I *want* you to work on the paper!"

She returned his gaze with steady eyes.

Skipper went on. "You'll work in every major section, the business side, production, news, circulation. You'll attend every key meeting, accompany me on trips, meet the staff."

"To what end?"

"To be my successor," said Skipper. "There's no one else in the family but you, Johanna."

Her eyes fell away. "There's Larry," Johanna said weakly.

"Larry's a child." Skipper seemed to struggle to say something further, but stopped. His lips were wet, and, as he shook his head morosely, a look of pain crossed his face. Johanna yearned to reach over and touch her uncle's hand.

He spoke gently. "We can go outside the paper and find some-one, Johanna. We can sell. We can surrender control. We can wait until you get married, and appoint *your* husband. We can do any one of a number of things. But we *don't* want to."

"My immediate, visceral reaction is no."

"I knew it would be."

"I don't have—"

"You don't have . . . *what?* You're a member of the family, Johanna. Your great-grandfather began the paper with *nothing*. Built the paper into a good one, maybe a great one. Your grandfa-ther built on what Frederic accomplished."

Skipper reached across the table and took his niece's right hand. "There's a tradition to be maintained here. You have a life inter-est in the family trust. It pays you—and will pay our children and *their* children—and, frankly, it seems to me you have a respon-sibility to that trust and to that family."

"If I'm incompetent, what happens?"

"You won't be."

"But if I'm—"

"You're not going to be publisher overnight, Johanna. It's years of training and commitment. It's 3 A.M. calls. It's a union crisis every other week. It's having to be a bastard. And being a woman, you're going to have to prove that you're tougher and smarter than everyone else, that you have balls."

He spoke more slowly. "If you're incompetent you can be re-moved. By a family vote."

The waiter interrupted. Skipper ordered a steak and salad, and another martini. Johanna asked for a chef's salad and tomato juice. They sat in silence.

"Who's replacing my father?" she asked distractedly, staring past Skipper.

"We're not sure."

Johanna closed her eyes. Three men at a nearby table burst into laughter. A waiter brushed past her, and she heard the tinkle of sil-verware in the crowded restaurant. The men were speaking nois-ily; one was repeating a story, laughing as he spoke.

Absently, Johanna brushed her fingers through her hair. "Would there be much opposition to me?"

"You're a young woman. Inexperienced. You'll be watched

very carefully. *Judged.* Eli Faber won't like it. The senior
people."

"When would you want me to begin?"

"As soon as school ends."

"I've always fought like hell to avoid the *Star.*" Her smile was
melancholy. "But all along," she said, facing him, "all along, I
knew."

*

Given directions by Howie Bishop, the taxi driver found the
Paley house on Beech Drive in Fairfax in less than twenty minutes. In its red-brick simplicity, the two-story house was indistin-
guishable from dozens of others.

Bishop paid the cab fare. Children, bouncing a basketball
against the hoop attached to a garage door across the street,
glanced at him and returned to the game. Bishop trudged up the
walkway, his black plastic travel bag slung over his shoulder,
glancing at the two waterspouts that showered both sides of the
lawn. It was a meticulously kept lawn, shaded by a single elm,
laced with a freshly turned bed of tulips, azaleas and hyacinths
that flanked the front path.

The bell chimed three times.

Maggie Paley opened the door, wiping her hands on the cotton
apron folded around her skirt. Wisps of gray hair, slipping out of
her tightly wrapped bun, curled over the sides of her forehead.

"Mr. Bishop . . ."

" 'Howie,' please . . .

"Something smells terrific," he said as he walked in.

"I had an inspiration today," she said, averting his eyes. "I
baked lemon meringue pie, which is my son's favorite, and now
I'm baking a whole wheat bread for Jerry. *His* favorite."

She was a pretty woman in her fifties, slim-legged, with a narrow waist that opened into an ample, plump bosom. Her slightly
crooked front teeth failed to mar a delicate attractiveness. She
spoke in a heavy New York accent.

They had met three times: twice at *Star* parties, when Jerry ran
the City Hall bureau, and at the farewell party in Barry Cohen's
apartment when Jerry left the *Star* to join Fitzgerald's staff.

Maggie Paley seemed older now. Her face was wan, her pale-
brown eyes dulled with lack of sleep, the skin beneath the lids

swollen. Her unease—hands fluttering at her side—suddenly vanished as Jerry climbed down the steps to greet Howie, who caught Maggie's sharp stare.

Jerry Paley welcomed Bishop with a handclasp and a broad smile, and showed Howie into his cramped study in the rear of the house, seating himself in a pine rocker.

"Maggie wants to give us some lemon meringue pie in a couple of minutes, but let's sneak a quick one in, okay?" As Paley fixed scotch on the rocks for both of them, he said: "Delighted you could come down, Howie. Help you in any way I can."

Howie Bishop watched Jerry.

"Would have met you in the office on the Hill, but believe me, if I went in to work right from the airport I would have been up to my ass in phone calls."

"You've been out of town," said Bishop. It was a statement.

"Got in this morning at ten, went right to the hospital at Bethesda, took my boy out, came home, made some calls, here I am."

"Panama?"

"Terrible place. Fitzgerald wanted me to go there. He's on Foreign Relations. All involved in the Canal." Jerry Paley was speaking too quickly.

Bishop said, "How's your boy?"

Paley handed him the drink and sat on a wing chair covered in a quilted bluebird and floral print. "Raise a kid, live a normal life, hope for the best and then bang-bang it's over. Just about killed her." He nodded toward the kitchen.

Paley's stomach rolled out of the cardigan, and his neck bulged with an extra layer of flesh. Veins showed beneath his flushed cheeks.

Piles of newspapers and books lay scattered on the cheap green-and-brown rug. Around the study—on the walls and bookcases—rested the mementos of Jerry's career. Pictures of Jerry with governors and senators, framed letters from two Presidents thanking him for his work in their successful election campaigns, a picture of Jerry shaking Skipper's hand, a photo of Jerry, Maggie and their son Mike, about nine or ten, on the deck of a fishing boat. Tanned and grinning. Maggie wearing baggy trousers and a woolen turtleneck sweater, her hair twisted in the wind. Happier days.

Jerry tasted the drink. "Mike is in and out of the hospital," he said. "This week it was terrible swollen feet and red scabs. Scared the piss out of us. Last year when that happened the doctors said that if it got worse they would have to amputate his *feet*. Jesus! What a time. Thank Christ it didn't get worse."

Jerry took a gulp of his drink. He's aged badly, thought Howie. His thinning gray curls were flecked with strands of milk-white hair.

"Four weeks ago, maybe it was five, it was fatty tumors all over his hands and neck. Horrible. A couple of weeks before then he was driving the car into White Flint to do some shopping, right? Out of the blue, he loses his sense of direction, kid doesn't know where the fuck he's going. Parks the car on the side of the road and begins to *cry*. Like a two-year-old baby.

"You know Mike used to lift weights, tough guy, he was on the wrestling team in high school. Now he develops little breasts like a woman. Suddenly, for two, three weeks at a time they appear, and then disappear. He loses big clumps of hair in the shower, gets bald, then it grows back after a month."

Bishop fixed his eyes on the moccasin slippers that held Jerry's white, hairless feet. "I'll tell you, in a way we're lucky," said Jerry. "Between you and me I pulled a string here, and with the help of some cops high up in the department in New York, he's now working at the Arlington Police Department, a desk job, no pressure, a decent job. A living."

Howie Bishop wanted to change the subject, but Paley was deep into it. Jerry finished his drink in two fast gulps.

"We've tried to sue, but the Veterans Administration won't budge," he said. "There's no connection, they say, between what Mike and hundreds of others are going through and the fact that they were in Vietnam and got sprayed with Agent Orange. Prove it, they say. *Prove* the connection. Those fuckheads."

Paley rose and poured another drink, glancing at Howie's to make sure he didn't need a refill.

"Three weeks before Mike went to Vietnam he eloped. Sweet girl. Parochial school. Nice family. He was in the Marines. A lance corporal. Six months after he gets to Vietnam, he sees them spraying a chemical over the trees while he's out in the field. And they kept doing it. He went into defoliated areas and the ground would be covered with this shit. He remembers even being sprayed with the stuff on patrol, and they would tell him and everyone else to cover their mouths and watch for the enemy. Don't worry about defoliants."

Jerry sat down. "So he gets a skin rash on the back and a tumor on the legs and feet that swell up like balloons and they say, Okay, give him an honorable discharge and a hundred and fifty-four dollars a month for service-connected disability and goodbye.

"So he comes back a wreck, a fucking wreck, and three children are born dead, three straight years in a row, and then comes little Angela," said Jerry Paley. "You have any kids?"

Bishop said no.

Paley went on: "Well, maybe it's a little hard for you to believe this but, like, little Angela, she's not so little anymore, she's ten years old, she was born with sixteen birth defects. A hole in her heart, a partial spine, deformed intestines, no rectum, missing bones, brain damage. She can't walk. Okay?"

Bishop nodded.

"But you know, Howie, you know—I love her. Can you believe that?"

"Yes, I can."

"Maybe it's hard to believe, but, Jesus, I love her. My granddaughter. Maggie said the priest told her it's perfectly normal. We love people in different ways. I *love* the child."

Paley drained his glass and glowered into it. Sighing deeply, Jerry Paley ran his tongue over his lips. He spoke without looking at Bishop.

"All right, Howie. You're doing a number on us."

"Why did you join up with Fitzgerald?"

Jerry looked up. "The gelt, for one thing. Fifty-two five is a little heftier than the thirty-eight I was making at the *Star*. Money was one reason. Here comes Davey Fitzgerald, a hotshot, smart politician, charismatic, as we say, possibly ready for the big one, and he offers me a job." Paley lit a cigarette. Bishop watched him.

"Reasons for joining Fitzgerald," said Paley. "I'm a fifty-two-year-old reporter with nowhere to go. How many fires have I cov-

ered in East Harlem? How many cutesy features have I written
about the first day of spring? How many? How many protests have
I covered by the blacks, the spicks, the women, the nuns, the bus
drivers, the taxi drivers, the gays, the parents of one-armed les-
bians. How *many?*

"How many times did I try to say something—with a little po-
etic flourish here and there—and have it butchered by some nitwit
on the desk who reads with his lips. Jesus, Howie, *you* know. By
the time I was thirty, I stopped reading my own stories in the
paper. Besides. . . ." Jerry's eyes went blank. "Your heart breaks
too many times when they all know that you still care.

"So. A long answer to your short question. I was bored. And
needed the money. And frankly, I dreaded the prospect of competing with the young hotshots."

Jerry Paley grinned. "It's a young man's game, Howie."

"I know."

"They should shoot all reporters over forty."

"Make it forty-five."

"Okay, forty-five. What the fuck does a guy do? They get
scared. They lose confidence."

"They get screwed," said Bishop.

"You see guys wearing toupees in the newsroom. Ridiculous.
You see some guys trying to fit into clothes that a twenty-three-
year-old wouldn't wear. Keep up the illusion. It's a great game for
kids, but after that . . ."

"Are the rumors true?"

"What are the rumors?"

"You're on the take."

Paley laughed. "You've got to be kidding. You've got to be out
of your fucking head. Who's telling you that?"

"I'm serious."

"You got the wrong boy."

"Okay."

"Ain't true. Ain't true one fucking bit. How am I involved? Tell
me?"

Bishop waited.

"Just tell me."

"Payoffs. You're involved."

"Cheryl."

"What?"

"I told the silly bitch she had no proof, nothing, but she doesn't give a fuck who she destroys. As long as she cuts up Fitzgerald."

"You banged her?"

"Who didn't?"

The door knock interrupted them. Maggie Paley entered, smiling, carrying a wooden tray with cups of coffee and slices of lemon meringue pie.

"You've got to try some of this, Howie," she said, placing the tray on the steel-and-glass table in the center of the room. Maggie brushed aside a layer of newspapers to set the tray down.

If she sensed the tension in the study, Maggie Paley betrayed nothing. Her smile was pasted on her face. She glanced at Howie, then her husband, and slipped out of the room, closing the door.

The strain in the room broke.

"You think I'm schmuck enough to play nickel-and-dime games, Howie? You think I'd sacrifice this?"—his right hand waved across the room—"for a few bucks? You believe some cunt who wants to get even with her boss—?"

Howie lifted the plate of pie, cutting a large chunk with his fork. Finally he looked up. "Did you ever take a bribe, Jerry?"

"Are you . . . ?" His voice cracked with anger.

"Did you?"

"*No!*"

They glared at each other. Bishop wolfed down his pie in silence. Finally he asked Paley to call him a taxi to take him into town. He was spending the night at the Mayflower. Paley sat absolutely still.

"Old Barry Cohen is pushing. Is that it?"

"Barry is pushing."

"Never liked Barry." Jerry Paley leaned back in his chair, his tongue sliding over his teeth. He let the comment linger.

"Good newsman."

"That shit he pulled in Vietnam. All those rumors. The way he won the Pulitzer. That fit Barry to a T."

"Whatever Barry wants, Barry gets."

Paley lit a cigarette. "Maury taking over? Evan's job?"

Bishop shrugged. "Rumors."

"Skipper still humping Sally Sims?"

"Yup."

"She still married to Charlie Queer?"

Bishop nodded.

"Odd fucking world."

Howie Bishop watched Jerry stand and phone for the taxi.

"Your man Fitzgerald still dropping his wick into anything over twelve and under seventy?" asked Howie after Jerry hung up the phone.

"He enjoys the ladies," said Jerry, suddenly somber.

"Still enjoying Mrs. Claiborne?"

Jerry Paley's glare unsettled Howie.

By the time the taxi horn sounded outside, Bishop and Paley were finishing off another scotch. Bishop walked out of the study, looking around for Maggie Paley to say good-bye.

The smell of camphor and fresh polish hung sweetly in the air, and Howie Bishop was reminded of his childhood in Queens. The russet floors shimmered.

"She's probably resting upstairs," said Jerry Paley, opening the door.

They shook hands, Howie staring into Jerry's tired, swollen eyes. He could smell the whiskey on Jerry's breath.

Gripping his shoulder bag, Howie walked toward the cab, aware that Jerry Paley was standing at the screen door behind him. He climbed into the cab and waved; Jerry lifted his right hand and nodded.

Across the street, the children were still playing basketball. As the cab moved off, Howie watched a tall youth in a numbered sweat shirt jump into the air, and gently thrust the ball, with his right hand, onto the backboard. The ball fell through the hoop.

Dusk lingered, shadows falling across the street, and a cool, wet wind brushed Bishop's face. Kitchen lights glowed on the suburban street. Howie rolled up the window, turned, and saw Jerry, still standing at the doorway.

Howie would call Barry as soon as he reached the Mayflower. He would meet Cheryl later.

Suddenly he despised this story, wished he wasn't involved. Howie didn't want to see Jerry Paley again.

*

Hold the calls. No goddamn calls.

Hugh told Francine to hold the calls except urgent ones. He

slammed the door, the underarms of his shirt covered with arcs of
sweat. It was five-fifteen, and he had twelve hundred words to
write, the lead of the paper. The foreign desk was screaming for
copy.

Okay. Okay.

The White House briefing had been vague. Yes, the President
was very concerned about the situation between China and Russia.
No, the President was not yet planning to negotiate . . .

Hugh's stomach knotted. Blood vessels pounded on the side of
his head. Five-twenty. He began typing on his video terminal.
"Administration officials said today that President Bergen has tentatively agreed to start private negotiations with China and Russia
in an effort to head off a major confrontation between the two
superpowers."

Okay. Okay. Hugh pressed the buzzer on his desk, and Francine
rushed in.

He demanded the morgue folder on the China-Soviet dispute.
Silently she walked out.

All right. Get the caveat in just in case. AP and UPI are leading
with the official White House comment and we don't want to
thrust ourselves too far out on the limb.

Second graf. "Although the White House said later today that
the President was not planning to negotiate, other ranking Administration sources said that the President had decided to do so following an early morning Cabinet meeting at which Bergen 'reluctantly agreed' to seek talks. Administration sources described
Bergen as 'very worried' about the deteriorating situation on the
China-Russian border."

Third graf. "President Bergen's decision came as the New York
Star learned that the Soviet command in the Far East had placed
all aircraft, ground troops and tactical missiles on twenty-four-
hour alert. A Pentagon spokesman refused to comment."

The door flew open. Francine stepped in, tossed the folder of
newspaper clips on his desk, and left. Hugh didn't look up.

Fourth graf. "Administration officials were especially concerned
about the buildup of Soviet troops and weapons in Mongolia. Estimates of Soviet forces ranged as high as two million troops eastward from Irkutsk."

Fifth graf. What now? Parsons had asked him to insert high up in the story a paragraph of Carl Ross's story from Peking, and a sentence or two of Ernie Richards' Moscow piece. The stories had been telecopied to the Washington bureau. The Hong Kong and Moscow stories were also on the front page, but Hugh's Washington piece, the main story, was serving as a roundup.

Hugh wrote quickly.

"Meanwhile, Western efforts to start Soviet-Chinese border talks were imperiled today by new and violent propaganda exchanges. The Chinese attack on Moscow was in the form of a dispatch from Peking by Hsinhua, the Chinese press agency, which attacked the Soviet leadership as 'the new Hitlers,' and said that the Russians were planning a 'deadly nuclear blitzkrieg' against China. China would repel such an attack 'with an ocean of humanity that will submerge the few million aggressor troops,' said the statement."

Sixth graf. "The Soviet government newspaper *Izvestia* said that China had provoked the border clashes, and that Peking had undertaken 'an extremely dangerous and menacing expansion policy.'"

Seventh graf. "After denouncing Vice Premier Phung for 'lusting shamelessly to absorb the Soviet Union's sacred territory,' the statement said: 'The peace-loving Soviet peoples must adhere to the doctrine that socialist countries have the right to interfere in one another's affairs if their own self-interest or those of others are aggressively threatened.'"

Eighth graf. "To State Department officials the Soviet attack was especially ominous since, according to Soviet analysts, similar comments were used in the past to justify Russian military moves in such countries as Czechoslovakia."

He heard the door open.

Francine said, "Your son is on the line, and Alvin Simmons called."

He kept typing.

"Tell my son I'll call him as soon as I finish, and tell Alvin"—damn, he wanted to speak to Alvin, feel him out, gently, about Pomerance—"tell him I'll call him tonight at home."

Beautiful, he thought, typing out the ninth graf. He was ahead of *everyone* in the Washington press corps. Everyone. He had this story by the balls and was squeezing.

The "Today" show was quoting "A report today from Washington in the New York *Star* . . ." The three networks last night were also quoting the *Star* . . . AP and UPI cited his reports . . .

Glory be. Glory be hallelujah. I am on a high, I am going to get that job. I am sailing along.

He was breathless now, tapping furiously on the video terminal. Twenty minutes to deadline, talking to himself, giddy.

And Pomerance. Let's find out about Pomerance. Let's sock a double exclusive to them in the next few days—the Russian-Chinese crisis. *And* Pomerance.

Pomerance!

What is *that* all about?

Maybe that's an even bigger story.

No. No *way*. China and Russia squaring off. A hell of a goddamn story.

But . . .

Pomerance in a White House car?

Why was Alvin Simmons out of the office the past two days? On assignment, the secretary said. Unavailable. Why hasn't Simmons returned his phone calls?

Maybe.

Maybe there's one hell of a story there too.

A big goddamn story.

An exclusive.

A big one.

*

Maury moved quickly to Ward's desk as soon as word reached New York that Hugh had begun filing his story. The newsroom, five forty-five, spun with energy. Telephones rang nonstop at empty desks. There were shouts of "Copy." Reporters, cupping phones against their ears, punched video-terminal keys with gusto. Reporters whirled up to the desks of editors, their shirts unbuttoned at the neck, ties askew. Copy boys and copy girls, gripping folders from the morgue, loped across the newsroom. Bursts of laughter rang out in one corner of the newsroom. In another corner some veteran reporters, assigned to oblivion writing obituaries, played poker.

"Good story," said Maury.

"Hughie's got a source," said Ward, rising out of his chair, lighting a cigarette. He wished Hugh Finch's stories weren't twisting his belly with rage.

Ward told Maury he wanted to make some staff moves for the next week. Send the Bangkok correspondent, Gordon Kahn, to Hong Kong. Get Lorraine Hudson in Paris to fly to Vienna to watch Eastern Europe. Have Freddie Fairchild in Cairo apply for an immediate visa to China.

Good old Freddie, Ward thought. Good old delectable Margo.

Skipper walked over, his left hand restlessly jangling coins in his trouser pocket. He wore a blue striped double-breasted worsted wool suit, the only one at the desk, and possibly the newsroom, to wear a jacket this late in the afternoon.

"Hugh is onto something," said Skipper, biting his lip.

Ward faced Skipper, then turned away, absently toying with a ball-point pen. Son of a bitch. Hughie's onto something big. Got his fingers on a good one. Front-page play. Byline. At this moment, at this oh-so-opportune moment when they're hunting for a managing editor, the little fucker turns into a star.

Ward heard Maury's strained voice. "We're deploying the staff, Skipper. Thought we should send Kahn from Bangkok to Hong Kong, and Lorraine to help out in Eastern Europe. Get Freddie Fairchild to push for a visa to China."

They were interrupted by a phone call from Carl Ross in Peking. Maury and Skipper listened in on extensions. It was nearly 6 A.M. there, and Peking's three major publications—*Jenmin Pao,* the official party and government newspaper, *Hung Chi,* the party's ideological journal, and *Chichfang Chun Pao,* the Army paper—had just issued an unusual joint editorial telling the people of central China to "realize and prepare for the enemy to launch a major war."

Ward calmly told Ross to file a story immediately for the first edition, then flesh out the story for later editions. He hung up.

Maury stuck a chewing-gum stick in his mouth. "Let's make this a new top on Carl's story. Keep Hugh the lead of the paper."

It was an order, gently stated but unmistakable. Skipper's eyes fell on Maury and Ward. Without a word, Skipper steered them several feet away from the foreign desk to a silent corner beside the water fountain.

"I want a list, Maury," the publisher said suddenly in a voice so low and tense that Ward felt his throat tighten.

"List?" said Maury, puzzled.

"Who's dispensable in the newsroom? Whom we can let go." Skipper turned to Ward, swallowing hard. "I want to pare down the foreign staff."

Anticipating Ward's question, Skipper murmured, "Contingency list, that's all it is." The publisher repeated, *"Contingency. May come to nothing."*

"Depends on the Guild," said Maury. "Frank Lazzarutti."

"Depends on the *drivers,*" Skipper corrected. "We can publish a paper without the Guild. Use the wires. Get editors to pitch in, cover stories. We can do it if the drivers work, if they cross the picket line."

Skipper drew in his breath. *"The Wall Street Journal* is snooping around, doing a story on us . . ."

"So is *Time,*" said Ward.

"I want this closely held, don't want it published."

Skipper opened his mouth, as if to continue, but stopped. He frowned and abruptly turned and walked off.

"God*damn,*" said Maury, more to himself than to Ward, watching Skipper walk through the newsroom.

Ward glanced at Maury, then returned to the foreign desk, surprised to see Ray Silver smiling at him.

"He's hungry for the job," said Ray.

"Who?" said Ward.

"Maury. Good old Maury. Telling Skipper, 'I thought we would send Kahn from Bangkok.' *I thought.*"

"The barracudas are out, honey," said Florence, ripping a sheet of paper out of her typewriter. The phone rang, and she picked it up.

Ward lifted Hugh's copy from Washington, his eyes distractedly wandering over the story.

So they were finally planning cutbacks, Skipper taking the plunge against Lazzarutti, squaring off against the unions, risking a strike. Bloody ominous it was, cutting back the staff, starting with a couple of kids and secretaries, moving on to the fifty-five-year-old clerks, then the reporters, the tired ones, the ones who had a modest talent years back, crushed now, knock them off and then target the oddballs, yes, every newsroom had them, offbeat characters that Ward found appealing, silent men who drifted on the fringes. Christ knows where they came from, who promoted them, shirts flopping out of the trousers, egg-stained ties, whispering to themselves, writing three- and four-paragraph stories on a jumper at Grand Central, a failed bank robbery in Rego Park, a drug heist on West 127th Street, a public-relations handout from the Urban League, the heart attack of a retired furrier on Central Park West.

No bylines for these jokers, not quite Woodward and Bernstein territory here, Robert Redford uninterested thank you, but well, maybe it's how we all end up, more or less, hacking away, dying a little with each story, struggling against the gods like Kaiserman over there, pissing in his pants because he's going to be chasing a fire in the South Bronx one day, just like twenty years ago.

"Fuck!"

Ray Silver looked at him solemnly. "Hugh's story *that* bad?" Florence raised her eyes. "What's wrong?"

Ward shook his head, aware that the thirst in his throat was somehow draining his entire body. His hands were shaking. He yearned for a martini, like the two at lunch, Gordon's gin, plenty of ice, a twist, not too much vermouth. Been a bad day, bad couple of days. It had been downhill since lunch, depressingly downhill. The realization, leaving ashes in the mouth, the stomach knotted, the realization that one is *not going to make it . . .*

What was it she said? Silly bitch! Marilyn Cheever from *Time.* I think you're too nice a guy, Ward.

Marilyn Cheever, New York bureau of *Time,* had called him on Thursday to interview him for a story they were preparing, about, as she put it, the fight to get Evan Claiborne's job. What fight? he said. Come on, she said. Cut the bullshit. Okay, let's have lunch, he said.

They sat in the upstairs restaurant of Sardi's, unfashionable, Siberia, far from the *Star.* The waitress, in a black tie and tails, served them bloody marys, and Marilyn opened her jacket to reveal an impressive pair. Marilyn comes on strong. You're much younger than I thought. Where did you go to school? Oh, really.

What year? You must know my older brother, Kenneth. Kenneth Cheever. He's a stockbroker in San Francisco. Wow. How interesting. Married? Oh. I see. In India. Out of sight.

Was Marilyn playing footsie? Was she gently rubbing the knee beneath her slit corduroy skirt against his dacron-and-wool draped foot? Was it purely an accident that the toe of her ankle-strapped pumps—is this what they're wearing now at *Time* Inc.?—seemed to be caressing his leg?

Was it his boyish, well-bred charm that drove her wild? The rather pedestrian good looks? The hint that wildness in the sack awaited her? Getting fucked by a married man?

Or was it something more mundane? The need to get a goddamn story for *Time*. Get some gossip. Get a job on the *Star*. (Yes, once before, a Philadelphia *Inquirer* reporter, a tall, frizzy-haired girl who listened to him with her mouth open, passed her phone number to Ward in the midst of chopped steak at Downey's and told him to phone anytime. He rationalized later that he had avoided calling her because there was no job for her on the foreign staff. Actually, her aggressiveness frightened him.)

Does one need complications like Marilyn Cheever? Isn't Florence enough? Isn't it enough to have a wife doing Yoga on a houseboat in Kashmir? Why, in Christ's name, did I ask to see Marilyn on Monday night?

Marilyn said, really, you're too nice a guy, Ward. I've spoken to Barry Cohen and Hugh Finch and they are tough cookies. Everyone says so. Those people are playing hardball, right?

Right, Marilyn.

The door to Evan's office was open, wide open, and they were struggling like hell to push through. Like a silent-movie comedy. Climbing over one another. A stiletto in the back, a sharp kick in the groin. A thumb in the eye. They all wanted it.

Hugh is pushing like crazy. A black managing editor. Perfect. Get the blacks on the staff to calm down. Maury. Frightened Maury. Groomed for it. Waiting for it. *Hungry* for it. Barry, good old Barry. Don't fuck around with Barry, what Barry wants, he gets. And Sally? Terrific choice. Do wonders for the paper's image. A woman managing editor. Christ almighty. There goes the women's suit against the paper.

Ward placed Hugh's story in the out-box, and leaned back in

his swivel chair. Glancing at the sleeve of his turtleneck, he flicked off a cigarette ash. The sweater wrist was frayed, worn away to its white cotton lining.

You want the job? Start wearing shirts, *ties*. You *want* the job. Always lurking in the back of the brain. *The job*. Damned good managing editor you'd be. Sensitive to the needs of the staff. Independent. Freewheeling. Maybe not as tough as Evan but . . .

Too nice a guy. Evan's replacement would be selected by the Steiners on the basis of what? Age, experience, talent, loyalty, adaptability, personality, *strength*. What, precisely, had Ward shown them? He was intelligent and pliant. Princeton. Was there anything substantial behind the WASP mask that Frieda found so charming?

Ward Parsons lit a second cigarette, ignoring Florence's frown. Was he accepting everyone else's lighthearted judgment of his shrewdness, his talents, his toughness? Was he merely adhering to the role that the Steiners—and everyone else—had thrust on him? Wasn't he, after all, a bit of a pushy son of a bitch too?

He shut his eyes and, quite suddenly, heard Alex Vikas' voice over the phone, good CIA source from Saigon days, shrewd bastard. Vikas had called him less than an hour before to say he'd like to speak to him about the Soviet-China crisis, the Agency's side. Translation: the Agency wanted to leak a story. Ward had patiently told Alex that editors usually pass up writing stories, and suggested that he call Barney Fischer, the White House correspondent, but through lunch with Marilyn Cheever the conversation with Alex gnawed at him. Yes, Barney was knowledgeable, he could handle this story, but why was Ward so generous, so *benevolent* about giving a front-page byline to someone else? Since when was warmhearted charity a rule of the trade?

Even as Ward's eyes flashed open, he felt a tremor of excitement in his chest. He *knew* what he had to do. A kick in the balls wouldn't hurt Hugh Finch. A little one-upmanship won't destroy Barry Cohen. Let's surprise Maury.

Fight!

Fight for the fucking job.

Editors on the *Star* were hardly barred from writing, especially the foreign editor. This story—the China-Soviet conflict—had enormous implications. Copy was flooding in. It was Hugh's story, *his* byline, but no single reporter ever held a monopoly over a single story. A breaking story is always up for grabs.

After all, it was for the good of the paper: competition makes better stories. Our readers benefit. Let's round out some of Hugh's fine coverage with some in-depth analysis by the foreign editor, take a step back, interview some intelligence source, find out what's *really* happening.

For the good of our readers.

You hypocritical bastard.

For the good of Ward Parsons.

He turned to Florence and said in a voice lit with excitement, "Get me Alex Vikas at the CIA."

*

Nancy Chang was in the bedroom. "God, you look tired," she said, kissing Maury Kramer as she fastened a gold necklace around her throat.

"You look beautiful," he said, dropping his jacket on the bed.

Nancy ignored him. "Why don't you rest?"

"I'll have a drink, take a shower. Feel better."

"Bad day?" she asked.

"Busy." He walked into the living room of their apartment on West Ninth Street. It was 7:15 P.M.

He dropped four ice cubes in a glass and splashed Bourbon over them, then kicked off his shoes and sat down in the rattan rocker that she had purchased several weeks earlier on Columbus Avenue. He closed his eyes.

She walked in and kissed him on the forehead.

"Let's not go," she said. "I'll run out and get a steak and . . ."

"With you looking like that, it would be a waste not to go."

She did look beautiful. She wore a mauve blazer with a narrow front-slit skirt. The one-button blazer, tied with a thin belt, opened broadly at her chest, reaching her rib cage. The outlines of her ample breasts were visible.

"Too sexy?" she said.

"Look. You could be wearing sackcloth and you'd look beddable."

" 'Beddable'? Is that a word?"

"My own adjective. Describes you."

Nancy sat on the sofa. "How was the factory today?" Fridays and Saturdays were her days off on the foreign copy desk.

"Finch has another exclusive. A good one. The President's decided to intervene in the China-Soviet dispute."

Nancy watched Maury, her lips set in a wan half-smile that seemed to mask some hidden sadness he could never fathom. When they first lived together, Maury attributed Nancy's mysteriousness, her silences, her half-smile to her being Chinese. Inscrutable girl, the stereotype fell into place, one never quite knew what lay behind that infuriating smile, those narrow hazel eyes sheathed in black lashes. Yet he soon realized that there *was* a sadness and passivity to Nancy that had nothing to do with her heritage, that made her cling to him with an intensity that Maury found dismaying and also pleasurable.

"We're deploying the troops," he said. "Kahn, Freddie Fairchild, Lorraine." Maury sipped his Bourbon. "Barry sent Linda to Los Angeles without informing Sally or anyone else on the national desk, without informing *me*."

"Up to his old tricks," said Nancy, frowning.

"Could be a wild-goose chase. Could be . . . interesting. Checking on the Vice President. Some weird rumors." Maury stared at her. "Come here." She did so.

"I want to kiss you."

"Free country."

"You taste good." Maury held Nancy's face in his hands.

"You look tired, darling," said Nancy.

"Mmm. That feels nice, very nice. Keep your hand there."

"Like magic. Just gets big."

"Ah!"

"Let's not go. Another dumb-ass benefit."

"But this is a Steiner benefit," he said, stretching the words with sarcasm. "Command performance. Everybody's got to show up—especially . . ." He paused.

"Especially if you want to be managing editor." Nancy stood up.

"You going to leave me like this?"

She smiled, that infuriating half-smile, and turned on her heels and left the room, leaving a scent of perfume.

They had lived together for nearly ten months. It felt like a lifetime, thought Maury as he shaved moments later, a stretch of days that blurred the years, the pleasant years he had spent with Sarah. Was it heartless not to miss Sarah? Was it wrong not to keep on grieving? The months of her agony had left his own senses numbed, his body aching and exhausted. By the time she died he was beyond grief; he was tired and relieved.

Maury had depended on Sarah to run his life outside the *Star*. She had paid the bills, attended the house in Riverdale, drove the children to school, worried about the orthodontist's bills, served as his hostess. She was a decent, bright, undemanding woman—and yet, and yet, hadn't their marriage, their relationship, their sex ground into ordinariness, into torpor, into the same kind of melancholy standoff that afflicted so many of their friends? He had the *Star,* and, like so many of his colleagues, the *Star* was family. Life revolved around the *Star*.

He had noticed Nancy Chang in the newsroom—could one avoid this dazzling Chinese girl, this copy editor with her crimson lips, her unruly shoulder-length black hair, her easy laugh that made her body shake. She wore tight jeans, trousers that clung to her narrow waist; men's shirts rolled up at the sleeve, unbuttoned to the chest. Gold chains. Dark glasses. Copy editors on the *Star* don't usually dress this way.

After Barry introduced them, Maury took her to lunch at a Japanese restaurant on Fifty-fifth Street, off Seventh Avenue, and the following day phoned to invite her for dinner. That night, after she had taken him to her favorite Chinese restaurant on Mott Street, they took a taxi to her apartment on Bank Street and, with little said, removed their clothes and settled into her queen-size bed. He had not made love in more than a year.

Maury was weak at the knees the next morning, short of breath, but in an ebullient mood after having sex with this woman, this beautiful woman, three times. In the next few weeks he was aflame with energy, and even his colleagues noticed this remarkable change in Maury Kramer.

His life pulsed with a new intensity. His need for Nancy was so powerful, so embracing, that the *Star* faded in importance. He spent odd moments on the uptown bus thinking of her, caught himself at front-page story conferences distracted by the thought of her. At luncheons with Skipper or a visiting foreign correspondent, Maury found himself lost in conversation, yearning to kiss Nancy's neck and eyes, yearning to make love with her—sometimes uncomfortable, sometimes frenzied love on the mattress with her fingers dug into his back. Love in the bathtub, in the shower, on the living-room floor, two pillows beneath her buttocks.

Whatever fantasies he had—and, Maury told her with a laugh, he had limited fantasies—she indulged. Is this happening to me? he once thought. Is this really happening?

They made love in a rented car in the Connecticut woods, in a pool in Bridgehampton, and once he made her come in a restaurant by massaging her with his left hand while eating snails with his right hand.

In bed, when she came, Nancy arched her back, opened her mouth and wrapped her hands tightly around his neck, her body pulsing and subsiding and pulsing again over endless minutes until he struggled to breathe free. Her needs and cravings seemed absolute.

And yet Maury sensed—and later Nancy made it obvious—that her moods were extravagant, and frighteningly unpredictable. On some evenings a shadow seemed to cross her face, her eyes tightened and turned inward. She would lie in bed, the palm of her hand over her eyes, and whisper that she wanted to be left alone, could he please sleep on the sofa, could he just shut the door and not say anything. The next morning he would awake to the smell of freshly brewed coffee. Smiling, somewhat distant, Nancy would bite into her toast in silence and say nothing about the previous night. By that evening she would seem fine.

She told him once that her father, in Hong Kong, was an alcoholic who beat her mother and the three children. A younger brother was in and out of jail. An older sister had tried suicide twice. Nancy said her dominant fear was replicating her parents' marriage, finding a man who abused women.

Nancy had fled to Toronto, where she worked on the *Globe* and *Mail,* married a reporter who, it turned out, was impotent and beat her too, had an abortion after an affair with an editor and finally traveled to New York. She lived on Bank Street, worked on *Newsday* on Long Island. One snowy night when the assistant managing editor of *Newsday* broke off their affair after three months, Nancy walked into the bathroom, removed the cap from her Valium bottle and methodically swallowed two dozen five-milligram capsules. Inexplicably she stepped into the kitchen for a glass of orange juice and, as soon as she placed the empty glass in the sink, Nancy began to weep slowly. By the time she phoned a neighbor who lived on West 115th Street, Betty Kennedy, who was night news editor of the *Star*, Nancy was incoherent.

Nancy spent two weeks at St. Vincent's Hospital, and began daily sessions with a psychiatrist on East Eighty-seventh Street, off Park Avenue. Betty got her a job on the foreign copy desk of the *Star*. Eight months later, after a brief relapse and an unhappy affair with Barry Cohen, Nancy met Maury.

"I'm trouble," she had said abruptly one night in the darkness after they had made love.

"You sound like Lauren Bacall in one of those movies."

"I'm serious."

"I know."

"Why do you like me?"

"You're kidding. I ask you the same thing."

"Oh, Maury." She raised herself and crooked her arm on the bed, turning to him. The fingers of her left hand grazed the hair on his chest . . .

"You're a handsome man."

"I'm fifty-four, for Chrissake."

"You're super in bed."

"You can get some stud half my age who can keep it up longer."

"You're sweet."

"I can be a bastard."

"Now, come on." She kissed him. "I like Jewish men."

"Why?"

"You're going to laugh."

"What is it?"

"They're more paternal. More protective. Not all, of course. Some are bastards too. But in the main . . ."

"I never quite heard that before."

"I confess," she said, locking her fingers behind her head on the pillow. "I need a father. *And* a lover. Totally neurotic on my part. Classic case."

"Jesus, what a fruitcake."

Maury turned and kissed Nancy. She draped her arms around his back, holding him, feeling the sticky warmth of his body.

"What did Barry tell you about me?"

"You like Jewish guys."

"Is that all?"

"That's all." He turned to her. "How long did you see Barry?"

"A couple of weeks. That was enough."

"You didn't like him?"

"No."

"Don't want to talk about it?"

"No."

"Can I kiss you?"

"Yes . . ."

He had shaved and showered, and was wearing a new double-breasted blue blazer, flared beige cord trousers, buckled Italian shoes and a striped brown-and-white shirt that Nancy had bought at Harre and Hudson during her last London trip. His tie matched, a heavy silk, walnut-brown tie that she had purchased in Liberty's. A white silk handkerchief nestled neatly in his breast pocket.

"You are stunning," she said, looking up as he walked into the living room. She placed her Iris Murdoch paperback on the table.

"Old enough to be your dad."

"Are you kidding?" she said, standing. "I better watch out tonight. Starlets, widows, society ladies are going to try to get their claws into you." She kissed him.

"You smell fantastic," he said. "We should see more of each other."

"You know," said Nancy, biting his ear, "I think I'm really falling for you."

"You always fall for the wrong guys." He was holding her, studying her face. "When I'm seventy, let's see, you'll be, what is it, forty-four. Prime of your life."

"Oh, Maury." She kissed him hard. "I think I love you."

*

In the annals of the New York *Star,* the precise date that Frederic Steiner's birthday party turned into a significant New York charity event remains obscure, but Frieda insists it was 1938 or, at the very latest, 1939. It was then that Frederic decided his annual birthday party for *Star* employees, usually held in Billy Rose's Diamond Horseshoe or the Rainbow Room, should center less on a celebration of himself and the newspaper than in serving others— specifically, Jewish refugees fleeing Hitler. It was inappropriate, Frederic knew, to selfishly dwell on his own personal triumph in America at a moment when persecutions against his blood kin had taken an alarming turn.

"The *Star* Party"—as it came to be known among the readers of *Women's Wear Daily* and a certain segment of New York society —therefore evolved from a rather select charity event at which Frederic Steiner invited *Star* employees, as well as the men who dominated Wall Street, the publishing world, the theater to a full-fledged gala (currently five hundred dollars a couple) which benefited a half-dozen charities and, coincidentally, earned the newspaper some free publicity. Despite Evan's death, the family had decided to go ahead with the party, partly because tickets had sold unusually well this year, partly because Frieda knew the charities had come to rely on the funds and would be hard-pressed without them.

On this night there was a hint of rain, the air seemed chilly and damp, but the sky over Central Park shimmered with stars as limousines and taxis began unloading passengers at Tavern-on-the-Green just off West Sixty-seventh Street.

Frieda climbed out of the rented Cadillac with Skipper and Lucy, moving beneath the balloons that clung to tree branches at the entrance of the garden. They braced themselves for the stares, the whispers, the awkward condolences.

"Chin up," whispered Frieda, as Lucy followed her out of the car. "Keep your head high."

Lucy absently smoothed her black-striped dress, ignoring her mother. Her right hand toyed with the row of brilliant emeralds falling over her chest.

Skipper sensed his sister's nervousness. "We'll cut out early."

Lucy, holding his arm, stared ahead at the Crystal Room through her dark glasses, the noise pounding her ears. She was nearly frozen in place by nervousness.

"Is that Ernie Dunlap?" Frieda's voice was low and sharp, as three photographers moved restlessly inside the Crystal and adjoining Elm Room, aiming their cameras at that blend of socialite and show business and hanger-on types that feed upon the newspapers and magazines.

"Treacherous," Lucy heard Frieda whisper. She turned, but Frieda was staring up approvingly at the Waterford and Baccarat chandeliers. "Lovely room."

Peter Fosdick moved toward them, holding a glass of whiskey. "Mrs. Steiner."

Frieda, genuinely pleased, kissed him on the cheek and waved to Eli Faber. A dance band began playing just as Lucy saw Sally Sims and her husband Charlie enter the glass-enclosed salon. The crowd surged into the Crystal Room, and Lucy slipped away toward David Fitzgerald.

He was sipping a glass of champagne, talking to the Dunlaps.

"My deepest condolences," said Ernest Dunlap, staring intently into Lucy's eyes. He was a burly man whose face struck Lucy as curiously taut and sensual, a face that Lucy knew appealed to many women but not to her. His slender lips crooked, inevitably, in a half-smile, and the nostrils of his broad flat nose flared as he spoke. Dunlap's gray-black hair, combed back, perfectly highlighted his widely spaced slate-gray eyes, startling in their intensity.

The fact that Ernie Dunlap stood perhaps four inches shorter than his wife hardly diminished his stature and seemed, in a curious way, to magnify his appearance, given the extraordinarily thin figure of Charlotte Garrison Dunlap, the socialite and art collector. Charlotte Dunlap glanced quizzically at Lucy, and placed her drink on the silk-screened tablecloth.

"Thank you," said Lucy, glancing at David Fitzgerald.

"He was a wonderful man," said Ernest Dunlap. Suddenly Lucy sensed that Dunlap was mocking Evan, and she stared hard at Charlotte until the woman turned. Lucy smiled and caught Dunlap's eyes.

"He *was* wonderful," she said, firmly.

Lucy knew that Frieda distrusted "the Dunlap boys," as they were known—Ernie and Charles—two of New York's major builders, Ernie now running the lucrative business while Charles, the older one, and ailing, lived in Palm Springs.

For a moment she tried to concentrate on what Frieda had once told her about the Dunlaps—some bit of ancient history about their father and Frederic, about the way Frederic had purchased the *Star* building. What was Frieda's comment?

Don't trust them. They're vipers. They hate us.

Lucy tended to brush aside what she termed her mother's paranoia about enemies, but in the case of the Dunlaps she sensed immediately that Frieda was absolutely correct.

Lucy was pleased when Ernie, obviously aware that she wanted to talk to Fitzgerald, touched his wife's elbow and they excused themselves.

For a moment, she watched them thread past Sarah Felger, the newspaper's medical writer, who chatted with Frank Lazzarutti, the Guild leader. Lucy stared dully at the crowd.

"Christ, everyone's here," she said.

"When can I see you?"

"You have my number, darling." She lifted her dark glasses.

"You're upset."

"I get the feeling, David, the peculiar sense that Evan's death puts me in an entirely new category for you, a difficult one. Not just another wife to fuck . . ."

"Stop it," he said sharply.

"You're hurting my arm."

"I live in Washington, remember? I'm . . ."

"Not just *another* wife to fuck, a wife whose family has something you need, but a widow, a woman who may want a certain commitment now, make *demands*."

"I'm at the Carlyle tonight."

"I'm tired, David."

"I *want* to see you."

Lucy stared across the crowded restaurant toward the Elm Room, near the entrance. Crowds gathered, drinks in hand, at the bar carved out of wormy chestnut and beneath the brass candle sconces on the walls. Lucy heard loud laughter; flashbulbs went off. "My apartment," said Lucy Claiborne, without a smile.

Barry Cohen stood at the Crystal Room bar, sipping champagne, watching Fitzgerald and Lucy Claiborne. He had worn a black tie for the benefit, an extravagant gesture that left him feeling overdressed when he walked into the party and saw men in an assortment of suits, sport jackets, velour outfits, cashmere turtleneck sweaters and even T-shirts. By the time the party grew, though, the clothes styles seemed to blur: there were dozens of men in black tie.

He was—as one woman told him—shockingly handsome, and Barry believed it. Almost daily he worked out at the Y, lifting weights, pressing pulleys high over his shoulders, performing pushups, running six-minute miles around the track, swimming eighteen laps. On weekends he jogged through Greenwich Village, keeping his body lean and muscled, staring at times in the mirror as he changed into shorts, examining his broad shoulders and chest and flat belly.

He had come to the benefit alone, part of a day's work. It was a Steiner benefit, and one appeared at Steiner benefits. There were enough people he knew from the *Star,* enough media and political types, enough available women to make it a pleasant evening. He watched the lights shimmer on Central Park South; the band was playing Rodgers and Hart.

Barry began moving toward Frieda. A woman touched his arm.

"Hi," she said. "I'm Marilyn Cheever of *Time.*"

His eyes narrowed. "You're doing the big fight. Is that what you called it?"

"That's what I called it."

"There's no big fight, honey. That lady over there"—he pointed to Frieda—"and her son and daughter are making the decision. Maybe they have already."

"They haven't."

"How do you know?"

"They told me."

He lifted two glasses of champagne off a waiter's tray and handed one to her.

"Are you a reporter?" asked Barry.

"In the New York bureau. We're doing this for the media section."

"What's your prediction?"

"Probably him"—she nodded her head toward Maury, who stood near the buffet table with Nancy Chang and Mary Phelps. "But we're not predicting. Everyone likes power games."

Barry watched her carefully remove a notebook from her handbag. Their eyes met.

"Still working."

"Got to call the office in the next hour."

"You folks work late on Friday."

"Friday night's a killer at the office."

"How late do you work?"

"Not too late," she said.

The singer onstage, swaying her shoulders, laughed, and picked up the band's tempo.

> *If my heart gets in your hair*
> *You mustn't kick it around—*
> *If you're bored with this affair*
> *You mustn't kick it around.*

Maury turned to Mary Phelps. "Dance?"

Mary grinned. "No," she said. "As they say, you kids do it."

"Go ahead, Mary," said Nancy.

Mary grimaced and moved onto the dance floor for the fox-trot.

> *Even though I'm mild and meek*
> *When we have a brawl*
> *If I turn the other cheek*
> *You mustn't kick it at all.*

Nancy felt a hand on her back. She shivered and turned. It was Barry.

"You scared me."

"I do that to a lot of women."

"Didn't I just see you doing a number on some frail little thing in a red dress?"

"She's as frail as a bulldozer. She just left me—temporarily—because Skipper is free. She wants a quote from him. She works at *Time*."

"Marilyn Cheever."

"Doing a number on us. The big battle on Fifty-first Street."

"It's Maury's. Should be his." Nancy raised her eyes to Barry. "He *deserves* it."

"Shit, we all deserve it."

"It would hurt Maury . . ."

"You're beautiful."

"You're drunk, Barry."

"Three glasses of champagne do it." He waited.

Sally and Charlie Sims moved past toward the buffet, waving at them. Nancy waved back. Barry ignored them, staring at Nancy.

"You miss me?"

"No."

"I gave you what you wanted."

"Fuck off, Barry."

"Christ, to think I gave you up."

"Barry, you didn't give me up."

"Yes I did, honey."

"I chucked you out."

"'I chucked you out.'" He mimicked her Hong Kong-English accent. "You enjoyed every fucking minute of it."

"You're drunk. And vile."

"Come back to me. A quickie. Anytime."

"Fuck off."

Maury, smiling and breathing heavily, returned with Mary Phelps, holding her hand. "Let's get some food," he announced.

Men in starched white aprons and high white hats doled out food from steaming silver trays—courgettes and carrots and string beans, spicy curry and saffron-scented goulash. A corner of the table was reserved for a chef, cutting thin slices of pink roast beef onto a wooden board. At the opposite end of the table, trays were piled high with tunafish salad, and lettuce and tomato pepper salad. Slices of smoked salmon lay on one tray; emerald-green asparagus, on another.

Charlie Sims nibbled at a slice of smoked salmon and some asparagus. Sally examined her plate of roast beef.

"Hungry?" he asked.

"Not particularly. Just tired."

"Everyone in the world is here."

Sally wished she were home. "There's David Fitzgerald. I should talk to him," she said. "Let's just say hello."

"You just say hello."

His tone struck Sally as odd. She looked up and watched Charlie slowly sip his drink.

Finally he said, "Dave Fitzgerald has about as much interest in *my* saying hello as he has in that waiter over there."

"You're being ridiculous!" She regretted the hint of anger.

"I'm your classic appendage, darling. Like a little housewife. Mr. Sally Sims."

In the night glow, Charlie's windburned face seemed unhealthily pink.

"This is absurd," said Sally. "I won't go over."

"I insist you see him," Charlie said gently. "If you don't see that fascist I will be very upset." Charlie set his plate on the table and touched her elbow. "Run along," he grinned. "You've got a reliable source to talk to."

"It's the China-Soviet business."

Larry Steiner, standing at the opposite end of the table, watched Sally leave. He approached Charlie.

"Hi," he said.

Charlie smiled at him. "Beautiful night."

"Beautiful morning."

Charlie's smile held, but his eyes darted around the Crystal Room.

"You're embarrassed, aren't you?" said Larry, cutting the chunk of goulash with his fork.

"I suppose I am."

"Different generations, aren't we?"

Charlie continued to smile.

"You want me to leave?" asked Larry.

Charlie nodded, turning his eyes to his plate.

Onstage, the singer's voice lowered to a croon. The crowd overflowed now from the Crystal Room into the Elm Room and Terrace Garden. The sixty-foot Elm bar swarmed with couples.

Eli Faber, with Frieda Steiner beside him, carrying champagne glasses, stepped into the Crystal Room. Frieda waved to Sally, who was threading through the crowd.

"Sally!" Frieda's voice was a command.

Flashbulbs went off around them, and Sally heard loud laughter at the center of the room. She saw Barry Cohen, several feet away, moving through the crowd, and for a moment, watching the faint smirk linger on his face, Sally was dizzy.

"Sally, dear, tell me about this California story. Linda Fentress," said Frieda.

Sally turned to the elderly woman. "I don't know. Ask Barry."

Sally stood perfectly still, feeling the burn rise in her cheeks, her anger sudden and intense.

Sally's eyes vainly searched Eli's for support, and then she turned once more to Frieda Steiner, whose face was silvery in the night light.

Not Frieda's fault that Barry stole the story, not Frieda's fault that Charlie, beautiful Charlie, was easily wounded, a frail bird. Not Frieda's fault, damn it, that she was sleeping with Skipper out of needs too painful—too vague—to understand.

Eli broke the silence, chortling, "Another turf battle in the newsroom, Frieda."

God, he's dreadful, Sally thought.

Frieda frowned and said, abruptly, that it was a wonderful evening for a party. "Evenings like this perk me up, New York at its best, don't you think?" she went on without waiting for a response.

"How's Charles?" said Frieda. She was a woman with proper manners who remembered names.

Charles was fine, said Sally, backing away, nodding. As Sally turned, she heard Frieda order Eli to find Barry, please.

Sally felt adrift in the jostling crowd, her knees so weak that she stopped and slumped her shoulders, as if to settle her body. Skipper was speaking earnestly to Ward Parsons and Florence. Charlie was locked in conversation with Larry Steiner. She thought she saw David Fitzgerald beside the bar, chatting with Ernie Dunlap.

Sally turned and awkwardly pushed through the swarm. Too tired to speak, to smile, to exchange pleasantries, she would fetch Charlie and go home.

A hand gripped her wrist.

"Talk to me."

"Barry. I'm tired."

"You're pissed off."

"I'm pissed off. And tired. Barry, please get out of my way."

"I wanted that story, honey."

"You *got* the story. Linda's out in California, you got it. It's yours. Stabbing and pushing, you got it, darling." She felt herself blanch and stood perfectly still, anger pounding her chest. "Your style, Barry. No class."

He swayed forward. "Come home with me, Sally."

"For Chrissake. You're drunk. Get out of my way."

"I want you."

She laughed. "You ugly prick."

He blocked her way. "Temper, temper. Well-bred girl like you. Upper class and all that. Always had it easy, Sally. Token woman. Everyone's token woman. Never struggled. Why should the noblesse oblige struggle?"

They stared at each other.

"You want me, don't you?" he gasped, and even as Sally began to laugh, Barry moved so close that she smelled his whiskey breath. "I'm not beautiful like him. Right? Old Charlie. Still fuck you, does he? Or is it all for the little boys?"

She raised her hand but Barry easily twisted her fingers downward. He kissed Sally on the cheek, catching the wetness of her tears, then turned.

Bitch, he murmured to himself, stupid goddamn bitch. He looked up and saw Marilyn Cheever watching, grinning. Barry walked toward her, but twisted his head furiously as a hand reached for his arm. His anger dissolved at the sight of Eli Faber.

"Frieda wants to see you, Barry." He spoke softly, cat eyes fixed on the city editor. Eli's lips twisted into a smile. "She wants to know about the California story."

Saturday

CHAPTER 10

Linda Fentress is dreaming.

A jungle. Vice President Tom Nelson, Linda, Barry Cohen—they are pushing through swamp. The muddy, swirling water reaches to their knees. Mosquitoes and giant fruit flies suck Linda's hair and face. I am afraid of snakes, she cries to Nelson, but he moves ahead through the rancid waters that now reach up to their waists. I am afraid of snakes, she screams, but Nelson ignores her—is he deaf? She grabs Barry's arm, but he flings her away, and she falls into the water.

Then she sees it—an enormous ivory python, black diamond marks sweeping down its body in an unbroken line, slithering through the water toward her, sucking the water, leaving whirlpools in its path, moving rapidly in the current that traps her, prevents her passage. OHMYGOD.

Nelson and Barry have disappeared. The snake's slanted coal-black eyes are planted on Linda, they mock the terrified woman, and within seconds the enormous body uncurls before her, surrounding her. She is trapped in an enclosing circle, one covered with razor fins. The reptile is enormous, ninety feet, one hundred feet, its body two feet high, fat, pulsing with life. It moves toward its prey inexorably, gently closing in on her, gently, ever so gently . . .

Linda awakes, trembling. Her throat is parched, her body covered in an icy sweat. She feels her heart pulse, her head and temples throbbing, so she fears a vessel will burst. Her fingers touch the soft mattress; she hears a sound outside, the whoosh of a truck on a rainy street.

She reaches to the table beside her, knocking over a glass, and finds the lamp switch. It is four-fifty. She turns off the light and lies down again, still breathing heavily. She covers herself with the sheet and closes her eyes.

She is fearful of plane trips, a claustrophobic fear dampened by vodka on the rocks. She began drinking last night at Kennedy Airport in a packed lounge, and she kept drinking on the TWA flight to Los Angeles. Exhausted, she checked into the Century Plaza. Upon her arrival, she had barely noticed Room 1811. She'd flung open the terrace door overlooking the two steel-and-glass office buildings that angled toward one another without touching. She had then walked to the telephone, dialed room service and ordered two glasses of orange juice and a large pitcher of ice water. Plane flights, besides frightening her, were dehydrating.

By the time Linda eased into bed it was 10:20 P.M.–1:20 A.M. in New York. She set the alarm beside her bed for 8 A.M. and fell into a listless sleep, marred only by terrifying nightmares.

By six-thirty Linda was standing on the terrace, watching a man and woman jog across the street beneath her. The Century Plaza office buildings beyond were covered in dense fog.

She went back inside, took out her envelope of files, a yellow legal-size pad, set the Olympia portable typewriter on the table beside the window. She opened the large brown envelope that the *Star*'s morgue had hurriedly prepared on Vice President Nelson.

The fog outside was lifting gently; the sounds of early morning traffic building.

The first step: *Research Tom Nelson.* Read the files and make notes. Names and places and dates. Who supports him in California? Who opposes him? Who hates him? The haters—political and personal enemies—are often the best sources. Is there a better source than a man or woman who has been defeated or humiliated or ignored or fired? *Who hates Tom Nelson?*

Nelson is the golden boy of California politics, a movie actor, a *good* movie actor; he played *heroes:* lawyers, teachers, sheriffs, Army colonels. A twenty-three-year movie career without a hint of scandal, not even a divorce. For twenty years he has been married to Fay Nelson, a second-string dancer who never reached the Cyd Charisse level at MGM, and who is now a law student at American University in Washington, a woman who declined to campaign for her husband because she was studying for exams.

The spate of stories and editorials that followed—as well as the Art Buchwald and Russell Baker columns—assured Nelson the vote of the women's movement. Two children—a fifteen-year-old son, a twelve-year-old daughter.

Background: Finances. Sex. Gossip.

Born in Santa Monica, the youngest son of a cross-country truck driver who was killed in an accident outside Denver when the boy was four. Mother worked as a cashier in the local movie theater and department store to support her children—the oldest son is a doctor in La Jolla; the daughter, divorced with two children, is a commercial artist in San Francisco.

Tom Nelson joined the Army after high school, served two years as a company clerk in Fort Ord, and, in a movie comedy about the Army that was filmed outside the camp, was hired as a movie extra by a Twentieth Century-Fox casting director. After the Army he attended acting school in West Los Angeles, played a series of bit parts in cowboy films and then was given a small speaking role as the younger son of a man (played by William Holden) who returns to Kansas to avenge the killing of his Indian wife. Although the film *Texas Blood* was only a moderate success, Tom Nelson's single scene with Holden—an emotional five minutes when the young man urges his father to forgo killing—immediately thrust Nelson onto the lists of promising young actors. His next film, a George Cukor comedy with Ava Gardner, won him an Academy Award Nomination as best supporting actor and launched his career.

By his thirties, Nelson was actively involved in Democratic Party politics, serving as fund-raiser, speaking out and campaigning for Democratic congressional candidates, appointed to federal commissions on mental health and support for the arts. A long-running television series, with Nelson as a New York City lawyer, strengthened the actor's visibility across the country and turned him into a regular on the Johnny Carson and Dick Cavett shows. By the time he announced his plans to run in the Senate Democratic primary against the incumbent, whose name had been raised in an FBI investigation of Arab influence and bribery in Washington, Tom Nelson had gathered the support of the Hollywood liberal community and a broad coalition of blacks and Chicanos, farmers, star-struck women, academicians, environmentalists. He swept aside his opponent, and defeated the Republican candidate in one of the largest pluralities in the state's history. Six years later —with a staunchly liberal voting record, except for a hard-line approach to law and order and criticism of the Supreme Court decisions limiting police search and seizure—Nelson won an even broader plurality. His selection to serve as Bergen's Vice President came as no surprise, largely because Nelson appealed to the constituency that eluded the far more conservative Bergen.

Linda Fentress scanned the xeroxed clips, underlining relevant sentences, one story catching her eyes. It was a brief Los Angeles *Herald-Examiner* article from San Diego during Nelson's first Senate campaign. At a news conference Nelson strongly denied his opponent's accusation that union leaders in San Diego linked to organized crime had been supporting him.

A sliver of misconduct; something to be stored away, remembered . . .

Finances.

As an elected official, Tom Nelson was compelled to reveal his finances each year under the Financial Disclosure Act. His last disclosure, like the previous ones, showed few surprises.

His years as a movie actor and television star had quite naturally made him rich. Nelson had shrewdly invested in municipal bonds and Los Angeles real estate, placing all his money in a blind trust upon his election as United States senator a decade before. He owned a house on Lasky Drive in Beverly Hills that was now worth an estimated $1.8 million, and owned a Washington home on Lowell Street in Cleveland Park worth an estimated $425,000. His two children had separate trusts in their names.

No surprises. Not a hint, in the clips, of financial shenanigans. In fact, his finances were blatantly straightforward. If Nelson were a Texan into oil, a lawyer, a big-time farmer, or merely an average politician scrapping for a campaign buck, his finances would be more intriguing. But he was a movie star who earned a lot of money and invested it wisely—in a rather traditional manner. No surprises here.

Sex.

Zilch. The clips yielded nothing. Happily married. Works as a partner quote unquote with his wife. Does the dishes. Two picture-book kids, the boy a football player, like his father, at Sidwell Friends in D.C. The girl plays the cello. The wife's chocolate layer cake is terrific.

There is a xerox of a crumbling gossip column item from the New York *Post,* fourteen years old, saying that Nelson and starlet Lois Barrie are "more than just partners." Period. That's all. Some smart, enterprising librarian in the morgue had filed the item.

All right. Linda writes *Lois Barrie's* name beneath her list.

Gregory Hamalian.

Old friend. Good source. Work with Gregory.

Elliott Hanley.

Directed Tom Nelson's first major movie. *Daily News* seeking him out. What did Gregory say? Your standard Hollywood queen director. Second-rater making a big splash. Blacklisted. Blacklisted by . . .

Joey Keefer.

Died five years ago. Former state senator. Son of late Majority Leader Merton Keefer. Brother-in-law of Dave Fitzgerald. At the end Keefer worked for . . .

Marcus Lynn.

Mean son of a bitch. Lawyer. Movie clients. Producer. Used to be Tom Nelson's buddy, had a falling out before Nelson became Vice President. Nelson's enemy.

Linda looked up. What the hell do they have on Tom Nelson?

Reporters gossip, travel in packs, eat and drink together, can't keep their mouths shut. Rumors surge like waves across newsrooms. There are few secrets. The past is an open book. Get some jerk's Department of Motor Vehicle license and you have his history—where it was issued, where he lived, what he looked like, his age. Check someone's mortgage records at the bank, and there it is: earnings, family income, jobs, references, education, past addresses, military background, marital status, children, the works.

There are few confidences. Everyone leaves a trail. Investigative reporting is finding the right document, the right *person,* after a dozen false starts. Manipulating and cutting deals. Knowing how to orchestrate sources, how to play one against the other. Knowing how to ask the right goddamn question.

Start with the enemies. Rule number one. They have the longest memories. Nasty sons of bitches only too pleased to spill every rumor and innuendo. Off the record, of course. Don't quote me. Strictly background.

Just plug in. Plug into the right source . . .

Marcus Lynn's office and home numbers were in the phone directory. She would call the publicity people at Fox and CBS—Fox to set up an appointment with Elliott Hanley, CBS to reach Lois Barrie, now the star of a television series playing the divorced mother of three teen-age girls. A ridiculous show with high ratings.

Linda rose from the chair and walked to the terrace. It was eight-thirty, and the sun had finally burned through the fog, leaving a thin mist in the Hollywood hills. The Saturday traffic below was moving lazily past the hotel. To her left, eight or nine windows away, a man and woman, both in jeans, holding cups of coffee, moved onto the terrace and gazed down. Linda watched them for a moment. The man, who was shirtless, placed his coffee on the terrace table and kissed her on the cheek. He was in his twenties. The girl smiled vaguely.

Linda slipped back into her room, closed the curtains and removed her clothes. She walked into the bathroom. Calgon bath oil beads and Ultra Max shampoo and bars of soap, lay in packets on the marble table. She turned on the taps for a bath, resting the bath oil and shampoo on a shelf beside the tub.

She weighed herself on the scale below the sink. One hundred and eight. Fine. She stepped off the scale, and looked into the floor-length mirror facing her.

Her legs were still firm, the knees trim, but the area around the thighs just a bit too flabby. Her hips and waist remained narrow, the ass slender and her tight, small breasts (a source of humiliation when she was a teen-ager) still inadequate, she felt, her weakest attribute. Linda's pale-green eyes—her best feature—coupled with her shoulder-length blond hair compensated for, and deflected from, what she felt was her critical flaw.

Viewing herself in the mirror, Linda Fentress could see the tiredness beneath her eyes, the blotched skin that came with sleeplessness, the stringy hair. Christ, she was ordinary; except for her figure, which was fine, she was drab beneath the makeup, tight clothes, tough walk, talk, and style that excited some men but threatened others. In fact, Linda Fentress was an attractive woman (some said beautiful), but she was without a shred of confidence.

She was an army brat whose father, a first sergeant, had hauled her mother and their three children—two older brothers and Linda —from Georgia to Texas to South Carolina to West Germany, and finally to New Jersey, where Linda took a typing and shorthand course in Trenton and stumbled into a job as a secretary in the classified ads department at the New York *Star* office in Manhattan.

The City Hall bureau chief, Jerry Paley, a gentle Irishman whom she met one night at Fritzi's, managed to teach her to become a reporter. He also slept with her at the same time, the first of a series of older married men who not only attracted but also educated Linda Fentress. Old Jerry Paley, Linda would say later, was her own Columbia School of Journalism.

Without a college degree—and uneasy about her dependence on Jerry and her lack of formal training and education—Linda left the *Star* for a job with the Associated Press, assigned first to the Santa Fe office and then to Chicago, where her work on a series involving the capture of "The Evanston Strangler" won her the Newspaper Guild Award and a nomination by AP for the Pulitzer Prize.

Her aggressiveness, her blond good looks, her tough style masked, she knew, a hundred hidden terrors that assailed her every day. Smart, college-educated women awed her. She knew she dressed like a whore because she felt those tits were hopeless, her face (without mascara and eye makeup and lipstick) was too ordinary. Having a family, raising children, frightened her—it was a commitment, it was being stuck in some tacky house with screaming kids like her mother. She knew it was irrational—she was not her mother—but the notion clung to her and, although she yearned for stability, the men she selected were either married or impotent or crazy.

She was restless and scared, could not remember when she hadn't been. Inexplicably, when she began to settle into a job, getting comfortable in it, she immediately yearned to leave, and sought an excuse to do so—either an affair with another reporter or editor, or an argument or dispute over a story with her boss—

something that forced her to quit. In the past few years she had worked at AP, the Washington *Post,* and Chicago *Tribune* before rejoining the *Star.*

"I've been to the top and it sucks," she was fond of saying.

Linda Fentress settled into the bath, opening the packet of bath oil and pouring it over the hot water. She sat back, letting the steam rise into her face and hair, the scent heavy and sweet.

She was thirty-four and felt it was time to settle down, commit herself to something permanent. Her options would soon start to diminish. Could she make it at the *Star?*

*

Eli Faber decided to walk that morning from his apartment on Park Avenue to the Steiners' duplex farther downtown. It was a perfect spring Saturday in New York; the azure sky, fringed with puffs of clouds, promised a splendid afternoon. The sun shimmered on the apartment windows and the cool air held a sweet, lingering touch of warmth.

He was a slight man, balding, with a hawk face, soft feminine lips and brown cat eyes covered by rimless spectacles. A dapper figure, Faber strode briskly across Eighty-sixth Street and Park, moving with his head tilted high, his mouth set in a frown, his right hand jangling coins in the pocket of his Italian brown whipcord trousers that Lenore, his wife, had insisted he purchase at a men's store off Piazza Navona the previous summer.

If Eli was a homely man, he compensated for his physical flaws by meticulous attention to his clothing and appearance. He purchased his boxer shorts at Brooks Brothers, his shoes at Bally and Gucci, his suits at Pierre Cardin or John Weitz or Brooks Brothers. His shirts were often tailor-made by Mr. Lee at the Mandarin Hotel in Hong Kong, or purchased at Bloomingdale's. His haircuts cost forty dollars.

For his meeting with Frieda Steiner, Eli wore a button-down, striped Arrow shirt and red silk bow tie flecked with blue dots. As it was Saturday, he wore a double-breasted blue blazer and new brushed pigskin loafers that still seemed somewhat tight at the toes as he stepped quickly across Eighty-fifth Street.

He had begun as a part-time messenger on the *Star* at the age of sixteen, and by the time he was twenty-three he was serving as

Frederic's aide, traveling companion, and in the old man's final years, financial adviser. Although Eli's schooling was limited—he eventually attended Columbia University with the Steiners' financial help—he was tough and street-smart, the oldest son of a family of Latvian immigrants who had settled on Broome Street in the Lower East Side and never moved out.

A lawyer and accountant, Eli Faber served the *Star* faithfully from Frederic to Jonathan, and now, to Skipper, keeping his eyes on union negotiations and what the competition was up to, watching the bond and stock markets, guiding the Steiners on personal taxes—although the family retained Price, Waterhouse for the newspaper—arranging tax shelters, creating trusts for the children and grandchildren, performing hundreds of small, and big, favors for the family that rewarded him with a sizable retainer each year. It was far from his only job—from his office in the Seagram Building, Eli Faber and his staff of financial consultants served as advisers to an international electronics company, a small South American nation, an entertainment conglomerate, an international computer corporation, and an airline with routes on the West Coast and in the Southwest.

If Eli's relationship with Skipper was hardly as friendly as it had been with Frederic and Jonathan, Eli remained a dominant player in the management of the *Star* because of his ties to Frieda Steiner—a fact of life that both men accepted within the strictures of a relationship that had grown more strained in recent years. Without quite acknowledging it, their philosophy and outlook toward the *Star* diverged sharply now, and the small signs of friction —the shrug, the tilted eyebrows, the heavy silence, the smirk, the sentence thick with innuendo—had dominated Eli's and Skipper's relationship in the past few years.

Eli sensed that Frieda's passing would, in every likelihood, sever his links to the *Star*. Skipper would ease him out and hire some Wall Street hotshot who would charge twice as much and fail to give the commitment, the *love,* that Eli had lavished on the newspaper. It was a concern—and not a minor one—but hardly something to worry about on this dazzling Saturday morning in April.

Eli was comforted in the knowledge that Frieda and Lucy retained firm trust in him, and that his ties to the Steiners reached beyond the adviser-client relationship. Frederic had virtually adopted him, Frieda had set up her own small education trust fund for Eli's two sons—smart boys, one of whom was a dentist in Westport, the other a lawyer in Atlanta. Eli, in turn, had attended the Steiner weddings and family parties and the funerals. Eli Faber was virtually part of the family.

And yet he was smart enough and certainly discreet enough to sense that he would always be a paid underling, part of the Steiners' retinue of advisers. And if he bristled at times at the family's behavior, if he felt slighted, he needed only Lenore to remind him that Frederic had plucked him out of poverty and sent him to school—merely because he liked the boy—and that Jonathan and Frieda had treated him, indeed, as a member of the family, and that Frieda, the most loyal of all, was a woman whose faith in him as a friend and adviser was complete.

By the time he reached the Steiners' apartment building, Eli Faber was perspiring. He nodded to the doorman, who knew Eli, and removed a handkerchief from his blazer, dabbing at his forehead and cheeks. In the cramped elevator he combed his hair and straightened his tie.

Frieda was in a blue-and-gold paisley dress, with a diamond choker that Eli recognized as a gift from Jonathan. Yes, Eli said, he would like some coffee, black, as he sat down at the oak table in Frieda's study. The morning papers were strewn on the thick floral carpet. Frieda flicked off the radio.

They talked about the party and how well Lucy seemed. Frieda asked Eli how his boys were doing, and when he replied fine, just fine, Frieda informed him that Johanna was going to start working on the paper and wasn't it a marvelous idea.

Eli winced, but quickly agreed, yes, it was marvelous.

Frieda pressed a cigarette into her holder, and Eli lit it for her.

"Eli. I am in a quandary about this managing editor business. Evan's replacement."

He sipped his coffee.

"I'm uneasy about Maury," Frieda said. "He's loyal, of course, which is not to be brushed aside. But I'm *uneasy*. He's older. Is he . . . strong enough?" Frieda watched the smoke pour from her lips and finally brought her gaze to Eli. She trusted him completely, his discretion, his judgment, his loyalty.

"After Maury, there's the younger group, an interesting group. Parsons, the foreign editor, well-bred, very charming. Yale man. The black fellow, Hugh Finch. Attractive, bright. Cohen, the city editor. A bit too aggressive for my taste." Frieda examined her oval-shaped diamond ring. "And Sally Sims, of course."

Their eyes met in silent awareness of Sally's relationship with Skipper.

"Whom does Skipper favor?" asked Eli.

"Maury," said Frieda.

"The vote is . . ."

"We're meeting on Tuesday. Skipper wants it that way." She waited. "What are your feelings, Eli?"

"Let me get to that in a minute, Frieda." He untied the middle button on his jacket and crossed his legs, carefully lifting up his trousers to reveal a shock of black silken sock. "*The Wall Street Journal*'s doing a story on us."

"So is *Time*," said Frieda.

"You know what they're going to say? They're going to say we're a troubled newspaper, on the decline."

Eli sucked his lips together as he spoke. "We're a family paper, privately owned. Not public. Don't have to make profit-and-loss statements to the stockholders. *We're* the stockholders, Frieda, we don't have to reveal to Wall Street that our losses are . . . growing, circulation going down." He swallowed hard. "When was the last time you sat in on a budget meeting with your son and department heads?"

The question puzzled Frieda. "A year, eighteen months ago," she murmured.

"Shouldn't you be ashamed of yourself, Frieda? Shouldn't this be your responsibility too?"

She set her coffee cup down.

"I suggest—and please don't take this as a rebuke—I suggest you take your job as a stockholder far more seriously. You and Skipper and Lucy have the majority shares. For God's sake, exercise your judgment, your will, your rights. *Forget* Bella Verde. *Forget* retirement. Forget you're a Steiner woman, and all that implies, and play an active role. Kay Graham does it. Dolly Schiff did it. Look at Buff Chandler. Stop playing the tottering grandmother. It's not the day and age for that sort of thing."

"I'm seventy-four, Eli."

"So what?"

"I'm out of touch."

"Bullshit."

She smiled. "Eli, I always felt you treated me like a glass figurine. I think I always resented it. You were so, how shall I say, careful with me, as if I were a child. You patronized me."

Eli shrugged. "It was a different time, Frieda. And I didn't patronize you."

"Water under the bridge."

"Frieda. I was frightened of you. I could deal straight with the old man. I dealt with your husband like a brother. Jonathan treated me as an equal. But you, Frieda . . ."

"You and Jonathan whored together. Your little trips to Los Angeles and London and Paris. Your dinners every month or so at the Harmonie that never seemed to end until three or four in the morning. My husband. I will never forgive you for that."

"Frieda . . ."

"He was his father's son. In the beginning that wasn't the case. Not at all. Do you remember how shy he was? The awkwardness? How frightened he was of Frederic?"

"I remember."

"He needed whores later on. He needed a different floozie every six months. I went through hell, Eli. I blamed myself. He got older and needed those women and you were his . . . procurer."

"That's unfair, Frieda."

"I thought he would die in bed with one of them. Just like his father. Thank God he didn't."

"Frieda, why on earth bring this up now? Why? Does it solve anything? You're an elderly woman, but a vibrant woman. Why poison yourself like that? I'm sixty-four. Do I dwell on the past? Forget Jonathan. Forget what happened. You're a Steiner and you have responsibilities to yourself and to the family and to the future of the *Star*."

"Eli, you didn't patronize me," she said, examining her hands. "I wanted it that way. I wanted to play that role. The wifely role. Let the men do it. Now I try to overcompensate. I meddle. I'm a pain in the ass."

He laughed. "Frieda, stay in New York for a while. Help pick the managing editor."

"Yes, Eli. Yes, I will."

Frieda stared at him with glittering eyes. "I'm *alarmed,* Eli. I look at the circulation figures, the advertising pages. We're . . . sliding."

Frieda took a deep sigh. "You've heard about the cutbacks in the staff. Skipper's starting . . ." Frieda gazed at him. "You didn't know."

"Skipper doesn't tell me everything, Frieda," Eli said coldly.

"Next week. Cutbacks start next week. Keep it secret."

With his thumb and forefinger Eli brushed a fleck of dust off his right trouser leg. "That's wise."

"He should have told you, Eli."

"It's unimportant." Eli struggled to smile. "What's important is the *Star,* what needs to be done. Cutting back is the first step."

"The first step to what?"

"A new *Star.*" His eyes widened. "A *new* paper that people will read. A paper that makes money, Frieda. Expand advertising. Reduce hard news. Limit international and Washington news. Cut out the heavy stuff." The smile stretched to a grin. "More photos. Features. How-to-do-it articles. Advice to the lovelorn. Yes! Exposés! Another page of comics. Breezy writing."

"You don't like my son," said Frieda suddenly.

"If I said yes, I'd be a liar. I don't like what he's doing to the paper."

"He'll object to what you say. Cutting foreign and Washington news."

"Then . . ."

"You want an entirely different paper, Eli."

"Then, we'll have to make certain decisions by ourselves." He waited a beat, catching Frieda's glance. "There are three votes besides Skipper's. Three other people make decisions about our paper. You. Lucy. And me." Leaning forward, Eli spoke tensely. "You have got to confront the fact that certain changes need to be made to keep the *Star* alive."

Frieda returned his gaze.

"News is important," said Eli, "but survival is even more important."

"We've cut the foreign staff, Eli, cut the national staff, we're cutting to the bone."

"Not enough! Not enough!"

"We've got a tradition, Eli . . ."

"We're losing money, my dear. We're *not* the *Times. Not* the Washington *Post* or *The Wall Street Journal.* We can't afford the luxury of a foreign staff, a big Washington bureau. *We're in trouble, Frieda!* We need a publisher, we need an editor, responsible to the needs of the paper now."

Frieda stared at him hollowly. "You know I always felt that had Jonathan died ten years later—he died so young—my daughter Lucy could have been publisher," she said. "But it wasn't the time and place for a woman to take over. Women, Steiner women, didn't run the paper."

"Lucy's still young."

Frieda absently opened a small silver box on the table beside her and removed a cigarette. She allowed Eli to light it.

"I need your help, Eli. Your support."

He reached over and grasped Frieda's cold, firm hand.

"Painful times," Frieda said.

*

By the time Eli Faber left the apartment house on Park Avenue and Eighty-first Street, it was eleven-fifty. He sniffed the moist spring air and felt good, strolling toward Madison Avenue in the glistening sunshine. He would talk to Lenore that afternoon about their August vacation. She was procrastinating between spending the month at their home in Easthampton or renting it and taking a trip to the Orient.

As he strolled toward Madison Avenue he pressed his hand into his pocket to make sure that he had the dimes and quarters for his phone calls at the booth on Eighty-third Street. First, he would call Senator David Fitzgerald, his close friend and client, to inform him of his pleasant and productive chat with Frieda Steiner. As was his practice, Eli Faber would phone David Fitzgerald from a phone booth, murmur his number and hang up. One minute later, David Fitzgerald dialed the number. A precautionary measure, of course, to avoid any nonsense about subpoenaed phone records.

After conversing with Fitzgerald, Eli Faber thought that perhaps he could take a cab to the Harmonie Club for a salad lunch. But it was Saturday and the club was probably crowded, too many bores who would hog his time grumbling about the stock market. Eli Faber was in no mood to chat about money.

Otherwise, he could take a walk to Parke-Bernet to see some Chinese glass paintings that intrigued him. Or else he could take a stroll down to Bloomingdale's to buy some ties—he needed some new spring ties to perk up his wardrobe. But on Saturday afternoon the men's shop was crowded and unpleasant and something to avoid.

Of course, he could call Shirley's house on Thirty-eighth between Park and Lexington. This was in the back of his mind anyway—he had thought about it last night when Lenore dropped off to sleep as soon as they returned home from the party, and he thought about it this morning when he left a note on the dining-room table saying he'd be home by late afternoon. "Seeing Frieda, going to the office, etc." Yes, etcetera. Lenore, who complained more and more of headaches and arthritis in her neck, always slept until at least eleven o'clock on Saturday and Sunday.

Eli visited Shirley's house at least twice a month now, paying her a hundred and fifty dollars a visit to spend an hour or so with Myra or Serita. Actually, Serita was his favorite, and she was probably on duty all afternoon. That was how they talked—like firemen or taxi drivers. On duty and off duty. She was a thick-lipped Dominican girl with heavy thighs, muscular arms and an open, ingratiating smile that hinted at mischief.

Shirley, who had known Eli for years, had selected both girls, Myra and Serita, for him about sixteen months before, fully aware that either one of the women would allow him to gain his pleasure in a way that Lenore, years ago, had rejected. Actually, it was an ordinary pleasure, but Serita's yelps of delight—as opposed to Myra's obvious theatrics and mock groans—endeared the Dominican girl to Faber.

He would phone Shirley to make sure that Serita was on duty and available and, if so, would buy her a little gift, perhaps a bottle of eau de cologne, on Madison and Seventy-fifth. Serita adored cologne.

Eli smiled at a young boy, perhaps six, and his older sister, bouncing a basketball, speaking animatedly as they walked along

Madison Avenue. He gazed at three pre-teen girls in jeans and sweaters, their small breasts bobbing as they giggled and rushed across the street toward Fifth Avenue. The eyes of one of the girls, a blue-eyed redhead with freckles, fell on Eli Faber, and he turned away quickly.

Such a pleasant Saturday morning in New York.

*

At that moment, in Room 806 of the Mayflower Hotel in Washington, Howie Bishop was signing the room-service bill. He watched the waiter leave and began pouring coffee. It was eleven forty-five.

"We want the diary, Cheryl."

The sun, splaying through the window, caught her sullen, kewpie-doll face. She lifted her big dark glasses atop her auburn hair, strewn in a sloppy knot behind her head. Her blue eyes were strained, her pale skin shorn of makeup, laced with an arc of blemishes on her cheek. She worked as a hostess at a private club called "charisma," with a small *c,* on K Street, between 8 P.M. and 3 A.M. The morning hours were not her best.

She crushed her cigarette in an ashtray. "Fifteen thousand dollars."

There was a small twitch to Howie's mouth. "That's an awful lot."

"That's an awful little," she said, frowning at the coffee.

"We don't bribe," said Howie.

Cheryl rolled her eyes. "Fish don't swim, planes don't fly." She let out a tense laugh. "Since when?"

Howie Bishop tasted the coffee.

"Cash on delivery," said Cheryl, lighting another cigarette. She eyed Howie through the flame on the match. "Tomorrow. Tomorrow afternoon. My place."

*

Seated in a wing armchair in his study, David Fitzgerald scanned the Washington *Post,* then folded the paper and dropped it on the Persian carpet. He had struggled to sleep on the halfempty morning shuttle from New York, but a Greek-American businessman on the aisle seat recognized the New York senator and engaged him in a conversation about Cyprus. A politician does not ask a constituent to kindly shut up, so Fitzgerald had listened as the DC-9 veered south and as Mr. Dimitri Padopolis, the owner of three luncheonettes in Manhattan and Queens, condemned the Bergen administration and Congress for lifting the arms embargo against Turkey and taking what he termed an anti-Greek stance. It was impossible to argue with Dimitri Padopolis.

Upon arriving home, he had kissed Celia, who was still in bed, taken a shower and then changed into sneakers, jeans and a gray sweat shirt. In his study Fitzgerald had begun writing on a blank envelope when the call from Barry interrupted. As soon as he hung up, Fitzgerald continued the notes to himself.

A busy day. He had phone calls to make through the morning, a six-mile run later from his home on Macomb Street to Rock Creek Park—the *Daily News,* the *Times* and the *Star* had published features over the past year on New York's "running" senator. Lunch at home with Celia, then a visit to Kitty White in Georgetown, back home, a dinner party at Pamela Harriman's.

Fitzgerald, with his felt-tipped black pen, wrote names on the envelope.

Lucy. She had been sleeping when he left her apartment at seven-fifteen. He would phone her later in the morning.

Belling. Check the China-Soviet situation.

Eli Faber. Hopefully, Eli would phone him any moment.

Marcus Lynn. Call him at home tonight in Los Angeles.

Jerry Paley. Have Jerry meet him at 9 A.M. on Monday.

Cheryl.

Cheryl. He closed his eyes. Cheryl. That stupid money-hungry bitch. Should have fired her after two weeks, but Celia pitied the girl, took her on as secretary, thank you notes and invitations, silly whore couldn't even manage that.

A knock on the door. He turned the pad over, hurriedly placing it in his desk drawer. Celia slipped in. She wore a cornflower-blue chenille robe and velvet slippers. Her streaked hair fell loosely to her shoulders. She toyed with her hair—a child's habit that exasperated him—as she spoke.

"Am I interrupting?"

"No, dear."

"I heard the phone ring."

"Just the office."

She smiled. "How was the party?"

"The party? You mean the benefit. Fine. The Steiners were out en masse."

"I should go to New York more, shouldn't I?"

"Not if you don't want to."

"It seems such an effort." She smiled. "I'm thinking of going away for about a week."

Fitzgerald looked up.

"Mary Haggerty is going to a farm near Warrenton," said Celia. "Horseback riding. Swimming. Silly things like picking apples. Get away for a little rest."

"Of course." He watched her. "Something wrong?"

She averted her eyes. "Just tired, dear. I'd like to get away from the city for a while."

As Celia aged, the resemblance to her brother, Joey Keefer, grew: the same high forehead and deep-set, liquid-brown eyes, the same oval-shaped face with stark, conspicuous cheekbones that made her once yearn to be a model or actress (until her father had ended that notion). Her appearance at a Washington diplomatic reception now guaranteed Celia's photograph the next day in the Washington *Post*.

Poor Joey Keefer. Dropped dead in Mexico City five years back. Heart attack, they said. Just like that. Bastard was pissing whiskey at the end, goddamn rummy he was, like Daddy. Celia never got over it.

"You're still beautiful, you know."

"Still? Thanks."

"I didn't . . ."

"It's a compliment. I know. I have a silly habit of turning aside compliments."

Her father, the late Senate Majority Leader Merton T. Keefer, Democrat of Florida, was a titan in Congress whose power spanned the Eisenhower to Bergen administrations until, three years ago, he died in an ambulance en route to the alcohol treatment center at the United States Naval Hospital in Bethesda, Maryland. Hours earlier, Keefer's wife had phoned the family physician in a panic after the majority leader began smashing liquor bottles in their famed fourteen-room Cleveland Park house —the Kennedys and Johnsons attended numerous parties there— and threatened to burn it down. In fact, Keefer's alcoholism was so

acute that, days before, he had peed on the floor of the Senate in
the midst of a debate on federally funded abortions for poor
women. (He was vehemently against the measure.) The incident
went unreported, except for oblique references in various newspapers to "a commotion on the Senate floor" during the debate as
well as "an unruly atmosphere" marking the vote.

Death was attributed to "congestive heart failure."

Celia, leaning forward, fingering her hair, told her husband, "I
shouldn't keep you, you're busy."

"What's on your mind?"

"The item in yesterday's Washington *Post*."

"I heard about it. What exactly did it say?"

"It said you were raising money, making plans for a presidential race."

"That's silly."

"Is it true?"

"I told you."

"I couldn't take a campaign, David. I couldn't do that. Physically and mentally—I'm sorry. That must distress you. My holding
you back that way."

"You're not holding me back."

"I'd become an issue too. You've thought of that, I'm sure. A
wife who drinks."

"Come on, Celia."

"Darling, I couldn't take it." Her face wrenched in pain. "Divorce me. I'll divorce you. The children are old enough. I don't
want the guilt of holding you back."

He saw the bluish pulse at the side of her forehead, and scented
the sweet mints she sucked after drinking her vodka.

"It's not as if our marriage has been made in heaven," she said
with a gentle laugh. "Far from it. Far from it. God knows."

"Come on, Celia." Fitzgerald spoke with an edge.

She stood and tightened the set-in belt on her robe.

"I need a cigarette."

"On the desk."

She lifted a cigarette out of the open pack. He lit it. Celia sat on
the leather sofa now, facing him. She crossed her legs.

"I *was* beautiful." She inhaled and shut her eyes. "I was quite beautiful when I was a girl." Celia smiled, her fingers touching her forehead. "Certainly I could have been a model except for Daddy. You remember that *Vogue* photographer at the party in New York, the fellow with the long hair. I told you. I knew him years before. He wanted me to work as a model. Stay in New York. I told you that. But it's over, isn't it? All over. Daddy put his foot down and said it would be unthinkable for a nice girl from a nice Florida family to work as a model in New York. Unthinkable." She puffed the cigarette, turning away from him. "Nice southern family.

"David, you didn't think that when you married me you'd get all this excess baggage," she said. "Ghosts and nightmares. The Keefers had the right connections, Washington connections, and a smart boy from New York could use Washington connections. That's why you married me."

She stared her husband down. He turned away.

"You're upset," said David Fitzgerald.

"I'm upset." She nodded her head. "You began screwing around on our honeymoon night."

He studied his fingernails.

"No. It was actually about ten days later," she said. "Ten days after the event, I found—you know what I found—I found lipstick on your shorts. Lipstick." She laughed. "But I'm just a dumb girl from Florida whose daddy kept a black woman in Tallahassee that everyone knew about. Daddy's other wife. Sweet Daddy. Beat my mother, beat *me* with a leather strap when he was drunk. And he was always drunk, my dear. Nice sweet Daddy. Had a union leader, Cuban fellow from Miami, who hated Daddy, had him eliminated. Body never found. Florida politics. Sweet Daddy."

Her head rolled against the back of the sofa, and tears wet her face.

"Jesus Christ," Fitzgerald murmured, rising and taking a step toward her as the phone rang. It was Eli Faber. They spoke briefly, and, after replacing the phone, he sat on the sofa and kissed her.

"Divorce me," she whispered. "David, please, I couldn't face a campaign. Honestly. A divorce would hurt you a bit but, God knows, you wouldn't have to worry about me."

Fitzgerald's fingers ran over her face, touching her lips.
"I'm frightened, David," she said.
"You still are beautiful, Celia."

*

Outside the Mayflower Hotel, Cheryl turned right on Connecticut Avenue and stepped quickly along DeSales Street. Tourists
marching toward the Mall and the cherry blossoms jostled her,
cameras slung around their necks. The heavy air promised
warmth, the westerly breeze was flat, lifeless. Cheryl stared up at
the white sky flecked with golden streaks, and, on Rhode Island
Avenue, placed the dark, oval glasses atop her hair over her burning eyes. She turned up her raincoat collar. She was shivering now,
shivering and perspiring.

At an outdoor phone, Cheryl inserted some coins and dialed
Jerry Paley's home. He picked it up with a slurred hello on the
third ring.

"Listen to me, honey," she said breathlessly. "I'm selling my
diary to the papers." She pressed the phone against her ear. "Getting out, Jerry. *Fleeing*. Maybe Panama. Maybe Rio."

"Which paper?"

"The *Star*."

"Who on the *Star*?"

"A reporter. Howie Bishop."

Jerry's voice dropped. "Howie Bishop."

"You know him?"

"Selling it to Howie. You dumb bitch. Selling it to Howie
Bishop." Jerry Paley caught his breath. "You know what Howie's
going to do?"

Cheryl spoke carefully. "Howie's gonna give me fifteen thousand dollars. That's what he's gonna do."

"And after that."

"After that he's gonna print the diary."

"He's going to burn the diary. Destroy it."

"Bishop promised—"

Jerry spoke in a fury. " 'Bishop promised.' Sweet Jesus! Bishop's
boss is a guy named Barry Cohen. Barry works for Fitzgerald.
You get it? So Bishop gives you the money. And you get out of
town. And the diary's not going to see the light of day. They're
playing you for a dumbbell."

Cheryl's voice shook. "Oh, no."

"They're screwing you."

"They're not screwing me. Take my word, I'll get even. That diary's gonna get published. It's gonna see the light of day. I'm making myself a copy. As simple as that. If the *Star* doesn't publish it, someone else will."

Jerry spoke after a moment. "Be careful."

"What are you saying?"

"Fitzgerald doesn't want the diary printed."

"I'm not scared of that bastard."

"You should be. You going to tell him?"

Cheryl thought for a moment. "No, I won't tell him." She spoke assuredly. "But I'll make sure he finds out."

*

Two miles away, in a corner of the Mall near the Hirshhorn Museum, a carousel crammed with children twirled slowly to the sounds of "Hi, lilli, hi, lo." The youngsters strapped onto wooden horses punctured the music with laughs and delighted shrieks. Parents and grandparents huddled beyond the fence, taking photographs, waving, oblivious to the two neatly dressed men that walked past the ticket booth toward the set of ripening cherry blossom trees a dozen yards away. One of the men spread out the morning *Post* on the damp earth, and they both sat down.

"Is this where you CIA guys always meet reporters?" asked Ward Parsons.

Alex Vikas smiled grimly. "We try not to meet reporters. I don't *like* reporters."

"Don't trust them?"

Vikas bit into his hot dog and roll, gazing at a jogger. "Opportunists. Hypocrites. Liars."

"Is that all?" said Ward.

"Vietnam soured me. Christ!—the brotherhood. Barry Cohen and Dorothy Faye and all you guys. Your generation's little war. Front-page bylines and French food at night. So sure of yourselves, you were. Wait till those North Vietnamese take over, those benign liberation forces." Alex's eyes searched Ward's face. "So what if they massacre peasants, if thousands of ethnic Chinese drown in the sea. If they liquidate political opponents."

Alex removed his jacket, his white shirt stained beneath the armpits. "What happened to that Vietnamese guy who won Barry the Pulitzer Prize? What happened to him? And you remember those Cambodians who helped Dorothy Faye? I'll give you one guess what happened to them." He shook his head. "You know the problem with you guys?"

Ward lit a cigarette.

"No accountability. A lawyer keeps fucking up, and his clients disappear. A doctor loses a few on the operating table, and his patients get a little nervous. A guy at Ford Motor Company screws in the wrong bolt, and he's out on his ass. A CIA case officer recruits the wrong fellow, and he's dead. But a journalist writes bad stories, false stories, hyped stories, and not only does the bastard survive, he succeeds. Wonderful. Nothing as old as yesterday's story. Last week's stories are forgotten. Jesus, would I love to read some of Barry's old stories from Vietnam. Or Dorothy's. Or all those other creeps."

Ward examined his cigarette. "Why are we sitting here, Alex, beneath a cherry tree?"

"Where do you want to sit?"

"An expensive restaurant. Tiberio's or Jean Louis'."

"I like the hot dogs outside the Hirshhorn. Good for the digestion."

Ward leaned back against the tree trunk.

"Your man here, Hugh Finch," Vikas said. "He's got some leaking sources."

Ward lifted a notebook out of his suit jacket as gently as he could.

"Let me guess who," said Ward playfully.

"You're absolutely right," said Vikas.

"Why would Belling leak to the *Star?*"

"Slimy son of a bitch he is. One of your Harvard intellects who managed the war but gave the impression he was really against it."

"Is it power? Washington power play?"

"You're getting warm, sonny."

"Power. Power means money. Money. Money means budget."

Alex studied his fingernails. "The budget. Eddie Belling wants to control the intelligence budget. *All* intelligence activities. CIA—sure. Also FBI, DIA, domestic counterintelligence. We're talking

about fifty, maybe sixty billion bucks. We're talking about a vast
. . . a *secret* bureaucracy. We're talking about power, unprece-
dented power, for a Secretary of Defense. *Independent* power. A
job that even the President, even Congress, cannot quite control."

"The President'll fight Belling on it."

"The President will *not* fight it. The President *needs* Eddie
Belling, my friend. The President is facing an international crisis,
one that's unraveling. You don't dismiss your Defense Secretary in
the middle of a crisis. Especially a Defense Secretary as shrewd as
Eddie."

"Yes." Ward watched Alex. "Belling's strong in Congress."

"And the press. Don't forget the press. Old Eddie Belling is a
great Secretary of Defense, according to you assholes. Voice of
sanity and moderation. Liberal voice in the midst of all us barbar-
ians. Angel of peace."

Alex's voice dropped to an angry whisper. "Why were we un-
prepared for the China crisis? Was there an intelligence failure? I
can see the front-page stories now. All you turds writing the same
carefully leaked garbage. You'll *demand* that Belling take charge.
Congress will insist. Give good, liberal Eddie Belling the job of intelligence czar."

"Belling's orchestrating it," said Ward.

"Like a virtuoso," said Alex, grinning angrily. "Toscanini."

"Extend his power into intelligence."

"With a little help from a friend or two."

"Like . . ."

"Like David Fitzgerald."

Ward concentrated on the soda can.

"They've cut their deal, Fitzgerald and Belling," Alex said.

"Two snakes."

"Coiled around one another. Waiting to pounce." Alex Vikas'
tongue nestled a shard of food in his back tooth. "If the President
drops out of the race for reelection—and you've seen the polls—it's
a free-for-all." He nodded his head. "Fitzgerald wants it."

Ward gazed at the slight tic at the corner of Alex's mouth. "So
does Tommy Nelson." Ward brushed a crumb off the sleeve of his
turtleneck. "You guys are supporting the movie star."

"Tom Nelson's the best we have," said Alex, starting to smile.

"We're most comfortable with Vice President Nelson running for President."

"And uncomfortable with Fitzgerald."

"Fitzgerald wins, and guess who gets most of the pie?"

Ward nodded thoughtfully. "Belling."

"Belling," said Alex. "Fitzgerald wins, and Belling emerges with extraordinary power. Defense. *Intelligence*. Foreign policy too. Belling runs it all."

Ward held Alex's eyes. "Why did you want to see me?"

"Get our side of the story."

"In exchange for what, Alex?"

"Front-page story."

"Come on, Alex. There's something else. Always something else."

Old Washington game. Trading information. Teasing, sexual. Give it to me and I will do it to you gently . . .

"The *Star* sent a girl out to California. Someone named Linda . . ."

"Fentress."

The tic stretched, quivered. "Keep me informed."

Ward held his stare. "You bastards," Ward finally said. "Great at spying on reporters, aren't you? Lousy at real spying."

Alex glanced at a plane overhead, lowering toward National Airport. Ward followed his gaze.

"Close the notebook, let's talk off the record," Alex said. "The Russian Ambassador, Mr. Grizenko, saw our boss last night. Asked what *we* know. When you got the Russians asking *us* for guidance, you know the world's upside down. We don't know what's going on. None of us. The Chinese are provoking the Russians and the Russians are scared."

The tic fluttered, stopped. "In the past three weeks we've picked up the Chinese digging like crazy in the Gobi Desert. *Digging*. Bulldozers. Tractors. Chinese know we're watching and tell us to lay off. First, they're digging for oil. Then they tell us they're building more civil defense shelters. We don't know . . ."

Ward's eyes lowered in blankness. So Vikas was onto Linda's story, Vice President Tom Nelson. What was Linda chasing? Why was the CIA interested?

Ward heard Alex's voice. "Meet me Monday, noon. The Pentagon boat basin." Ward looked at Alex, who smiled faintly. "Monday we find out what's in those tunnels the Chinese are digging." There was a small twitch to Alex's mouth. "Now you can open your notebook, Ward. You want a story for Sunday's paper, don't you?"

*

Francine Miles, Hugh's secretary, was shopping at the supermarket, and Hugh Finch, barefoot in khaki trousers and white T-shirt, dialed Alvin Simmons' office at the old Executive Office Building. He sat on Francine's bed, the pink sheets tangled in a heap on the floor. Her perfume lingered on the bed. He rubbed his unshaven face and lay back on two pillows.

After reaching the Secret Service switchboard, he finally heard Alvin's voice.

"You have been elusive, baby," said Hugh.

"Been busy." Alvin let the words linger.

"Let's get together," said Hugh, sensing the strain over the phone. "Tonight?" He had tickets to the Bullets game, but would cancel the evening with his children.

Hugh heard Alvin's intake of breath. A moment's pause.

"Faye's taken the kids to Durham to see her mother." Reluctance, uneasiness, finally yielding to friendship. "Sure. Why not?"

"Omega about eight?"

Hugh hung up the phone and yawned; the pressures of the past forty-eight hours had drained him. Leading the paper two days in a row. Two first-class exclusives. A reporter from *Time* magazine —somebody named Cheever—had called to interview him about his prospects for appointment to managing editor. He was elusive with her blunt questions—"Do you think being black helps or hurts your chances?"—but the badgering interview, the glances of people in the bureau, the series of exclusives, the item in Friday's "Ear" column stirred an uneasy buoyancy. (*Our own Sweet and Super Hugh Finch is being mentioned, earwigs, for a Big Job in the Big A. Hugh has given up* most *of his pleasures to work, work, work and impress the Powers.* Most *of us would be bereft when Hugh withdraws. Heh-heh-heh.*)

Was it actually possible that Hugh Finch could be managing editor of the New York *Star?*

Hugh placed his arm over his eyes. He dreaded the phone call to Lila and the children, canceling the basketball game. He would take them to an afternoon movie instead, and out to a fast-food place—they'd enjoy that. He'd buy them gifts next week. Take a day trip with them next Saturday or Sunday. Drive to Mount Vernon, maybe even Williamsburg. Speak to Lila . . .

Lila.

She was avoiding him now. When he appeared at the house in Wesley Heights, Lila was never there. She was shopping, or studying, or taking a bath. Or at school. The kids were there with Teresa, the sullen housekeeper. Or with Lila's sister, whose eyes were daggers and who always said tightly that Lila wanted them back at a reasonable time, and please not to stuff them with junk food, but give them a *decent* meal, and please not to take them to a violent movie like last time.

Christ!

He heard the door unlock, Francine dropping packages on the kitchen table. She stepped into the bedroom, smiling. A pretty girl, a gap between her front teeth, soft auburn hair.

"Kiss me," he said.

She sat on the bed, kissing him hard, her hands resting gently against his cheeks. Hugh's two hands enveloped her head, pressing her face onto his.

"Not now," she said tightly. "My mother's coming in on the Metroliner at noon. Remember?" He nodded. Francine asked him what he wanted for breakfast, and slipped out to make it. Blurred visions of Lila and his son Terry, and his daughter Marguerite. He heard Francine moving noisily in the kitchen.

Alvin Simmons.

Pomerance!

He would start with Alvin. Dig it out. Maybe it was nothing, probably nothing. Start with Alvin. Then move on to Pomerance. Dig it out. What the hell was Alvin doing at National Airport picking up Pomerance?

And the China story. Tomorrow, Sunday, Vice President Nelson on "Meet the Press." Belling was on "Face the Nation." He'd cover them. And Monday. Kamchatka. The Kamchatka Peninsula.

Pomerance. Dr. Seymour Pomerance. The White House car. Alvin meeting him at the airport. Suddenly Hugh heard the voice of *Time* magazine's Marilyn Cheever, her words sending an echo through his body.

Does being black help or hurt your chances?

*

It was Kitty White's view that Georgetown hostesses were divided into two castes: those born into money and those who married money. Although the passage of time blurred the distinction for outsiders—hostesses were, after all, a select breed—each caste viewed the other with contempt. The old-timers were snobs and elitists, according to the opposition, women with petty bigotries who scorned Italians and Jews and Irish (until the Kennedys), women comfortable with a certain breed of Washington lawyer, with State Department mandarins and columnists and bureaucrats who sprung from good families, and had a fine education and were sending their children to the "best" schools. It was somewhat curious that some of these hostesses (who were now Episcopalian) had Jewish forebears and had emerged somewhat unscathed from backgrounds that included a surprising number of suicides, nervous breakdowns among their children, and other discreet scandals.

The newcomers were viewed, perhaps correctly, as *arrivistes,* women who married real estate developers and lawyers and oil speculators, who surged triumphantly onto the Georgetown scene with plenty of money, an instinct for self-promotion, and a zealous awareness of the ways to flatter society columnists and party reporters with invitations and gossip. Although some of these women retained old-fashioned class and religious bigotries, most of them were deeply committed to the notion that power in Washington is ephemeral and it didn't matter if a Californian had a dumpy wife, or a New Yorker wore old suits, or a Georgian went to Nowhere University or a Texan had no class. Background, Kitty White was fond of saying, is irrelevant. What counted was power. Now. Who controlled the levers of government. And if someone's father was a saloonkeeper or his mother a maid, if someone ate with his goddamn fingers and wore white socks and vinyl belts and spoke with a funny accent, more power to him. If they were powerful, they counted. Besides, some of those lawyers and mandarins and columnists were pompous bores.

There was one further distinction between the two castes, per-

haps the major one. Although the old-timers had traditional backgrounds, the newcomers emerged from worlds that seemed at best
glamorous, at worst tawdry. The newer women—often long-
legged, honey-blond, southern and throaty-voiced—were former
Las Vegas chorus girls whose husbands found them at the Desert
Inn or the Sands Hotel. One or two were former beauty queens
whose affairs with Iranian diplomats during the Shah's regime,
Kuwaiti and Abu Dhabi princes and even a king (who set one
girlfriend up in an apartment on Avenue Foch) marked them as
party girls before they surfaced as the wives of lobbyists, senators
and real estate developers. Two were even rumored to have been
high-paid prostitutes in London and Beverly Hills before settling
on P Street and Volta Place, respectively, with their husbands, one
a senior partner in a well-known law firm, one an oil lobbyist.

Kitty White had lived on Q Street long enough to straddle both
castes; she was an outsider, a former fashion model from Houston
married to a Texas senator who had died three years earlier in an
air crash on a snowy night outside Denver. He left her stocks, municipal bonds, insurance, part ownership of a Dallas television station, a sizable ranch near Houston, co-ownership of an apartment
building in downtown Houston, as well as the Georgetown home.
The fact that Senator Leroy Reynolds White was about to be indicted for tax fraud, bribery, and stock manipulation before his
death was virtually forgotten now, except among her competitors
on the Georgetown party circuit. Kitty called them the "hags."

"Saturday afternoon in April is not my best time," said Kitty,
pecking David Fitzgerald on the cheek as he closed the door in the
parquet-floored hallway.

"Why?"

"Wisconsin Avenue is mobbed. You have to fight your way
through. It's the season—the tourists from Peoria are in town." She
smiled. "I'm a goddamn snob, right?"

"You're goddamn beautiful."

He placed his arm around her narrow waist and they walked
into the living room. Sunlight filtered through the coarse plaited
glass that hung over the window grilles, bathing the room in a
soft, filmy glow. Chintz draperies, which Kitty lowered during parties, were knotted to the wall.

"You look casual," she said. "Our jogger in the Senate."

"Four miles," he said, sitting on the white-and-floral sofa. "Drink?" She ran her fingers through her streaked blond hair.

"Scotch and water. Plenty of ice."

Kitty walked to the liquor cabinet and poured two scotch whiskeys and water. Fitzgerald watched her, an elegant woman in boots, corduroy jeans, and a cream-colored silk shirt. A gold chain dangled between her breasts.

"You look terrific."

"Always the politician, David."

"Would I kid you?"

"Would you kid me?" She mimicked him. "What can I do for you?"

She sat and faced him.

He began slowly, studying his drink, then watching Kitty.

"I'd like you to arrange a couple of dinners. Discreetly. First, some of your Texas friends. Some of the money men. A couple of Wall Street people that Leroy knew so well." He let the words linger, gazing at her eyes.

"Discreetly."

"Right."

"Then a dinner with a couple of people from the *Times,* the *Post,* the L.A. *Times,* the bureau chiefs. The standard crew, and some *Time* and *Newsweek* and *U.S News* types. Some columnists too."

"And then?"

"Some Senate people and congressmen. Maybe a visiting governor or two. I know most of the people in Congress, of course, but it's different when you're breaking bread. Mix it up with some of the big Democrats in town, the lawyers, a couple of pollsters. Some people from the AFL-CIO."

"The brokers."

He nodded. "The brokers." He sipped his drink.

"I understand," she said. He knew she did.

"Soon?"

"The sooner the better."

"I see." Kitty wet her lips. "One question."

"Yeah."

"What's in it for me?"

He watched Kitty. "I didn't expect that."

"I didn't think you would, David."

Kitty stood, and found a silver cigarette box on the carved walnut center table beside the draperies. She slipped the cigarette into her holder. Fitzgerald watched her lift the silver lighter on the table.

"David, I know, or hope I know, who I am," said Kitty White, flaring the lighter. She sat in the wing armchair, gripping her cigarette holder with her thumb and forefinger. "I'm not an educated woman. I'm not a smart woman. I'm not even pushy, like a lot of women here. I don't have to be, I guess."

She leaned back and inhaled. "Unlike most women here, I had the good fortune—the very good fortune—for someone whose mother was one quarter Indian, probably black, and whose father was a Swede who wanted to go to California but wound up, like the fool he was, in Texas." She tasted the drink. "You're probably thinking, Why in God's name was I fortunate, right?"

Fitzgerald sat perfectly still, waiting.

"For the first thirteen or so years of my life I thought I was pretty goddamn *un*fortunate. In fact, I was miserable. And poor. And lonely. Okay? But after thirteen or fourteen, fortune struck, as they say. Because you know what happened? The combination of this illiterate Indian woman, with beautiful caramel skin, and this drunken Swedish father with blond hair and blue eyes, this combination produced a rather stunning little girl. And when she developed into adolescence she wasn't lonely anymore. Do you get it, David?"

She stood and splashed whiskey in her glass. "Houston. New York. Hollywood for a year and back to Houston. I wound up marrying that bastard, and he was, you know, a rather stupid bastard, but rich. He left me alone, which was nice, and died quickly, which was even nicer. He also left me rich. Not rich rich. But rich enough."

She sat on the armchair and crossed her legs.

"As I told you, I'm not smart." She lifted her hand. "Don't contradict me. I'm not smart. It's a hang-up. I never even graduated from high school. Don't pass that around, please. The hags would love that one. I struggle. Christ, I read the news magazines cover to cover. The New York *Times,* the Washington *Post,* the New York *Star, The Wall Street Journal.* Every goddamn day. I make the effort. But I *know,* I'm aware of the fact, that I didn't get ahead thirty years ago and I *won't* get ahead on my brains, but on something else."

"Your looks."

"Jesus, you're old-fashioned. In a manner of speaking, yes. My mama, who spoke from experience, gave me one bit of advice. You're a pretty girl. Do nothing for free. Nothing. With a man. With a woman. Nothing for free. There's no free lunch. Got it?"

"There's no free dinner."

"Right."

"What do you want?" said Fitzgerald. The lids of his blue eyes narrowed.

"Respectability." She lifted her chin. "You want to run for President, David, and I guess you have a chance. I don't know what you plan to do about Tom Nelson, but that's *your* problem. You start running for President and you want to use me to help start a little groundswell—meeting some of Leroy's bankrollers, the media, the power brokers in town." She gulped her drink with a sigh. "I want a job in the campaign. I want to be somebody. Do you understand?"

"Sure," he said easily.

"I want a job in the *White House.* A paying job. Something I could do. I want to be taken seriously. Do you understand?"

"I understand."

"No, you don't. I want a piece of the action. A permanent piece of the action. And, David?"

"Yes," he said.

"I want ownership of you."

She stood and walked to the window, untied the rope that held the draperies, and they swept down, blanketing the windows. The room was suddenly dark.

She tossed off her boots and unbuttoned her silk blouse, then turned at the same moment that she unfastened her bra. Her breasts were strong; her nipples hard. He stood.

"All right," she said. "I still turn you on, I see."

"You still turn me on," he said.

"Now I want you to fuck me hard, David," Kitty said.

She grabbed the sides of his face and pressed his mouth onto her lips, then began to unfasten his jeans.

"Kitty," said Fitzgerald, his hands clenched on her buttocks. "I need fifteen thousand dollars."

"When?" Her voice was hoarse.

"Now." The fingers of her right hand circled the zipper on his trousers.

"Later, David."

*

Linda Fentress studied the list that she had typed earlier on her Olympia portable. She placed the yellow sheet beside the phone, and glanced at her watch. Twelve-fifteen.

Why was she always too aware of the three-hour time gap between New York and California? Three-fifteen on a Saturday afternoon in New York. She would have completed her exercise class at Lotte Berk and, depending on the weather and her mood, walked home, along Central Park South and uptown on Broadway. Shopped on Seventy-third Street. Gone out to dinner with Chris Fuller, a writer at *Sports Illustrated* (divorced, father of three, wife walked out on him and living with a twenty-nine-year-old premed major at Columbia). Chris has the children three days; Maria has them four.

Poor, sweet, uptight Chris. Another guarantee of what her shrink termed a relationship that would go nowhere.

She had read Tom Nelson's file twice, underlining names and phrases to check out. She had made her phone calls. The Hamalians would see her for brunch tomorrow morning in Malibu. They'd have Lois Barrie there, in from location in Hawaii.

Fox said Elliott Hanley would personally return the phone call by late afternoon, or leave a message. Refused to give his home phone. (Is there anything worse, thought Linda, than a self-important publicity type who works on the assumption that she's doing you a favor by letting you interview some half-assed movie director?)

After phoning Marcus Lynn's office, and informing his secretary that she was a reporter on the *Star* working on a piece about the Vice President, Marcus Lynn's office yielded results. Linda had said she was working on a background piece—the phrase was meaningless, but somehow heavy with implication—about Tom Nelson. Could she see Mr. Lynn quickly?

Ten minutes later, the secretary phoned and asked Linda to

meet Marcus that day for lunch at La Bella Fontana in the Beverly Wilshire. One-fifteen.

A faint skip of the heart. Opening wedge.

Linda had put on a cherry-red leather skirt, a black angora sweater. Hooped earrings. Tinted glasses.

She shrugged. Jesus, why was she so nervous? Only another goddamn story, chasing the *Daily News*. And what the hell are *they* doing today? She took a Valium and glanced, once again, at the pile of xeroxed clips on Tom Nelson. It was twelve-thirty.

What was it that Jerry Paley had told her years ago when she was struggling with some idiot post-Watergate investigation: reporters, good reporters, have got to know how to gather information, organize it, analyze it and draw their own conclusions. It also helps if you're a prick, because, inevitably, the people you're investigating turn out to have crippled wives, or retarded sons, and are really lovely guys just trying to make a quick buck. It's not easy working on stories that are going to send people to jail or destroy their careers, or force them to send their children to the University of Hawaii.

There was a difference between the reporters who smelled stories, picked up leads, built up fat files, plowed through court files, checked bank records, mortgages, financial holdings, met sources at two in the morning, worked the telephone like virtuosos, *worked their asses off*—and those reporters who called themselves "investigative," like the ones from some of the big papers, and were handed files from the DA's office or an organized crime squad or congressional investigators who didn't have enough evidence to push for an indictment and manipulated the press to write bullshit leads justifying six months of work, saying, "The District Attorney is quietly investigating . . ." No skin off anyone's ass. Except the target of the aborted investigations. *Fuck* him.

Just beat the competition.

She walked out onto the balcony, a soft breeze brushing her face. *Don't oversell yourself,* Jerry said. *Don't cut deals. Don't overreach. Too many goddamn reporters oversell themselves to their editors, and, in their panic, hype stories, fabricate, pipe quotes from anonymous sources. Bullshit stories.*

Rule to remember, according to Jerry: *institutions don't fuck people over as much as other people fuck people over. If you find welfare mothers being crowded into rat-infested hotels at fifty bucks a night, find out who owns the hotel. Find out where the furniture is stored, how much it's costing the government to store it. Find the owners and which politicians they contribute to, which law firms handle their legal work, which insurance agencies write their policies. Nine times out of ten, you'll find out that what costs the public money benefits* someone *powerful.*

The place to start was, of course, the public records.

She would begin Monday at Los Angeles County Courthouse. In her notebook Linda wrote: *Deeds, tax assessments, SEC reports, contribution lists, etc.* Interviewing blindly was not the first step. It was a dumb step. *A dumb, half-assed, amateurish step.* A foolish waste of time. She was panicking because Pirota and Farrell were in town.

She closed her eyes. Jerry Paley said never, never interview the principals until all research is completed. If you talk to them early you just get jerked off and give them a chance to burn files and destroy public records. Wait until the end when you can go in with a stacked deck, simply asking for confirmation or denials or situations or facts that you have already documented. Wait. *Don't panic.*

And then squeeze. Squeeze painfully. Scare. Threaten. Jerry had told her of the droshky approach. A droshky is a Russian sleigh, and in the late-nineteenth century a popular lantern show toured the country in which the following scene took place.

It is a Russian winter. Fierce snows. Howling winds. Hungry wolves.

A Russian family boards the droshky, the droshky moves through the snowy woods, wolves appear, the family panics. The wolves give chase, gaining on the droshky and the rapidly tiring ponies.

Finally, in an act of desperation, the father takes the youngest child, or the weakest or the least favored, and throws him off the back of the droshky into the mouths of the wolves.

The wolves are satisfied. The family flees.

There usually comes a time in investigations when you'll have to use the droshky approach, Jerry said. *Go to a marginal figure and threaten that you'll focus on the silly bastard, expose him, unless*

*he gives you information or documents you need to finish the job
on the guy you're actually going after.*

*You'll be surprised at how quickly politicians, banks, com-
panies and girlfriends will throw their buddies off the back of the
droshky.*

Twelve fifty-five. She glanced at herself in the mirror once
more, made sure her notebook and a half-dozen pens were in her
handbag. Linda would leave her tape recorder in the hotel.

You *have* to start with blind interviews. You have to make an
ass of yourself. Talk to Nelson's enemies (like Marcus Lynn),
old girlfriends, ex-wives, landladies, ex-agents, people that all-
American Vice President Tom Nelson may have stabbed in the
back on the way up.

How can you start investigating someone when you're not precisely sure what you're investigating?

What the hell was the Daily News *investigating?*

*

"The lobster is a specialty," said Marcus Lynn.

Linda Fentress sipped her bloody mary. "The lobster is fine."

He ordered two lobsters without looking at the waiter, and ran
his finger along the wine list, lifting his tinted, framed glasses as he
did so. He settled on a 1971 Vouvray, "Le Mont" Moullux,
handed the wine list to the steward, who said, "Thank you, Mr.
Lynn." Linda saw the pinky ring on his left hand, a diamond circled by grains of rubies, and the gold, wide-bracelet watch.
Marcus Lynn's fingernails were carefully polished, his hands
scrubbed pink.

"You come here often?" Linda asked, eyes darting around.
Pompeiian fluted columns and red velvet covered walls. A cherub
stood on one leg atop a gurgling marble fountain in the center of
the room.

"Two, three times a week."

Cool it, Linda, stay calm, don't push, it's L.A., folks are laid
back, do it easy, avoid the gangbusters approach.

Marcus was swathed in clothes almost exquisitely tasteful—
suede lace-up shoes, fawn silk suit with cotton shirt and square
gold cufflinks engraved ML, silk crepe tie.

He sat absolutely still, pale skin stretched taut over a slender
face whose delicacy was broken by a broad, swarthy mouth. Days

later, Linda would recall shuddering at the mouth and its hint of menace. His voice was faint and very low.

"Always enjoyed reading the *Star* back East," Marcus said. Linda was aware of his intense gaze beneath his tinted glasses. "We don't get it here, of course. We get the *Times* and *The Wall Street Journal*. Gather the *Star*'s in some trouble."

"Lots of newspapers are." Let him do the leading, Linda, start with small talk.

"Couple of reporters from the *Daily News* saw me Thursday."

Linda tasted the bloody mary, bracing and tart.

Marcus said, "They wanted to know about Vice President Nelson's past. His movie career. Who gave him his early break. Etcetera. Etcetera."

Linda's finger fondled the spiral notebook in her handbag, placing it on the table. "Etcetera. Etcetera."

Marcus Lynn said, "They told me they were doing a background piece on Tom Nelson"—he let the words linger—"just like you."

"You don't like Nelson."

He smiled. "I despise him."

"Personal? Ideological?"

"Both," said Marcus Lynn. "Where are you from, Linda?"

The question disarmed her. "Nowhere. I'm an Army brat."

"Married?"

She shook her head, No.

"Where's your family?"

"Fort Hood, Texas. Killeen. The armpit of the free world."

"You have brothers? Sisters?"

"Two older brothers. One died in Vietnam." Linda tried to smile. "You married?" Playing dumb she was, but that's okay. Let him lead you by the hand. She knew Marcus was unmarried, divorced from the Mexican actress Davita Lopez. One child, a daughter.

Marcus shook his head, No.

The waiter placed breadsticks, a freshly cut loaf of brown bread, and butter on the table. And the steward, hovering behind him, carried the bottle of wine in an ice bucket. He began uncorking it.

"Why do you despise Nelson?"

Marcus tasted the wine, gurgled it in his mouth, and swallowed. After a moment, he finally looked up at the waiter and nodded. The waiter poured the wine in their glasses.

Linda saw Marcus' eyes fasten on her face. "He took a very beautiful young girl once, and destroyed her life," he said.

Linda whispered, "What did he do?"

"Took advantage of her innocence, her beauty." He ran his forefinger over the rim of the wineglass. "My daughter."

Even after the maître d' approached and apologetically told Marcus Lynn that there was a phone call from Washington, D.C., and would he care to take it now, Linda sat utterly still. She heard Marcus ask him to take the message.

Marcus lifted his chin to Linda. "Eli Faber asked me to cooperate with you. I've known Eli for years."

Linda drew back in surprise.

Marcus murmured, "Said I should help the *Star*. Help *you*."

She had met Faber a half-dozen times. Greasy little man, she thought. How does he get in on all this?

Linda felt her heart pulse. "All right, Marcus, help me. Now. What should I dig after?"

Marcus' voice softened. "What's the greatest musical film ever made?"

Another disarming question. Christ! She knew little about films. "*The Sound of Music*."

A smile lit his face. "Not the greatest money-making musical, the greatest . . ."

Linda shrugged. The heart pulse quickened. She felt her cheeks flush. "I don't know, Marcus, *The King and I?*"

"*The Wizard of Oz*. You're Dorothy. In the land of Oz. You're on the yellow brick road. And at the end of the road, at the very end, are *films*. Black socks films."

Linda narrowed her eyes, puzzled.

"Black socks films," he said. "*Porno* films."

Linda felt her lips part. She began to speak, but caught her breath.

"Have you seen them?"

"Paul Brock has a copy."

She wrote the name in her notebook with trembling fingers.

Too easy, Linda. Too simple. Stories don't happen this way. Falling into place too quickly . . .

"Paul Brock," said Marcus, "is a producer with the largest porno collection in town."

So after all these years, Linda, they're unveiling alleged porno flicks of Nelson. Suddenly *now*. It's too perfect. And what's this story about Marcus Lynn's daughter and Nelson? And Marcus is a friend of Eli Faber. Too many connections here, connections to the *Star,* Marcus trying to show he has some muscle, what does Marcus want? . . .

Linda stood up, excusing herself, to go to the bathroom; actually to write down her notes quickly, notes and quotes to be used someday. *The Wizard of Oz* quote, *terrific,* grist for the mill, so far perhaps Marcus assumes it's a conversation, unintimidated he is because she's not taking notes in front of him.

Old Jerry Paley rule: *don't fuck around with a notebook and pen like Lois Lane if the subject wants to be a pal, a source. Potentially he'll be scared off by the tools of the trade.*

Old Jerry Paley rule number two: *no matter what the women libbers say, honey, in a male-female situation, especially with your looks, play coy, play innocent, play ga-ga, and don't come on like Bella Abzug. If the bastard wants to cop a feel, let him. You'll get a front-page byline out of it.*

It was only when Linda nodded to the maître d', as she stepped out of the restaurant, that the brief exchange between him and Marcus came back to her.

Glancing around the lobby, Linda Fentress walked to the ivory-shaded house phone and lifted it.

You want to be a hotshot investigative reporter, Linda, do it, do it with a vengeance.

"Excuse me," she said. "This is Marcus Lynn's secretary." She spoke a little too breathlessly. "He just had a caller from Washington, left a message. Can you pass it on to me, please?"

"Ah, one second, dear, here we go. Yes, Washington, D.C. . . . The message is from Cheryl. No last name. Just said, 'Giving a copy of the diary to Jerry P.' That's the message."

Linda swallowed hard, feeling the heat in her eyes.

Who's Cheryl?

Linda was certain she knew who Jerry P. was.

*

In Washington, Cheryl put the phone down and remained seated in the twenty-four-hour post office across from Union Station. She smiled to herself, faintly triumphal, despite a chill that made her shoulders quiver.

Giving a copy of the diary to Jerry P.

Marcus would now phone his buddy, David Fitzgerald. Pass on the urgent message that Cheryl had called him at the Beverly Wilshire to say she was giving a copy of the diary to Jerry.

So there are two copies. And it would be foolish of Fitzgerald to try anything violent now.

Cheryl stood up, feeling the coldness spill over her entire body. Her fingers tugged at her throat. Her heart pounded.

*

In the Saturday stillness of the newsroom, Sally Sims tried to read a Washington *Post* editorial calling for a Camp David summit between the Russians and the Chinese. She set the newspaper aside and glanced at the crammed manila folder that her secretary had left. Letters asking for jobs, letters of complaint from someone saying he had been misquoted, letters from furious readers, memos from Maury and Skipper and Frieda that had to be answered.

Saturdays were, for Sally, a day to deal with the paperwork of the national editor's job, a day to sit quietly at an empty desk in the newsroom, leaving the day's editors to deal with incoming copy and the Sunday and Monday pages. A weekend crisis, a major story, and she took over the national desk, of course, but there was no important story on her desk, Sally suddenly thought with a metallic taste in her mouth.

Absurd, wasn't it? Every Saturday, she came in and had to find an empty desk in the newsroom like some goddamn stringer, because the editors had no cubicles or offices to do their private work.

She opened the folder, feeling a slow surge of anger lift from her chest. An hour, perhaps ninety minutes of work, with code words penciled atop each paper (except the memos from Frieda, Skipper, and Maury) so that Rose Tyler would respond with letters that were dutiful, personable, and pro forma. Sally began to read, but the words blurred.

Should have taken the offer years ago from the *Times,* a wealthy paper, prestigious and classy, a paper that treated editors with *respect.* The L.A. *Times* had nibbled too, years back, asked her about working there, *that's* money, no shortage of private offices there. But she'd hung onto the *Star,* falling star it is too, hung on *because* it wasn't the *Times* or the L.A. *Times, because* she as well as Ward and Maury and Hugh and, yes, Barry, feed on the competition, need the beleaguered sense of clobbering the giants, yearn to prove they're somehow superior to the titans. Were they, in fact, losers, all of them, terrified of success, craving to remain outsiders, David versus the Goliaths? Refusing to abandon this rickety ship and board a glistening ocean liner, smoothly sailing, bilge-free, not a crack in sight.

Damn it, they needed the Star, *all of them!*

She deserved the job as much as anyone. All right, there's Maury. But she was as good as the others, *better.* News judgment superb, always was. Got along with the staff, she was trusted, wasn't competitive with them or personally involved, like Hugh. Not ferociously ambitious, manipulative, like Barry. As for Ward, well, was Ward *too* nice? Would he have the balls to make a decision that's painful? Like Kaiserman—Ward's ulcer bleeds every time he sees Mark Kaiserman.

All right, she was initially intimidated at the thought of the job. Question number one: how could the family appoint her if she was sleeping with Skipper? Question number two: could they appoint a woman? Question number three: was her own personal life a bar to getting the job, which was a combination of one and two?

It was Barry who had stirred her, Barry with his arrogant theft of the California story, deploying Linda Fentress just like that, making brazen cracks about her and Skipper with that meanness last night. Charlie.

Stiffening, Sally placed the folder in her leather case. She'd do the paperwork later, tomorrow.

Damn it! She *did* want the job. And she could get the bloody job if she took steps quickly. First of all, stop the relationship with Skipper. She couldn't have the job while sleeping with Skipper. And then work it out with Charlie. Resolve her personal life at once and push, push like hell.

*

Barry was on the phone to Linda when the intercom rang. It was 4:20 P.M. He told Linda to wait and walked into the kitchen to pick up the earphone.

Carlos, the doorman, spoke in cracked English.

"It's Miss Marye."

"What?" said Cohen impatiently.

"Miss *Marye* is here to see you, Mr. Cohen."

Barry heard her voice in the backdrop. "It's Margie."

"Miss *Marye*," Carlos repeated.

"Send her up," said Cohen.

Barry walked to the phone and told Linda to call him again Sunday night. The porno connection was intriguing.

"You sure you don't need help?" he asked.

"No, I don't need help," she said. "I don't need help at all."

It was a meaningless question, Barry knew, because no reporter ever wanted help. The competition is too fierce for someone to "help out"—send in a second person and there's conflict between the reporter on the scene, eager to protect his turf, and the "helper," equally eager to move in.

If the story got too big he would send her help, order staffers to Los Angeles, deploy people like a commanding general. In the meantime it was Linda's, and Linda's alone.

He hung up as the doorbell rang.

She wore a navy-blue cotton-knit pullover sweater and a skirt and sandals. Her hair was tied behind her head.

"Hello, stranger," said Barry.

She turned away.

"I left my lipstick here, right?"

"Right. It's in the bathroom."

She walked past him, and Barry locked the door, stood against it and waited.

Within a moment she returned.

"Thanks, Barry."

"You're pissed off at me."

"You're not a nice guy."

"No one said I was."

"Took me to the party and dropped me. Like *that*. Sniffing around that bitch from *Time*. I'm sure she went home with you."

"She went home with me."

"I'd like to leave now."

"No."

"You're kidding."

"I'm not kidding."

Margie glared at him, her mouth trembling. "I would like to leave."

"Why?"

With his right foot he lunged toward her in a single step and laughed. Margie backed away.

"Unlock the fucking door." Her voice quivered with fear.

Smiling, Barry moved his left foot forward and whispered, "Come on, Margie, come here." He was laughing.

Furiously, she picked up a glass ashtray. "Goddamn it, I'll kill you."

"No, you won't."

He prowled around her, lurching his shoulders and open hands like a fighter seeking to feint his opponent. He thrust at her with both hands. Margie lost her footing for a moment and stumbled back, her elbow brushing against a table lamp that toppled to the floor.

"You rotten bastard. You rotten motherfucking bastard. I hate you. I hate you. I hate you, you miserable bastard. You are a fucking animal, a fucking dog."

He gripped her arms tightly. "That's enough," Barry said hoarsely. He placed his right hand firmly on the back of her neck and thrust her face toward his, kissing her fiercely, struggling to move his tongue inside her mouth.

As he did so, he seized her fragile wrist and tightened his fingers around it. The ashtray dropped to the floor.

Awkwardly, he thrust her on the sofa and lifted her skirt. His fingers probed the wetness, and when his thumb and forefinger slipped the panties to her knees, and then the floor, she dropped her shoulders and lay back mutely, as if surrendering. Her eyes were shut.

The phone began to ring. It would be Howie Bishop calling from the Mayflower. He was supposed to call before five. Howie would have to call back.

"Forget it. Forget it," he whispered as he kissed her firmly on the lips, the neck. He kicked off his running shoes, awkwardly thrusting his trousers and underwear to the floor.

Barry entered into her easily. Margie gasped, opening her mouth, while his body probed hers. She dug her fingers into his neck, pressing them beneath his shirt, arching her body to meet his. She felt his fingers fumble beneath her sweater, lifting it above her breasts.

His lips bit her right nipple while he roughly massaged her left breast. "Yes," she whispered, "yes," wrapping her arms around his neck. "Yes, yes . . ."

But his body stiffened now and he came, too quickly, groaning and shuddering and kissing her neck.

"Stay with me," he whispered. "Stay tonight."

Margie's eyes remained shut. She began stroking the hairs on his chest.

*

By dusk the darkening sky promised showers in Washington. The air was damp; the westerly winds were laced with rain and chunks of swirling sand. Heavy clouds moved rapidly overhead.

Hugh and his two children, engulfed in the crowd leaving Tenley Circle, moved slowly out of the movie house onto Wisconsin Avenue. Hundreds more were waiting in an unruly, noisy line inside the lobby to catch the five-thirty show.

"The last James Bond was better," said Terry. He was a handsome, confident twelve-year-old in sneakers, jeans and a windbreaker marked "Sidwell Friends."

"This one was creepo," said ten-year-old Marguerite, who always agreed with her older brother.

They walked across Van Ness Street to Roy Rogers for dinner. As the two children chatted about James Bond—it was evident that they adored the movie—Hugh's mind wandered. He had to call the office, he had to shower and change to meet Alvin, talk to Francine.

Weekends were ostensibly reserved for the children, but work interfered. Always. There were morning news conferences on the Hill, interviews, meetings, stories, lunches, dinners. Washington was a working town, not a fun town, not a hip town; in fact, it was still a small southern town, but everyone in Hugh's world worked hard, relentlessly, 7 A.M. to 9 P.M., working lunches and dinners, setting aside three hours on Saturday or Sunday for the kids.

He was lucky to see them once each weekend, speak to them a couple of evenings on the phone. Hugh struggled now to listen to them, to talk to them about the movie or school or the Bullets or Redskins . . . but he was unable to ignore work, especially now, unable to separate himself from the job to pay the kind of attention that he knew his children, especially the boy, needed.

Terry was a smart kid, sophisticated, good in school, no problem there, nice friends, but so *distant,* so remote, every feeling hidden beneath layers of silence. When Hugh told him that, unfortunately, they could not go to the Bullets game that night—a game that he knew the boy desperately wanted to go to, probably boasted to his friends that he was going to—Terry merely shrugged and turned away. Yet his eyes were filled with deep hurt.

He would make it up to the boy, of course. Buy him a gift. Take him to another game. The kid understood that journalists keep crazy hours, cancel out, get phone calls in the middle of the night. But . . .

Lila had told Hugh in her blunt way: "The *Star* is not family. Don't treat it that way. You'll get screwed too. *You've got your family.*"

She was correct, absolutely correct, but there was no going back now. He had his hands on one helluva story, courtesy of Edward Belling. The other story, Pomerance, was elusive, but damn it, intriguing. *Two* stories.

Didn't that gal from *Time,* Marilyn Cheever, tell him over the phone that, yes, he was one of the *chief contenders.* Her words.

Terry and Marguerite carried trays loaded with chicken, cole slaw, french fries, apple turnovers and milk. He paid the cashier and they sat on wooden stools at a long veneered table. The restaurant was packed with children and their fathers: divorce night at Roy Rogers. Hugh sipped black coffee.

Terry waved to a classmate at the opposite end of the table. Marguerite happily tore apart the chicken wing. Hugh leaned forward and said he had to make one call, a quick one, to the office. He'd be right back. One afternoon in two weeks with the kids and I can't leave the goddamn office alone. They'll tell Lila, of course, and she'll nod happily: of course, of course. There's only two things he cares about—the office, making it, making it big; and screwing white girls. That's your father. No—she wouldn't say that. She doesn't talk like that in front of them. She doesn't twist the kids against him like some wives. But, Christ, she believes it. She believes every word of it, and she's right, she's goddamn right, and *I can't help myself.*

Sam Hunter, the deputy bureau chief, was working the desk.

"I've been trying to call you," he said.

"What's up?"

"We got a story from Washington slugged China. Leading the paper. I didn't know a goddamn thing about it. I checked. Ward Parsons filed it."

"Parsons." Hugh felt dizzy.

"He quotes authoritative sources. Says the United States received reports this morning that the Russians had entirely closed down this new railroad line . . ."

Hugh shut his eyes.

". . . because of major guerrilla attacks. Parsons says it's a quote new development in the rapidly deteriorating situation on the China-Russia border unquote."

Rain started to pelt the booth. Hugh swallowed hard. "Anything else?"

"Says the CIA believes the railroad attacks on the Baikal-Amur Mainline are a major escalation of the conflict. Quotes one intelligence source saying quote the Russians choke to death without railways unquote. Good quote."

"Terrific."

"He goes with that, some background stuff, the Russians need the railways to get food and provisions to troops, to get timber and coal through Siberia to Pacific ports. Then there's one graf, an intriguing graf, about, let me see, about ten grafs down. Let me read it. 'Authoritative sources predicted stepped-up border tensions in the next few days, and said Monday may prove pivotal in the crisis. The sources declined to discuss possible events on Monday. The White House, meanwhile, was reportedly locked in emergency meetings through the day to deal with the situation.'"

Hugh slumped in his seat. The childlike insecurity that lingers dormant in most reporters, including Hugh, engulfed him now, knotting his belly, filling his throat with a tightness that left his tongue dry. He could barely speak.

"That bastard," Hugh said.

"Leading the paper," Hunter repeated.

"That miserable cocksucker."

"I guess," said Sam Hunter, "he wants to get into the act. He wants to get his front-page byline too. Ward's stabbing you in the back, baby, stabbing and twisting."

Hunter continued, "I guess he wants to impress the powers that be. Ha. Ha."

Hugh said quietly, "What's Maury's home phone?"

Hunter said: "Maury's home phone in New York. Okay." The home phone of every key editor in New York, as well as members of the Washington bureau, were beneath a hard glass plate on the copy desk. Hunter gave him the phone number, and Hugh hung up, then phoned Maury, using his telephone credit card. Nancy answered as there was a clap of thunder.

"Is Maury there, Nancy? This is Hugh Finch."

"One sec. Where are you calling from? Is it raining?"

"I'm calling from the parking lot of Roy Rogers on upper Wisconsin Avenue. We're about to be washed away in the flood."

"Dear, dear. It's lovely here."

"It always is, Nan."

"Here's Maury."

Hugh struggled to control his voice. "I have a story for the second edition," he said. "A good one. This new railroad, the Baikal-Amur, this new railroad's been shut down."

"Hugh."

"Sources say the attacks on the railroad are a major escalation . . ."

"Hugh, we *have* that story tonight."

"You're kidding."

"Ward Parsons wrote it. Didn't he inform you?"

"Inform me of what?"

"That he was coming down."

"Afraid not."

"Oh, shit. He was supposed to."

Through his rage Hugh heard Maury's uneasiness. The fact that one reporter was obliged to inform another that he was moving

onto his turf for a front-page story was a ritual that was largely ignored on the *Star*.

Hugh tried to control his voice. "All right, if Parsons wants to
play those games, let him."

Maury sighed. "Look, Hugh—hey, where the hell you calling
from? It sounds like incoming."

"I'm outside Roy Rogers on goddamn Wisconsin Avenue. I just
heard from my desk that Parsons filed on my story. *My story*. I've
had this fucking story for the past few days. He gets a bug up his
ass to file a Sunday front-page story. Wonderful. So he comes in
and jerks off a few of his CIA buddies and we got a story."

"Calm down."

"Don't tell me to calm down. You're the *acting* managing editor. Right? What are we playing? Columbia Journalism School?
This is *my* story and you tell him to keep his fucking hands off."

"Hugh."

"Yeah."

"Hugh. Listen. Parsons is foreign editor. He can do whatever
he likes. If he wants to write a story, he'll do it. I read the story
and thought it was a good story and okayed it. *I* okayed it. It was
a goddamn exclusive and I'm not holding out an exclusive because
your nose is gonna get out of joint. We're a daily, my friend.
We're competing with the *Post* and *Times* and a dozen other
papers, and I don't give a shit *who* comes up with an exclusive. If
it's a good story, we print it, we print it, you hear me, and if
you're pissed off, then that's too fucking bad."

Hugh felt a sickly taste in his mouth.

"I hear you."

"What?" said Maury.

"I hear you, I *hear* you, Maury." He inhaled. "Everyone's
pushing for that fucking job, right?"

"Right," replied Maury. "Look, you've done a terrific job.
You've beaten . . ."

"Hey, man, do me a favor, cut the shit, okay? Cut it. I don't
want no Boy Scout talk. Everyone's playing rough games. Okay. I
play rough games too."

"There's enough stories for everyone, Hugh. Christ, there's
enough stories . . ."

Hugh laughed.

"Talk to me tomorrow. Call me tomorrow morning."

"Sure, boss."

"Come on. Goddamn it. This story is only starting."

"Okay, partner, call you tomorrow." He hung up the phone.

By the time Hugh and the children climbed into his Volvo to drive toward Wesley Heights, the rain had subsided to a drizzle. He drove in silence along Massachusetts Avenue. Only as Hugh slowed for a red light as they approached Dexter Street did Marguerite finally lean forward and whisper to him:

"Daddy, will we see you tomorrow?"

Hugh grasped her hand. "I'll try, sweetheart. I will. But I'll have to work all day. I'll speak to you over the phone if I can't come."

She sat back, and Hugh sensed her disappointment. He peered into his rearview mirror and saw Terry staring blankly out the window.

He's twelve years old, and I don't know him. His protective layers are thickening. Christ, when I was twelve years old, Daddy was long dead, we had moved to a half-dozen cities, we scrounged. Christ, the humiliation of wearing Salvation Army hand-me-downs, shoes and socks too big, the kids laughing at school, the goddamn underwear with holes in it, too embarrassed to take my pants off for swimming class because of my underwear. I wanted to die. *You walk straight,* said Mama, *you keep your head high and take no truck from no one. Be proud. Take no truck.* And Terry? Four thousand dollars a year tuition at Sidwell. Everything in the goddamn world at his fingertips. No holes in *his* underwear. Music lessons. Tennis lessons. Sports camp in the Poconos costing a minor fortune. Wants to be a doctor. Has everything except his goddamn father, whom the kid needs. The girl is young enough, innocent enough, to hurl her disappointment at her father's face, pout in anger, expose her fierce hurt. But the boy just stares out the window . . .

"Look, I'll try to see you tomorrow, folks."

"Mommy's upstairs," said Marguerite. The front bedroom light was on in the two-story red-brick house.

"I have the key," said Terry sullenly.

Lila gave the boy the house key to avoid confrontations with her ex-husband. Inevitably, when he returned the children home, the upstairs light served to underscore the dual facts that Lila was home and that it was unnecessary for Hugh to come into the house.

He kissed Marguerite and shook Terry's hand. He promised to get seats for an Orioles game in Baltimore the following Saturday.

"Can I go too?" said Marguerite eagerly.

"Aw, come on," said Terry. "Since when do you like baseball?"

"Why not?" said their father. "We'll all go."

The exchange brightened the two children, who walked up the leaf-strewn entrance to the house. He watched Terry open the door. Marguerite turned and waved.

It was six forty-five. He would pick up Alvin Simmons at the old Executive Office Building at 8 P.M. Hugh told Alvin that he would probably be a couple of minutes late; he had another appointment at seven-fifteen.

Saturday evening at the Deadline Bar is, perhaps, the quietest night of the week. The husbands are home in Vienna, Virginia, or Falls Church or Bethesda or Chevy Chase. The bachelors are preparing to take out dates to dinner parties in Georgetown or Cleveland Park or Capitol Hill. The tourist trade is minimal. Except for a journalist or two on duty, who may stop off for a nightcap before journeying home, the bar is rather sedate and lined with only five or six reporters. It was hardly unusual, then, to see Hugh Finch, the Washington bureau chief of the New York *Star,* sitting at the bar on H Street, nursing a Bourbon and water, chatting with a *Newsday* reporter who covered the White House, two blocks away.

Hugh had nearly finished his drink—it was 7:20 P.M.—and, certainly, the *Newsday* reporter, or anyone else in the bar, hardly noticed when Hugh excused himself to walk into the bathroom. Perhaps two minutes later, a bespectacled man in his mid-thirties, with a trim beard and a carefully scissored mustache, folded his copy of the sports page of the Washington *Post* and placed it on the counter at the end of the bar. He rose from his stool, stubbing out his cigarette in an ashtray. The man straightened his cashmere charcoal-gray turtleneck sweater over his pleated trousers, a shade softer than the sweater. He wore a navy-blue sport jacket and black tasseled loafers.

The man's half glass of beer, his Kents and disposable lighter, and the folded copy of the Washington *Post* rested on the counter, assuring his return. He was merely going into the men's room.

Hugh stood at the urinal, and the man with the mustache stood two urinals away. The man glanced behind him to insure that no one was in the stalls, and, satisfied, removed an unmarked white envelope from the breast pocket of his jacket and handed it to Hugh. In turn, Hugh's hand reached into his trouser pocket and he removed an envelope, handing it to the man, who nodded.

Hugh zipped up his pants, flushed the urinal, placed the envelope in his jacket pocket and left the bathroom without a word. The man walked into a stall, locked it, and opened the envelope.

By the time the man had left the bathroom to return to his beer, Hugh Finch had departed the Deadline Bar.

It was a straightforward exchange: in Hugh's pocket now, as he climbed into his Volvo, was slightly more than three grams of cocaine. In the man's pocket, an envelope, containing three hundred dollars in twenty-dollar bills.

Hugh was now prepared for his evening with Alvin Simmons.

*

Years later, when he recalled that Saturday night in April, Hugh was uncertain if he consciously set out to get his friend Alvin Simmons drunk and high that night. It was not unusual for him to purchase the cocaine at the Deadline Bar. They would have eaten and drunk too much—they often did when they met downtown for dinner. Perhaps the evening would have unraveled in precisely the same way. Perhaps . . .

But Ward's front-page story had jolted Hugh. It stirred ripples of rage and left him unhinged, frightened. The story had opened a chasm of doubt and confusion and insecurity that Hugh assumed he had sealed years earlier. Scratch a reporter, Hugh would say, and you find a child needing affirmation. Needing applause. Needing the prompt ego satisfaction of a byline to publicly assure the reporter that, yes, the talent is there, the skills are on target.

Was Hugh any different? Was his confidence as slippery as everyone else's? Was he any less vulnerable? Was being the Washington bureau chief of the *Star* any different from serving in New York like a kid writing obits or working the police beat, always jittery, always groping, always keeping an eye over one shoulder to insure that the new kid on the block isn't better or smarter or pushier?

Having lost the China story for one day, Hugh was determined not only to regain it but to drive even harder. He had assumed, stupidly, that the story was his, a big story, an important one, a story that could have a bearing on his own career. *His story*. But this story, like any other story, was up for grabs. *Ward was pushing*.

All right, Ward, push. Push *hard*. We both push hard. Barry is pushing and politicking too. He's got his own stories. What the hell is this California investigation about?

And Sally. An operator. If they want a woman to run the paper, there's Sally. Can she have a better rabbi than bedmate Skipper?

And Maury. Waiting . . .

The downtown traffic was light that wet Saturday evening, as Alvin and Hugh drove down Pennsylvania Avenue past the White House, turning onto New York Avenue toward R Street. They had decided to have a drink first at the Foxtrappe, a black club that Hugh had joined years ago, a club for lawyers, doctors, government officials and middle-level professionals in their thirties and forties.

The two sat in the amber-lit downstairs lounge; Hugh sipping a beer, Alvin ordering scotch and soda.

"You're quiet tonight," said Hugh.

Alvin said he was tired.

"Busy week." Alvin nodded his head, and grabbed some peanuts off a dish in the center of the table. He ate the peanuts slowly, distractedly.

They listened to the disco sounds that filtered down from the bar upstairs.

"Cheer up, man, it's Saturday," said Hugh.

Alvin smiled, and gulped his drink.

They drank for an hour and twenty minutes, watching the crowds moving into the club, listening to the laughter upstairs and the pulsing music, chatting quietly even as Alvin started to loosen up and get drunk. By the time they left the Foxtrappe, Alvin was humming softly and leaning on Hugh's arm as they walked to the car, which was parked on Sixteenth Street.

Hugh drove to Columbia Road, stopping on the way to buy two large bottles of cold beer and a bottle of Red Label scotch before arriving at the Omega, which was packed and noisy. They shared *misitas de puerco* and *asapao,* finishing off the beer as Alvin began reminiscing about his eighteen months as an MP in Saigon, about a Corsican restaurant off Hai Ba Trung that he would take girl-friends to. Alvin was not quite drunk by now, but he was laughing and guzzling beer and speaking loudly above the din.

They left the restaurant by eleven-thirty and Hugh drove to Ed Murphy's Supper Club on Georgia Avenue, where Alvin drank more scotch.

Was it Hugh's imagination that Alvin seemed agitated, a bit too giddy? Anxious to get drunk? Was the steady flow of whiskey and beer, which Alvin freely consumed that night, unable to wash away whatever was bothering him?

Hugh was fully aware that, under pressure and anger, Alvin drank too much, couldn't quite control it. Hugh had seen Alvin drink at home, especially after a tense trip with the President, who had a politician's habit of surging into crowds to shake hands. A Secret Serviceman's nightmare.

Now Alvin was drinking swiftly, gulping down one scotch after another, welcoming each order. One moment he seemed sullen; the next moment he was laughing too noisily.

By midnight, Alvin's voice was slurred, his eyes hollow. He cradled the back of his head against the front seat of Hugh's car, starting to laugh as Hugh drove downtown over Memorial Bridge toward Alvin's home in Arlington.

Alvin handed him the house key and Hugh unlocked the door, grasping Alvin's waist and gently pushing him into the living room, where the Secret Serviceman dropped onto the Chesterfield sofa. Hugh removed Alvin's jacket, heavy with the .357 magnum that he always carried, folding it over a mock-leather footstool be-side the window. He kept his own jacket on.

Breathing heavily, Hugh poured a quarter of a glass of scotch and handed it to Alvin.

"Hell. I shouldn't," said Alvin.

"Why not?" said Hugh. "We're home."

Alvin laughed, and sipped the drink. His hands were cold.

Hugh stood over him.

"I have a present," he said.

Alvin looked up.

"Some coke."

Alvin studied him and laughed. "Beautiful."

Hugh walked into the kitchen for a teaspoon. When he returned, Alvin was humming softly. Hugh's hands trembled.

Come on, Alvin, come on, come through. Talk to me.

Hugh walked to Alvin and crouched on the floor at his friend's feet. He then removed the envelope from his breast pocket. Spooning out some particles of cocaine, Hugh watched Alvin snort the cocaine, pressing his finger against one nostril as he did so. He inhaled once, briefly, then a second time, expansively. He opened his mouth and exhaled. Then it was Hugh's turn.

Alvin shut his eyes now and tasted his drink. Hugh stood, wobbly for a moment, then eased himself into the rocker, facing Alvin. They sat in silence. Hugh was drowsy and chilled. His heart was pounding.

Finally, Hugh rose and turned on the radio to some rock music. He handed the spoon to Alvin, who snorted the cocaine through his other nostril.

Hugh walked into the bathroom, peed and washed his face and neck with cold water. He returned to the living room and sprinkled more cocaine onto the spoon, handing it once more to Alvin.

Alvin snorted it through both nostrils now, then returned the spoon to Hugh, who flicked the powder back into the envelope.

"More whiskey," said Hugh, pouring scotch into the glass. Alvin was mumbling, his eyes shut.

"I saw you, Alvin," Hugh finally said.

"What?"

"I saw you. At National Airport on Tuesday. You were meeting a friend of mine."

"A friend of yours?" Alvin's eyes remained firmly closed. He barely moved his lips.

"Dr. Pomerance. That guy from New York."

"You know Dr. Pomerance? Nice guy."

"Here, take some more."

Hugh placed the spoon into the envelope, handed it to Alvin, who snorted slowly, pleasurably now.

"Feel better?" said Hugh.

"Much better," said Alvin. "I feel nice."

"How's Pomerance doing?"

"Oh man . . ."

Alvin closed his eyes. He began to sleep. Hugh waited four minutes.

He got up and walked to the footstool, where he had placed Alvin's jacket. The revolver rested in his left breast pocket. In his right-hand pocket lay the notebook that Hugh wanted, the thin, flat pad that Hugh had seen Alvin and every other Secret Serviceman use to jot down their schedules each day, expenses, times of arrival and departure. The Secret Servicemen called it "the bible."

Hugh, turning to Alvin, who was mumbling now, lifted out the notebook. He turned to Tuesday and read: *Office 7:55. Meeting 8:30. Depart for National 11:30. Pick up Pomerance 12:20. National. Eastern shuttle. Arrive Walter Reed 12:55. Pick up Pomerance 5:25. Walter Reed. Arrive Madison 6:18. Phone calls: 30 cents.*

Hugh turned the page. Wednesday.

Pick up Pomerance, Madison, 8:15. Arrive NIH 8:55. Depart NIH 1:27. Arrive WH 2:05. Depart WH 5:15. Arrive National 5:50. Pomerance. 6 P.M. shuttle. LaGuardia. Lunch NIH $2.55. Phone calls, 45 cents.

Hugh Finch slipped the notebook back into Alvin's jacket. Alvin groaned quietly, a broad smile lingering on his face. Hugh watched him.

"Here's some scotch," said Hugh loudly, pouring more whiskey into the glass.

"Thanks," whispered Alvin. His eyes remained closed.

"I saw old Pomerance at Walter Reed," Hugh said quietly. "What the hell was he doing there?"

Alvin repeated, "What the hell was he doing there? What the hell. Oh man. Oh *man.*"

"Hey, I saw him at the White House too. Thursday afternoon. We had a talk." Hugh struggled to keep his voice steady.

"Did you? Did you have a talk?"

"We had a *nice* talk."

"I'm glad, baby." He rolled his head and took one more gulp of whiskey.

"Hey. Did he talk to you, really talk to you?" said Alvin. He finally opened his eyes, but they stared blankly past Hugh.

"Of course he did," said Hugh.

Hugh leaned forward. With two trembling hands, Hugh grasped Alvin's wet shirt, moving so close to him that he smelled the sweet-sick mix of whiskey, food, beer and cocaine.

"Tell me," said Hugh tersely.

"What?"

Hugh pulled Alvin closer, their faces inches apart. Rage and panic shrouded Hugh's words.

"Tell me. Tell me. Talk to me. Tell me. Goddamn it. Tell me. My friend Pomerance. My buddy Pomerance. Why is he here?"

Alvin shrugged. "Didn't he tell you? Didn't he talk to you?" He nodded his head. "Oh Christ, man. Didn't he tell you? The President's *dying*."

Sunday

CHAPTER 11

"Actually, President Bergen has, in all likelihood, smoldering leukemia—or what we call 'aleukemic anemia.'"

Dr. Pomerance spoke carefully, watching Hugh open his notebook and start writing.

"Perhaps I should explain," said Pomerance. He seemed elegant even in his unusual outfit: Puma Fast Rider running shoes, blue-and-gold striped nylon shorts, a loose-fitting gray sweat shirt.

Pomerance had apologized to Hugh about the outfit. Sunday afternoons were set aside for a five-mile jog around Central Park, rain or shine. The doctor said he tried to run at least three days a week.

Pomerance, the odd smile fixed on his face, opened an office door so carefully and discreetly painted that Hugh had failed to notice it.

It was on Fifth Avenue and Seventy-fifth Street, as befitted a highly paid cancer specialist who had treated film stars, politicians, the wives of millionaires and, now, the President of the United States. A bold Rothko painting—black, white and red—dominated the spacious room.

"Mr. Finch. I have never particularly enjoyed speaking to newspaper reporters," said Pomerance, handing Hugh a Seven-Up. Pomerance gripped a glass of white wine, and stepped behind the desk.

"I should tell you," said Pomerance, glancing up, "the White House is very, *very* upset that you're here."

Hugh said nothing.

"The President is very upset," Pomerance went on.

Hugh tasted the soda.

"This is precisely what we wanted to avoid. A newspaper leak. Sensational stories. That sort of thing. We hoped to avoid that by assessing the President's illness first and then, of course, making the announcement at the proper time."

Pomerance frowned. "Now we're still operating in the dark"— Hugh began writing—"please don't write this, Mr. Finch. We're *still* not sure how to handle a newspaper story."

Pomerance stiffened, seeming to catch his anger. "I'm not talking about a cover-up, please understand me." He studied the wineglass. "I'm talking about understanding the President's illness. We have not come to any conclusions about it."

"We?"

"Myself. Doctors at NIH and Walter Reed. We're still studying the tests, and we'll be taking more tests in the next two days. We're having a doctor fly up from Dallas, a specialist, to join our team. We're still *unsure,* Mr. Finch, quite unsure, and that's why a newspaper story is premature."

Hugh had waited until nine-ten Sunday morning to phone Pomerance, leaving word with the doctor's answering service that he wanted to speak to the doctor urgently. He also had phoned the White House and asked the operator to reach Danny Fraser, the President's press secretary. It was an emergency.

Sorry, Alvin, thanks buddy. Got your shoes off, tucked you under the quilt at 2:15 A.M., and was home by 2:50, drifting into waves of sleep, myriad images of you, Alvin, of Terry and Marguerite, of Francine, of that son of a bitch Ward Parsons, of my father, merging, twisting through my head. 4:20 it was, bolted out of bed, gagging, arms and legs bathed in sweat, heaved the dinner in the toilet bowl, flushed and felt the tears, hey, I am sorry, man, had to do it that way, had to get that story, need that byline.

Pomerance returned the call within ten minutes. Hugh spoke rapidly. Was it true that tests diagnosing that the President was suffering from leukemia had been conducted at the National Institutes of Health? Pomerance said, "Mr. Finch, I have *nothing* to say. You will have to phone the White House."

While Hugh waited for Danny Fraser to return his call, he weighed his strategy. He would phone Maury promptly after Danny's call. How the *Star* would play the story—what precisely Hugh wrote—depended, of course, on the White House comment.

Hugh saw three White House options. The first was confirming the news; privately informing Hugh that the disease had been discovered early enough to destroy the malignant cells. The President is carrying on his duties as usual and is, of course, undertaking delicate negotiations with the Russians and the Chinese at this very moment. Concerned but not overly concerned. First option—and a hell of a story, a Pulitzer. Guaranteed, friends, to place Hugh Finch on the fast track leading to Evan Claiborne's vacant office.

The second option: stonewall, no comment whatsoever. You go ahead and print whatever you want, but it's your ass, sonny boy. We will not talk about this *rumor*. We will say *nothing*. And if you're wrong, fella, and print a story, if you got the facts twisted, then *your* credibility and *your* paper's credibility are destroyed.

The third option, of course, would be total denial. The President is in good health. Jesus, what'll you guys think of next?

The phone had rung at five minutes after ten. To Hugh's amazement, it was the robust voice of White House Chief of Staff Barton Taylor, who only returned phone calls to reporters from the Washington *Post,* the New York *Times* and the Los Angeles *Times*. The New York *Star* was on the second-string list, reserved for Taylor's aides.

"You fellows never stop. Sunday's another workday," Taylor said lightly.

Bastard's scared. Old establishment Bart Taylor. Metropolitan and Cosmos clubs. Little Hughie's got Barton by the short hairs. Gonna do a story someday about the Bart Taylors of Washington.

One of the capital's half-dozen top lawyers, Barton Taylor was a pudgy, bespectacled figure whose white wavy hair and gentle smile somehow enhanced his reputation as an utterly reasonable liberal Democrat serving and advising dozens of major corporations and at least four Presidents. After his White House appointment, *Time* magazine called Taylor "the quintessential Washington insider whose legal savvy and razor-sharp mind had successfully guided numerous industries through a minefield of court cases and consumer-oriented congresses." In other words, while Bart Taylor's credentials were impeccable—he was a board member of the American Civil Liberties Union, an unpaid adviser to the Urban League—he also represented automobile makers seeking to kill a piece of safety legislation, the airline industry hoping to block low-cost fares, pharmaceutical companies plotting to wreck controls on prescription drug prices.

Barton Taylor coughed and lowered his voice. "Just spoken to Danny and, ah, some other people about your phone call."

Hugh bent forward, picking up the first paper he could grab— the sports section of the Washington *Post*.

"Dr. Pomerance doesn't want to talk to you, but we have told him to see you on one condition."

Hugh swallowed.

"That you not publish anything today."

"I can't . . ."

"We're still getting—look, I am talking to you off the record, right?"

"Right."

"We're still getting other medical opinions. Other evaluations. Pomerance will talk to you on an off-the-record basis today and tell you what he knows."

"This is ridiculous."

"What?"

"This is crazy. The President is seriously ill and you want to orchestrate the announcement."

"The President is *not* seriously ill. If you want to write a story that says the President *is* seriously ill, then go ahead. But it will be denied up and down the line. The President is *not* seriously ill. I don't know who your sources were on this—and we're looking into that right now—but the President does not have a confirmed case of leukemia, as you indicated to Danny. No confirmation. And if you write that the President is suffering from leukemia, well, then, it's your reputation. I can't believe a paper of the *Star*'s standing would print a rumor like that."

"Why do you want Pomerance to see me?"

"To discuss what the President *does* have. It's confusing to all of us. It's still under debate. We're flying in specialists from Dallas and Atlanta. We can deny that he has leukemia. Let's avoid speculation and gossip. Let Pomerance talk to you."

"And then?"

"Give us twenty-four hours."

"Why?"

"To get further diagnoses. To speak to our allies. To cope with the diplomatic and political fallout. Good Lord, we have a crisis between the Soviets and Chinese. We have a sick President. You'll not lose your exclusive in twenty-four hours."

"What if I print something tonight?"

"Based on what? Rumor? Gossip? Based on *what?* The President is somewhat ill, and we have specialists flying in."

"A good story. A terrific story."

"You won't have Pomerance's detailed knowledge of what's wrong with the President. You won't have the White House staff at your disposal."

"And I would if . . ."

"If you wait twenty-four hours."

"It'll leak tomorrow. It'll leak *tonight*. You can't keep this quiet."

"*It will not leak,*" said Barton Taylor quietly. There was a five-second pause.

Taylor finally said: "Hugh, this places all of us in a difficult, perhaps impossible, position."

Hugh exploded. "It places *you* in a difficult position. It's *my* decision."

"And Skipper's." Barton Taylor said it in an offhand manner.

"I see," said Hugh Finch.

"No, you don't."

"What?"

"No, you *don't.*"

Barton Taylor's voice glowed with confidence.

"I think you're facing a problem, Hugh. Print some rumor-filled story tonight, and do you know what happens in the next few days? You're isolated. Totally isolated. The story becomes a one-day wonder for you. But the New York *Times* starts getting exclusives and details about the President's condition from well-known medical sources. The L.A. *Times* and Washington *Post* and AP and the Chicago *Tribune* and Boston *Globe* get briefings, selective briefings—we *do* that, you know—selective briefings on the President's condition. And the New York *Star* is not there. *Not* there. Not invited to any of the briefings. No exclusives in the New York *Star*. And in the meantime everyone else, every competitor, gets exclusives. Even an interview with the President. The *Times* and Chicago *Tribune* interviewing the President about his *condition,* and the New York *Star . . .*"

"Fucked."

"Exactly."

"I got the story, and you're threatening us to keep it out."

"For twenty-four hours."

"You'll talk to Skipper anyway, won't you?"

Bart Taylor waited a beat. "I owe him a call." As Taylor spoke, Hugh shut his eyes. "When can I see Pomerance?" he asked.

*

"We're still evaluating the President's condition," Pomerance said slowly. "More tests are being conducted tomorrow. I'm flying down to Washington in the morning."

"What exactly is 'smoldering leukemia'?"

"It's also called 'preleukemia.' Three names are associated with it: smoldering leukemia, preleukemia, aleukemic anemia. What is it? It is, uh, how shall I say, a series of clinical designations for hematologic abnormalities which may precede the development of overt leukemia."

" 'May'?"

Dr. Pomerance faced Hugh. "Yes, *may.*"

"What are the prospects of it turning into overt leukemia?" Hugh crossed his legs, keeping his notebook resting in his left hand.

"That's a difficult question to answer. I can't give you a simple answer. For one thing, details about preleukemia are still surprisingly obscure. It's only in the last couple of years that we've given attention to this disorder, which is probably far more frequent than we thought."

Hugh waited.

"All right," said Dr. Pomerance, folding his hands atop his curly gray hair and leaning back. "You asked about the prospects of it turning into acute myeloblastic leukemia. By definition, the term 'preleukemia' implies that AML is inevitable. In practice, it's not. Certainly the risk of leukemia is high. But frankly, we don't know how often these abnormalities appear in patients who never progress to overt leukemia. There's evidence that chromosome abnormalities, like the President's, may remain stable for years and years without turning into AML."

"What are the symptoms of preleukemia? When did the White House call you?"

"The symptoms are fatigue, some weight loss, pallid skin. The President has been tired lately and his physician, Admiral Linders, thought quite rightly that he was working too hard. He was jogging at the White House last Wednesday and became breathless, his heart beating heavily. Nearly collapsed. Linders gave him a blood test and found a very low hemoglobin count, 6.8."

"A normal count is . . ."

"Between 14 and 16. The 6.8 count was very low."

"So you were called in."

"I flew down Thursday."

"What did you find?"

He stared at Hugh. "I've been told by Barton Taylor to speak to you candidly, so I will. I want to emphasize as strongly as I can that there's an element of uncertainty in this case—extreme caution is warranted about making hard and fast judgments. He *probably* has preleukemia. He doesn't have AML, we think."

Dr. Pomerance leaned forward and opened a folder on his desk. "What we found caused immediate concern. About 42 percent of his cells were abnormal. Besides the 6.8 hemoglobin count, his platelets numbered 35,000. His white blood count was 1,400 with 23 percent granulocytes."

Hugh, writing quickly, said: "What does that mean?"

Dr. Pomerance sighed. "The hemoglobin carries oxygen in the blood. A low hemoglobin count—too few red blood cells—forces the heart to overwork and, unless it's diagnosed early on, could result in congestive heart failure."

"What did you do?"

"We gave the President blood transfusions."

"The platelets are what?"

"Platelets are cells that cause clotting. Essentially, it prevents you from bleeding to death if you get a shaving cut. Some people have platelet counts as high as 400,000. Low normal would be 160,000. The President's 22,000 was very, *very* low."

"And the white blood count?"

"A normal count would be 4,000 to 10,000 WBCs, with 45

percent to 75 percent granulocytes. These are the principal fighters against infection. The minimum level of safety is probably 500. With a count of 500, the body probably can repel infection. Probably. Less than 500, the patient is endangered. The President's granulocyte count was 322."

"Was he endangered?"

"I would say, uh, yes, he was."

Hugh gazed up at Pomerance, who was studying him with a frown. The doctor sipped his white wine and waited.

"Where were these tests given?"

"The NIH."

"Secretly?"

"I suppose so. I suppose you could say that."

"Why was it kept secret?"

"Ask Barton Taylor."

"Because of the Soviet-China conflict?"

Dr. Pomerance paused, then smiled.

"Ask Barton Taylor."

"Where is the President now?"

"At the White House."

"Is he . . . functioning?"

"Yes. He's working."

As Hugh turned the page of his notebook, he asked why the disease was called preleukemia. Pomerance responded that there was an element of doubt over the diagnosis, that if President Bergen were a typical leukemia patient his marrow would be packed with leukemia cells, he'd have malignant cells in the blood, he'd have such symptoms as bleeding from the gums, a fullness in the belly resulting from an enlarged liver or spleen.

Dr. Pomerance looked up. There were no myeloblasts or malignant cells in the blood, he said. Only in the marrow.

"Is he being treated? With chemotherapy or something like that?"

"We've decided to do nothing. So long as there are no blasts in the blood, there's no clinical evidence that early treatment is beneficial."

"And if there were blasts in the blood?"

"We'd have no choice. The President would have to undergo chemotherapy immediately."

"Could chemotherapy be conducted secretly?"

Dr. Pomerance shrugged. "If you're talking about the President, no. Certainly not. The effects on his skin, his hair, his weight would be evident to anyone. I assure you, Mr. Finch, the President is not undergoing chemotherapy at this point."

"What will you do now?" asked Hugh. Pomerance responded that doctors would take more tests and a bone marrow, watch and wait and see "how the disease declares itself."

"If it spreads?"

"We place the President on chemotherapy to induce a remission."

Hugh's right arm ached and his fingers, clutching the pen, trembled. *"Will* it spread?" Hugh asked firmly.

"There's no way for me to respond to that question, Mr. Finch."

"Fifty-fifty?"

"I don't like these journalistic games."

"Are you evading my question, Doctor?"

"I suppose I am. I'm used to dealing with patients and families. I try to be candid with people under circumstances where it's often quite difficult, personally, to be candid. I try to be honest because that's what people want, what *most* people want. I'm not used to dealing with the media about the physical condition of the President of the United States."

"If we were not dealing with the President but a relative of *mine,* what would you tell me?" Hugh paused. "Will it spread?"

Dr. Pomerance weighed his words. "There are some indications that leukemia becomes evident within about six months in about one third of the cases, and within one year in about one half. There are some indications that by two years perhaps three quarters of the patients have unequivocal evidence of leukemia."

He paused and swallowed. "But . . . *but* . . . and please keep this in mind . . . the preleukemic syndrome is known to last five years, ten years, twenty years. There are cases of people with this condition living quite normal lives for thirty years. And even more important, Mr. Finch, the term 'preleukemia' has been criticized because it infers progression to leukemia and is therefore assumed to be fatal. It's *not.*"

Dr. Pomerance leaned forward. "There are large numbers of

people with the same symptoms as the President who will *never* evolve into leukemics. We assume, too, that preleukemics will die of other causes before leukemia sets in. And we assume that there are people with the same condition as President Bergen who have been diagnosed by their physicians under a variety of illnesses that may include 'refractory anemia' or 'hyperspleenism' or 'aplastic anemia.'"

"Are you worried about the President?"

Pomerance's eyes darted uncomfortably around the office. "Of course."

*

Barton Taylor, seated in the den of his home on Highland Place, heard his wife in the kitchen talking to the family cook. Sunday lunch was a tradition in the Taylor home—three hours of Washington gossip spent over rare roast beef or a loin of pork washed down with Nuits St. Georges "Les Boudots," or the other burgundy he preferred, Pommard 1976 (Bullot-Milot). The men would then retire to the den—Rollie Evans and Art Buchwald and Ed Williams and Bob Strauss and sometimes even Henry Kissinger.

It was old-fashioned, of course, but Barton Taylor always said with a smile that he and his wife were old-fashioned folks.

He had just shaved and dressed when the agitated call came from Danny Fraser about Hugh Finch. Should we inform the President? asked Danny. His voice squeaked when he was nervous.

No, no, let's not bother the President with this *now*. He's up to his neck in China and Russia—enough difficulties confronting him. Let me take care of this. *This* is what he was paid for at the White House (quite inadequately, mind you), fixing and smoothing over and advising and using the network of classmates and contacts and friends in every corner of the government and the media.

Barton Taylor lit his pipe, sucking it harshly as he circled the tobacco with the flame of his silver lighter. The sweet scent mingled with the pleasant aroma of the food—yes, it was roast beef today and braised carrots and apple pie.

He smiled. Why not give Skipper a call? Haven't seen Skipper in a while. Since that nasty business with his son Larry three years ago, maybe it was four. Sordid affair. Messy. Not any more sordid

or messy than other little episodes involving, say, the Supreme
Court Justice's wife and the chauffeur—that was an ugly one because of the blackmail. Or the senator and the fourteen-year-old
girl, or the heroin habit of the cabinet officer's son, or the minority
leader who kept stealing women's underwear at Woodward and
Lothrop. Episodes dealt with quite discreetly. But the thing involving Skipper's son was so *public*. In Central Park. Was it five
or six others arrested?

Well yes. Of course. Skipper did owe him one now. Perhaps it
was time to call in the chips. What was it that Skipper said when
he had phoned in the middle of the night? He did not want to appeal personally to the police commissioner and wanted as few
people as possible to know, but perhaps Barton could quietly
assess the situation and help out the Steiners. Wouldn't the New
York *Post* or the *Daily News* wallow in a sordid story about Larry
Steiner arrested in an orgy, for God's sake, in the Ramble. In an
assortment of positions, with at least three of the participants (including Mr. Steiner) naked from the waist down, their trousers at
the knees.

Wasn't it fortunate then, extremely fortunate, that the police
commissioner, James T. Wagner, a bright Vietnam veteran who
was first in his class at Fordham Law School, had been quietly
negotiating to join the firm of Thompson, Taylor, Morrison and
Stewart. James T. Wagner had six children, three of them in Catholic high schools, and he simply could not afford their college
costs on his $56,500 salary.

So Barton Taylor flew to New York and met Commissioner
Wagner for breakfast. I'll have to be perfectly candid with you, it's
the Larry Steiner incident last night. You know about it, of
course. The boy's father has been a close friend for years. The
boy is obviously disturbed. You're a father, aren't you? Six children. Well, you *certainly* understand. Children can do foolish
things, irrational things. Not only hurt themselves but their parents. You understand, I'm sure. Children get involved with the
wrong kind of people who want to exploit their—how shall I say
it?—naïveté.

And, Commissioner, let's face it. The silly incident will not only
damage the boy's father *personally,* but it will damage the *Star*
too. Humiliate a fine paper whose editorials on the police, and the

police commissioner too, carry some influence. Mind you, some strong editorials and nice stories applauding *your* fine work, Commissioner, could certainly be helpful to you, ah, personally.

If the deal was arranged, it was left unspoken. James T. Wagner had nodded solemnly and agreed that perhaps Larry Steiner had suffered enough.

And late that afternoon, seated in his office in Washington, Bart Taylor received a phone call from the police commissioner, who said quietly that, ah, the matter we discussed has been taken care of. Taylor said, "Thank you very much, Commissioner, and by the way, can you come down for lunch next week to meet the senior partners here? They're quite eager to sit down and have a chat . . ."

Barton Taylor now lifted the White House phone on his desk, telling the operator to reach Mr. Skipper Steiner, publisher of the New York *Star*. The White House switchboard could reach anyone, at anytime, within several minutes, and it took exactly three minutes and twelve seconds before Barton Taylor's phone rang and the White House operator informed him that Mr. Steiner was on the line.

"Skipper, how are you? We haven't spoken in years. All I get from you are those wonderful Christmas cards. How's everything? . . . Good . . . And how's, uh, Larry?"

Six minutes later, after setting the phone on its cradle, Bart Taylor was suddenly struck by a marvelous idea. He had to tell his wife to invite the Wagners next week to lunch.

James Wagner had become such an able partner.

*

Skipper hung up the phone and stared at Sally, who sat on the Chesterfield sofa, her feet tucked beneath her buttocks, looking at the *Star*.

"Important?" she said, turning a page.

Skipper had walked across the drawing room and stood at the high, unadorned window, with a vista of Central Park below.

His hair was fringed with gray now, and the outline of his stomach, through his V-neck sweater, made her aware that he was turning just slightly flabby. He wore cavalry twill trousers and an open-necked shirt beneath the woolen sweater. His tasseled loafers with brass eyelets gleamed.

"What?" said Skipper vaguely. He was staring out the window. "The White House call." Sally waited. "What's wrong?"

Skipper lit a cigarette. "Too many things happening at once." He avoided her eyes. "Frieda called this morning. She's not going back to Bella Verde, she's staying in town." He looked up. "She said she had an interesting conversation with Eli Faber."

"Uh-oh."

"The slimy son of a bitch."

"One of Frieda's untouchables."

"I think Eli's fantasy was that *he* would run the paper one day," said Skipper, pouring himself a glass of scotch.

"Publisher?" Sally lit a cigarette.

"It's not that farfetched. Eli was Frederic's surrogate son. Eli was *nothing,* but he was smart—probably smarter than Uncle Arnold, maybe even smarter than my father. And loyal, ambitious."

"He knows the paper."

Skipper turned to her. "Knows every corner of the paper, better than I do, better than Frieda. He's worked in virtually every department. Probably knows every employee over forty-five. Knows where all the bodies are buried. Old Eli's part of the woodwork."

She stared at the curled black hairs on his wrist and fingers. His voice—his soft, calm voice—assured her. She yearned to touch his arm, but held back. She wanted his hands on her, the strength of his hands over her. *Hold me. Just hold me.*

"I think Eli had certain notions," Skipper was saying. "When Uncle Arnold died there was a moment when Frederic wavered. Could have made Eli his heir. But Frieda fought it. Got my father to go to Frederic and offer himself."

She watched his lips, her eyes fixed on a razor cut beneath his nostrils. One day without shaving, and he resembled the swarthy fishermen that Charlie had photographed during their vacation two summers ago in Mykonos.

Charlie . . .

Golden Charlie . . .

"My father barely made it at first," Skipper was saying. "But with Eli beside him, guiding him, and with Frieda behind him, pushing him, he made it."

"Eli resented your father," Sally said.

"Resented my father, and sure as hell resented me," said Skipper. "When my father had his stroke, the only heir apparent was *me*. I was young, without experience. Lucy, being a woman, was out of the question then. Eli was trustee. He was close to Frieda. He knew the paper better than anyone."

"But he wasn't a Steiner."

"Exactly. He wasn't a Steiner. And now we're getting Johanna to come down from Cambridge to work on the paper . . ."

"Who does *he* want to be managing editor?"

Skipper winced.

"Who do *you* want?" Sally persisted.

Outside, the distant muffled sound of a police siren lingered on Fifth Avenue.

"Maury." Skipper spoke as quietly as he could. "I'm sorry," he said, watching her.

Sally smiled.

"He deserves it," said Skipper.

"Of course."

"Did you want it badly?"

"I wanted it, Skipper. I wasn't going to move heaven and earth to get it, but I *wanted* it."

"It's time we appointed a woman to the job, is that what you're saying?"

Sally was struck by the coldness in his voice.

"Do you actually want to be appointed because you're a woman? Affirmative action? Is that what you want? Look at the men we're considering. Maury deserves it. He's worked his ass off for the paper, a loyal, decent man. Barry Cohen, a Pulitzer Prize. We care deeply about the Pulitzer Prize."

"It's nonsense."

"Of course it's nonsense. I know it's nonsense and you know it's nonsense, but the paper, as an institution, takes the prize with deadly seriousness and we *reward* our winners. Besides, Barry knows the paper too. He began as a copy boy. He's worked on every desk. Why not Barry?"

"Because Barry is . . ."

"One second. Hugh Finch has been brilliant in the last couple of days on the China story. Wonderful reporter. And black. Yes. Why not Finch? And Ward Parsons. A superb foreign correspondent. The best foreign editor we've had in years. Inspires tremendous loyalty. What *about* Ward?"

Sally stood up, ignoring his eyes, and slowly walked across the uncarpeted bleached floors into the study adjoining the living room. She opened the liquor cabinet and poured herself a Bourbon and soda, adding two cubes of ice from the silver bucket.

She sat on the banquette in the study and sipped her drink.

Skipper came in.

"I like this room," said Sally, staring at her drink. "Guess I want to be alone."

Skipper moved beside her. "What do you want to do on the paper? Any job. It's yours."

"Except . . ."

"You want it that badly?"

"I think I'm bored, Skipper. Maybe a little tired. That's a hell of a sales pitch to be managing editor. I'm bored and tired and I think . . ."

"Yeah?"

"I think I'm a little lonely."

Tears filled her eyes. "Oh Christ. Oh Lord. Why do I have to do this?" Her right hand flew to her face. "Just like everyone else. The paper, the goddamn paper, is the only thing we have. It's mother and father and lover."

He kissed her on the neck, and his lips and tongue glided gently around her left ear. "You're lovely," he whispered.

"We've got to stop."

"No, no," he said, licking her neck now.

Sally thrust up and held his face in her hands, kissing him fiercely. "I want the job, Skipper. I want it!" Their eyes locked. "If it means the end of us, the end of *this,* that's okay too. I *want* the job."

Skipper struggled to draw back, but Sally's fingers tightened over his hair.

"It's *that* important?" he said.

"I want to be treated just like them," Sally said quickly. "Ward. Maury. Barry. Hugh. No better, no worse. Take me seriously, Skipper. Give me a chance."

Her voice wavered. As Skipper lifted his left hand and gently ran his fingers over the side of her face, Sally felt her strength ebb.

"You have a chance," she heard him say. "There's two days left."

"A chance!"

"I want you," he said, lifting her sweater and easily unfastening her bra. He massaged her breasts, kissing her on the neck and lips and hair. Then he held one breast in his hand and sucked.

"Stop. Please!"

"I want you, darling. I need you."

She closed her eyes, arching her neck back, smelling his hair and sweat, feeling his soft cheek on her chest. Tears stained Sally's face. His mouth moved over her stomach, his tongue probing. She felt his strong hands on her thighs and hips, and swiftly Skipper was crouching on the floor, unfastening her trousers, removing her sandals. He lifted her legs now, tossing her trousers away.

Her hands stroked Skipper's hair as he kissed her, biting gently, chewing. She wanted to pull him up, but he kept her legs apart as he probed with his mouth: she lay back on the sofa and surrendered to his hands and lips and tongue. He was caressing her now with two fingers and thumbs, and Sally gasped, the slow, twisting movements of his fingers now leaving her wet and yielding, her belly and throat tight with tension. She began to weep. Flames flickered from her crotch into her stomach and neck. Skipper had stopped and was standing now and she heard him unzip his trousers and, opening her eyes, she saw him unfasten his plaid shirt and drop it on the floor. She stared at his broad chest, then took hold of his penis.

Skipper groaned, gazing down at her, and then closed his eyes as she lifted herself up and guided him closer to the sofa.

*

Linda Fentress dreaded the prospect of renting an Avis car. Taxi service was haphazard in Los Angeles, you had to have wheels. The freeways frightened her: the seventy-mile-an-hour traffic, her own confused sense of direction, the inability to think but just to drive—*drive*—on this flat maze of highways, left her wet with perspiration and trembling, yearning for the Broadway-IRT subway line or the bus on Central Park West.

Gregory Hamalian had offered to pick up Linda and drive her to his house in Malibu. Linda accepted, grateful for the one-day respite from having to drive herself. This is dumb, she thought, foolish, I've got to rent a goddamn car.

Linda picked up the phone and ordered one, then she swallowed a Valium and made sure a new notebook and at least three pens were tucked into her brown leather shoulder bag. She left the room to meet Gregory in the lobby at nine-thirty.

Everything about Gregory Hamalian seemed to have shrunk—his abundant belly had disappeared, his luxuriant beard was now carefully trimmed, his shoulder-length hair was now reduced to a rather soberly cut French style that accented his wide cheekbones and narrow mouth.

"Jesus, you're gorgeous," said Linda, kissing him.

"Midlife crisis. Male menopause."

"What have you done?"

"Swimming every day. Running along the beach at least three times a week. Stopped heavy drinking, stopped eating crap."

"What else have you stopped?"

"Except for one or two things, practically everything."

She grinned. "Is this what happens to guys in California who reach a certain age?"

"Sshh," said Gregory. "After forty you're supposed to disappear into the ocean. I'm lingering past my time."

They walked to his battered Dodge Colt at the hotel entrance. A soft rain had left the empty street damp, and Linda shivered as she climbed into the car.

It was the loneliness that seized her on the road; the empty hours in hotel rooms, too much drinking in bars, eating on the run, the alarming sense of rootlessness, migraines.

Linda took a drag on her cigarette. "This is not my kind of story, Gregory. Up against Pirota and friend from the *Daily News.*"

"Irwin Roth from the *Times* called."

"*Fuck.*"

"He's at the Bonaventure."

"What did you tell him?"

"Zilch."

"We got the *Daily News* guys, then Irwin Roth—who's better than both of the *News* guys together—probably the full resources of the L.A. *Times* and Christ knows who else working on the same story. Wonderful," Linda said.

He stopped at a light on Wilshire Boulevard.

"Tell me about Lois Barrie," said Linda.

Instinctively, she removed her notebook from her pocketbook and pressed down on her ball-point pen. Gregory watched the light turn green and started the car.

"An old friend," said Gregory. "I directed her in a couple of TV shows in the early sixties. Floundered for years. Never made a dime until 'The Fraser Family.' "

"Did she sleep with Nelson?"

He shrugged. "I think Lois slept with a lot of people."

"Did you sleep with her?"

"Lois Barrie slept with a lot of people."

Lois Barrie had won four Emmies, been a regular on the "Johnny Carson Show" and appeared on the covers of *People* and *Newsweek* as a result of her long-running comedy series about the working, divorced mother of three teen-age children. "The Fraser Family" had been among the top ten television shows for the past four years and had dealt, with unusual candor for television, with such subjects as illegitimacy, masturbation, abortion and teen-age sex.

Gregory said, "She's seeing you because I told her you were a reliable, honest journalist and not a jerk."

"Thanks."

"Told her she can trust you."

Linda nodded.

"Did some checking, made a couple of calls about Elliott Hanley."

Linda quickly turned the pages of her notebook. " 'Your standard Hollywood queen director.' That's what you said."

"He signed some dumb-ass petitions in the late forties. He was on something called the End Jim Crow in Movies Committee. He edited a documentary about the heroism of the Russians in the Battle of Leningrad."

"And he was blacklisted?"

"For five or six years. By this guy Keefer, Joe Keefer. State senator. Ran a miserable little witch-hunt on the industry."

Linda started writing. "Elliott Hanley was a buddy of Vice President Nelson."

Gregory said, "Hanley gave Nelson his first big job. Knew Nelson when he was a struggling actor. The interesting thing"— Gregory stopped at another light on San Vincente and turned to Linda—"the interesting thing is that Marcus Lynn produced that film."

"I had lunch with him yesterday. Scary." She lowered her voice to a whisper. "Hear anything about our Vice President making porno movies years ago?"

Gregory shook his head.

"Marcus Lynn passed it on as a fact," Linda said.

"Jesus!"

"Marcus said I should get to someone named Paul Brock."

"The Cecil B. De Mille of the porno industry."

"I left two messages at his office," said Linda.

"He discovered quote unquote that fourteen-year-old girl who played a whore in that disaster by Bertolucci. April Talbott."

"The one with the mother, the beautiful mother, who looks like she's twenty-five?"

"The mother is forty. He's done both of them. Together. Threesomes. Mother, daughter, and Paul."

She glanced at him.

"I shock easily," said Linda.

Linda turned to the back flap of her notebook and began writing another list:

Elliott Hanley—director, first break.

Lois Barrie—girlfriend?

Joe Keefer—dead. State senator. Blacklister. Brother-in-law of David Fitzgerald. Name keeps coming up.

Paul Brock—porno king.

Marcus Lynn?

Linda spoke intensely. "Got to find out Nelson's early addresses. Where he lived. What he *did*."

Her eyes scanned the names.

"If he was making porno films, if he was doing anything *weird* like that, it was just after he got out of the Army, maybe while he was still in the Army, those early years when he was scrounging around."

Linda lit another cigarette. "We have all this junk in our
morgue, all those bios, that just kind of wash over those early
years. No one really checked."

"You sound like 'Police Woman.' "

"A guy I once knew in New York, an editor, taught me: 'Good
reporters think the worst of people.' "

"Guilty until proven otherwise."

"Exactly." She shook her head. "It's odd. Nothing about those
three or four years, except that he was a struggling young actor.
Nothing about what he did, where he lived, how he struggled."

A curtain of fog blanketed Pacific Coast Highway. Gregory
switched on the car's low lights, driving slowly along the wet road.
Linda heard the sound of waves, gulls close by. She opened the
window full, allowing the cold, damp air to lap her neck and forehead.

Gregory veered the car into the driveway of his pale stucco
house. A half-dozen Ficus trees and an arbor of logs covered the
entrance. A silver-gray Rolls-Royce was parked in the pebbled
driveway. The California license number was LB-1.

Gregory said, "That's not my car, honey."

"I've always wanted to meet a movie star."

*

The telephone was ringing, startling Lucy awake.

"Lucy, are you up? You sound sleepy." It was Frieda.

"What time is it?"

"Eleven-fifteen."

"My God."

"Darling," said Frieda. "Skipper wants to see us. Both of us,
this afternoon. He suggested one-thirty."

"What's it about?"

"What?"

"I asked, What is it about?"

"Skipper said it was quite important—those were the words he
used, 'quite important.' " Lucy winced at the agitation in her
mother's voice.

"I'll be there at one-thirty," Lucy said.

*

On Sunday, the *Star*'s newsroom awakens slowly and lingers,
through the day, in a pleasant torpor. Even the clatter of the AP,

UPI and Reuters machines seem muffled, as if the chaos of events in the nation and abroad had somehow drifted into an abrupt lull before Monday's outpouring of news stories. Sport shirts and jeans and unshaven faces are visible, whereas during the week the newsroom maintains an unspoken decorum (Evan frowned at reporters without ties).

The weekend staff is, in fact, a curious mixture of men and women on the way down or up, bewildered ex-foreign correspondents seated beside hungry twenty-six-year-old reporters craving front-page bylines; once powerful political reporters and men in their fifties and sixties—talented journalists and elegant writers swept under by age, melancholy, fury at the newspaper for consuming their talents and energies and discarding them in favor of the newer breed—doomed to the humiliation of writing obituaries now, and covering empty press conferences in Queens, and serving as a "leg man" for some new hotshot recently hired from *Time* magazine. Precisely what they did thirty years before.

Younger reporters are especially attracted to weekend work. Press conferences and features and news stories, normally handled by the front-line staff during the week, are left, for two days, in the hands of the weekend staff, affording them the opportunity to get a byline on a decent story, to write a feature, accompanied by a picture, guaranteed to get a nice play in the paper and a note in your mailbox from Barry Cohen saying that was a fine job or excellent story or salutations or we really beat the competition on that one.

Shortly before twelve-forty on this Sunday, Tony Lazzarutti, the foreign desk clerk, rushed into the near-empty newsroom, head down, lips firmly pursed, loping to the copy desk, trying not to actually run. He carried a paper bag, wet at the bottom, with a container of black coffee and a danish pastry.

"Good afternoon, Tony." It was Nick Simons, the city desk clerk, about five yards away. Nick's words were edged in sarcasm.

Tony's eyes fell on the news copy and messages strewn on his desk, waiting to be sorted.

"In your prolonged absence I took a few calls," Nick said. As usual, Nick had arrived at work an hour early. Clean-shaven, starched white shirt, even on Sunday. Nick had once told Tony that he would be named managing editor one day.

Tony sat down at the desk, trying to concentrate on the messages and copy. He had fifteen minutes, perhaps twenty, before the first two editors would arrive.

"Your father called at twelve-fifteen," said Nick Simons. "And Ward Parsons called."

Tony turned, startled.

"Twice."

"What?"

"He called twice. Twelve-fifteen. And about twelve thirty-five."

"What'd you tell him?"

"I told him you were banging Raquel Welch on the newsroom floor. What could I tell him? I told him you were probably stuck on the subway. The IRT. You know. It's bad on Sundays."

Oh *fuck*. Tony turned and picked up the phone, found Ward Parsons' number on a list of editors beneath the glass cover on the desk.

Could he help it if every goddamn Saturday night his two roommates on 112th Street had to invite what seemed like all of Columbia Law School and every weird girl north of Ninety-sixth Street to their house. BYOB—Bring your own bottle. Could he help it if the flood of beer and cheap wine and pretzels left him physically incapable of even turning off the alarm clock at eleven o'clock on Sunday morning to dress and throw some cold water on his face and crawl downtown to the newsroom.

He could lie to Ward—the IRT broke down at Seventy-second Street, someone jumped on Ninety-sixth Street—but as soon as the foreign editor picked up the phone he blurted out the words:

"I'm sorry, Mr. Parsons. This is Tony Lazzarutti. I'm sorry. I just got in late."

Ward sighed. All he wanted was the Soviet-China copy. Any summaries? Any messages?

"Give me five minutes and I'll call you right back."

Tony hung up, began leafing through the papers and wire stories piled on the desk, and turned on his video terminal.

The phone rang. It was his father.

"Dad, look, let me call you later. I got in late . . ."

"I know. You're supposed to start working at noon, right?" Frank Lazzarutti, chairperson of the paper's Newspaper Guild unit, had been an accountant in the *Star*'s auditing department for twenty-three years, and had never been late for work.

"Right, right. Look, I'm swamped," said Tony. "The China-Russia story."

His father sounded annoyed. "First of all, if you're supposed to start working at twelve you should be in by twelve, you should be in at *five* to twelve. Second of all, the reason I'm calling is to tell you to please call your mother. You haven't phoned in five days . . ."

"Dad, I'm . . ."

"It's her birthday."

Christ! His mother's birthday! Completely forgotten. He would phone later.

Get the Soviet-China copy fast.

Dad was turning off the oven right now. The Sunday ritual. Between 12:45 and 1 P.M., turning off the oven and allowing the loin of pork or the ham to simmer. Listening to the WINS news—Dad listening to the news all day—humming softly, impatiently glancing at his watch, waiting for Mom and the girls to return from St. Theresa's.

Dad, I'm not screwing up.

Sunday lunch Dad would grumble about the *Star,* the owners and Eli and their Ivy League henchmen, the new breed, dismissing loyal employees who had given fifteen and twenty years to the paper, calling them irrelevant, replaced by machines, the heartless sons of bitches.

Marie Lazzarutti would grin and say, "Oh come on, Frank, you love it, you love the paper, you love working there. You run the union like a Mafia don or, better yet, like a tough parish priest in the archdiocese."

"I did love the paper," Frank would say, "when the old man was there."

Hard to believe, thought Tony, leafing through the copy, that the Steiners and Faber detested and feared Dad, that his own father was a figure of some awe, especially among the older employees, his own father . . .

He had heard the stories so many times as a kid on Sunday afternoons: how Dad forged his birth certificate at fifteen to work as Frederic Steiner's personal messenger, a scrappy kid from Little

Italy, Mulberry Street, whom the old man—then in his waning days—took under his wing.

How Frank went to Frederic Steiner one afternoon, nervous as hell, and said if you don't mind me saying so, sir, no one reads the *Star* in my neighborhood, in Little Italy and in Chinatown, the parents read the *Daily News,* and in high school we get the *Times* cheap, and if I can suggest, sir, a lot of my friends go to parochial schools. So Frederic looked at him puzzled, and Frank said, You hire some Irish and Italian boys as salesmen. You go to parochial schools. First you offer the school a little gift for its fund-raising drive for a new gym. They're always having a fund-raising drive. A little gift for the school from the *Star.* Then, a week later, your salesman offers a free copy of the *Star,* including the Sunday *Star* to each teacher if the class takes the *Star* at a cut rate. Sir?

Yes.

I think you could get every Catholic school in Lower Manhattan to do this. And the kids bring the paper home for Mom and Dad to read.

That's interesting, Frank.

I've been thinking about it, sir.

Do you know Eli Faber? My son, Jonathan?

No, sir.

Both of them are working on circulation. We're not too successful in certain, well, ethnic parts of the city.

Yes, sir.

You be here this afternoon at five o'clock. This office. I want you to talk to Eli and Jonathan.

It was Frederic's intent to find tough, able youths, totally loyal to the New York *Star,* and guide their careers within the organization. Two decades earlier, at the peak of his career, Frederic had hand-picked Eli Faber. Now, seven years after Arnold's death, as Frederic's life visibly drained, the Lazzarutti boy suddenly stirred him.

Frank plainly reminded the old man of Arnold. If the Italian youth was taller than Arnold, with broader shoulders and a trimmer waist, he had, nonetheless, the same wide, black eyes and wavy hair. A firm handshake and open smile. The same exuberance with other employees, the same quality that evoked confidence among employees. A gifted leader. Undevious. Tough.

Intelligent. The boy has a *future,* Frederic would say with a grin whenever Frank left his office.

But Frederic's death in 1952, and the ascension of his son Jonathan, had abruptly severed Frank's career on the management side of the *Star.* Jonathan, hardly a vindictive man, had grown increasingly resentful of the old man's outpouring of affection for Frank, of stories about Frank Lazzarutti's street-smart ways and his fierce work habits and his "leadership qualities." And only nineteen years old. A hell of a quick learner.

Rationally, Jonathan Steiner's fear of his father's office boy made little sense. Frank was hardly a threat to the future publisher of the *Star.* But the old man's gleeful stories about Frank Lazzarutti, his obvious pride in him, the offhand comparison to Arnold, left Jonathan Steiner seething. The void left by Arnold's death was being filled by this boy.

It was many years later that Frank had finally pieced together the full story of the events that followed Frederic Steiner's death, the events that had left him puzzled at the time, and hurt, and finally furious.

Frieda Steiner had understood her husband's unspoken fears. Totally supportive of Jonathan, keeping a wary eye on any hint of competition, Frieda listened in alarm to her father-in-law's stories about Frank Lazzarutti. *It was cruel to Jonathan, not fair.*

Even before Frederic's death, Frieda had decided that she detested Lazzarutti. Pushy. A wise guy. No class. And within hours after Frederic's collapse in Helena Standish's bed, Frieda sat with Eli Faber in her living room, saying perhaps it would be best, after all, to bring in an entirely new staff in the publisher's office. Start afresh. Transfer the secretaries to other departments. Redo the offices. Place Frank Lazzarutti in something more suitable to his talents, like the accounting department.

And Eli, who was fond of Frank but understood the inchoate anger stirred by the innocent youth, the threatening nature of Frank's presence to Frieda and Jonathan, said, yes, that was a fine idea.

Within two weeks Frank was informed by Eli Faber that he was being promoted to the accounting department as a trainee, an opportunity that pleased him, although Frank told Eli about ten days later, when they met in the elevator, how much he missed working in the publisher's office.

It was a story Tony Lazzarutti had heard so many times, yet its full meaning eluded him until he was hired as foreign desk clerk. (As Newspaper Guild Chairman, Frank had demanded that the *Star* hire the children of union officials with the same priority that they employed the Ivy League kids whose fathers knew Skipper.) Witnessing his father's power and broad popularity among employees, Tony suddenly realized that the energy, the toughness, the ambitions that Frank Lazzarutti deployed against the Steiners could have so easily shifted the other way; that fate, and Frieda Steiner and some of the tricks of his life had turned Frank into a union boss when, at the same time, he could so easily have emerged as an executive on the *Star*.

As foreign desk clerk, Tony sorted the incoming copy, keeping wire-service stories neatly filed in slots on a wooden shelf beside him. He answered phones, placed calls overseas for the foreign editor, and sent messages abroad at the behest of the day and night foreign editors and slotmen.

Unlike Nick Simons and the other clerks in the city room struggling for promotion, Tony had no desire to remain in the newspaper business. He wanted to work in public-interest law, although his father had firmly suggested a more lucrative field. Yet the newspaper job and people fascinated him—the frenetic tempo of the work close to deadline, the easy camaraderie of the copy editors on the desk, the odd fervor of these anonymous men and women who edited each story to an allotted amount of space, who fit headlines over the story, who retained an impressive and arcane knowledge of dates and events and personalities.

Nameless people they were, the copy editors who groaned at a reporter's syntax, spelling, writing gimmicks and sloppy use of facts. They read incoming messages, knew of the reporter's marital problems, his bouts of influenza, his conflicts with the foreign ministry or the landlord or the American Embassy. There was a vicarious element to reading the incoming messages each day. No privacy, Tony thought, as he glanced at a message from Cairo:

PARSONS INFORMATIVELY APPLIED FOR CHINA VISA AND AWAITING WORD FROM INSCRUTABLE VISA OFFICER WHO ACKNOWLEDGED REQUEST BEING SENT PEKING. AM TAKING TWO DAYS OFF AS HAVE

COME DOWN WITH WHAT CAN ONLY BE DESCRIBED AS DELHI BELLY
IN CAIRO ALLBEST FAIRCHILD.

Tony placed the message beside the telephone: anything linked
to the China-Soviet conflict would be set on this separate pile and
read to Ward Parsons. He leafed through the other messages.
From London, Larry Lake said that he was surprised and, quite
frankly, upset that his story on the role of the Royal Family in
British life had not yet run in the *Star.*

INFORMATIVELY I HEAR TIME AND NEWSWEEK PLANNING
LONGISH PIECES AND SUGGEST WE RUN MY STORY SOONEST.
REGARDS LAKE. (Tony knew the message would be greeted with
laughter on the foreign desk. It was a common ploy among foreign
correspondents to claim that their stories should be published immediately because *Time, Newsweek,* the New York *Times,* the
Washington *Post* or *someone* was about to print the same story.)

Lorraine Hudson was arriving in Vienna Monday, staying at the
Intercontinental, and had set up appointments with East European
watchers for a reaction story on the China-Soviet dispute.

Marty Kaplan had arrived in New York from Buenos Aires,
staying at the Plaza.

From Moscow, Ernie Richards said that rumors were sweeping
town of a major Chinese nuclear test on Monday in Asia. Could
the Pentagon or State Department people check this one out.

There were other messages that Tony glanced at, placing them
on the "A" pile—to be read to the foreign editor—or the "B" pile.
He nearly placed the one from New Delhi marked "urgent" on the
"B" pile. He read it quickly and, since it said nothing about China
and Russia, was about to place the sheet of paper in the secondary
group. But he read it again.

WARD HAVE BEEN TRYING TO REACH YOU FOR TWELVE HOURS
BUT PHONE LINES HAVE COLLAPSED OR SOMETHING. PLEASE PHONE
ME AS SOON AS YOU CAN AT THE HOUSE. VAL IS VERY ILL. DOCTORS
SAY POSSIBLE MENINGITIS. AM WORRIED. ALARMED. PLEASE REACH
ME. KAREN.

"Sir, there's an urgent message from your wife," said Tony, moments later, over the phone. He read it slowly.

Tony thought he heard a slight gasp over the phone, followed
by an eight-second pause. The foreign editor finally said he would

come down to the office immediately. In the meantime, Ward wanted Tony to send an urgent message to Karen.

"All right. One sec, sir." Tony swiveled to the video terminal. He cradled the phone against his ear.

Ward spoke quietly, hesitantly. "Karen, is there anything to be done at this end? What about departing New Delhi? Please send more detailed message of Val's illness. I will make immediate checks with doctors here. Extremely worried about all of you. Speak to you in the next hour. Regards Ward."

"Is that it, sir?"

"Uh, change it," said Ward Parsons. "Change the last word. Instead of regards make it love. Love Ward."

"Okay, sir."

Tony Lazzarutti hung up the phone and saw Howie Bishop, gripping a valise and typewriter, move to his desk in a corner of the newsroom. The paper's star investigative reporter. Tough, abusive, bullying.

Tony watched Bishop lift the phone and start dialing. Howie Bishop's sandy hair, flecked with gray, spilled over his forehead. His striped button-down shirts were inevitably rumpled and rolled up at the sleeves, his collar button open and his tie loosened to his chest. His baggy trousers fell beneath his waist, leaving his shirt draped loosely over his belt. Often his shirttail flopped out.

Three weeks earlier Tony had read an article in *Esquire* magazine about Howie Bishop and two other investigative reporters—a woman on the Chicago *Tribune* and a kid on the Philadelphia *Inquirer*. The magazine called the reporters "the nation's new folk heroes. America's watchdogs."

"Tireless. Relentless. Obsessed with the truth."

That's what the magazine said.

"Like his city editor and mentor Barry Cohen, Howie Bishop has a sense of outrage. A compulsion to lay the villains low."

*

Barry Cohen was reading the sports section of the *Star* when the phone rang. He got up from the sofa, scenting the freshly brewed coffee that clung to the apartment. Lifting the phone, he heard Margie in the kitchen.

"Bishop here." It was Howie's urgent voice. "I'm back in town, Barry. In the newsroom." Howie waited. "Don't like the story."

"Don't *like* it?"

"Two hours after I talked to you on the phone, Barry, an envelope's delivered to my room. I look inside. Fifteen thousand dollars."

"So? It's for Cheryl."

"I *know* it's for Cheryl, Barry. I know and it stinks." Howie took a tremulous breath. "You're pushing too hard. Too fast. Get someone else. Deliver the money to Cheryl . . ."

"Getting soft, Howie?"

Howie ignored him. "Fitzgerald's one thing. Don't mind going after that son of a bitch. But Jerry . . ."

"Jerry's what?"

"One of us," Howie said through clenched teeth. "We *know* him. Jerry's the fall guy, you know that, Barry."

Barry's voice was very cold. "Where I go, you go, Howie. Remember that."

"Besides, he's got the kid, little Angela. Jesus."

"I'm promoted, so are you, Howie. I'm kicked out on my ass, you are too. We're together, fella." Barry's voice fell to a whisper. "Took you from nowhere, Howie, real estate news. Can drop you right back in there. You want to write obits, do transportation news, go on to rewrite? I'll *do* it, Howie. You want to leave the *Star*? Get another job? Try it, Howie. The Washington *Post* has got kids half your age doing it better. The *Times*? No way. You're a bad egg in the business. You smell a little bit. Got a reputation, loose with the facts. A bit of a thug."

"Under your guidance," said Howie Bishop dryly.

"You're going to fly back to Washington and get the diary from Cheryl tonight, and *I'll* see Jerry tomorrow. I'll take care of Jerry. And tomorrow night we're going to have one hell of a front-page package, you from New York and Linda from L.A."

"You want it too much, Barry."

"And Howie, if I get the job, if that miracle does take place, you know what? You're going to be my deputy."

Howie closed his eyes. "Thanks."

Barry slammed the phone down as Margie walked into the dining room from the kitchen. She placed an electric coffee pot on a mat in the center of the round oak table beside a white marble tray with a chunk of Cheddar cheese, and a ball of Edam surrounded by three toasted bagels.

"Why do you like me, Margie?"

She turned away. "I always fall for the wrong guys. A personality flaw."

"Where do you live?"

"Uptown. Eighty-eighth Street, near Columbus."

"You live alone?"

"Sometimes." She knifed off a chunk of Cheddar, placing the cheese on her plate. With her thumb and forefinger, she picked up the cheese and ate it. "I'm alone now. The guy I've been living with is out on the Coast. An actor." Barry watched her. Margie's auburn hair fell to the shoulders of her blue sweater. Her narrow hazel eyes stared blankly at the coffee cup.

"You like rough stuff," he said quietly.

She shrugged, "Whatever," and lit a cigarette.

"Where you from?"

"Pennsylvania. Steel mill country. Bucks County. The unfancy part. *Very* unfancy." Margie's eyes flickered on Barry, then returned to the coffee cup.

"Big family?"

"Too big. They're either in the church or the steel mill." She sucked the cigarette. "One brother's a priest. Two of my sisters are nuns. Yeah. The older and younger one. I even thought about it for a while. Can you see me as a nun?"

"No," said Barry quietly.

"Another brother works in the steel mill," she said. "He would have been a priest too, but he got fucked up in the war. Got a head wound. Can't concentrate."

"Vietnam?"

"Yeah." She placed the cigarette in an ashtray, watching the smoke curl in the air. "Everybody went to Vietnam in my town." She shrugged. "My high school class. About eight of them didn't come back. One guy's a quadriplegic." Margie shook her head.

"Were you in Vietnam?" she asked.

"For the *Star*. Yeah."

"I saw a photo in the kitchen. Up in the cabinet when I was getting cups. You and some guy. Is he Vietnamese?"

"His name is Chan. He called himself Charlie Chan. Some idiot photographer once told him that he spelled his name like Charlie Chan, so that's what he called himself." Barry poured coffee into his cup, then stirred the brew silently. "His real name was Nguyen Vo, Nguyen Vo Chan. He was our bureau's reporter, translator, go-between, everything."

"What happened to him?"

Barry stared past her. "Left behind when Saigon collapsed."

"You think he's alive?"

"No." Barry sipped his coffee and listened to an ambulance screaming past the house. "Someone who worked in the bureau, Dorothy Faye, she got a note from his brother a couple of months ago."

"Saw her on Dick Cavett. She wrote that book."

Barry nodded.

"He was sent to a reeducation camp near Hanoi. Got a fever and died."

Maggie crushed her cigarette in an ashtray. "You miss it?" she asked.

"Miss what?"

"Vietnam."

"No one ever asked me if I missed it."

"I am."

His eyes lingered on the coffee cup. "Suppose I do. Suppose a lot of guys do. Dorothy does. We all miss it. It was the high point, honey."

Barry walked into the living room and picked up the ringing phone. Margie lifted her shoeless right foot on the chair, folding her hands around her ankle. She heard Barry on the phone, making another appointment to visit the Carlyle.

CHAPTER 12

By the time Frieda arrived at Skipper's apartment, Lucy was already there sipping coffee. Frieda greeted her son with a kiss on the cheek, and over his shoulder scrutinized the steaming mug in Lucy's hand with a frown.

Frieda knew that she tended to complain and babble nervously at moments like these abrupt business conferences in Skipper's apartment. What in God's name was the emergency on Sunday morning? Not that she minded. Not at all. She could see Lucy and Skipper and later, perhaps, tell Skipper about her conversation with Eli Faber. Skipper resented Eli and vice versa, but Eli certainly seemed to have some valid points about dealing with the unions now. Teach them a lesson. That dreadful man who now ran the Newspaper Guild—Lazzarutti, Frank Lazzarutti. Dreadful. Ingrate. Rabble-rouser. His predecessors were, at least, pliant or dumb or quietly bought off by Frederic and then Jonathan. Some cash gifts once a month, some stock in a child's name never hurt anyone. There was even one union leader who received his payments in a Zurich bank account. Small payments, mind you, but worth every cent, a guarantee that come September and October the Guild won't decide to push for *unnecessary* pay and health and security benefits, threatening to close the paper at the height of the advertising rush, the moneymaking season.

Frieda heard her son and daughter speak of Johanna. Although Frieda had lost hearing in her right ear, her vanity barred the use of a plastic device. I'm just an old, deaf woman, she suggested to an author who wanted to write a book about the *Star*. I meddle, but, frankly, dear, I have no power. She believed it, she *wanted* to believe that her power was marginal, that the men traditionally controlled the paper—had always controlled the paper—leaving her, quite naturally, in a vaguely defined, subordinate role. Frieda resented any implication that she had extraordinary power; she knew the gossip, but it was totally off base. If she had been raised in a different way, at a different time, if she had built her life on certain assumptions that it was perfectly normal for women to work, she would have exercised the kind of power that Dolly Schiff and Katherine Graham and even Buff Chandler had applied. She *could* have been the formidable figure that people believed she was. But she was not formidable. Despite what Eli Faber said. Her role was . . . meddling . . . carping . . . prodding . . . She was a foolish, slightly deaf woman with poor vision in her right eye, a touch of rheumatism in her shoulders and old-fashioned ideas. She missed Bella Verde and the bougainvillea and

potted cannas and kangaroo vines and Kohleria. She missed her
spice garden.

Frieda closed her eyes for a moment. And yet . . . and yet . . .
Eli was absolutely right. She could hardly ignore her responsibility
to Jonathan and the Steiner family and the New York *Star*.

Eli had phoned her on Sunday morning, just as Frieda was
stepping out the door en route to Skipper's apartment. *Can I see
you on Monday?*

Well, yes, of course, Eli, she said. *Is there anything . . . special?*

*Frieda, let's talk at lunch. I'll meet you in the Russian Tea
Room.*

The phone call had disturbed her. Two meetings with Eli in
three days. It was as if she were participating in secret, conspir-
atorial meetings about the *Star* and her son's management of the
family paper; as if, somehow, she was engaged in negotiations
against Skipper's interests.

She would inform Skipper. Tell her son what Eli had said about
the paper's finances. Do we actually need to fly three foreign correspondents from their home base because of this border crisis?
Aren't expenses, especially overseas, getting out of hand? The
paper is so lean now, advertising's fallen off, circulation's dropping, the cost of paper and print are rising . . .

Yes, she would tell Skipper this morning about her meeting
with Eli on Saturday. Let's keep this aboveboard, even if Skipper
resented Eli, didn't appreciate his loyalty and value to the paper.
Let's be adults, not children. Let's forget petty squabbles. What
counts in the end is the *Star,* the future of the *Star,* and let's not
get bogged down in personality conflicts.

Skipper was refilling her mug, and her son and daughter were
still chatting about Johanna coming to New York. Joining the
Star. Frieda gazed at her son. A handsome man, she thought. Always handsome. Thank God he took after the Steiner side of the
family. Taller than Jonathan, though, heftier, the same shoulders
and torso as Frederic. The same body and appetites of his grandfather. Not quite as blatant, not quite as aggressive, but he enjoyed women in the same way. The same grin, the same hands and
fingers, the hairy fingers, the same as . . .

Arnold.

Her husband's brother, Arnold Steiner.

Frieda watched Skipper. Her hands were trembling now, as she stared at the coffee mug. This grotesque mug. He has this exquisite French porcelain china in the house and he uses . . . mugs. She was breathing heavily now, and her eyes widened on Skipper's hands.

Arnold's hands.

She was an old woman and would go to her grave soon. At long last, freed. The knowledge buried with her, like a candle's flame quashed—that it had been Arnold's seed that had flourished in her body and had produced Skipper. Not Jonathan—not her husband. His brother. No one knew, no earthly being, and if there was a God, He had punished her enough for those two weeks in 1933, two weeks when she had deceived her husband, two weeks when she had shared her marriage bed with her husband's brother.

Arnold had had the wisdom to stop the affair. He said it would wreck her life and destroy the Steiner family. She knew he was absolutely correct—the lovemaking, the passions, alarmed her, were too frightening. She had to end the affair and resume her life with the man she had married only five weeks earlier. That was her real life. Mrs. Jonathan Steiner.

She had married too hastily. *My dear, he is your last chance* —that's what her mother had said. *Let's face it, dear, you're not as pretty as your sister.*

It was only on the night before the wedding, after a party at Otto Kahn's Italian Renaissance palace at 1100 Fifth Avenue ("Uncle" Otto was a cousin of her mother's and lived just down the street from the Warburgs, who were distantly related to her father), that Frieda, unable to sleep and twisting in her bed, sensed that her impending marriage actually had remarkably little to do with Jonathan Steiner.

Marriage would not only free her from her parents and sister, it would prove to them, finally, that men, or at least a man, desired her. She was *not* as odd and unattractive as they had whispered for years. She would marry Jonathan Steiner and wrest herself free from her own family. And, in the process, in ways that she could not imagine, she would hurt them.

The honeymoon at the house on Eden Road that Frederic had purchased two years earlier (and sold in 1942) was marred by storms and unseasonably chilly weather. They played solitaire and listened to the radio and struggled to read popular books and were invited to bridge games and cocktail parties at the nearby home of the Schiffer family: the Lehmans, the Littlesons, the Stralems, the Stroocks, the Warburgs, the Schiffs. It was made perfectly plain to Frieda that Frederic Steiner's family had not been invited before into these homes, and that Frieda's marriage to the son of this *arriviste* (these nouveau-riche Russian peddlers, these Oriental types, are the dregs, my dear, and give our people the worst name, sniffed one of her mother's friends who had tea with Frieda) had shaken the elder German-Jewish aristocracy.

Frieda was too bewildered to care. Her first night with Jonathan was a disaster. Alone in a suite at the Plaza Hotel, before boarding a Florida-bound train in the morning, the newlyweds awkwardly embraced in the darkness, breathing heavily, fumbling at the tangle of pajama buttons and lacy knots on the double bed. Jonathan's hands were so cold that Frieda jumped as he touched her.

During the rest of their honeymoon, Jonathan struggled to perform well, but he trembled and perspired as he lay beside her. She was inexperienced and frightened.

Two weeks after the honeymoon, the painters and carpenters had completed the apartment on Madison Avenue—and five weeks after the honeymoon, Arnold had appeared at his brother's door one lunch hour, with his wedding gift to Frieda: a squealing Yorkshire terrier.

Frieda had gasped in delight, lifting the terrified animal into her arms and rubbing her cheek against its soft head. She apologized for the mess in the apartment, and invited Arnold into the kitchen for lunch.

She found herself speaking too rapidly, as he walked into the kitchen and placed his country tweed jacket, with suede elbow patches, over a chair and sat down. As Frieda chopped the celery and chicken on a salad board, she said that a full-time maid and three-day-a-week cook were scheduled to start working the following week.

By the time they sat down at the kitchen table, Arnold had laid out papers on the living-room floor for the puppy. He placed a blanket over the dog, who lapped at a bowl of milk and slowly, grudgingly, lapsed into sleep.

Arnold ate hungrily, explaining that he had played football early that morning in Central Park and was en route to the *Star* to work in his father's office. He was spending his two-week Easter vacation at the *Star* and said he loved every minute at the paper, speaking to the printers and compositors and phone operators and reporters, watching a new paper born each night. Just think of it, he said, what an extraordinary feat of imagination and skill to produce a big newspaper every day, and we all take it for granted.

It was his gusto, his exuberance that stirred her. He was handsome, with a mischievous smile, but this, she thought later, seemed irrelevant, or was at least overshadowed by his enthusiasm.

How's married life? he abruptly asked.

She shrugged and nodded, staring at her half-eaten salad.

I'm not going to get married until I'm thirty-five, he said. *I want to travel to Europe and Asia. I want to see the world.*

She nodded. *That's a wonderful idea, Arnold.*

She watched him finish his lunch, eating two slices of black bread slowly.

She said, *I'd love to go to Paris myself.*

Oh, you will, he said. *You and Jonathan would have a wonderful time there.*

The mention of Jonathan's name forced her to smile. She saw Arnold's dim resemblance to her husband: the same high forehead and narrow, charcoal eyes, the same jutting chin. They were brothers, and yet . . . it was as if a shadow had blurred Jonathan.

Frieda's lunch with Arnold Steiner—an hour of conversation, shy glances, trembling fingers—left an imprint on her that, instead of fading, inexplicably sharpened with age. At sixty she abruptly recalled the smell of the fresh canary-yellow paint in the kitchen when they sat, Arnold's heavy breathing as he spoke, the careless way he ripped apart the bread and hungrily bit into it. She recalled the blackness of his eyelashes, the small hairs flaring from his nostrils, the lilt of his voice . . .

At seventy, the memories flooded her mind. One evening she *felt* the soft hair of the dog against her cheek. Smelled the sweet-sick mixture of paint and chicken and mayonnaise. She recalled the precise too-strong taste of the coffee blend, the tiny freckles flanking the bridge of his nose, the way he bit his lip when she spoke. For the first time in forty-five years she scented again his shaving lotion. Beads of sweat broke out on her forehead—just like then, *just like then* . . .

He asked her if there was milk in the new refrigerator and she replied yes, of course, and he rose from his chair and stepped past her, brushing against his sister-in-law in a flicker of a second. It was an innocent gesture, a touch, but it stirred her. She began weeping.

Arnold turned. *Frieda!*

She stood and rushed into the living room. He walked behind her.

What's the matter?

I'm just tired.

She was standing at the curtained window, her back to him.

He asked nervously, *Is there something I can do? What's wrong? Are you feeling sick?*

No. No.

She wept into her hands. *I'm sorry, Arnold,* she said. *Excuse me.*

Let me help you. He touched her shoulder.

As if waiting for this gesture, she turned and buried her face in his shoulder. He cradled the back of her head with his hand.

I am sorry, Arnold, she whispered. She placed her arms around his firm shoulders. She was dizzy and lost and frightened, she was fevered . . . Her hands reached the back of his neck and, even as Frieda pressed her lips onto his mouth, she repeated to herself, *Oh my God, I am lost.*

Her hands and mouth devoured him. She was in a dream trance, her mother and her sister and Jonathan swimming in the shadows that darkened as Arnold, stunned at first, then trembling, said yes, yes, yes, guiding her, half-carrying her into the bedroom, unbuttoning her blouse, unzipping her dress with her help.

Later, much later, Frieda accepted the fact that she had seduced Arnold out of needs impossible to understand, out of lust, out of loneliness, out of an eerie desperation. It was, she sensed, her one moment of freedom, total freedom, the first and last. She was purged. She accepted the secret that her lovemaking with this man had left her guilty enough, terrified enough, of her own desires to settle into the role demanded of her for the rest of her life.

Three months later, when the doctor confirmed that Frieda was pregnant, she nodded and smiled and *knew* that Arnold was the child's father. Her desire for him, her craving, had been so complete that, with her pregnant now, it was incomprehensible that Jonathan's seed, as opposed to Arnold's, would have flourished in her body. Her certainty was total. *The child was Arnold's.* It was a secret that would die with her. And when the nurse brought the eight-pound three-ounce infant into her arms, after the six-hour ordeal in the delivery room at Doctors Hospital, she wept with joy, rubbing the infant's soft cheek against her own, just as she had brushed her face and chin over the squealing puppy that Arnold had presented to her.

*

"Mother, I wanted to talk to you . . ." Skipper was saying. He had returned to the sofa after opening the window that faced Central Park. "We're getting some visitors in fifteen, twenty minutes."

Skipper saw Frieda search his face.

"The editors of the paper are coming," Skipper said. "And so is Bart Taylor."

Lucy asked, "What on earth is going on?"

"Taylor will explain," said Skipper, lighting a cigarette and watching his mother turn away. She was lost in thought. Vacant-eyed, Frieda twisted the diamond on her finger. Skipper's eyes met Lucy's.

"I'm frightened," Frieda suddenly said, her voice dropping. Skipper started to speak, but his mother lifted her chin in a gasp. "Memories," she whispered. "You get old and the past and the present and future blur." Tears streamed over her cheeks. "Too many memories."

Skipper stood perfectly still, aware that his mother had probably not heard him say that Bart Taylor and the editors were coming.

"We were once so powerful, so confident," Frieda went on. "We've got to survive." She leveled her eyes on Skipper, and swallowed hard. "I was talking to Eli. We've *got* to face the unions. Cut the staff. Cut costs. Reduce expenses."

Frieda stiffened in her seat. "Is it too late to stop foreign travel? Stop those three foreign correspondents that Maury wanted to move?"

"No."

"Stop it. *Stop* it."

*

One-forty. On the foreign desk Ward was on the phone to Ernie Richards in Moscow.

"Look, Ernie, look at it this way. I understand. Christ knows, I understand. But we *can't* let you leave on vacation in the middle of this crisis. The story is *primary* now. There's no one else on the staff with your expertise. . . ."

Ernie's voice slurred with tiredness. "Oh, fuck the story. Fuck the goddamn story. I haven't seen my kid in ten months. She's looking forward to this. I haven't seen Francoise in *four* months. Four months and ten days." Francoise was Ernie's girlfriend, an Air France stewardess.

Ward stiffened as an ulcer pain knifed his stomach.

Ernie was shouting now.

He shut his eyes, waiting for the phone connection to New Delhi and Karen, hearing the echo of her voice. Dear God, the kid is seriously ill . . .

The phone was ringing, and Ward watched Tony pick it up. It was Norman Walker, Jr., the Paris bureau chief. Ward grimaced, put Ernie on "hold," and reached for the phone to Norman, who informed Ward that he had spoken to Frieda Steiner. She had agreed it was a good idea for Norman to write a news analysis on the China-Soviet situation for Tuesday's paper, to use his *experience* . . .

Ward leaned forward. That son of a bitch.

"You shouldn't make end runs, Norman."

"What? What?"

"Nothing." Ward dampened his lips. "Keep it tight." He slapped the phone down.

"Your wife's on the line," Tony said.

Ward lunged for the phone and heard the soft hiss, like flowing water, of the overseas link. Voices were blurred, accents of an Indian woman—"Please go ahead."

Abruptly, Karen came on the line. "Karen, this is Ward. Where's Val?"

"At the British hospital. Miraculously, we got her in as an emergency. Hold on. Let me light a cigarette." He waited. In the silence Ward heard the flowing water, the distant tangle of voices. Karen said, "Thanks. God, it's hot. It's suffocating."

"What's happened?"

She began speaking rapidly, and Ward felt his forehead burning. By the time he had left Delhi, she had wasted into fragile thinness. The bones bulged beneath Karen's neck; her wrists had shrunk. Her eyes, narrow and liquid, rimmed pink with exhaustion, engulfed a fiercely chiseled face.

"When I left Kashmir, Val had a cough, a slight cough, but I thought, well, everyone is coughing with air conditioners and swimming and the heat and everything, and that she would get over it."

It had taken three days for the telegram from New Delhi to reach her in Kashmir. Valerie had begun running a high fever, neck was stiff and—what had alarmed the Kesslers, the American Embassy family the child was staying with—she seemed confused. The Kesslers called friends at the British Embassy, and were able to get Val admitted to the hospital on the British compound.

"It's absolutely illegal, I guess," said Karen. "We're not allowed to use the British hospital because we're not diplomats. We'd have to use one of those Indian pits, and I have a fear, a *thing* about Indian hospitals since Lacey died."

Ward blanched. "What do the doctors say?"

"They've given Val spinal taps . . ."

The pain in his belly had drained away, replaced by a tightness beneath his chest that left him short of breath.

". . . and they've diagnosed it, tentatively, as H. flu. It's a bacterial meningitis. Affects children."

"How serious is it?"

"Well, Jesus, it's serious. Very, *very* serious." She was struggling to control herself. "It can be *fatal.*"

Ward's eyes were shut tight.

The British doctor had urged that they fly to the Children's Hospital on Great Ormond Street in London, and they would do so on Tuesday or Wednesday. In the five-second pause Ward knew, with an absolute certainty, that Karen wanted him in London, needed him there.

Ward finally spoke, and he sensed her disappointment. "I'll get the London bureau to help."

Karen replied quietly: "Thanks."

. . . Steiners vote on Tuesday, can't possibly leave, besides Alex Vikas is starting to leak, hell of a source, remote possibility, dear, slender chance, oh-so-slender that the Steiners will not opt for Maury or Barry or Hugh or Sally, but will . . .

"I'll call you tomorrow night, your time," Ward said, pressing the phone tightly against his ear. He felt the cold sweat on his chest and back; his turtleneck sweater clung. He had to rush uptown, shave and change his clothes. Couldn't appear at the publisher's apartment in a floppy turtleneck.

Ward thought he heard Karen say good-bye before the click. Tony said Ernie Richards was still on hold, and Ward stared blindly at the clerk. Ray, examining a message from Larry Lake in London, groaned. Ward stood up, seized with a surging anger at himself, at Norman and Ernie, at Frieda, at the bloody goddamn paper. At Karen.

He turned on his heels and walked out of the newsroom.

*

As soon as Ward stepped into Skipper's apartment, he heard Barry's unmistakable laugh—a shrill, high-pitched cackle that struck Ward, almost physically, like a slap.

"What the hell's going on?" Ward said to Sally, who was standing at the open doorway.

"Don't know," she said as Maury walked over.

"Story worked out fine today," said Maury. He wore, like the other men in the room, meticulously casual clothes—a muted brown tartan shirt tucked over a beige turtleneck sweater that elegantly matched his suede lambskin jacket and cavalry twill trousers.

"You look like a goddamn Park Avenue gentleman," said Ward.

Maury grinned. "My normal Sunday outfit."

Skipper stepped beside Ward. "What can I get you?"

Quickly, Ward glanced around the room to make sure the others were drinking, then he asked for scotch and water. As Skipper moved away, Ward's eyes fell on Frieda Steiner, seated on the sofa beside Hugh, who was somberly making a point with both hands. Ward heard the word "China."

That son of a bitch.

Barry was standing in a corner of the room, beside an uncurtained window overlooking Central Park, with Eli Faber and Lucy.

"Why are we here?" Ward asked Maury.

As Maury lifted his shoulders and shrugged, Ward heard Frieda laugh. He watched the elderly woman, smiling and nodding her head, place her fingers on Hugh Finch's hand and tap him affectionately.

Skipper handed Ward a drink, and was about to speak when the doorbell rang. Abruptly he turned, Sally, Ward and Maury gazing at one another.

They heard the door shut, then the sound of muffled voices. A hush settled on the room and it took exactly five seconds before Ward saw the familiar round face, the luxuriant crown of white hair, the tinted spectacles that cartoonists had caricatured so often. Ward squinted, staring hard until he recognized the guest: Barton Taylor.

Accompanied by Skipper, the White House Chief of Staff moved around the silent room, his eyes absorbing every face, his handshake oddly limp and moist. Skipper said firmly, "Let's all sit down."

Barton Taylor was handed a drink. Carefully folding his white linen napkin beneath the glass, he said, "I don't know how much Skipper has told you . . ."

"Nothing," Skipper said.

"Fine. That's fine. I phoned Skipper this morning and we decided that it would be best for all of us if I came here and talked to you all face to face.

"Skipper felt—and I couldn't agree with him more—that all of you, the owners of the *Star,* and the editors, should learn certain information firsthand, directly, and then make your decisions based on that information." He settled back on the sofa. "All right, first. Needless to say, this is off the record. My trip is a secret. And what I'm about to tell you is not to leave this room. I need your promise on this." Taylor's eyes roamed the room.

Sally and Maury and Eli nodded. Barry bit his lip, and shook his head affirmatively. Ward murmured, "All right." Only Hugh said nothing. His black eyes were fixed on Barton Taylor. Skipper said, "I think we all agree with that."

"Fine," Taylor said. He inhaled deeply, then leaned forward and took a sip of the bloody mary, gulping it quickly, then taking a deeper swig of the drink. "Well, all right. In recent months President Bergen has been very . . . tired. I've noticed it, Mrs. Bergen has noticed it, so has the staff. Tired and pallid. He's had some loss of weight. Well, all of us thought the President was just working too hard," said Taylor. "The President's physician said he was in fine shape but needed some rest, a change of scenery. As you may know—*you* certainly know, Mr. Finch—the President was supposed to go to Palm Springs this weekend. But that was canceled because of the current, ah, situation between China and the Soviet Union."

Taylor's voice lowered. "The other day the President was playing tennis with his daughter and he, uh, fainted—or nearly fainted, I should say." He spoke the words rapidly. The room was silent. Frieda, seated beside Barton Taylor, turned her head and stared at him.

"The White House doctor found that the President was anemic, *very* anemic, and suggested we get a rather well-known specialist from New York to come down and see him."

Barton Taylor cleared his throat. "Well, a series of tests were conducted and . . ." Taylor leaned forward and paused. ". . . and the illness was diagnosed as something called preleukemia."

"My God," said Frieda.

"Now, Mrs. Steiner. It's *not* leukemia. Your reaction was precisely what mine was: 'Oh my God, the President has leukemia.' But the President has *pre*leukemia, which means—and I'm no doctor, of course—that the President has a good chance, a *very good* chance, of survival. People who have preleukemia lead quite normal lives. With the right treatment, and the right care, the President *will* survive."

As Barton Taylor spoke, Ward saw his eyes flickering and staring beyond Frieda and Skipper. The man wants to believe what he's saying.

"This was just one diagnosis from a prominent physician from New York, by the way," said Barton Taylor. "That's just his opinion. Not that we don't have faith in this doctor, but in the next few days we're getting other opinions. Doctors are flying in today and tomorrow from Atlanta and Dallas.

"Now . . ." He cleared his throat. "President Bergen has been facing, as you well know, this crisis abroad between the Chinese and the Russians, this crisis that has taken some very serious turns. I don't want to talk about our intelligence data, but, as you can see from the front page of your own paper, the situation is escalating and causing us some—well, I don't want to use the word 'alarm.' But you understand, you fully understand, here are two superpowers, two countries facing one another on hostile borders. Two nuclear-armed countries. I don't want to go into details here, I can't, but suffice to say that we have some indications that in the next two days, the next three days, the situation between these countries may even worsen.

"The dangers are extraordinary. *Extraordinary*. Not just the dangers of one side attacking the other. That, in itself, is an alarming prospect. I mean the dangers, the *inevitable* dangers of the United States getting involved in such a conflict."

Taylor swallowed the last drops of his bloody mary. Skipper stood and lifted the empty glass. "Just a bit lighter on the vodka," Barton Taylor said, staring at the table.

"The scenarios we face . . ." he said slowly, allowing his eyes to fall on Hugh, then Barry, then Sally Sims, finally Lucy, ". . . the scenarios are frightening. All pointing to the dangers of a nuclear war that spreads from the Soviet Union to China to the United States."

The silence in the drawing room was broken by the distant blare of a car horn outside, a persistent honk. Taylor said slowly: "Anyone who's convinced that a war between China and the Soviet Union can be limited to those countries is a damned fool. A war like that is *uncontainable*."

Skipper returned with the bloody mary, placing it on the lacquered table at Barton Taylor's knees.

Frieda said, "This is all quite alarming."

"You're absolutely right, Mrs. Steiner. Quite alarming," Taylor replied quickly. He inhaled deeply and repeated, "Quite alarming.

"Early this morning," he said, "we received word that President Kopeikin and Premier Phung have agreed to come to the United States to start talks at Camp David."

"When?" Hugh asked.

"Talks are scheduled to start Tuesday. It will be announced this afternoon, simultaneously, in Moscow, Peking and Washington."

He gazed at Frieda. "This is one bit of good news, a ray of hope. For all we know, it may be the last chance. Premier Phung—and I'm going to have to remind you all again that this is totally off the record—refused to come at first, categorically rejected the President's messages, said the Soviets could never be trusted. It was only the President's personal intervention, a personal phone call to Phung, that opened the way to the summit."

"What did the President say?" asked Ward.

Taylor nodded his head. "The President said the good faith of the United States was on the line and he would guarantee, *personally* guarantee, that the Soviets would comply with an agreement."

"He trusts the President," said Lucy.

"Absolutely. *Absolutely,*" said Taylor. "As majority leader, Bergen led the fight for arms sales and technology sales to China. The President has written extensively—and favorably—on China. He's opened the way for everything from major scientific and cultural exchanges with China to the training of Chinese military people at Fort Benning and Fort Hood. The President has been *pivotal* in developing the ties that we now have with China."

Taylor cleared his throat. "This morning I received a call from Danny Fraser, the White House Press Secretary, asking if it were true that the President has leukemia." He gazed at Hugh, and quickly turned away.

"To be perfectly blunt about it, I was shaken. There are very few people in Washington who know. This is *very* closely held. Danny Fraser didn't even know. And what was so upsetting about this is that I saw everything unraveling. *Everything.* Including prospects for peace."

Ward watched Taylor's performance—his eyes flashed in anger now, his voice clenched with rage. "*Unraveling.* For one thing, the word 'leukemia' is like a red flag. Well, it's not leukemia, it's *pre*leukemia, it's a condition that people have had for ten years, twenty years and nothing has happened to them. The President is not dying, he's very much alive. There's no chemotherapy, no radiation involved. The doctors are just watching him. The President is alive."

Taylor gazed at Maury. "Once something is published in the New York *Star* or the Washington *Post* or the New York *Times* or whatever, all the medical statements in the world will not correct the erroneous impression given that the President is *dying*. But beyond this, far more important than this, if something is published now, then the prospects for peace are, if not shattered, then seriously undermined."

"Are you asking us to suppress publication of the news of the President's illness?" asked Maury.

"I'm asking you to delay publication."

"Delay?" said Maury.

"One week."

"That's absurd," said Maury.

"Goddamn it," interrupted Hugh. "It'll leak, Mr. Taylor. Jesus! The President is sick. You think that won't leak out in the next forty-eight hours? You can't keep that under a lid."

"Do you want to bet, Hugh?" asked Taylor calmly. "There are probably ten, at most twelve, people in Washington who know about the President's illness. They won't talk."

"That doesn't make sense," said Sally Sims. "If Hugh found out . . ."

"It won't happen again," said Taylor, compressing his lips.

"What happens if we publish?" said Skipper. "What happens . . ."

"Damn it," said Hugh, rising and staring at Bart Taylor. *"Damn it.* You ask us not to publish anything for twenty-four hours and we don't. And now you're asking us for a week. You . . ."

Bart Taylor interrupted. "I asked you not to publish anything for twenty-four hours so the paper could at least get the story accurate and have you speak to Dr. Pomerance." Taylor faced Frieda. "Finch spoke to Dr. Pomerance, a specialist who treated the President . . ."

"I've heard of him," said Frieda.

". . . He spoke to Pomerance on the proviso that the *Star* not publish anything for twenty-four hours."

"I knew about it this morning, Mother," said Skipper. "So did Maury."

Hugh stood beside the window, glowering. Frieda watched Hugh, then turned to Barton Taylor.

"What happens if we publish?" she asked quietly. "What happens if we simply publish the facts. The President has been ill and it's been diagnosed . . . as . . ."

"Preleukemia," said Lucy.

"You can publish what you like, Mrs. Steiner," said Barton Taylor. "But the implications of publishing this now, on the eve of the summit, are not in the interests of the United States. *Not* in the interests of peace and would . . ."

"That's nonsense," Hugh said.

"May I finish, please," said Barton Taylor evenly. "And would create conditions that make the prospects of war imminent."

Sally, Lucy and Hugh all began speaking, but Frieda lifted her right hand to quiet them. "How?" she said.

Taylor sighed. "Word leaks out that the President has been ill, has something called preleukemia. Do you think Premier Phung would agree to accept the good faith of the United States from a President who's ill, who may, or may not, have a fatal illness? Do you think the Chinese would agree to negotiations, knowing that Tom Nelson may take over?"

Frieda said, "The Chinese don't like Nelson?"

"They can't abide him," said Barton Taylor. "They think he's pro-Soviet, superliberal, anti-Chinese. It's a simpleminded, inaccurate view of Tom Nelson, but the Chinese adhere to it and we can't change their minds."

"Even if we delay for a week," said Sally Sims, "what difference does it make?"

"It may not make any difference in the world, Mrs. Sims," said Taylor. "It may mean nothing. But the hope is that after a week of talks at Camp David, intense round-the-clock talks, after a week the *momentum* for peace, or at least a settlement, will have begun. Did anyone think Sadat and Begin would . . ."

Skipper, studying his pipe, interrupted. "Barton, you're asking us to delay publishing a major story, a major exclusive story . . ."

"For one week," said Taylor.

Hugh said in a choked voice: "And then two weeks and three weeks. You're asking us to cover something up for your own ends." He moved toward the circle. "All right. What about the public's right to know? Doesn't the public have a right to know that their highest elected official is sick, seriously sick, despite what you say?"

"Hugh. I *detest* that concept," said Taylor. "There's no such thing as the public's *right* to know. Legally, it's unheard of. It's nonsense. It's something used by newspaper lawyers. The public's right to know. Self-serving nonsense. The First Amendment talks about freedom of speech and the press and religion and the right of people to peacefully assemble. Nothing about the public's *right to know*. I think you're being a little self-serving. The public's right to know is a high-flown way of saying, Let's publish it before the Washington *Post* or the New York *Times* or the L.A. *Times* gets onto it. You're interested in the exclusive, the story, and to hell with the implications."

Hugh stared at Taylor, Frieda gazed at her son. Skipper finally said: "If the President is dying, you can't keep that quiet."

"Even for one week?" said Barton Taylor. "Even on the issue of war and peace? A nuclear confrontation. Even for one week?"

Lucy said quietly, "Could you take us to court?"

Taylor smiled. "I doubt that. I don't see a court case here. I see a case of restraint on *your* part. In the national interest."

"You're asking us to censor ourselves," Sally said.

"You're always censoring yourselves, Mrs. Sims. You censor yourselves a dozen times a day. Isn't that the way newspapers and newspaper reporters and editors operate? If anything, isn't it the responsibility of a free press to engage in self-censorship? Isn't the freedom of the press assured precisely because you engage in self-censorship?"

Frieda turned to him. "Are you saying that we would be endangering our press freedoms if we fail to censor ourselves here?"

"Baloney," said Hugh.

"I don't buy that," said Sally.

Taylor sighed. The telephone rang. "I'm saying that the consequences of publishing this now could seriously injure the newspaper. And newspapers throughout the country."

Ward watched Skipper stand and walk quickly to a black lacquered writing table in a corner of the room that held a black phone.

Taylor looked at Frieda. "I'm saying that the backlash against you, by other newspapers, by the public, by Congress, could be damaging indeed if you publish now and the talks collapse. I'm saying . . ."

Skipper interrupted. "Barton, it's the White House." Taylor gazed at Skipper, then arose. Skipper pressed the "hold" button on the phone and escorted Taylor out of the drawing room into the hallway. Ward heard a door close. Within seconds Skipper returned.

"We're going to make this decision today—all of us," he said, frowning. "I want to take a vote."

"A what?" said Frieda.

"A vote. I want to see your positions."

"Skipper. Is that necessary?" said Frieda.

"Yes, Mother, I think it is." He spoke firmly. "The *Star* belongs to all of us. The best interests of the paper are served right here. By everyone in this room."

"It's a family decision," said Frieda impatiently.

"No, Mother, it's a decision made by *all* of us." He turned to Hugh. "Should the paper publish now or wait?"

"Now," said Hugh.

"Sally?"

"Now."

"Ward?"

"Wait."

"Maury."

"Now."

"Eli?"

"Now."

"Barry?"

"Wait."

"Lucy?"

"Wait."

"Mother?"

"Wait."

"All right. Myself. Wait. Reluctantly. It's five to four to wait."

Maury, his eyes fastened on Hugh, said slowly: "I don't think we should overlook the fact that Hugh got this story—and one hell of a story it is—and we're committed to publish his story."

"Absolutely," said Skipper. "Hugh, in no way, in no way at all, is this a lack of confidence in you."

Maury looked at Hugh. Christ, don't let him be a wise ass. Hugh said nothing.

Taylor slipped back into the drawing room and stood beside Skipper. His chest heaved a heavy sigh. Ward saw Taylor's right hand grasp the sofa, then loosen and tap his fingers as if playing a fast run on the piano.

"There's been an assassination attempt against President Kopeikin," he said, struggling to keep his voice calm. "Total news blackout. The Soviet armed forces have been placed on highest alert."

Rapidly, Hugh dug into the breast pocket of his sport jacket to remove a narrow spiral notebook. With his right hand he found a pen.

"We don't have any further information except that Kopeikin is alive, but several ranking Soviet Air Force officers were killed."

"Where did it take place?" said Ward.

"Visiting Soviet troop installations in the Chita area. C-H-I-T-A. Siberia. We have early reports of a bomb or grenade. Some kind of explosion. Don't know which." Taylor stared at his watch with a frown.

"Did anyone see Dave Fitzgerald on 'Issues and Answers'?" he said quietly. Lucy turned to him. Barry looked around the silent room and said, "No."

Taylor said solemnly: "I gather he criticized the President in strong terms. Said the current crisis is an intelligence failure by the Administration. Blamed President Bergen's lack of leadership, said he seemed oddly paralyzed. That was the quote read to me. It's on the wires."

Taylor's lips framed a smile. "Fitzgerald's a brawler. Likes to mix it up. Has fantasies about next year."

"Barton." Skipper spoke up. "The feeling in this room, the feeling within my family, is to wait."

Taylor nodded, Frieda caught his eyes. "I'm quite uncomfortable about waiting," she said. "I don't like being in the position of suppressing news, good *or* bad. Years back we did it without any qualm, but times have changed. We were used. Every paper was used. So I'm doing it, but I don't like it at all. And Skipper?"

"Yes?"

"I think we should hold this on a day-to-day basis. I don't like this one-week commitment. I think we should commit ourselves day by day for one week. Monitor the situation and decide day by day."

*

Alvin Simmons heard the phone ring in the bedroom as he smeared shaving lather onto his chin. Cursing, he left the bathroom slowly, his forehead still pounding, the taste in his mouth—despite the icy orange juice and the two cups of steaming black coffee—metallic.

The caller identified himself as Frank Kirby of the Office of Special Investigation at Treasury.

Alvin slumped at the edge of the king-size double bed.

"We've been ordered to give you a polygraph test as soon as possible. I'm wondering . . ."

"By who?"

"By the White House."

It was the voice that enraged Alvin. Calm. Officious. Controlled. A lingering hint of nastiness. Alvin felt his chin tighten. Now look, motherfucker, look here, don't use that tone with me.

"Tomorrow morning. Eight forty-five. Treasury Building. Third floor." Kirby's words commanded, recited a room number.

Alvin dropped the phone on the cradle and fell back on the bed. His stomach ached. Shutting his eyes, Alvin crooked his arm over his face.

Oh Christ, man. Didn't he tell you? Didn't he tell you? The President has leukemia.

Shirtless, wearing only shorts, Alvin began shivering.

Tell me. Talk to me. Why is Pomerance here?

Awkwardly, Alvin twisted the quilt over his chest, keeping his eyes shut, dangling his icy toes over the side of the bed.

No dream. No hazy nightmare.

Foxtrappe. And the Omega and Ed Murphy's Supper Club. *Talk to me.*

He lurched out of bed and stumbled into the living room, finding his jacket crumpled on the footstool. His fingers, shaking now, reached into the left breast pocket. The checkered wooden stock on the .357 magnum chilled his fingers.

He rested the two-pound weapon in his right hand, letting the forefinger on his left hand glide over the nickel-finished barrel, the serrated front sight, the shimmering, six-chambered cylinder, the slender guard beneath the weapon's grooved trigger.

Alvin's thumb lingered over the guard. His eyes fixed on the weapon as he clasped his two hands over it, grasping the revolver firmly. A ribbon of ice pierced his neck and spine.

Hugh. *Hugh.*

Tears smeared Alvin's face. Hugh. Oh Hugh. Jesus! I trusted you, man. You were my *brother.* I loved you, man. God*damn!*

*

Less than fifteen miles away, in the red-brick house on Beech Drive in Fairfax, Maggie Paley quietly shut the door of the upstairs bedroom facing the street and tiptoed downstairs to the living room.

"Asleep," she whispered to her son Mike, who was seated on the beige floral sofa. "Fell asleep like a little angel."

Jerry crushed his cigarette in the ashtray on the Plexiglas table in front of the sofa. Scattered sections of the New York *Star* and the New York *Times* and the Washington *Post* lay on the table.

"You hear what Angela said to me the other night? You hear about it?" said Jerry. "When I got back from Panama and called up and spoke to your wife—you were still at the station house—I said to Doreen, 'How's my baby Angela,' and Doreen gave Angela the phone and she said to me, Angela said to me, 'Grandpa, where you been. I missed you.' How do you like that? 'Grandpa, where you been?'" He grinned, nodding his head.

Maggie sat on the armless love seat. "Take something for the road," she murmured to her son.

"Not hungry," said Mike Paley distractedly.

"Where is the funeral?"

Jerry watched his son push back his chair and walk to the bathroom in the hallway. Mike's hands dug conspicuously in the pockets of his brown glen plaid sport jacket. "Outside Philadelphia, near Allentown," said Mike over his shoulder.

The door slammed.

Maggie and Jerry stared at each other in silence.

"He's lost weight," Maggie finally said. "Tumors on his fingers again, every ten days. More coffee?"

"No, thanks."

"Bit chilly in the house."

"Is it?"

Maggie examined her hands. "I met the boy who died. Kenny. Same outfit as Mike. Nice boy. Came here on a visit after he was discharged. He was sick then. Came with his son. The little boy was okay, he had the boy before he went to Vietnam." Her voice cracked. "Kenny got sprayed too." Maggie stared at her husband.

"What's the matter?"

"Nothing's the matter."

"Don't be angry with me."

"I'm not."

"Is something . . . the matter?"

"I told you, no."

"Is everything okay at the office?"

"Everything's fine."

"Was Fitzgerald good on the television show?"

"He's always good on TV."

"He reminds me of Jack Kennedy. A bit."

"Every Irish politician reminds you of Jack Kennedy."

"Every handsome one, that's true."

"He's not Jack Kennedy."

"I didn't think so. Jerry?"

"Yeah."

"I didn't like that Bishop fellow."

"Howie Bishop? I don't like him either."

"Mean face. Mean eyes. Something nasty about him."

"Nasty guy. Hell of a good reporter."

"Really?"

"Uh-huh."

"I guess you have to be mean to be a good reporter."

"No. Not always. That's not true."

"Anything special?"

"What?"

"Anything special that he wanted?"

"Bishop? No. Nothing special."

They heard the noise of the toilet flush.

"He's got so skinny," Maggie whispered. "Mike has."

"Skinny, yeah."

She forced a smile. "I still have a picture in my bedroom dresser. Mike and Doreen going to the high school prom. Just before he enlisted."

"I remember."

"He must have been a hundred and ninety pounds."

"At least. All muscle. Big chest," said Jerry.

"You remember he spent every dime on clothes, the boy did. Before Vietnam. Trousers had to be perfectly creased. Spent a bloody fortune on sweaters and shirts and haircuts."

"Drove me crazy," murmured Jerry Paley.

"Drove who crazy?" said his son, stepping into the room.

"Talking about you and your clothes in high school," said Maggie, lifting her eyes to her son and then turning away.

Mike shrugged. "Not like now."

He was bald now, his skin eerily pale. Purple blotches marred his cheek and forehead.

"Doreen seemed upset at St. Malachy's this morning," said Maggie gently.

"Doreen's always upset," said Mike.

"That's not fair," interrupted Jerry.

Maggie asked, "Is there anything I can . . ."

"What can you do?" flared Mike.

"For Chrissake," said Jerry.

"Well, what can you do?" said Mike, turning to his father. "What? Can you stop *this*?"

Mike lifted his hands from his pockets. His mother turned away.

Jerry said fiercely, "Cut it out, Mike. Your mother's only asking."

Mike's eyes darted to the floor.

"You have a long drive, Mike," said Maggie softly. "Perhaps you should . . ."

"I lose my temper too much," Mike said. "Doreen's upset because she went to some doctor who treated the kid of a friend of ours. This friend, Stewart, nice guy, black guy, was a helicopter pilot for the First Air Cav. Helicopters were used for close-in spraying. Unfriendly areas near hamlets they didn't want to hit. The helicopters flew without doors so they could return ground fire. The helicopter blades would kick up the spray right into the faces of the crew. The cockpit was filled with the shit."

Mike smiled. "The guys were told not to wear masks. Can you believe it? Told by their officers that Agent Orange wasn't harmful to human life. But they had to use old planes because the spray peeled the paint off. And they were told not to spill any on their fingers because it would burn like acid. But don't worry, boys, it's not harmful to human *life*.

"Stewart comes home and gets the usual symptoms. Loses weight, tumors all over his body. Impotent most of the time. Then nineteen months after he gets home, his wife gives birth to a little boy."

Mike Paley paused. "Multiple birth defects. Cleft palate. A blind, deformed right eye. No right ear. Bladder extrophy. Split penis. Imperforated anus. Deformed jawbone. Nice, ain't it? You know what the VA told Stewart? You know what those fuckers told him? 'You have no service-connected disabilities.'

"Well, Stewart's wife has a good government job and, naturally, every cent and more that they have is going to the kid, who's a little difficult now. So the doctor suggests putting the kid in a special school, a *home,* somewhere in North Carolina. They see the kid now every couple of weeks, right?

"Well, Doreen sees the doctor, who says, like, 'Well, Mrs. Paley, your little girl, little Angela, was born with pyloric stenosis.' I mean the bottom of her stomach was open and whatever she swallowed she threw up. Little Angela was born without a rectum, she was born with a hole in her heart. She was born with every organ in her body defective—defective spine, defective bladder, deformed hands. She has one vagina, which changes off into a second vagina, and two cervixes, and Christ knows how many ovaries. She's an eight-year-old kid in puberty.

" 'I mean, Mrs. Paley,' the doctor tells Doreen, 'little Angela is a freak.' That's the word that motherfucker used. 'I mean Angela is a classic case of Agent Orange,' the doctor says. *'Put the kid away.' "*

"Mike. He's only one goddamn doctor," said Jerry.

"Tell that to Doreen," said Mike in a gasp. "She hears a doctor talk like that and she panics. They're going to take Angela away. The social workers and the doctors . . ."

The telephone was ringing.

"Doreen thinks they're gonna take Angela away from us."

Maggie rose and lifted the phone on the side table beside the sofa. She listened, then turned to her husband. "It's Barry Cohen."

Jerry stared at her. "I'll take it in the study," he said, walking out. Maggie held the phone loosely to her ear, then placed it down as soon as she heard her husband's voice.

"What does Cohen want?" asked Mike.

She shrugged.

"Never liked that guy since Vietnam," said Mike Paley. "You remember how he won that big Pulitzer Prize in Vietnam? You remember that?"

"No, I don't," she said distractedly.

"Dad'll tell you the story someday. That bastard. Do anything for a story."

"A lot of journalists are like that," she said as Mike buttoned the center of his sport jacket. Maggie eyed the sores on his hands before he pressed them back into his pockets. He edged toward the hallway.

"I wish you could have taken the Volvo," said Maggie. "It's so much pleasanter on these long trips."

"The Chevy's okay, Mom," said Mike.

"Supposed to be tuned up tomorrow at the garage in Arlington," said Maggie. "Ridiculous. Garage mechanics getting to be like surgeons."

"What's wrong with the car?"

"Just age. A little knocking here and there."

Maggie brushed slithers of lint off his jacket. "You're staying tonight with . . ."

"Tony. My buddy Tony. We called him Tony the spick. Tony's got it too."

"My God," said Maggie Paley as Jerry returned to the living room, and the three of them stepped outside.

"How's the job, Mike?"

"Got one hell of a big haul on Friday night. Four guys and three women run this warehouse. Drugs and weapons. Jesus! Like L. L. Bean, you order what you want and you get it. Heroin. Cocaine. PCP. Hash. Anything. And the weapons. You name it. .38

specials. .41 and .44 magnums. Browning high-powered pistols—beauties. Colt Pythons. P-38 Walthers—the Germans used that one. Ruger .22's. Rifles."

"Are you selling the weapons?" said Jerry Paley.

"Hoarding them," said Mike. "We're cataloguing them."

Maggie put her hand on the sleeve of her son's jacket. "I'd be happier if Doreen drove. You get so dizzy . . ."

Mike shook his head. "Doreen's been to two funerals so far in the last year. That's enough."

Jerry let his cigarette fall on the driveway, ground it out fiercely with his heel, then reached into his pocket and removed a fistful of carefully folded cash. He counted out six one-hundred-dollar bills. Maggie watched her husband's hands, then lifted her eyes to his face.

"Jesus, Dad," said Mike.

"Take it. For Kenny's kid," said Jerry.

"Thanks." Mike gripped his father's hand. "Thanks." He opened the car door and sat behind the wheel.

Maggie stepped away. "That was kind of you, Jer . . ."

But Jerry was already climbing the steps, leaving Maggie standing alone in the middle of the street as Mike drove away. The smile drained from her face.

Best not think of the bits of conversation overheard, she said to herself. Not . . . *think*. The two or three hundred dollars he pressed into her hand every few weeks, the envelopes he slipped to Doreen and Mike. The clothes he turned up with for Angela. Besides paying the hospital bills, the doctor's fees, the medicines. Ordering the hand-made bed. The special toilet. Building the ramp in the house. Tens of thousands of dollars.

What are the rumors . . . you're involved . . . Howie, you think I'm corrupt . . . corrupt . . .

Drinking fiercely the last twenty-four hours, the worst in years. Nothing like it since you split up with that girl Fentress, Linda Fentress, the blonde. You always liked the blondes, always took them under your wing—paternal, weren't you, and it was her or me, Jerry, I told you that. The blond cupcake or me. And you stayed with me but you punished me for it, you got stinking drunk that night, just like . . .

Last night.

As soon as Howie Bishop left, you started drinking. Two six-packs of beer, maybe three. Finished a pint of Smirnoff's and three quarters of the scotch.

Jerry.

Grilled a porterhouse last night, rare on the inside, baked potatoes with melted Cheddar, your favorite. Two forkfuls and you stop. And you got up, neatly folding the napkin, and walked into your study, firmly closing the door.

If you only talked. If you only . . . believed. If you only had faith in the light of God. The peace and exaltation of prayer. O Sacred Heart. O sweet Jesus.

The screen door slammed behind her, and she heard Jerry in his study gently close the door as soon as she entered the house.

*

"I'm at the post office near Union Station," said Cheryl. "Now listen, Jerry. I just sent a copy of my diary. It's yours. Anything happens to me and you give it to a newspaper reporter, someone who's honest, who'll nail Fitzgerald to the wall with it."

"All right, Cheryl."

"They're going to try to pin it all on you, Jerry. You're the fall guy for Fitzgerald and the whole rotten crew. Be *careful,* Jerry."

He started to laugh. "Too late to be careful, honey."

CHAPTER 13

It was only after two bloody marys and a joint that Lois Barrie lifted her oval-shaped dark glasses, placing them atop her curly black hair. Lois looked older than she did on television.

Her stockinged feet nestled beneath her buttocks, Lois fixed her eyes on Linda Fentress. "All right, my dear. I hear you're doing Tommy Nelson."

"We're looking at his background."

"What does that mean?"

"His early career . . ."

Lois interrupted. "His early career was *spectacular.* Unlike most of us, he struggled for about three minutes. Less. It was the Army. They found him at Fort Something-or-Other."

"Fort Ord," said Gregory.

"It was the face," said Rita Hamalian.

"It was his *eyes,*" said Lois Barrie. "Smoldering eyes. Dark, beautiful eyes. That's what Tommy had."

"Interesting face," said Gregory.

"Nonsense," said Lois Barrie. "The face was bland. Bland and beautiful. The eyes smoldered, but behind them—nothing. No sex. No mystery. Nothing. That's why he was a half-assed actor and a good politician."

"Going to be President," said Gregory, smiling.

Lois snorted. "Last time I saw Tommy was when he came to town for the Jean Hersholt Humanitarian Award."

"Brunch," announced Rita.

Lois spoke in a hoarse voice. "The day after the award I was in Ma Maison, and who walks in but Vice President Tommy Nelson and his henchmen. Well, my dear, Tommy walks over in the middle of lunch and kisses me on the cheek and tells me how much his *children* love my program. All noblesse oblige. That prick."

"Lois likes Nelson," Gregory said.

As Linda walked onto the patio, she caught a last glimpse of the sputtering fire in the living room's massive fireplace. It was built like a grotto, driftwood limbs and grapevines clinging to the volcanic rock that framed the blaze.

Lois Barrie had talked without pause for forty-five minutes and barely acknowledged Linda. She had gossiped about the costs of a new Francis Ford Coppola movie, the weather in Hawaii, the food at the Royal Hawaiian Hotel, a new yogurt and grapefruit diet guaranteed to remove a pound a day.

Linda's mood veered between fascination and impatience, even anger, at the actress' babbling self-absorption. Maybe this is the way they are in L.A.

Gregory passed around baskets of croissants and home-baked black bread, cheese, salad.

"Miss Fentress," said Lois.

"Call her Linda," said Gregory.

"Linda, my answering service said there were three calls from someone named Pirota of the New York *Daily News* and a Mr.

Roth of the *Times*. Do they want to see me about the same thing?"

Linda nodded.

"I don't give many interviews, Linda, except under the most *intense* pressure from the network," said Lois Barrie. Her right hand was crooked over the cane-backed chair. "People ask dumb questions and write dumber articles. I don't *need* that. I don't think the ladies who read *McCall's* or the *Ladies' Home Journal* need my wisdom. They have Dinah Shore and Carol Burnett and all those *nice* ladies. I'm not nice."

Linda spoke up. "Just want to talk to you, on background, about the Vice President."

"Jesus, I still can't believe it," said Lois. "Vice President of the United States. Jesus! Who ever thought that cocksucker would amount to anything but a middling movie actor who aged well." She grinned. "Darling, give me one more joint, please."

Gregory reached for the tortoiseshell box on the table, flipped it open and handed the cigarette to Lois, then lit it with a match.

"I'll talk to you," Lois said slowly, "if you don't use my name. The only reason I'm here is because you're a friend of Rita and Gregory. They cared about me when I was *nothing*. They are friends."

Linda nodded. "I won't use your name."

Give me a lead, Lois, let's start, need a beat on this story, it's getting tangled. Pirota and Irwin Roth competing, Barry impatient, give me a break, Lois . . .

"Who discovered Tom Nelson?"

"It's common wisdom that Elliott Hanley discovered Tommy. Gave him his first break in a William Holden thing. Well, I adore Elliott. He's a friend, a lovely man, destroyed by the blacklist, finally making a comeback. But in point of fact, the person who actually discovered Tom Nelson while he was still in the Army was a man named Marvin Conrad."

"Never heard of him," said Gregory.

"Died eight, nine years ago. Tommy sent flowers to the funeral."

"Who was he?" asked Linda.

"A casting director and then assistant director on some drecky movies, and then poor Marvin was called in by the same state committee that destroyed Elliott Hanley. Sort of low-grade House Un-American Activities Committee. Investigating subversive activities quote unquote in the film industry. Run by this scumbag Joe Keefer."

"He's dead," said Linda.

"Who?"

"Joe Keefer."

"Dropped dead in Mexico City about five years back. Unfortunately, it was a heart attack. I was hoping for something more painful."

Keefer. Brother-in-law of Dave Fitzgerald. Worked for Marcus Lynn.

Linda was writing quickly, aware that the jigsaw was adding pieces, nothing quite falling into place yet; the story, instead of simplifying, became more entangled and murky.

"Marvin Conrad refused to inform on his friends and colleagues," Lois was saying. "He was uncooperative. Overnight he lost everything. Couldn't get a job cleaning the toilets at MGM. The poor bastard wasn't big enough in the industry to work under a false name or go to London. He was small-time. A *nobody*. So he and Elliott scrounged . . ."

"He and Elliott?"

"Elliott and Marvin were hotsy-totsy for a while," said Lois. "Then they split up and Marvin opened an acting school in Anaheim that was closed down when Disneyland took over. Then he worked in an acting school on Wilshire, and then the poor son of a bitch dropped dead."

Linda blankly watched Rita push back her chair and lift the pot of coffee to refill everyone's mug. "Marvin discovered Tom Nelson, and Elliott Hanley cast him in that movie," said Linda.

Lois Barrie took a deep and final drag on the joint and crushed it in the ashtray. "If it wasn't for Marvin and Elliott, Vice President Tom Nelson would have been . . . what? An insurance agent in Pasadena."

Nothing in the official bios, nothing in the *Star*'s morgue, that two old queers discovered Tommy Nelson.

"You know anything about porno movies?" blurted Linda, catching Lois' hard stare.

"I've seen a few."

"Anything about Nelson appearing in them?"

Lois Barrie spoke through stiffened lips. "Haven't heard that."
The sound of the telephone in the bedroom broke the tension.
Gregory left. "Speak to Paul Brock," said Lois. "He has the best
collection in town."

"I've called him twice," said Linda.

Lois Barrie reached into the tortoiseshell box and lifted another
joint, then lit it with Gregory's lighter.

"Who else are you seeing?" she asked quietly.

Linda shrugged. "Nelson's early years intrigue me."

"What about your scrapbooks?" interrupted Rita Hamalian.

"That's right, my scrapbooks." Lois Barrie inhaled and
coughed. "My scrapbooks. Once upon a time I kept scrapbooks
of all my clips, my appearances, publicity pictures, gossip items,
etcetera. Dating back to the last century, which means the
nineteen-fifties in Hollywood. Historical memorabilia. I mean
some of the children running studios now weren't even *born* when
I began," said Lois, turning to Rita. "I'm a relic of the good old
days."

"What was your first film?" asked Linda.

"You've never heard of it, dear."

"Wasn't it *The Robe?*" asked Rita.

"That's what my publicity people say. Actually, my first film
was as an extra in something called *He Ran All the Way,* which
had the distinction of being John Garfield's last movie. You don't
remember him, I'm sure. That was my first. It was followed by *The
Kid from Cleveland, Montana Belle, The Naked Jungle, Cat-
women of the Moon*—major films, you see—and then, finally, my
appearance as a maiden in *The Robe.* My *official* debut."

"Why do you hate Nelson so much?" Linda stopped writing.
Lois swayed in her chair, stared for a long moment at the half-
filled glass of orange juice and raised it to her mouth. Her voice
was slurred now.

"I don't *hate* him, honey," she said. "Tommy just used me,
that's all. He's no better or worse than about two thousand other
people in this town. He used me. Now he's this great fucking liberal. Cares about the blacks and the Hispanics and poor people.
Well, Tommy doesn't give a rat's ass about those people. He's
using them too. Who are his real supporters, his money men? The

Marcus Lynns, the Paul Brocks of the world. He's got Las Vegas money, the teamsters in San Diego. He's the CIA's favorite liberal. I know nothing about politics, dear, but what does that add up to? That he's a hypocrite. No, not a hypocrite. A whore!"

Gregory slipped back into the dining alcove and sat down. Linda and Rita sat silent, watching Lois. "We were kids together," she mumbled. "He was twenty or twenty-one. I was about seventeen. We were both scared. Didn't admit it, of course, but we were scared out of our minds. Scared and hungry." She tried to laugh. "Like Judy and Mickey. 'Hi, let's put on a show.' We read plays together. Acted out the parts in bed. For Chrissake, we even read Shakespeare. We were kids and, well, I kind of loved Tommy Nelson."

Linda blinked twice, lowering her eyes to the jonquils on the table. Gregory lit a joint. Rita watched Lois.

"Well, Tommy made it fast," said Lois. "There he was. Big-time agent at William Morris. Contract at MGM. Academy Award nomination. The works. And I went from bit part to bit part. Decided to go to New York. Joined Actors Studio. Two Broadway plays that flopped, one of them closing in Philadelphia. Some very good off-Broadway, which at least got me some TV work in New York, commercials to pay the bills. Never *quite* making it.

"Tommy became a big star and old Lois was still beating at the door. All right. More power to him. But soon old Tommy was so establishment, so Mr. Jean Fucking Hersholt Humanitarian Award that he was too important, too prominent to be seen with an aging starlet.

"Well, I came out here to do the series which, believe me, I thought would last about three minutes. I was actually reluctant to do it, but Max, my agent, bless him, *bless him,* said, Lois, this is going to make it. It was the first series about working mothers, the first, and after six months we're the number-three show in the country.

"Well, I try to reach Tommy, just say, 'Hello,' but after leaving four messages with his answering service I get the picture. Tommy does not want to speak to me. All right. But I'm hurt and puzzled. Why is Tommy treating me like a leper?

"So four, five months later I am invited to a party at Marcus Lynn's—Marcus gives two parties a year at his palace up near

Bedford Drive, and an invitation is comparable to a federal subpoena. One is ordered to attend. So who is there? You guessed it. He kissed me on the cheek, and when I say to him, in my usual subtle way, 'Why the fuck haven't you called?' he tells me that he's interested in running for senator and there are a lot of people in California suspicious of liberal movie actors running for office and he has to clean up his act first—those were the words he used, 'clean up his *act*'—and he can't possibly be seen in public with someone like me. It would hurt his Mr. Clean image. *Someone like me.*

"Don't you love it, dear? I am Eva Perón. I am Mrs. Hitler. Someone like me. He makes it clear that he couldn't be seen in public with me, but every now and then he could certainly drop over for a quickie. And being a fool, of course, having a strong instinct for self-delusion, I agree. Why not? I'll do my Joan Crawford back-street number, even after he gets married to Miss Goody Two-Shoes and has his All-American family, even after he becomes senator. Why not? Let's see each other on the sly, and let me be available whenever he wants. Like an aging groupie."

Her voice cracked. "After three months I decided to end it. Let's be grown-up, Lois, I say to myself. The bastard's married, which doesn't bother me, but he's embarrassed about me, which does. Do I need this? I've been through a lot of guys, have seen plenty, and I'm into meaningful relationships now, and the last thing I need is to feel lousy about myself. Right? So I call Tommy and ask him to meet me and he says, 'Let's have a drink,' and I agree, and he tells me to meet him at the Polo Lounge at five. I was going to end it on my terms. And I felt terrific.

"Well, I show up at the Polo Lounge at five. And you know that scene. Well, maybe you don't, dear, but it's not a place to sit alone. Everyone sees you. Everyone in the business is there. And I have gone to Michael, my hairdresser, and I have on my Chanel suit and my two-toned slingbacks—it's the early seventies, remember?—and I look gorgeous. I've finally started to make money. I'm prepared for my little scene *looking great*. Right?

"So I wait. Ten minutes, twenty minutes, an hour. By six-fifteen I'm onto my second Valium. By six-thirty I get up and go to the bathroom. Looking like death. I throw up over my little Chanel suit and break down and start to cry."

"He never showed?" said Rita.

"Never showed. Never called. *That's* how Tommy ended it."

"Was that the last time you spoke to him?" asked Linda.

"Last year. When he met me at Ma Maison and told me how much his kids loved my program. Two hours later he called me at the studio and invites me up to his suite at the Hilton. He's there for a Democratic fund-raiser.

"I'm sure he's thinking, 'What the fuck.' May as well fuck a tried-and-true veteran like me while he's back in his old hometown." Lois tasted her coffee. "So I go up there. Don't ask me why, but I go up there. In about four seconds Tommy starts unzipping his pants. As if I've been waiting for this moment for fifteen years.

"I said, 'Tommy, why didn't you show up at the Polo Lounge?' He looks at me and says, 'Oh.' Just like that. 'Oh.' He says to me, 'I got kind of busy that afternoon.' "

Lois Barrie lifted her eyes to Linda. "I waited for him to take his pants off, and then I picked up the phone and asked for the front desk. I said to them, 'This is Lois Barrie in the Vice President's suite, and the man is trying to rape me.' Tommy runs over and grabs the phone and hangs it up and said, 'You're crazy,' or something like that. And I said, 'Tommy, I've been through a lot of shit, but I'm a big girl now. I earn at least eighteen thousand dollars a week, with residuals, and I've got a two-picture contract at Fox that, if I'm lucky, will earn me nearly a million bucks. I'm not one of your one-night stands every five years. And besides that, I'm going to do everything, *everything* I can to hurt you. I despise you.' " She paused.

"That's the word I used," said Lois Barrie. " '*Despise.*' I walked out of there with him, quite literally, holding his cock in his hand. The manager of the hotel was pacing outside the suite, and these two Secret Service boys didn't know what the fuck was going on, and I said, 'Don't worry, fellas. Nothing happened. He couldn't get it up.' "

She smiled vacantly. "So I suppose, as you say, I do hate him."

"Marcus Lynn hates him too," said Linda, digging her razor-point pen into the notebook beside her plate, etching tiny circles. Gregory and Rita watched Lois.

The actress turned to Rita. "Darling, may I have just one more glass of orange juice. Some ice. A touch of vodka. Big glass." Rita nodded, and walked to the oak sideboard beside the window.

With a gentle flick of her forefinger, Lois pushed the dark glasses over her eyes. "Marcus and Tommy were friends. Marcus guided Tommy's career, was politically important. It was Marcus who raised the money and organized Tommy's Senate campaigns. They were friends until . . ."

"The daughter. Marcus' daughter. What happened?"

Lois Barrie's voice dropped. "The tragedy of Marcus' life. Maria. He's never been the same since Maria went mad. She tried to . . . smother her infant daughter."

"Good God," whispered Rita, turning.

"Never heard that before," said Gregory.

"You wouldn't," murmured Lois. "Marcus and the Beverly Hills police hushed it up, and Maria is confined to a mental hospital near Carmel."

Linda was writing quickly. "What's the name?"

"Haven. Something Haven. *Rose* Haven." Lois removed her glasses, contemplating Linda. "It's closed to the general viewing audience, dear. No one goes there without Marcus' consent, and not even Marcus goes there." She began to laugh, but stopped. Her voice grew heavy. "Actually, the poor girl gets one visitor. Her grandmother. Illiterate Mexican woman who lives in Marcus' house. Speaks no English. The woman and Maria pray together."

Story's slipping away here. Focus on Tom Nelson and the films and his past. Don't get tangled in marginal stories . . .

"Gorgeous girl, Maria was," said Lois.

"Like her mother?" asked Gregory.

"The same skin, same hair, same eyes."

"What happened to her mother?" asked Linda.

Lois examined her fingernails. "Davita Lopez was a Mexican actress who Marcus tried, and failed, to make a star. Kept casting Davita Lopez as nuns, starry-eyed virgins, which was casting very much against type. Since Davita was screwing anything over the age of twelve."

Slowly Lois began twisting the diamond-and-platinum dome ring on her pinky. "By the time Marcus threw Davita out, he had grown obsessed with Maria. She was beautiful, just like her mother, but she was *not* going to turn into Mama. Marcus sent her to convent schools, private tutors. The child was protected. To be kept innocent. Or, if not innocent in this day and age, away from the influence of Hollywood. He was molding Maria to perfection."

Rita set the glass of orange juice and vodka before Lois. "Maria was eighteen, maybe nineteen. Marcus sent her to work that summer in the office of Senator Fitzgerald. David Fitzgerald of New York, a buddy of his. Naturally, the girl is told to look up the family's dear friend Tommy Nelson, *Senator* Nelson.

"The child falls for Tommy. Only an eighteen-year-old convent girl would fall that way. The first passion in her life. Grand love! And it's not some jerk-off football player on the high school team, but United States Senator Tom Nelson, whose family is safely tucked away in Martha's Vineyard."

Lois sipped her drink. "Marcus hears about the affair and flies to Washington. He arrives in late afternoon, and by the time he gets in and calls Maria's apartment, her roommate tells him that she's out. No idea where Maria is. Calls Tommy's office and a secretary says he's at some restaurant near the Capitol. Well, Marcus goes into the restaurant, sees them both together, and, I would say, goes mildly berserk."

"Jesus," said Rita, setting down her coffee cup. Gregory lit a joint.

"He slaps the girl across the face, calls her a whore, grabs her and leaves. Outside the restaurant he slaps her some more. The girl's hysterical by now. Crying like a baby. They get on a night flight to L.A. and by now the girl is silent. Doesn't say a word. They get home and she locks herself in her room for a week, maybe two. Stops talking. Starts acting weird. Suddenly, one morning, she disappears."

A question flickered across Linda's memory and vanished. Something utterly logical. Simple. A pivotal question.

Lois was speaking quietly now. Linda bit her lip hard.

"Well, Marcus is frantic. And guilty. He has cops and private detectives looking for her. Two months pass, four months. Six months. Nothing. Then he gets a phone call from a private detective. Can Marcus meet him at a movie theater off Sunset. A porno house. Marcus and the detective pay their five bucks, or whatever they pay now, and there, in living black and white, under the name of Maria Lopez, is Maria starring in something called *Blow Dry*. Made in Mexico City."

"What did Marcus do?" said Gregory.

"Marcus flies down and traces the girl. She's pregnant. The final days. Pregnant and frightened. Marcus begs Maria to come back. Breaks down and apologizes for the incident in Washington. He's guilt-ridden, contrite. Says nothing about the porno film. He *wants* Maria and the baby."

Linda saw Lois' eyes blur, the marijuana and whiskey shriveling her voice. "Too late for Maria to fly back, so she stays in Mexico City to have the baby. Wants her grandmother to stay with her, so Marcus flies the old woman down. Maria seems scared but normal and she has the baby, a daughter.

"Marcus has a nursery all set up in his house. He's joyous! A grandchild. Maria will be *fine,* they'll start again. It will all work out. Maria leaves the hospital and starts to pack up. Wants to see her mother, who lives in a resort down there, wants to say good-bye. So the grandmother takes the child to L.A. to Marcus' house. Maria will follow in several days. They'll start a new life together, Marcus thinks.

"Maria returns to L.A. perfectly calm. On the first night she's back Marcus hears a noise in the nursery late at night. Slips out of bed, thinks, perhaps Maria's in there feeding the infant. Opens the door and she's smothering the child with a pillow, crying hysterically Maria is, trying to *kill* the infant."

Rita gasped. "How horrible."

"Ten seconds later and the child would have been dead. Maria, herself, had swallowed a big enough overdose to kill a horse and was rushed to Cedars of Lebanon."

"Does anyone know why?" asked Gregory.

"Who was the child's father?" said Linda impatiently.

"Why? The girl's mad. Obviously possessed. The child's father?" Lois' eyes darted from Gregory to Rita to Linda.

"Who is he?"

"There were rumors that it was some Mexican boy in one of her porno movies," said Lois slowly, draining her drink. "And there are rumors, just rumors, that the child is Tom Nelson's."

Linda felt her lips part.

"That's a new one," said Rita.

A nasty taste filled Linda's mouth.

What did Jerry Paley used to say? Investigative reporting is like sex: you get better with practice and it's not done enough. Ha. Ha. If it were only true. Only true. Why is this one so . . . twisted. Confusing. Corruption is one thing. Good old-fashioned corruption. Check the recorder's and tax assessor's offices. Check deeds and mortgages and SEC reports and bank files and land purchases. Find a mistress who's been kicked out on her ass and eager to talk. Cut a deal with a prosecutor: you tell me what you have, on background, and I tell you what I have. Okay? It's not kosher. But that's the way we play ball. Hardball. But this one . . .

A Vice President's past. Did he make a dirty movie? And how do you prove that? Does he have an illegitimate child? Is that what we're looking for? And who are these people? Aging movie stars, blacklisted directors, a girl in a mental hospital. What does it all add up to? Muck. Gossipy muck. No Pulitzer Prize here. Sorry, Barry. No goddamn Watergate here . . .

"Linda?" It was Gregory. "The phone call before was from a friend of mine who works at the L.A. *Times* morgue. Said he'd be there in about an hour."

She struggled to smile. "That's great."

Have to reach Paul Brock. Biggest porno collection. Call Elliott Hanley, Tom Nelson's first director. Read the files on Keefer, Joe Keefer, tinhorn witch hunter, brother-in-law of Dave Fitzgerald, name keeps cropping up, the bastard's dead, Joe Keefer.

"Joe Keefer died in Mexico City five years ago," said Linda suddenly.

Lois was moving shakily toward a pine rocker. "It made my day."

"What was he doing in Mexico City?"

Rita, who was pouring more coffee, stopped and stared at Lois, who eased into the rocker.

"Keefer was Marcus' errand boy. Flunky. A hopeless drunk in the end, a rummy that Marcus employed because of Keefer's connections."

"Brother-in-law of Dave Fitzgerald," said Linda. "Marcus and Fitzgerald are friends."

Lois Barrie's eyes went blank. "Believe me, honey, it gave joy to plenty of people in this town to see Joe Keefer crawling, delivering Marcus' messages."

"What messages were there in Mexico City?"

Lois seemed lost in thought. "He would deliver monthly payments to Davita Lopez. Marcus supported her, spent a fortune on that whore."

"Maria's mother," said Linda, staring at her notebook. "It was the same time Maria had the baby, wasn't it? Keefer's death . . ."

"The same time." She breathed a heavy sigh and shut her eyes, and almost immediately seemed to fall into a daze. The sweet smoke hung heavily in the air.

"How do you know all this?" whispered Linda.

Lois Barrie kept her eyes closed. "Because I was sleeping with Marcus. And, my dear, that's what we mostly did."

Linda turned to Gregory and asked to make a phone call. He pointed to the bedroom.

Linda dialed the Century Plaza for messages. Barry Cohen had called from New York, leaving his home phone number. Elliott Hanley's answering service had called to say he was unavailable for interviews. Linda opened her notebook to a clean page, wrote the director's name on the top line and dialed his number.

Hanley answered the phone on the second ring. Linda explained that the *Star* was planning a story about Tom Nelson's early years in Hollywood and wanted to see people who knew him.

"Didn't my answering service reach you?"

"No." Linda struggled to sound pleasantly dumb.

"I'd rather not speak to you."

She was seated on the king-size bed, staring at a row of conch shells on the rattan chest of drawers beside the window.

"Only fifteen minutes," said Linda.

"I have nothing to say."

"Can *I* judge that, Mr. Hanley?"

"I'm afraid not, Miss . . ."

"Are you trying to hide something?"

"I don't think that's necessary, Miss . . ."

"Fentress. Linda Fentress." She heard the phone click.

That son of a bitch. That faggot son of a bitch.

Raging, Linda dialed Barry's phone number, using her telephone credit card. The line was busy.

Fuck it.

Fuck the whole rotten business. Fuck Barry Cohen and the *Star* and Pirota and Farrell and Irwin Roth.

She dialed Barry's phone number again, barking the numbers on her telephone credit card to the operator. Still busy.

She lay on the bed, gulping hard, shutting her eyes. Some stories fit together beautifully. Find the jigsaw pieces and fit them. Some stories demand balls and Linda's got them. Staking out a grand jury. That's Linda's specialty. Knocking on the door of a guy under investigation who doesn't answer phone calls because he's scared. Show up at his house. Embarrass his wife, his kids. In front of the neighbors. Fuck 'em. Talk to me. Off the record, on background, you call it honey, but talk to me, talk to me right now because I need a story and you're gonna get nailed to the wall unless you talk to me. Now!

Linda's got balls. That's what the guys in the newsroom say. Linda's got a pair. A tough broad. Anything for a story. Call up a guy at three in the morning. Show up before breakfast while the kids are having their Cheerios and the old lady's still in a housecoat. Linda is tough. Linda is . . .

Scared.

Always scared.

Barry's phone was ringing now. "How you doing?" he asked.

"Confused!"

"You got anything yet?"

"Been out here twenty-four hours!"

"I'm kidding, honey."

"No you're not."

"I hear Irwin Roth is there."

"You hear correct. Irwin is here. Pirota and Farrell. Christ knows who else."

"You need help?"

"No!"

"Howie Bishop can help."

"Howie Bishop sucks."

"Linda, I don't want to get beaten on this . . ."

"You keep *saying* that, Barry. Christ!"

"Maury is pissed. We stole the story. *I* stole the story. It's not a city desk story, remember? California's not our turf. It's a national story. Sally . . ."

"I'm pushing . . ."

"We don't show results fast and Maury gets antsy. Tells Sally to take the story."

"You're both up for it?"

"What?"

"The job."

"That's irrelevant."

"You ever see *Pinocchio?*"

"You're a bitch, Fentress."

"Your nose is getting very long."

"If we move fast on this one, if we show results, beat the shit out of the competition . . ."

"When does the family decide?"

"Tuesday."

"So you want me to write something by . . ."

"Tuesday."

"Something fake," she said. "That's the only way."

"Something to stake our claim on this story," said Barry.

"Not sure about this story," Linda finally said. "It's not just porno films."

"That's the story I *want.*" His voice had a knife edge.

Linda tightened her free hand into a fist.

"Why should Howie come out here?" asked Linda quietly. "Isn't he working on Son of Watergate?"

"He's on third base heading for home," said Barry. "He'll be ready to write tomorrow. We hope."

Tuesday. No, Barry. Can't get a story by Tuesday.

"You going to nail anyone?"

"Maybe a big fish. Or maybe a little one." He added softly, "You're not going to like this, Linda."

She felt her heart skip. "What are you talking about?"

"Jerry Paley."

"Jerry?"

"Up to his ass in payoffs."

"*Jerry?*"

"Potential Pulitzer," Barry was saying. "Hell of a story. Like yours. I smell *Pulitzer.*"

She removed the phone from her ear and examined the instrument with dismay.

"What's it about, Barry?"

Keep calm, Linda, you're a pro, okay, don't unravel here, distance yourself . . .

"Big bucks," murmured Barry. "Arabs. Lobbyists. A diplomat or two."

"Is Fitzgerald involved?"

Linda caught the two-second pause.

Suddenly her eyes riveted on the pad clutched between her fingers, the pad of notes and phone numbers. Linda opened her mouth, as if to speak, but felt dizzy. She was leafing through the pages, knowing precisely what she was looking for.

"Fitzgerald's *helping,*" Barry finally said, but Linda didn't care. She had found the words: the message that Marcus received at the Beverly Wilshire.

"Got to run, Barry," she said. "Speak to you later."

Linda hung up before the city editor said anything further, rushed into the dining room, catching the startled gaze of Rita.

"What's wrong?" Rita said.

"Who's Cheryl?" cried Linda, walking up to Lois.

Giving the diary to Jerry P. Cheryl.

"Cheryl," said Lois drowsily. "Darling, you look like a wreck."

"Who's Cheryl? Does Marcus know someone named Cheryl?"

Lois lowered her eyes. "Cheryl is some Washington bimbo that Marcus sleeps with. Someone who works for . . ."

"Fitzgerald. Dave Fitzgerald. Is that it?"

"Yes," said Lois Barrie, smiling. "Fitzgerald and Marcus are quite close."

Linda looked away. "Something's *wrong,*" she said, and turned and saw Gregory's puzzled face. She stared past him. "I think I'm working the same story as Howie Bishop."

*

The phone rang in Jerry Paley's locked study. He took a deep pull on the vodka in his glass and reached for the phone. It was Fitzgerald.

"I think, perhaps, a, uh, another trip to Panama is necessary."

"That's fast. I just got . . ."

"I know, Jerry, but there's some pressing matters down there that need our attention."

"How soon?"

"Tonight?"

"There's a seven-fifteen flight to Miami. I'll catch the first plane out of there tomorrow morning."

"Back here in the afternoon?"

"Late."

"It's going to be hot down there," Fitzgerald said.

"At least a hundred."

"Hotter."

"A hundred and twenty-five?"

"Yes."

Jerry drained his glass of vodka. Grasping a tissue off the desk, he wiped his forehead and cheeks and neck, twisting the wet, filmy paper cloth into a ball and flinging it backward toward the straw basket, a foot and a half away. He missed.

"Thanks, Jerry," said Fitzgerald, hanging up the phone before Jerry said good-bye.

Jerry heard footsteps upstairs, the sound of Maggie in little Angela's room directly overhead. The spill of toys on the floor. He opened his eyes and faced the pile of bank statements, canceled checks, deposits, receipts, bank books. He found his phone book beneath a bank statement.

A woman answered Barry's phone.

"Is Barry there?"

"No. He just left."

"My name is, uh, Jerry Paley. Can I leave a message?"

"Sure."

"Got a pencil?"

"Yeah."

"Who is this?"

(A pause.) "My name is Margie."

"All right, Margie. Can you tell Barry to meet me tomorrow night, Monday night, and not in the afternoon. Tell him to be at The Four Seasons in Georgetown at eight o'clock. The lounge."

As Jerry hung up the phone, he heard Maggie's voice as she wheeled Angela downstairs. "We're going to get you some nice juice and cookies, we are. And we'll see Grandpa later."

Jerry Paley was drunk now, and he whispered, "We'll see Grandpa later," as he picked up one bank statement and tore it apart, letting the pieces drop to the floor.

*

It was Latief Kwame's poor luck to have an exam scheduled Monday morning at nine in the course "Monetary Theory and Policy 1," to be followed by another exam at twelve o'clock in the course "Shakespeare and Chaucer."

Two spring examinations in one morning.

Granted, it was exam time at George Washington University, but wasn't it unusual to face two tests in a single morning? Unusual and *unfair.* He thought of complaining last Thursday to his faculty adviser, a black man named Ferguson who taught physical education, but the last time he saw Mr. Ferguson and grumbled about the heavy workload, the faculty adviser said, rather unpleasantly, that this is the way American universities work, and if it was too difficult, then perhaps Latief Kwame should return to Lagos.

So Latief Kwame sat at his desk behind a wooden panel in the lobby of 1820 P Street, his notebooks and three texts piled in front of him. At least he had time to read on the job, unlike his younger brother Togo, who worked for Diamond cabs, or his cousin Olugu, who worked for Barwood cabs. Better money driving a cab, of course—in some weeks Togo cleared two hundred and fifty dollars, even three hundred dollars, which he sadly wasted on clothes and movies—but no time for schoolwork. At 1820 P Street, Latief Kwame indulged in the luxury of being paid to read, a job that he was especially grateful to have at moments like this when exams loomed. He could study his preface to *King Lear,* his favorite, and then move on to *Hamlet* and *The Merchant of Venice* and, hopefully, *Antony and Cleopatra* by the end of the evening.

The cardboard sign in the lobby read, in bold blue letters, ALL VISITORS MUST BE ANNOUNCED. And Ezra Tucker, the building manager, had warned him about robberies on P Street, and Twentieth and Twenty-first streets, and not to be afraid of asking a stranger entering the lobby where he was going.

There are a lot of creeps around this neighborhood, Mr. Tucker said, a slight white man with a chicken neck who walked with a shuffle and broke into small, twisted grins as he spoke.

At first, Latief Kwame solemnly accepted Mr. Tucker's comments; he even stood inside the door entrance to keep careful watch on visitors. But after stopping three people in the first week and being told somewhat angrily by two of them that they had lived in the building for many years—the third was a maid who had worked for the same woman for seventeen years—Latief Kwame retreated behind the desk and avoided confronting the stream of people entering the lobby. He merely watched. And he adopted the rule, voiced to him by the Pakistani student who worked at 1810 P Street, that any well-dressed white man or middle-aged woman, black or white, who walked into the lobby was hardly up to any mischief. It's a matter of common sense, said Abdul, who told him with a gleeful smile, revealing terrible yellowed teeth, that there were plenty of American girls in these buildings who made themselves available.

In seven months of part-time work in the building, Latief Kwame had met no available American girls, and he concluded that Abdul was either a liar or an extraordinary playboy, which seemed unlikely, given Abdul's teeth and terrible mouth aroma.

Yet Latief Kwame was not quite willing to write off Abdul's remarks, since Latief knew that he was painfully shy with American girls, and the one or two that he noticed, especially the new tenant on the sixth floor, entertained men with such frequency it only seemed a matter of time before he would, hopefully, receive a smile from her in return for his persistent grin whenever he saw the woman enter the lobby and walk quickly to the elevator.

Latief Kwame glanced up now and smiled. The gray-haired woman who lived on the fourth floor passed through the lobby, gripping a brown bag of groceries. "Good afternoon," she said. "Looks like we'll have some more rain." Latief nodded. "Yes, ma'am." The lobby door opened and a bearded fellow with an earring, who lived with another bearded fellow on the sixth floor, walked in with a third bearded fellow. Smiling and nodding, Latief watched them step into the hallway. Some odd fellows in the building.

Opening his textbook, Latief Kwame turned to a study of *King Lear* by an Oxford professor. It was a risk to review only several plays, but Latief sensed that Professor Stevens, a lady who spent considerable time talking about women in literature, would ask at least one question about Shakespeare's female characters. Undoubtedly, there would be a question about Shakespeare's "craft."

Latief glanced up and smiled. The long-haired fellow who lived on the first floor waved as he stepped through the lobby to the entrance. Nice chap. Friendly. Works as a guitarist in a Georgetown nightclub. As always, the fellow was wearing a khaki jacket and an old hat—this time a black top hat.

Latief watched him open the door and hold it for a stream of people: the elderly woman from the second floor, a man—a white man, quite well-dressed, a stranger in sunglasses who nodded to Latief Kwame and walked briskly into the lobby heading for the elevator. Followed by a woman, attractive, also a stranger, in a beige coat and sunglasses.

Latief opened his book, glimpsing the visitors one final time as they stepped into the elevator.

Odd. Not much sun today.

Moments later the elevator door creaked open at the sixth floor, and one of the visitors stepped toward the apartment and rang the bell. The eyehole flashed open for at least eight seconds. Finally, the visitor heard the door unlock, watching the handle turn.

"What do you want?" Cheryl whispered, half her face pressed against the opening.

"I want to talk to you."

"Not now."

Down the hallway a door slammed.

"Just a few minutes."

"I'm busy," she said, keeping the chain on the door lock.

"Now?"

"I'm expecting someone soon." Cheryl hesitated, though, gazing intently at the visitor.

For reasons never fully explained—the pleading look in the visitor's eyes, the tone of urgency, perhaps—Cheryl cast her face down to the floor, weighing her next move. She finally glanced up at the visitor, her eyes and lips framed in puzzlement, and unfastened the lock. Shrugging, Cheryl opened the door and allowed the visitor to slip in.

According to Latief Kwame's sworn testimony to the police that night, at about 7:15 P.M. a man who identified himself as Mr. Bishop of the New York *Star* entered the lobby and asked to see

Cheryl Thomas. There was no answer in her apartment. Bishop waited approximately forty-five minutes and said he would return at nine o'clock. When he came back, there was still no answer in the woman's apartment and Bishop demanded that they open Miss Thomas' door.

At that point, Latief Kwame phoned the home of Ezra Tucker, the building manager, who agreed to have Latief unlock the door of the apartment only after Bishop had threatened to call the police.

The apartment was perfectly still, although a light glistened in the kitchen. It was warm and musty, with the scent of cigarettes and greased fish and bacon choking the air. Newspapers and magazines littered the floor. A pair of sequined shoes lay on the stained grass-green carpet beside the sofa. Close by, next to a half-open window overlooking a courtyard, a round oak table held several dishes covered with crumbs and specks of cheese, a cup with muddy coffee and an open container of milk.

For a moment, Latief Kwame frowned and nodded his head at Howie Bishop, momentarily satisfied that the woman was not home. Latief saw the white curtain billow against the window. He yearned to say something clever to the extremely rude newspaper reporter.

Latief saw her first. Taking a step toward the kitchen, he stopped and, catching sight of the outstretched hand beside the bedroom door, let out a cry. He heard Howie Bishop rush beside him and, moving warily past the sofa, saw the body.

Cheryl was lying face upward, her hair twisting over the floor in a golden halo. The woman's frozen blue eyes stared at him fixedly, accusingly, the eyes of a dead fish. Catching his breath, Latief flung his left hand to his open mouth.

Her milk-white skin was unblemished except for the trickle of blood that seeped from her mouth and congealed at the corner of her lips. A drop of blood quivered on her chin.

And then Latief saw that her entire navy rib-necked sweater was turning an eerie purplish color before his eyes. On Cheryl's collar, at the center of her neck, was blood.

Latief was momentarily sickened, the smell of stale food and decay choking his throat. He grasped the edge of the sofa, gulping air, dimly aware that Bishop had removed a notebook and was writing with a pen that scratched against the paper.

Latief tried to concentrate on the floral pattern of the sofa, on the brown stains blotching the carpet. His lips began jabbering until Bishop grabbed his arm and walked him out into the hallway. He saw Bishop press the buzzer for the elevator and thought, for a moment, that he was perfectly all right until the elevator door creaked open.

Grasping the icy rail as the elevator moved downward, Latief Kwame was suddenly seized with the memory of Cheryl's blue eyes gaping at him.

It was then that he fainted.

Although the police disclosed later that the victim sustained four wounds to her body—one bullet entered the chest and severed a major vein, one entered the back and punctured a kidney and a lung, one went into the right arm and one into the palm of her hand—although the police said there was "an obvious scuffle," the two bearded men who lived next door, who happened to be entertaining the third bearded man, said nervously that they had heard no signs of trouble all day in the apartment. Miss Thomas was a perfectly pleasant neighbor who once used their hair dryer.

Howie Bishop was questioned by the police for two hours. He told them that he had an appointment with Cheryl Thomas to discuss her two years working for Senator David Fitzgerald. Under questioning, he said Cheryl Thomas had numerous friends in Washington's political and diplomatic community, but he had no idea what the motive for this murder could have been.

Latief was questioned far more intensely for more than four hours on Sunday night, and ninety minutes on Monday morning. He informed the police that the victim often had men visit her, but he failed to recall their names. Mostly people from the Middle East. Well-dressed men. Once or twice an African arrived in a limousine.

According to Latief's account, the woman had phoned him on the intercom at about two-thirty to say she expected a visitor shortly and to allow him upstairs. Otherwise, he would have stopped the visitor. Of course. It was the policy of the building's management to announce all guests, and Latief adhered to this policy *except* when tenants informed him beforehand. Like the woman.

Latief Kwame told the police that he saw an olive-skinned man —"like an Arab"—step into the lobby shortly after three in the afternoon. The man said, "Miss Thomas' apartment" (in what seemed like a foreign accent) and walked directly to the elevator. The man departed thirty minutes, perhaps forty minutes, later. Walked toward Dupont Circle.

Describing the visitor, Latief Kwame said he wore gray trousers, a navy blazer and a white button-down shirt and striped tie. Bald. Heavyset. Looked a bit like "Kojak." And he wore sunglasses. Big sunglasses over his eyes.

Actually, the killer passed through the lobby in a blur, and the description that the frightened Nigerian handed to the police was a blend of fantasy and deceit. In fact, Latief Kwame had no idea what the killer looked like.

Two days later, when the police found out that the wires in the intercom to Cheryl's apartment had been short-circuited for at least three weeks (the woman had complained twice to Ezra Tucker), Latief Kwame was hastily dismissed from his job by the building's owners for allowing visitors in unannounced. In fact, the owners of the building, the Gold-Fleischer Realty Corporation, hastily hired two retired police officers from the Arlington police force to manage security at the building on P Street, which served as a focus for a spate of feature stories in the Washington *Post* about increased violent crime in the northwest section of the city.

Unhappily, Latief Kwame could only find a job driving a Diamond cab. Not a difficult job, but certainly not as easy as the one sitting behind the desk at P Street. And for weeks after the murder, whenever Latief drove past the building in his taxi, he silently cursed the bad luck that had led him to allow the stranger with the dark glasses into the house.

Monday

CHAPTER 14

On her mornings in New York, Frieda Steiner usually ordered only the New York *Star* from the doorman, but as she stepped toward the intercom on Monday morning, she requested all the papers. It *was* a waste of money, Frieda thought as she stepped into the living room to open the heavy silk drapes and gaze outside at darkened, rainswept Park Avenue. A waste of money, but she had awoken too early and had too much time to spare.

Despite a brandy late last night, she had slept poorly in the bed that Frederic had purchased in the nineteen-thirties. It came from a dealer in London, a seventeenth-century Roman paneled and gilded bed made for Pope Urban VIII and used in the Barberini Palace. An enormous piece of handiwork, dominating a room whose paneled doors and overdoors had been painted by Tiepolo for the Palazzo Rezzonico in Venice, whose Chinese silk wall coverings and draperies, once part of a Florentine villa, lent a dark and gloomy and, for Frieda, ominous tone to the room.

She carried them into the kitchen, put on the teakettle, then glanced down at the top paper on the pile. The *Daily News* headline read:

SOV TROOPS, TANKS, NUKES
RUSHED TO CHINA BORDER

Lower down the page, a grainy photograph showed a blond girl in sequined tights standing behind a table between two men. The girl's hands rested on the shoulders of the two men, a bored, vaguely hostile smile marring her pretty face.

The caption read: *"Ex-Senate Aide Slain. Cheryl Thomas, former aide to Senator David Fitzgerald (D–N.Y.), flanked by uni-*

dentified Saudi Arabian businessmen at Charisma Club in Washington, D.C. The 26-year-old hostess and former stewardess was found slain last night in D.C. apartment."

As Frieda placed the *Daily News* on her tray, and stepped toward the kitchen cabinet for a cup and saucer, her eye caught the front page of *The Wall Street Journal,* now lying atop the *Star* and *Times.* She felt a shock; her left hand flew to her hair, she began stroking invisible strands from her forehead.

She read and reread the headline atop the left-hand column on the front page:

A FAMILY PAPER
Troubled New York *Star*
Faces Cost Squeeze, Tough Unions
As Readers Flee to Suburbs

———

Competition from TV, Rivals,
"Just like *Herald Tribune.*"
Comics, Gossip, Recipes Added

Frieda sat down and read:

NEW YORK—Like an aging dowager fallen on hard times, the New York *Star* is nervously facing an unpredictable future that demands some drastic—even embarrassing—sacrifices if the venerable institution wants to survive.

An independent, family-owned newspaper that has managed to keep afloat in the always turbulent New York publishing world, the *Star* is now facing an array of difficulties that makes the outlook for one of the more respected and complete papers in the country "very troubled indeed."

"It's like the *Herald Tribune,*" said one newspaper analyst. "Hemmed in by the competition in a declining market. Advertising and circulation are on the slide. Union demands are out of sight for a struggling paper. There's competition from TV, from suburban papers, even from home video terminals. Newsprint prices are skyrocketing. At some point, the *Star* will face the inevitable."

Frieda's cold fingers brushed her lips as she read a quote attributed to Skipper—"We have problems, sure, but these are endemic to any big city newspaper." Her eyes caught isolated phrases: "Skipper's appointment had seemed a classic case of corporate nepotism . . . Skipper has surprised people . . . transformed the paper into a livelier daily designed to appeal to younger and suburban readers . . . With the *Star* building, Skipper's critics maintain he has moved too slowly and indecisively, failed to 'bite the bullet' against the unions . . ."

Frieda read slowly now:

Sources inside the paper say Mr. Steiner is preparing to confront the feisty Newspaper Guild chairman, Frank Lazzarutti, with a plan to terminate the employment of nearly 150 reporters, advertising salespersons, artists and other white-collar employees in an effort to scale down expenses. Mr. Lazzarutti, a popular and articulate trade union figure with national ambitions, would inevitably pick up the gauntlet and force a showdown.

Precisely how poorly the *Star* is faring can't be ascertained. A closely held private company, the *Star* discloses neither profit nor revenue. But industry sources say the paper's circulation has now slumped to 400,000, the lowest point in years. Revenues this year are estimated at $120 million, an increase of 8 percent over last year. Costs—which include newsprint, ink and new equipment—are expected to increase 12 percent.

In its heyday in the 1940s and '50s, the *Star*'s circulation was a respectable 600,000, and the paper made money as New York's "second-best" daily. But sluggish management by Jonathan Steiner, rising costs of production, excessive settlements with unions and recurring strikes, together with the middle-class exodus to the suburbs, have taken a heavy toll. Beyond this, television has obviously played a role in the decline of papers like the *Star*.

Profits sank to the break-even point in 1978; then, in 1979, the paper ran in the red. It has been losing money ever since, with the paper expected to lose nearly $2 million this year.

"It's an unfortunate truism of the industry that the only real way to cut expenses, for a paper like the *Star,* is to hold down editorial spending and trim the staff," said one Wall Street newspaper analyst. "The trouble is, once you start cutting the editorial side, the product diminishes. And once the product diminishes, circulation and then ads drop. It's a vicious cycle."

Frieda felt the pounding in her ears now as she read quickly. Isolated phrases, sentences sprang alive.

Tragic death of Evan Claiborne . . . Maury Kramer, a respected low-keyed deputy favored to succeed . . . Other contenders include Barry Cohen, the feisty city editor who has developed a first-rate investigative staff . . . Ward Parsons, the foreign editor . . . Sally Sims and Hugh Finch . . . If appointed, the first woman and black to run a New York daily . . .

The sight of her own name in the next paragraph made Frieda wince. She reread the words.

> Although Skipper Steiner will play a key role in selecting the managing editor, the family figure dominating the paper remains the publisher's mother, Frieda Steiner. At 72, Mrs. Steiner remains the *Star*'s largest single shareholder, controlling an estimated 45 percent of the voting stock.
>
> Despite her protestations to the contrary, Mrs. Steiner oversees the editorial side of the paper with a barrage of memos and phone calls that have earned the gray-haired matriarch such nicknames as "The Iron Lady," "Evita," and "Mommie Dearest."

Frieda's hand touched her chest. She was gasping for air. Once again she read the paragraphs, and then her eyes scanned the words that followed:

> Mrs. Steiner, responding to a phone call from *The Wall Street Journal,* emphasized that she had little day-to-day control of the paper, although she conceded: "I meddle a little bit." She declined to say anything further about her role on the *Star.*
>
> Other stockholders within the family circle are Skipper Steiner (29 percent) and Lucy Steiner Claiborne, the publisher's sister (19 percent).
>
> A longtime family friend and trustee, Eli Faber, who advised Jonathan Steiner and is reportedly close to Frieda Steiner, holds 7 percent of the company's stock. Mr. Faber, mentioned a decade ago as a possible publisher of the *Star* when Jonathan died, is rumored to have bickered with Skipper about the direction of the paper and its content.
>
> Many observers date the decline of the *Star* to the death of its founder, Frederic Steiner, in 1952 at a time when the paper was starting to face financial difficulties. His heir, Jonathan, a low-keyed, almost reclusive figure in contrast to the flamboyant Frederic, was forced to economize while such competitors as the *Times* and *Daily News* were expanding.

"In point of fact, my father did what he could, given the situation in New York," said Skipper Steiner. "Our problems are hardly unique. The metropolitan area has declined and, with it, our difficulties have increased."

Frieda nodded as she read that many of the *Star*'s problems were beyond its control. Unions were fighting the introduction of labor-saving production equipment. Distribution was costly and complicated; newsprint prices, which represent almost 30 percent of the paper's costs, had climbed over 80 percent in the last five years. The flight of the white middle class from inner cities had devastated the retail industry, the newspaper's major advertiser, and had a pronounced impact on circulation . . .

Narrowing her eyes on the article, Frieda read that papers such as the *Star* viewed current trends in the industry with nervousness. Recent polls showed Americans spending fourteen minutes a day reading papers, compared with twenty-two minutes a dozen years ago. Despite increased education and higher income in the country, newspaper circulation has declined steadily since 1945.

How the troubled New York *Star* deals with its problems is being watched with interest on Wall Street and across the newspaper industry. Despite Mr. Steiner's strenuous efforts to keep so-called "hard" news dominant in the paper, there are persistent rumors that the *Star* is planning to eliminate more of its foreign business, cut back traveling by overseas and national reporters and concentrate increasingly on "bread and butter" local stories appealing to New York readers.

The penny-pinching mood after years of declining ad revenues is visible at the *Star*. Its dimly lit, stark newsroom has bare tile floors and stained walls and ceilings. Editors grumble about everything from mice to a lack of private offices in which to carry out personal conversations. The toilets periodically overflow, and the cafeteria has been dubbed "The Gulag." Given the problems, however, the paper's aggressive staff speak with intense feelings about the daily.

"The *Star* is like family, it's Mom," said Maury Kramer. "You complain about her, you scream at her, but in the end you're loyal to her because no matter how terrible she's been to you, no matter how destructive, you still love her with a passion."

Newspaper analysts claim that the *Star*'s money-saving measures, including staff cutbacks, are merely "Band-Aids," and fail to come to grips with the more rooted problems facing the *Star*—problems that just may be insurmountable. Analysts predict that in the long run, if the paper survives, the *Star* will "inevitably" fall the way of other independent family newspapers facing cost pressures: it will sell out to a conglomerate seeking to diversify into the newspaper market.

Such a step is "not in the near or distant future," Skipper Steiner said heatedly, although *Star* sources report that a California conglomerate sought to buy the newspaper. Two key reasons are offered for selling the family paper: rising costs, including investment in new technology, as well as crushing inheritance taxes which the Steiner estate will have to pay once Frieda Steiner dies.

Frieda took a choking breath. She was exhausted and felt the urgency of thirst. But she sat rigid in the chair, unable to move, leveling her eyes on the final paragraphs.

At present, independent newspapers are being bought out by chains rapidly, at a rate of fifty to sixty papers a year. Three out of five of the nation's newspapers now belong to chains, while less than half were under group ownership five years ago.

"Although a conglomerate can provide great resources for a newspaper," said Skipper Steiner, "they have also chopped budgets, held investments down and wrung papers dry of profits. It takes five or six years of pouring money into a paper to make it really first-rate, and few corporations are going to wait that long to show a profit margin.

"If we sell out, as some people want," added Mr. Steiner, "the *Star* will most certainly survive, but it would not be the paper that Frederic Steiner and my father would have been proud of."

One newspaper analyst said the Steiner family now faces two major options if it doesn't want to die: selling the paper for a probable hefty sum; or "going for the jugular," setting out on a five- to ten-year commitment that would mean losing money initially but eventually recouping its investment and turning the corner.

"We're at a crossroads now, and we've got some hard choices ahead of us," said Skipper Steiner. "I assure you, we're going to endure. We're going to make it. Frederic Steiner came to this country with nothing and built up this paper, and we're not going to allow it to die."

*

"That was Mother. She's upset," Lucy said, stepping into the dining room.

"She should be," said Fitzgerald. The morning papers lay strewn on the dining table. Lucy watched him push *The Wall Street Journal* aside, and place the *Star* beside his coffee cup. Fitzgerald's starched white shirt was open at the chest, revealing a triangle of black-gray hair that coiled to his collarbone. He sipped coffee.

Lucy gripped her velour robe at the breast and watched him.

"So awful about that girl," she said.

"Cheryl? Tragic."

He sighed. "My office issued a statement last night. Made the late editions."

"You're going to run for President."

He looked up. "With your help."

"*My* help? You mean the *paper's* help. The *Star*." Lucy's angry tone surprised him.

"I *need* the paper, Lucy," said Fitzgerald, watching her.

"That's why you want me to vote for Barry."

"What's the matter?"

Lucy contemplated him, and Fitzgerald moved toward her, vaguely menacing.

"I heard Kitty White's on your team too, David. I've heard rumors. I'm pleased for you, David. I'm sure Kitty White's invaluable too." Lucy paused.

"Evan slept with her too."

"Kitty slept with a lot of people."

"She wanted something. She wanted us to cover her parties, to make her credible, give her access to New York. She wanted publicity and I think she wanted a column, a once-a-week Sunday column on the social scene in Washington."

Lucy knew her cheeks were burning. "I respect the woman. I do! She knows precisely what she wants and goes after it. It's admirable. I wish I had that kind of . . . *strength*."

Fitzgerald placed his hands on her shoulders, but Lucy drew away. "She uses people so effortlessly, David." Lucy lifted her eyes to his face. "Just like you."

*

Charlie Sims saw the headline in *The Wall Street Journal* as he poured water into the kettle shortly before 7 A.M. Placing the ceramic kettle on the stove, Charlie lit the flame beneath it, and then sat down on a kitchen chair to read.

"Guess what," he said, walking into the study a few minutes later.

"Sshh," she said. Gnawing at her fingernail, her eyes fixed on the television screen, Sally watched a reporter standing on the White House lawn. The reporter spoke breathlessly: "There's a crisis atmosphere this morning at the White House. The President is having breakfast with his crisis team, including Secretary of Defense Belling, Secretary of State Victor and Vice President Nelson."

An anchor man in the New York studio broke in to ask whether there was any chance that the Camp David talks would be canceled because of the assassination attempt against President Kopeikin; the response from the White House reporter was that both the Russian and the Chinese leaders were still scheduled to arrive at Camp David Tuesday morning.

Sally looked up at Charlie. He tossed the newspaper on the sofa. "There's an article on the front page you may be interested in." Sally stared at the headline.

"Oh Christ," she whispered, then read, " 'Like an aging dowager.' " Glancing at Charlie, Sally said, "Ouch. That hurts."

"It gets better."

"Is it terrible?"

"Interesting. Brutally accurate."

"Oy vay."

"I'll start the coffee."

Humming softly, Charlie placed the paper filter atop the melita and then ladled out four spoonfuls of Italian and French roast that he had purchased Sunday afternoon at Zabar's. And then, still humming—it was a familiar Rodgers and Hart song that he had probably heard at the party at Tavern-on-the-Green on Friday—he closed the flame under the simmering kettle.

No. It was the Rodgers and Hart song he had heard on Larry's stereo yesterday afternoon. Seated on the living-room floor eating caviar (purchased, too, at Zabar's at some reckless price, caviar and egg and Macon blanc), listening to Ella on the stereo. Charlie was aware that Larry's faint smile and wide, imploring eyes begged and waited for him. Larry said, *I want to make love to you*

now. Charlie? I need you. Now. Please . . . Larry, listen to me.
We can't see each other. It's foolish. It's too close, incestuous. I
like you, Larry. You're generous. You have so much . . . so much
to give. But it's dangerous for us, and I will not leave her. My life
is orderly now. And sane. And I do love her in my way. It's hard
for you to understand. I know you can't understand because
you're twenty years younger than I am, and you're a different gen-
eration, and so much freer and more honest. And Larry, you
know, Larry, I just can't hack that kind of thing. I can hack the
one-night stand in Key West and the quickie in the afternoon with
a Greek boy in Mykonos, but Larry, I don't want the commitment,
I don't need it, and I'm sorry, I'm really not . . .

He shut his eyes, breathing in slowly as the memory flickered;
the buttons twisted open, the zipper being pulled down, Larry's
warm fingers and mouth, Larry's head moving back and forth, up
and down, the fevered sounds engulfing the living room as he lay
and writhed on the floor . . .

Sally, walking into the kitchen, murmured, "It's going to hit the
fan now."

He turned, startled. She smiled. "You're miles away."

Charlie nodded. "Miles away."

Lifting the kettle, Charlie said, "The story was *kind* to you,
Sally."

"A little patronizing! The token woman."

"You're too sensitive, love."

Sally swallowed orange juice in a single gulp. Her irritation at
him ebbed and flowed with alarming frequency. One smirk, one
acid-tipped comment, left her enraged. She yearned to sound lighthearted, but her voice was strained. "Home all day?"

Charlie glanced at her. "Except at five-thirty. I'm meeting Felicity for drinks at The Four Seasons." Felicity Hager was Charlie's
agent.

"I'll meet you at Dorothy's, then?"

Charlie asked if the usual players were going to be at Dorothy
Faye's house.

"Some new ones. Marty Kaplan's in from Buenos Aires. He'll
be there."

"More Vietnam memories." Charlie rolled his eyes.

"And Patrick and Michael and George and, of course . . ."

"Billie." He smiled.

"She *is* dreadful, isn't she?" said Sally, watching him. Her anger, so palpable only a second before, yielded now to fear. She loved Charlie, needed him.

"Billie would be dreadful even if she weren't a rich radical. A *People* magazine radical who stars at Elaine's and summers at Martha's Vineyard. Writes about the oppressed peasants in Asia and Latin America from her six-room co-op on Park Avenue. Some radical!"

Sally smiled. "Don't be mean. She's Dorothy's dearest friend."

Charlie lifted his eyes to Sally. She began to speak but suddenly held back, startled at the tension on his face.

"She ignores me, dear," he said. "I guess that's why I detest her so much. Treats me like nobody."

"Charlie!" Sally took a step toward him, but he turned and lifted the coffee pot; in profile, a serenely handsome man in a blue knit shirt, painter's white cloth pants and slip-on moccasins without socks.

"Charlie, dear. Billie's a fool."

He ignored her words. "Sally, I'm not one of those chic husbands you read about in *New York Magazine*. I . . . I guess I find it difficult to handle your success." He grinned. "I think I know the way a housewife feels when she goes to a party with her big-shot husband."

Charlie poured coffee into his mug, then stepped to the kitchen table and sat down beside her. "Sorry," he said. "Didn't quite mean it that way. I guess Billie brings out the worst in me."

Sally reached over to take his hand. "Let's not go tonight. The only one I really want to see is Marty Kaplan, and I'll take him to lunch." He turned to her. "Charlie, let's just stay here. We never have dinner alone. I'll cook."

"No, I'll cook. You bring wine."

"Charlie." She touched the shoulder of his blue knit shirt. "Charlie, I do want us to be happy."

"Me too."

"It's complicated."

"Very."

"We're not as sophisticated as we think we are."

"Two kids from the Midwest conquering Gotham."

Sally grinned. "You still make me laugh."

"You still make me happy, Sally." He leaned forward and gently kissed her.

"Why is it so complicated for us?" she whispered.

"You keep saying that."

"Charlie?"

"Yes."

"I want to be managing editor."

He swallowed. "Go after it, then. Push! Play politics. Do your Barry Cohen number."

He kissed her on the cheek, and Sally let her fingers touch his eyebrows and slither over the outline of his nose.

"Charlie," she whispered. "Let's try."

"I need you," he said.

Sally felt her lower lip tremble. "I've got to . . . I've got to work things out, but I want us to be happy with each other."

"I need you," he repeated, staring at her somberly.

*

When Maury Kramer awoke, he lay in silence, inhaling, listening to the soft breathing of Nancy beside him. His toes touched her knee, and he pushed himself close to her, letting his left hand fall on her shoulder.

When he kissed her, the smell of perfume seeped into his nostrils, a smell that stirred him, aroused him. Nancy buried her hair in his chest.

"What time is it?" she whispered, snuggling in to him, allowing the cool, long fingers of her right hand to fall gently beneath his ear.

"Ten after six."

"Jesus!"

"Can't sleep."

"Nervous?"

"I guess so."

"Don't be." She spoke in a hoarse whisper, rubbing her thumb and forefinger onto his earlobe, kissing his chest.

"You're exciting me," he said.

"That's not my intent. Not at six in the morning. I like the way you smell. Sweaty and hairy."

"Thanks."

She smiled. "Take it as a compliment. A man's smell."

A delivery truck had stopped outside the brownstone, its radio sounds breaking the silence with Barbra Streisand.

"Your friendly newspaper deliverer," said Maury.

"Can't you talk to those guys?"

"Me?"

"You're powerful. You're managing editor."

"*Acting.*"

"Don't quibble with words. You're the boss man."

He kissed her neck, pressing his hands firmly around her shoulders. Her fingers twisted into his hair.

"Maury, sweet . . . If you get it, you get it. If not . . ."

"You'll throw me out."

"I'll be secretly overjoyed because I'll have you more. You'll have more time for the crazed Chinese female."

He kissed her right nipple.

"I want it," he murmured. "I want that damned job too much."

*

Thunder woke Eli Faber with a jolt. He sat up in bed, short of breath, feeling his head pound violently. In the dawn half-light, he tried to recall the dreams of the night that merged with the phone calls, Dave Fitzgerald's anguished voice.

Cheryl's dead. Christ! Don't know who did it, Eli. And there's no word, there's no bloody word on the diary. Cops have sealed the apartment. Yes. And what we know, what we're sure of, is that the stupid bitch mailed a copy to Jerry Paley. It's gonna unravel, Eli . . .

He had calmed Fitzgerald, wondering whether the senator's distress was just a little bit disingenuous. Knowing, of course, that Fitzgerald had every reason to want the girl dead.

I'm not a fool, Eli had thought with a trace of anger, even as he spoke soothingly to Fitzgerald. Dave, we'll get what we want in the end. You and me, we'll do it, we'll get it . . .

And so will the Dunlaps, Eli thought. Charles and Ernie Dunlap. Millionaire New York builders, his dear friends. Threading in and out of the Steiners' lives, showing up at Evan's funeral, at the party at Tavern-on-the-Green. Lurking like a dark shadow.

Frieda hating them with a passion her children failed to understand, a passion borne of guilt. The Dunlaps were waiting.

Eli climbed out of bed, still dizzy from the dreams, feeling the rise of passion in his groin. He walked to the window to stare down at darkened, rainswept Ninety-first Street, the sensation in his body at once pleasurable and uncomfortable. He turned and looked across the room at his wife Lenore, curled in bed, snoring with a faint whistle. He touched himself.

He would call Shirley's house later, get the thick-lipped girl, Serita, to satisfy him.

Eli gasped, startled out of his trance by a bolt of lightning. He was fully awake now, his face very cold. Suddenly, as he stepped back and heard the thunder crack ominously close, Eli saw the misty figures that had floated through his dreams. Shirley and Serita. Cheryl.

Harry Laxman.

He hadn't thought of Harry in years, dead and buried Harry was, murdered too, like Cheryl. Her death had triggered the dream, stirred the connective links.

Eli listened to the rain, the wheels of a car swishing past. He was locked in place, eyes wide in fear: he saw Harry's taunting face.

Harry Laxman.

It was Harry, a shrewd, ambitious Lower East Side gangster who had introduced the young Eli Faber to Frederic Steiner, got Eli the job. It was Harry who had worked for Frederic, then grew rich on gambling casinos and real estate. Made few mistakes in his criminal career, but he had made one while still in his twenties: one fatal mistake. He had stirred the rage of the Dunlaps while fixing the sale of what is now the *Star* building to Frederic Steiner.

CHAPTER 15

Over the three previous decades, the West Fifty-first Street site—now known uniformly in the city as "the *Star* building"—has been lauded in architectural studies of New York as a "cast-iron building of importance . . . cast iron at its grandest . . . an urban masterpiece . . . a robust and lyrical triumph on the West Side . . ."

A corner building, it is ten stories tall, with solid columns two stories high sustaining round arches over spacious plate-glass windows. Rope molding extends across the face of the edifice at every floor, and circular medallions appear in the spandrels above the columns. The building's exterior is painted bluish-gray, with a long arcade of cast-iron arches framing windows and doorways at the street level.

On the tenth floor, where the *Star* executives keep their offices, in the wall vault of Skipper Steiner, rests the fading and yellowed deed of sale of the building. This document bears two signatures: the shaky scrawl of a Texan named Morris Dunlap, who had built a small real estate business in New York, and the firm, straight, almost printed signature of Frederic Steiner.

In 1935 Morris Dunlap, prematurely withered and paralyzed by a stroke, and overwhelmed in Depression debt, sold his jewel, the West Fifty-first Street building, to Frederic Steiner for a mere twenty-five thousand dollars. The sale, according to Dunlap's sons, Charles and Ernest, killed their father, who died ten days later in his sleep.

Morris Dunlap and Frederic had been introduced to one another a year earlier by Harry Laxman, a brawny youth who had led a Lower East Side gang and had performed some violent tasks for Dunlap in the Texan's takeover of several buildings in the nineteen-twenties. At the same time, Harry Laxman served as an associate to Frederic Steiner, a publisher facing some especially troubling trade union organizers, one of whom, a Greek youth from the Bronx, was later found shot to death in a Buick on a side street in Coney Island. (It was widely assumed that Laxman organized the murder, although the killers were never found.)

Like numerous gangsters in New York at the time, Harry was exceedingly brutal, but, unlike many of them, he was also very smart. He later grew rich developing gambling casinos in Havana and, in the process, gained a veneer of respectability through his marriage to Sarah Schiffer, the daughter of a prominent German-Jewish financier and younger sister of Frieda Steiner. (Laxman's wife later changed their last name to Lake. Their son, Larry, became London bureau chief of the *Star*.)

Although Laxman worked for Morris Dunlap and gained his trust and although he had grown fond of the Texan's two teen-age sons, he plainly saw his future tied to Frederic Steiner and promised him that the building he craved, which happened to be owned by Morris Dunlap, would fall into the hands of the Steiner family.

Accordingly, Laxman, with a lawyer and an accountant ostensibly serving Morris Dunlap, shrewdly worked out an arrangement that benefited everyone—except, of course, the Dunlap family.

Other bids on the building hovered around eighty-five thousand dollars, but Laxman, with the lawyer and the accountant, informed neither Morris Dunlap nor his sons nor his wife, who had taken solace in drink because of the family's misfortunes. Thus the twenty-five-thousand-dollar check that Frederic Steiner handed Morris Dunlap on a blustery March morning in the builder's apartment was reluctantly accepted as the reasonable price (given plummeting property values) for Morris' prize building. Frederic Steiner received title to the building that night.

As Frederic Steiner departed and closed the apartment door, the Dunlap children, seated in their bedroom, stared silently at one another. And then, within seconds, they heard the choking sounds of their father in his study—sobs so piercing that Ernie Dunlap, even now, shivers when he recalls that moment so long ago.

It took two years for Morris Dunlap's sons to learn that on the evening of the deal an envelope actually containing fifty-five thousand dollars was given to Harry Laxman, who, according to previous arrangement, paid out 20 percent of his "finder's fee" to the lawyer, and 10 percent to the accountant.

At that time the Dunlap sons were in their teens and working as office boys at the *Star*, where they had developed a close friendship with an eager clerk from the Lower East Side named Eli Faber. They vowed eternal vengeance against the lawyer and accountant, and vengeance against Frederic Steiner.

Fortunately, Charles and Ernie Dunlap had inherited their father's business sense as well as his ruthlessness. To their mother's distress, they shunned college, and with the help of bank loans, mob money, and quiet financial guidance from Eli Faber, they emerged as one of the major prewar and postwar property developers in New York.

Wealth, marriages to women from socially prominent families, and the passage of years had diminished their rage. But Frederic Steiner's death in 1952 suddenly stirred them. Instead of burying their vengeance, instead of accepting the fact that the participants in the fraud so long ago were aging and probably ill, Frederic's death kindled a deep elemental fury in both men. *Why should the wicked die peacefully?* The memory of his father's sobs destroyed Ernie's sleep. He and his older brother had promised to avenge their father, and they would not cheat themselves now from a duty that seemed inescapable. It was a matter of personal justice.

Eight months after Harry Laxman was found shot to death in Las Vegas, the *Daily News* carried a story detailing the especially grim gangland slaying of Angelo Corolla, a retired accountant with mob connections who had suffocated in a locked pine coffin, which was swept ashore on a July morning at Orchard Beach in the Bronx. The knuckles of the old man's hands were crushed, evidence of his desperate efforts to lift the lid. According to the *Daily News,* police informants speculated that the murder was apparently the result of an old vendetta against the accountant, who began his criminal career working for Jewish gangs on the Lower East Side. It would have taken a surprising, perhaps extraordinary, leap of the imagination for the *Daily News* and the police to have connected the deaths of Angelo Corolla and Harry Laxman.

Three months after that, the *Daily News,* the New York *Times* and the New York *Star* carried front-page stories about the murder of Strobe McWhirter, the former chairman of the New York Bar Association, a legal adviser to virtually every New York City mayor since 1946, a Dartmouth trustee and senior partner in one of the most prestigious and largest law firms in the country.

Like Angelo Corolla, Strobe McWhirter died in a particularly brutal way, although only the most strenuous police work would have linked the deaths. McWhirter's throat was cut and he was dumped into a bathtub filled with icy water in the bathroom of a brownstone on Thirty-eighth Street, between Park and Lexington avenues.

The fact that the brownstone was a well-known brothel known

as Shirley's house, was ignored by the press at the time, and unsuspecting readers were informed that Mr. McWhirter was "visiting a friend's apartment . . ."

Publicly, the police said robbery was an obvious motive, and a spokesman reported that known narcotics addicts in the vicinity were being picked up and intensely questioned. Privately, the police were puzzled by the brutality of the well-planned murder, which involved two masked men in their twenties sweeping into the house, locking the girls and their startled customers in a bedroom, and then savagely killing the elderly man after whispering something in his ear.

Had Strobe McWhirter been an ordinary man murdered in an expensive brothel, the New York City police would have been far more dogged on the case. But within twenty-four hours after the killing, rumors spread that officials high in the city government, including the mayor, had placed a veil of secrecy over the investigation, which was unusually discreet and, in retrospect, skimpy.

Had they examined the obituary in the New York *Times,* for example, the police would have found that Strobe McWhirter had founded his law firm at the peak of the Depression, one year after graduating from Harvard Law School. According to the *Times,* Mr. McWhirter had accumulated his earnings to start the firm while working as a lawyer for the late Morris Dunlap.

Had the police used aggressive tactics, they would have threatened and possibly beaten Shirley Buchanan into informing on her clients, which included Ernest Dunlap as well as Eli Faber, who often visited the house together. These facts would have intrigued any policeman seriously examining McWhirter's murder for possible clues.

Two months later, as Eli and Ernie dined alone in the Dunlap apartment, the phone began ringing. It was Charles, who was recovering from a serious heart attack at his home in Palm Springs. The two men chatted about their families and Charlie's health, and the weather in Palm Springs and New York, until Charles interrupted and whispered hoarsely, I'm still not satisfied.

Ernie understood. He examined the palm of his right hand. Neither am I, he whispered, looking up at Eli Faber.

CHAPTER 16

Just in from Buenos Aires, Marty Kaplan was seated at a table in the Plaza Hotel's Edwardian Room when he saw Ward step toward him. They shook hands warmly.

"Our foreign correspondent," said Ward. "Don't you look the part."

Marty wore a khaki bush suit, a short-sleeved shirt, two open buttons at the neck, with two breast pockets and side vents, as well as narrow vents on his left-hand shoulder sleeve for pens. The shirt hung over a pair of khaki pants.

The two men had worked together on AP in Saigon—their first assignments abroad—and shaped a surprisingly intense friendship that, like so many Saigon ties, endured for a year or so after Vietnam but then faded rapidly as reporters followed separate paths.

They sat now in silence as the waiter placed two glasses of juice on the table.

"You going to cut back the foreign staff?" Marty asked, his eyes studying his cup.

"Don't believe everything you read in the papers."

"Interesting article this morning," said Marty. "You read it?"

"Line by line."

"Is it true?"

Ward watched Marty. "You *can't* cut back the foreign staff without slicing into bone pretty quickly. What do we cut now? Moscow? Peking?"

"Buenos Aires," said Marty Kaplan.

"Can't cut all of Latin America," Ward said quickly.

"Why not?"

"Great potential story down there."

"That's what everyone says. Great potential. The great untold story. Latin America?"

"You sound bitter."

Marty Kaplan shrugged. "Hell. I'm not bitter. Too old to be bitter. Just . . . amused. I get the feeling everyone's eyes glaze over when they see those datelines—La Paz, Rio, Santiago, Quito. Buried inside the paper, nice and comfortable beside the panty ads."

"So what do you want to do?" asked Ward, still smiling but watching him.

"I want to go to Paris or London."

Ward tapped his fingers on the table. "I'd love to send you. . . ."

"But . . ."

"But there are no openings. If there are, Ernie Richards gets first crack. He's been in Moscow four years, almost five. Lake in London and Norman Walker in Paris are unmovable, period. Frieda's boys."

Marty Kaplan examined his coffee cup. "All right, Ward. I want to come home."

The smile faded from Ward's face. "You're out of your mind."

"I'm tired, Ward. *Tired!*"

"Take two weeks off. Take a month."

Marty shook his head. "The legs go first, just like a baseball player. You can't run as fast as the younger guys to catch the one plane in Gabon that leaves each week for Nairobi. The hands go too. They shake a little when you're typing a story under deadline on the Reuters telex in Kampala. You start drinking a little earlier in the afternoon and get to know the names of the bartenders and the girls in Intercontinentals. Too many Intercontinentals, Ward, too many PTT offices that close down at 4 P.M., and consulates that work from ten to twelve and crummy airports and delayed flights and one-night stands with flakey Pan Am stewardesses." He turned away. "You remember I went to Beirut last year. The usual gang was at the Commodore. But, Ward, there was a new gang. AP reporters and UPI stringers who were ten years old when we were in Vietnam. Jesus! They looked at me the exact same way that we used to look at those old warhorses in Vietnam. We used to laugh at those guys. And pity them. Hey, Ward. Hey. I'm burned out."

Ward felt the heat on his face. "You'll come back to New York and do what? You'll be working for Barry Cohen. You'll be chasing false alarms in Queens while Mark Kaiserman—"

". . . chases fires in the South Bronx," laughed Marty. "He told me it's the one thing he's worried about."

Ward glanced up as the maître d' appeared at the table. Mr. Kaplan has a phone call in the lobby; Ward watched him leave the table.

Wonderful! Two of his prize bachelors, Ernie Richards and Marty Kaplan, were restive. Always the way. The guys you want to keep fixed in one place are unhappy, and the guys you want to move, like Larry Lake and Norman Walker, won't even be bombed out.

He would end this meeting with Marty, take a cab to the office, work for an hour, then go to LaGuardia Airport for the Washington shuttle and the appointment with Alex. Pain clenched his stomach.

Spasm of guilt, that's what it is, Ward; ulcer's sending the message. Stop playing games with Alex Vikas. Stop fighting like a scorpion to get that damn job. It hurts, friend—Christ, it hurts, you're as meager and groveling as the others. Cutting deals. Agreeing with that oily son of a bitch Bart Taylor not to publish Hugh's story in order to stop Hughie, elbow him off the track . . .

Kaplan returned to the table.

Whores, me and Barry, voting the way we did. Brothers under the skin, but there's a price, friend. I don't know Barry's price, but for old Ward it's the pain shooting across the stomach, the perfectly calibrated ulcer that gnaws with clockwork precision as the self-hatred works over the belly. The meetings with Alex, the vote, the half-crazed wife and perhaps dying kid en route to London. And meanwhile you're diddling your secretary and hoping to get diddled tonight by a *Time* magazine groupie while you're politicking like a son of a bitch to get the job . . .

Marty said, "It was Sally. I'm meeting her for lunch."

*

Eight forty-five. Four taxies had careened past Sally Sims on Central Park West, and now a downtown bus, belching black smoke, barreled down the street, crammed with traffic that seemed to slow and deepen on rainy mornings.

Damn! Should have left at eight-fifteen, even eight o'clock, to start the day in a reasonably sane frame of mind.

A taxi, its on-duty sign aglow, slowed to a halt on Seventy-second Street. Breathless, Sally ran against the red light and flung open the taxi door to step inside. She was trembling with excitement.

After the Monday 11 A.M. editor's conference in Skipper's office on what was coming up this week for the city, national and foreign desks, Sally thought, I'll slip away, grab a cab for Bloomingdale's, and buy Charlie something wonderful: a Geoffrey Beene silk crepe tie, a Lanvin cotton shirt, a handwoven voile sport shirt by Cerutti. Something special.

Yes, Charlie. Let's try, my sweet. Let's try.

She would drop the gift off at the apartment and then meet Kaplan for lunch. Perfect! So smart of Charlie to have suggested she phone the foreign desk to find out that Marty was staying at the Plaza. Such perfect timing that Marty was still having breakfast there, so that she could arrange lunch with him and not bother to go to Dorothy Faye's tonight. Just perfect.

*

The buzz of the intercom startled Frieda, who was sipping tea and watching an interview on the "Today" show with Defense Secretary Belling. "Yes," he had been saying, "the Administration had recently bolstered its Sixth Fleet forces in the Pacific and our forces around the world have been placed on red alert, but this is perfectly natural in view of the crisis. We're watching this very closely, of course, we're quite concerned and . . ."

As the intercom sounded, Frieda instinctively looked at her watch: it was eight fifty-five.

Salvatore's voice came over the intercom. "Mrs. Steiner, your son is on the way up."

Frieda hurried into the bathroom, flung her unflattering but comfortable quilted bathrobe on the bed, and quickly struggled into her underwear. Opening the closet door, she reached for the pale-blue silk kimono whose color brought out the blue in her eyes and softened her skin. Thank God she had finished her morning Lazlo routine, Frieda thought as she thrust pearl earrings on and found, in the closet, her backless high-heeled slippers.

Breathless now, she walked to the mirror to comb her hair, ignoring the sound of the chiming doorbell until she was satisfied that the flattering wave behind her ear was in place. She stepped to the door to unlock it.

"You've seen the article?" Skipper said.

"Yes."

He walked in and began to pace the room.

"It's a damaging article, Mother."

"The first time I read it—I was angry, insulted." Frieda spoke slowly, emphatically. "The second time I came to the conclusion that it was more or less accurate."

"Psychologically it'll do *wonders* for us on Wall Street," Skipper said, ignoring what she'd said.

"That *Journal* reporter wanted to speak to me," Frieda said. "Persistent. Kept calling. I spoke to him once briefly. Finally told him that I do not like to talk to reporters writing about *my* paper."

" 'The Iron Lady.' "

"I wasn't amused."

Skipper caught the tension in her voice. "Who leaked it, Mother?"

"Leaked what?"

"The cutbacks. You told Eli."

"I thought he already knew."

"It was a secret, Mother. Just the family, just us. Eli is *not* the family. He's responsible for leaking that garbage to the *Journal*."

Skipper's mouth twitched. "The comparison with the *Herald Tribune* was odious."

"Odious, but true," said Frieda.

"*Not* true, Mother."

"It *is* true." Frieda seemed to rise in her chair. "We're not talking about tomorrow. We're not talking about next year. We're talking about five years from now, ten years. We're talking about the children. And *their* children."

Frieda stopped, aware that she had heard these words before from the lips of Eli Faber.

"What do you suggest we do, Mother?" Skipper's mocking tone was starting to annoy Frieda, who stared at her son.

"I suggest we *fight*. Fight for our lives. Face reality and take action. Maybe *drastic* action."

"Cutbacks are drastic enough, Mother."

"Cutbacks are the first step," Frieda said quickly. "We're going to survive. We're going to *change*. Give readers different coverage. *Livelier* coverage."

She stood and walked toward the fireplace. "Our decision yesterday not to publish Hugh Finch's story was wrong. It's going to haunt us." As Frieda spoke, the force of her words seemed to embolden her. "Ten years ago, twenty years ago I wouldn't have *dreamed* of publishing that kind of news. Especially when the White House begs, no, threatens us. Wouldn't dream of it. But times change." Her voice dropped. "We're in a competitive business, Skipper. If we have a story, we publish it."

"It's dollars and cents, isn't it?" Skipper spoke sharply.

Her eyes held his, then she said: "I want the *Star* to survive. I will do *anything* to make it survive. I am legally bound to insure that it doesn't die." She reached for the silver box, took a cigarette, her hands shaking as she held a lighter to it.

"What does that mean, Mother?"

"It means that we make decisions *together*." Frieda reached for the chair beside Skipper and sat down. "You and I and Lucy."

Watching his mother, Skipper picked up *The Wall Street Journal*.

"Eli leaked this garbage, Mother. Look at this. 'Sources on the *Star*.' 'One insider at the *Star*.' It wasn't me or you." Skipper stared at Frieda. "Don't you see what Eli wants?"

"He wants what's best for the paper."

"He wants to get rid of me."

"That's absurd!"

"He wants to take over."

"What is this business about a conglomerate?" She spat out the words. "Do I have to read in another paper what's going on at my own paper?"

"Oh Christ, Mother. They came here four, five months ago. A California conglomerate wanting to expand to the East Coast. They worked through Eli, and didn't even make a firm offer. I told them flat out we weren't interested. We're a family that wants *control* of the paper. That ended that. Until I read this article."

Frieda watched Skipper pace the living room, finally halting at the window to stare at the stream of morning traffic on Park Avenue.

Frieda's voice was surprisingly gentle. "Whom are you voting for tomorrow?"

"Maury. And you, Mother?"

"Still not sure." Frieda crushed her cigarette in the ashtray. "The layoffs frighten me, Skipper."

He turned. "Me too."

"They're a perfect excuse for Lazzarutti to call a strike." She wet her lips. "I've always been alarmed at strikes. They lead to nothing but . . . heartbreak. After every strike a paper folds. Even when I say the word, even when I *think* of it, I get nervous."

"The drivers hold the key, Mother. If they cross the picket lines we will get the paper out, and break Lazzarutti."

As if anticipating Frieda's next question, Skipper nodded. "They're amenable to . . . an arrangement."

"Eli knows them," Frieda said. "He's paid them off for years. Talk to him, Skipper. Talk to him this morning. He'll *do* it. Trust him." She stiffened.

Frieda stood up, her eyes pleading. "We've got to work together, Skipper. All of us." She stepped toward her son. "We've got to survive."

*

Frank Lazzarutti woke up each morning at precisely 6 A.M., without an alarm clock, a habit that dated back to his boyhood when he delivered newspapers in Little Italy.

By eight-ten he was in the *Star* cafeteria, seated in a corner. The table was known throughout the newspaper as "Frank's table," and if a newcomer or visitor mistakenly sat down at the four-seat table, he was told, somewhat gruffly, by the two busboys that the table was "reserved" and to please move to another one.

It was from this table that Frank Lazzarutti held court, and if employees had the slightest grievance about their work hours, about their transfer from one department to another, about losing a day's pay for illness, about being unfairly passed over for promotion—if they had a question about the Guild scholarship or health benefits or vacations—they knew that Frank Lazzarutti was on hand after eight o'clock each morning to listen to them. In most cases the grievance was resolved within twenty-four hours.

In successfully resolving employees' grievances, Frank not only assured his reelection by overwhelming majorities every two years

as the *Star*'s Guild chairman, but he earned a reputation across
New York's newspaper industry as a union leader, one of the few
in the business, who relentlessly intimidated the *Star*'s management and worked fiercely for his union brothers and sisters. He
had a tight grip over the hearts and minds of union members, who,
in the words of Eli Faber, "would follow the son of a bitch into
the Hudson River if he asked them to."

He had risen through the union ranks until his insurgent slate
had crushed the team who controlled the *Star*'s Guild unit for
years, fattening their pockets with payoffs from management—
payoffs which had been handled discreetly by Eli Faber to thwart
labor troubles on the *Star*.

"So what do you want to do when you grow up?" Marie asked
her husband on a snowy night this past January after he had appeared on a television discussion of New York's labor problems.
Frank had been introduced by the host, a Columbia University
labor economist, as "one of New York's rising labor leaders."

"What do you mean?" he asked. Frank was seated at the
kitchen table, chewing a sandwich.

"Come on, Frank. As they say in the movies, I'm your wife."

"All right, Marie," he said slowly. "You remember the hacks
who ran the *Star*'s Guild before we took over? Remember them?
Well, the guys who control the New York Guild now are their
blood brothers."

"So?"

"So I want to run against *them*. Insurgent slate. I'll get people
from the *News* and *Times* and *Post*."

"You'll win."

He nodded. "I know."

"And then? Big shot in the AFL-CIO."

"One step at a time."

"When are you taking your next step?"

"When Skipper takes *his* next step."

It was time, Frank knew, to make a move against the *Star,* a
move to challenge not only Skipper and Frieda and Eli Faber but
the aging New York Guild leadership. They were fearful of
Frank's ambitions, intimidated by his hard-line tactics, his control
over *Star* employees, his growing popularity among the restless
rank-and-file on the other papers.

The leadership knew, of course, that Frank sought an issue on which to confront them and, possibly, topple them. And on this Monday morning—with *The Wall Street Journal* in front of him—Frank knew he had found his issue.

In the cafeteria, Frank read the story about the *Star* quickly, then read the story again, slowly, line by line, and felt his stomach knotting.

Start dismissals. Reduce the work force by 10 percent. Cut back every department.

Frank's eyes tightened. *Strike!*

Eli and the Steiners and the Wall Street boys want to cut back! Get rid of the fifty-five-year-olds who've given thirty years to the paper, tired and broken and used. Get rid of some deadwood, dismiss the kids. *Cut back.*

One dismissal, one threat, and the New York *Star*'s Newspaper Guild chapter walks out, 987 employees. With the printers and the newshandlers and the stereotypers and, yes, the drivers. *Strike.* If the Steiners and Faber play hardball, the local will match them. And crush them.

And the *Star* local, headed by Frank Lazzarutti, will demand support from the New York Guild. *No more bullshit.* One dismissal from the *Star*, and the Guild strikes every paper in the city. One dismissal, and the drivers will join them.

And if the Guild leadership equivocates—if the hacks crumble under pressure from the publishers—then Frank Lazzarutti will form a rebel slate and call a special election, finally, to lift the Guild out of its torpor, to topple the bastards.

It was time to act. It was time to move in fast and take over the union. It was time to . . .

Strike.

Strike.

Strike!

*

"They think the motive was robbery," said David Fitzgerald, lifting the silver pot of coffee. "Someone said Cheryl had cash or jewels. Coffee, Eli? I issued a statement last night."

"We got it in the late editions," Barry Cohen said.

They were seated in Fitzgerald's suite at the Carlyle, at a room-service table in the center of the living room.

"What did I see this morning, Eli?" said Fitzgerald, glowering. "Didn't I see somewhere that a *Star* reporter had an appointment with Cheryl?"

"Howie Bishop did," Barry said. "We didn't get the diary." He was aware that both men were staring at him.

Eli's appearance at the door when Barry entered the suite had startled the city editor. But in the next few moments, as he exchanged handshakes, Barry pieced it together with sudden ease. Eli was a friend of Fitzgerald's. It was *Eli—Eli*—who would maneuver Barry into the job.

Fitzgerald opened a bucket, lifted two chunks of ice with his right hand and dropped them into a glass. Barry heard the ice crack as Fitzgerald poured a quarter of a glass of scotch.

"Diary's out of our hands." Fitzgerald was tightening the top of the whiskey. "Cheryl's dead. Without her, the diary was meaningless."

Eli spoke up. "Just a bunch of names and dates and figures."

"No one *knows* about the diary," said Fitzgerald. "Except us . . ."

"And Jerry," Eli murmured.

"What's important is to deal with Jerry *quickly*," said Fitzgerald. He saw the alarm on Barry's face. "I don't mean anything violent, for God's sake."

"We mean a story," said Eli. "A story in the *Star*."

"A perfectly good story. A *hell* of a good story." Fitzgerald lifted the glass to his lips. "It's Pulitzer material. Your *second* one. Jesus, there can't be too many guys around with two Pulitzer Prizes." He took a deep gulp of his drink.

"It's painful for me, Barry, painful to talk about because it involves someone we both know and respect."

Barry lifted his spiral pad out of his pocket.

Fitzgerald coughed. "I've had my suspicions for a while, of course. It's not overnight. We've been keeping an eye on him."

Eli interrupted. "You understand, Barry, that Dave wants to help you. And I think he *can* help you. Both of us can help you."

Barry's eyes moved between the two.

"And he's perfectly aware that you *need* a story now, a good story."

Fitzgerald looked at his drink. "This black fellow, Hugh Finch, seems to be getting some . . ." He lifted his face to Barry. ". . . some major stories, exclusives. He's certainly in the running now."

"Parsons also, don't forget Ward," said Eli. "He's pushing hard."

Fitzgerald said with a smile, "We want *you* to get the job." He downed his drink, keeping his eyes fixed on Barry.

"Start at the beginning, Dave," said Eli, watching Barry open his notebook.

Fitzgerald stood up to pour another drink. "You understand, as soon as I heard the *Star* was making certain queries, that Howie Bishop was working on something, I began my own probe. Checking files, snooping around." Fitzgerald turned to Barry. "I was shocked."

Walking to the table, clutching his drink, Fitzgerald sat down with a sigh. "You'd think Jerry would be *smarter*." He shook his head. "Now, Barry, the facts are all there *waiting*. And I can—how shall I say—*guide* Howie Bishop."

Fitzgerald's voice grew strained. "Perhaps Bishop can uncover the details and then, just as you publish them, he can phone me . . ."

"For comment," said Eli Faber. "Perfectly natural."

"Yes. Ask me to comment." Fitzgerald smiled awkwardly. "And then I'll ask the Justice Department for a full-fledged inquiry into my employee."

"And then we print a story that says the Justice Department is investigating Jerry Paley," Barry said.

"At the behest of Dave Fitzgerald," said Fitzgerald.

Barry's thumb clicked his ball-point pen in and out. "Investigating Jerry Paley following the *Star*'s investigation."

"Exactly," said Fitzgerald. He spoke firmly. "We *help* one another. Prosecutors and reporters do it all the time."

"Makes the *Star* look *quite* impressive," exclaimed Eli. "Hell of a story for you, Barry." He tapped Barry's hand. "I think you know, if things work out as we expect, as we expect *now*, I think you know where this can end."

Fitzgerald, in the meantime, had stood and walked to the sofa. Barry watched him turn the combination lock on his leather case, then lift out two legal-size manila folders. "Gentlemen, bring your coffee over here.

"I hired Jerry Paley because he's smart, he's a pro, he knows his way around New York. I hired him to run the staff and keep me smart. I hired him because I didn't want to look like a dummy."

Fitzgerald sighed. "Jerry's got a problem. He likes money." His voice dropped.

"I suggest your reporter find someone at the City Federal Bank on Twenty-first and L Street in Washington. Have a reporter check the date and time of visits to the safety deposit vault in the name of Jerry Paley." Fitzgerald paused. "Perhaps your reporter should compare the time of the visits to City Federal with trips to Panama that day, usually an hour or so later."

Barry's eyes widened. "Panama!"

"Quite natural for us to be interested in Panama," said Fitzgerald quickly. "Signing of the Canal treaty. Mutual defense."

"It's a question of knowing where to look," said Eli. "Where to *look*."

Fitzgerald spoke up. "I think your man would be well-advised to take the time to visit a lawyer down there . . ."

"Aleman," said Faber. "Domingo Aleman."

"Insofar as I know, he's a partner in a rather substantial law firm. Do we have an address, Eli?"

Faber removed a small black notebook from the breast pocket of his suit. "Calle Roberto. That's R-O-B-E-R-T-O. Number six."

Fitzgerald cleared his throat. "Perhaps Bishop should inform the lawyer that he wants to form a company just like Mr. Paley's. I'm sure Mr. Aleman will be able to assist you."

Suddenly Barry was seized with a spasm of anger so intense that for a moment he felt breathless. Finally he spoke. "Paley has his own company in Panama? What's the name of it?"

"Angela. Angela Enterprises."

Barry stared at his notebook. "Mr. Aleman, I assume, has the details."

"A safe assumption," said Eli, leaning forward. "Perhaps your reporter should ask Mr. Aleman to help him set up a corporate account at Credit Suisse in Panama."

"The money's transferred to Geneva," said Barry.

Eli nodded. "Zurich."

Barry said, "Where's the money coming from?"

"Trying to piece this together now," said Fitzgerald. "Checking memos that Jerry sent to me urging me to vote this or that way. Votes in committee or on the floor. Not big votes, mind you, not front-page stuff."

"What kind of votes?"

"A vote in defense appropriations, of which I'm chairman, to rebuild barracks in West Germany. Have a firm out of L.A. do it. Big job. Tens of millions of bucks. Sponsor a private immigration bill for two Saudi businessmen. Members of the Royal Family. Princeton graduates." Fitzgerald chewed his lower lip. "Support an air taxi route between Miami and Nassau. New Florida airline. Vote on the floor to support an oil depletion clause. Here's a couple of memos that may be of some interest to you."

"Thanks."

"You didn't get them from me."

"I know."

"Perhaps someone should compare the dates of some of my votes, my letters, with Jerry's visits to the City Federal Bank. That's what the folks at Justice will do."

"Cash on delivery."

"When I made these comparisons I was . . . shocked. That's what I'll be telling the Justice Department. Shocked. Disbelieving. I want to wash my hands of this . . . quickly."

"He kept the money in the safe deposit box and then went down to Panama . . ."

"When the time was opportune. Always on committee business."

"You're not allowed to take five thousand dollars out of the country," Barry said.

Fitzgerald shrugged. "Who's going to stop a United States Senate employee?"

"Dave, you didn't mention Long Island," Eli said.

Fitzgerald found a sheet of paper, handing it to Barry with a faint click of his tongue. "Copy of a memo that Jerry sent to me last year, urging me to introduce a bill. Take a look at it."

As Barry read in silence, Fitzgerald loosened the top button of his shirt. "Gonna be a hot fucking summer, Eli," he said. "If spring is this hot . . ."

Fitzgerald spoke even as Barry continued reading. "The Navy owned this land for years. Eight hundred and seventy-five acres. Three miles, more or less, from Islip. Not far from MacArthur Airport. Beaches and dunes. Still have some World War II barracks up there. Used it for training, a lookout for German subs. I get this memo urging me to support the sale of the property to the county—not unusual, mind you, not unusual at all. I check with the Navy and the Pentagon—they want to get rid of it. So the property goes to Suffolk County. Two provisions. That the land be used for recreation and that the government could reclaim it if a national emergency occurred. Which seems unlikely, since I don't see Russian subs landing on Long Island, although with this turkey in the White House I wouldn't be surprised."

He started to laugh.

"A conglomerate leases it. Eli, what were the terms?"

"Ninety-nine years, and an option for a ninety-nine-year renewal. They pay an annual rent—forgot the figure—and pay 5½ percent of gross receipts to the county for the first forty years, and 5 percent thereafter."

"So Jerry urges me to support the lease to this company named . . ."

"Argosy, Inc.," said Eli. "Dallas-based."

"I even wrote a letter to the Suffolk County Board of Supervisors supporting Argosy's bid," said Fitzgerald. "Got a copy of the letter right here. And got copies of Jerry's memos."

"What was Jerry's interest?" asked Barry.

"Jerry happened to buy a cheap plot of land out there. The Argosy people needed that land." Fitzgerald smiled at Barry. "Perhaps Howie Bishop should check the real estate records in Long Island."

"Jerry's got a piece of the action," said Barry.

"I think Howie Bishop's going to find that Jerry Paley's plot of land turned very, *very* valuable," said Fitzgerald.

The three men stared at one another until Eli spoke.

"The Argosy people are planning an amusement park out there. Space Age East. A little Disneyland."

"I've heard about it," said Barry dryly.

"Controversial," said Fitzgerald. "Environmentalists don't like it. Say it's going to turn the place into Coney Island."

"What's wrong with Coney Island?" said Barry, a smile tightening his face.

"That's my feeling too," said Fitzgerald.

"Precisely," said Eli.

"Some people are going to make a bundle on this deal," Fitzgerald said, rolling a chunk of ice in his mouth.

*

Seated in the kitchen of his apartment on Kalorama Road, Hugh Finch had read *The Wall Street Journal* article quickly just after Francine's call had awakened him at eight twenty-five.

Now he lifted the wall phone to dial Alvin's home number again. Still busy. Furiously dropping the phone on the hook, Hugh winced at the nausea that rose in his throat. He had dialed Alvin's phone number until two-thirty in the morning, when he had finally asked the operator to try it. Was it off the hook? That's possible, sir, came the bland reply. By three-ten Hugh had fallen asleep.

Yet now, as sunlight trickled onto the kitchen floor, Hugh's exhaustion gave way to impatience and anger at Alvin's elusiveness—an anger mixed with fear.

He would apologize to Alvin. Calm him, lie to him. Hey. That was quite a night. I was lit up. Swacked. What did we do after ten o'clock? I was in-tox-i-cated. Jesus! I was blind.

Hugh scanned the front page of the *Star,* and not finding his name, furiously tore into the paper until page twelve. There was his byline.

By Hugh Finch, Jr.

He read the headline and the subhead.

POLITICS AND THE CRISIS
Fitzgerald and GOP Attack Bergen
Conflict Seen as Election Issue

It was a slapdash news analysis, a thumbsucker that he wrote in New York after the vote in Skipper's apartment. Had to get his name into the paper, had to see the byline. Maury understood, of all of them; *Maury . . . knew.*

I'm not going to get the job, am I, Maury?

They were riding in a taxi from Skipper's apartment to the *Star.*

No, said Maury.

Will you?

Ask me Tuesday.

Would the story have made a difference?

If it were published tomorrow, it could have, Maury said. *Sure. It could have made the difference.*

I'm competitive, Maury.

Insecure's the word. Nature of the business.

I carry on like a twenty-two-year-old. Need to see my name in the paper five times a week. Otherwise, I think I'm slipping. I'm forty-two and still need those bylines.

Hey, Hugh. If you weren't competitive, if you weren't a little crazy, if you weren't born poor and a little hungry, you wouldn't need the Star. *None of us would.*

Hugh reached for the phone and dialed again, hearing the click and the busy signal. Then, with a force that seemed beyond his control, a rage that frightened him, he flung the instrument against the wall.

Alvin.

*

Barry was sprinting down Madison Avenue now, his chest and thighs soaked with sweat. On the verge of breaking two stories. Linda's and Howie's. His staff. *His stories!* And even if the odds against him were absurd at first, the job was his. He was laughing. *His.*

*

As Ward reached his desk, Florence ripped a sheet of paper out of her typewriter, the daily list of correspondents and their whereabouts.

"Everyone's talking about the *Journal* article," she said.

"What are they saying?" Ward stared at the note, marked PER-SONAL, stuck in his typewriter.

"That the situation is *scary.* Comparing us to the *Herald Tribune.*"

Dear Ward:

Name of the doctor who'll take care of your child is Norman Scott-Thompson, one of the world experts on bacterial meningitis. I phoned him last night and he's pleased to handle the case. Call his office immediately with details of Karen and Valerie's

*flight. I'm listing below his office and phone number on Harley
Street and his home phone and address in St. John's Wood. Good
luck! Sarah.*

Ward looked up and saw, in the newsroom's northwest corner,
the sharp-featured face of Sarah Felger, the *Star*'s medical correspondent. She was a skinny spinster just under six feet tall, with
gray hair rolled into a bun and tortoiseshell spectacles tied on a
cord knotted around her neck.

A reporter for twenty-six years and one of the *Star*'s institutions, Sarah treated *Star* employees with a maternal loyalty, a love
that years ago displaced whatever personal life Sarah had. She
lived with her mother, Ruth, a retired psychoanalyst, on West End
Avenue and Seventy-fourth Street, but spent virtually every waking hour at the *Star*.

Ward had phoned Sarah at home on Sunday night to talk about
Valerie's illness. When he had mentioned meningitis Sarah had
said quietly that it *appeared* that the British and Indian doctors
had treated the child correctly, but that she thought Karen was
perfectly sensible in wanting to leave India for the hospital facilities on Great Ormond Street in London. Now let me take care
of some of the details, Sarah Felger had said.

Florence leaned forward. "Forty minutes, Ward."

He glanced up at the wall clock: nine thirty-five. He had to
catch the eleven o'clock shuttle to Washington for his appointment with Vikas.

He reached for Carl Ross's story summary from Peking, and
saw Nick Simons, the city desk clerk, toss a sheet of wire-service
copy to Pat Donlon, the deputy city editor. Barry's chair was conspicuously empty.

"It's Moscow on the phone," said Florence. "Ernie Richards."

Ward lifted the phone. "Good morning." He found a ball-point
pen on the desk and grabbed a sheet of copy paper.

Within eight minutes, Ward had filled the sheet.

Ernie's key source, the German Ambassador's wife, had told
him that diplomats in Pakistan were picking up rumors of a Chinese nuclear test in the Kamchatka Peninsula. Meanwhile, the Soviet Defense Minister, Georgi Malenkov, a hard-line SOB who
favors confrontation with the United States, return to the cold

war, even a couple of nuclear strikes against China's military, is rumored to be leading the opposition in the Politburo to President Kopeikin's trip. And *Pravda* this morning bitterly attacked the United States, saying the Soviet Union had limited its missile forces on the good faith of the United States, while the United States was secretly arming the Chinese. Playing the China card.

That's my lead, said Ernie, with the Malenkov business in the second or third paragraph.

Ward started to ask about Ernie's vacation but stopped, hung up, opened the center desk drawer and removed a Maalox tablet.

"Ulcer acting up?" Maury leaned over his desk.

"Should have gone into insurance," said Ward, swallowing.

Maury pulled up a chair. "When you get to Washington, keep Hugh informed. He's turf-conscious. Doesn't enjoy visiting firemen."

Maury lifted Ward's coffee to his lips. "Why did you vote against publishing Hughie's story?"

Ward brought his gaze to Maury's face. "I'm a son of a bitch, okay? I just didn't want Hughie to get that story."

Maury said, "I'm disappointed. That's something Barry would do."

"Maybe Barry and I are more similar than you think."

"You prick."

"I want the job, Maury."

"So do I," said Maury. "I *deserve* it."

Ward stiffened. "What you deserve and what you get are two different things. You know that better than I do. Even if you *get* the job, what does it mean, really? In the end you're chewed up anyway. Like Evan. Like any one of a dozen guys stumbling around the newsroom. It's the nature of the ball game." He struggled to smile.

Except for the slight quiver on his right eyelid, Maury showed no reaction. He waited several seconds, then pushed back his chair.

"I want Hughie to cover the Camp David talks. I want him to be chief reporter. You work it out with him today about who else covers what, and I want a memo to show Skipper by five o'clock."

Maury, turning, started to walk away, but then swung around. "Good luck, Ward," he said.

Ward compressed his lips. "Good luck, Maury."

Ward looked over at Florence, who began typing. "While you were talking to Maury you got a telephone call," she said. "Someone named Marilyn Cheever. *Time* magazine. Asked if she could meet you tonight at eight-thirty instead of eight. Same place, she said. Broadway Joe's." Florence tore the sheet out of the typewriter.

Ward avoided Florence's face and watched her fingers straighten some papers on the desk. He finally said, "I'm sorry, Florence."

"Nothing to worry about." She inserted the second sheet into the typewriter.

"Yes, there is. I was going to cancel."

"Honey, don't cancel. Why should you cancel? For *me?* Don't you *dare* cancel."

Florence finally looked at him, a glitter of tears in her eyes. "It's the goddamn lying. 'I'm going to stay late in Washington. May even sleep over.' *Lying.*" She tossed her hair back. "I mean, I knew this wasn't a permanent arrangement. I knew that. Maybe I had fantasies but . . ." Florence blinked hard, staring him down.

"You know, Ward, Mary Phelps over there. Evan's lady. She's older than me, of course. Been around longer. I had lunch with her one day just after I was hired. Years ago. In the cafeteria. She told me, *Don't* get involved with any one man in the newsroom. *Don't!* Because in the end you got . . . nothing. Like her. Look at her. She gave years to that son of a bitch. *Years.* And for *what?*"

She took a deep breath. "It's not *your* fault. It's *mine,* for Chrissake. She told me to quit once I got involved. Get another job. Don't hang on." Tears ran down her cheeks. "*Fuck this place.* Jesus, this is just what I need. Monday morning weepies in the newsroom."

The phone was ringing. She got up and grabbed her pocketbook off the floor.

Tony Lazzarutti stared at her. At the city desk, Nick Simons turned. Florence, her cheeks wet and pink, rushed off.

"Lovers' spat," called Nick with a grin, loud enough for Florence to hear. Ward's face paled.

"It's your wife," said Tony, holding the phone, avoiding Ward's eyes. "From New Delhi."

A peal of laughter erupted from several reporters clustered around Nick's desk. In that moment Ward felt that his hatred for Nick Simons was so intense that, had his hand not grasped the phone, he would have gone over and smashed that kid with a killing force. But the phone, like a magnet, held him, as Ward heard the echo of rushing water on the overseas line.

"Hello, Ward, is that you?" It was Karen.

"Yes, Karen. How is it going?"

"We're leaving tomorrow morning at 4 A.M. British Airways. Flight 900. It's Delhi to Frankfurt to London. We get in at eleven-fifteen in the morning British time." He scribbled the details on an empty sheet of paper.

She sounded exhausted. He recalled dimly lit Delhi Airport, the scent of jasmine and cow dung hovering in the predawn darkness, the mobs of Punjabis swarming around the check-in counters, families embracing and weeping and touching.

"Dr. Fuller said we *have* to have someone travel with us. A nurse. I'm sorry. A nurse. Val has to have intravenous line. Penicillin. Dextrose and water."

"All right."

"We'll have to go first-class. I'm sorry. It's going to cost a bloody fortune."

"Don't worry."

"I'm not *worried*. I'm just telling you. I'm not worried. It's not as if I've been spending your *money* here. We've been living frugally."

"Come on, Karen."

"I'm sorry, Ward. Sorry. I'm just at my wit's end." Her voice dropped. "I am very scared."

"I know. I know."

Dear God, don't let her start crying too.

"Now look," Ward said. "We have a doctor. I'll reach him immediately with the flight number."

"What's his name?"

"Scott-Thompson. I think it's Norm . . ."

"Wonderful. Dr. Fuller here says he's *the* expert. Fuller has been trying to reach him."

"Well, we have him, courtesy of Sarah Felger. An ambulance

will meet you at Heathrow and take you to the hospital." Ward glanced up and saw Ray Silver return to his desk.

"The London bureau called this morning," said Karen. "I'm booked for two weeks in an apartment hotel on Hill Street. Fortynine Hill Street."

"Terrific."

"Ward? Can you meet us there? Is there any way?"

He bit hard on his lower lip. "I wish . . . Look, I wish I could."

"Shouldn't have asked."

Ward heard himself say, "How's Val?"

"Very dehydrated. Looks awful. That's why she needs all this intravenous stuff. But Dr. Fuller says we *seem* to have caught it in time."

Ray Silver signaled Ward, tapping his watch—he would barely catch the eleven o'clock shuttle unless he left immediately.

"Karen, look, I'll call you tomorrow."

"You're busy."

"Got a plane to catch."

"You better go." Anger and hurt chilled her voice.

He saw Florence thread her way back through the newsroom, returning to the foreign desk, tinted glasses covering her eyes.

"What time is it there now?" asked Ward.

"Midnight. Five after."

"Get some sleep."

"Still got to pack. Ward, call me tomorrow. In the morning. Call me, please."

"I will."

"I'll be glad to get out of here," said Karen. "Better go now."

Ward stood up as he set the phone down. Speaking softly, he instructed Ray Silver to phone Dr. Scott-Thompson with Karen's flight number. Then, lifting his leather attaché case, he turned on his heels and left the newsroom.

*

Barry bounded into the bedroom, draping his jacket over a chair, flinging his tie on the bed. Take a shower, *get . . . clean.* He unfastened his shirt, aware of a tightness in his chest. His heart was pounding.

The job was his.

The dryness in his mouth drove Barry into the kitchen for orange juice, the sweetness of the liquid serving, strangely, to calm him. He started to laugh. Little Barry. Got that job. How far he'd come to get it, how long the journey from the Bronx, from Tessie and Max.

Max: *There was such promise when I came to this country, but it just went wrong. You work and work. You work your ass off. For what? I can't find the way, Barry. Something's wrong. I wanted to teach the violin and I wind up working in a fucking delicatessen. God plays vicious tricks. Smell my hands! Pickled herring and lox and carp. I stink of garlic. I spend an hour each night washing my hands and I still stink.*

Barry: *You needed the money, Dad.*

Max: *Don't tell me! She needed the doctors the minute you were born. Doctors cost money. First they say it's normal for a woman to be depressed after giving birth. Fine and dandy. So I wait. I'm still waiting. Ten years! Permanent depression. What the fuck. I'm depressed too.*

At six, he sees her on Bainbridge Avenue, her stockings circling her ankles, her kinky, red-black hair streaming over her face, her eyes darting up and down the street to cross. She whispers to herself.

He hides.

When he is seven, Tessie refuses to leave the house. Max returns home tonight and cooks scrambled eggs for dinner, cursing his fate. Little Barry, carrying a list of food and five dollars clenched in his fist, shops three times a week.

My mother is sick.

Uncle Jerry wants to take him to Great Neck. (Look, Barry and Marty are the same age. They get along. Let him stay with us for a while. Get him away.)

No!

At eight, he returns home from school at three-fifteen. Pours a glass of milk and finds a chocolate chip cookie. Her door is closed. And then . . .

A choking gasp in the bathroom. A groan that terrifies him.

Ma? Ma? Are you all right?

He hears her cry. He opens the door.

She is on her knees, gripping her stomach, her mouth twisting.
An open bottle of lye rests at her feet.

He lifts the bottle and pours the liquid down the toilet bowl.

She is taken, once again, to the crazy house in Staten Island;
mesh-wire windows and shrieks beyond locked doors and the hideous smell of disinfectant and vomit and shit.

A growing boy.

He steals pencils from Woolworth's and cuts classes to go to the
Paramount. He shoots crap in the schoolyard and wins. Other
boys, he senses, weaker boys, would be crushed, humiliated. Not
Barry.

At fourteen he gets a job after school delivering for the supermarket on Jerome Avenue. He meets the policeman's wife.

What's your name, she asks, after Barry places the cardboard
carton, crammed with food, on the kitchen table. She opens her
pocketbook and removes a bill.

He tells her. She is wearing a blue kimono and furry slippers.
The kitchen stinks of bacon. Frankie Laine blares on the radio.

You're a handsome boy.

He has never had a woman before. He has seen pictures, heard
talk.

Come here.

She twists off his belt, removes his trousers.

Don't be scared.

She thrusts his shorts to his feet, and crouches to the floor. She
kisses and licks the tip of his penis. She opens her mouth wide,
bobbing her head, twisting her tongue deep over his throbbing
cock. His legs tremble fiercely when he comes and he watches, fascinated, as she rises and swallows.

Now I want you to do something for me, Barry.

She hands him his belt with her left hand. The fingers of her
right hand fondle his balls, gently.

I want you to hurt me.

She unfastens her kimono, falls back on the bed. She spreads
her legs, allowing the fingers of her right hand to stroke and massage herself. Her smile reveals a gap in her front teeth.

He is hard again, his penis arcs in the air.

Hurt me!

Barry stares at the curly black hair on her crotch, at the moist and flushed woman. Fiercely, she grabs his left leg.

Hurt me!

The leather slaps her stomach. Her nails pierce his leg. Her eyes are wild.

Hit me! Hard!

His heart pounds, his stomach clenches in a tight ball. He shuts his eyes and swallows hard . . .

. . . Tessie sits in the kitchen, biting her knuckles. His father sobs. *What do I give you, Barry? Good times? Your mother's a crazy woman.*

God, he hates her.

He hits the policeman's wife with a force that frightens him, the buckle crashing her thigh. She gasps as her body stiffens. Her eyes, dull with fear, widen on Barry. A small weal of blood trickles onto the bed.

Now, Barry, give it to me. Now!

He moves on top of her.

He sees the policeman's wife on many afternoons.

Years later he works nights as a copy boy on the *Star*. He sits in Fritzi's on his dinner break, reading the early edition of the *Daily News*. An item on page five catches his eyes: "The wife of a Bronx policeman killed herself last night with her husband's .45 caliber revolver, according to police authorities. The woman placed the weapon to her mouth after an argument earlier in the day with her husband . . ."

He feels nothing.

There is no one.

. . . Until Chan.

Like a brother.

They met in 1968, Barry stealing Chan from AP. Every American newspaper and magazine had a Duc or a Phung or a Tai or a . . . Chan. Someone to change money. To bribe exit visa officials and cover the ARVN briefing and find expensive girls for visiting firemen. Someone to pick up rumors at Givral's and La Pagode, and take photos in the field and fix appointments with President Thieu's assistants and translate the Saigon newspapers and work tirelessly six days a week, sometimes seven, for the Americans who were adored and hated, sometimes at once.

They are in Cheap Charlie's late one night, eating baked crabs and smoking pot. March 1975. Barry has flown in weeks earlier from his post in Bangkok, and just filed that An Loc has been abandoned. Tay Ninh Province is collapsing. Next morning they are leaving on a Beechcraft Baron—shared with *Time* magazine and the Baltimore *Sun*—for I Corps. Tens of thousands of Vietnamese are streaming along Route 1, abandoning Quangtri and Hue, seeking refuge in Danang. They have been together, inseparable from the start. Chan ferrets out details, extraordinary bits and pieces, exclusives for Barry.

Chan smiles. He sips his whiskey.

I am scared, Barry. I am scared for Mai and the children. The Communists are no fucking good. They will destroy me and destroy my family. So help me, Barry. I will not go on the blacklift like the others. I will stay on to help you, Barry. I will stay on until the end and help you, help you. But, then, in the end, I trust you will help me.

The television networks and the news magazines and the major newspapers had begun a blacklift smuggling Vietnamese and their families out of the country aboard C-130s and DC-8s.

Barry pays five thousand dollars to immigration officials to get the *Star* Vietnamese office staff out.

All except Chan.

Barry, shall I go? Like my friends at NBC and AP?

Stay, Chan. I'll take care of you and Mai. I need your help. The final days are going to be an incredible story. The biggest story in years. Stay. I will get you out in the end. I will not abandon you.

I trust you, Barry.

He was alone now in Saigon. Covering the collapse of Saigon by himself. Marty Kaplan and Dorothy Faye had left the previous weekend on Barry's orders. It was too dangerous for all of them, and he wanted the story himself.

A reporter's dream story. Once in a generation a story that assured a Pulitzer Prize to some lucky bastard. The fall of Saigon!

For days he is sleepless, rushing through the streets of the city to interview frightened politicians and ex-generals and shopkeepers, badgering Embassy officials, typing in a frenzy at night while Chan bribes and cajoles the Reuters teletype operators to rush the copy to New York, while Chan brings him French bread

and salami and warm Coca-Cola, while Chan mops his neck and
forehead with wet towels, while Chan massages his shoulders to
keep him awake. The air conditioner collapses in the offices and
Chan, miraculously, finds a fan.

Chan feeds him rumors from Givral's and Broddard's and La
Pagode, picks up gossip from his cousins in the military command,
types out pages of color and quotes each day that no one else has.

Stay with me, Chan.

Sixteen Communist divisions tighten their grip around Saigon,
moving to cut off Route 15, the city's only escape to the sea.
Barry hears the artillery at the air base at Bienhoa. Big 122-mm
rockets crumple streets in Cholon and the center of the city; one
of them, crushing the penthouse of the Majestic Hotel near the
Saigon River, leaves the office lights quivering. Barry smells dust,
hears screams on Tu Do. A child wails.

Shortly before midnight, Barry receives the phone call from a
CIA friend: All eligible Vietnamese are to be in front of the USIA
compound on Le Qui Don at 9 A.M. for evacuation.

Chan sleeps on the sofa.

Yes, he will inform Chan.

He types thousands of words that night, finally waking to rush
his copy to Reuters, sending Chan into the damp, eerie streets at
dusk to gather quotes, thrusting him in the midst of the growing
crowd at the American Embassy.

(According to *Time* magazine's press section the following
week, the coverage of Saigon's death throes by New York *Star* bureau chief Barry Cohen, who has worked in Southeast Asia since
the late nineteen-sixties, was probably the most perceptive and
devastating by any American correspondent.)

This is fantastic, Chan. Fantastic quotes.

URGENT AND IMMEDIATE COHEN BARRY YOUR COPY IS MARVEL-
OUS STOP OUR HEARTS ARE WITH YOU ALL BEST SKIPPER STEINER.

Eight o'clock. Chan has returned from the swarming gates at
Ton Son Nhut airbase, reeling off quotes and impressions. Yes,
ARVN soldiers and policemen are emptying their guns. Yes,
South Vietnamese A-37 pilots, who had defected to the north,
struck the airbase and destroyed several planes on the ground.
One pilot has slit his throat.

Mai sits on the sofa in the office with three of their frightened children. The fourth, a six-month-old boy, crawls on the floor and plays with a wastebasket. Four battered suitcases, wrapped in belts, nestled at Mai's feet.

Eight forty-five.

Chan!

Yes.

Barry shuts his eyes and swallows. Blood pounds his forehead. Nausea wrenches his throat. The VHF radio tuned in to the mission warden's control center (code-named "Dodge City") sputters. "U.S. Embassy in trouble. Marines to the gate as soon as possible."

A swelling and frightened crowd has gathered at the American Embassy—the crowd tearing at the latticework on the front gate and struggling to climb the ten-foot wall. Begging to enter. Shaking sheets of white paper . . . I am Mr. Anh. I have worked for the American Government for fifteen years. I am Catholic. I will be murdered by the Communists . . .

The sky is filled with clattering Cobra gunships.

Hysterical women seek to thrust their infants over the Embassy wall.

The mob surges forward. A youth shrieks in pain, his right hand clawed in the barbed wire strung atop the wall.

United States Embassy in trouble.

Chan! Get to the Embassy.

The words linger, like thickening smoke, in the air.

Chan lifts a notebook and pen from the desk and rushes out before Barry murmurs . . .

No.

It is eight fifty-five.

His hands trembling, Barry rolls a sheet of paper into his Olivetti.

Urgent. New lead. Saigon.

The infant on the floor sees a mouse dash past the file cabinet. Alarmed, he wails, and Mai lifts him to her chest.

A rocket lands, with a thwack, in the slums beyond the Saigon River.

The child seems to hold his breath. The other children huddle together. Mai weeps softly.

At the thunder of the 130-mm artillery, chunks of cheap office plaster drop on Barry's desk.

He is shaking now, his lips and chin streaming sweat, his fingers swollen, unable to grip the typewriter keys.

He will rush to the Continental to pour whiskey into his belly, to wash up, find some food.

Perhaps . . .

He will find out about the evacuation plans for Americans.

On Le Loi, the pulsing sun blinds Barry. The armed policemen on Lam Son Square eye him menacingly. The iron gates on stores are locked shut, black eyes peering at him.

On Tu Do he sees Ward Parsons of AP running out of the Continental, lugging a typewriter and shoulder bag.

What's happening?

Everyone's leaving. Evacuation. Guys from the Washington Post *and the* Times *and* Newsweek *just left. Get the hell down to the river. The statue of Trang Hung Dao. The assembly point.*

Barry whispers, *What about your Vietnamese?*

Ward stares at him. *They've all been evacuated, Barry.*

Of course.

The plane trees, overhead, sway in the heat. Incense and nuoc-mam stir the air. Cobra gunships circle Lam Son Square. Barry turns, the sun stinging his face.

Runs back to the office and Mai.

Listen to me. Tell Chan to take this copy to Reuters and to keep filing. Keep filing. Use my name. File everything. Color and quotes. Everything. At 4:30 go to the USIS building and Le Qui Don. Your name is with the guard. Your name and Chan's name and the children. They will take care of you and you will be evacuated.

Somehow Barry believes it.

And he picks up his portable typewriter and an overnight bag.

And runs.

And later, as the helicopter rose up into the cloudless sky, he sees long, long rows of trucks moving down the Bienhoa highway toward Saigon. A vast North Vietnamese Army convoy.

And that night, in a bunk bed aboard the U.S.S. *Blue Ridge,* listening to the Chinooks thump across the deck, Barry stares wide-eyed in the darkness, drained and shaking.

Goddamn it, Chan will find his way out. Wily little bastard. Knows every trick in the book. He'll make it.

Mai had smiled at him—no, it was a grin—Mai had grinned at him as he left, and shouted something in Vietnamese to the children. And they had all abruptly laughed. And when his eyes fell on Mai for the last time, Barry saw a narrow-boned face obliterated with grief. Yet, Mai laughed with the children.

Yes, Barry, he will keep filing the story.

And just as Barry lapses into sleep on the U.S.S. *Blue Ridge,* there is a sharp knock on the door. He opens it and sees a Navy ensign in a T-shirt. The youth hands Barry some wire messages.

The one from Skipper reads: BRAVO. YOU HAVE MADE YOUR NEWSPAPER PROUD AND WE ARE DEEPLY GRATEFUL FOR YOUR TALENT AND COVERAGE IN THIS TRYING TIME.

And Evan's message says: THAT'S ONE HELL OF A STORY AND IF YOU DON'T GET A PULITZER I WILL EAT MY HAT.

Barry rips the messages apart, crumpling the shards of paper in the fist of his left hand. Then he walks to the deck. A hard westerly wind, flecked with salt and spray, laps his face and chest.

Shivering, he flings the ball of paper into the South China Sea . . .

Now, in the kitchen, Barry pushes his chair back and steps into the bedroom, his feet cold and a little numb; he removes his shorts. Moving into the bathroom he starts the shower and suddenly sees the face of Jerry Paley. Sorry, Jerry! Barry tries but can't erase the image, even when he climbs in and lets the water slap his face. Grasping the soap, Barry starts to scrub his arms and neck.

*

Skipper received the phone call from Harry Watson, the vice president in charge of labor relations, at nine forty-five.

Lazzarutti had scheduled an emergency Guild meeting at noon to empower him to call a strike if layoffs began. Skipper asked about the drivers, and heard Watson's slight intake of breath. "The drivers are meeting right now with Lazzarutti," said Watson.

"What does that mean?" asked Skipper quickly.

"Don't know."

Watson's tone—usually suffused with platitudes and glib assurances—alarmed Skipper. In the past, Billy Weldon, the drivers' leader, had been cooperative, amenable to Eli's bribes, keeping the drivers at work. If the drivers supported the Guild, a long strike loomed.

Skipper heard the doorknob turn and lifted his eyes as the familiar rangy figure of his secretary, Geraldine Heaney, entered.

"That confidential memo to department heads," Skipper said.

"Already typed, Mr. Steiner."

He leaned forward. "Distribute copies at nine tomorrow morning. Hand-carry them yourself."

"Yes, sir."

"The last person who laid off employees was my father," he said dully. "And it killed him. Call Johanna in Cambridge. Ask her to come down immediately. Tell her to be prepared to stay for at least a week. Let her stay in the family apartment. Frieda's scheduled to leave tomorrow."

"Yes, sir."

"And call Larry," he said. "I want to have lunch with him today. Let's say, ah, The Palm. One-fifteen."

"Sir. Larry is a vegetarian. You remember?"

"Oh *Christ*. Yes. Where should we, ah . . ."

"One of his favorites is The Ginger Man."

As Skipper nodded, their eyes locked briefly. "Mr. Steiner, Miss Sims called while you were on the phone. She wants to speak to you."

He glanced at his watch.

"Tell her to come right up. Maury can wait a minute."

"Yes, sir."

Miss Heaney turned and took two steps.

"Did you read the article in the *Journal?*" Skipper asked.

"Yes, sir." She faced the door. Skipper waited.

"Perhaps I'm speaking out of turn," Miss Heaney said.

"Go on," said Skipper.

She turned and stared at him. "Be careful, Mr. Steiner."

Skipper's eyes searched her face. She took a tentative step toward him.

"There are people who don't like you, don't wish you well," she said.

He leaned forward. "Like who?"

"Like Mr. Faber."

To Geraldine Heaney's surprise, a faint smile lightened Skipper's face.

"You and I are the only ones who never trusted Eli Faber."

"He *used* your father. He was jealous of him." She spoke quickly. "He's doubly jealous of you."

"He wants the paper, Miss Heaney."

"Always, Mr. Steiner. Always. Always wanted the paper." She stepped back, but kept her eyes on Skipper.

"Mr. Steiner, is it true about . . . wanting to sell to a conglomerate?"

"No."

"Difficult times," she finally said, nodding.

"That's why I want my niece here," Skipper said. "That's why I want to see my . . . son. Difficult times."

As Miss Heaney left, Skipper turned to face the chinoiserie lacquered commode that stood against the northern wall of his office. On it were photographs—some of them fading and yellowed, others awkwardly posed by inept Park Avenue society photographers; even now the portraits still moved him and stirred memories of his childhood and youth, when life's possibilities seemed as endless as the Hudson.

A formal Bacharach photograph of Frederic Steiner served as the centerpiece of the collection—a photograph taken late in life, the tired eyes, white hair and bland smile contrasting sharply with the picture on its right of a younger Frederic Steiner, in the prime of his life, his chest expansive, his chin jutting out, his blue eyes lively, almost impish.

To the left of Frederic was a fading picture of Jonathan's brother—Uncle Arnold, at Fort Polk, Louisiana. Wearing a khaki uniform and boots, a helmet tucked under his arm, Arnold stood in front of a tank, grinning mischievously. His carefully written scrawl, in the corner of the photograph, read: "To my favorite young man in the whole world, Skipper. Uncle Arnold. 9/7/43."

Skipper stared at the photograph. Uncle Arnold had sent him letters each week, detailed one-page letters about basic training, and learning to shoot at targets with an M-1 rifle and .45 caliber pistol. Arnold wrote about his excitement because he was going overseas to fight the Germans.

Then Skipper had returned home from school one afternoon, surprised to see his father seated in the living room, staring gravely at him. *Your Uncle Arnold is dead.* He saw his father's strained eyes and turned away, refusing to watch him cry, abruptly angered that Uncle Arnold's letters would stop coming now. *Mother is in the bedroom and to be left alone. You will have dinner at Aunt Sarah's house with Lucy.*

He was aware of the phone ringing that crisp autumn afternoon, of closed doors and whispers, aware that his mother's grief was secretive and mysterious in ways that puzzled him.

Even more clearly, Skipper recalled the late evening that Frieda had walked into his room after the family had returned from Washington and Arnold's funeral. The children had been left behind in New York in the care of maids.

Frieda's perfume smelled sweet and powerful, and he gazed at his mother, fully expecting her to dissolve into weeping, as she had over the past week. She grasped his hand as he lay in bed. Her voice was surprisingly firm and clear and intense.

Keep his letters. Keep every one of them. And the photographs. Put them in a scrapbook and save them because they will be your lasting memory of Arnold . . . of your . . . Uncle Arnold.

The following afternoon, when Skipper came home from school, he found a brown leather scrapbook wrapped up on his bed, its plastic pages clamped and opening only on the firm twist of his fingers. He spent the evening inserting Uncle Arnold's letters and pictures into the album. The next morning, his father gave the boy the letters that Arnold had sent to him, but when Skipper asked his mother if she had anything for the scrapbook—he called it "Uncle Arnold's scrapbook"—she answered quickly, no, no—she had nothing at all . . .

Skipper glanced now at the picture beside Arnold's—a formal photograph of Frieda and Jonathan on their twenty-fifth anniversary—and then examined the photograph that he had taken years before, his son Larry playing frisbee on the lawn at Bella Verde.

The boy was then probably ten or eleven. And even then, so distant, so skinny, so . . . unmasculine. Why? *Why?* His wife had blamed Skipper, and Skipper had blamed her. Mutual neglect and guilt. Margo had told him, If only he had spent less time on the *Star* and chasing women, and more time with his son, then Larry would have been *just fine*. And Skipper told Margo that if only *she* had spent less time playing bitch mother and pitting the boy against his father, if only she had cared about him enough to show some love for the boy—and not leave him to a shifting cast of nannies—then he would have turned out normal.

Mutual neglect and guilt.

"Hi."

He turned, startled. It was Sally.

"You were somewhere else," she said, smiling.

"Looking at my collection here."

She walked toward him.

"This has always been my favorite picture of you, Skipper." She grasped the left edge of the ornate metal frame.

"Ensign Mark Philip Steiner," he said, smiling.

"What sort of plane is that?"

"It's an F-9 Panther. Straight-wing, single-engine attack plane. Long since gone."

"We never talked about combat."

"War is hell."

"Come on. Did you see much fighting?"

"A little. More than a little." He grinned. "North Koreans. Tough SOBs."

"Where was this taken?"

"The U.S.S. *Philippine Sea*. Off the Korean coast. Forget where. Probably late fifty-one. Squadron U.F. 111."

"Skipper, you were so handsome. You must have had a girl in every port."

"As a matter of fact, I had a girl in Pensacola. Not a girl, really. She was a sailor's wife. Poor bastard was on a destroyer in the Mediterranean, while his wife did her number in Florida. I had a girl, an unmarried girl, at Corpus Christi. And I had a wonderful girl in Tokyo."

"Tokyo?" said Sally. "Japanese?"

"Japanese. Her first name was Fumiko. Very, very lovely. I met her in a department store around the Ginza. Mitsukoshi. I was buying a kimono for Frieda. Fumiko was the salesgirl."

"It was serious," said Sally, surprised.

"I almost married her."

"Skipper, you never told me."

"I haven't told you a lot, my dear."

"Why didn't you marry her?"

Skipper glanced away.

"It was very innocent," he said quietly. "She was a very solid middle-class girl learning English. She showed me around Tokyo. One weekend she took me to Kyoto. Another weekend to Hakone. I guess I didn't marry her because . . . well, because, I didn't have the guts. It was like the Navy. I *loved* the Navy. I loved the life. I loved flying. I wanted to stay in. Make it a career. But again, no guts."

"Skipper, you had to come back and run the paper. There was no one else."

"Eli was licking his lips for the job. Or they could have trained Lucy. It would have salvaged her life. Or they could have sold the paper."

"Oh Skipper. You don't sell a newspaper that your grandfather and uncle and father . . ."

"And mother. Don't forget mother."

"And mother," Sally laughed. "You don't sell a paper that they spent their lives struggling to make great."

"So I was trapped." He walked to his desk and sat on his swivel chair.

"And the girl?"

"I knew she would be unacceptable to the family. I knew it would be very difficult for me. And for *her*. I knew that I would have to work very hard to come to terms with Frieda. So . . ." He shrugged. "Couldn't face it. No guts. And so I did the next best thing. I found a woman who was the complete opposite of Fumiko, and married her. Now Larry, my son, is paying for it, somehow."

Sally moved toward his desk, hesitating for a moment before sitting on the leather wing chair that faced him.

"Skipper, I wanted to talk to you now. Before the vote." She studied his eyes. "I want us . . . to take a break. It's difficult for me to talk like this. I wish I had something in my hands. A drink."

"Do you want one?"

"At ten-thirty in the morning? Christ, no. Skipper, listen. Listen. I've got to *try* to make my marriage work. I'm not a woman who can live with one person and sleep with another. I don't do it well. Skipper, I'm sorry. I'm not expressing it well. I just . . . I just want to try again with Charlie."

His eyes softened. "Sally, I care for you very much."

"I know you do, Skipper. And I . . ."

The intercom sounded, and Skipper picked up the phone impatiently.

"Tell Maury to wait."

"I should go," she said, not moving.

"Stay."

"Skipper, darling. I care for you. I do. But it's tangled up. You're my boss. I work for you. I have a marriage that seems . . . pointless, and yet I *love* him. I love Charlie. I want to make my marriage work. It would be so easy, Skipper, so easy, if I didn't love him."

He stood and walked behind Sally, kissing her hair. She held his warm fingers on the back of her neck.

"You're a lovely woman, Sally."

"Please understand," she whispered.

"I do."

"I need a chance with him," she said, twisting her face to his. "I *want* a chance with him."

She kissed his fingers, and for a moment she allowed her cheek to rest against his hands. Then she stood and smiled and walked out.

*

Five floors below in the newsroom, Larry Steiner picked up the phone at his desk in the drama/films department. It was ten thirty-five.

He dialed, heard two rings, then a click, and then the familiar voice.

"Can you talk?" Larry said.

"I'm kind of busy," Charlie Sims said. He spoke sharply.

"I'm at work. Monday morning blues. How are you?"

"Finished my piece, thank God! And my agent just called. *Travel and Leisure* wants me to do something on Yugoslavian vacation places."

"Fantastic!" Larry watched Sarah Felger, about ten feet away, cradle a phone against her right ear, scribbling notes on a yellow pad. He closed his eyes.

"Charlie, can I see you today?" Larry's voice was pleading.

There was a brief pause.

"Larry, why don't we cool it awhile? I just . . . well, look, my life is complicated. I'm trying to uncomplicate it."

"It's somebody else, isn't it?"

"No. Well, maybe. Yes."

"Who?"

"Sally."

"You're kidding."

"No. I'm not kidding. I'm not kidding at all."

In the center of the newsroom, Frank Lazzarutti and several reporters huddled beside an empty desk, the union leader gently pounding his fist into the palm of his hand as he spoke.

"Can we meet one more time?" Larry asked softly.

"Why?"

"Why?" He struggled in vain to sound lighthearted.

Charlie paused. "Well, what about lunch? Today."

"Damn. I can't. Just made a lunch date with . . . a friend. What about now!"

"*Now?*"

"I mean, I can leave in twenty minutes. Let me just . . . see you one more time. Old times' sake." Larry's heart thundered in his ears. It always ended this way, in pleading, humiliation. "If you don't want to, I understand. I do."

Charlie Sims sighed. His voice was strained. "Come on over."

*

Maury watched Skipper's hand shake as he flicked the silver lighter for his cigarette.

"It's a game I play," Skipper said with a shrug. "Two puffs and that's it. Expensive habit."

Maury smiled. Geraldine Heaney had phoned him an hour earlier, summoning him to the appointment on the tenth floor. Now Maury sat on one of the two leather chairs that flanked the publisher's desk. Skipper leaned back on his swivel chair, locking his hands behind his head. His shirt was unfastened at the neck now, his tie loose.

He asked the status of the investigative stories, and listened impassively as Maury told him that Barry Cohen's staff was about to wind up one big one—corruption on Dave Fitzgerald's staff: specifically, Jerry Paley's murky plunge into influence peddling, payoffs, illegal bank accounts.

"Stupid bastard," Skipper said, glancing at Maury. "What about this Hollywood story? The Vice President? That story's competitive."

Maury nodded. "The *Daily News* is out there too, so is the *Times*. Linda Fentress is on it. We'll know more by tonight."

Skipper leaned forward. "I *want* these stories."

Maury nodded. "I understand."

"I want them *badly*. We . . . *need* them. *We* need them. What was the word that the *Journal* used today?"

"Sluggish."

"Right. Sluggish investigations. Sluggish. Let's show the bastards."

Skipper pushed back his chair and walked to the window. "You think we did the wrong thing yesterday. Voting not to publish." It was a statement, not a question.

"It's going to leak, Skipper, sooner or later. You can't put a lid on a story like that."

"But Maury. It's *wrong* to publish."

Maury stared at Skipper's coffee cup, emblazoned NEW YORK STAR. "I have problems with right and wrong. If you've got the news, you print it."

"At whatever cost?" said Skipper.

"At whatever cost," Maury said slowly.

"Despite the consequences? For the newspaper? For the country?"

"Whom are we trying to protect?" said Maury. "The country? Or the President?" He waited. "Or Bart Taylor?"

Skipper winced. "Maury, I owe Bart Taylor a favor. He saved my family a great deal of pain. He saved *me* from a nightmare of humiliation, public humiliation, because of my son. Granted." Skipper nodded. "But there's another consideration."

Maury watched him, silent.

"There are limits to what a newspaper, a *responsible* newspaper, publishes," said Skipper. "We don't print everything. *You* can vouch for that. We know far more than we print. And there are times when you *have* to hold back. Damn it. *You have to hold back.*"

"Why?"

"We're dealing in war and peace."

Maury began speaking, but Skipper interrupted.

"Don't give me an argument about freedom of the press, Maury. Don't give me high-minded platitudes. What we have here is a story, a good story, a *scoop*. It'll boost circulation for a couple of days and knock the hell out of our competitors. That's all we have, Maury, a story, and the only reason we print the story is because we're competitive sons of bitches, and to hell with the prospect that we *can* affect war and peace."

At the sound of the telephone buzzer, Maury jumped. Skipper walked to his desk to lift the phone, and Maury settled back in the leather chair, listening to his own heavy breathing. He was aware that his struggle to remain cool and managerial in the past six days, to somehow prove to Skipper and the staff that he was suited to serve as managing editor and was not merely a second man, had taken its toll. As the Steiners neared their decision, his body seemed to tighten and clench. He ate food quickly, but tasted nothing. His ribs ached, his mouth was dry with tension. Perhaps most alarming, his hands and feet trembled so that he had started to develop moves to mask the shaking: gripping his thighs with both hands, wrapping his arms around his chest as if he were freezing. He was exhausted.

"That was Harry Watson," said Skipper.

"Problems with Lazzarutti?"

"He's picking up rumors . . ."

Their eyes locked.

"Drivers will *support* the Guild."

"Jesus!" Maury said. "I thought . . ."

"Strike would be crippling."

"I thought we had . . . *assurances* from the drivers."

"Just a rumor," said Skipper, lighting a cigarette. "Everyone's jittery. In the past the drivers have always been . . ." He stared at Maury . . . *"amenable* to us."

Suddenly the tall case clock beside the doorway began to chime.

Skipper's voice was heavy. "I want you to be managing editor, Maury."

Maury heard the echo of a car horn. He swallowed hard.

"We vote tomorrow," said Skipper. "There are four of us. I'll try to make it unanimous."

Maury nodded. "Thank you," he whispered.

"You deserve it."

The triumphal moment passed without a hint of exhilaration. Then Skipper said, "We're going to face a rough stretch."

*

Sally Sims's secretary, Rose, switched off her electric typewriter as Sally sat down at the national desk.

"Marty Kaplan called," said Rose. "Set for lunch at twelve forty-five. The Russian Tea Room. The Pentagon people are coming up right now . . ."

"*Damn.* I forgot. The missile briefing."

". . . And Peter Fosdick said he would have to leave the briefing early."

Sally turned to stare at Rose. "Tell Peter *I* will have to leave early. Tell him that I would . . . prefer he stay on. No. Tell him I *want* him to stay on. Tell him his goddamn Monday morning squash games are a pain in the ass."

"I'll omit that," said Rose, straight-faced. "I like your dress."

"That bastard. Thanks, Rose. He wouldn't try any of that shit if I weren't a woman."

Rose set the phone down. "That was Senator Fitzgerald's office. He invites you to lunch on Friday."

Sally looked up.

"They didn't say what it's about," said Rose.

"He's running for President. That's what it's about."

Sally glanced at the sleeve of her dress, pleased that Rose, who parceled out her compliments carefully, had noticed.

Rose said, "You should've seen the cafeteria this morning. Everyone buzzing about the article in *The Wall Street Journal.*"

Instead of answering her, Sally Sims unexpectedly leaned forward and whispered: "Don't tell a soul, but I'm cutting out early to buy Charlie a gift. Bloomingdale's, I guess. A lovely gift to surprise him. And tonight we're going to have a wonderful dinner. Alone. I sound like I'm seventeen. Rose, we just don't do those things."

*

Kitty White opened the door of her Q Street home and waited until David Fitzgerald stepped inside to kiss him firmly on the lips. Then she locked the door, escorted him through the living room into the library. It was an extraordinary room that the late Senator Sam White, Democrat of Texas, had personally decorated—the motif was French, the groin-vaulted ceilings and walls were adorned with trumpet-wielding angels and centaurs that were once ornaments of an eighteenth-century villa in the Italian Piedmont.

"Quite a room," said Fitzgerald.

"Sam always had the taste and money for expensive schlock," said Kitty, watching him. She smiled. "What about that girl?"

"Cheryl? Tragic." He lit a cigarette.

Kitty lifted her chin. "Did she know a lot?"

Fitzgerald exhaled, keeping his eyes fixed on the smoke. "Enough."

"Who did it?"

"The police suspect some drug addicts."

Kitty made a clicking sound with her tongue. "Give me a cigarette, David." He handed her a pack, watching her insert one into a gold-tipped black holder. As she leaned forward to catch his match, the two stared at one another.

"All right, David," said Kitty, smiling. "We are about to embark on our adventure. And it *is* an adventure. I have arranged some private gatherings—drinks, dinner—with some gentlemen from Texas and one from Alaska and several from Nevada and Florida whom you've undoubtedly heard of, gentlemen with a great deal of money who have an interest in getting the *right* person into the White House. Unlike the one we have now. These gentlemen are quite busy and they know why they're coming and some of them are flying in to meet you because Sam White's widow called them and some of them are flying in because Kitty called them."

She held the cigarette holder, unsmiling, between her thumb and forefinger. "I have also arranged for a Saudi Arabian gentleman, who actually lives in London and Paris but also has interests here, as well as a South African friend and a Libyan. They want to have some private chats with you. Separately, of course. They all know who you are. And I think they can be of some help. I think you've heard of them too."

Kitty examined her long painted fingernails.

"Now, what about the lady in New York?"

Fitzgerald stared at Kitty.

"The merry widow," she said.

"Lucy Claiborne."

"Drop her."

"I am."

"When?"

"I need her for . . ."

"For what?" Kitty blew a smoke ring.

"I need that paper in New York, Kitty. I don't have the *Times* or the *Daily News*. *I need that paper.* Tomorrow they're voting on who's going to run the paper. I want one guy . . ."

"Who is it?"

"A guy named Cohen, Barry Cohen."

"Never heard of him."

"You will. He's going to get that job."

"With your help. You and the merry widow."

"And some other people."

"You will have the *Star* in your pocket."

"Yes," he said.

"That's good," she smiled. He looked at his watch.

"What time is it?" she said.

"Eleven-thirty."

"Busy day?"

"Very."

"Oh, the busy life of a United States senator."

"We've got a couple of votes on the floor. And Christ knows what's going to happen abroad."

"I think it best that you stay here for a while. Mr. Busy Senator," Kitty said, tapping his hand.

She got up out of her chair and unfastened her cord belt, dropping it on the floor. As her beige linen twill jacket opened, revealing her firm breasts, Fitzgerald stood, grabbed her by the waist, and with a grunt pulled her toward him, arching his face down to meet hers. Firmly holding her buttocks, he licked her right nipple while his thumb and forefinger massaged her body.

Kitty groaned, slipping her long fingers through his hair, over his ears and neck. Closing her eyes, she put her hands on top of his head and pushed down as his tongue snaked her stomach and dug into her navel.

He fell to his knees, dropping his jacket, loosening his tie, all the while licking her. Shutting his eyes, he nibbled and chewed, his tongue darting into the soft, damp folds, pressing relentlessly inward. His hands shot up blindly, finding her breasts and firmly massaging them as his tongue and lips and mouth consumed her.

"*Now. Now.*" Kitty repeated. A low, husky groan lifted from some hidden place, Kitty grasped his head, her body reared up, and then, with her eyes tightly closed, with her body, a single, pulsing muscle, she came with violent shudders.

Her legs trembling, she lifted his face to hers. "Let's go into the bedroom."

*

A stately elm shaded the house on Q Street, and when Fitzgerald opened the door fifty-five minutes later and walked hurriedly down the steps to the Diamond taxi that Kitty had called, he nearly stumbled over the outcropping of aged tree roots that had sprung through the sidewalk cracks and enveloped the curb.

Across the street, a Dominican housekeeper and a four-year-old boy in a Spiderman sweat shirt, walked toward the park at Dumbarton Oaks. Two gray-haired women, their arms locked, chatted and strolled toward Wisconsin Avenue. They stopped briefly to smile at the child.

The elder of the two, whose fragile legs moved reluctantly, stood firmly on the pavement, watching the child and resting.

Suddenly the older woman jerked her head so abruptly that her companion instinctively tightened her fingers on her friend's arm. The younger woman followed her companion's eyes.

A woman emerged out of the shadows of an alley separating two brownstones. She wore a trench coat and wraparound sunglasses. She was in her late thirties or early forties, her hands pressed into the coat's side vents, her face, beneath the collar and spectacles, remarkably frail and, to the older passerby, suffused by fear.

What stirred the elderly woman—a Georgetown resident for fifty-two years whose late husband had served as one of F.D.R.'s original brain-trusters—was an eerie sense that the woman in the trench coat had been waiting in the alley for hours, staring at the house across the street, and had stepped out abruptly, as if in a trance, ignoring the passersby who faced her.

The woman in the trench coat walked firmly toward Thirty-first Street.

Watching her, the younger of the two women, the widow of a well-known columnist, observed that the trench-coated figure looked somewhat familiar.

Her elderly companion, who was ailing and spent most of her days in the sitting room of her home on R Street reading the daily newspapers, women's magazines and Gothic mysteries, said, yes, wasn't her picture in a recent *McCall's?*

Puzzled, the two women turned and, arm in arm, walked slowly toward Wisconsin Avenue and lunch at the Georgetown Inn.

Actually, the photograph had been in the Washington *Post*.

The woman was Mrs. David Fitzgerald.

CHAPTER 17

At the Pentagon boat marina, Alex Vikas fell in behind Ward at the food counter. "Let's put the hot dogs in a cardboard box," said Alex, "and get out of here."

They walked to Alex's Volkswagen Rabbit and drove off, Ward glimpsing the Pentagon through the dense curtain of dogwood and red maple.

They drove over Memorial Bridge onto Rock Creek Parkway. A motorboat cruised gently up the Potomac. Ward peered up at the Kennedy Center and the Watergate.

"Where are we going?" he asked.

Alex pressed his foot down hard on the accelerator. "Let's take a ride."

"Are we being followed?"

"Probably."

"By whom?"

"Suspicious folks."

Ward loosened the wrapping around his hot dog. "Like the Pentagon?"

"Smells good."

Ward passed a hot dog to Vikas. "They don't trust you."

"Never did. Old Eddie Belling."

"They know you leaked the story."

"Jesus, I hope they do. If they don't we're in trouble. Any six-year-old in this town knows who's leaking what to whom."

A half-smile creased Ward's face. "And Belling's leaking to Hugh Finch. Defense and CIA are playing us, Finch and me—one against the other." Ward reached into his jacket pocket, and removed his notebook. "Who's telling the truth?"

"We're both telling the truth. We're both telling lies. It's a process of *selection*." Alex twisted the car onto the Massachusetts Avenue ramp, eyes fixed on the rearview mirror.

"And we print it?"

"You guys eat it up."

"Belling's a pro," Alex finally said. "Orchestrates his leaks. This week it's the New York *Star*."

As the car stopped for a light at the corner of Thirty-fourth Street, Ward peered over Alex's shoulder to the guard shack and the barrier leading up to the Vice President's turreted residence, partly hidden by red oak and pine on the seventy-two-acre Naval Observatory site.

"It was the President's hope to settle the Soviet-China crisis quietly, avoid going public, avoid Camp David," Alex was saying. "Hugh Finch's stories—his Pentagon source, Mr. Belling—*forced* the President to go public and begin talks. The President doesn't *want* to do it . . ."

"The President's dying," said Ward.

"I know," said Alex, not missing a beat. He turned up Thirty-fourth Street.

Ward's gaze slid to the line of pockmarks on Alex's chin. The handsome Mediterranean face had grown puffy since Saigon. Alex had aged: but then, who hadn't?

"This reporter, Linda Fentress," Alex suddenly said.

Ward saw the faintest flicker in Alex's lower eyelids.

"In California," said Alex Vikas.

As Alex drove, gazing fixedly ahead, his fingers lunged into his breast pocket and removed two folded sheets. Ward opened one

of the papers, and emblazoned on top was a purplish stamp: TOP
SECRET.

Ward looked up with a hollow gaze as Alex spoke softly.
"We'll talk about Kamchatka in a minute. Quite a story." He
chewed his lip. "Tell me about Linda Fentress first, what she's
found in California."

*

On the foreign desk, Tony Lazzarutti received the phone call
from Ward at twelve twenty-five.

"Take this summary now and get a copy to Maury, fast." There
was an edge in Ward's voice. Tony slid his chair up to a video terminal.

Ward said firmly, "It's *exclusive*. Get a copy to Skipper, and
send one to the Washington bureau. Hugh Finch. Ask for reaction. Tell Ray Silver to get a reaction from Ernie Richards in
Moscow and Ross in Peking."

"All right, sir."

"The dateline is Washington."

"Washington."

Ward began: "China comma in a surprise development comma
has conducted its first long-range tests of a new and highly accurate mobile intercontinental ballistic missile with mobile warhead
comma Administration officials said today period. The Chinese
missile test comma which stunned . . ."

"You're going too fast, sir."

Ward spoke slowly. He said the test, which stunned American
officials, had dramatically advanced Peking's nuclear capabilities
and appeared to place the Chinese virtually on a par with the
United States and the Soviet Union. The test had been monitored
by CIA reconnaissance planes and satellites in the western
Pacific's Kamchatka Peninsula. Six reentry vehicles, Ward said,
fired from tunnels in the Gobi Desert, impacted five thousand kilo-
meters away in a near-perfect hexagon, plainly indicating that the
Chinese had developed missiles of extraordinary accuracy.

"Sir?" said Tony. "One second. Maury is here. He wants to
talk to you."

"Ward," Maury said. *"Hell* of a story."

"Thanks."

"Just called Skipper. He's coming downstairs. Are you coming back this afternoon, or filing from Washington?"

Parsons winced. Finch was turf-crazy, like everyone else. Filing from his bureau would upset the bastard.

"I'll catch the two o'clock shuttle."

Maury gave the phone back to Tony.

"Mr. Parsons?" said Tony Lazzarutti. "We're up to . . ."

"Here goes . . . What disturbs officials here is potential Soviet reaction to China's test which comma for the first time comma places the bulk of the silo-based Soviet missile arsenal in jeopardy period."

Ward paused. "You got that, Tony?"

"Got it."

By the time Ward completed dictating the story, the back of his turtleneck was damp with sweat. He slammed the phone down, and flung open the door of the booth on Connecticut Avenue.

"Good story?" said Alex dryly.

Ward ignored his faintly mocking tone.

"It intrigues me, Alex, your interest in Linda's story."

Alex ignored him. "There'll be better stories in the next seventy-two hours." He lit a cigarette. "I'll drive you to the airport."

Ward stood still. "The Vice President? Porno films?"

Alex examined the cigarette between his thumb and forefinger. "Call me at the office . . ."

"There's more to Linda's story, right? Something else. You're worried, Alex. Worried about Linda. Worried what she'll find."

Alex's lips shaped a wan smile. He turned on his heels and walked to the car, Ward beside him. "What is it, Alex? How are you guys involved?"

Alex held the door for Ward, who slid inside. Then Alex stepped to the driver's side. Ward stared ahead, speaking quietly.

"Tom Nelson's always supported the Agency. Always supported you guys. As senator, as Vice President. An unlikely friend."

"We got all kinds of unlikely friends," said Alex Vikas.

*

When Frieda Steiner walked through the revolving door of the Russian Tea Room, she saw Eli Faber immediately. At the bar, grinning, he placed his bloody mary on the counter and stepped toward her, awkwardly reaching for Frieda's arm and kissing her.

"You smell wonderful," he said.

"Oh, *Eli.*"

"And you *look* wonderful," he said, standing an arm's length away from her at the crowded entrance.

They were escorted quickly into the dining room. As she sat down, Frieda closed her eyes and sighed. "It's so marvelous to go out, Eli."

"Let's have a drink."

She lifted her arm. "No, I . . ."

"I insist," he said. "Let's have fun, Frieda."

She laughed. "You've talked me into it."

Eli ordered two bloody marys.

Frieda nestled against the red banquette, glanced at Eli, then let her eyes wander over the crowded restaurant. "I haven't been here in so long," she said. "*So long.*"

This was New York, the New York she adored, pink and golden, handsome men and lithe, beautifully dressed women, the sound of laughter, the voices, the glorious restaurant smell of perfume and flowers and nutmeg and garlic. The dancing eyes. The kiss on the cheek. And the colors here, the glorious flamingo-pink table linen, the shimmering lanterns on each table, the paintings and samovars crowding the lush green walls, the sconces and chandeliers that seemed to bathe the restaurant in a ruby glow, so comforting, so . . . sensual.

It had been so long since anyone had taken her out like this, treated her like this. Eli . . . *knew.*

He said, "I won't even ask if you read the *Journal* article this morning."

Frieda avoided his eyes.

"The truth hurts," he said.

Frieda finally looked at him. "We are *not* the *Herald Tribune,* Eli. We are *not* dying. We have problems, of course, but . . ." She shrugged. "*Every* paper has problems."

He placed his hand over hers. "Frieda, my dear. What are you saying? I *know* what our problems are."

She sipped her drink. "Skipper said you were the main source for the article."

Eli smiled grimly. "I'm surprised Skipper's not blaming me for the Chinese-Russian border war."

"What do we do, Eli?"

His voice was low and firm. "Two things. First, we name Barry Cohen managing editor." He waited a beat. "And we publish what we know. *Tonight.*" Frieda saw the veins straining in his neck.

"We publish whatever Finch has," said Eli. "We publish!"

"Eli, we've decided . . ."

"Change the decision. It's not engraved in stone."

Frieda crushed out her cigarette in the ashtray, slowly raising her eyes to watch a waiter glide past the booth.

"Frieda, our job is not to preserve national security. Our job is not to sit in judgment of news. Our job is to print what we know. Every time, Frieda, every single time a paper decides not to publish, it backfires. Look at the Bay of Pigs. Frieda, my dear . . ." He leaned close to her and whispered, "What if the President dies tomorrow and we haven't published? We've humiliated ourselves. How do we know how serious this illness is? *People ought to know.* What happens next year if he's still alive? Our job is not to sit on news. Our job is to *publish.*"

Frieda examined her nails. "Eli, dear, Skipper felt strongly . . ."

"It's your paper, too, Frieda. *Yours.* You've given *your* blood to it. Don't you see, Frieda? We're at a critical point. The *Journal* is absolutely right. We face extinction in two years, five years, certainly ten, unless we act now. Publishing this would be a first step, Frieda, a signal to the industry. The *Star* is going to make it. We're not afraid to take chances. Not afraid to tackle the government. We'd get tremendous publicity in the next week. The television news shows, magazines, papers around the country. It would give us a shot in the arm and, more important, Frieda, advertisers would notice, readers would notice. We publish this tomorrow, Frieda, and by next Monday our circulation and advertising are up five percent."

Lifting her spoon, Frieda allowed her forefinger to linger over the grooved edge. "I can't go against my son," she said.

Eli frowned, then lifted his attaché case off the floor, placed it on the banquette and snapped it open. Removing a sheaf of long, white papers stapled together, he hastily leafed through the document.

"Jonathan's will," he said. "Page twenty-one." Eli began to read. "'I have so designated my wife, my son, my daughter and my longtime associate as executors and trustee hereunder because I have absolute confidence in their integrity and business judgment. Accordingly, it is my expressed hope that my wife, my son, my daughter and longtime associate serve as members of the board of directors.

"'It is also my expressed hope that the board:

"'Nominate and appoint my son Mark Philip Steiner as president and chairman of the board of the New York *Star* Company.

"'Nominate my wife Frieda Schiffer Steiner as executive vice president.

"'Nominate my daughter Lucy Steiner Claiborne as executive vice president.

"'Nominate my colleague Eli Faber as controller.'"

Eli coughed, stared at the document and read slowly.

"'If my son Mark Philip Steiner, or any member of the board, shall fail for any reason to qualify or, having qualified, shall perform a negative or imprudent act counter to the interests of the New York *Star* Company, I would not expect the board to retain this person in office.'"

"Unthinkable!" said Frieda, twisting her ring.

Eli ignored her. "He goes on to say that the board shall elect a family member as replacement *unless* the best interests of the *Star* are served by an outsider."

Eli struggled to sound calm. "I think Skipper's decision was *not* based on the best interests of the paper. I think it was based on . . . personal considerations. I think Skipper owes a great deal to Barton Taylor."

"Larry!"

"I think," said Eli, "that Barton Taylor will go to any length, including blackmail, to stop us from publishing. Skipper knows that."

"Our enemies would love to print a nasty story about . . . the incident with Larry."

"My dear, they'd love even more to print a story that we withheld news—critical news—because we owed Bart Taylor a favor.

Wouldn't some investigative reporter have a field day with that one?"

Eli leaned so close to her that she scented the mixture of tangy aftershave lotion and powder that he dabbed on his face.

"Let's show New York, show the industry that we're *not dying.*"

Suddenly Eli looked up and exclaimed, "Marty!" Marty Kaplan stood before them.

"Just wanted to say hello. I was at the bar and saw you." He spoke rapidly. "How are you, Mrs. Steiner?"

"I heard you were back on home leave," said Frieda. The lines crevicing his eyes and lips, the flecks of gray in his hair, startled her. Such a bright young reporter—Marty was getting older.

"Just got back the other day."

It had been a tradition, when Jonathan was alive and during Skipper's first years as publisher, that each foreign correspondent have an appointment with Frieda before the reporter went abroad or returned home. As Frieda moved into retirement, the tradition faded, leaving her friendly only with the older correspondents.

"You're looking no worse for the wear, Marty," said Frieda. Silly lie, she thought. Stop babbling like a schoolgirl. "Marty, I'd love to see you, love to hear about South America," she said. "It's so rare that I . . . Please call. We'll have lunch."

"I'd be delighted," he said, still smiling, leaning forward as a waiter brushed past.

Eli said, without a hint of enthusiasm, "Join us for a drink?"

"Sorry, I can't," said Marty Kaplan. "I'm waiting for Sally. Sally Sims. I'm a bit early." He nodded and, after a few final words, shook hands and left.

Frieda and Eli drank in silence until Frieda said, "I want to know the reporters again. Talk to them. Like the old days." She straightened up, folding her hands firmly on the table.

"Now tell me, Eli," she said in a pulsing voice. "Why should I vote for Barry Cohen?"

"Because Barry will cut costs," said Eli quickly. "Kick out deadwood. Knock heads together. Provide a new product for us . . ."

Eli's words at the apartment yesterday echoed. *A new* Star. *Reduce international and Washington news. Cut out the heavy stuff. More photos. Comics. Advice to the lovelorn . . .*

"Get some new columnists," Eli was saying. "Cut out some of the old ones."

"Like?"

"Sarah Felger."

Frieda was stunned. "Eli! She's one of our most popular columnists."

"Of course," he said. "Among our readers. Average age forty-two. Average income thirty thousand. An elite group. What about the youth market? Sarah doesn't speak to them. Get a young doctor. Get one of these young, hotshot women who write for *Cosmopolitan* or *McCall's*. Barry will give us excitement, Frieda. He's tough and mean and . . ."

"Aggressive. So aggressive."

"He's not an Ivy League smoothie, Frieda. He's not *nice*. But, my dear . . ."

"Yes."

"Wall Street and Macy's and Gimbels and Bloomingdale's and Saks don't give a *damn* about niceness. The people who pay for classified ads—and we can make *money, real money* on those ads once the paper starts to grow—they could care less if the managing editor went to Harvard. These advertisers want *results,* and Barry will give them results."

"Skipper wants Maury."

"So?"

"So he's the publisher, Eli," Frieda said icily. "It's his decision."

"Like suppressing the news of Bergen's illness is his decision." Eli stopped as the waiter appeared at their table with luxuriant plates of blinis, caviar and sour cream. A second waiter poured vodka over ice.

"Rumors all over the building this morning. Rumors that Lazzarutti and the drivers have reached an accommodation."

Eli winced. "Don't believe rumors, Frieda."

Eli's eyes narrowed and, as he turned to Frieda, she caught a look of such coldness that she started. "Frieda, we're going to call his bluff. Finally. Break the son of a bitch. Give him the strike he's always wanted."

"He's shrewd. If the drivers support him . . ."

"They won't."

"But if they *do?*"

"We face a long strike."

"A deadly strike." Frieda blurted out the words. She frowned and shut her eyes tight.

"Why didn't Skipper tell me about the offer the conglomerate made? Why did I have to read about that in *The Wall Street Journal?*"

"It was a good offer." Eli drained his vodka. "Perhaps Skipper thought you'd be interested in selling."

"Don't be absurd."

"It was a *splendid* offer, Frieda. By the way, it's a standing offer too. I *assumed* Skipper would pass it on to you."

"Don't make those assumptions, Eli." Her fear and confusion had now given way to rage. Frieda was shaking with anger—at Eli and Skipper and herself.

*

Anatoli Rosenstein, a Kiev-born émigré who arrived in New York, via Vienna, in 1971 and began driving a taxi one year later, turned to his passenger, who returned his glance.

"Do you mind if I smoke?" asked Sally.

"Me? I don't mind," he said, shrugging elaborately.

They were locked in traffic on Sixtieth Street between Madison and Fifth avenues. It was twelve thirty-five. Crosstown traffic at midday is always a bitch, Sally thought, and she never learned. Never. She had stayed at Bloomingdale's too long. Wandered the quiet first-floor aisles and gone slightly mad with presents for Charlie. Instead of two or three small gifts, she began to buy compulsively, filling up three shopping bags, barely able to carry the load.

Charlie would adore this, she kept saying. And she bought the gifts. A cotton-and-silk long-sleeve pullover. A navy cable-ribbed crew-necked sweater. A tie. A dusky-blue Yves Saint Laurent shirt. A mustard-yellow windbreaker that would look glorious on Charlie, a perfect jacket for their home in Bridgehampton.

She closed her eyes now, listening to the blare of horns. He would love the gifts, he always did, like a child, gleefully opening each box. Charlie always responded to surprise presents, signs of affection, signs of love. Oh, Charlie, let's be happy together, finally, let's try . . .

She *could* change her plans. Drive to the Russian Tea Room now, be there five minutes early, check the load of packages and wait for Marty. It would make more sense. But then, someone would see her with these shopping bags and she would have to explain and it was nobody's damn business, after all, that she had slipped out of work early to go on this shopping spree. And besides, she wanted to surprise him in the apartment *now* and watch him open a gift or two and then taste his mouth, locking her fingers over his neck and smelling the sweetness of his hair.

As the taxi finally surged across Fifth Avenue toward Central Park West, Sally glimpsed the Plaza Hotel, the sun piercing its white glazed brick, its green-tiled mansard roof glowing. On their first date, Charlie had taken her to the Oak Bar; it was dusk on an autumn afternoon, and she had sipped Dubonnet on the rocks and, inexplicably, fallen in love with this beautiful man, so blond and lithe, with an endearing cowlick, his smooth, narrow face unblemished and perfect except for the eyes, little blue eyes that darted from side to side, the eyes sometimes of a frightened animal.

Sally had sought so little from him, she knew. Separate lives. Separate journeys. Whether or not Charlie knew about Skipper was a lingering question to be deferred until the question itself faded. It was irrelevant actually. She loved Charlie, and he loved her, and as her career spiraled, as his sputtered, their mutual loneliness had deepened.

She needed him now.

The taxi sped north, twisting past steep banks of ripening azaleas, the air unseasonably warm, a hint of rain once more. Sally opened the window full.

Let's try, Charlie darling. Let's try . . .

Sunlight glowed off the Dakota's buff brick walls and terra-cotta trim.

As the taxi halted at the gatehouse, Sally told the driver that she was leaving in ten minutes for the Russian Tea Room. Could he wait?

Anatoli Rosenstein shrugged and nodded. Sure. Why not?

A tremor of exhilaration stirred her as, breathless, she bit her lip. Why am I so goddamn nervous? Dizzy, her eyes misting, Sally slumped against the wall of the creaky elevator, the taste on her tongue metallic. Her fingers twisted tight over the shopping-bag handles.

She unlocked the apartment door and rushed into the two-story living room.

Except for the sound of her heavy breathing—except for the distant echo of a car horn and a police siren—the apartment seemed eerily silent.

"Charlie?" she called. Then raising her voice: *"Charlie?"*

Disappointment turned to frustration. He was probably out to lunch on Columbus Avenue, or jogging.

Gripping the packages, she began climbing to the balcony level, disheartened that Charlie was out, that her tantalizing surprise had fizzled.

She grasped the doorknob of his study and walked in. The smell of fresh-brewed coffee lingered. On his mahogany partners' desk Sally saw a white sheet of paper in the typewriter carriage. He had stopped in mid-sentence.

Sally removed the packages from the shopping bags, placed them atop the desk. She found a sheet of lined, legal-size yellow paper and picked up his felt-tipped pen. Quickly she scribbled: "Surprise! Surprise! I Love You," and placed the sheet between two of the boxes. Smiling now, she left the study and began walking toward the stairway. But a glance at her hands changed her mind. She would wash up, phone Marty from the bedroom to say she was late, then return to the cab.

Twelve-fifty. Not too bad.

She opened the door, and met Larry Steiner's wide eyes.

Crouched on his knees in the double bed, naked, resting on his elbows, Larry Steiner curled beneath Charlie, whose penis was thrust into him. They looked so grotesque that she wanted to laugh, but instead, she stood absolutely still for a moment, her mouth frozen open.

Charlie's head, arched back, whirled toward her, his lips ridiculously twisted apart, his violet-blue eyes wide with terror, a stage performer in a comic double take.

She was aware that her legs were sagging, that vicious needles seemed to stab her brain. Her eyes fixed on Charlie's buttocks and the soft layers around his belly. Charlie's gaining weight, she thought, quite insanely.

She knew she had to turn slowly and leave the apartment. She must not faint here. It was a question of *concentration*. Clamping her eyes shut first, turning, then opening the eyes. Walking. She had to stay controlled. One step at a time.

Yet she was unable to move. Her entire body seemed weighted to the spot. Suddenly her eyes caught Larry Steiner's face. Skipper's face. Skipper's hair. She stared at him and, as Charlie eased himself out of Larry, Sally stepped back without a sound. In that moment she felt a wave of nausea so intense that her only movement was to lift her right hand and steady herself against the wall.

Sally heard a sob and realized she had begun to weep. She saw Charlie reach toward a navy-blue sheet at the foot of the bed and fling the cover over the bodies. But her eyes dissolved and, as she turned and walked down the steps, grasping the banister, she heard a howl—an animal howl—followed by muffled cries. The sound struck her like a whiplash.

She stopped at the bottom of the staircase, listening intently to the sounds in the bedroom, her body shaking.

Charlie was crying.

Then she ran.

CHAPTER 18

From the moment Nick Simons appeared in the newsroom as a copy boy, he ran harder, spoke faster, and thrust so many story ideas on Barry that the city editor finally told the kid to calm down and to suggest only two, perhaps three stories a week.

In fact, Barry Cohen, who eagerly sought new, feisty talent, was impressed with Nick, and, when the previous desk clerk grew restless and joined *Newsday,* Barry promptly promoted Nick Simons. It was only one step below reporter, and Nick, who was the youngest and most aggressive clerk on the paper, was obviously on the ascendant.

It was 1:20 P.M. and Nick looked up, surprised to see Barry thread toward the city desk holding a cardboard tray from the cafeteria. Like Sally Sims and Ward, Barry rarely ate at his desk.

Nick Simons grinned and started to speak, but caught sight of the slight quiver on Barry's lips, the flush on his cheeks. Just as Barry reached his chair, the phone rang and Nick grabbed it.

"It's Howie Bishop." Nick saw Barry's eyes tighten.

"If Linda calls," said Barry to Nick, "don't let her go."

Nodding his head, Nick watched Barry lift the phone. Two biggies they were working on, corruption in Fitzgerald's office and Nelson's porno films, Howie Bishop and Linda, stories that left Nick Simons aching with envy.

Jesus, he was better than Howie, younger, tougher than Linda too. All he needed was a break.

"Where are you?" Barry was saying.

"Riverhead, Long Island. Your sources were absolutely right, Barry. We got Jerry Paley by the short hairs." He spoke without fervor.

Barry watched Nick Simons swivel around to avoid appearing to eavesdrop. Nick overheard Barry's conversations with the same intensity that Barry, as a clerk, had overheard Fritz Pratt, the old city editor.

"Got hold of the deeds, tax stamps and mortgages," said Howie. "Pulled the land maps. Company called Reliable Enterprises. Set up in Wilmington. Bought ten acres of land eighteen months ago up near Islip. Mostly potato farms. About six thousand dollars an acre." Howie sighed. "Well, as you probably know, some very fortunate things happened to Reliable Enterprises. Seems that right beside the potato farms there was a big tract of government land . . ."

"Eight hundred and seventy-five acres." Barry spoke to himself, writing down the figure.

"Empty for years. Used by the Navy during World War II. Well, about six months ago the land was rezoned. Changed from agricultural zone to commercial zone. And you know what else happened? You know what? Senator Fitzgerald sponsors a bill approving the lease of the government land nearby to a company down in Dallas."

"Named?"

"Just as you told me, Barry. Argosy. Seems Argosy is planning this amusement park, one of the biggest in the state, perfect spot, leasing the land from the government. But . . ."

"But," said Barry tensely.

"The major access road into the park from the Long Island Expressway, the crucial piece of property that the Argosy people needed, that piece of property was owned by Reliable Enterprises."

Barry was writing on the pad. "How much did they sell it for?"

"Fifty an acre."

"Right. The price went from six thousand to fifty thousand bucks an acre." He whistled.

"I called our stringer in Wilmington," Bishop said. "Got him to check the corporation records on Reliable."

"And?"

"Margaret Donovan is president and . . ."

"Margaret who?"

"I called our personnel office. Asked them to pull Jerry's file. And . . ."

"Maggie."

"Her middle name."

Barry swallowed. "That stupid bastard."

"The son is secretary-treasurer," murmured Howie. "Mike Paley. The money went to Mike and Maggie." Whatever anger had remained in Bishop's voice had softened to sorrow.

Howie said: "Those memos, Barry. The ones from Jerry to Fitzgerald. Urging him to sponsor the bill. They *destroy* Jerry." Howie sighed. "I'm leaving for Panama in two hours."

Barry saw Nick Simons motioning to him, mouthing the words, "Linda Fentress."

Barry cupped his hand over the phone. "Tell her to wait."

"Got an appointment tonight with that lawyer you suggested. Keeping his office open for us."

"I want the story tomorrow, Howie."

"Sure." Howie Bishop waited. "We'll need a reaction from Jerry."

"I'll get it," Barry said.

"The diary's a dead issue," Howie said.

"Like Cheryl."

"Wonder what happened."

Barry caught Nick staring at him across the desk.

"The diary's buried and gone," Barry said distractedly, watching Nick. The same hunger. The same fevered ambition. There was even a vague resemblance in their curly hair and deep-set eyes. Barry glanced at the flickering light on the telephone extension. Linda was waiting. "Call me tonight, Howie."

Barry hung up, turning to Nick.

"Get Jerry Paley. Tell him I want to see him tonight. About ten-thirty. Book me for the night into The Four Seasons. Tell Jerry . . ." Barry pressed the extension button on the telephone console and lifted the phone. ". . . I have to see him."

As Barry began talking to Linda, Nick Simons started leafing through the Rolodex beside him for Jerry Paley's number. Suddenly a pang of jealousy struck Nick with a force that made his heart skip.

Would be nice to get a biggie before the strike; maybe even a byline, make everyone sit up and notice.

Probably one hell of a story in that diary . . .

*

Linda Fentress opened the telephone booth door, inhaling the salt breeze on Washington Street. Story tomorrow. Bastard wants a story tomorrow.

Recounting the last twenty-four hours to Barry had filled Linda with a sense of futility. "What's to show, Barry? Unanswered phone calls, a story not quite . . . *right*.

"First of all, the guy who has the biggest porn collection in town, who knows everything about the business, is a movie producer named Brock. I've left about twenty messages at his office and home. Then, there's a director named Elliott Hanley, who gave Tom Nelson his first break. Elliott is stonewalling me, refuses to talk. Don't know why. A guy's name keeps cropping up in the L.A. *Times* clips: Bernstein, Paul Bernstein. Nelson's agent. Then he disappears. Checked the Screen Actors Guild and Directors Guild and there's no record of a Paul Bernstein. The phone book has about forty Paul or P. Bernsteins, and I may have to go that route. Anyway, I want Tom Nelson's early addresses, right? So I call MGM—which, I've been told, has terrific back records, they've kept everything—and tell them who I am and who I work for and it's an emergency and blah-blah-blah and since Tommy worked on three films for them in the early fifties they still had copies of tax withholding forms and what-not and the nice man there gave me two addresses listed for him in West Hollywood. The first building was torn down. The second building is just past Hollywood Boulevard, place called Whitley. Landlady's been there like twenty-five years, but she remembers the people before her—called them white trash—a mother and a daughter. The mother was, essentially, a hooker, who was later killed in a car accident on La Braya, but the daughter, a young kid then, maybe fifteen or sixteen, always had pictures of Tom Nelson on the wall, the daughter had a crush on him because he was a movie actor and she wanted to be some kind of actress and he took her to the studios and what-not. The daughter was a link to Tom Nelson, right? The landlady remembers the last name was Garrett. To make a long story short, we checked the Screen Actors Guild and we got the name Cindy Garrett at the Whitley address in 1956, and then we put the name through a check of the Department of Motor Vehicles and miraculously, yeah, they came up with this address in Venice. About a block away . . ."

She had avoided questions about Jerry Paley. Dear God, didn't want to hear anything at all about Jerry. Or Cheryl. Or Fitzgerald. Or . . . Maria.

Tragedy of Marcus' life. Maria. He's never been the same since Maria went mad. Tried to smother her infant daughter.

Lois Barrie's words had haunted her sleep.

Rumors, just rumors, that the child is Tom Nelson's.

Don't labor over . . . connections, Linda. L.A. story is puzzling enough without Maria. Don't get sidetracked on *her,* and besides (*who are you kidding, Linda?*), what happens if you tell Barry there's an illegitimate kid that may be Vice President Nelson's. Barry pees in his pants and sends out Howie Bishop to help quote unquote. So stick with the porno angle. Just take the story, block by block, build the structure, that's what Jerry used to say, and if the stories intersect, if the cast of characters merge, then and only then would she lay it on Barry.

Walking now, Linda watched two remarkably pretty girls in tight denim shorts and lettered T-shirts, roller-skate effortlessly—almost defiantly—toward the beach. Linda's fingers clawed into her handbag for her spiral notebook; she leafed to the last page and the list of names.

Marcus Lynn.

Daughter—Maria (Rose Haven Mental Hospital).

V.P. Nelson.

Lois Barrie—early girlfriend.

Elliott Hanley—directed Nelson's first major film.

Marvin Conrad. Died. Casting director. Discovered Nelson. Blacklisted.

Joey Keefer. Died (heart attack, Mexico City). State Senator. Fitzgerald's brother-in-law. Led blacklist investigation, destroyed Hanley, Conrad, etc.

Paul Bernstein—agent.

Brock—major porno producer in town.

Linda added the name "Cindy Garrett."

She looked up at the low white stucco apartment building on Strongs Place.

Please, Cindy. Help.

The door opened behind a chain, and Linda saw the outline of a face staring at her, anxious, piglike blue eyes, and straw-colored hair tied in a knot. The woman sucked a cigarette and said, "You from Welfare?"

"I'm not from Welfare. Are you Cindy Garrett?"

The woman held her stare and said nothing. The smell in the hallway churned Linda's stomach, a vapor of urine and garbage that clung to the walls.

"I'm a reporter. A newspaper reporter. From the New York *Star*. My name is Linda Fentress." Linda waited. "I'd like to talk to you about . . . about Tom Nelson."

The woman lowered her eyes. "A newspaper reporter. New York." Linda caught her puzzled stare as she unfastened the chain with her right hand, and motioned with her chin for Linda to follow her in.

Cindy Garrett wore flip-flops and a loose-fitting pink-and-white housedress over her heavy body. A charm bracelet dangled on one wrist. Silver and turquoise rings covered fingers on both hands, which, given her bulk, were unusually long and delicate. Her fingernails and toenails were painted pink.

The heavy scent of perfume laced with fried food weighted the air. Linda saw a single room cluttered with faded furniture; a television set flickered now with a soap opera. Movie magazines, *TV Guide* and newspapers lay strewn on a low wooden table in front of the sofa.

Cindy Garrett switched off the television set.

"I got coffee or Tab," she said.

Linda asked for coffee.

"Newspaper reporter from New York," said Cindy, walking to the farthest corner of the room and an open door leading to a kitchen. "You live in New York?"

"Yes," called Linda. Her eyes darted around the room.

"Never been to New York, love to go someday, always wanted to go to the Radio City Music Hall," said Cindy from the kitchen.

"I've never even been there," said Linda, eyes darting to the opposite wall as she removed a notebook and ball-point pen from her shoulder bag. A picture of Marilyn Monroe clung to the peeling white plaster. She was in a tight, barebacked dress, turning her head over her shoulder at the camera, her eyes distant and heavily shaded, her smile wistful but her face a mask of solitude.

Linda stood and stepped toward the wall when Cindy Garrett returned, carrying two cups of coffee.

"That's my Marilyn picture, my favorite one," said Cindy Garrett. "Taken on the set of her last movie. Just before she died."

"I've always identified with Marilyn," said Linda quickly. It was a lie, appropriate to the moment. Cindy sat on the sofa and curled her feet beneath her buttocks, revealing plump thighs and copious breasts.

"You won't believe this, honey, won't believe it at all," said Cindy, lighting a cigarette, "but people said I looked like Marilyn. Don't laugh. I mean, look at me now. But, I mean, then, back then, I had the looks."

Linda watched her taste the coffee. "It's weird," said Cindy. "She was born on June 1, 1926, and I was born on June 1, 1934. The same birthday. Geminis." She grinned. "I saw her once at Grauman's Chinese. God, she was gorgeous. That skin! That hair! The figure! Look, I mean I knew I wasn't quite up to that. It was the life. That fucked-up life. Father abandoned her. Living in foster homes. Orphanages." Cindy stared hard at Linda. "I mean,

like, I *knew* Marilyn. I know what that's all about. And the men.
The creeps. How they used her. Used her and abused her. That's
what I say. Had she stayed with DiMaggio, it would have worked
out. He was the best. But, Jesus, she couldn't hack it with one
guy."

Cindy held her cigarette with an elegance that surprised Linda.
"When I lived in L.A. I used to drive by the house in Brent-
wood," said Cindy. "Fifth Helena Drive. Still remember. 12305
Fifth Helena Drive. Ranch house. Nothing grand, nothing like
you'd expect. I always thought—oh, it was crazy, I know—but I always thought that the last night, August 4, that last night when she
was alone reaching for the phone, that if she had a friend, a *real*
friend, a woman friend that she could trust, someone to talk to,
not one of those bloodsuckers, that it would have saved her."

Linda tried to control her voice. "Tell me about Tom Nelson."

"Handsome. Handsome as sin. Knew he'd make it. Not quite
like he *did*." As Cindy laughed, Linda caught an echo of unexpected bitterness. Or was it her imagination?

Cindy spoke very quietly, avoiding Linda's eyes. "When he was
elected Vice President, I sent him a letter and I got a beautiful
response—framed up in the kitchen. I'll show it to you. 'Thanks
very much for your kind sentiments and I wish you the best wishes
for the New Year!' "

"How long did he live in the house on Whitley?"

"Awhile," shrugged Cindy Garrett. "Basement apartment. We
would sit and talk about movies, and he promised me that if he
made it, I would make it too." She started to smile. "And here I
am."

Linda glanced up from her notebook.

"Can't blame Tommy Nelson," said Cindy. "Kept my looks for
about ten and a half minutes. Once he started working the following year, he invited me to the set at Fox. Jesus, that was terrific.
Then, when he really began to make it big—he had moved away—I
would get some calls from the studio and he'd put me in crowd
scenes. Paid my way for two years to the Screen Actors Guild.
Then . . . then it all kind of collapsed. I got involved with the
wrong guys, including my mother's boyfriend. That was a scene. I
got pregnant. And gave the baby away. I left L.A. for a while.
Went to Honolulu. Met Joey over there. Terrific guy. A spade.

Younger than me, but what the hell. Beautiful guy. In the Twenty-fifth Division. I got pregnant again but I wanted to, I wanted to have his kid, and he went to Vietnam, and two days before I gave birth I got the telegram saying he was dead." Her lips trembled and she struggled not to weep, all the time staring at the cup. "That tore me up, honey, that did it. So I came back here and I'm working as a waitress downtown and trying not to get too fat."

"And what about the kid?"

"The kid's wild. Uncontrollable. Doesn't go to school. Runs around the beach. Fourteen years old. The kid needs a father. Not some strung-out blonde telling him what to do." She shook her head.

Linda heard herself whisper, "My brother was killed over there too."

"You understand then, honey." Cindy glanced at Linda sideways. "What are you doing? A story about Tommy?"

"About his past. The early years."

"All the way from New York."

Linda held Cindy's gaze until the woman turned away.

"Did a guy named Bernstein, Paul Bernstein, ever visit Nelson?"

Linda saw the faintest flicker around Cindy's mouth. "No."

Then she said, "Do me a favor, honey. Don't put my name in the papers."

Linda nodded, watching her.

"Funny. So long ago. Tom Nelson. I see his picture in the paper now, and it's like I never knew him."

"What sort of guy was he?"

"A charmer. What Tommy wanted, Tommy got." She tried to smile, and now Linda was certain that the bitterness was real.

"You don't like him?" Linda said.

"Don't dislike him. Just a guy."

They stared at one another.

"Did he ever get any visitors?"

"I could never tell."

Linda's eyes narrowed in puzzlement. "How do you mean?"

"Well, the friend got visitors, the guy who lived on the first floor."

"The friend."

"Yeah, the guy who supported him. Tommy didn't have any money. He scrounged for at least a year."

Linda tightened her fingers on the pen. "The guy who supported him. Who was that?"

"I don't remember the name. Very quiet and nice man. Also in movies, kept to himself. Mama always said that he was a true gentleman. Always paid the rent for both of them on the first of each month."

"Was it Brock? Paul Brock?" said Linda.

"That name doesn't ring a bell."

"Think," pleaded Linda. "Who was the guy?" Linda's fingers tore through the notebook and the interview with Lois Barrie. "Was it Marvin Conrad?"

"That's familiar, hon, but not . . ."

Linda stiffened. "Familiar," she said impatiently.

Linda's voice rose. "It was Elliott Hanley, wasn't it?"

"That's it," said Cindy Garrett, staring at Linda blankly.

*

Sally ran out of the entrance of the Dakota, stopping at the curb, watching the taxi inch toward her. "Russian Tea Room?" said Anatoli Rosenstein, peering up through the passenger window.

She saw his puzzled expression, and wanted to assure him, yes, everything was fine. Sally began to speak but let out a groan instead. She swayed and knew her control was slipping.

"Something wrong, lady?"

"Please!"

Her eyes darted down Seventy-second Street toward Broadway. She must get away. Twisting open her bag, Sally fumbled for her wallet, lifted out several bills with her left hand and, seeing one of them was ten dollars, flung it through the window.

"Hey! You already gave me money," said the taxi driver. He shrugged and, with the money between his fingers, returned the bill through the window. "*Take* it." He spoke gently. "Take it, lady."

I want to die.

"Come on, lady, here's your money back."

By now, Alonzo, the doorman, was stepping toward them, eyeing the driver suspiciously. "Is something wrong, Mrs. Sims?"

Now she began to cry. Trapped between Alonzo and the taxi driver, Sally backed off, her pocketbook open, her hair matted and wet on her forehead.

Suddenly the sun disappeared, blanketing the street in grayness. A woman across the street had stopped to gape. It was raining. Sally turned and ran west toward the Hudson River.

*

The latticed façade of the house on Edgeley Road, its red tile roof glistening in the afternoon sun, was laced with ivy, and bougainvillea. As Linda Fentress walked to the door her first thought was that the house seemed buried under foliage, that even in the heart of Westwood, Elliott Hanley had nestled himself inside like an animal awaiting winter. She pressed the bell, counted to fourteen, and watched the door open.

He was a large-featured man, with a thatch of thinning gray hair that fell over his wide forehead. His tinted spectacles hung loosely over his nose. In his right hand Elliott Hanley held a bound movie script, his index finger holding a place near the center. Impatience curled his mouth.

"Mr. Hanley. I'm Linda Fentress of the New York *Star*."

Hanley winced. "Miss Fentress," he said sternly. "I don't know where you come from. I don't know where you learn your manners."

Linda raised her head. "I have to see you, Mr. Hanley," she said fiercely. "I *have* to see you."

He began to shut the door, and she pitched her body forward against it.

"Miss Fentress, I . . ."

"Look!" gasped Linda. "You throw me out and I camp outside the house. You call the cops and I make a scene in front of the neighbors. You go to a dinner party and I show up. You go to a movie and I sit behind you. *You won't know what hit you, honey.*"

She heard the scrabble of feet and turned to face a muscled Japanese youth, barefoot and shirtless, in white trousers, emerging from an open doorway.

"I want to talk to you, Elliott," she said, as the youth advanced toward her.

Hanley lifted his hand. "Fuki, no." The youth's eyes narrowed on Linda, then looked toward the older man.

Hanley carefully removed his spectacles to stare, frowning, at Linda. After a moment, he folded the glasses into his safari jacket and asked Linda to come inside.

"Fuki, bring us some Perrier—I assume that's all right with you, Miss Fentress. We'll be on the patio."

Linda followed him into the sunken living room—a sleek expanse of polished oak flooring that held leather and tubular chrome armchairs. Silently Hanley opened the french doors that led to a narrow deck and patio.

Linda settled in a wicker chair, fumbling for her notebook and pen.

"Now, Miss Fentress . . ."

"Linda."

"Linda. All right. How did you find me? I'm not listed."

"I had your phone number," said Linda. "I knew you lived in Westwood. I called Twentieth Century-Fox, got a secretary in the publicity department. Told her I was a reporter from New York, had an appointment with you at your home in Westwood—had your phone number to prove it—but I had misplaced the address."

"I guess I never understood newspaper reporters," said Hanley, watching her. "Aggressive. Superficial. Not very accurate. What happened yesterday is instantly forgotten. Gullible."

Fuki appeared and placed the tray with two glasses of iced Perrier and lime on the garden seat between them.

Hanley lifted a cloth napkin from the tray to dab his brow. "I know very little about Tom Nelson," he said. "I know what I read, just like you."

First off, let them lie, Jerry taught her, babble away, comfort themselves with the assumption that you're naïve and don't know, and then . . . strike. Clean and surgical.

"I knew him early on, of course. He was in a film of mine, a Western . : ."

"*Texas Blood.*"

Linda caught the stare of his gray eyes. His face was oddly shaped: flabby, almost bulbous, but with a line of mouth so delicate that his otherwise unremarkable features were softened into gentleness.

"Yes," said Hanley. "Tom Nelson was dazzling."

"After that?"

"After that, we went our separate ways. Onward and upward for Tom." Hanley tapped his hand impatiently on his knee. "Haven't seen Tom Nelson since, oh, since the fifties."

Linda drew two small triangles on a blank page in her notebook. "Heard you were friendly with him."

"Tom Nelson? My dear, I knew him as a young actor. There are hundreds of young actors and actresses who pass through your life in this town. Very intense for five or six months, and then you don't see them for a dozen years. He was hardly a friend."

She faced him. "Then, why did you pay his rent for more than a year?"

Hanley's smile lingered, but shadows seemed to blacken the sockets of his eyes. His left hand, grasping the drink in midair, froze.

"I think that's overstating the case considerably." He swallowed hard. "I didn't . . . I just helped him."

"I want to know about Nelson's early life."

Hanley ignored her. "Actually, very few people are aware of the fact that I helped Tommy Nelson." He smiled. "Least of all Tommy, who's probably repressed it. If it wasn't for me . . ."

He leaned forward. "If it wasn't for me . . ." Hanley's smile vanished. "I wouldn't dare ask how you . . . *got* your information. That's not done, is it? Or what the information means to you. Or what you're going to print. I mean, what does it all add up to? That Tommy was broke and I paid his rent. What does that mean?" His chin trembled. "Well, this calls for a drink, Linda. Yes! Let's have a little pick-me-up."

Linda watched him walk to the open door leading to the living room. He called Fuki and ordered scotch on the rocks. Linda asked for Campari and soda.

"*Why* did you support him?"

"That's irrelevant."

"To you. Not me."

"My dear young lady. It's buried. The past. It can't destroy me. I'm sixty-one years old." He laughed softly. "Linda, years ago I was in trouble. I had to get out. Flee! And if you're broke and alone in L.A. and in trouble, you head north. I wound up in the

Santa Lucia Mountains in Big Sur. A cabin there. Actually, a
shack. Walked over granite rocks and sea stacks for hours. Extraordinary fogs that kept you wet. Walked on the chaparral. It
was velvet. Beneath Santa Lucia firs. Certainly one of the most
beautiful trees in the world. Exquisite. And I was high. High and
happy. And Linda, I decided then and there that somehow the
past would *not* destroy me. It won't, it won't, *it won't* destroy
me."

They watched each other in tense silence until Fuki stepped
onto the patio, placing the tray before Linda.

Hanley paused. "Fox was making a movie about soldiers. Marvin Conrad went to Fort Ord to find some extras. Marvin was
casting director, and a thoroughly decent, sensitive and naïve
thirty-year-old child with whom I happened to be living. He found
Tommy Nelson in a soldier show. Tommy was about to be discharged from the Army and was, in fact, planning to come up to
Hollywood. Marvin cast him in the film and told him to call when
he got to Hollywood, which Tommy did. He cast Tommy whenever he could—crowd scenes, bits—and we both got to know him."

"How well?"

His face seemed to wither in the glinting sun. "If you're asking
if one or the other or both of us slept with him, the answer is no.
N-O. The subject was never raised, and Marvin was thoroughly
protective of Tommy. He—Tommy—was hungry and looking for
work and Marvin and I were sort of . . ." He shrugged.

"Godfathers," said Linda.

Nodding, he whispered, "Godfathers. Yes. I like that. Godfathers." Elliott Hanley smiled abruptly, but his lower lip trembled.
"I mean, Tommy had talent. And ambition. And a kind of boyish
vulnerability."

"I see," she said.

"No, you don't," he said harshly. Astonished at his own anger,
Elliott Hanley drew back.

"The studio tried like hell to get a young star for the William
Holden film. They begged Monty Clift. Others. Chuck Heston, I
think. But the part was too small or the actors were busy and I
told Marcus—I pleaded with Marcus Lynn, the producer—to test
Tommy Nelson. Well, he did, and the rest, as we say in Holly-

wood, is history." He lifted his drink, as if making a toast, and brought the glass to his lips.

"That was the year you got blacklisted." He grimaced. "Must we go into that? Really, dear." Hanley's fingers raked his hair. "I was nobody. Marvin was nobody. *That* was the difficulty. I mean, *I* was not about to undermine the American republic with Grade B Westerns and silly comedies. Marvin was about as political as, well, Fuki over there. We signed a couple of petitions. Spanish Civil War refugees. Jewish refugees. Russian refugees. We attended an anti-bomb rally at U.C.L.A. Marvin, fool that he was, *fool that he was,* registered as a Communist in the Los Angeles primary election in 1944. He didn't vote, but that was enough."

A telephone was ringing inside the house.

Linda's lips were gummy with the tart Campari taste.

Glancing at the empty page in her notebook, Linda asked quietly: "Elliott, what do you know about porno films?" She stared at him firmly. "About Tom Nelson and porno films."

Was it her imagination that his body stiffened, almost inadvertently? She saw a small, pink blotch surface beneath his lip. "I never heard of that," he said.

She leaned forward, about to repeat the question another way, but a glance at his face stopped Linda. Suddenly Fuki appeared to inform Elliott he had a phone call. The three exchanged looks as Elliott pushed back his chair. In the silence the air seemed electric with tension.

Porno films . . . Marcus' daughter Maria appeared years later in a porno film, then tried to smother her baby, Tom Nelson's child. Dear God, there's a link here, a thread that connects . . .

Linda asked if there was a second phone in the house she could use to make a call, and Hanley told Fuki to take her into the kitchen. She dialed the Century Plaza. Paul Brock had phoned at noon. He would be available between 1 and 3 P.M. at his cabana at the Beverly Hills Hotel. It was now twelve-forty.

*

Hugh Finch caught a glimpse of the Washington Monument, blurred by the filmy curtains of Secretary of Defense Edward Belling's office.

"Ironic, isn't it?" Belling was saying. "We seem to have been caught up in a power struggle on the New York *Star*. The *Star* sounds more Byzantine than the Pentagon."

Hugh began to grin but was stopped by Belling's cold stare.

"I assumed *you* were writing the China story," said Belling. "Instead, it's Parsons."

Hugh crossed his legs, right foot over left, a deliberately casual gesture. He was, he sensed, beyond exhaustion. For a tantalizing moment he had *nearly* succeeded in publishing the story. *His* Watergate. *His* Pentagon Papers. *His* Pulitzer. And yet . . . it dissolved so quickly. Appeared and disappeared. One minute you're on top, and the next minute you start sliding. And once the slide begins, it's bottomless, sonny, the nature of the business.

"I'm still on the story," said Hugh, fixing his eyes on Belling. "Several of us are. It's called creative competition."

Belling forced a smile. "Parsons seems especially creative. It's unfortunate. He'll have only half the story." Belling crouched forward, frowning at Hugh. "Alex Vikas' half."

"What's *your* half?" asked Hugh.

Belling sighed. "China conducts a startling nuclear test. Alters the balance, the equation. We're caught by *surprise*." Belling's voice lowered in indignation. "Whose U-2s and satellites watch China? Who's manning the listening posts in Pakistan? Whose job is it to know what's going on at China's test site in Lop Nor? At China's nuclear facility at Lanchow? Who? The CIA. Alex Vikas and his boys, right?"

"An Agency failure."

"An Administration failure."

Hugh waited a beat. "You want to be *President*."

"That's absurd! The worst-kept secret in town is that I'm supporting David Fitzgerald."

"But he may falter," said Hugh. "That murdered girl. Whiff of a scandal there. Not going to help Fitzgerald."

Belling examined his cigarette. "Stumbling a bit, isn't he?" There was a slight twitch to Belling's mouth. "Well, now, we can't let Tom Nelson take over the Party, can we?"

Their eyes met and, in that moment a tremor went through Hugh. "You *knew?*"

Belling said impatiently, "What? Knew what?"

"About the President," Hugh whispered.

"Good God, of course we *knew*. How could we not know? Come on, Hugh, you're a smart fellow. You fellows amaze me with your naïveté."

Hugh spoke in a rush of breath. "Barton Taylor said only four people knew besides him—the President's wife, Dr. Pomerance, the White House physician, Admiral Linders and . . . and the Secret Serviceman." Hugh said stiffly, "Did Alvin tell you?"

"Alvin Simmons didn't tell me, although the evidence is rather circumstantial that he *did* leak the news to you. Or at least you stumbled onto it through him. That's what the Treasury people and FBI believe, and they're taking care of him."

Hugh shut his eyes. "What's happened to him?"

"Christ!" said Belling dryly. "We won't tear out his nails. He'll be transferred. Quietly. One of the Service's outlying bureaus. Keeping an eye on the idiot mother of President Bergen in nowhere Indiana. Sad business. I gather he had a future."

Hugh closed his eyes, hearing Alvin's voice, as if in an echo chamber.

Didn't he tell you? Didn't he talk to you?

Hugh opened his eyes, but the words shrieked.

The President has leukemia.

Belling walked to the window, his back toward Hugh.

"We're facing an international crisis . . ."

"With a dying President," said Hugh.

"Intolerable," said Belling.

Hugh laughed bitterly. "Intolerable. Tell that to Barton Taylor. It's not going to work. Taylor's going to tough it out."

"Nonsense," said Belling smoothly.

Hugh ignored him. "The President's going to make it to Camp David. Gonna *succeed*. Mark my words . . ."

Belling finally turned and spoke quietly.

"The President is ill, seriously ill. Our respected national leader is covering it up in the hope, the *fantasy,* that he will solve this crisis quickly and leave an administration that smells like a rose, leave the mantle of power to Tom Nelson. Nelson will take over the Party and the country. And this, my friend, is unthinkable."

Belling sighed. "In a little less than two hours, at six o'clock, my aide Colonel Walker will call in representatives of the major newspapers and the wire services. At the off-the-record meeting this medical report"—Belling lifted a sheet of paper off the center of his desk—"will be distributed."

Belling raised his chin a fraction, his face cold with disdain. "By tomorrow, Congress, the American people—shaken by the news, fully aware that President Bergen is a lame-duck President whose personal guarantees are obviously worthless—by tomorrow I expect the House and Senate to demand that someone else step into the breach. Someone who has the trust of the Russians and . . ."

Finch said, "You. *You.*" He stood up, pleading. "Give it to me first. We *will* print it."

*

Linda Fentress returned to the patio to find Elliott Hanley crouched before a flowerbed of daisies and marigolds. He examined the flowers and spoke very quietly. "Garden beauty is meant to be shared—that's what Mother always said. We lived in Glendale. Our garden was shared by the entire neighborhood." He stood up with a sigh. "That phone call. Two gentlemen from the New York *Daily News.* Persistent, like you."

"I'll be fair, Elliott." She tried to sound comforting, but her tone pleaded. It was a statement she had used many times before. Linda swallowed. "You've been waiting for this for thirty years."

The disdain in Hanley's face turned to blankness. "Sit down," he said. "Put away your pen."

She followed Hanley and sat on a wicker chair.

"In the early fifties Joe Keefer slithered up from under a rock and hit California politics. Former FBI man. A Southerner, from a political family in Florida. The Keefers. He became a state legislator here, with his father's help.

"Joe learned fast. The only way to grab the headlines was to hunt subversives in the movie industry. Actually, it was a low-grade House Un-American Activities Committee. I mean, *they* handled the big boys and girls while Joe was given the crumbs. But Joe had ambitions. Mean but clever, that was Joe Keefer. Used FBI connections. Knew the tricks of the trade. Developed a network of informers, people who gave him information in exchange for keeping his mouth shut."

"Blackmail," said Linda.

"Well, yes, of course." Elliott drained his drink. "Joe used tra-

ditional tactics. Confessions guaranteed to get a headline. Public
humiliations. Naming friends. The standard things.

"We were all living in a very precarious state during the reign
of terror. The industry was in turmoil. We—Marvin and I—didn't
have resources. Just a casting agent and a second-rate director
who, by the way, had a mother to support. Foolishly, *foolishly,* we
thought we would escape the terror. We were *nobodies.*"

He spoke rapidly. "Well, Joe Keefer knew that Tommy was on
the way *up.* Keefer knew of Tommy's *association* with known subversives in the industry. Keefer wanted . . . wanted *desperately* to
get Tommy to inform. And Tommy became—how shall I say—a
cooperative witness, a witness only too pleased to inform on his
friends. What we said, what we signed, what we laughed at. He
named Marvin Conrad. He named me. He named others. By the
end of Tommy's secret testimony we had the start of a Com-
munist-homosexual conspiracy poised on taking over the film industry."

"Secret testimony," said Linda.

"Tommy managed to find a shrewd lawyer . . ."

"Named?"

Hanley smiled. "Marcus Lynn. Himself a Communist in the late
thirties. A popular lawyer in the fifties for the victims of the terror. Marcus and Keefer agreed that in the interests of Tommy's
career, his testimony should remain secret. And it was. It *was,* my
dear. Joe Keefer flogged the conspiracy briefly—even got some national coverage—and he had fantasies of running for senator, turning into a prominent figure, the California Joe McCarthy. But
then, thankfully, he disappeared, slithered right back under a
rock.

"Don't look so puzzled, dear," Elliott said. "Beneath Joe
Keefer's layer of evil, he was only a twisted little man. Frightened.
A rummy at heart who Marcus eventually . . . destroyed."

Elliott Hanley narrowed his eyes. "Marcus has a gift, a special
gift that only the most successful of us manage to utilize. He
exploits weakness. He sniffs it out. He *knows.* We're all vulnerable. He taps that vulnerability. Only the most successful lawyers
and businessmen and movie directors and, I suppose, newspaper
editors"—he laughed—"have that gift."

"What was Keefer's weakness?"

Linda watched Hanley's tongue dampen his lower lip.

"Joe Keefer had what I can only say is a peculiar weakness. More peculiar than most, although, dear, I'm old enough to feel that my weaknesses are quite evident and fairly peculiar. But Joe's, well, Joe's weakness was he liked children."

For a moment Linda watched a bee sway languidly over a branch of the lemon tree, beside the Ficus. The bee settled on a ripe, wet lemon whose skin glistened.

Hanley seemed to frown. "Children. Yes. Little girls. Not too little. Not eight or nine, although I wouldn't quite put that past him. But twelve or thirteen."

"Jesus," she whispered.

Hanley said, "Given Keefer's friendship with the police and the FBI, his powerful family, it was a problem that seemed manageable. He was smart enough to pick little black girls or poor white girls, children whose families were often pleased to receive a three-hundred-dollar or five-hundred-dollar token of appreciation, families easily intimidated."

A tense silence had fallen over the patio. "What happened?" said Linda.

"Keefer was drunk with power. Insane with it. Threatened to run for senator. And he would have won, dear, *he would have won.*"

"He had to be stopped," murmured Linda.

"Keefer began threatening Marcus and . . . Tommy. Threatened to go public. Ask Tom about his friendship with two fags. Two subversive fags. Would have shattered Tommy's career. Threatened to call Marcus to the stand about *his* past . . ."

"Unless . . ."

"Unless Marcus supported him, ran his campaign, raised money."

"Joey was blackmailing them . . ."

"Until Tommy Nelson . . ." Elliott stared at Linda with dead eyes, ". . . found a young girl."

"How young?"

"Twelve, maybe thirteen. Quite a pretty little thing. Blond. And Tommy and Marcus set it up discreetly. Got the girl to hang around Keefer's house, and before he knew it . . ."

Linda felt her heart thudding.

"Who was she?"

Hanley shrugged. "Daughter of our landlady. Had a crush on Tommy. Tommy told her he would help her break into the movies if she cooperated."

Linda's mouth fell open.

"Films were taken by a hidden cameraman," said Elliott Hanley. He turned away. *"Me!* I took them. Poor Joey. Didn't know what hit him. Didn't know that Marcus and Tommy had set him up. Stupid bastard. Thought it was the girl's mother who wanted the films. He didn't know."

Elliott paused. "Keefer was informed by the girl's family lawyer that the rape of a minor was punishable by five years in prison. Of course financial arrangements could be made with the child's mother *not* to press charges. But that was the least of it." He smiled faintly to himself. "Given the nature of the films, Marcus advised the Keefer family that Joey should retire from public life, not seek public office lest Keefer's numerous enemies got their hands on the films."

Linda spoke slowly, eyes widened on Elliott. "So Keefer ended up working for the man who betrayed him."

Hanley glanced at her. "It was in the interests of Keefer's family, of Marcus and Tom Nelson, of Joey's FBI sources to keep him shut up. Kept under wraps. Controlled. His family didn't want him in Washington. Joey was an embarrassment, you see. He had nowhere to go. He was drinking, making a spectacle of himself. He was broken. So Joey was informed that if he worked for Marcus, if he kept clean, the FBI would take him back one day. The fool believed . . ."

He smiled at Linda. "So far as I can tell, Joey never found out that it was Marcus, the man he worked for, who had destroyed him."

"Lois Barrie said Joey was Marcus' flunky," said Linda impatiently.

Hanley took a deep breath. "One almost pitied the bastard. Brought Marcus his morning coffee. He helped with the groceries. Delivered messages. Served as a chauffeur, drove Marcus' daughter Maria . . ." Hanley stopped and studied his drink. ". . . Maria to school."

Don't get sidetracked, Linda, Maria's not the story, not yet, target Nelson and the films, that's priority number one, yet . . . why, why does Maria hover like a dark presence, wherever you turn there's Maria . . .

"Why did Maria try to murder her child?"

Hanley's voice dropped. "No one knows. Not even Marcus."

"I don't believe that."

Hanley stared at her. "Don't pursue that story, my dear. Don't! You'll hear rumors all over town that Tom Nelson's the child's father."

"Is he?"

"Don't pursue it, Linda."

"Why?"

"Because Marcus will kill you."

They stepped from the patio to the silent house. "Aren't you enraged, Elliott?" He looked at her puzzled. "Nelson informed on you. Blacklisted you. He destroyed you for years."

"No, I'm not enraged, Linda. I have my share of . . . guilt. And, besides, *besides*"—Hanley shook his head. "Besides, I loved Tom."

Linda turned away, pressing the point of her pen against her notebook, drawing tiny triangles imprisoned within rectangles. Got to forget Maria, go to see Paul Brock, the porno guy, got to see him soon before those bastards on the *Daily News* do. She looked up. Hanley had placed the tinted spectacles over his eyes. She thanked Elliott, and congratulated him on the Neil Simon film.

She walked to the door. "Lois didn't tell you that she got me the job. A loyal friend. Rare in this town. Lois is bent on rehabilitating me." He stopped. "I'm an adequate director, Linda. Not especially good, not terrible. But on the strength of this one film my career seemed to be taking off." He smiled impassively.

She started to speak, but Elliott lifted his left hand with difficulty, a gesture that implored Linda not to persist.

Distractedly, he asked her where she was going, and Linda responded, "The Beverly Hills Hotel."

"Do you know Paul Brock?" she asked. It was an afterthought and a way to change the subject.

Hanley stiffened a little, as if surprised. "Everyone knows Paul Brock," Elliott murmured. He caught his breath and said, "Haven't seen Paul in many years."

One more question for the road, Elliott, just one . . .

"Tom Nelson's first agent. Paul Bernstein. Where is he?"

Hanley stopped and stared at her. "My dear, Paul Bernstein *is* Paul Brock."

*

A harsh breeze on Seventy-second Street and West End Avenue struck Sally's face. There was a faint odor of decay on the street, and the sight of an overturned garbage can, its lid clattering toward Sally, disgusted yet fascinated her. She stood perfectly still, staring fixedly at the empty milk cartons, eggshells, used tea bags, smeared grapefruit rinds that seeped out of the bin and zigzagged toward Broadway.

Out of the corner of her eye she saw a bolt of lightning streak the sky, and then there was silence. Darkness cloaked the street, thick chunks of warm rain started slowly. From the apartment houses lights glittered in windows. Sally saw people running. She knew this lull would yield to the full force of the storm, but in those flickering seconds Sally's fear locked her against the car. It was impossible to move.

A violent gust struck her. Sally's hand flew to her face. She turned on her heels, the wind and wet, slippery curb making her tilt forward and lose her balance. Her handbag fell in a pool of water. Bending low, suddenly trembling at the knees, Sally was aware that the storm was smashing her body, weakening her muscles. She toppled to the pavement, moaning aloud.

Sally felt the painful sting in the palm of her left hand, and winced when she saw the blood running over her wrist. Lifting the shard of glass that had sliced her palm, Sally heaved it in the gutter with all her strength. The rain plastered her hair, seeping over her shoulders and chest; Sally lifted her injured hand to her face.

Warm blood smeared her lips and curled over her chin. Sally was gasping for air, suddenly alarmed as the wall of water drenched her. Trying to push herself up, Sally felt herself sway, then pitch forward.

Oh, Charlie, she gasped, tasting the salt of her tears. And then she saw the pool of headlights stop beside her. Sally looked up, alarmed, and heard the taxi driver's Russian accent even before she saw him.

Lady, lady . . .

Cursing in Russian, he reached toward Sally. His hands roughly grasped her arms. He was attempting to pull her into the safety of the cab.

Sally felt herself crumple. She wanted the rain to hammer over her, to soak her to the bone, to wash her away.

Charlie my sweet!

She was howling now, weak at the knees as the driver lifted her. Sally opened her mouth, but gagged as the rain slapped her throat. The strength of his hands, tight on her arms, was strangely comforting. Suddenly she had an impulse to laugh.

But she shrieked. *Charlie!*

Alarmed, the cab driver dropped his hands. For a moment Sally concentrated on the water streaming over his hair and nose. Then she touched his arm and pushed herself into the cab. Sally was shivering with cold, but calmer.

Charlie.

She whispered his name one final time.

*

"Maury! Listen to me! I'm at the Pentagon. We've got a little more than two hours. Two hours to decide whether or not to print my story. They know. Belling knows about the President. He's gonna leak the story at six o'clock. Do you hear me? He's gonna leak the story tonight *unless* we publish."

"For Chrissake, Hugh. Belling will leak it to whom?"

"To the Washington *Post*. The *Times*. The L.A. *Times*. The wires. You still there?"

"Still here."

"I got a copy of the medical report, Maury. *Pomerance's* report. Listen! Quote. The low white count, the low platelet count, represents a form of leukemia. The disease could most certainly accelerate at any time. What we need to be concerned with are the following: sudden changes in the platelet or white count, episodes of bleeding or infection, worsening of anemia and the presence of blasts in the peripheral blood. Unquote. You still there?"

"Christ. Stop asking me that. I'm . . . *thinking*."

"Listen. Here's my lead. The President of the United States is seriously ill and quote may have a form of leukemia unquote according to a secret medical report obtained by the New York *Star* today. *That's* the lead. The story!"

Maury spoke quietly. "You still got your notes from Pomerance's session with us yesterday?"

"They're at home. You remember Bart Taylor's argument—that the President is the only one to negotiate with the Russians and the Chinese, so we can't publish. Remember? Well, listen. A secret message went to the Chinese this morning. Third-country channels. Asking if they were amenable to a meeting with *Belling*."

"Son of a bitch."

"Shuttle diplomacy," Hugh said. "That's the plan—that the Chinese and Russians welcome Belling. The first step. He'll shuttle between Moscow and Peking. Negotiate. When both sides are finally ready to meet, face to face, Belling flies them to Camp David. Belling has an aide. A colonel. Walker. Chinese know him. Trust him. They've agreed to Belling's immediate visit."

"And the Russians? Kopeikin?"

"Under pressure from his own hardliners not to welcome Belling."

"We'll get Ernie in Moscow. Check his sources." Maury's voice dropped. "*Good* story."

"It's *brilliant*."

"Get your copy ready. When you hear from me, you'll call Belling and tell him *we'll* print it. It's *our* story. I'm seeing Skipper in four minutes." He spoke emphatically. "We've *got* to print it."

"And if Skipper says no?"

"I quit."

"Me too," said Hugh. He heard Maury laugh.

"What's so funny?"

"Someday I'll tell you," said Maury.

Hugh thought a second, then said, "Congratulations."

Hugh next dialed his office in the Washington bureau. Francine Miles answered on the first ring.

"Francie, I'm at the Pentagon. Going to my apartment now to write. No interruptions. Maury knows where I am. It's important, honey. It's . . ."

"That story."

He was breathless.

"You got a problem," she whispered. "Your kids are here."

"My kids."

"You remember. Terry. Handsome boy. Sports freak. Marguerite. Adorable. Smart as a whip. Your *kids*. They said you promised that . . ."

"Oh *fuck*. I *forgot*. I promised them. The Orioles. I *promised*."

"That's obvious," she said. "Listen, you may be in luck. It's supposed to rain. I think they would settle for pizza and the Clint Eastwood atrocity on Connecticut Avenue, or that *Star Wars* clone uptown."

"Do me a favor. Take them downstairs. Put them in a cab for my apartment. Give Terry your key, just in case they get there before me. Oh fuck. *Fuck*."

"I've got a better idea," said Francine calmly. "Why don't I come with them. You write your big story, as we say, while Francine and the kids play Monopoly and Scrabble. When we get bored, we'll have sex."

"Don't be a wise ass. There's only one person you have sex with."

"Since when?"

"Since now. We'll talk about that later."

She lowered her voice. "We'll see you soon."

"What would I do without you, Francie?"

"Find someone else," she said lightly. "Just like me."

*

"Where's Maury?" asked Ward, catching sight of Florence stepping toward the foreign desk.

"Went up early to see Skipper. Before the front-page conference."

Ward looked up at the wall clock. Six minutes before the daily session in Skipper's office. The meeting with Alex Vikas in Washington D.C., the packed shuttle flight to LaGuardia, the crawl through midtown traffic had drained him.

Ward heard Tony Lazzarutti's voice interrupt. "Incoming message from your wife, sir. 'Departing Delhi in the next half-hour . . .'"

Florence Malley had returned and was speaking to Ray, avoiding Ward. "Rumors all over the newsroom. Drivers are *supporting* the Guild."

Ward heard Ray's voice. "Strike. Jesus Christ!"

Ward closed his eyes. "No way," Florence was saying. "Skipper'll cave in. Wait and see. *No* cutbacks."

His eyes met Florence's. By tonight she would pack up and return to her apartment on Eighty-seventh Street. Sweet, loyal Florence who deserves better, deserves a guy out of this business, a lawyer, a doctor or a dentist, a Wall Street broker, a sane guy who values her and not . . . not a goddamn newspaperman.

Lost Florence.

Lost . . . Karen.

Ward stood, his face burning. Karen was departing Delhi right now. Karen *needed* him, but how could he leave? He had a story, a goddamn story, Alex's front-page story. Wasn't that always the way? Isn't that always the priority? How could he yield the story now, the byline, when the prospect remained, ever so slight, that he would be managing editor?

*

Two hours.

Climbing two steps at a time, Hugh ran into the five-story building on Kalorama Road. Francine and Terry and Marguerite would soon be there; he would shut the study door and start the story, waiting, *waiting* for the call from Maury, the call that he *knew* was imminent. Go ahead, Hugh, call Belling. The story is . . . yours.

Skipper. Frieda. Lucy.

It was their paper, their decision, and they would publish. No other way now. No options. They had to publish his story. And by tonight, as the first edition rolled into the delivery trucks, as the desk editors on AP and UPI and all the other papers stared, shaken at the eight-column headline across the New York *Star* over the byline Hugh Finch, he would know, *yes,* that the struggle, the broken marriage, the bruising competition, the loneliness, the betrayal—yes, even the betrayal of Alvin Simmons, was worth it. The story was *his,* the culmination of a career, the pinnacle. Pulitzer, baby, and it *was* worth it.

As he turned the key and pushed open the door, Hugh suddenly stopped in midstep. Something was wrong.

Francine, in a beige raincoat and gripping a black umbrella, stood at the opposite end of the hallway, Terry and Marguerite beside her. The children, in canary-yellow anoraks, turned and stared gravely at him.

Marguerite's fingers fumbled at the top button of her jacket, a movement that caught Hugh's eyes. It was only then that Hugh looked over the child's head to the figure looming at the entrance of the living room. It was Alvin.

Slouching against the wall, his hands pressed into his pockets, Alvin smiled. His eyes, rheumy and stained pink, widened.

Hugh felt shivers crawl over his scalp.

"Welcome home," Alvin said.

"How did you get in?" Hugh looked away, regretting the words as soon as he said them.

Alvin laughed. "Shit, I am a trained Secret Serviceman. Armed and trained."

"Tried to reach you."

"Well, here I am, Hugh boy. In living black and white."

"You drunk, Alvin?"

"Fuck no, I'm not drunk."

Francine murmured, "Why don't we leave? Me and the kids'll take a walk." The children eyed her quizzically.

Sunlight bathed Alvin in an eerie bluish glow. He nodded several seconds before speaking. "Maybe you better stay here, honey."

The smile unsettled Hugh. "Hey, look, I tried to reach you. I'm gonna work things out."

"Sure." Alvin grinned.

"No shit. I'm going to work things out. I *know* the Secretary of Defense. He'll take care . . ."

"You motherfucker," Alvin whispered, still smiling. "I want to kill you."

The pulse at the side of Hugh's temple began to beat visibly. He struggled to sound calm.

"Perhaps they *should* go." He pointed with his chin to Francine and the children.

"Perhaps they should stay."

"Hey, Alvin . . ."

Quickly Alvin thrust his fingers into his suit jacket and removed a revolver. Francine, white-faced, shrank back, groping for the hands of the two wide-eyed children.

"I want to kill you," whispered Alvin, the smile gone, his face absolutely desolate.

"Oh my God," Francine whispered.

"Give me the gun." Hugh struggled to keep his voice controlled. He took one step toward Alvin.

Alvin stared at the ceiling, his face blotched with tears. Hugh spoke firmly. "Give me the gun!"

Two more steps. Hugh caught the smell of whiskey and sweat, keeping his eyes fixed on the butt of the revolver.

Francine pressed the children to her side.

Alvin's chin sagged to his chest, his mouth agape. For a moment his eyes widened. And then it happened.

Hugh lunged for the weapon. Francine saw Alvin twist his face, releasing a weird hissing sound and then stiffening his body. As Hugh grabbed his arm, Alvin seemed to rise off the floor. He flung his right arm backward, the barrel and cylinder aglow in the sunlight that streamed through the living-room window.

What shocked Francine was the rage that propelled Alvin's body. She knew, instantly, that there was no contest here. Alvin's anguish and defeat had given way to immense fury. She heard Alvin grunt and watched, fascinated, as the revolver, twisting sideways, moved in an arc downward, smashing over Hugh's ear with a cracking, terrible thud. Hugh let out a high-pitched gasp and crumpled to the floor.

Francine saw a trickle of blood seep onto Hugh's hair. In the next moment the blood spurted silently over his ear, misting his hair in an eerie purplish fluid. Francine gasped. Marguerite's whimper was buried by the hands that covered her face. Terry, his lips twisted, on the edge of weeping, gaped at his father.

Alvin stared calmly down at Hugh, who struggled to lift himself up, but shaking his head as if puzzled, fell forward.

"Oh my God," whispered Francine.

Wild-eyed, she stared at Alvin. The revolver, firmly planted in his hand, was pointing downward at Hugh's head, Alvin's index finger resting on the trigger. Hugh lifted himself to a seated position, his back toward Alvin, shaking his head, the sound of his uneven breathing filling the silence.

"They wanted me to take a lie detector test," said Alvin through his teeth. "Well, I went to a lawyer. He said, 'No way. Don't have to take no lie detector test if you don't want to.'

That's the law, man. Career's finished, though. All over. That's what the man said too."

He swallowed and shook his head. "That's okay. Just a job anyway. Other jobs around town. Not bad. Security man. Doorman. Night watchman. Shit, that's what I deserve to do anyway. Night watchman. That's what I'll do except . . . except . . . I'm going to kill you."

Hugh turned to Alvin. Francine stepped back. Alvin took a half step, the sole of his right foot pressed against Hugh's leg. The gun, firmly in Alvin's hand, hovered two feet away from Hugh's head.

Alvin cocked the trigger.

"Don't," whispered Hugh.

"You destroyed me," said Alvin.

"My God! Please!" Francine shut her eyes.

"Beg me," said Alvin.

"What?"

"*You beg me.*"

"Don't kill me. Please. Don't kill me."

Alvin nestled the revolver against Hugh's temple.

Hugh shut his eyes. "Please don't kill me. Please don't kill me. I don't want to die."

"Hate you, motherfucker," said Alvin.

"I don't want to die." Hugh was weeping now, his shoulders hunched, his body twitching. "I don't want to *die.*"

Francine said softly: "Please, Alvin."

Hugh shuddered and stopped weeping. But then he gasped, twisted his mouth open and howled.

"Big man," whispered Alvin.

Hugh's body seemed to shrivel. "Please!"

"Sorry, baby," said Alvin. He jerked the weapon onto the back of Hugh's head. Francine saw him extend his index finger around the trigger. She shrieked as he pressed the trigger. The revolver clicked. Hugh's body crumpled, his breath a high birdlike whimper.

It took several seconds before Francine heard Alvin's laugh. Hugh turned, his face wrenched in anguish.

"Big man," Alvin said. He contemplated the gun in his hand,

then glanced with a frown at Francine and the children. Finally he placed the revolver in his shoulder holster.

Ignoring Hugh, Alvin slowly turned on his heels and walked to the door. But then he twisted around and stared at Hugh, catching his eyes.

The sound of the door closing seemed to charge Hugh's body. He began to shake as soon as the door shut.

Francine rushed toward him. "Let me help. I'll get some ice . . ."

He released a single, harrowing sob. "Get *away*."

She ignored him and said nervously to the children, "Go get some ice. In the kitchen."

"GET AWAY. GET OUT. PLEASE GET OUT."

She reared back. "Hugh!"

"EVERYBODY. GET OUT."

"Hugh. Darling. You've got the story . . ."

He turned to her, his face contorted in agony.

"Get out. Out! *Out*."

*

"Eli. I had a wonderful time," Frieda said.

"We will do this more often," he said gravely. "From now on."

"From now on," she said. "I think . . ." She faced him. "I *know* this is going to be a turning point, Eli. For me. For the *Star*. For us."

He lifted his vodka glass. "To us," he said.

She lifted her glass of tea. "To us," she said. Frieda tasted the tea and sighed. "Time for me to see Skipper," she said.

The woman who brought them to the table approached and told Eli he had a phone call. Puzzled, he glanced at Frieda and excused himself.

Frieda settled back on the banquette.

A turning point. The words echoed.

Frieda had felt such contentment in the past ninety minutes that she was amazed at the tremor of fear that stirred her as soon as Eli left. The contagious excitement only moments earlier, the sense that she was embarking on an adventure, a bold and perilous adventure, had yielded to a tension that left her stomach knotted.

Suddenly she was angry at herself. The *Star* had to survive, that was her first priority. One had to eliminate jobs in the newsroom, one had to move toward more entertaining human-interest stories and gossip, one had to cut the foreign staff and get some young blood to replace people like Sarah and even Norman Walker, Jr., painful as that would be.

What unsettled Frieda, she knew, was what Eli didn't *quite* say. Inheritance taxes and capital-gains taxes made selling to a conglomerate a . . . possibility. Eli had raised the subject before, over the years, pointing out that newspaper groups and conglomerates were buying at high prices, that independents like the *Star* were a vanishing breed.

He suddenly appeared at the table, his face pale.

"The drivers just announced that they will honor the Guild pickets. The Guild's prepared to strike indefinitely. Strike starts tomorrow night."

Frieda stood up unsteadily, grasping Eli's hand, and waited as he signed the bill.

It was Eli who noticed Marty Kaplan, still at the bar.

Frieda said: "Good God. Have you been here all along? Haven't you had . . . Where's Sally?"

Marty Kaplan's tie was loose, his right hand grasped a bloody mary. "Stood me up." He shrugged. "Don't know where she is."

"That's *unlike* Sally." Frieda touched his arm. "Haven't you had lunch?"

"Three bloody marys and some peanuts. I've had far worse."

"Marty, I'm going over to the office. My car is outside. Join me."

Her authoritative tone was unmistakable. It was an order from Frieda Steiner. As Marty quickly paid his bill, he wondered why on earth Frieda Steiner wanted to speak to him.

*

Maury Kramer sat at the edge of the leather sofa in the waiting room outside Skipper's office, keeping his eyes fixed on the steel-and-glass table at his knee. His right shoulder ached; the throb in his chest constricted into a piercing pain that quickly subsided. His hands trembled, and he hungered for a cigarette, an addiction that Nancy abhorred and a habit that he had sought to break, without success, since his wife's death. He shut his eyes, as if willing his nervousness to end.

Would this moment of triumph, this moment he had prepared for all those years, burst and disintegrate in an absurd twist of fate? Would it end before he began?

Skipper *had* to publish Hugh's story.

And if he refused to publish, well, the new managing editor would have to resign. And wouldn't that be a bitch, wouldn't that be a goddamn laugh!

Maury stiffened as the door to Skipper's office opened. Harry Watson, gripping a sheaf of papers, stepped out; behind him, Skipper, in shirtsleeves, glanced at his watch. Geraldine Heaney stopped typing.

"Something wrong?" asked Maury, standing up.

Skipper said, distracted, "Sally's disappeared. That sounds more melodramatic than it is. Probably stuck in traffic. Or something. I had a lunch date with my son and *he* didn't show up. Have been trying to reach him. Christ. When it doesn't rain . . ." He glanced at his watch. "We've got five minutes. Come on in."

Just then Maury heard sounds behind him. He turned. In the doorway stood Frieda Steiner, with Lucy hovering beside her.

"We've interrupted, haven't we?" said Frieda, without a hint of remorse. "Good afternoon, Maury."

Maury smiled uncertainly, suddenly aware of the growing resemblance between Lucy and her mother.

"Five minutes before the front-page conference," said Frieda to her son. "Can we see you *now?*"

Skipper turned to Maury and asked him to wait. Barry entered the reception room, stopping cold, breaking into a puzzled grin at the sight of Frieda and Lucy. Skipper told Barry the front-page conference would be delayed.

Holding out his arm, Skipper ushered his mother and sister into the office. As he turned to close the door, he caught sight of Ward Parsons entering the reception room.

Skipper flicked on the desk lighter and held it for Lucy, bringing his gaze to her face. "To what do I owe this sudden visit?"

Lucy inhaled, saying nothing. Frieda's voice broke the silence.

"Lazzarutti's called a strike for tomorrow midnight, and the drivers are supporting him. What are we going to do?"

Skipper stared at his mother. "Talk to him. We're meeting him late this afternoon. And tonight. And all day tomorrow. See if we can work out some . . ."

"Skipper, he's not interested in compromise," Frieda said impatiently. "He *wants* a strike and he wants to humiliate us."

"True."

"So?"

"So. We'll cancel layoffs at the last minute."

"Why?" said Frieda, tightening her lips.

Skipper spoke evenly, almost as if to a child. "Because we can't afford a strike, Mother. A strike would shatter us. The *Star* doesn't publish, and our competition does. We'll die."

"Jonathan used the same argument," said Frieda. "Can't afford a strike, so yield. Give in to the unions. Don't bite the bullet now. Wait. Do what's expedient in the short run. Forget that we have deadwood all over this building. Forget that we need to economize in order to survive, in order to pay for all those computers and lasers and new technology that we *need.*"

Skipper and Lucy gazed at their mother, startled at her vehemence.

"I . . . we . . . have decided, Skipper, that we *must* publish Hugh Finch's story. Can't afford not to. I want it published tonight."

Frieda twisted the emerald and diamond ring set in platinum on her pinky.

"And Skipper," she said, staring past him, "I think it's in the best interests of the paper that we appoint Barry Cohen managing editor."

Except for the red flush that lit his cheeks, Skipper betrayed no emotion. His voice was controlled.

"I think that's impossible."

"Impossible?"

"I told Maury this morning that he was my choice." He waited. "I *want* Maury . . ."

Frieda spoke in a gasp. "*You* want him. *You.* What about *us.* What about *me.* It's *my* paper. I'm not dead yet, Skipper. When I'm dead and gone you can do what you want. In the meantime the paper is *mine.*" Frieda's voice shook with rage. "It is my *life,* Skipper. It's been my life since long before you were publisher. I may behave like a silly old woman, but, Skipper, I'm not. I'm *not.* And *I run this paper too.*"

Skipper spoke softly. "Traditionally, Mother, the publisher selects his managing editor, and the stockholders go along."

"I want to forgo tradition."

He turned to Lucy. "Do you agree?"

She nodded.

"It's Eli," said Skipper.

"Yes, it's Eli," Frieda said coldly. "It's Eli and it's *The Wall Street Journal* and it's the reality of what we face here in New York. It's deadwood that we can't fire because we're afraid of Lazzarutti."

"And Barry will change that?" said Skipper evenly.

"He's tough and he's mean," Frieda replied. "He may not be my type personally, but perhaps that's the trouble. Perhaps I should care less about my personal tastes and care more about competing. That's my fault, Skipper, not yours."

"And Maury?"

"Perfectly decent man. He'll stay on as Barry's deputy."

"He'll quit."

"So be it."

"You're taking over, is that it, Mother?"

"No, Skipper. *We're* taking over because it's life and death. As simple as that. It's *survival.*"

"And publishing news of the illness assures our survival."

"It's a symbol, Skipper," said Frieda, lifting her chin. "We're starting anew. We're an investigative paper now. We're going to be lean. Cut ourselves to the bone. Tomorrow morning we begin."

Skipper pushed out his chair and walked to the window. Lucy lit another cigarette.

"I'm sorry about this," Lucy finally said to no one in particular.

Except for the faintest flicker in Skipper's eyelids, his face looked perfectly calm. "I want a formal vote tomorrow on the managing editor's job, and then I want *you* to inform Maury."

"Whatever you say," said Frieda.

"And Mother?"

"Yes." Frieda glanced at her fingernails.

"I resign."

Frieda's eyes darted to Skipper, standing in profile, facing the window, a ray of luminous light casting a soft, filmy glow over his black hair and face. *So beautiful, she thought. So like Arnold . . .*

Lucy said, "Skipper!"

"Don't be a child," said Frieda.

Skipper spoke firmly. "Hugh will write his story tonight and we will publish it in tomorrow's paper. Tomorrow we vote. Two o'clock."

He stared at Frieda. "We will issue a formal announcement after that naming Barry Cohen managing editor of the New York *Star*. We will issue a second announcement through the public relations department saying that I have resigned, effective immediately, to pursue other business interests."

Frieda inhaled deeply, her face suddenly pale. "You're a fool."

Skipper struggled to smile. "Now I think I better start the front-page conference," he said. "We're late as it is. I'll inform our editors that we have decided to publish Hugh's story. Better get Hugh on the phone."

He glanced at Frieda. The mask of desolation on his face—his calm, perfectly reasoned voice—stirred Lucy. She blinked hard as tears wet her face.

"Skipper, please!" she said.

"Busy few days we have," he said, gazing out the window. "We have Hugh's story. The China-Soviet crisis. Howie Bishop's investigation. Linda Fentress, I gather, is finding out some interesting details about the Vice President, and there may be a substantial story there in the next twenty-four hours. Frenetic time, Mother."

"Skipper," said Frieda quietly. "*Why?*"

"Perhaps . . ." He stared at Lucy, then examined his desk. "Perhaps it's my declaration of independence."

"You never wanted to be publisher, did you?"

"It was preordained, Mother. My divine right. I had no choice."

"No choice," she whispered. "You blame me."

He fixed his eyes on Frieda, and spoke so softly that Lucy leaned forward to hear.

"I blame you for controlling this paper from the moment that Jonathan took over. I blame you for refusing to let go, at any cost. I blame you for instilling the fear of God, the fear of your own wrath, on the editors of this paper. Crippling *them!* I blame you for being a hypocrite. Cut out the deadwood, right? What about

Norman Walker, Jr.? What about your fool nephew Larry Lake? Keep lazy incompetents and hangers-on and court jesters like Eli around to fawn over you and make you feel young and like the beautiful girl you never were."

Frieda tried to smile. "Your resignation is accepted, Skipper. You can leave immediately if you like. You hate me for being what I am, and I accept that. I plead guilty. I'm guilty of controlling the paper and controlling my children's lives. Frieda is too strong, isn't she? Frieda meddles. Queen Frieda. Well, Frieda dominates because she has to dominate. Because she had the misfortune of marrying a weak man and having a weak son who wanted her to take charge."

Frieda narrowed her eyes. "What do you blame me for? Is it the Japanese girl? You blame me for that? Do you think I would have leaped off the Empire State Building if you brought her home and married her? I would have *respected* you, Skipper. *Yes!* You were too weak to marry her. *You* were frightened. Don't blame *me* for your not being a man."

Frieda stood up. "There's only one reason you don't want a strike, my dear. You're *terrified* of facing Lazzarutti. And you know why? He's tougher than you are, and you know it."

Frieda gripped Skipper's desk. "We will have the formal vote tomorrow on Evan's replacement."

"And Barry Cohen's job," said Skipper quietly. "Who's going to be the new city editor?"

Frieda said, "I had an inspiration this afternoon. I think Marty Kaplan would be a fine choice."

CHAPTER 19

At the Beverly Hills Hotel, Linda found a phone booth beside the Polo Lounge and called Gregory Hamalian. He had just left an envelope for Linda at her hotel, crammed with xeroxed Los Angeles *Times* clips on Joe Keefer. The files on Marcus Lynn had been voluminous—folders and folders on Marcus defending blacklist victims, Marcus as a Democratic National Committeeman,

Marcus as a movie producer, Marcus as a lawyer, Marcus as chief executive officer at Transcon.

"Who owns Transcon?"

Gregory replied that the items on Marcus' company were vague, worth further checking. Linda chewed her lip.

As if anticipating her next question, Gregory said in a low voice: "There's nothing at all on the daughter. Maria."

Linda nodded, about to thank him, when Gregory said:

"Caught an interesting article in there. Intrigued me. One of the blacklisted guys Marcus defended was an old boyfriend of Lois. Named Gus Heller. Filmmaker from New York. Spent the last fifteen years making porno films in Mexico and L.A."

"Gus Heller," said Linda, scrawling the name on the back page of her notebook.

"Something about the name rang a bell. Got out Heller's clips in the *Times* library. Just out of interest and . . ."

"Yeah?"

"Murdered in San Diego about five years ago. I remember the story. Found in a car that was set afire with gasoline. Mission Bay Park, right near the zoo. Beaten to death. Police said it looked like a gangland thing."

Linda narrowed her eyes on the name. "Five years ago," she said.

"I called Lois," said Gregory, waiting. "It was Gus, Gus Heller, who produced the porno film with Maria."

Linda flinched. "When was Gus murdered? Specifically."

"Lois said Gus was killed a day or two *before* Maria flew to L.A. She remembers they were preparing the nursery at Marcus' home . . ."

Linda spoke in a single breath. "Gus Heller, the guy who made Maria's porno film, is murdered in San Diego. A day or two after *that,* Maria flies from Mexico to L.A. and tries to smother her infant." Linda began turning the pages of her notebook. "In the meantime, the guy who blacklisted Gus Heller, the guy they all hated . . ."

"Joey Keefer."

"Keefer drops dead in Mexico City," Linda said. "All in the same week!"

Linda absently wrote Maria's name on a blank page. Exasperated, speaking to herself and to Gregory, she murmured, "Why does this story always come back to Maria?" Linda's eyes lifted as the words came to her. I've got to see her.

Linda thanked Gregory. She had one more quick call to make before meeting Paul Brock.

One more favor. One more chip to call in.

Linda found Sandy Jaffe's direct line at his law firm in Washington.

Linda and Sandy had met at a party at Hugh Finch's apartment during the early days of Watergate when Sandy was at the Justice Department. Sandy proved to be the perfect source: talkative and reachable anytime, a source that later provided most of the details of her investigations of Nazis in the United States when he moved on to the Immigration and Naturalization Service. The fact that she was a young blonde with a superb figure helped.

Linda had slept with Sandy three or four times during the summer while his family was in Nantucket, and the relationship had, quite happily, dissolved into an uncomplicated friendship in which reporter and source fed and assisted one another—in exchange for publicity. The fact that Sanford M. Jaffe was prominently mentioned in Linda's stories served him perfectly at a point in his career when two of his three children were about to enter college and his bank account totaled $14,500. Largely on the basis of Linda's stories, Sandy accepted a partnership in a prestigious tax and litigation firm at Sixteenth and L streets. Now his three-hundred-dollar suits, his haircuts with tinted gray sideburns, his luncheons with Linda at Lion D'Or, bespoke his success. She had not spoken to him in nearly six months.

"Sandy, darling. I need help."

"Where are you?"

"Beverly Hills."

"Nazis in Beverly Hills?"

"It's not Nazis, honey. That's the *only* thing I'm sure of. It's . . . well, I don't know what it is. I need a small favor. Can you, or one of your minions, go to the SEC and run a check on Marcus Lynn? He's director of a corporation named Transcon. Conglomerate into everything. Real estate. Movies. Cable TV. The works."

"We'll pull the files on subsidiaries too."

"Bless you. And keep this between us."

"Top secret," he said. "Linda, I don't like you out there alone. All those horny producers and casting directors."

"Don't worry, love, I'm saving it all for you."

"You're just after my money."

"Absolutely. Send my best to the wife and kids." She was shaking.

Panic gets you nowhere, Linda thought as she set the phone down. That's what Jerry always said. Let the story *flow*, take its natural course.

Jerry! Why, hon. Oh Jesus! Was it money, was it the kid and Mike? That's the reason. But Jerry, you should have known, you dumb bastard, now Howie and Barry have got the story and they're going to chop you to pieces . . .

Paul Brock's yellow-and-white striped cabana in the Beverly Hills Hotel overlooked the diving board at the deep end of the pool. Except for three children splashing noisily at the shallow end, the glistening turquoise pool was empty.

As Linda climbed the steps toward the cabana, she saw a woman in a bikini, her smooth skin bronzed, her white-blond hair cut short, a zigzag fringe above her eyes. She was bending over an aluminum-and-glass table, intently pouring salt over a lettuce and tomato salad.

Linda saw Paul Brock seated at the table, examining an inside page of the *Hollywood Reporter*. A chunky man with gray-black curly hair, Brock wore two gold chains around his throat and a narrow navy boxer bathing suit that fell below his stomach. Dark-blue hopsack espadrilles rested between his feet.

"Hi, I'm Linda Fentress."

He lifted his sunglasses for a moment, then dropped them back to the bridge of his nose. The woman ignored her completely.

"Of course, of *course*. The New York *Star*." He held out his hand without rising. "Would you like a drink? Some lunch?"

Linda asked for a Perrier.

Brock said: "I expected a hag. *Old*. You're a starlet. Come on, sit down." He introduced her to the woman, called Ingrid, and ordered Linda's drink.

Linda was aware that Brock's eyes did not leave her face.

Linda thanked Brock for seeing her.

He shrugged. "I try to be helpful, honey. I'm a transplanted New Yorker. I get the New York *Times* every Sunday."

His gaze was like a powerful ray, unsettling Linda. "My sources told me why you're here."

"Sources?" She was puzzled.

"It's a small town." He scratched the tuft of hair beneath his left nipple and smiled.

She removed her notebook. "I'm glad you know why I'm here, Mr. Brock."

"Paul. Please. I'll call you Linda."

Linda found it difficult not to fix her eyes on his swarthy lips. She explained that she was writing a story about Vice President Tom Nelson.

"Were you his first agent?"

"I was . . ." Paul Brock turned to Ingrid. "Honey, order a bottle of white. Three glasses. Tell them to bring the Perrier with it." His eyes back on Linda. "I was Tommy's first agent. Yes. My previous incarnation. I was fat and married and my name was Paul Bernstein. I lived in the valley. I was going to a Freudian shrink. I performed sex in the missionary position. I was *very* unhappy."

Linda smiled. "How did you meet him?"

"One day this guy in an army uniform walks into my office on the Strip. I was known around town as one of the few agents to look at unknowns. Well, he was hungry for work and he was another handsome kid wanting to be Jimmy Dean and I told him, 'Look, when you get out of the Army come up here and see me.' "

Linda looked up from her notebook and caught Brock's stare. "So after he leaves the Army, I worked with him for about a year. He gets some little parts through Marvin Conrad. And then we split. Haven't seen Tommy since then."

Linda said, "Haven't seen him?"

"Quit the agenting business. A friend of mine came out from New York. Gus Heller. Brilliant filmmaker." Linda wrote the name. "Began working with Gus. The production side."

"Gus Heller. Familiar name," said Linda, playing dumb.

"Gus? Film buffs know about his horror films. Brilliant son of a bitch. Movies were his life. He would have been the second Hitchcock."

"What happened to him?" She studied her notebook.

His voice dropped. "Murdered about five years ago. Down in San Diego."

"He made porno films," said Linda.

"Great porno films," said Brock dully. "Not out of choice, honey. Not because he got his kicks that way. Gus was trapped in this inquisition by a son of a bitch named Joe Keefer. Gus was about as political as Lassie. But he was a New York Jew, signed a couple of petitions—like me, you know, end fascism, down with the Ku Klux Klan—and that was enough for Joe Keefer. The atmosphere was . . . *scary*."

Linda stared at Brock, suddenly aware that his square, chunky face, his voice, the way he held his chin, reminded her of Jerry Paley. "Gus and I became outlaws for a while." He shrugged. "Like we had to eat. We had kids. We were *devastated*. I had the contacts and he had the talent. He applied the same energy, the same *genius,* to his porno films that he used in his horror movies. Technically they were brilliant. Beautiful films. If some of them were around today, they'd be shown at the Museum of Modern Art."

"The films aren't around?"

"Virtually all the best ones, the ones he cared about, the earliest ones, were destroyed when Gus died. He had ten, maybe twelve. Original prints. The car was wrecked and burned. They identified Gus through teeth marks."

"Who killed him?"

Paul Brock turned and stared at the pool.

"Come on, Paul. He made the film with Maria. That's the last film he made. Right? *Right?* So who killed him?"

Brock was examining her. "There were rumors and variations of rumors for a while. Then it stopped. You're asking if Marcus killed him? No one knows."

Her eyes scanned his legs, the bulge in his bathing suit, his chest and face. Their eyes met. He smiled.

"You're very pretty," he said.

Linda compressed her lips. "Virtually *all* the films." She stared at him. "*Virtually*. What does that mean?"

"It means that there's one that wasn't in the car. His first one."

"Who has that one?"

"Me."

A waiter appeared with a bottle of wine in a bucket. Reaching toward the tray, Linda poured the Perrier.

"Why weren't copies made of the originals?"

"No need to make copies," said Brock, leaning over to pour wine. "Gus made those films years before. *Years before*. They were kept in a bank vault in Mexico City. Never released." Their fingers touched as he handed her the wineglass.

Linda leaned forward. "Why not?"

He tasted the wine. "Because Tommy Nelson didn't want them released."

Linda heard the children's shrieks in the pool, an eerie echo as if lost in a tunnel. Laughter trickled from the cabana next door.

"Tom Nelson *appeared* in those films," she said. It was a statement.

Why is he telling me this? Why now?

Paul Brock's forefinger ran over the rim of the wineglass.

"Gus came to me and says he's got this offer to make a porno film. We're beggars. We take what we can get. But Gus, being Gus, wants to be creative. He asks me if I have an interesting actor. New faces. I look through my file and give him some names, including Nelson. Still in the Army."

Linda was writing his words in a fever, the notebook pressed on her lap.

Too easy, Barry. Shouldn't happen this way.

As Brock leaned forward, Linda watched the sun glisten on the gold chains draped around his neck. "Gus used the same care, the same sensitivity, on these films that he used on his early movies."

"I don't understand . . ."

"You're a very pretty lady," Brock repeated.

Linda persisted. "Tom Nelson didn't want them released, so you didn't . . ."

Paul Brock gulped his wine. "Marcus Lynn didn't want them released. Tommy's lawyer. They were friends. Marcus and Tommy. Tommy made it big overnight and got *scared*. These were the films he made with Gus. Films about to be released. So Marcus calls Gus and asks him to lock up the films in his safe. Don't release them. Marcus was Gus's lawyer, and my lawyer too. Represented all of Keefer's victims. So Gus agrees."

"What did Gus get in return?"

"Put down your pen. He got a decent cut of Nelson's salary." Brock removed his glasses.

Linda was aware of the sun pulsing on her hair and burning her neck. She lifted the wineglass to her lips and drank, meeting his heavy-lidded brown eyes. Linda's heart thundered. It was the heat and the wine. She felt drawn to Paul Brock.

"Did Tom Nelson have a child with Maria?"

His eyes flickered. "That's the rumor."

"Why did Maria try to kill the kid?"

Brock cast a glance toward Linda. "Stay away from Maria. It *upsets* Marcus."

"Is Marcus a friend of yours?"

He smiled crookedly. "Marcus despises what I do. He's highly moral. Goes to church on Sunday. I'm a pariah in this town, but who cares? Each one of my movies makes more money than the phony, patronizing crap that's being produced."

"Why are you telling me all this?"

"Because I want to go to bed with you."

"*Why* are you telling me this, Paul?" She gripped her wineglass firmly. Ingrid opened her right eye, gazed at her, then twisted her head to face the full blast of the sun.

"Because Marcus asked me to."

"But I thought . . ."

"Marcus despises me but we still talk. He's still my lawyer. He asked me to . . . help you when you finally show up."

"Are you helping anybody else?"

"You first. My secretary says there are calls from two guys on the *Daily News,* a guy from the New York *Times,* and a woman from the Washington *Post,* who I'm sure isn't as pretty as you."

"Why is Marcus being so nice to me?"

"Perhaps you should ask Marcus."

"It's the *Star.*"

"I think you're getting warm."

"Fitzgerald."

"Quite warm."

"We publish a story about Tom Nelson's porno films, and he's finished. Presidential campaign goes down the drain. Fitzgerald takes his place."

"Something like that."

"And if we don't publish it . . ."

"Someone will," he said.

"The film. Can I see it?"

"Anytime."

"*Now*."

*

As the front-page conference ended, Maury Kramer rushed into an anteroom, his hands digging into his breast pocket for his black leather telephone book. He dialed Hugh's number in Washington. Hey, we're on. They want the story. It's yours, baby, go ahead. Incredible to believe, but Skipper simply walked in and announced that he had changed his mind and decided to publish . . .

On the fifth ring, Maury hung up and dialed the Washington bureau, lighting a cigarette as he did so. It was only when Imelda Lincoln, the bureau's telephone operator, told him that neither Hugh nor Francine Miles were there that Maury's stomach tightened. He asked to speak to Sam Hunter, Hugh's deputy.

Maury's voice was controlled. "Where's Hugh?"

"He's home, Maury."

"He's *not* there. No answer." Maury lost control. "He *told* me to call. He *told me*. Supposed to be home. Where the fuck is he? He has less than an hour to call Belling, or else we lose the story. *Where the fuck is he?*"

Sam spoke in a quavering voice. "It's unlike Hugh to do this. I'll send a copy boy up to his house. I'll call Francine's house. Jesus!"

Maury winced at the needle-pain piercing his shoulder blades. "I'll call you back in five minutes." He stood and walked quickly into Skipper's office. It was empty.

Rushing into the reception room, he asked Miss Heaney, "Where's Skipper?"

"He's gone."

There was something about the tremulous pitch of her voice that made Maury even more nervous.

"*Gone?*"

"Something's wrong," she said. "He left. Just walked out. Said he would speak to me. Didn't say he would see me. Said he would *speak* to me."

"He'll be back," said Maury. The pain in his shoulders made him wince.

Skipper had behaved oddly, lost in thought, distracted. Frieda and Lucy departed so quickly.

Something's happened.

He backed off two steps and turned.

Got to find Hugh.

The story's yours.

Yours.

*

The film began rolling.

Linda saw the face of a man in a devil's mask fill the screen, a grotesque mask with distended eyebrows, disfigured nose and mouth, a mask that seemed encircled in flames. The camera reared back to reveal the man standing naked, twisting his hands in anticipation of eerie pleasures.

The fifteen-minute drive from the Beverly Hills Hotel in Paul Brock's silver Porsche had calmed Linda until the car swerved past the stone figures and pre-Columbian statues that flanked the white-columned entrance to Brock's home. As the car stopped in front of the house, Linda felt her heart thud.

Too easy it is, Barry, too perfect: the film ready and available courtesy of Paul Brock, end to the journey, clean and simple. But Barry, come on, it's not the end but the beginning, just one layer to be stripped away atop layers that grow murkier. In one week five years ago back events collided with mysterious violence. Gus Heller, who made Maria's film, is murdered brutally in San Diego. Joe Keefer, the guy who blacklisted Heller, who blacklisted them all, who Marcus and Nelson destroyed through his taste for little girls, drops dead in Mexico City. And Maria, who had an affair with Tom Nelson, who probably had Nelson's kid, flies to L.A. and tries to smother the infant . . .

The scene in the film blurred to a blond girl in her teens, dressed as a child in white apron, pushing a doll carriage amid a haze of clouds that could be heaven or hell. The word "Hollywood" appeared on the screen followed by a close-up of the girl, nestling the doll against her ear, smiling sweetly.

It was Cindy Garrett.

The devil appeared, grinning, allowing his fingers to linger over his flaccid penis. Mock horror twisted the girl's face. She began to flee in the swirl of smoke, but the devil, whip in hand, lashed the weapon onto the floor and the girl stopped, as if trapped. No, no, no, whispered the girl. The devil shook his head and moved toward her.

Again he lashed his whip and two naked figures appeared through the clouds. A man and a woman. The devil grinned and, with his whip, beckoned the couple toward a bed. The camera panned their young faces and bodies.

At first Linda failed to recognize what her eyes saw. *She knew the man.*

It was Elliott Hanley.

Her eyes fixed on the screen, Linda watched the bizarre charade unfold. The devil ordering the couple to tie the girl to the bedpost with his whip. As the devil lay on the bed, the couple flanked him and fondled him, the woman, a young, quite beautiful Hispanic, placing his penis in her mouth. Elliott sucking his nipples, then reversing, the camera focusing on Elliott's mouth around the devil's penis, and the woman—her long, lean body draped over the bed—tonguing his nipples and licking his chest.

Linda stared blankly past the screen. End, please end. She covered her mouth as if in disbelief, inhaled deeply once, then twice, tasting the salty wetness of her tears. Her eyes darted toward the black ceiling and then, nowhere to rest, focused back on the screen. Beside her on the sofa, Paul Brock coughed.

The devil had mounted the girl now, his hairless buttocks heaving high in the air, close-up shots of his penis sliding into her. Elliott fondled the devil's balls; the woman, her legs spread apart over the girl's head, was kissing him deeply. Quickening his movements, the devil thrust into her as the camera focused on the girl's face, drained with ecstatic tension. She pounded his shoulders. The camera held the orgiastic scene now—the participants fondling and kissing, the devil rapidly surging to climax—when, abruptly, the girl removed a knife from beneath her pillow.

As the devil arched his shoulders and twisted his neck in pleasure, as his body tensed, the girl plunged a knife into his back repeatedly; the blood spurted over the screen in a startling—and horrific—climax. The final scene revealed the three survivors standing over the blood-soaked body, solemnly facing the camera.

Linda kept her eyes shut even after Paul Brock turned on the lights.

"Rated PG."

"Nelson was the devil."

"Very perceptive."

She glanced at Paul. "That's it?"

He nodded.

"The mask. We can't prove it's Nelson."

"Marcus can prove anything he wants." Brock lit a joint. "Did it turn you on?"

"No."

"Does this turn you on?"

She grasped the joint between her thumb and forefinger and sucked it. "A little."

"Do *I* turn you on?"

"A little."

He kissed her neck. Linda shut her eyes, aware that his hands were caressing her body, his fingers expertly unbuttoning her shirt to find her hardened nipples. She reared her head back. "No," she whispered. She was drifting, floating, even as he removed her trousers and dropped to his knees.

Tears swept Linda's cheeks. His tongue found her clitoris, and the moment of connection loosened a burning flow that soared through her body. Grasping, she wrapped her hands over his head and pressed him fiercely into her. She groaned as his tongue lapped and slithered toward the spot from which her body flamed. She tensed, digging her fingers into the back of his head; she lay back, forcing him with her. His hands ran over her breasts and belly and settled on her thighs. He kissed her navel, her breasts, he licked her stomach, his tongue an instrument of exquisite pleasure.

Roughly, Brock opened her legs and, crouching over her, burrowed inside her with his mouth, chewing, tasting, kissing, licking. She gasped, her body twisting beneath him, abandoned to his mouth. His hands, grasping her buttocks, lifted her firmly to his tongue, and now her body was wrapped in a pleasure beyond control. She was enflamed. She arched her shoulders and held her breath. And in the infinity of release, as shoots of pleasure engulfed her, freed her, Linda's face dissolved and she wept without control.

He pushed up and lay beside her. "What's wrong?" he whispered.

"Nothing," she said. "Everything." Linda placed her hand on his chest. "I'm scared. Shouldn't be doing this."

"Doing what?"

"Going to bed with you. I don't usually fuck around with sources the first time out."

"I like you."

"You're not telling me everything, you know."

He kissed her.

"Hold me," she said hoarsely. "Just hold me."

*

Ward and Barry sat across from Maury's desk, watching him cradle the phone to his ear. Maury's voice rose. It was his third call in ten minutes to Sam Hunter, the deputy Washington bureau chief. *"Got to find Hugh."*

Barry turned to Ward and whispered: "Where can the crazy bastard be?"

Maury's anger at Hugh had given way to exhaustion. "For Chrissake, *I do not want to lose the fucking story.*"

He dropped the phone, like a heavy burden, on the hook. Maury's body seemed to shrivel, and Ward noticed his face was gray.

"Something's happened," said Ward. "An accident. Car crash."

Barry began pacing. "The Steiners want the story. Okay, then. We've got to salvage it."

"Hugh has the notes. Hugh has all the details." Maury's voice seemed faint.

"Barry's right," said Ward. "Let's get someone else, someone in the newsroom to start . . ."

Maury interrupted. "He's finished. His career's over. The best story of his life." Maury stared at the floor. "Silly bastard. He blew it."

*

They lay silent in the bedroom, listening to the violent gusts of wind, the rain.

"What time is it?" she finally said.

"Five after four," said Paul Brock.

He kissed her fingers. The odor of sex and sweat filled her nostrils. "I needed that, Paul."

His hand moved downward, but she held his fingers and placed them over her navel. "No. I have an appointment at five."

"See me later."

"Paul. That film disgusted me."

"They were hungry," he said quietly. "Hanley. The blond kid. Even Tommy Nelson. When you're hungry and scared, well . . ."

"You do anything."

"You humiliate yourself in a dozen ways."

Linda sat up, curling a sheet around her shoulders. "Can't write this story. Can't prove the masked guy was Nelson."

"Someone will," said Paul Brock. He pushed up, lighting a cigarette for both of them. "Marcus'll see to it," said Paul, eyeing her through the flame of the lighter.

Linda listened to the harsh wind. "He's blackmailing Elliott."

Brock shook his head. "Marcus is into favors, not blackmail. Paid-up debts."

"After all these years . . ." said Linda.

"Marcus calls in his chips," said Paul Brock. "It's *time,* Marcus told Elliott, time you told the truth about Tom Nelson. Elliott's going to stay anonymous. Deep throat. Leak the sordid details about the film, about Tom Nelson."

"And if Elliott doesn't agree?"

"He will," said Brock. "Marcus knows he will."

"So long as Marcus and Nelson were friends, the film stayed locked up," said Linda.

"But then Marcus' daughter slept with Tom Nelson," said Brock, lying back in bed. "Marcus turned against Nelson with a fury."

"Marcus wanted to get even with Nelson. Destroy him. Use this old porno film that Nelson made thirty years earlier." She examined Paul Brock's face in puzzlement. "Marcus wanted to take revenge on Nelson just because he slept with Maria."

Suddenly the question that had seemed so basic and crucial to Linda's story—the unasked question that had plagued her since the session with Lois Barrie—reached her lips.

"Someone told Marcus about his daughter, *informed* him about Maria and Tom Nelson. Who?"

"David Fitzgerald," Paul replied, watching Linda.

Linda sat back and whispered more to herself than to Paul Brock. "That's where my story begins."

"No, honey, that's not where it begins." Paul's voice was low and tense. "It begins when a son of a bitch named Keefer got Nelson to inform on all of us."

*

Hugh Finch watched sunlight linger on the floor. Every moment was painful. He lay in bed. The gash at the base of his skull burned, a trickling of blood ran down his neck and smeared the pillowcase. A foul smell soaked the air. Raising his arm now, he winced and held his breath, glaring at his watch.

Ten to five. The phone rang once more, strangely comforting now, a symbol of life in the dead room, so near, so absolutely within reach and yet so distant. Humiliation and self-hate had given way to a not unpleasurable sense of drift. He closed his eyes. A sharp knock on the door startled him, followed by the sound of angry voices. He swallowed hard, puzzled at the noise, tasting the blood that had seeped from his nostrils. Pressing the palms of his hands to his ears, Hugh waited. Like a child, he thought, hiding. The phone and pounding on the door stopped simultaneously.

Outside, he heard the distant blare of car and truck horns on Connecticut Avenue. He groaned softly as he turned and faced the wall, staring into the darkness.

*

Maury walked through the newsroom, which vibrated now with predeadline fever. It was this hour, approaching dusk, that shaped his day, the hour around which his life had revolved for so long. Even as a copy boy, thirty-four years earlier, he had secretly adored the deadline hour and the exhilarating mood of completion, *finality,* when the paper was locked up and running off the presses.

Maury stood beside the city desk now, breathing heavily. Two phones were ringing simultaneously and Maury watched Nick Simons lift one, ask the caller to wait, then press the flickering extension on the second phone. Maury dug his fingers over the cold steel edge of Barry's chair.

"You okay?" said Barry, turning quickly.

"I'm okay." Maury's voice tightened with irritation. The pain eased. He asked Barry if Howie Bishop had landed in Panama.

Barry stood up. "Expect to hear from him in the next two hours."

"If we publish the story tomorrow I want full reaction from Paley." Maury saw Nick Simons cup his right hand over the phone and turn to Barry.

"It's Frank Rosales downtown." Nick Simons eyed Maury and spoke to Barry. "The cops have no news, nothing, on Sally Sims. Checked hospital records. The only jumper in the last six hours was a white male, age sixty-seven, in the garment center."

The three exchanged glances. "Keep checking," said Barry stiffly.

Barry turned to Maury, saying that he planned to fly to Washington that evening to see Jerry Paley. Poor bastard, thought Maury, eyes darting across the newsroom, sensing in that very moment that Nancy was rushing in.

She wore black velvet pants and a white satin-glossed crepe with mandarin collar around which hung a strand of glowing baroque gray pearls. He had bought her the pearls only two weeks before at a jewelry shop in Soho.

It was impossible actually to smell her rich, heavy perfume and the sweetness of Nancy's hair, but somehow, inexplicably, he did. Maury was smiling, watching her run to the foreign desk, tumble into her chair, wave to Ray Silver and mime the word, "Sorry."

His eyes turned to Barry, who watched him with amusement. Maury heard Barry say, "Linda's filing her story. *Tomorrow!*"

Maury stiffened at the spasm of pain across his shoulder blades. He started to speak, but now the memory of Skipper's sudden departure—Maury had tried to ignore it over the past thirty minutes—possessed him with a force that alarmed him. His head was pounding.

He edged away from Barry, distracted, trying to concentrate, immerse himself . . . Hugh Finch's disappearance . . . the Chinese nuclear test and Soviet reaction to it . . . the Jerry Paley story (somehow it gnawed at Maury, it wasn't quite *right,* were

they pushing too quickly to publish?) . . . Where was Sally? . . .
Linda Fentress' investigation was Pulitzer material *if* it worked out
. . . the strike, Christ, maybe the whole thing would go up in
smoke tomorrow at midnight . . .

But now, walking past the foreign desk, the reminder of Skipper's departure made his legs tremble. Mustn't panic, he thought.
Skipper probably dashed out in search of Sally. There was a family problem somewhere. The boy, Larry, was in more trouble.

The job was his. *His.* He had given his life to the paper. *It was
his job and they would not take it away.*

He bent low at the water cooler and allowed the liquid to cool
his lips and drip off his chin. Phones rang across the newsroom.
Maury lifted his face and walked toward the office, keeping his
eyes fixed on the open door. He turned, impulsively, and glanced
at Nancy, who was busily scanning a video-terminal screen.
Maury smiled, curiously calm and lightheaded.

The first spasm struck his chest as he passed Ward's chair. He
halted and waited. He felt dizzy and perspiration broke out on his
forehead. His hands tingled. He grasped the edge of the chair. His
chest was burning. He moved his mouth but no words came. Another spasm, violent and painful, exploded across his chest, and as
he fell to the floor, Maury heard shouts. Someone was screaming
to call Sarah Felger. Call an ambulance.

He saw a blur of hands and feet and faces, and he caught a
glimpse of flowing gray pearls on a white backdrop before
blackness descended.

*

As Linda turned the car onto Benedict Canyon Drive, she
smelled the piney scent of poplars and wet grass. The rain had
stopped, leaving the air damp and chilly. The sky, gray and ominous only an hour before, now glistened like a pale, sea-blue can-
vas with pumpkin-colored streaks. Sunlight pricked the windshield.

Seeing Lois Barrie's scrapbooks would yield little, she knew.
But Rita's gentle persistence surprised Linda, and when Linda
phoned in the morning to thank the Hamalians, Rita told her that
Lois' offer to show her scrapbooks should not be ignored. It was
an unusual gesture, almost as unusual as Lois' candor about her
personal life.

Linda hesitated before pushing the buzzer. It was a modern white house with stainless-steel doors at the entrance. To Linda's right, through the wet trees, she caught the smoky, gray vista of Los Angeles.

Her impulse was to flee the silence, return to the hotel, swallow a Valium, read the clips on Joe Keefer and soak herself in a hot bath before planning her next move. *She had to see Maria.*

She was exhausted: the trip to Venice and her interview with Cindy Garrett, the session with Elliott Hanley, the grisly film, the sexual interlude with Paul Brock, the rain, Barry's incessant calls, the pressure to produce a story—it all had drained her. She yearned for the oblivion of sleep, the stillness of a hotel room to review her notes and try to sort out the tangled threads of this story.

There was silence behind the door; perhaps Lois Barrie had forgotten. A bluebird chirped overhead, and Linda watched it flutter from beam to beam. After five seconds, Linda turned and took half a step; then she heard the doorknob twist. She whirled around, and caught her breath at the sight of Lois Barrie.

Shards of blond hair fell loosely on Lois' forehead and cheeks. Her skin was pale. Lois swayed forward, gripping the door for support with her right hand. Linda caught the stench of whiskey.

"You killed him." The voice was hoarse, almost comic.

"Killed who?" Linda wanted to laugh. A trickle of water from the roof beam hit Linda's forehead.

"Elliott's dead."

Linda recoiled as if struck. "Dead!"

"Scavenger! Scavenger! You *disgust* me. You *killed* him. You! Prying around with your notebook. Opening wounds. All for a story. A story in your bloody paper." Lois' wild and accusing eyes dissolved in tears.

"What happened?"

Lois spoke through taut lips. "After your little interview, Elliott told Fuki that he wanted to drive to Big Sur. Fuki saw that he was upset and begged Elliott not to go alone. Fuki would drive. Elliott said, 'No.' He wanted to be by himself. Somewhere around Ventura, a police car began chasing him. They said he was going at least seventy miles an hour. By the time he lost control, he was going ninety. He sideswiped a truck, skidded and the car flipped over. Broke his neck."

Linda swayed and started to shiver.

"I didn't kill him, Lois. Please. If it weren't me, it would be someone else. There are a half-dozen reporters chasing this story. What about Marcus? What about *him*? He's orchestrating this. What about him?"

"Marcus handed you the gun and you pulled the trigger. Marcus . . ." Lois smiled and cried. "Marcus . . ." She let out a hysterical laugh. "Marcus is eaten up with passion. Yes, passion. A passion for revenge. Destroy Tom Nelson at any cost before he gets to be President. Maybe it's insane or misguided. But there *is* passion there. What do you care about, honey? What? The *byline? What?*"

"Help me," pleaded Linda. "I've *got* to understand the story. Why did Fitzgerald tell Marcus about Maria?" Linda stepped so close to Lois Barrie now that the scent of whiskey was repellent. Linda spoke feverishly.

"Who killed Gus Heller in San Diego?"

A shadow darkened Lois' face, framing her eyes in a wide, almost mysterious glow. "Joey Keefer died in Mexico City, then Maria flew to L.A. and tried to kill her baby. Why?" Linda felt the wild drumming in her heart. "Why? It's all linked. It's all part of my story. *Help me!*"

*

At 8:10 P.M. the telephone rang in Dorothy Faye's Bank Street apartment just as her eight dinner guests had moved into the living room with plates of the Vietnamese chicken and spiced crab that had been prepared in the cramped kitchen by Mr. Dinh, who actually worked for Dorothy's closest friend, after Sally Sims, Billie Dawson. (Billie had found Mr. Dinh in Ramuntcho's, a Saigon restaurant that she favored during the fourteen months that she researched her book on Vietnamese peasants.)

Dorothy picked up the phone in the kitchen.

"Hi," Sally Sims whispered.

"Sally! Christ! Where are you?"

"Staten Island."

"What?"

"Staten Island. I'm at the ferry terminal."

"Oh God," said Dorothy. "Sally. Everyone has been . . . *frantic*. Skipper called twice. Three times. I mean, I think he's called the *police*. We thought something *terrible* happened. Oh, I'm so relieved. Sally, you're alive. I shouldn't say that."

"Yes, I'm alive." Sally laughed softly.

"What happened?"

"Long story," said Sally. "Dorothy, can I stay with you tonight?"

"Of *course*," said Dorothy. "Thank *God* you called. Now, look. Get into a cab and come up *right now*. Dinner has just started."

"Dinner?"

"My dinner party. For Marty Kaplan."

"Marty. Oh Lord." Her voice cracked. "Oh *God*."

Dorothy spoke quietly, pleadingly. "Sally, let me come down and get you. I'll meet you at the ferry. They don't need me here. I'm just the hostess."

Sally laughed. "No."

"It's Charlie, isn't it?" Dorothy whispered. She listened to Sally's intake of breath.

"It's not Charlie. It's me," Sally murmured. And then she repeated the words, *"It's me."*

Dorothy heard Billie's voice in the living room. She pressed her lips to the phone.

"We were so alarmed. Everyone. Poor Rose has been beside herself. She's still at the office. Skipper was . . . *panicked*. I know he called Charlie . . ."

"Oh God."

"He *had* to. Darling, we have been scared. And I had to worry about this goddamn dinner party."

"I'll go back to the office."

"What?"

"Rest on the sofa. Maury's office. I'll come down later tonight. I can't face those people."

Dorothy waited, then said gravely, "Are you all right?"

"I'm all right."

"Do I have to worry about you?"

"No."

"Will you take a cab to the *Star* and stay in your office?"

"Yes. I'll call Rose."

"And Skipper."

"No," said Sally. "I can't. Phone him and tell him I'm safe. Please. Don't tell him I'm staying at the *Star*. Tell him I'm staying with you. Can't see him tonight."

Dorothy Faye nervously dialed Skipper's home phone. When she heard his voice and blurted the good news that Sally was safe, she knew immediately that her lips could no longer restrain the truth.

"Skipper, she didn't want me to tell you and she'll probably kill me, but she's going to spend the next few hours in Maury's office and I think she would *adore* seeing you, I think she *needs* to see you."

*

A hazy light enveloped the sun room. Lois Barrie tucked her feet beneath her buttocks on the wicker sofa, slowly sipping vodka on ice. Linda sat facing her.

"Help me," she said. "There was no reason for Elliott to die. Not now. After all these years. For Elliott's sake, *help* me."

"I had the strangest conversation with Elliott this afternoon," said Lois. "Poor bastard was crying. He said the truth would come out. And I said, Elliott, for God's sake, so be it. Let the truth come out. If Marcus wants to destroy Nelson, let him. If Marcus wants to use you to destroy Nelson, fine. If the great American public becomes aware that you have appeared in a porno film, what are they going to do to you? Burn you? Lynch you? Hell, it's one more spicy chapter in your biography.

"Elliott said I didn't understand, and I asked him what he meant by that, and he repeated the words, 'I didn't understand,' and then he hung up." She glanced at Linda.

"I don't know why he killed himself. Shame? Humiliation? I don't know."

Linda said, "Who murdered Gus Heller?"

Lois' voice was faint. "Maria just appeared in Gus's office in Mexico City one day, and said she needed the bread and offered her services. He didn't know her. After all, Maria went to convent schools and Gus was not exactly the kind of person that Marcus would allow in the house."

Lois looked up. "Gus, who usually got hags or deadbeats, was only too pleased to use this ripe little number."

She stared at Linda. "Marcus sees the film, hears who produced it and is crazy with rage. He confronts Gus Heller, who is, to say the least, stunned that Maria is Marcus' daughter. Gus didn't know, kept saying he didn't know he was using Maria Lynn. Well, Marcus believed Gus, but . . ."

Linda stopped writing in her notebook.

"Marcus wanted revenge. Revenge on *Tommy*. He had to destroy Tom Nelson."

"The baby's father."

"The man who started Maria on the path that led to . . . the films." Lois' eyes widened. "Marcus hit on a plan. He told Gus to take Tommy's films out of his vault in Mexico City. Marcus would destroy Tommy with the films he had made thirty years ago. Told Gus to take them and fly to L.A., where Marcus would offer them to newspaper reporters."

Lois drained her drink and spoke quickly. "Foolishly, Gus told Marcus that he would stop en route at his studio in Tijuana and burn Maria's films. Destroy every reel."

"He did . . ." began Linda.

"He destroyed her films, maybe a half dozen, and then began the drive to Los Angeles. Tommy's films in the trunk." She paused. "Gus always kept films in the trunk."

Linda saw the slight tremor around Lois' lips.

"Murdered that night," said Lois. "Police said Gus was beaten to death by repeated blows to the head. Probably a wrench. The car was demolished, the trunk open. The films . . . destroyed."

"You loved Gus," said Linda.

"Killer never found." Lois gasped, struggling to control herself.

"Who did it?"

"It was open, the trunk was open. That's what the cops said."

"What are the rumors, Lois?"

She heaved her chest. "Tommy Nelson somehow *heard*."

"Nelson!"

"Heard that Gus was carrying the films to L.A. *Tommy had to stop delivery.*"

"Nelson killed Gus."

"Got one of his thugs in San Diego to do it."

Linda stared at Lois Barrie.

"Every reason to kill him," said Lois impatiently. "Gus had the films. Gus *knew*. Gus collected part of Tommy's salary for years. "Christ!" Tears stained Lois' cheeks. "Gus didn't pocket the money. Gave it to Elliott Hanley, who *needed* it. Gave it to some flakey blonde in Venice, who needed it."

Lois shut her eyes, tossing her head back. "Feel better now. Takes just a few minutes and I feel . . . swell. Pot, coke and vodka. Wunderbar. Coke cuts the alcohol. Makes me pleasant. Makes me *forget*."

Linda persisted. "With Nelson's films destroyed, with Gus dead, Marcus needed Elliott Hanley."

"Needed Elliott to talk to reporters like . . . *you*," said Lois. "Provide details about Tom Nelson's career. Elliott was going to serve as the major source for the destruction of Tom Nelson."

Linda caught the ice in her voice. "Perhaps I can see your scrapbooks."

*

In the newsroom the following message was nailed to the center of the bulletin board.

MAURY KRAMER'S CONDITION IS STABLE. HE HAS SUFFERED A "SERIOUS" HEART ATTACK. DOCTORS AT ST. CLARE'S HOSPITAL ARE ALLOWING A FEW VISITORS TOMORROW. WHEN WE WILL HAVE MORE DETAILS.

MARY PHELPS.

Twenty-five minutes to deadline.

"All commercial lines to Moscow are out," said Tony Lazzarutti, slapping the phone down.

"The bastards have pulled them," said Silver.

"Call the State Department," ordered Florence, glancing up from her typewriter. "I'll get the girls upstairs to reach operators in Finland and Stockholm and maybe Warsaw." The girls upstairs were the *Star*'s phone operators to whom Florence, wisely, sent three bottles of cognac every Christmas, courtesy of the foreign desk. If anyone could pierce the Iron Curtain, it would be the girls upstairs.

"Any more AP?" said Ward coldly, staring at the yellow sheet in his hand, rereading the words for the third time.

"I'll check in the wireroom, sir." Tony left.

Again, Ward glanced at the AP "Bulletin."

MOSCOW—RUMORS SWEPT MOSCOW TODAY THAT THE SOVIET UNION WILL CANCEL PRESIDENT KOPEIKIN'S VISIT TO THE UNITED STATES FOR PEACE TALKS WITH CHINESE PREMIER PHUNG.

THE REPORTED DECISION, FOLLOWING AN ALL-NIGHT POLITBURO MEETING WOULD DASH DEFENSE SECRETARY EDWARD BELLING'S LAST-DITCH EFFORTS FOR A PEACEFUL SETTLEMENT TO THE INCREASINGLY BITTER BORDER FIGHTING BETWEEN SOVIET AND CHINESE FORCES.

-MORE-

Ray leaned over, blinking wildly. "Told the Washington bureau to check the Pentagon one more time."

As if anticipating Ray's next question, Ward said, "My source at the Agency has nothing."

Tony returned. "Zilch, sir."

Ward fixed his eyes on Florence long enough so that she turned to him. Her eyes flickered, she frowned and then thrust a sheet of paper into her typewriter.

It was his imagination, perhaps, but the newsroom's noise seemed muted, and except for the occasional shouts of "copy," the creak of the coffee wagon, the sound of phones ringing, a layer of heavy silence blanketed the cavernous room. Reporters stood in clusters, chatting, nodding, shaking their heads. There were no card games now, no peals of laughter since Maury's collapse.

Ward's fingers picked up the sheaf of neatly folded messages on the desk, but he shut his eyes for a moment. *Twenty minutes to deadline.* He turned to Ray Silver. "Let's prepare to use the wire story on the front page with a precede saying all phone lines to Moscow are down."

Ray shrugged. "A bitch." They abhorred using wire-service stories on the front page from cities in which they had reporters. What was the purpose of having a reporter overseas if they were compelled to use an AP or Reuters story?

Ward leaned toward Tony and whispered: "Do me a favor. Call *Time* magazine. Someone named Cheever. Marilyn Cheever. The New York bureau. Tell her that I can't make it tonight."

Florence's blue eyes met his, her lips set in a frown. "Don't do it for me."

"I'm doing it for *me.*"

The phone was ringing. "It's not going to work. With or without this Cheever character. It won't work," she said, struggling to smile.

Ward watched her intently. Tony was dialing the number of *Time* magazine. Florence lifted the phone, holding her hand over the receiver. She spoke quietly.

"You can't have everything, honey. Me. Wife and kids. Marilyn Cheever. You want it all. Like you're sixteen. Sixteen going on forty-two. You can't manage it that way because . . ." She nodded . . . "You hurt too many people."

Florence pressed the phone to her ear. Ward rubbed his thumb and forefinger into his swollen eyes. He had not eaten since breakfast with Marty Kaplan, but his hunger was dulled by tension and a not unpleasant exhaustion. He felt surprisingly calm.

"It's Ernie!"

Florence's voice stunned them. Ward bolted up in his chair and grabbed the extension.

"Where the hell are you?" shouted Ward. "What? The German Embassy. How . . . The Ambassador's wife? I won't ask you what you had to do. Don't tell me. Don't want to know. You sordid bastard. Hey, this is a terrific line. Trust the Germans. The vile fuckers are *efficient!* Okay, now, what do you have? Russians have placed all troops on alert and . . . what? . . . began moving some people into shelters just like the Cuban missile crisis. Jesus! Hey. *What?* The Germans have heard that Kopeikin has *accepted* Belling's initiative. Hard-liners what? *Trust* the son of a bitch to take an even-handed approach. Christ! Rumors of a major Chinese test. Yeah. We got that firm, it's true. Who did the story? *Me!*" Ward was laughing. "Thanks. Now listen. *You* have a hell of a story and you got a working phone. Stay in the Embassy. Do whatever she wants you to do." He held the phone away from his ear with a smile, as Ernie's curses charged the air. "You're doing it for the story, for the *byline,* kid." Laughing again, Ward said, "You have a Pulitzer tumbling right into your hands. You're the only one, only one tonight with the full story. It's worth the sacrifice, you silly bastard. Every sacrifice. What? She wants you to do *what?* Oh *no. No!* Kinky krauts. Well, you just keep it up, Ernie. *Keep it up.*"

By now a crowd had gathered around the foreign desk. Ward twisted in his chair. *"We got it!"*

*

Barry Cohen, watching the spin of activity on the foreign desk, turned to catch the eyes of Nick Simons.

"What do you hear, Nick?"

The youth shrugged. "I hear you're gonna be managing editor."

"Who told you that?"

"Just gossip."

Barry examined Nick's leonine face. "Gossip." He smiled faintly. "Copy boys. Clerks. Pick up everything. Always. When I was a copy boy, Nick, me and my cousin, Marty Kaplan, and Mark Kaiserman and Ray Silver. One group. We knew everything too. We were *hungry*."

"Hungry?"

"Just like you, Nick. Hungry. Wanted to make it. Worked our asses off. We were nothing, nobodies, poor kids from nowhere. Didn't wear the right clothes. Just like you, Nick." Barry laughed. "Didn't go to the right schools. Try starting at *Time* or *Newsweek* without going to the right schools. Didn't have the right names. But we had talent and energy. Energy to burn. And this paper appreciated that. It *still* does."

The phone was ringing. "How long you been on the desk?"

"Sixteen months."

"Long enough. Starting Monday, you're on tryout as a reporter."

Nick Simons' mouth fell open.

"Hey, the phone's ringing," said Barry, watching the clerk lift the phone and say, "City desk.

"It's Howie Bishop in Panama."

Barry reached for the phone.

Nick felt the sweat start on his face. To his puzzlement, at the moment of abrupt triumph—the moment he had craved for so long —he slumped in his chair unable to savor the moment. He fixed his thoughts on . . . Howie Bishop.

Damn!

His heart was pounding.

Another biggie Howie had, nailing Jerry to the wall. Front-page byline, that son of a bitch.

So he had finally made the staff—big fucking deal—it would take years to get Howie's biggies.

Best job in the world Howie had. Number-one investigative reporter on the *Star*. After Howie comes Linda. No room at the top
for Nickie, neither Howie nor Linda known for generously parcel-
ing out stories to the younger folks.

Nick gnawed at his lip. He would get there. Not tomorrow or
next week or even next year, but *he would get there*. Work harder
than Howie. Days and nights, weekends, vacations. *Work!* He
would probe deeper, be more of a prick. He had energy to burn
while Howie was getting older. He was tougher. He would dazzle
Barry . . .

Barry pushed back his chair. Leaving for Washington, he said
to Pat Donlon.

. . . going to make it big, Barry, you wait and see, bigger than
you ever think. Nick Simons, reporter. Nick Simons, *city editor*.

*

Frieda and Lucy watched the evening news in silence, seated in
the library of the Steiner apartment. Blurred, grainy newsreel images flickered on the screen: Soviet President Kopeikin and Defense Minister Malenkov; the scene abruptly shifted to the White
House lawn, and Barbara Simpson, a blond television correspondent, saying, in her faint southern drawl, that the White House
neither confirmed nor denied rumors sweeping the capital of a
Chinese nuclear breakthrough, but Administration officials were
increasingly concerned about the prospects now for a . . .

Lucy coughed. "That's one of David's friends . . . one of several."

Frieda ignored her, watching the news intently. "We have that
story of the Chinese test. Ward Parsons has it."

"She's pretty. Younger than she looks. Twenty-eight or twenty-
nine."

"Darling, we're going to have quite a paper tomorrow."
Frieda's voice shook with excitement. "*Quite* a front page. The
President's illness. The Parsons story. An exclusive by Ernie Rich-
ards. Way ahead of the television people."

Frieda turned to Lucy, who watched a shadow fall across her
mother's face.

"You were saying. Barbara Simpson . . ."

Lucy spoke impatiently. "Barbara Simpson is one of David's
girlfriends. She's pretty."

"Not that pretty."

"And young. Younger than I."

Frieda stared at her. They had said nothing about the events in Skipper's office since returning to the apartment. Except for a brief flurry of conversation when Mary Phelps phoned and informed them of Maury's heart attack, both women had made it a point of eluding one another in the large apartment.

Now Frieda examined her ruby ring. "Are you unhappy with David?"

"I told him it would be best if we stopped. It was a silly interlude, Mother. Made little sense." She stood and stepped to the television.

"You saw the item in the paper this morning?"

"The *Daily News*." Lucy angrily switched off the set. "I saw it, but it hardly made a difference. I've known about Kitty White for the past few days. I'm sure Kitty White will serve his purposes. Everyone does." She spoke gently, with only a hint of rancor.

"He'll be President someday."

Lucy lifted a cigarette out of an ivory box. "No, he won't, Mother. He wants it too much."

Frieda watched her daughter light the cigarette. "You're upset about this afternoon."

"Aren't you?"

"Perhaps it's for the best." Frieda rubbed her hands. "Of course I'm *upset*. My own son. Of *course* it grieves me. But we have a newspaper to keep alive. We have work to do, and if he . . . if he . . . feels as strongly as he does, then I respect his decision."

"What will we do now?" asked Lucy.

"Appoint Eli publisher. Do we have any *choice?*"

"The day-to-day operations of the paper would be in the hands of an outsider."

Frieda's voice rose. *"There's no choice!"*

"What about Johanna?"

"Come now." Frieda shook her head. "Johanna's a *child*. Don't be absurd. Ten years, twenty years from now, yes. I can see Johanna, with the proper training. Yes! But not now. At this critical moment. When we need experience and a steady hand."

"Frieda, she's smart. And tough. Tougher than I am. She's like you. You and Frederic. It would take time, Mother. But she could do it." Lucy's almost pleading tone surprised her mother.

Frieda snapped a cigarette into her holder. "Eli *expects* it and *deserves* it." She stared at the blank television screen. "The paper is not well, dear. Frederic built it, and Jonathan kept it going through good times. Well, times have changed and we're standing on quicksand."

Frieda bit at her cigarette holder. "Frederic, brilliant as he was, could hardly foresee any of this, and I wonder . . . I wonder if *he* wouldn't sell to a conglomerate."

"Mother! Eli wants you to sell!"

"Eli has made the suggestion. I'm not *about* to sell. It's just one option that we have."

"Who wants to buy?"

"A California conglomerate. Group of investors headed by a movie type. Marcus Lynn."

Lucy stood shakily. She yearned to sound calm, but her voice cracked.

"I better go now, Mother. I don't want to stay anymore. I'm tired." Lucy picked up her handbag, avoiding her mother's eyes.

"Stay!"

"Mother, no. I'll see you tomorrow at the office. We're appointing Barry, right? I'll want to visit Maury first. Perhaps I'll take Johanna with me. She's coming in." She was weeping. "Mother . . ." Lucy turned. "Mother, I haven't amounted to much, have I? Haven't done too much with my life. I was born a little too early. One generation too early. I could have played a role on the *Star,* Mother, a *real* role. I could have made a contribution. Instead, I just went along. Silly, vapid Lucy Steiner."

Angrily, she wiped her eyes. "I love the paper, Mother. Love the paper more than you think. I had ideas, but who on earth would accept them from someone like me? So I went along. All these years. Never wanting to upset you. Agreeing with you even when you were wrong. Following you like a child. Yes, maybe that's the way I wanted it. But no more. I *break* with you, Mother. I *break* with you on Eli!"

Frieda tightened her fists. "Do I have any other choice but Eli? Tell me. Without experience, Johanna would fail *completely.*"

Lucy laughed and wept. "Mother, oh, Mother, you *want* her to fail, don't you?"

Frieda reared back. "Don't be a fool!"

"You couldn't bear it if Johanna succeeded. All these years, Mother, you've been the only businesswoman in the family. Frieda Steiner. Queen bee. You scared the men and bulldozed your decisions through. And carried on this pretense of being supportive, secondary to the men. You ran the show, Mother. And you knew it. And you loved it. And any other woman who came along threatened the hell out of you, Mother, *including* me."

Lucy grabbed her raincoat off the sofa. "You're the queen. You quashed me, Mother. And now you're doing the same to Johanna. If Johanna succeeded, it would make you irrelevant."

Frieda opened her mouth but no words came out. The two women stared at one another for a few seconds, then Lucy turned and left.

*

By the time Linda Fentress reached Lois' third and final scrapbook, her fingers were so flecked with dried paste, her eyes so strained with fatigue, that she nearly overlooked the picture.

On the bottom of the third to the last page—beneath two lengthy stories of the Emmy Awards in the Los Angeles *Times* and *Variety*—a darkened wire-service photo was fastened against the paper with Scotch tape.

The caption read: "EMMY AWARDS: Arriving at post-award dinner Sunday night at the Beverly Hilton, winner Lois Barrie is flanked by mogul Marcus Lynn and Maria Lynn, Mr. Lynn's daughter. Also, Joe Keefer, a former state senator."

An anonymous AP photographer had caught them unaware in a remarkable tableau. Lois gazed at the camera, her mouth open. Marcus to her left had turned in profile, his right hand slicing the air, chatting with someone out of camera range.

Maria stood at Lois' right. She wore a simple plaid blazer and skirt, a sweater and blouse tucked beneath the jacket. Her crown of black hair was braided high on her neck. She was the shortest figure in the photo and, despite the contrast to Lois—a blond figure who towered above her—Maria dominated the photo.

At first glance, Maria seemed like a serenely beautiful Mexican teen-ager, her honey-colored skin matched by heavy-lidded eyes, her face thin and shaped by high cheekbones, her mouth curved in a vague, half-sensual smile.

At second glance, there was obviously something odd, perhaps off-key, about Maria. Trapped by the photographer, caught in this unguarded moment, Maria stared at the camera, her lips frozen in a forced smile. Her remarkably firm chin jutted forward. Linda stared at the photo, and suddenly the notion struck her why the picture seemed so curious; Maria's face was a mask of rage.

Linda looked at Joe Keefer. He stood to Maria's right, his head lowered, a sickly pallor evident on the newspaper reprint. He had been a slight man, just an inch or so taller than Maria. His thin, gray hair was cut short, almost as a crewcut.

His face was remarkably average. He could have been a bank clerk. Years earlier, he had perhaps been ugly, but the face in the photo had a softness around the corners of his mouth, his jaw. His eyes—at second glance—looked vacant, stunned.

Linda examined the picture further. Keefer seemed so pale, so frightened, resembling the shadowy men that hovered in doorways on the West Side, men that appeared so harmless, and yet Linda hurried to the other side of the street whenever she saw one. She turned the page but returned to the photo, bending low and close, peering at the grainy faces. Perhaps it was that fleeting second when the shutter clicked, perhaps the photographer caught Maria so unaware that her face, in that moment, was distorted beyond recognition—the balance of mouth and nose and eyes and forehead helplessly twisted—but no. The face glowed with defiance.

She closed the scrapbook, then reopened it and turned to the photo, examining the date. It had been taken six months before Maria left for Washington to work for Fitzgerald. Squinting, Linda suddenly realized that the photo had been cropped.

Years ago, Linda had worked on the *Star*'s photo desk as a clerk, answering phones, dashing into the lab for negatives and contact sheets, filing prints, watching editors with L-shaped rulers lift red marking pencils and crop prints as deadlines neared.

Was it absurd to hunt down an AP photographer who wouldn't recall what he did last week, no less five years ago? Was it equally absurd to get a print of the full negative, which would probably reveal nothing new? Was she hunting for meanings, even symbols, in photographs that were, in the end, worthless? Was it all a time-consuming, pointless chase?

Yes, of course.

No!

Before Linda left, she asked Lois Barrie about the photo, but the actress shrugged. Marcus often took Joey Keefer along as a safe escort for Maria.

Twenty minutes later, Linda was in her room at the Century Plaza. She phoned Gregory's house and spoke to Rita Hamalian. Could Gregory try to get a copy of the full negative of Lois Barrie at the Emmy Award party that was published in the L.A. *Times?* AP would probably have it in their files under Lois' name.

Perhaps it's important, Rita.

She was exhausted by now, but Linda knew she had to see one more person before night fell.

Marcus Lynn.

*

When Sally awoke, her body was stiff with cold. A square of light shimmered through the window. She twisted away, hands thrust over her eyes. Then she heard another noise, a sharp, unmistakable knock on the door.

Sally stood up, flung herself at the door and opened it. The light in the hall seemed blinding, and she failed in that second to recognize who was in the doorway. Then the hazy image merged into reality; it was Skipper.

She moved toward him, held out her arms, and with a half step he lifted her up.

"Oh my God," she said.

"I woke you up."

"Where am I?"

"Evan's office," he said.

She caught the smell of whiskey on his breath. The hair on his chest, through his open shirt, brushed her cheek.

"Evan's office." Sally twisted her hands around his hips. "Just hold me for a second. Just hold me."

Then she asked, "What time is it?"

"Ten-twenty."

"I fell asleep. Terrible sleep. Bad dreams. I remember coming here. Rose Tyler. Sweet Rose. God. She brought me a thermos of chicken soup from the cafeteria. Can you believe that? Chicken soup, and then she gave me some cognac. Skipper, that's a glorious combination." She laughed. "I didn't want you here, darling."

"I know."

"Dorothy told you. She's impossible."

"Sally, dear, look. I . . . *know*. I know about Charlie and Larry."

"Oh God."

"Larry told me."

Skipper's fingers touched her hair; he kissed her gently. Wordlessly, she followed him to the Chesterfield sofa that she had sat on so many times in the past, facing Evan.

"You look as bad as I feel," she whispered.

Skipper started to smile. "I quit today. Better yet, I was ousted. Mother and Eli have taken over." He spoke calmly. "They're going to change the paper, cut the foreign staff, cut national news. Get rid of Sarah Felger and the old-timers. Confront Lazzarutti. They're selecting Barry as managing editor."

"Skipper. Sweet." She stared at him. "What will you do?"

He shrugged. "Take a break. Think. Try to work out my life."

"Poor Maury," Sally whispered.

Skipper winced. "Maury's had a heart attack. Sounds bad . . ."

"Oh my God."

"He was my choice. You knew that."

"Yes."

"I wanted him to groom Ward. Maury was an interim choice." Skipper touched her face. "I wanted Ward to be . . ."

She saw the glitter in his eyes.

"I need you, Sally. Move in with me. Divorce Charlie. We'll get married. If you want, we'll have a kid . . ."

Sally compressed her lips firmly, as if this would stop the flow of tears.

"*Damn*. That would be so easy, so nice."

"Yes."

"I can't, Skipper."

"Why?" His voice pleaded.

"No, no, I can't."

Sally's eyes widened and she stared at him. She saw the dark stubble on his haggard face, the tangled hair.

"What will you do?" he asked.

"Divorce Charlie . . ." Her face, her mouth, wrenched with strain. ". . . leave the *Star,* leave the city."

*

Marcus Lynn's Tuscan-style estate off Bedford Drive was an imposing mansion—the kind of Beverly Hills home that Linda had read about in movie magazines as a teen-ager—guarded by iron gates and a walled and spiked fence partially draped by eucalyptus and elm and jacaranda trees.

Marcus opened the door himself. "I've been expecting you."

He seemed taller than the first time they had met, over six feet, and the impression he gave was of deepening, almost permanent, weariness.

He stepped aside, allowing Linda to enter the huge, richly paneled entrance hall, glistening beneath a crystal chandelier. Beyond a Regency table, which held a porcelain vase with multicolored, long-stemmed silk flowers, curved a wide staircase.

They turned right, walking beneath a Louis XVI tall case clock that chimed once. It was six-fifteen. Their footsteps echoed in the hall, until he abruptly touched Linda's arm and turned right again into a leather-paneled room that, Linda assumed, was the library.

Linda placed her handbag on the floor, removing her notebook and pen. No more pretense of hiding the tools of the trade.

"I compliment you, Linda," he said. "You're ahead of your competitors. You have the story all wrapped up." Marcus' eyes fluttered. "You've seen the film. When can we expect a story?"

Linda spoke quietly. "They had masks. He was not identifiable. I can't print a story based on that." Linda's fingers brushed over her hair. "Marcus, why did Elliott kill himself?"

He stood, gazing at her. "A drink first. Or are you into something else?"

"Diet soda."

Marcus walked toward the liquor cabinet. "I asked Lois if her scrapbooks were helpful to you, and she said she wasn't sure."

"Neither am I." She watched him open the ice bucket.

"What exactly are you looking for, Linda?"

She opened her mouth but said nothing. Finally she examined her notebook and spoke. "I don't know, Marcus. I know there's a story here, but it's not the one you want me to print. That happens. Someone thinks they're leaking one story, and a totally unexpected story comes out of it."

He splashed scotch whiskey over the ice in his glass. "We've got people from the *Daily News* and the *Times* and the Washington *Post* and the L.A. *Times* interested in this story, Linda. Someone's going to print it. You're going to lose your exclusive." Marcus handed Linda her drink.

She shrugged. "*My* problem. You were so certain, Marcus, so certain that Elliott would serve as your . . . deep throat."

Marcus walked to the windows, gazing through the pale curtains. "Just wanted Elliott to be on hand for reporters like you. Off the record. Identify Tom Nelson. Let the reporters do the rest."

"You had something on Elliott, something besides the films. You *knew* he would do it."

Marcus stood completely still. Linda persisted.

"Paul Brock said you were calling in your chips. What *were* your chips, Marcus? You were *threatening* Elliott. Threatening him with what?"

Marcus turned and glared at Linda. "Elliott Hanley was a fool living in some thirty-year time warp. Obsessed with guilt."

"*Why?*"

"Elliott was an informer. He informed on his boyfriend Marvin Conrad. He informed on Lois and Gus Heller and Paul Bernstein. He informed on Tommy Nelson."

Linda caught her breath. "But I thought . . ."

"You thought *what?* Tom Nelson informed on his friends? He *did.* It was only after Elliott's testimony, Elliott's *secret* testimony, that Joey Keefer called Tom Nelson. Elliott *worked* for Keefer."

Marcus moved to his chair, sipped his drink and glanced up at Linda's startled face. "It was to Keefer's advantage to catch a rising star like Tommy, a potential box-office name. Someone to blackmail for years and years. Elliott Hanley was irrelevant to Keefer, but Tommy . . . well, Tommy was someone to be used."

Linda saw the flicker in his lower eyelids.

"Keefer told Tommy that he would keep his name secret—keep the fact that he was an informer secret—so long as Tommy supported him, raised money for him in Hollywood, so long as Tommy *served* Keefer."

"You destroyed Keefer."

"Joey Keefer was a miserable little pervert," said Marcus. "Drunk with power." He tasted his drink, watching Linda. "We dealt with him in a rather vicious way."

Linda said quietly, "Why did Elliott inform?"

Marcus contemplated his drink, then drained it.

"Keefer threatened to expose Elliott's sexual predilections, which, at that time, were taboo. It would have destroyed his career and, more important for Elliott—and this may sound laughable—it would have destroyed his mother."

Linda stared dully at the glass in her hand. "Not laughable," she said.

"Elliott was perfectly content to play the roles of martyr and informer so long as Keefer kept the secret."

"No one knew?"

"Except me."

"And Elliott was terrified . . ."

"The truth would come out."

Linda spoke firmly. "So thirty years later you called in your chips—is that it, Marcus? You told Elliott that unless he talked to reporters about Nelson's porno films, you'd expose him as Keefer's informer. Elliott Hanley cared. After all those years he still cared."

Marcus' handsome face was perfectly still, his eyes so clear and cold that Linda lowered her gaze. The phone rang twice, but Marcus ignored it.

"Hanley sat there and cried," he said. "Just a couple of hours ago. Cried and cried. Kept babbling that he had betrayed the only people he really loved, Tom Nelson and Marvin Conrad. Said he betrayed his own lover, Marvin Conrad. Betrayed Lois and Bernstein."

Marcus stood up and walked to the liquor cabinet, where he started to pour another drink. The clock chimed. Six-thirty.

Linda turned at the sound of footsteps. A Mexican woman moved quickly past Linda and bowed low to whisper to Marcus. For a moment Linda caught a full view of her face: wide, coal-black eyes set in honey-colored skin that seemed to glisten. Her nose was flat, and her delicate mouth revealed large, milk-white teeth. She resembled a beautiful peasant woman and seemed just slightly incongruous in her starched white apron over a black dress that came below her knees. Her low black shoes, shiny and new, squeaked as she walked. A crucifix hung on her chest.

Frowning, Marcus stood up, telling Linda he would return shortly. Linda watched them leave, catching a remarkably distinct smell of soap as the woman stepped past her. Linda stared at a Gauguin portrait over the Georgian-style fireplace, then her eyes dropped to the marble top covered with an eighteenth-century Siamese buddha and a set of T'ang and Wei figures.

She was calm, almost lightheaded with fatigue. Hazy images and blurred voices swept over her: a woman in Venice, Elliott Hanley's desolate face, Paul Brock's laugh and New York accent and the fierce, pleasurable grip of his fingers over her arms, the film splattered with memories and joylessness . . .

Marcus returned to the library and seated himself on the sofa, facing Linda.

"That was Paul. He's seeing some fellows from the *Daily News* tomorrow. Other reporters are calling."

"Marcus, I need one more day," Linda said. "One more. I'm keeping my editor in New York on tenterhooks. He keeps calling me. I need twenty-four hours. I have to see one more person."

"Who?" He was mildly interested.

"Maria."

Except for his lips, which drained of color, Marcus' face was impassive.

"That's impossible."

"I know where she is, Marcus. I've got to . . ."

"She has nothing to do with this."

"Marcus, I think she has everything to do with this."

He stared at her and spoke in a tight voice. "She has *nothing* to do with this. She's sick. Very sick."

Linda spoke softly. "Marcus, her affair with Nelson started this. Had there been no affair . . ."

Marcus stood. "I think you'd better go."

Linda lifted her handbag and notebook and slung her tape recorder over her shoulder.

"I think you're a fool, Marcus. I don't think you want to know the truth."

"I know the truth." His face was inches away from Linda's. "I *know* what happened."

"It was Dave Fitzgerald who told you about Maria and Tom Nelson."

He stepped back as Linda spoke.

"You told Fitzgerald to watch your daughter, and the next thing you knew he was on your doorstep saying your daughter and Nelson . . ."

"It was *Keefer.*" He spat out the word, turning to Linda. "Keefer played me *tapes.*" Marcus' voice cracked. "It was Keefer. Fitzgerald and Keefer came together."

"What did Keefer say?"

"There were rumors all over Washington about my daughter and Tommy Nelson. Fitzgerald was afraid to tell me. Joey said he had to find out himself. He made tapes of them. I burned the tapes and I thought the sounds would burn out of my mind. But the sounds are sharper now. More intense. Every day, every waking moment, and now in sleep, even in my sleep I hear those sounds."

"By destroying Nelson you destroy the sounds."

Marcus looked at her blankly. "For five or six months I wanted to murder Tom Nelson. I knew if I were alone with him I would do something . . . irrational. Nelson betrayed me. Exploited her innocence." He sighed. "Well, the murder phase is over, Linda. I want to get even. And I *will.*"

She grasped his arm. "Marcus. I've got to see Maria."

"Impossible."

"It began with her, Marcus. Your hatred for Nelson. The films. Gus's murder. Your revenge. Even Elliott's suicide. *It's her!*"

Marcus spoke coldly, "The only one Maria asks to see is her grandmother."

"Her . . ."

"The woman who served us. My wife's mother. A deeply religious woman. Brings Maria chocolates." He smiled, but his face was drained. "Prays for the salvation of her daughter and granddaughter."

Linda stared at him blindly. "The woman in the film I saw at Paul's house. Not the blonde."

"A small-time Mexican actress. Davita Lopez."

"Your first wife."

From an upper floor a child screeched with laughter. Linda felt her stomach knot.

Marcus spoke as if not hearing. "Fell in love. Beautiful girl. A primitive beauty. From the south. I wanted to save her from that life." He struggled to laugh, but emitted a short, furious snort.

"Please, Marcus," groaned Linda, seething with anger at herself for begging. But she continued. "I've *got* to see Maria."

"*No!*"

Linda stared at Marcus' face. Suddenly his eyes glittered at the sounds upstairs—a bike creaking followed by a child's shout.

"No," he whispered once more, turning to Linda, who knew, at that moment, that she was going to see Maria Lynn.

*

Seated in the lobby phone booth, Barry dialed the Century Plaza, using his telephone credit card, and left a message for Linda Fentress to call him at The Four Seasons Hotel in Washington.

Then he walked to the reception desk of the hotel and registered quickly, asking the clerk to send his tote bag and typewriter —he always carried a typewriter, even on overnight trips—to his room. Barry told the clerk that he would be in the Garden Terrace.

He walked through the lobby and stood for a moment at the entrance to the crowded lounge, his eyes darting across the room. Three Japanese men sat on sofas, sipping tea and biting hungrily into pastries. On a gray leather chair he saw a blond woman whom he recognized as Kitty White, the Washington hostess, sipping wine with an Arab in white-and-black robes, and another man.

Five yards away, on a velvet sofa, leaning forward and gulping his scotch and soda, was Jerry Paley. Barry stepped toward him quickly.

"You look good," said Jerry, remaining firmly seated and shaking Barry's hand.

"You too," said Barry, grinning.

"Liar. I look like hell."

Barry sat on the sofa, facing Jerry, and leaned close, tapping his fingers on the wrought-iron and glass table between them. "Who's that?"

Jerry Paley turned and squinted.

"That's Kitty White. Georgetown hostess and whore. She's into power."

"The guys."

"The Arab is Sheik something or other. From an oil emirate. Throws money into causes quote unquote. Rumored to help some politicians. The other guy is an old-time Kennedy liberal."

Barry glanced around the room. "Hey, it's interesting here. More interesting than New York."

"No, it's not. How's the New York *Star?*"

"Surviving. Barely."

A waitress appeared, and Barry ordered scotch on the rocks. Jerry asked for another scotch and soda.

"Heard about Maury," said Jerry Paley. "Poor bastard."

"He'll make it. Knock wood."

"He's banging that broad too much."

"A lot to bang."

"You should know, boychick."

Barry smiled.

"Where's Bishop?" said Jerry Paley.

"In Panama."

Barry glanced at Jerry and thought he saw a tremor around his lips.

"That's my stomping ground. Panama City. Fitz sends me down for the Foreign Relations Committee. Jesus, ain't much in Panama."

The pianist was playing the theme from *Dr. Zhivago*. Barry noticed Jerry's remarkably delicate hands, his nails bitten to the quick. He caught Jerry's vacant stare.

"You're in trouble," said Barry.

Jerry's eyes fluttered.

"I hate to do this . . ." began Barry.

"No, you don't."

Barry said, "This story hurts."

Jerry Paley sighed. "Spare me the sorrow. It doesn't hurt. You know that. A story doesn't hurt. A story is a story. Beat the competition. Fuck the implications. Get a Pulitzer. Whoopee. You're a little guilty, Barry, that's all . . ."

"Guilty about what?"

"Guilty about making whatever arrangements you did with Fitzgerald. What are they? What did he promise you?"

"Cut it, Jerry," said Barry.

"Cut it," said Jerry laughing. "Oh boy."

Barry stared at his swollen face, the eyes stained pink. "We have a story. Howie's got it. We're going with it tomorrow night."

"And what did Howie discover?" Jerry Paley tasted his drink, as if it was his first of the night.

"We *know*, Jerry."

"*What* do you know?" His voice sharpened.

The Japanese men turned, eyeing the two Americans.

Barry spoke softly. "We know about Panama. All about Panama. Listen to me. Howie walked into an office in Panama City this afternoon. Law firm by the name of . . ." He removed the notebook from his breast pocket, folded to a middle page. "Herrera, Diaz and Ortega. Howie said he wanted to form a company just like Mr. Jerry Paley. A company that deals in securities abroad, a company with subsidiaries. Mr. Herrera, Diaz and Ortega referred Howie to a partner in the firm, a gentleman named Aleman, who was only too delighted to form a company *just like Mr. Paley.*"

As Jerry lifted the glass to his lips and drank, Barry thought he saw two red welts surface on Jerry's forehead. Barry's eyes returned to his notebook.

"It seems a company was set up, Jerry, a company named Angela Enterprises. Mr. Herrera, Diaz and Ortega nominated the officers to the company, who just happened to be employees of the law firm."

Barry leaned forward. "Then a funny thing happened, Jerry. As soon as the company was created, they resigned. Just like that. Resigned as incorporating officers and directors. They assigned bearer shares to *you.*"

Jerry Paley seemed to be listening to the piano player. "And then what happened?" he said dully.

"It seems Angela Enterprises began a corporate account at the local branch of a Swiss bank. Deposits into the account—and there are some hefty deposits—are immediately transferred to the bank branch in Zurich. Banhofstrasse. Famous street."

Barry nodded. "Someone once described Switzerland as a country where very few things begin, but many things end. That's what happened. It ended right there."

Jerry examined his empty glass. "Clever. Got it all wrapped up. Neat little package. You and Howie."

Barry ignored him. "The question, of course, isn't what you did with the money but how you got it. That's the lead of the story, Jerry. *How you got the money.*"

Barry watched Jerry order another drink. Inexplicably, Jerry Paley smiled, fixing his eyes across the lounge.

"We *know*, Jerry," Barry said.

"You know nothing."

"Okay," said Barry impatiently. "We know nothing. Nothing about the deal in Long Island. Zoning change. That's nothing, right? Six thousand bucks an acre to fifty, right? All in the name of Margaret Paley."

Jerry Paley winced twice at the sound of his wife's name. Barry spoke through clenched teeth. "Nothing about the sale of the land to a company called Argosy, Inc., Dallas-based property developers. Just a coincidence. You bought those potato fields cheap, then got Fitzgerald to support the zoning change."

Barry's shaking hand turned the page. "All kinds of coincidences. A *pattern* of coincidences, Jerry. Five trips to Panama this year, and each time, Jerry, just before you leave, you coincidentally drop into your bank in D.C. for a visit to the safe-deposit box. Coincidences pile up."

Even before Barry stopped talking, Jerry whispered, "What was Fitzgerald's line? Let me think. 'I depend on Paley. He's my eyes and ears. I had total *trust* in him.'"

"What are you saying, Jerry?" Barry spoke coldly.

"I'm saying you don't have the story."

"Here's the story, sonny boy," said Barry, pointing his finger at the notebook. "We *got* the story. We got the memos . . ."

"Should have known," said Jerry, trying to grin.

"The memos, right? All kinds of memos." Barry lifted his cowhide case to the table and quickly unfastened the combination locks. Snapping the lid open, his fingers plucked out a white folder that held a small pile of pages.

"Here's one, Jerry," he said. "Some new barracks for our troops in Germany. You remember that one? Armed Services

Committee is squabbling where to build the barracks. One faction wants the barracks in Kaiserlautern, west of Frankfurt. Big contract. What to do?" Barry looked up. *"What to do?* You give Fitzgerald a very persuasive memo, Jerry, on the advantages of Würzburg. Strategic location. Troops need it more. Facilities worse. You tell him everything except one detail. You're cozy with a certain Delaware company that wants to build the barracks in Würzburg."

Jerry's hollow smile puzzled Barry at first, then enraged him.

"You want more, Jerry, we got it," he said. "The close-support Air Force fighter. You remember that one. The one the Pentagon didn't even want, but Congress pushed it. Close vote. That company in Texas pulled out all the stops and you got Fitz . . ."

"Always wanted the memos," said Jerry softly, smiling. "Insisted I send the memos. It's beautiful." He was staring across the lounge. "Me and Cheryl. She's dead. Poor, silly bitch."

"Cheryl passed on the money to you, and you put it in the safe-deposit box," said Barry. "It was a mistake, Jerry. Dumb mistake. The dates you visited the bank coincided within twenty-four hours with the dates on the memos."

Jerry Paley's smile turned into a sickly grin.

"Then, before you went down to Panama on official business, you took the money out of the box," said Barry. "It's illegal to leave the country with more than five thousand dollars. Have to declare it. But, hell, no one's going to stop a Senate aide."

"Dumb, wasn't it?"

"Maybe you wanted to get caught."

Jerry Paley shrugged. His lips drained white, an eerie smile was fixed on his face.

"My word against his. And yours."

"How much money was there, Jerry?"

"I'm a messenger—you know that, Barry." He stared across the room. "The money *disappears.* Transferred to Switzerland. Twenty-five percent stays in my account. Seventy-five percent disappears into another one. Guess who?"

"I don't believe you."

"Don't believe me," sighed Jerry Paley.

"He's going to the Justice Department," said Barry.

Jerry shrugged. "So what do you want from me, Barry? Reaction? A good quote to round out the story?" He gazed at Barry. "Take this down. This is a lesson in the new journalism. Shade the truth. Don't worry about the consequences. Fuck the facts. May get in the way of the story. Don't dig too hard. Yeah. Because if *you* dig, Barry, you're going to slam into the source of your story."

Jerry Paley crouched forward. "What kind of deal did you make with him?"

The two men turned to watch Kitty White leave the lounge. A waiter approached and told Barry that he had a phone call in the lobby.

Barry stood up and told Jerry he would be right back. Paley fixed his eyes on the table, saying nothing, the sudden pain in his face so acute that Barry lingered for a moment before threading his way out of the lounge.

Linda Fentress was on the phone. "Not sure what I have, Barry, not sure what I'll *get*, but I'll have a story tomorrow night."

"You saw the film! That's the story."

"Listen to me, Barry. That's *not* the story. Something here I've got to unravel."

"I want this story tomorrow." He spoke angrily.

"You'll get it."

"File early."

"I can't file early."

"Why?"

"I'm going to Carmel. Up north. I've got to see someone there."

Moments later, Barry slammed the phone down, almost frozen in place by his fury at Linda. He yearned to gain the staff's trust and affection but, more important, he needed *control*. And Linda, feisty and unpredictable, was stubbornly determined to remain independent. Her singleminded determination, her energy, her zealousness in unraveling a story—the very qualities that made him hire her—enraged him now. Once she returned to New York, he would punish her—cold storage for several months.

Walking toward the lounge, Barry suddenly remembered he had not eaten dinner. He glanced at his watch. Ten-twenty. He would find a restaurant in Georgetown after finishing the session with Jerry. Important now to get a reaction, good quote, an on-the-record quote, from Jerry to insert high into the story. Yes! Round out the story.

The piano player had begun a medley from *Hair*. He knew something was wrong even before he reached the sofa.

Jerry Paley was gone.

*

Eli Faber stepped rapidly up Park Avenue, the soft, westerly breeze brushing his face. It was 11:50 P.M., but the traffic, swirling uptown and downtown, seemed unusually heavy for Monday evening. He stopped at a red light on the northeast corner of Seventy-fourth Street.

The breeze picked up, tingling his body, still chilled from the hot and then cold shower at Shirley's. He had toweled himself too quickly, leaving his hair and shoulders damp, wanting to leave the brownstone as quickly as possible.

He had decided to visit Shirley's on a whim, having remained at his office at the *Star* to wait for the first edition, to chat with David Fitzgerald, to clean up paperwork and prepare for tomorrow.

The paper was *his*.

Events had moved so rapidly, so *exquisitely*. The years of waiting, the years of fawning over Frieda, the years of bowing and scraping to Jonathan and Skipper, humiliating years while the paper dawdled and stumbled, those painful years had paid off in a set of bold strokes.

The paper was his.

Crossing Seventy-fifth Street, Eli smiled to himself.

Once they resumed publishing after a long, bitter strike, once they resumed publishing with Barry at the helm, they would transform the paper. Kill the foreign staff, pare down Washington news. Fill the pages with gossip, with crime stories, with spicy writing. Flashy investigative stories. Yes! And at the appropriate time, well, there would be plenty of opportunity to sell the paper . . .

He had wanted to celebrate the triumph in his own personal way, and had phoned Shirley at ten-ten to see if Serita was available. Be here before eleven, said Shirley.

But the girl, who normally welcomed him with a wide, mischievous smile, whose half-open negligee instantly aroused him as he stared at the triangle of dark, luxuriant pubic hair, seemed tired.

Her flat lips forced a grin. She fell on the bed, burying her face on the pillow, awaiting him and, as he entered her, as she arched her back and buttocks, her squeal of delight seemed forced and theatrical, almost a mockery of pleasure.

Angered, he came quickly, then climbed out of the bed. Eli scrubbed his body with grim perseverance, hating this whore, knowing that he would visit her again and again like the others until Shirley found a new dark girl for him.

Then he had taken a cab uptown from the brownstone, but his restlessness led him to get off at Seventy-second Street. A twenty-block walk, on a cool, clear night, would calm him, ease this foolish anger at Serita. And it did.

As Eli strolled uptown, nodding to doormen and smiling, the breeze buoyed him. Perhaps the world was collapsing, at least facing a major crisis, perhaps misery and sorrow loomed in darkened corners close by. Yet New York never seemed more luminous.

The *Star* was his.

His.

Walking toward the familiar gray-and-brown awning on Eighty-first Street, he glanced up to the eighth floor. He had expected to see darkness, but the apartment's windows glowed. He kept walking. At the corner waiting for the traffic light, he turned and stared again at the living-room and bedroom windows that gleamed—quite dramatically, he thought—in a building encased with darkened windows.

It would be absurd to visit Frieda now, even phone her, to ask if something was wrong. Absurd and panicky. He turned and stepped rapidly across Eighty-second Street, aware that his legs were trembling. The wind was cold now. Eli listened to the sounds of car horns and tires slapping on Park Avenue. His heart pounded.

Nothing was wrong. Nothing at all.

*

Maggie Paley awoke with a start at the sound of a garage door closing. Her hand reached the night table and she found her watch. It was eleven-twenty. Jerry was home, at last, and soon enough he would climb upstairs and slip in beside her, his heavy body warming the bed and comforting her. She smiled and sighed deeply.

In the ten seconds before she lapsed back into sleep, Maggie Paley wondered whether perhaps she should wander downstairs and chat with him while he ate the cold chicken leg and salad that she had placed on a plate under the plastic wrap in the refrigerator. He ate so chaotically now: always on the run, drinking too much, far too much, and eating too little. They would sit and talk, and Maggie would tell him that Mike had returned in the early evening, exhausted from the trip and the funeral in Pennsylvania, burning with grief and outrage—his friend dead, another victim of the war, and if that wasn't horrible enough, his child a victim too, just like little Angela.

Jerry, you should have seen little Angela. Mike took her home, God bless her, and she came up and puckered her lips and kissed me and said, Thank you, Grandma, you're wonderful.

Can you imagine, Jerry? Little Angela talking like that!

Maggie would tell him in the morning. She was tired now and pulled the quilt up to her chin. Comforted in the knowledge that Jerry was finally home, exultant at little Angela's choice of words, Maggie Paley smiled. She would tell Jerry and he would grin—Maggie saw his wide grin right now—and shake his head and whisper: "That little sweetheart."

It would make Jerry's morning.

*

Jerry turned the ignition key, and the Volvo's starter engaged the engine with a healthy thrust. He relaxed for a moment, aware that the sounds in the sealed garage were amplified mightily, ricocheting from wall to wall.

On the way home—over Key Bridge and along Route 50—Jerry Paley had gripped the wheel of the car, pleasantly surprised that the garage tune-up had quelled the unhealthy whine and smoothed out the carburetor kinks that had afflicted the aging vehicle. Spark plugs had been replaced, carburetor parts cleaned, new points, condenser, rotor, and distributor cap had been installed. The car ran beautifully.

He had locked the garage door and, after settling into the driver's seat, opened the window. An acrid smell of gasoline and garbage stung his nostrils. He had turned the key, startled by the powerful sound of the igniting fuel-and-air mixture in the cylinders. He listened and swallowed hard. The rigid steel and flexible-hose fuel line along the chassis was gurgling now, the burned gases moving out of the cylinders into the exhaust pipe, the muffler and resonator silencing the gases surging through the tailpipe. It was better this way, thought Jerry, inhaling deeply, wondering why his cheeks were stained with tears. He smelled the sweet, stinging vapor within seconds.

*

At that moment, Linda lifted the ringing phone in her room at the Century Plaza. She was smoking a joint and sipping orange juice, barefoot in her jeans and khaki shirt. The curtain on the open terrace flapped in the warm breeze. Linda had just opened the envelope left by Gregory, containing copies of the newspaper clips on Joe Keefer.

Linda heard Sandy Jaffe's low voice.

"Thank God it's you, Sandy," she whispered. "Not the prick who calls himself my city editor."

"I thought you'd be out with Warren Beatty."

"Not my type. I like rich Washington lawyers."

"I'll remember that." He told Linda that his office had checked the files of the Securities and Exchange Commission for Transcon's ownership.

Linda grabbed the envelope containing Joe Keefer's clips and began writing on the back portion.

"Most significant holdings in Transcon are held by something called Morris Trust, Limited," said Sandy Jaffe. "Headquartered in St. Martin, Netherlands Antilles. Registered down there."

Linda let out a whistle. "It smells."

"I called a friend at IRS," said Sandy. "The bottom line is they've got a paid informant in St. Martin who's checking on the ownership of Morris Trust. Should know tomorrow."

"Bless you, Sandy."

"You win a Pulitzer Prize, and I want to . . ."

"Sandy, darling, we're *beyond* that. We're friends. What else do you have?"

"Checked with a guy from Justice. Very reliable. Now, you didn't hear this from Justice Department sources."

"Promise."

"You know, of course, that Transcon's chief officer is Marcus Lynn in L.A."

"Yes."

"They've got a major subsidiary down in Dallas. Argosy, Inc. Land developers. They've got a bunch of people on the board. But the guy who actually runs it, controls it, the money man who's not listed, is someone named Eli Faber."

Linda felt a cold sweat start on her lips. "My, my . . ."

"Eli's been the source of a couple of Justice Department investigations," said Sandy. "He seems to be a close friend of a certain New York senator. Eli's also an executive on a certain New York newspaper."

"Eli and Fitzgerald and Marcus and . . . Transcon," said Linda.

"One big happy family," said Sandy Jaffe, laughing.

*

Frieda wandered into the living room after watching the late-night news, leaving the television set on in the study to fill the silence. She sat on the suede living-room sofa and picked up a new best-seller by an English mystery novelist.

Through the evening, she had forced herself to concentrate on separate tasks—preparing lamb chops for dinner, phoning her sister afterward, calling the *Star* to find out the makeup of the front page. It was self-deception, she knew, to carry on as if nothing had happened through the day, as if life had not taken a frightening, perhaps irrevocable, turn.

Now her body was gripped with an almost lightheaded burst of energy. She yearned to breathe the cool night air, to walk outdoors and burn the tension from her chest. She stood and walked to the window.

Glancing down onto Park Avenue, Frieda stared at the stream of lights flowing noiselessly in either direction.

Tears wet her cheeks.

Was she jealous of Johanna?

Had she crippled her daughter?

Frieda let out a sob, covering her face with her hands.

Was Skipper right? Did she allow hangers-on and incompetents and court jesters to fawn over her and treat her like the beautiful young woman she never was?

Skipper!

Arnold!

God, she hated this apartment. Its shadows breathed, its memories lurked in every corner.

Arnold!

She recalled the words in his last letter with amazing clarity.

Arnold!

She gave a gasp.

At night, it's difficult to sleep . . .

The words in his last letter flowed to her lips with amazing ease, the letter buried in a trunk in the cellar at Bella Verde, the letter that she had failed to give to Skipper out of some grasping need to hold onto one enduring shred of Arnold Steiner. She closed her eyes and recalled the words precisely.

. . . You know, Caesar's armies fought the German tribes here. Caesar called it the Ardennes, "A place full of terrors." And that's what it is. Skipper must be such a big boy by now . . .

Never, *never* would Skipper know.

She gazed up at the ceiling, then heard her howl of despair.

Never!

＊

David Fitzgerald suddenly woke up.

Seated in the library of his big, yellow stucco home on Macomb Street, Fitzgerald opened his eyes at the sound of voices outside, teen-agers laughing and the loud throb of rock music from a car radio.

He glanced at his watch. One-thirty.

He recalled sitting in the rosewood armchair around ten-forty waiting for Celia. It had been a long day, starting with last night's press calls about Cheryl's death, the meetings with Eli and Barry Cohen, the shuttle to Washington and Kitty White. Senate business, more reporters badgering him about Cheryl's death, phone calls, the gossip that Eddie Belling was making noises *himself* about running for President.

Fitzgerald sat, listening to the soft wind creak the windows of the house that Senator Merton Keefer had bequeathed to them, a splendid house, a house marked by three cantilevered octagonal stairways that whirled into the cupola above.

Strange that Celia hadn't woken him when she came in. He had slept deeply even through horrible dreams. Was he awake when the door opened, or dreamed that he was awake? Had Celia stepped into the living room and stood over him? Or was it one of the dreams?

Celia! She was still beautiful but so frail, tortured by fears difficult to understand. She had turned into a virtual recluse, ignoring dinner-party invitations until they stopped, even pleading illness when President Bergen invited them to the state dinner for the Israeli Prime Minister. She seemed perfectly content to lock herself in this house with its antebellum artifacts—he was gazing at a walnut secretary that had once served as a plantation post office —and blurred memories of her thug of a father and twisted older brother.

David Fitzgerald eased out of the chair, switched off the lamp and left the study, walking up the stairwell. The house was eerily silent.

He would slip into the master bedroom, where she slept on a huge bed, chintz cascading in billows from the canopy. Kiss her gently on the forehead. Then slip into his own bedroom down the hall. Several years ago they had given up all pretense of sleeping together.

Reaching the top portion of the stairway, Fitzgerald heard the faraway sound of an ambulance. He glanced upward at the cupola, and a beam of light from a street lamp caught his eyes, blinding him for a flickering second.

Suddenly he stopped. His hand grasping the rail was slippery with sweat. Fitzgerald lifted his foot onto the final step, stricken with alarm. His entire body was shaking.

He ran the seven steps to the master bedroom and flung open the door. The scent of perfume and pink soap caught his nostrils. The shutters were open, light streaming through and enveloping the fringed Mexican rug at the base of the bed.

Celia wasn't there.

Tuesday

CHAPTER 20

Fitzgerald awoke startled when the telephone rang.

"Is this Senator Fitzgerald?"

The male voice was just slightly high-pitched, with a Virginia drawl, thick with nervousness. Suddenly Fitzgerald was furious.

"Yes. Yes. What is it?"

"I'm terribly sorry to disturb you at this hour, sir. This is Captain Bender at Second District Headquarters on Idaho Avenue. I thought you should know, sir—your wife was apprehended about ninety minutes ago. On the verge of jumping off Key Bridge."

David Fitzgerald closed his eyes.

"We took her into custody, sir, and in the course of a routine search of some of her belongings we found a, ah, .38 caliber revolver in her possession."

Inexplicably, Fitzgerald began to nod. He heard the policeman take a heavy breath.

"Sir, in the course of a routine ballistics check we found evidence indicating the weapon was the same one used in connection with the homicide of Cheryl Thomas."

Fitzgerald wanted to laugh, but coughed instead.

"She's confessed, sir. Your wife has confessed to the killing. We've charged her with second-degree homicide."

Fitzgerald lay on the bed, his mind an absolute blank. The grayness of dawn seeped through the folded window curtains. He thought he heard Captain Bender go on to say that Mrs. Fitzgerald had been given an opportunity to call a lawyer, but that she asked to speak to you, sir.

*

Seated in the last row of the 727, Hugh heard the change in engine pitch as the shuttle started its descent into LaGuardia. The dried wound over his left ear was swollen and pulsing, incredibly sensitive now to the touch.

The West Indian doctor who had cleaned and bandaged the wound last night at Sibley Hospital's emergency room had ordered him to see his personal physician this morning first thing, get it cleaned once more and rebandaged.

"You must be careful with this, Mr. Finch," the doctor said in his singsong accent. "These bathroom falls are so *common*."

Hugh closed his eyes as the plane shuddered through a belt of white clouds, descending.

Got to go to New York first, Doctor. Call Maury, meet him in his apartment. Resign. No questions, please, Maury, I just have to . . . quit.

At a telephone booth, just inside the terminal, he dialed Maury's number. Nancy picked up the phone on the fourth ring.

"Nancy, is Maury there? It's Hugh."

"Hugh?" She sounded a little dazed.

"Is *Maury* there?"

"Hugh. Maury's in the hospital." Her voice was so low that Hugh barely caught the words. "Maury's had a heart attack."

"Oh Jesus! How bad?"

"Bad." Her vacant tone implored him to stop questions.

"I'm so sorry," he said softly.

Gently, Hugh started to bang his head against the phone booth. "My fault," he whispered. "My fault. My *fault*."

Maury had fought for him, depended on him to write the story, gone to the mat for him. He had failed Maury—no, he had betrayed him, just as he had betrayed Alvin. And he was certain that the betrayal had struck Maury down.

He would go home now on the next shuttle, write his letter of resignation to Skipper. Disappear for a while. Sort out the debris. Salvage what he could.

End it with Francine.

End it with the life that consumed him and destroyed those he loved.

Start with the kids, thread his way back into *their* lives. Be a father. Got to be *human*.

He heard Nancy whispering, "It wasn't your fault, don't be absurd."

"Hey, look!" Hugh spoke in a choked voice. "I'd like to send him a note. What's the hospital?"

"St. Clare's. But Hugh, I'm sure he'd like to see you."

"No, he wouldn't."

Nancy spoke calmly. "Hugh, he's proud of you. I'm sure he is. That was a terrific story. You're being quoted on the 'Today' show. It's going to make Maury so proud . . ."

"What the hell are you talking about?"

There was a pause. "Have you been smoking something? What I'm talking about is your *story*. The lead of the paper."

"I haven't seen the paper."

"Well, there's a story there under your byline, about the President of the United States. You *wrote* it, didn't you?"

"Hey, listen. Got to go. Thanks."

He ran to the newsstand, and even before he lifted the top copy of the *Star* he saw isolated words in the headline . . . *Bergen Ill . . . Leukemia . . . Curtailed Activities . . . by Hugh Finch . . . New York* Star *Staff Correspondent.*

They had written the story with his byline. They had . . . saved him.

Quickly he scanned the story. *Saved him.*

Standing in the midst of a crowd swarming around the newsstand, Hugh breathed slowly and tried to concentrate on the front page.

Beside that story was one by Ward Parsons, on China's surprise development of a mobile intercontinental ballistic missile; a three-column photo covered the center of the page: Defense Secretary Belling, climbing up the stairs of an Air Force 727 at Andrews Air Force Base, chatting with Colonel Walker. That story was written by Barney Fischer.

Secretary of Defense Belling, calling the Chinese-Soviet border conflict "a grave threat to international peace," departed Washington last night in a surprise diplomatic mission to Moscow and Peking that seeks to create a "dialogue" between Soviet and Chinese leaders and lead to face-to-face peace talks under Belling's aegis.

Again, he stared at the byline that led the story atop the front page.

By Hugh Finch

He was suddenly aware of a thirst that seemed extraordinary, as if all the liquids and poisons within him had emptied, leaving his mouth parched.

Opening his eyes wide, Hugh folded the paper, and only then caught the headline on the bottom left of the front page, and the grainy photo of Jerry Paley.

SENATE AIDE KILLS SELF:
BRIBE INQUIRY CITED
By Howard Bishop

"Poor bastard," Hugh said. His eyes widened, once more, on the byline.

By Hugh Finch

He dug his fingers into his pocket and paid for the paper, and, bending low, he suddenly felt his eyes turn moist. Hugh concentrated on the trickle of water gurgling out of the fountain, and felt the tears on his cheeks.

When was the last time he had cried like this? So long ago, he thought, at his father's funeral at Bebee Memorial. In the darkness beneath his eyes, Alvin Simmons' face emerged.

He turned and, holding his sides, aware that people were staring at him, walked out of the terminal to find a taxi for St. Clare's Hospital.

*

As the policeman opened the door, David Fitzgerald saw Celia look up. She was seated at a wooden table in the center of the room, her face waxen. Her eyes pleaded with him.

"I wanted to die," she said.

He sat down on a chair that creaked. "You killed her."

There was a faint odor of decay in the room, masked by disinfectant. It was incredibly warm. He saw scratch marks and peeling on the lime-green walls. His eyes darted to the locked and barren window at the far end.

"I went to her," Celia said softly. "I wanted her to kill me. I begged her." She stared at her hands. "I couldn't face a campaign, David. Couldn't do it."

Celia was sweating. David Fitzgerald wondered why he hated his wife so.

"I've destroyed your career, David." She turned away.

"I suppose you have."

"I wanted to give Cheryl the gun, wanted *her* to kill *me,* but she laughed."

"Laughed?"

"She said I was a fool. Said your career was over. You'd be going to jail because of her. Because of her diary."

Fitzgerald heard male shouts outside the room. He struggled to control his voice. "Cheryl told you about a diary?"

"Showed me the diary, pages of names and numbers, pages and pages. Said this was evidence that could finish you. It was her laughter. She was screaming. She said she despised you, told me to get out with my gun, told me I was a fool, like my daddy, like my brother was a fool, like Joey . . ."

She stared at him. "David, she waved the diary. Said it was going to finish you. Dredge up the past."

Celia wept softly. "Kept calling my brother a *pervert,* like Daddy. Said she had been to bed with Daddy and Joey and they sickened her. She was waving the diary at me all the time, laughing. Waving the diary and I had to have it. With all my strength I had to have it."

"You fought," he whispered.

"I didn't want to kill her."

Fitzgerald heard a car door slam. "You have the diary," he said.

"Begged her. 'Stop laughing.' "

"You have the diary."

"At home."

His lips parted. "Do the police know?" said Fitzgerald.

"Know what?"

"About the diary? What have you told them, Celia?"

"I told them I killed Cheryl. I told them she was screaming and laughing when I asked her to kill . . ."

"You said nothing about the diary?"

She shook her head.

"Where is it?"

"I came home, David, and you were sleeping in the study. I wanted to kill you. Would have been so easy to kill you and then sit and wait for the police to come. But I spared you, David."

"Why?"

Celia looked at him, then lowered her eyes. "To punish you, David. You'll live. That's your punishment. You'll live knowing that I wrecked your chance to be President." She smiled. "The diary's in your bedroom, David. I left it there. And then I walked to Key Bridge."

Celia's voice was surprisingly sharp. "I've saved your life, David."

"Thank you," he replied dryly.

"Now I want you to help me die."

He returned her stare. "Don't be a fool," said Fitzgerald.

"You will help me die."

"I'm getting a good lawyer for you. I've asked Eli to find one. They're charging you with second-degree homicide, Celia. But you were obviously insane . . ."

"If you don't help me die, I'll tell the police about the diary."

Fitzgerald drew back.

Celia said: "I won't endure a trial." She tilted her chin up. "I've never seen you look helpless, David. Until now."

*

Frieda Steiner walked slowly to the gray-stone mausoleum, listening to the pleasant sounds of a hummingbird. She had risen at six-ten, with a yearning to go to Woodlawn Cemetery.

Yesterday had exhausted her. The article in *The Wall Street Journal,* lunch with Eli, Skipper's decision to quit, confrontations with Skipper and Lucy. Barry's ascension . . . Maury's heart attack . . . Lazzarutti's deal with the drivers . . . Hugh Finch's story . . . stories unraveled by Howie Bishop and Linda Fentress . . .

Now she moved hesitantly, nodding her head. They would vote this afternoon at three. Quickly. It would clear the air. Eli appointed, Skipper resigning. Barry named managing editor. Then meet Johanna in late afternoon to map out plans for *her* to start learning the business of running a newspaper.

Frieda saw the edifice of the mausoleum—S T E I N E R etched atop the grated door.

It was here, in this building snaked with ivy, that the Steiners rested forever. Yes, in death as well as life, Frederic has controlled them. Selecting the locale and the simple Italianate stone that seemed to darken each year and sink in the perpetually moist flat drifts on which Frieda stood twice, sometimes three times, a year, and cried softly.

From a brown paper bag, Frieda removed a pruning knife and a pair of shears. One must clip the roses gently, just above the bud. Prune.

Quite suddenly, Frieda was cutting now in a fever, tears streaming, the wall of roses blurred, the smell horribly sweet.

Skipper's words—her son, *his* son—had stung her. *The beautiful woman you never were.*

Yet somehow it was Lucy's rage, her cold-eyed fury, the years and years of daughter and mother anger, jealousy, love, hate that struck her now with an almost physical force.

Frieda Steiner buried her head in her hands.

They both despised her. Her daughter. Her son.

His son.

She stared at the smear of dirt on her knees, then raised her eyes to the mausoleum. Suddenly she felt the tensions within her drain away, yielding to an almost lightheaded calmness. Her trembling stopped and, for the first time in days, perhaps longer, perhaps the first time since Evan's death, the pall of loneliness and confusion lifted.

She knew what she had to do.

*

Maury Kramer lay in the hospital bed, his face gray, his eyes dull. Two prongs feeding oxygen were thrust into his nostrils; four electrodes clamped with adhesives clung to his half-shaven chest. The electrodes were linked to a wire atop the bed that reached into a cardiac monitor, and made faint bleeping noises.

"You stupid bastard," Maury said. "How'd you get in here?"

"I told them I was your son," Hugh said.

Maury smiled.

"I'm sorry, Maury. Sorry about yesterday."

Maury stared at the ceiling. "That's all a century ago."

Hugh swallowed. "Someday I'll tell you what happened."

"Can hardly wait."

"You saved my ass, Maury."

"We all saved your ass, sonny," Maury said. "Your lady friend called."

"Francine?"

"Francine. Said you were in trouble. That's all. You were in trouble. If someone's in trouble, you help. Barry and Ward and I sat down and typed up all we could remember from the meeting with Dr. Pomerance at Skipper's house. Barry called Pomerance and did a number on him. Got some terrific quotes. Ward called Belling. Told him we were printing the story. *Your* story. We fed everything to Marty Kaplan, who wrote it up."

"Thanks."

"Thank *them*. Your colleagues."

"Maury, forgive me."

"Fuck it. Just a story. Forget . . ."

"No. *No*. Not the story. This." He waved an arm at the hospital room. "It's my *fault*. I knocked you out of the race."

"You didn't do a thing to me, kid." Maury looked at him. "Maybe I wanted this to happen. Maybe . . ." Maury shrugged and smiled. "Maybe I really didn't want that job in the first place."

Hugh heard the door open behind him.

"Five minutes are up, Mr. Kramer," the nurse said to Hugh.

Maury blinked twice, then smiled. "You son of a bitch. Told them you were my son."

"Your *adopted* son. In a manner of speaking . . ."

Maury turned to the nurse. "Two more minutes, Miss," he said. "The boy came all the way from Washington."

She eyed both of them, obviously puzzled, a little suspicious. "*One* minute," she said firmly, turning on her heels and leaving the room.

"What are you going to do when you grow up, Hugh?" Maury asked.

Hugh shrugged. "Want to get away. Get away from Washington. Maybe go abroad for a while. Maybe even take my kids." Hugh moved close to the bed and held Maury's hand.

"And you?"

"The paper's changing. Someone's got to come in fast and shake up the place. Be a son of a bitch. Not me. No way."

"Who'll get the job?"

Maury shrugged. "Probably Barry. Told him this morning that he better take care of me when I get back. I don't want to cover fires in the South Bronx with Mark Kaiserman."

They smiled.

"Hear about Jerry Paley?"

Hugh nodded.

"That hurts." Maury bit his lip. "Something went wrong, Hugh. Shouldn't have happened."

"We pushed too fast," said Hugh solemnly. He looked at Maury. "Fitzgerald was Barry's source, wasn't he?"

Hugh didn't wait for an answer. "I think I understand why Belling leaked the stories to me," he said. "Fitzgerald asked Belling to do it. Fitzgerald used my stories to put pressure on Cohen. Made Barry move fast. Print the Jerry Paley story quick. Beat me out in order to get Evan's job."

Maury turned away. "We get hungry for the story."

The nurse announced his minute was up; the phone began to ring.

As the nurse reached for it, Maury tightened his grasp on Hugh's hand.

"You look like hell," Maury said.

"*You* look terrific," said Hugh, grinning.

The nurse frowned at them. "It's Nancy," she said, handing the phone to Maury. "First and last call of the morning. No more."

*

Linda glanced at her watch. Five fifty-five. Golden Gate Airlines Flight 450, scheduled to depart for Monterey at six-thirty, was now scheduled to leave at six-fifty.

Two men carted rope-bound copies of the Los Angeles *Times* to the newsstand five yards away.

. . . You'll get the story, Barry, a story you never quite imagined. Not just Tommy Nelson and his porno films, but Joe Keefer and Fitzgerald and Eli Faber and the blacklist and . . . and Maria, Maria Lynn. Sitting out there in the funny farm, waiting to fit the jigsaws into place . . .

Linda had not seen a newspaper in two days, had ignored the television news. Nothing mattered except the story. The story absorbs you, like an alien spirit, seizing every pore, knotting your belly, stabbing your bowels. The story.

Never a story quite like this one, Barry. I'm involved. Committed. Got to see this story through. It's my story and I'm into it.

She stood: she would buy a newspaper and concentrate on the front page for the next hour—studying the headlines, absorbing each story, ignoring the baffling pieces of evidence that had made sleep difficult all night. It was evidence brought by Gregory, evidence that now rested in the eight-by-ten envelope in her leather shoulder bag.

Gregory had arrived at midnight, drunk and glassy-eyed. He had auditioned badly at ABC, choked up when he saw the casting director and associate producer of the series, flubbed his lines and finally stomped off without a word. Drove to the Los Angeles *Times*, picked up the uncropped photo of Maria and Keefer and a copy of Keefer's obit. Then he went to a Mexican bar and drank margaritas until 11:45 P.M., when he stumbled to the Century Plaza where Rita Hamalian and Linda were waiting for him.

At ten minutes to one, the women helped Gregory to Rita's car —Gregory would pick up his car in the morning. Linda turned to Rita and repeated her instructions.

Have Gregory call Rose Haven in the morning, first thing. Imitate Marcus' voice. Say a friend of Maria's is coming in from New York and it's all right for her friend, Linda Fentress, to see her.

Linda had watched them drive off and then had returned to the room. Lighting a joint, the flame of the match heating her face, Linda sat on the bed and lifted the glossy print of Maria and Joey Keefer out of the envelope. What had been cropped from the photo was instantly evident.

Their hands were touching, fingers clasped like awkward children.

Linda held the photo beneath the lamp, studying Keefer. His shoulders hunched in a baggy black jacket, his thin lips smiling, Joey stared hollowly at the camera. He looked pathetic. Beside him, Maria stood perfectly still, her slender face held high. So strong. Strong and willful, and beautiful.

Linda dug out the copy of the obituary: a pro forma job, skeletal, probably written by a bored rewrite man.

Mexico City (AP)—Former State Senator Joseph T. Keefer, 58, who briefly led a statewide probe of subversives in the film in-

dustry in the 1950s collapsed and died today while on vacation. Police listed the cause of death as an apparent heart attack.

In recent years Mr. Keefer, who was the son of Merton Keefer, the late Senate Majority Leader, had worked as an aide to Marcus Lynn, the chief executive officer of Transcon Corporation and a prominent Los Angeles lawyer and businessman. Mr. Keefer's sister, Mrs. Celia Fitzgerald, is the wife of New York Democratic Senator David Fitzgerald . . .

Gregory had included a copy of another AP story, a six-paragraph story with a Sarasota, Florida, dateline about Keefer's funeral. Linda scanned the story, then returned to the photo. Here were Joe Keefer and Maria, flesh and blood, figures whose clothes, eyes, lips and hands, whose wordless expressions, revealed far more than a wire-service story buried in the Los Angeles *Times*.

Linda switched off the light after leaving a wake-up call for 5 A.M. The hotel had booked her on the flight to Monterey, arranged a rental car at the airport, reserved one night at the Pine Inn in Carmel.

Just as sleep was about to envelop her, Linda bolted up with a start. Turning on the light, she lifted the two stapled sheets off the floor, her eyes examining the last paragraph of the obituary, words that had seemed so ordinary that their impact had eluded her only moments before.

Among those attending the funeral were Senator and Mrs. Fitzgerald, Marcus Lynn, the Los Angeles businessman, and Mr. Lynn's daughter, Maria, an actress.

Linda stared again at the glossy print.

Bits and pieces, Barry. Evidence trickling in. Holding hands they were, Maria and Keefer. She went to his funeral. Why? She returned to Mexico City, then visited her mother in Zihuatanejo. Then flew to L.A. and . . . placed a pillow over her infant's crying face.

What happened in Mexico City? Who did Maria see? What had her mother said?

*

Now, stepping to the newsstand, Linda Fentress caught sight of a row of chocolate boxes, cellophane-wrapped with pink and blue ribbons.

Maria's grandmother always brought her chocolates.

She bought a box and settled it carefully in her shoulder bag, bought orange juice, two glazed doughnuts and coffee. Returning to her seat in the lounge, she was abruptly aware of a man across the aisle wearing aviator glasses.

Thinning black hair; strong face perfectly tanned; lips slightly bulbous and sensual. The man crossed his legs and shifted in his seat ever so slightly, his eyes beneath the spectacles still fixed on Linda. She thought she saw a faint smile.

Fuck off, honey.

She stared at the eight-column headline.

WHITE HOUSE CONFIRMS BERGEN ILLNESS
PRESIDENT "CARRYING ON" DUTIES
IMPACT FEARED ON CHINA-SOVIET CLASH

Christ! Always the way, isn't it? Bust your ass on a story, bury yourself in it, and who'll give a damn?

She sighed and read the Los Angeles *Times.*

Confirmation of the President's illness, which stunned the capital, followed a copyrighted story in the New York Star *by Washington Bureau Chief Hugh Finch . . .*

Linda bit her lip hard. Son of a bitch *did* it.

She would send Hugh a telegram later in the morning: CONGRATULATIONS BABY STOP OH WHAT A STORY STOP ITS A PULITZER STOP LOVE LINDA FENTRESS.

She looked up, and saw that the man in the aviator glasses was on the phone, his back toward her. He was slimmer than Paul Brock, his shoulders broad and muscled like a football player.

Frowning, she turned the page to pick up the lead story on A12, but the picture on A13 stopped her: a photograph of Jerry Paley. Her mouth opened in astonishment at the headline.

SENATE AIDE FOUND DEAD
EX-N.Y. *STAR* NEWSMAN

For a moment Linda felt sick. She started to sway, her eyes fixed on the third paragraph.

It was the second tragedy within a week to strike the office of Senator Fitzgerald, a potential presidential candidate in next

*year's election. On Sunday, Cheryl Thomas, a former receptionist
in the senator's office, was shot and killed by an unknown assail-
ant in her apartment in northwest Washington. Police declined to
speculate on the cause of death, and said they doubted there was
any link between Miss Thomas' murder and Mr. Paley's apparent
suicide.*

As Linda rose shakily, she saw the man in the glasses glance
up.

She went to a phone. Jerry's number at home came back to her
with a clarity that astonished her. She had not dialed his home
number in eighteen months, perhaps two years.

Linda felt the raw grief knot her stomach as she whispered her
telephone credit card number to the operator. The line was busy.
Stay calm, stay *calm*. She tried once more.

Dear God, let it ring.

Maggie Paley picked it up on the second ring.

"It's Linda Fentress, Mrs. Paley. I am so horrified."

"What do you want?" Maggie Paley said coldly.

"I'm so sorry," Linda whispered. She swallowed hard. All right,
she had slept with Jerry years ago. But the brief affair had evolved
into a closeness, a friendship that had enveloped Mike Paley too,
when he returned home from Vietnam. Like Linda's brother,
Blaine, buried in Columbus, Georgia, Mike was a victim of the
war.

"Why did he do it?"

"Ask Barry Cohen," said Maggie Paley. "Ask Bishop—Howie
Bishop. Your colleagues. Ask Dave Fitzgerald."

"Is Mike there?"

"Mike's gone. Been trying to reach you."

"*Me?*"

"He's going to New York. Says he has something for you,
Linda. Something . . . Jerry left for him to give to you."

"I'm in California," Linda whispered. "Carmel. Staying at the
Pine Inn. P-I-N-E. Tell Mike to call me there."

"If I speak to him," said Maggie. "Good-bye."

A crowd was gathering at the departure gate. Linda quickly
phoned the city desk; Nick Simons answered.

"Nick, it's Linda. I'm expecting an important call from Mike

Paley. Jerry's son. Tell him to call me at the Pine Inn. If I'm not there, leave a message. It's *important!*"

Linda asked for Barry, who picked up the phone immediately. She wanted to talk about Jerry Paley, but instead closed her eyes and whispered: "When's the vote, Barry?"

She had no idea why she asked the question except to move onto a neutral landscape. Jerry was dead. Barry and Howie had killed him. Linda thought she heard Barry say three o'clock.

"What happened to Jerry?"

Barry was saying, Jesus, you do a thousand stories and no one kills himself over it.

Jerry, you're gonna be unhappy leaving the Star. *You bitch and moan, but you're gonna be miserable leaving the business* . . .

Listen, honey, I got a son who's permanently disabled, walking wounded, and I got Angela, little Angela. That costs money, and I want to give her the best, nothing but . . .

Linda heard the final call of Flight 450 to Monterey. Suddenly she hated Barry. She wanted to hang up the phone, board the flight to Monterey, meet Maria, complete the story, return to New York and just quit. Leave the *Star.* Come out here to Los Angeles, maybe Denver. Atlanta.

Barry was talking about the follow-up in tonight's paper. Good, decent story, Linda. We got Marty Kaplan working on a feature about Jerry, the kind of special guy he was, the tragedy.

Linda tasted the tears on her mouth.

"I've scheduled your story tonight," he said.

"Don't," she said.

Barry coughed.

"I don't have the story, Barry. Don't push me."

"There's a porno film, right?"

"That's not the story."

"Don't tell *me* what's the story. Nelson made a porno film . . ."

"There's *more,* Barry." Linda spoke in a gasp. "Answer a question. Tell me about Jerry Paley. AP story in the L.A. *Times* says that the Justice Department was investigating Jerry at Fitzgerald's request. Quotes Senate sources. Land deal in Long Island. Payoffs by a company in the Southwest. Company officials and cooperating with . . ."

"Jerry was in trouble," Barry interrupted. "The Long Island deal was only *part* of it."

"The Senate source was Fitzgerald!"

She wanted to laugh at Barry's silence, was about to say goodbye, but for reasons that she could not fully understand, Linda asked one more question.

"What company was it, Barry?"

There was a pause so long that Linda thought the line was disconnected.

Barry finally said, "Something called Argosy. In Dallas."

"Dallas!"

"Heard of them?"

"No," said Linda.

Of course I've heard of them, you silly bastard. Faber's company was paying off Jerry, and now company officials are cooperating with federal authorities. It's a laugh, Barry, a scream. Fitzgerald and Faber gang-banged Jerry, is that it? The fix was in on poor Jerry . . .

Linda said she had to catch a plane, hung up, walked toward the gate. She walked as if in a trance, with an odd lightness.

A man was boarding the plane. Almost immediately she sensed something was wrong, but her mind and body could only absorb one shock at a time. She knew with certainty that the stories were threading together in a way that frightened her.

Jerry Paley and Fitzgerald and Eli . . .

Eli's company nestled in Marcus' Transcon Corp . . .

And the mysterious money men. Morris Trust Ltd. in the Netherlands Antilles. The link that held Transcon and Argosy . . .

And . . . and . . .

Maria!

Chaining, Marcus and Joey Keefer and Fitzgerald and Vice President Nelson . . .

She found her boarding pass in the pocket of her bag and pushed through the gate, the last passenger on the plane.

As she ran, Linda glanced ahead to the open plane door and saw a man boarding.

The same man who had sat across the aisle from her.

Suddenly a revelation struck Linda so forcefully that she stopped short and caught her breath. He had waited at the gate, watching her on the phone, and had stepped on board only when he was sure that she would too.

He was following her.

*

Pat Donlon, the deputy city editor, watched Barry slam down the phone. "Schedule Linda's story," Barry finally said without looking up. "Slug it porno."

Frowning, Donlon started writing with his fine-tipped black pen on a yellow legal-size pad. Later he would type out the city desk story schedule on his video terminal.

Years ago Jonathan Steiner had tapped Pat Donlon, a former political reporter, as a possible city editor on the *Star*. But an early bout with alcoholism, coupled with a certain diffidence that was misinterpreted as a lack of toughness, had crushed his prospects. Now he was a permanent second man—spotting wire-service stories that had to be covered, assigning reporters, insuring that Barry offered to the managing editor a full package of stories each day.

The phone rang and Nick Simons picked it up.

"Slug it 'exclusive,' " said Barry to Pat. "Let's say, 'Investigation uncovers link between Vice President and early porno films.' " Barry examined the palm of his right hand. "Add another sentence. Say 'FBI and Justice Department stepping into probe!' "

Nick Simons said, "It's *Time* magazine. Gal named Cheever."

Pat Donlon compressed his lips. "*Have* they stepped into the probe, Barry?"

Barry lit a cigarette. "Call the Washington bureau, Pat. Tell them I want Justice and FBI reaction to Linda's story."

Barry caught Pat Donlon's stare. He knew Pat had been a friend of Jerry's; Pat's cold, wordless disapproval of the city editor was evident, always, in his narrow-eyed gaze, the faint twitch on his chin.

"Give the story some muscle, Pat."

"Maybe we're hyping it."

Nick Simons leaned forward. "Cheever's doing a story about, ah, Jerry's death."

Barry opened his mouth but, on second thought, shook his head. "I'll call her later."

Nick's eyes met Barry's. "She also hears rumors that you got the job."

"That's all they are," said Barry, suddenly annoyed. *"Rumors."*
His gaze returned to Pat Donlon, who was rolling out a sheet of
paper from his typewriter. "If they're not investigating the story,
they *should* be, right, Pat? We're *helping* the fuckers. Calling
them. Getting reaction. They say they'll investigate what *we're* investigating. And we got a front-page story. The FBI and Justice
are investigating . . ."

Pat Donlon tossed the paper on Barry's desk, turning away as
he did so. Angry at the gesture, Barry blindly read the note.

"TO THE STAFF. BECAUSE OF THE POSSIBLE STRIKE AT MIDNIGHT
TONIGHT, EARLY SUMMARIES AND EARLY COPY ARE MANDATORY."

Barry signed the paper and lobbed it to Nick, asking him to
post it on the bulletin board. Nick read the note as he pushed
back his chair.

"Lazzarutti and Watson and Faber are meeting on the tenth
floor now," said Nick. "Just saw Big Mama go upstairs a minute
ago."

Barry watched Nick thread his way toward the bulletin board.
"Just promoted him."

Pat nodded. "Nick's got a future in journalism." His voice was
flat and dry.

"Are we gonna have a strike, Pat?"

Pat Donlon shrugged, still avoiding Barry's gaze. "Drivers are
supporting the Guild. A switch. Interesting . . ." Pat Donlon
scowled at his yellow pad, speaking softly.

"We got City Hall covered. The courts. Kaiserman's filing on a
killing in Yorkville. Tailor on Eighty-seventh Street shot by some
kids."

Pat turned to him, swallowing hard. "Congratulations, Barry."

Barry stared into Pat's blank eyes. "Vote's not until later."

"Congratulations anyway," said Pat, lifting the pad. He
coughed. "Follow-up on the killing in Washington? Cheryl . . ."

"Get the bureau to handle it."

Pat nodded. "Another overnight story. Some fires in the South
Bronx."

Nick returned as Pat spoke, picking up the final four words.
The phone was ringing. Nick laughed. "Get Kaiserman!"

Even Pat Donlon smiled as he lifted the phone. "After interviewing kings and prime ministers . . ."

"Use rewrite," said Barry.

Nick Simons cleared his throat and leaned across the desk. "There's a rumor . . ."

Nick's rumors were surprisingly accurate, largely because the source obviously was his bedmate, Lois Malamud, who worked in Skipper's office.

"Sally's quit," said Nick.

Barry heard Ray Silver, on the foreign desk, speaking excitedly over the phone. "Speech *tomorrow* night?"

"Even better rumor," Nick said, pressing his face forward and glancing to his left. Pat Donlon was busy on the phone.

"Skipper's quit."

Barry felt his chest go shallow. Each step closer to triumph seemed slippery. Victory loomed, yet events somehow teased him.

Stay *calm!*

Barry dialed his apartment, listening to the two rings before the click.

"Margie, honey, meet me at Fritzi's at one. Want to celebrate something. Don't ask me now. Just *be* there."

It was a command, she accepted.

Barry slammed the phone down, suddenly angered at himself for his almost willful plunge into self-doubt. The job was *his.* Natural to be uneasy, even a little paranoid, as the vote neared.

A torrent of voices reached Barry's ears. Peter Fosdick, on the national desk, was shouting to the picture desk that Dr. Pomerance, whom *Star* reporters had staked out, had just left his apartment building and stepped into a government limousine, apparently en route to LaGuardia.

At the foreign desk Ward Parsons was yelling into the phone, Ray Silver and Florence and Tony Lazzarutti watching him.

"Ernie, I can't hear you, the line keeps cracking. Speak slow. Belling has . . . what? He's offered to take you to Peking? His plane! Just you and AP and the guy from the *Times. Jump* at it. What? Your kid in Paris. Oh Jesus! I said, *Oh Jesus!* Well, look, Ernie, you gotta. Yeah, you gotta cancel the kid. Cancel the kid's trip. Delay it. Sorry, but look, yeah. I know. I know, I *know* but you gotta. I am really sorry, but . . ."

Barry struggled to smile. There were shouts across the newsroom, phones ringing, even a peal of laughter from the mail desk. The sullen mood that veiled the room because of Jerry's death had abruptly burst, and the aisles flowed with reporters and editors and clerks moving through the aisles.

Barry glanced up, saw Pat Donlon's chalk-white face as he dropped the phone.

"What's wrong?" Barry asked.

"That was Howie Bishop," Pat Donlon whispered. "The police just charged Mrs. Fitzgerald with the murder of Cheryl Thomas."

Ward noticed at once that a crowd was gathering at the bulletin board beside the mail desk. He glanced at Ray Silver, then Florence.

"Too early to announce," said Ray. "They're supposed to meet at three."

Florence bit her lip. "Maybe it's Maury. Something's happened. He's . . ."

"Spoke to him ten minutes ago," said Ward.

He leaned over to Tony Lazzarutti, who was setting the overnight messages in a single pile, and asked him to go check.

"Like Chinese wall posters," said Ward, keeping his eyes fixed on Florence. "You look . . . different."

"Same old me."

"It's the hair. The curls."

"The hair and the makeup. New dress too." She smiled reluctantly. "You like it?"

"You're beautiful," he said quietly.

"Beautiful I'm not. Pretty, yes. Hairdresser says I look ten years younger. I think I look like an Irish Barbra Streisand." She turned away. "We can't work together, Ward."

"No."

"Barry's got the job. That's the rumor."

"I've been a bastard." He saw the glitter of tears in her eyes.

"It's my fault, honey," said Florence. "It's the pattern. That's what the shrink likes to say. The pattern of my life. Relationships bound to go nowhere." She laughed. "For a son of a bitch, you're okay, Ward."

Ray Silver spoke even before he hung up the phone. "President's going on the air tomorrow night. White House calls it a major speech."

"*Fuck!*" said Ward. "We'll miss it if there's a strike."

Florence began, "Maybe there won't . . ."

"There's *going* to be a strike and we're going to miss covering the speech. Miss the speech *we* brought on. The President is reacting to *our* story, not a story in the *Times* or the Washington *Post.* Reacting to *us,* and *we're* missing it. It hurts."

"Like sex without a climax," said Florence.

Tony stood beside the desk. "Two-line announcement. 'Mrs. Frieda Steiner is temporarily assuming control of the *Star* until further notice. All news decisions are to be handled by Mrs. Steiner's office.' "

"Jesus," said Ray Silver, slumping in his swivel chair.

Betty Kennedy joined them, agitated. "The word on the strike is *bad.*"

Betty was a bulky black woman in her forties with russet skin and slanted coal eyes that lent a touch of drama to her face, now crowned by a sedate Afro. Although night news editor of the *Star,* she demanded, and won, the right to serve as deputy chairman of the Guild under Frank Lazzarutti, a concession reluctantly accepted by Skipper.

"Eli's playing hardball," said Betty, shaking her head. "The bastard *wants* a strike. No concessions. Says every department's gotta cut back 10 percent. Refuses to budge. Strike starts at midnight. Period. Where's Skipper?"

They stared at her.

"Didn't you see the bulletin board?" asked Ward. Barry Cohen and Peter Fosdick walked up.

"Mommie dearest has taken over," Florence said.

"Jesus," said Betty.

"We've got one more paper," Ward said firmly.

"But we'll miss Bergen's speech," Betty said. "It breaks my heart."

Florence reached for the ringing phone. "Maybe there's an early draft, a text we could steal." She spoke with a shrug, lifting the phone.

Ward stared at her. "Text," he whispered. His eyes met Barry's.

"It's Hugh on the line," Florence said.

"*We gotta get that text,*" said Barry. "He *must* have an early draft."

Ward turned to them, placing the palm of his right hand over the receiver. "He's at LaGuardia. Going back to Washington. Just saw Maury."

Barry, Peter Fosdick and Betty fell silent and watched Ward, who spoke excitedly.

"Hey . . . don't worry about that, Hugh. We got *another* paper, tonight. Forget it. It happens. What? Don't thank me. It was Barry's idea. Yeah. Barry the bastard. *Forget it.* Hey, look. Listen! The President's making a speech tomorrow night. He's reacting to *your* story. We're sure as hell going to miss it if we have a strike. We *need* an early copy of that text."

Peter Fosdick shrugged. "Unheard of."

"We'd beat every paper in the country," said Betty Kennedy.

"Who can we reach at the White House?" said Ward to Hugh.

Telephones were ringing across the newsroom. Over the loudspeaker, Nick Simons announced: "Early copy, *please*. A reminder."

"Not a bad *idea*." He looked up at his colleagues and mouthed the words, *Barney Fischer*.

Ward set the phone down. "Our White House correspondent."

"God's gift to women," said Florence, grinning.

"Banging the First Lady's press secretary," said Barry. "*And* social secretary."

"It's the blond hair and the pipe," said Florence.

Ward said, "If Barney Fischer has to steal or grovel or fuck his way to that speech . . ."

"We'll need a good political story too," said Ward breathlessly. "Who'll take over the Party in the next election. Nelson? Fitzgerald?"

Betty said, "If Belling comes out of this smelling like a rose, don't tell me *he's* not a contender."

"We got a hell of a story on Fitzgerald," said Barry suddenly. They stared at him.

Inexplicably Barry smiled. "His wife is being charged with the murder of that girl."

The stunned two-second pause gave way to a babble of voices until Barry lifted his hand. "Don't have the details," he murmured. "Howie's working on it."

"That knocks out Fitzgerald," said Betty.

"I'm not *sure*," said Barry, his voice strained with an anger that puzzled Ward. "Wait till you see what we got on Tom Nelson."

"Linda's story!" said Betty Kennedy. The phone rang, and Florence lifted it.

"That's a biggie," said Barry. *"That's* dirty stuff. That's a *Pulitzer* for us. The Fitzgerald story may be a one-day wonder. Who knows? Looney wife. Temporary insanity. Fitzgerald gets a good lawyer and plays his cards right and quietly puts the old lady away and he'll get the *sympathy* vote."

"Linda filing today?" asked Ward.

"She'd better," said Barry.

Betty and Fosdick drifted away. A spot of sun caught Barry's hair, and Ward stared at him, suddenly surprised to notice a gentleness and delicacy about Barry's mouth. His lips were a thin line in a strong, tired face.

Ward spoke quietly. "You saved Finch's ass last night."

"We all did, Ward."

"You voted against publishing it the day before. The way I did."

"That was all a century ago," said Barry.

"You changed your mind because you knew Finch was out of the running. *You* had the job." Ward spoke without rancor.

"Nothing's sure. Nothing's ever sure," Barry said. He swallowed and stared at Ward, who was startled at the desolation in his eyes.

"Hey, tonight, after the vote, let's go out, you and me." Barry struggled to smile.

"I . . ."

Florence interrupted. Larry Lake was on hold.

Barry ignored her. "Never liked you, Ward. Always so . . . golden. Things always came easy to guys like you."

Barry stepped close to Ward. "We're gonna have a new paper, Ward. Exciting. Competitive. *Alive.* You'll be part of it. Let's talk tonight."

Ward spoke with difficulty. "Can't, Barry. Like to, but I . . . I'm catching a plane for London." Ward was aware that the people on the desk behind him—Florence and Ray and Tony—had suddenly twisted around in their chairs.

"Kid's sick. Very sick. Got to see my wife."

"Bad time to leave," said Barry. "The strike. The story. You're running with a hell of a story."

Ward nodded. "Always a hell of a story."

Barry suddenly grinned. "I guess that's why I . . . hated you, Ward. Always had class." Barry lifted his head. "I think I respect you, Ward."

"No you don't," Ward said.

*

On the tenth floor, Geraldine Heaney started to lift a cup of tea to her lips, but her hand shook so violently that she set the cup down on the saucer. Despite Skipper's absence this morning—despite the whispers in the elevator, the alarmed calls earlier from the gossiping secretaries in the newsroom—Miss Heaney had sensed that the turbulence ensnaring the newspaper would leave her untouched. Her feelings toward Skipper—however complicated and unrestrained—were cloaked by the primness and stern professionalism that had carried her this far. She would show no grief at Skipper's departure (at least publicly). She would carry on.

It was only when she finally opened the newspaper to the front page, and saw the story of Jerry Paley's suicide, that her knees quite literally buckled. She wept quietly.

Jerry! He was the only reporter she actually knew, except for Sarah. He had made her smile. Years ago, Jerry had told her she reminded him of his younger sister, a nun. The last lunch they'd had together at Fritzi's, he was drinking too much, and had confessed that he was taking his new job in Washington because of the good salary. He had Mike to support now, and little Angela, *little Angela,* and it was a fortune to keep her at home, but worth it, Geraldine, God knows it's worth it.

On the spur of the moment, Jerry had invited her out one Sunday afternoon to the house in Forest Hills to see little Angela before they all moved to Virginia. Oh, the sweetness of the family, Jerry and Maggie, and little Angela. The *love.*

The child's deformities seemed erased by the love they bestowed upon her, a love that amazed Geraldine Heaney. And in the months and years that followed, Geraldine Heaney was repeatedly invited out to Virginia for weekends and holidays with Jerry and Maggie—a respite from work, a respite from her vile aunts and cousins in Queens whom, she knew, snickered about the old maid Geraldine, who was rumored to have squirreled away money and stocks over the years that would certainly go to them.

And one Monday morning, after a Thanksgiving weekend with Jerry and Maggie, Geraldine phoned her lawyer and directed him to change her will from her family to Angela Paley, a child who needed the money.

And because Geraldine Heaney had developed an avocation of buying and selling gas, oil and utility stocks—she had a shrewd knack of buying utility stocks at precisely the right moment, and she had built up a considerable portfolio—Angela Paley would one day emerge a reasonably comfortable woman, a woman without need of charity, whose permanent nursing and medical bills would be paid as a result of a chance invitation that her grandfather, Jerry Paley, had offered to a secretary on the *Star* who reminded him of his sister.

Geraldine Heaney glanced up.

"Good morning, Miss Heaney."

"Good morning, Mrs. Steiner."

"Has my son called?"

Geraldine Heaney avoided Frieda's eyes. "Left a message with the operators. Unreachable. Said he did not want to be interrupted."

"Please call Eli Faber," said Frieda.

Geraldine Heaney said, "He's in negotiations with Mr. Lazzarutti in the conference room."

"*Please* call Eli Faber," said Frieda, her voice tense. "And tell him I would like to see him at once in Skipper's office."

Frieda Steiner walked past the desk, trailing a flow of expensive perfume whose sweet scent charged the air.

Miss Heaney stared down at the six-button pink telephone console on her desk and saw a light flash. Frieda had picked up the phone.

For a moment, Geraldine Heaney was possessed with a yearning to lift the receiver and eavesdrop on Frieda Steiner, but she called Eli Faber instead.

*

Frieda heard the familiar voice of Bethel Washington, a telephone operator at the *Star* for twenty-four years.

"Bethel, dear, I'd like to speak to Johanna at the apartment."

"Yes."

"And then Ward Parsons. And Hugh Finch in Washington.

Then call Bella Verde. Tell Louisa that I'll be coming back tonight." Frieda glanced at her watch. It was ten-forty.

"Mrs. Steiner, all right. And I've made your reservations. One o'clock. La Grenouille. I've told Mrs. Claiborne."

The intercom sounded, and Frieda pressed the switch. "Mr. Faber is coming in," said Geraldine Heaney, just as the door flung open and Eli faced Frieda.

*

On the foreign desk, Ward asked Florence to try to reach Alex Vikas as well as Sally.

"Larry Lake called before. Remember?" Ray Silver said.

Ward draped his sport jacket over his chair. "I didn't ask you about that."

"I noticed," said Ray. "But hold tight to your seat. Surprise. He called and said he changed his mind. He'll go to Belfast for a couple of weeks. As long as we want. Those were the words. 'As long as we want.' "

"Jesus," said Florence. "The Queen just ordered flags at half mast. Larry Lake's leaving London for two weeks."

"What happened?" asked Ward.

Ray said: "He called Aunt Frieda, who said—get this—who *said* that if he's ordered to go to Belfast, he better go there. If it's in the interest of the paper . . ."

"Amazing," Florence said.

Ward watched her dial the phone. "Something's happening," he said. "No one's behaving . . . predictably."

"Including you, dear."

Ward smiled at her. "Decided I had to go to London to see Karen, the kids."

"Admirable," said Florence. "Totally out of character. Wish I could understand you, Ward."

"Me too."

"Do you love her? Still?"

"Maybe."

Utterly pointless to linger with Barry taking over. Get away for a week, flee to London and avoid the embarrassed glances reserved for losers. As an editor he was no longer in the Guild—he would work through a strike—but the absence of a newspaper would make defeat even more painful. No newspaper, no crisis in which to bury his loss. No solace in the foreign desk's tempo. The paper would be stilled. Besides . . .

He had to see Karen. Had to struggle to pick up whatever fragments remained of their marriage.

Florence said, "Vikas' secretary said he's not there, and no answer at Sally's."

"What's with Sally?"

Florence shrugged. "Quit. Don't ask me why."

"The Irish Mafia knows."

She smiled vaguely. "The Irish Mafia has only heard. Something to do with her husband."

"You never liked Sally."

Florence looked at him. "Women like her have it so easy, Ward. Never struggled. Great feminist, of course. Except when it comes to patronizing us little folks."

"You're being unfair."

"Besides, she loves you too."

*

Eli Faber stood at the doorway, smiling.

"Good morning, Frieda. A pleasant surprise. A *very* pleasant surprise."

He kissed her on the cheek. "You look lovely and, as usual, you smell lovely."

"I don't look lovely, Eli. I'm tired. I'm going back to Bella Verde tonight, thank God."

The sun caught Eli's pink face as he sat in the leather chair facing Frieda. Was it her imagination that his lips seemed tight with tension?

"It's not going well, Frieda." He clamped a cigarette into a small gold-and-black holder and lit it. "Not going well at all."

"Lazzarutti's stubborn," she said.

"Insists we rescind our order to cut back," said Eli. "Or *else*."

"Or else," whispered Frieda, her eyes falling on the pale-gray carpet. "And the drivers?"

"Those bastards," said Eli, a bit too loudly. "Two-faced. Obviously, Lazzarutti has cooked up a deal with them."

"Obviously."

"What's the matter, dear?"

Frieda felt the sweat start on her forehead. "Jerry Paley's death has upset me."

"Horrible," said Eli.

"It's our fault. *Our* investigation caused this."

"Who's blaming us?" he asked.

"*I* am."

He leaned forward, glaring at her.

"Frieda, listen to me. It's tragic . . ."

"Eli, he was one of our *own*. And his son. That little girl. Eli . . ."

"It's not our responsibility to worry about the impact of what we print. We have something, we *print* it."

"Everything's gone too fast for me, Eli. Too fast." She stood and walked to the window, gazing outside.

"I'm an old woman and I want the love of my children. They hate me, Eli. They see me in ways that make me . . . despise myself."

Frieda shut her eyes as the sun flecked her face. "I'm old, Eli, *old!* I don't want them relieved to see me die." She chewed her lip. "I went out to Woodlawn Cemetery this morning, Eli. Had to do it, had to make my peace with the family. Kept thinking of Frederic, wanted to *see* Frederic. I saw him, Eli, saw him as he was. Brilliant and cruel and very hard. He sacrificed Dora, resented Jonathan because he wasn't Arnold. He twisted our lives. But Eli . . ." Frieda turned, eyes pleading. "There was a love. Intense, consuming, painful, but Eli, it *was* love. A love for family. A blood love that's . . . *died.*"

"What are you saying?" said Eli.

"I'm saying I want Johanna to be publisher," said Frieda.

"That's impossible."

"Eli, you'll teach her . . ."

"*Impossible!*"

Eli reached over and grabbed the ringing phone. "Miss Heaney, Mrs. Steiner and I are busy now. She'll call Johanna later. And Mrs. Heaney, please hold all the calls."

Frieda spoke through stiffened lips. "You have no *right* to do that."

"Of course I have no right," said Eli smoothly.

"I make the decisions." Her voice was tight.

"Yes, you make the decisions, Frieda. And you will decide at 3 P.M. this afternoon to appoint me publisher." He crushed the cigarette butt in the ashtray. "Sit down."

"I think I'll stand."

"As you please." Eli lit another cigarette, sucking in the flame, his hand shaking ever so slightly.

"I've waited too long, Frieda, *worked* too long. The paper's mine." His eyes widened. *"Mine!"*

Frieda spoke in a voice that, she sensed, was too haughty.

"You seem to forget, Eli, that I'm the major stockholder. I will not . . ."

"You will do what I say."

"How dare you!"

"You will do what I say . . ."

"Or? . . ."

"Or I'll inform Skipper that Arnold Steiner was his father."

Frieda reached blindly for the back of the chair for support.

"You *knew.*"

"I heard it from Frederic," Eli said. "Sit down, Frieda."

She ignored him. "How did Frederic know?"

"Arnold told him."

"And Jonathan?" she whispered.

"Jonathan hated you, Frieda."

"Jonathan knew?"

Frieda took one step, then two, and eased herself into the chair, facing Eli.

"There's no way, no way on earth, that Skipper would believe you," she said.

"Don't be a fool," said Eli. "Think of the humiliation of a court fight. The publicity. Wouldn't some competitors have a field day with that one? Me challenging the Steiners. Challenging Skipper's *right* to run the paper because he's not Jonathan's heir."

Frieda put her hand to her throat. *Why did Arnold tell his father?*

"And even if you had won the battle, my dear, you would have lost the war," Eli was saying. "Look at the cost, Frieda. The human cost. To think all these years your life was a *lie.* How would Skipper take it? Or Lucy? Your grandchildren?" He waited.

"Perhaps you'll have the paper, Frieda, but my dear, oh my dear, you'll have destroyed your family."

"Who else knows?" Frieda gasped.

"No one." He smiled faintly. "Dora knew. Frederic told her. And that woman, that whore he shacked up with."

"Helena Standish."

Frieda heard the sound of fire engines in the distance. She shut her eyes. "You're hateful, Eli."

"Took the secret to their graves."

"All these years I trusted you."

His voice was low and tremulous. "Years and years. All those years. Holding Jonathan's hand, training Skipper. Being court jester and yes-man. *Groveling*. Keeping my mouth shut."

Frieda stood perfectly still.

He stared past her. "Watching them stumble along, watching the *Star* sink when I could have made the paper *rich*."

"Oh Eli." Frieda wanted to laugh at him, but her whole body was shaking. "You would have destroyed the paper, cheapened it. Skipper was right."

Eli's mouth twisted into a smile. "Frieda, you're the smartest one in the family, you've always been the smartest, but you're a fool. You believe all this nonsense about the greatness of the *Star*. Your responsibility. *Tradition*."

His voice gained strength.

"It's a struggling paper in a declining market, a declining industry," Eli said. "We're a fading species. The newspaper! The *Star* isn't great like the *Times*. Not big and fat like the L.A. *Times* or the Washington *Post*. We're just a paper that wants to survive. One of dozens. And it's mine, Frieda, *mine,* and it *will* survive."

"At any cost?" said Frieda.

"Any cost." Eli spoke gently. "You'll be fine, Frieda. Adequate settlement for the family. Skipper will land on his feet. After the strike . . ."

Her eyes flared open. "You *want* a strike!"

"Of course I want a strike. A long, savage strike, like the *Herald Tribune*. A strike that will make it absolutely necessary for you to sell the paper at a surprisingly decent sum to a California conglomerate that will take over and give me total control of the paper. Permanently."

"Lazzarutti played right into your hands. And the drivers go to the highest bidder," she said, turning away.

"After the strike, and after certain changes in management, their leaders will be . . ."

"You'll take care of them. Is that it, Eli?" Her panic had drained away, yielding suddenly to choking anger. "How fortunate, Eli. It all happened too quickly. All came together . . . at *once.*"

Suddenly Eli stood and walked to the window, fixing his eyes on an excursion boat surging northward. He spoke intensely.

"I *want* the *Star,* Frieda."

Frieda wondered why she felt so calm. "Fitzgerald. You and Fitzgerald. Barry Cohen. You all . . . need each other." She frowned and looked down. "Poor Jerry Paley."

Eli turned and caught her glance. "Don't look at me like that, Frieda. It happens all the time. A senator or congressman throws his aide to the wolves. The big boy is shocked, *appalled* at the revelations in the press."

Frieda bit her lip. "Barry's to be your managing editor," she said.

Even before she finished, Frieda heard the heavy single gong echo across the office. She turned and contemplated the hands of the clock. It was eleven-thirty.

Eli spoke impatiently. "City labor mediator is set to arrive any moment. Ira Moskowitz. Mayor is sending him . . ."

Frieda ignored Eli's words. "It's sad."

"What's sad?"

"Barry would have been my choice anyway."

Frieda lifted her eyes to the Degas pencil drawing, examining the smooth flow of leg and arm and outstretched hand of the faceless dancer. She was aware of the ticking of the grandfather clock.

"Our final paper, tonight," she said.

"Quite a paper it is too. Big story from Los Angeles."

"Story by Linda Fentress," said Frieda.

"Shocking story. Sordid. Guaranteed to make life *very* difficult for Tom Nelson."

"It all fits," Frieda whispered. Suddenly she was very tired. "I'm finally starting to understand . . ."

"I think it's a Pulitzer Prize story," he said somberly.

"We're opening the way for Fitzgerald!"

The intercom sounded.

Circling the desk, Eli said: "That must be Ira Moskowitz from City Hall."

He flicked the button, and Frieda heard Geraldine Heaney's high voice.

"Mr. Moskowitz and his aides are here, Mr. Faber."

"Thank you, Miss Heaney," said Eli.

Frieda watched him smile faintly and, just as Eli moved to switch off the intercom, she heard Geraldine Heaney's voice quaver.

"And Mr. Faber, there's an urgent message from Barry Cohen. Please phone him at once in the city room."

Eli's smile lingered, but Frieda saw him stiffen ever so slightly.

"Three o'clock," he said firmly, turning with a frown.

As soon as he shut the door, Frieda slumped in her chair, the fatigue that struck her moments earlier suddenly yielding to a physical sensation that she had never felt before, frightening at first but then remarkably pleasant.

All her energy was draining out of her body. She held her breath, as if to quell the flow, but her strength, her vitality, seeped from every pore in a slow, unyielding tide.

It was the onset of old age, she knew. Surrendering to the natural rhythms of her body, the beginning of death.

CHAPTER 21

He had filled the gasoline tank at the station on Route 50 and now, easing the Chevrolet into the police lot, Mike Paley glanced down at the fatty tumors on his fingers. Take the pills, man, and wear the soft, furry gloves. Hide the ugliness. Hide the impotence. Hide the skin blotches on the chest and crotch and back and legs that itch *so bad,* so bad you want to die.

Die.

Like Dad.

He had to flee Mom's house, come to headquarters, flee from Maggie's stunned eyes, from the relatives and neighbors that descended on them, oh Lord, oh Mother of God, why did Jerry do it? Watching Mike, waiting for him to . . . crack in front of them. Wouldn't that be a scene, something to talk about, just unravel in front of them because he was sick and crazy anyway, sick since Vietnam, sick since he got sprayed.

Shit, man, got to deprive the VC of cover, got to root out the fuckers, got to defoliate, wash the jungles and forests with Agent Orange, pleasant little name, containing 2, 4, 5-T, which creates a poisonous byproduct 2, 3, 7, 8 tetrachlorodibenzo-p-dioxin—dioxin for short, perhaps, the most toxic synthetic chemical known, dioxin, shit we never even used masks, we drank the bitter water . . .

Sick since he got sprayed and had the little girl, little Angela, his fault, his sick sperm, flooded with poison, creating this . . . child.

Maggie had phoned him in the middle of the night, Arlington police already there. Dad's dead, locked himself in the garage and started the car. Dad's *dead*. She was breathless, whispering that he had left an envelope for you, Mike, something to be given to Linda Fentress, an envelope Maggie would hide from the police. Please come here, Mike. And suddenly Maggie was groaning that he was murdered, murdered by Barry Cohen and Howie Bishop. *Murdered!*

Calm. Remain calm. Walk into the station. Tell his buddy at the desk that he had to complete the detailed catalogue of the weapons haul on King Street. Spades and radicals stockpiling arms for the revolution.

Sign out the key to the lock-up room.

Accept condolences from the captain.

Wouldn't be working several days, sir, want to finish up the job before Dad's burial and take care of some personal matters. Just got a few more weapons to list. Jesus, sir, they had some classy weapons, the kind the I.R.A. uses in the old country . . .

Captain knows he's a little touched in the head, anyway, victim of that fucking war.

He knew the gun he wanted: the snub-nosed PPK Walther.

*

Sally stood at the half-open window, eyes fixed on the pale-green terrain of Central Park glistening with the wetness of yesterday's rain.

It was the first day of spring weather, that moment when the park wrests itself free from winter, when grayness lifts and yields to the softening shades of green and taupe and gold. Sally smiled faintly and examined the outline of the orchestra shell, and the balustrade steps leading to the brick terrace circling the Bethesda Fountain. She shut her eyes and waited for the ringing of the phone to stop.

The bedroom's scent was unfamiliar, a faintly doughy smell braced with the sharp tang of furniture polish. Was it her imagination that she caught the odor of soap, harsh and purging, over the stench of vomit? Her dry lips tightened, and she swallowed hard.

So much to do in the next few hours. Pack up. Take money out of the bank. Phone Rose Tyler. A farewell drink with Dorothy Faye, who would insist on accompanying her to Kennedy Airport. But, no, Sally wanted to depart alone.

Suddenly she was seized with fear. She was embarking on a journey that alarmed her, leaving this newspaper that she adored, this city that had nurtured her. Leaving Skipper.

Charlie!

She turned and stared blankly at the pristine linens perfectly set on the double bed, the hansom wall lamps and rattan furniture drenched in sun.

Once more the phone began ringing.

*

Ward Parsons watched Florence slip the telephone onto the hook. "No answer," she murmured.

"Where else can we try?"

"Nowhere else." Florence tasted her coffee. "Dorothy said if we can't reach her now at the Dakota, we won't be able to find her. Sally's *out*."

The telephone rang on the desk, and Ray Silver pressed the flickering extension button. Ward turned to Florence. "You busy for lunch?"

She examined the freshly painted pink fingernails on her right hand. "As a matter of fact, Burt Reynolds just canceled."

Ray Silver interrupted. "It's Ernie Richards. Just arrived in Peking."

Ward leaned toward Florence. "We're on."

"Wants to talk to you, Ward," Silver said. "Says Belling told them on the phone that the Russians just accepted a seventy-two-hour cease-fire. Prepared to go to Camp David."

Ward whispered to Florence before lifting the phone. "Call Alex Vikas."

"We've left three messages."

"Leave a fourth."

As Florence leafed through the Rolodex for Alex Vikas' phone number at the CIA, she caught sight of Barry Cohen locked in conversation at an empty rewrite desk, with Eli Faber seated beside him. She began dialing the WATS line to Washington, fully certain that Alex Vikas' secretary would say that he wasn't there. But Florence abruptly set the phone down. Her eyes glittered.

"Ray, can you join us for lunch?"

Ray Silver looked up, puzzled.

"Gonna be my farewell lunch." Florence said it loud enough for Ward to hear. He squinted at Florence, telling Ernie Richards over the phone to wait. Facing Florence, Ward said, peeved, "What the *hell* . . ."

"Got a new job, dear. Cable TV. Wave of the future." She tried to laugh. "Didn't want to tell you. Childish of me. Planning to write you a note while you were in London. Nice and neat. No scenes! Just a little thank you and farewell ha-ha letter. But then superstar Sally Sims has to flake out, so instead of taking her to lunch, you take me. And I realize how can I *not* tell you. So . . ." She turned to Ray Silver. "Join us, Ray. *Please!*"

*

"Clearly a case of temporary insanity," said Eli Faber, settling back on the swivel chair and crossing his feet on the desk.

"What was she going there for?" asked Barry.

"Wanted Cheryl to kill *her*. Silly bitch." He examined his glistening black wing-tip shoes with a frown.

"And the diary?"

"The diary . . ." Eli nodded. "The diary is where it belongs."

"You *know* what's in the diary?" said Barry, his voice strained.

Eli's tongue found a shard of food nestled between two teeth on the lower-left corner of his mouth. "Don't look at me with those incredulous eyes, Barry. Of course I *know*."

"You wouldn't have run the story."

"What story?" Eli spoke impatiently, fixing his gaze on Sarah Felger, across the newsroom, only the top of her head visible behind mounds of paper. "There's *no* story." He twisted his face to Barry. "*Jerry* was the story. Poor Jerry. The story's over."

Barry said calmly: "No, not Jerry Paley. Smart Justice Department investigators would have found certain discrepancies. The amount of money Cheryl took in and handed over to Jerry." Barry leaned so close to Eli that he saw the narrow shaving cuts on his throat. "And the amount of money that finally landed in Jerry's Swiss account. That's it, right? The disparity? The money that was laundered in Panama and the money that wound up in Switzerland. Paley didn't keep it all, right?"

"Ironic," whispered Eli. "The diary is *safe*."

"Most of the money went to Fitzgerald," said Barry.

Eli ignored him. "You'll inform Howie Bishop to drop his investigation. The story's over."

Barry waited a beat. "And if we don't, Eli?"

"If you don't, you're finished, Barry." Eli held his gaze. "What's come over you, sonny boy? Guilt? Jerry turns on the gas and suddenly you're a responsible newspaperman?" He drew forward. "You know how many guys out here are waiting to move into your place if you drop out? You'll be trampled in the crush. You know how many would do precisely the same thing as you? Make a deal. Cut some corners. Shade the facts. Or *worse*."

Eli loosened his tie knot. "You're Watergate babies. Do anything for a flashy story. Do anything to make it big."

"You're cynical, Eli."

"*You're* the cynical one. Bullshit stories and fake quotes and committed journalism. You know who the innocents are? Sarah Felger out there. Pat Donlon. Workmanlike, solid, accurate, unflashy. They're innocent and doomed, Barry. *Finito!*"

A telephone was ringing at an empty desk beside the aisle. Eli's dark eyes glittered, searching Barry's face. "You made your bargain with us, Barry. You going to keep it? You want the job?"

Barry nodded.

"Then you have your work cut out. Going to be a strike tonight. Best if we had that story tonight from Linda."

"I've told Linda . . ."

"You tell Linda, please to have that story on Tom Nelson."

Eli's eyes wandered over the newsroom. "Get Howie Bishop moving, get him to call Fitzgerald. Dave'll talk to him, on background, of course. Tell Howie what happened. Seems Celia tried suicide several times. Went to Cheryl's apartment and Cheryl refused to kill her. They fought over the gun and, quite accidentally . . ."

Barry leaned forward. "Howie'll want to pursue the diary angle."

Barry watched, fascinated, as the red glow on Eli's neck lifted like a tide to his face.

"I don't think that's wise, Barry," he said calmly. "Cheryl had her diary, and we know she sent a copy of it to Jerry Paley. And they're both dead. I don't think we have to worry about the diary, do we? Do we, Barry?"

Eli was grinning pleasurably, and Barry wondered why, in this moment of strange triumph, he was seized with such intense alarm that his fist touched his chest as if to quell the pounding.

*

At National Airport the noon shuttle to LaGuardia was departing twenty-five minutes late. Seated in 10D, Mike Paley clutched a brown envelope on his knees. He reached beneath his jacket, and his right thumb and forefinger found the metal-reinforced tab, curved to contour with his hip and tucked into his waistband.

As the plane swung into place, Mike felt the comforting coldness of the revolver's alloy frame, the creviced stock, the barrel, the slide stop button, the delicately curled trigger. He closed his eyes and wanted to laugh.

So simple. Hold up the badge and flash the Arlington Police card to the fat dude at the plane's security. Show ID. Sign a paper. Keep steady. Cool. Smile, man, no headaches, no shakes, no Agent Orange shit . . .

Steady and cool.

Slipping into enemy lines armed with a stolen badge and this lovely PPK Walther.

Call Linda first. Got to reach Linda with . . . the diary. Dad's instructions.

Mike's fingers grasped the brown envelope on his lap.

Dear Mike. Give this to Linda Fentress, and only Linda. It's a copy of Cheryl's diary. The only copy. All the money we took in for Dave Fitzgerald. Tell Linda that if the Star *won't touch it, then to pass it on to a newspaper that will do something with it. Give it to her quickly. Love, Dad.*

It was one-fifteen.

He would call Linda from the airport, and then climb into a taxi.

Find Barry.

By three o'clock he would reach the *Star,* and his war would finally end.

*

Ray Silver spoke even before Ward replaced the phone.

"Larry Lake's sources at the Foreign Office say the Chinese are rejecting a cease-fire."

Ward, pointing his chin toward the phone, said with annoyance: "That was Ernie. *He* said Belling was confident of a cease-fire."

Ray Silver leaned close toward Ward. "While you were talking to Ernie, Barney Fischer called."

"Barney Fischer would give his left nut to be Washington bureau chief," said Ward.

"May I finish," said Ray Silver. "Barney said he will try like crazy to get the President's text for the first edition."

"Watch out," said Florence.

"Don't knock the bastard," said Ward. "We *need* the speech."

"Barney's adorable," said Florence. "Sleeps with his sources. Who's giving him the speech? The President's secretary? His mother?"

"That's disgusting," said Ray.

Ward said to Ray: "Belling had a backgrounder on the plane. Told a bunch of reporters that the President's illness finishes Bergen's political career."

Ward, smiling faintly, said: "Belling told them he supports Fitzgerald, but if he—Belling—manages a cease-fire and gets the Russians and Chinese talking at a Camp David summit, if he works out a border agreement, then the dynamics within the Party may change. That's a quote."

"What does that mean?"

"It means Belling wants to run for President."

"Belling," Silver exclaimed.

"Told Ernie off the record, that he, Belling, *can't* support Fitzgerald now, because Dave's a loser! We've elected Presidents with crazy wives, Belling said, but never a wife that's murdered someone."

"Bunch of barracudas," murmured Florence.

Ward saw a rush of activity at the "copypersons" cubicle beside the wireroom. Luisa Rodriguez, one of the new copy girls, emerged through the crowd gripping a sheet of wire-service copy.

"Anything on Vikas?" Ward asked, watching the girl move past the city desk.

"His bitch secretary said he hasn't returned to his office," replied Florence.

"It's a lie," Ward said.

Suddenly Ward was aware that Luisa's eyes were fixed on his face; she was rushing toward the foreign desk.

Tony Lazzarutti leaned forward to glance at the bulletin.

For a moment the newsroom's noise seemed to ebb as reporters and editors looked at Ward.

"Bulletin from Reuters," said Ward, loudly. Barry and Peter Fosdick were stepping toward the foreign desk.

"From Peking," said Ward. "Peking radio just announced that the government has agreed to Belling's request for a seventy-two-hour cease-fire."

"Belling's doing it," said Barry.

"But Larry Lake's sources said the Chinese were rejecting—" began Ray.

Florence interrupted. "Larry Lake hasn't had a reliable source in three years," she said, rolling a sheet of paper in her typewriter.

"You're going to miss us," Ray Silver said, grinning.

*

In his office on the seventh floor of CIA headquarters, Alex Vikas turned in his swivel chair and gazed outdoors at the white-tailed deer and rabbits scampering on the woodlands below. He kept a pair of eight-power binoculars in the center drawer of his desk, and on lunch hours when he ate in the office Vikas often watched the wildlife around the gray-white concrete building nestled in the pine and elm forest in Langley, Virginia.

He heard Miss Tien's four staccato knocks, then listened to the door open.

"Amazing," he whispered, the binoculars pressed to his eyes. "Spotted sandpiper. Distinctive flight."

"What?"

"Distinctive flight. There it goes. Wings flap in a shallow arc." Alex's eyes met Mai's.

Mai Tien, the daughter of a South Vietnamese Army general and a French woman who ran a hair salon on Tu Do, had been his secretary at the American Embassy in Saigon in the late nineteen-sixties, and then followed him to posts in Bangkok, Hong Kong and now Washington. In the process she had married and divorced a State Department officer, and now lived in a house in Springfield with her mother and eight-year-old son.

"He called again," she said.

"Who?"

"Parsons. Very persistent."

Alex watched her glide past him and place the tray of food on the windowsill. He set the binoculars on his desk.

"What's this?"

"Egg salad. Ice tea."

"I don't like egg salad."

"You sound like my little boy. It's healthy, Alex. Keeps you strong and thin. Five pounds. That's an order."

"Come with me. We'll get a suite at the El Presidente."

"You're booked two nights."

"Join me. Make it four."

"What about Parsons?"

"What about him?"

"Keeps calling."

"I'm out of the country."

"You SOB. Don't need him anymore." Mai smiled.

"Come on. Come with me."

"I've got to man the fort, dear. Isn't that the right expression?" She shook her head. "Mr. Parsons will be upset."

"Mr. Parsons will understand. He'll call again. Next month. Next year. We need each other." He grinned. "Like me and you."

"The car will pick you up at three-fifteen," she said, placing a ticket envelope on his desk. "Flight leaves at four-twenty from Dulles. Connecting flight from Atlanta. Gets in at eleven thirty-five."

"We'll have dinner at Delmonico's. There's a terrific little restaurant on San Luis Potosi. Wonderful pâté. Go dancing at the Villa Fontana."

"Official passport and health certificate are with the ticket," said Mai Tien. "Your name, by the way, is Victor Wilhelm."

"You're breaking my heart, Mai."

"And in the trunk of the car"—she paused and stared at him—"in the trunk of the car is a Pan Am carry-on bag with five reels of film. As you requested." She lifted her steno pad. "The film people said, because you were in a hurry and expressed no preference at all, they came up with five extra reels in the lab. Something called *Great Moments in Sports*. Also, the Miss America Pageant of 1977. An FBI film, *Know Your Enemy*. One of our own training movies on underwater demolition, and a television documentary on the Cuban missile crisis."

Alex watched Mai examine her notepad. "The Ambassador has already been informed that you're stopping over on a brief inspection of our facilities in Latin America. Dick Thompson will meet you at the airport."

Twisting in the straight-backed chair, Alex contemplated his luncheon tray with a frown. Mai cleared her throat. "Terry Schachter just called," she said. "That girl's rented a car at Monterey Airport."

Alex Vikas lifted a cigarette from a pack on the sill, and lit a match.

"Fifteen minutes ago Marcus Lynn arrived at L.A. Airport," said Mai. "Got into his private plane. Heading north."

"Monterey," he said dully. Vikas watched the flame flicker before easing the match to the tip of the cigarette.

"Checking the flight controller," she said.

He sucked the cigarette. "Damn!" He spoke so quietly that Mai failed to hear.

"What?" She stepped forward.

"Call Dick Thompson," he said.

"He's at a reception at the Soviet Embassy. Trade union delegation from Cuba."

"Like to speak to him as soon as possible," Alex said.

The phone rang and Mai Tien reached for it. Alex stared disconsolately at the egg salad, opened his lower desk drawer and removed a nut-covered candy bar. Carefully unwrapping the paper, he lifted the candy to his lips.

"You have the salad." He smiled as she set the phone down. "Too healthy for me. Who was that?"

"Terry Schachter," she said.

Alex stared at her.

Mai Tien stepped toward the desk and lifted the tray. "Linda Fentress is booked at a hotel called the Pine Inn."

*

As the bellboy set Linda's valise on the rack beside the brass bed, she glared once more at the telephone message that the receptionist had handed to her, and dialed Sandy Jaffe's number.

He picked up the phone on the second ring.

"You haven't heard this from me," said Sandy. "Quote government sources."

"Promise."

"This friend of mine at the IRS got one of their informers down in St. Martin to check Morris Trust Ltd. . . ."

The fingers of Linda's right hand numbly curled around her pen; she was twisting the notepad open.

Sandy said: "We know that Morris Trust is the major shareholder in Marcus Lynn's company, Transcon. Well, Morris Trust is a dummy company owned by a couple of guys named Dunlap. D-U-N-L-A-P. Ernie and Charles. Real estate types in New York. Connections with the mob. That's all my friend had, but it piqued my interest."

Linda was writing in a fever. Sandy's voice dropped. "So I called a guy I know at Justice. Told him I knew a *Star* reporter who was interested in the Dunlaps. Asked him to check. Turns out this guy knows all about the Dunlaps. And he tells me it's kind of funny—the word he used was 'ironic'—kind of ironic that a *Star* reporter is doing this story. It seems the Dunlaps have some other dummy corporations in the Cayman Islands, Liechtenstein . . ."

Sandy coughed. ". . . They made a couple of offers on the *Star* years ago. And what this guy hears is that they still want the paper."

Linda was leafing through her notebook, straining her eyes on the writing that filled each page.

She found what she wanted in the center of a page.

Transcon's major subsidiary: Argosy Corp. Land developers in Dallas. Controlled by Eli Faber.

Barry! It's weaving together, merging. And, incredibly, it's coming right back to us. Eli Faber working with the Dunlap brothers! Hear me out, Barry. The Dunlaps, money men for Dave Fitzgerald, the bastard's major supporters, control Marcus' company. Eli's buried in there too. The Dunlaps and Eli want to take over the paper. And somehow, in a weird way, Jerry Paley and the girl in the mental hospital and Vice President Tom Nelson and Joey Keefer are tied in to it . . .

Sandy Jaffe said he would call Linda later with more information on the Dunlaps that his friend was gathering. By the time Linda set the phone down she was breathless with excitement.

Glancing at her watch—it was twelve-fifty in New York—Linda dialed the city desk and asked for Barry.

"He's celebrating at Fritzi's," said Nick Simons, his voice giddy. "His soon-to-be promotion."

"Wonderful," said Linda, dryly. Why did she detest this wise-ass kid whose hunger to make the staff seemed so offensive?

Linda's left hand dug into her leather case and lifted out the box of chocolates.

"Any word from Mike Paley?" She examined the pink-and-white wrapping, the purple bow.

"Nothing."

She heard, beyond Nick's voice, the blurred sounds of the newsroom. Telephones, the clatter of typewriters. A ripple of laughter. Christ, she missed it.

After hanging up the phone, Linda held the candy box against her chest. She moved, as if in a trance, dropping the door key and her notepad and pens into her leather case.

Linda's story was reaching a finale.

*

As Nick Simons hung up, the second of five extensions rang on the city desk. It was Howie Bishop.

Nick said: "Barry's been trying to reach you. Urgent."

"Like I'm at the arraignment of Mrs. Fitzgerald. What's urgent?"

At the opposite side of the desk, Pat Donlon pushed back his chair and stood up to leave as Ray Silver and Mark Kaiserman approached. "Going to Fritzi's," Pat mouthed. The lunchtime exodus.

Nick said, "Barry left a message."

"How does the strike look?"

"Gloom and doom. Everyone's out drinking lunch."

"And Barry's prospects?"

"He's pissing champagne. Celebrating right now with his . . . ah . . . lady friend. Here's the message. 'Forget the diary!' That's the whole message. 'Forget the diary!' "

Nick saw Ward Parsons and Florence thread through the city room. Over the phone, Howie's voice was edged with anger.

"Forget the *diary?*" Howie said. "Is Donlon there?"

"Out to lunch. Even Pat went out to get plastered." Nick waited. "You just have me to kick around. Tricky Nickie." His laugh was cut short by Howie.

"Where's Barry? At Fritzi's?"

"No."

Nick stiffened in amazement at his sudden lie, the words blurting from his lips.

He heard Howie murmur something about calling back later, but Nick listened vaguely, feeling his stomach knot. Yes, he resented Howie, hated the bastard for his success, yearned to be chief investigative reporter someday. But no reason to *lie* to Howie, a petty lie, difficult to understand.

Nick stared at the sheet of paper beside the phone.

Forget the diary.

He began to crumple the paper. What diary?

He crushed the sheet in his palm and flung the ball of paper into the far wastebasket, a perfect shot. Then Nick shrugged and lit a cigarette.

His euphoria since Barry had informed him yesterday of his promotion to reporter, had given way to a strange sense of foreboding. Instead of excitement, Nick was seized with nervous, almost angry, impatience. Officially, Nick would start his job in a week, once he trained a replacement. But a strike loomed, and the newspaper was in turmoil.

Even beyond this, Nick knew that the struggle had just begun; he had finally moved onto the track, but look at the reporters already loping ahead of him. He was just another young reporter, hungry for a front-page story, scavenging for that byline.

What diary?

*

In the last week Lucy Steiner Claiborne had grown accustomed to the surprisingly genuine outpouring of sympathy offered by relative strangers, and now, entering La Grenouille, she smiled as Madame approached.

Lucy knew precisely what to expect as soon as she saw the familiar signs: the widened eyes, the slumped shoulders, the slight tilt of the head.

"My deepest condolences, Mrs. Claiborne."

Lucy nodded. The room's broad mirrors shimmered, the pale, pea-green walls with their familiar oils were pleasantly aglow as sun streamed through the entrance curtains. Roses and jonquils and anemones and tiny white chrysanthemums seemed to flow over the room, with a scent Lucy found bracing.

As if to ease the sorrow, Madame escorted Lucy to the choice second table to the left, usually reserved for prestigious fashion designers, movie stars and socialites. It was a gesture that pleased and amused Lucy, who had told Johanna only an hour earlier that the less she cared about the right table, the more she was offered one. The less she cared about the most chic party, the latest restaurant, the newest designer, the more she threatened and confused people, as if in the very act of *not* caring, of extricating herself, Lucy had finally turned into that elusive woman whom she had struggled to create in vain all those years.

She ordered Perrier and, as the waiter slipped away, glanced at her watch. Unusual for Frieda to be late. Then Lucy was aware, quite suddenly, of a hunger that was intense and pleasurable, the first genuine craving for food in months. Perhaps it was the redolent scent of garlic and melted butter softened by the sweetness of flowers. More likely, it was her sense of triumph; she had decided,

finally, to confront Johanna at the family apartment. It was a decision made abruptly at eight-ten while Lucy completed her third-
lap jogging around the Central Park reservoir.

Either sever the relationship entirely or start anew. There was
simply no more time for guilt or conflict in her life. There was no
point, ever again, in lavishing friendship and understanding and
love, even on a daughter, without a modicum of respect in return.

By nine-thirty, Lucy Steiner Claiborne had been seated in the
leather sofa in the living room, staring at her daughter, telling her
of Skipper's decision to quit and Frieda's move to place control
of the *Star* in Eli's hands.

*I wanted you to take over the paper, Johanna. The paper
should be* yours.

Lucy saw her daughter's face turn white.

*We've got to endure Frieda's tragic mistake, Johanna. Yes,
tragic. She'll live to regret it. I'm sure of that. In the meantime,
you're the heir, Johanna, the future, and so long as Eli keeps the
Star on a steady course, so long as he and Frieda don't do anything shocking . . .*

Shocking?

Like sell to a conglomerate . . .

I can't believe that, Mother.

*Skipper is alarmed about the possibilities. He's heard rumors.
We may have to go to court. Skipper and I may have to go to
court to fight Frieda. A public court battle that would wreck the
family . . .*

Lucy had whispered, *I want you to understand, Johanna. Understand my rage at you. I've refused to pity myself through the
ordeal with your father. If I pitied myself, as you wanted me to, I
would have absorbed all the guilt that you flung at me. But I'm
strong, Johanna, stronger than I ever imagined. Perhaps it's the
Steiner blood. I refused to pity myself, and because of that and
because of motives difficult to understand, I stumbled into an
affair with Dave Fitzgerald. I regret it. And if you want to judge
me in a simple, self-righteous way, so be it. If you want to ignore
your own father's affairs—and they were humiliating, dear, humiliating and quite public—if you want to scorn me and my style of
life, if you choose to remain aloof from the family yet live in chic*

student poverty with your quite substantial income from the Steiner trust, then you're an unpleasant hypocrite.

She finally met Johanna's wide hazel eyes, and saw the pink glow flush her cheeks. *It's too late for me to reconstruct my life, Johanna. I was the wealthy wife of a talented and famous man. I wasn't raised to be a brain surgeon or a physicist. I had limited boundaries, and I think it's rather cruel for you or anyone else to scorn me. In a sense, my dear, it says more about you than me.*

Lucy's eyes locked on her daughter's face. *I have my home and a few close friends. I'm thinking, just thinking, of learning much more about art. It's the one thing we Steiners care about. Going back to school. Seeing if I have the confidence to study and take exams and . . . compete. I don't have much confidence at all, Johanna. Who knows? Someday, if I work hard enough, if I take myself seriously, I may end up in the* Star's *art news department.*

Johanna whispered, *I loved Daddy.*

Lucy grasped her daughter's cold hands. *You blamed his death on me. You had to! Otherwise his cruelty and insanity made your love meaningless.*

You've judged me unkindly, Mother. You always have. How could I live up to you and Frieda. Your beauty and Frieda's strength.

The eyes of mother and daughter met.

We've got to start again, Johanna, without judgment. Without judgment on my part or yours. Either start again or remove ourselves from each other's lives. Oh Johanna, I'm willing to start. Are you?

Johanna tightened her fingers in Lucy's firm grasp and leaned forward, her lips compressed. *Can I join you at the vote this afternoon, Mother?*

*

From her restaurant table, Lucy saw a rustle of activity at the bar as Madame glided past with a woman that Lucy recognized as Charlotte Garrison Dunlap. It was only then that Lucy caught the profiles of two men at the bar: Ernie Dunlap and his son Mark, whose photograph had appeared in the morning's *Daily News* as a potential candidate for Congress. They were laughing. Lucy steepled her fingers, watching Charlotte tilt her long, narrow face, her ash-blond hair upswept in a delicate crown, and kiss her husband on the lips with a soft smack, mouthing the word "Congratulations."

Lucy watched, fascinated, as Madame, picking up their exuberant mood, grinned and escorted the three of them from the bar to the center of the restaurant, out of sight.

It would have spoiled Frieda's lunch to sit near the Dunlaps. They were never to be trusted, Ernie and Charles. They detest us, dear. Bad blood between us.

Lucy glanced at her watch. One-fifteen. She felt a vein pulse at the side of her neck, a gentle skip of the heart. She looked up, a bit dazed, as Madame escorted an elderly woman into the restaurant.

The woman moved with difficulty, almost a shuffle, her shoulders stooped, her hair slightly strewn by the wind.

Lucy stared intently at the row of double pearls draped over her velvet-trimmed black jacket and, as Madame neared, chatting with the woman, Lucy turned with a smile to the empty banquette beside her.

It took five seconds. Lucy looked up and her smile froze. She heard the tinkle of laughter. The woman was within three feet of the table when Lucy's mouth twisted open. She tried to say the accustomed word, but the sight of this desolate figure choked her speech.

Finally Lucy leaned forward.

"Mother," she whispered.

*

Before Linda Fentress reached the crossing of Wildcat Creek and Highway 1, the sun dipped behind the clouds on the coastal range. Rain spat on the windshield.

She pressed her foot on the accelerator, thrusting the car into low gear as the road climbed steeply into hills that rose and fell away, the cypresses on either side worn pale by spray and wind, the redwoods towering beyond, drifting in fog.

From the rearview mirror, Linda caught sight of the carved vista of coast, the waves crashing beneath flocks of seabirds perched silent on crags.

She was strangely calm.

This is where the story ends, Barry, on a fog-draped canyon overlooking the Pacific.

High up on a slope of the hill, fringed with young redwoods, Linda saw a white building glisten and stand oddly isolated before a moss-draped pine forest. She slowed the car, but suddenly a carpet of fog blocked her vision, casting darkness over the entire canyon. Startled, Linda fumbled for the light switch. Ahead the road twisted around the mouth of a creek, and at a sudden fork Linda saw the hand-painted sign with its directional arrow pointing to the right: ROSE HAVEN.

Linda felt the flush rise in her face. She had phoned Gregory just before leaving Carmel. Yes, he had called Rose Haven and given a terrific performance imitating Marcus Lynn's slow, nasal drawl. A friend of my daughter will be arriving today to see her, he had said, all the way from New York.

She drove on.

You'll get the story, Barry; you'll get the story and nail Tom Nelson, nail the son of a bitch the way you nailed Jerry Paley. You'll get the job, and I'll get the byline, and that's what it's all about.

She pressed her foot down hard on the accelerator, the headlights casting zigzag streaks on the eerily bleached wildflowers nestling beside the road. A lush fragrance, grape and wild currant, filled the air, and, swerving the car, Linda saw a wedge of pale-blue sky that suddenly opened before her.

She was out of the forest, climbing over a narrow concrete road. At a dip in the road, less than thirty yards to her left, she saw Rose Haven. It was a low, three-story structure whose white stucco walls were banked with windows and cantilevered balconies. Nestled firmly between two flat crests, like the base of a triangle, the building was entered by a wooden platform that served as a footbridge to the second floor.

The windows were screened and, on the second floor facing the road, they were covered with bars.

*

"Something wrong, Mother? You don't look well."

"Don't feel well. What time is it?"

"One thirty-five."

"I'm so tired. I just want to finish the vote and go back to Bella Verde."

"I saw Johanna this morning."

"I want to stay in bed for a while. Sleep."

"She'll be at the vote."

"What?"

"Johanna will be at the vote. She's looking for an apartment in New York."

"No!"

"Mother!"

"No! No! Please! Johanna will *not* be at the vote. Tell her to go back. Go back to Cambridge. Find a life there. Don't look at me like that, Lucy. It's all over, dear. Barry Cohen is the managing editor. *Please* don't look at me like that."

*

"My name is Eva Kaiser," said the doctor behind the reception desk. Her eyes settled on a point somewhere beyond Linda's shoulder. "I am the associate director of Rose Haven. Maria will see you shortly. I should warn you, Miss Fentress, that Maria receives very few visitors. She has made progress at Rose Haven, but she's still *quite . . .* ill."

Linda detected an unpleasant defiance in Eva Kaiser's voice, the trace of a European accent, probably German or Austrian. The doctor's tiny slash of mouth, with protruding lower lip, her pug nose and slender ears seemed to shrink into a fleshy face whose slanted violet eyes—the only interesting feature to this woman—burned with suspicion. Dr. Kaiser's uniform was tight, bulging over her body.

Linda took a step back, suddenly aware of her own khaki linen blazer, white shirt covered with a string of chest-length amethyst-colored beads, and brown linen pants.

"You'll have to give me your necklace, Miss Fentress. Necklaces can be pulled off. So can earrings. We don't wear anything provocative, but some of our patients get abusive. If a patient comes up and says he wants to kill you, please don't take this lightly. Inform us at once."

Linda heard the faint tick of a clock. Beyond the window, Linda saw a sweep of green fields encircled by hills of cypress.

Eva Kaiser spoke sharply. "What's that?"

Linda stared at the package in her hands. "Chocolates."

The doctor frowned. "Frankly, we were quite surprised at Mr. Lynn's phone call." She looked up. "He said you were an old friend and wanted to visit. We asked Maria this morning, and she said she was quite pleased to see you."

Linda darted her eyes past the doctor's intense stare to concentrate on a Matisse print on the wall, two women seated in a café.

Without warning the door flung open, and a nurse walked in.

"This is Sandra Graves, Miss Fentress." Eva Kaiser kept her eyes fixed on Linda. "Sandra oversees the six patients in Maria's unit."

Linda smiled, almost absurdly pleased at the nurse's California prettiness, a vivid contrast to Eva Kaiser.

"Sandra will escort you to Maria," said Eva Kaiser.

*

Barry Cohen and Margie were lifting glasses of 1971 Dom Perignon in the crowded backroom restaurant at Fritzi's.

On an Eastern Airlines shuttle, Captain Scott Hanson received clearance from air traffic control at LaGuardia to start his descent over central Long Island.

At the enclosed sidewalk café of The Ginger Man, on West Sixty-fourth Street, three women—Mary Phelps, Rose Tyler, and Sarah Felger—had settled in for a last gallows lunch before the strike. Suddenly Mary leaned forward to stare at a corner table. There Skipper Steiner sat, intently examining the checkered tablecloth, listening to his son Larry talk.

Sixteen blocks to the south, on Fifth Avenue, a clerk in the Pan Am office slipped a bulky ticket into an envelope and smiled perfunctorily at the woman in glasses. "Have a nice trip, Mrs. Sims," said the clerk, gazing up at the wall clock. It was one forty-five.

In Mexico City, Richard Thompson, a United States Embassy official listed as a labor attaché, was just stepping into the pulsing heat of Paseo de la Reforma after an unproductive morning that had started with a breakfast reception at the Hilton coffee shop with a middle-level official of the Trade Union Congress. Walking toward the taxi stand, Thompson heard the honk of a horn and the familiar voice of Charlie McQueen, the official listed as Embassy narcotics officer.

Thompson's shoulders sagged. He knew, instantly, that his plans for the afternoon—tennis at the American Club with his wife Anita, a swim and a light lunch before returning to the Embassy—had just collapsed.

Charlie was smiling from his blue Toyota. "Climb in," he said, pushing open the door. "Uncle Alex wants to talk to you. Urgent."

As Richard Thompson slumped in the seat of the car, a Cessna 150 cruised northeast at 115 miles per hour toward Monterey. Glancing at the directional gyro and airspeed indicator, Marcus Lynn turned to his left and looked down on the bowl-shaped valley of San Luis Obispo, beyond which rose the jagged, wooded slopes of the Santa Lucia Mountains and Cuesta Pass. Sunlight fell on the square red velour box of chocolates on the passenger seat.

In Washington, D.C., Myron (Mike) Goldfarb sat in a wing chair in the Oval Office, watching the President of the United States gently place a sheaf of papers atop his carved oak desk less than two feet away. The thickly bespectacled twenty-four-year-old, who grew up in Shaker Heights and began writing speeches for then Senator Bergen even before graduating at the top of his class at Harvard, heard the President whistle, then saw him arch his eyebrows and nod to Bart Taylor, who stood behind Goldfarb.

"That's one hell of a speech, Bart." Myron watched the President lower his face and suddenly saw the eyes of the President of the United States glisten with tears. Myron tried to concentrate on the photo of the First Family beside the desk: the President and his wife; their son Tim, a pediatrician in Columbus, Ohio; and their daughter Joanne, a twenty-three-year-old who lived at the Watergate, was studying photography and was the delight of gossip columnists and party reporters. In this historic moment Myron Goldfarb wondered why Joanne Bergen would never give him the time of day.

Less than two miles away, on his sixth-floor condominium off Dupont Circle, the New York *Star's* White House correspondent, Barney Fischer, removed his jacket and tie just as the doorbell rang. Barney cursed his nervousness as he flicked on the stereo set beside the window and heard the overture from the musical show *Gypsy*. It was the same music that he had deployed successfully in conquest of the British Ambassador's secretary only two nights before.

In his office, President Bergen was speaking quietly. "Except for us, and *only* us, no one is to know what's in this speech." And then he added a phrase that made Bart Taylor wince. "Us—and my family, of course."

Back at Barney Fischer's apartment, Joanne Bergen had removed her raincoat and smiled as Barney struggled with the champagne cork. "Do all you journalists have champagne for lunch?" she asked, startling him with her self-assured gaze.

In Dr. John Carlson's office on Foxhall Road, the intercom rang just as the internist snapped his attaché case shut and prepared to leave. Although the well-known northwest Washington physician was late for his daily round of visits to patients at Sibley Hospital, John Carlson eagerly accepted the call when the nurse informed him that Kitty White was on the line. If Kitty's request was not quite what he had anticipated—Dr. Carlson had hoped, of course, for another dinner party invitation, which inevitably resulted in placing one more ambassador or senator's wife on his list of distinguished patients—his voice betrayed absolutely no disappointment as he dutifully obliged Kitty's request for a prescription. It was only moments later, while driving along Nebraska Avenue as a soft drizzle fell, that Dr. John Carlson suddenly wondered why Kitty White wanted one hundred Seconals. Hadn't he filled Kitty's order for barbiturates last month? The thought flickered and vanished as John Carlson glided his Jaguar into the hospital parking lot, just as Hugh Finch was climbing into his Volkswagen.

John Carlson gently honked his horn and waved: the bureau chiefs of several distinguished newspapers and news magazines, including the New York *Star,* were among his patients. He wondered whom Hugh was seeing at the hospital, perhaps a VIP, someone John Carlson should know.

In fact, Finch had only visited a doctor on duty, one with a Pakistani accent, a doctor who perfunctorily stabbed Hugh's left arm with cholera and tetanus vaccine and told him to expect some discomfort this afternoon.

Hugh turned the ignition key, cursing the numbness that enveloped his shoulder. Driving slowly out of the parking lot, Hugh kept the car in first gear, turning left up Nebraska Avenue.

Ward Parsons' routine memo yesterday had asked the staff to update their passports and vaccination records in case more reporters were needed overseas on the China-Soviet crisis. But Hugh was aware that the memo hardly applied to him—he ran the Washington bureau, he had no experience overseas, he was a little too old. They usually plucked some bright kid out of the newsroom and offered him the chance.

Besides, he was tired now, burned out, forty-two going on sixty. *Don't have the heart anymore for the job, Ward. Something died yesterday, that morsel of ambition, that hunger to make it, the craving for a . . . byline. You guys salvaged me, propped me up, but please understand the deadness inside. The emptiness . . .*

You take over the Washington bureau, Barney. It's yours, you deserve it, you'll do anything for a story, you'll get Bergen's speech, friend, through hook or crook, you'll get the speech and the front-page byline, and that's what counts. It's your chance, friend, and you'll do it, you're the new wave, Barney. The wave of the future . . .

The talk show on the radio had given way to the one fifty-five news . . . Mrs. David Fitzgerald charged with second-degree murder . . . Senator's office declines comment . . . President Bergen preparing major speech for tomorrow night . . . The Chinese government has reportedly accepted Defense Secretary Belling's plea for a seventy-two-hour cease-fire . . . Around the nation and the world there was reaction to the Chinese nuclear breakthrough. In Rome, Pope Joseph IV issued a statement . . . The weather today, light rain with patches of . . .

His mind wandered to the morning flight to New York, Maury's hospital room. Something had been said, an innocuous exchange of words had intrigued him. But the memory blurred and had disappeared until now. Instead of vanishing from Hugh's consciousness, disjointed words suddenly flickered back, as if a provocative and subtle message had been offered and finally accepted.

He saw Maury hanging up the phone. And the nurse approaching. And Maury remarking that he would miss the farewell party for Frankie Webb, chief of security.

Frankie Webb.

Hugh veered so abruptly into the left lane that the black limousine behind him braked, tires screeched. But Hugh didn't care. He drove the entire circle quickly; he would stop at a phone booth on the American University campus and call Skipper Steiner.

In Georgetown, less than three miles away, Kitty White glanced out the sitting-room window of her home on Q Street while pressing the phone to her ear. She spoke quietly. "The pills will be ready in time for your three o'clock visit to her, David."

*

At five minutes after two, Nick Simons slipped a message into the carriage of Barry's Smith-Corona.

Howie Bishop called twice. I informed him, as you said, to forget the diary. He seemed a little pissed off. Nick.

He returned to his desk, lifting a ball-point pen and writing the word "diary" on his yellow pad. One more paper before the strike, and wouldn't it be sweet to get a front-page byline in that last edition. *By Nick Simons.* Beside Linda Fentress and Barney Fischer and Ernie Richards.

"Why are you smiling?" Pat Donlon wove unsteadily toward the city desk, glancing at Nick.

"Fantasizing," said Nick, eyeing Donlon. Pat's days were numbered on the city desk. Without Evan's and Maury's protection, with a new city editor (rumored to be Marty Kaplan) to take over and hire his own team, Pat would soon be shuffled into a nondescript job editing transportation news until his retirement.

Pat slumped in his swivel chair. "You're going to be a star, Nick. Bigger than Woodward and Bernstein. Bigger than *Howie.*"

Nick's eyes fell on his yellow pad.

Diary.

Suddenly Nick said, "I sent a message to Jerry Paley's wife . . ."

"That's kind of you, Nick."

". . . Expressing my condolences."

Their eyes met. Nick wondered why he was lying, what motive led him to ingratiate himself with Pat Donlon, a mean drunk and a loser. Someone who could do nothing to advance his career, or to get him that front-page byline.

A phone rang on the foreign desk, and Nick watched Tony Lazzarutti answer it. Reporters and editors were straggling back into the newsroom after lunch. A smile stole across Nick's face.

"Tell me, Pat," said Nick, keeping his voice low, "tell me what you know about Cheryl's diary."

*

As Nick Simons and Donlon were talking, Ira Moskowitz, New York City's chief labor mediator, sat at the head of a granite conference table on the ninth floor, examining Frank Lazzarutti's face; then he turned to Eli Faber. Moskowitz, whom newspapers inevitably termed "dapper and bespectacled," spoke in the accent of his Brighton Beach boyhood. "Stop the clock! Let's negotiate, not argue. Stop the clock. Midnight tonight. Keep the paper going. Let's keep *talking*. You're playing with fire, my friend. A strike's going to *kill* you."

Eli Faber clasped his hands together, gently striking his lower lip. "So long as Frank stubbornly insists that we can't start layoffs, I see no point in extending the agony . . ."

"Damn it, Eli," Moskowitz said tensely. "Frank's *willing* to stop the clock. Willing to *talk*. The Guild won't strike until you start layoffs, and what I'm asking is . . ."

"Let him strike," said Eli, smiling, gazing steadily at Moskowitz. "We'll *break* him."

"You son of a bitch," Frank Lazzarutti said.

"Gentlemen, let's lower the temperature a bit," said Moskowitz, loosening the knot of his burgundy silk tie.

"What's the point, Ira?" said Eli Faber. "Frank has been itching for a strike and we're going to *crush* the Guild."

"And the paper too," said Ira Moskowitz calmly. "You're going to crush the New York *Star*."

Suddenly the room was silent. Ira Moskowitz watched Eli's face, perfectly composed except for a rhythmic twitch at the left corner of his mouth.

Abruptly, Eli pushed back his stainless-steel-and-leather chair. "There's a phone call I have to make," he said.

Ten blocks east at La Grenouille, Madame approached a table at the center of the restaurant and announced a phone call for Mr. Dunlap.

Lucy caught a glimpse of Ernie Dunlap threading his way through the restaurant. She had eaten her meal in silence, Frieda slumped beside her.

"It's two-ten, Mother."

"I've been a fool."

"What?"

"Forgive me, Lucy," she said softly. "*Forgive* me."

*

Seconds earlier a stewardess on the Eastern shuttle to New York had stepped quickly up the aisle, her head turning left and right, her eyes scanning the passengers to insure that seat belts were fastened.

The stewardess heard the flaps move and the delicate shift in engine pitch just as she caught sight of the passenger in 10D, his right hand slipping beneath his jacket.

She moved forward. No point asking 10D if he needed assistance, she rationalized, they would be on the ground in four minutes. And besides, she was very tired and the baby up front had been sick and that passenger seemed a little weird anyway.

Mike Paley heard the undercarriage rumble and drop, and the engines throttle their power. A sting of pain knifed his ears. He shut his eyes tight, hoping to ease the agony, and kept his lids closed even as the wheels bounced over the tarmac at LaGuardia Airport.

*

"There's Maria," said Sandra Graves. The screen door slammed on the terrace behind Linda Fentress, who turned to the nurse, almost reflexively, and caught a deadness in her eyes.

A dozen patients were clustered in groups on deck chairs overlooking a forest of Monterey cypress, the branches gnarled and misshapen by ocean winds that swept from the unseen Pacific three miles west.

Maria Lynn sat alone at the edge of the field, staring blankly at the cliffs below. Except for her hair, which was scissored in an oddly misshapen masculine cut, and except for a thinness in her face that sharpened her high cheekbones, Maria looked precisely the same as she had in the photograph at the Emmy Awards.

Linda struggled to ignore the patients, but suddenly a woman in jeans and sneakers stood and flung herself at Sandra Graves. "Help me, Sandra," she cried, glancing suspiciously at Linda. "I have these five babies. Carrying them twelve months. When will I deliver? Twelve months, Sandra! Listen to me! Victor is sending shocks to my brain. Hates my guts! Sending shocks to my brain that cast spells over me, forcing me to ask twenty-five people hideous questions. Isn't that ridiculous?"

"It's ridiculous," said Sandra quietly.

"When will I deliver my babies?" the woman pleaded. "If I don't deliver them I'll die."

A male nurse was approaching. "Victor, perhaps Phyllis should return to her chair," said Sandra Graves. "This is Miss Fentress, Victor. She's visiting Maria."

The woman stared at Sandra, an expression of betrayal on her face. "God, I hate you, Sandra," she said, turning and walking to her chair, ignoring Victor.

"Phyllis has been pregnant for four years," said Sandra, smiling. Just then Linda's eyes caught a flicker of movement behind a second-story window overlooking the field. As the curtain fell, Linda thought she saw the heavy figure of Eva Kaiser step away.

*

The phone was ringing on the city desk and, just as Pat Donlon started reaching for it, Nick signaled that he would answer. He heard a man's voice.

"Is Linda Fentress there?"

Nick frowned. "She's out of town."

"I've been trying to reach her," said the man. "It's urgent."

"Give me your phone number," said Nick. "I'll pass it on to her."

All phone calls to the investigative reporters were urgent, 98 percent of them from fruitcakes. Nick Simons and the other clerks were under orders *never* to inform a caller of the whereabouts of an investigative reporter.

"Is Pat Donlon there?"

Nick stiffened. "No," he said quickly.

Years later, Nick Simons would still recall that moment of fear, when he inexplicably lied again, this time to the caller. It was a foolish lie. Pat Donlon *was* there. And yet . . . there was that tone of urgency in the caller's voice, and an awareness that he obviously knew the city desk, the sense that he had a story for Linda Fentress. She wasn't there, maybe it was a good story, maybe a hell of a story, maybe a front-page byline which would mean so little to Linda anyway . . .

"Can I help you?" said Nick.

"This is Mike Paley."

Nick bit his lip.

"Sorry about your father," Nick said.

"I need to speak to Linda."

"She's out of town, Mike. This is Nick. Nick Simons."

"I've got to get a message to her. Urgent message."

"Give it to me, Mike." His voice was soothing.

"Can I trust you?"

"Of *course*."

"I know what's in Cheryl's diary. I got a copy. All the names and dates. I got it."

"I'll pass the message on."

Nick's fingers shook. He saw Pat rise and walk toward the bulletin board where Betty Kennedy had just tacked up the latest Guild report on negotiations. A crowd was gathering.

Nick said, "Sounds like a good story, Mike."

"Dad wanted me to give it to Linda. Only Linda. He said she'd know what to do."

Nick Simons kept his voice even. "Call me in fifteen minutes, Mike," he said. "I'll try to reach Linda. Give her your message."

He heard the phone click and listened to the dial tone. "You can trust me, Mike," Nick whispered as he gently replaced the receiver.

*

Maria gazed up at Linda. "I've been expecting you, Miss Fentress." Maria's smile revealed a slight gap in her front teeth that lent an unexpected innocence to her face. Her voice was low and flat, the words spoken emphatically.

"Come and sit down. Victor . . ." She turned. "Bring Miss Fentress a chair. Sandra?"

As the nurse took a step toward Maria, Linda thought she saw Sandra's lips tighten.

"Sandra, I think you can leave us alone. I'm sure Victor will keep an eye on me."

"I've brought you some chocolates," Linda said.

"How *nice!* Look at this elegant ribbon, Sandra. Oh look! It's silk. And the velvet flower. Thank you."

Linda turned and saw Victor approaching, hauling a white deck chair.

"I receive so few visitors," Maria was saying as she lifted the box of chocolates. "Grandmother comes once a month. We talk about the weather, we talk about God. She prays. She prays for my salvation."

Maria's scornful laugh annoyed Linda. Maria, sensing Linda's displeasure, shrugged.

"A sweet woman but a . . . peasant."

Linda eased into the deck chair, shuddering at the coldness of the wooden planks.

"No more than twenty minutes," Sandra Graves said. Linda watched Maria glance at the nurse with disdain.

"Don't be jealous, Sandra," said Maria, teasing. "We're old friends, aren't we, Linda? Aren't we? We have a lot to talk about." Maria's eyes darted from Sandra to Linda, her smile fixed.

Linda was amazed. That single photograph of Maria—with Joe Keefer and Marcus and Lois Barrie—coupled with the eerie story of her plunge into insanity had created a mental portrait of a frail creature buffeted and finally overwhelmed by storms so savage that Linda was prepared to absorb, to *accept,* the shocking act that had placed Maria in Rose Haven.

Not like this, though, Linda thought—so controlled, so powerful and knowing.

Sandra Graves said, "Twenty minutes," backing away. Linda saw Victor watching them and thought she caught, in that second, the rustle of curtains once more on the second floor.

"Who are you?" Maria asked, smiling.

"I'm a newspaper reporter. The *Star* in New York."

"It's so pleasant to see people from outside. I'm surprised Marcus allowed you in."

"I wanted to talk to you, Maria."

"The wondrous thing about being locked away is that madness and sanity are invisible to the eyes. I *look* perfectly normal. I'm not a lunatic like . . . like Phyllis over there having her baby. I *sound* normal. You don't know if I'm mad or not, do you?"

Linda stared at Maria.

"Or if I'm telling the truth or not."

She's beautiful, Linda thought. Maria's copper skin stretched over those remarkable cheekbones, and her broad, flat jaw gave strength to an otherwise delicate face. Her narrow, almost oriental eyes were violet-blue, her firm nose flared abruptly at the nostrils.

As Maria leaned forward, Linda saw that her body was supple, her waist narrow but her breasts surprisingly ample. Her off-white corduroy slacks and shawl-collar sweater over a ribbed gray turtleneck were strangely demure and limiting. The over-all effect was incongruous: perfectly ordinary clothes veiled a figure of grace and strange sensuality.

"Why did you lie?" Linda asked. "We're not old friends."

"We could be," said Maria. "Why did *you* lie?" She spoke through a smile. "Marcus didn't call. I don't believe Marcus called. Marcus would kill you if he knew you were here. No one's allowed to see me, Linda. No one! Except my grandmother. *No one can see me!*"

Maria's eyes narrowed. "They're watching us. Eva Kaiser and Sandra and Victor. They're watching. They don't *trust* you."

A soft wind, scented with salt and ocean, brushed Linda's face. She watched Maria pull down her sweater, noticed her nails, cut short and painted pink.

"Victor protects us from one another," Maria was saying. "Eva and Sandra . . . protect *me*. One word from me and they come running. You're here at my whim. I'm in control."

"Of course you are."

"Don't patronize me!"

"You've always been in control, Maria."

"Not always." Maria turned her face toward the forest of redwoods and Monterey cypress sloping westward.

"The soil is so poor," Maria whispered. "Erosion! You can *see* the erosion. We keep getting heavy rains. The adobe soil sucks the water. Becomes a liquid. Just slides down the forest. The earth isn't sharp. Turns into molecules like sand. Just *slides*. We add new soil. Every two or three months we deposit new soil in the ground, but the rains keep coming."

"You tried to kill your baby."

Maria's eyes flickered twice, and turned blank. She avoided Linda's face.

"*Who* are you?" said Maria.

"I'm Linda Fentress of the New York *Star*."

"What do you want?"

"I want to know why you tried to kill your baby."

Maria's fingers twirled her hair. "Adobe soil sucks the water," she said. "Becomes a liquid. Just slides."

"I'm not here to hurt you." Linda struggled to control her voice. "I want to know the truth. Nobody knows the truth. Not Eva or Sandra Graves. Not Marcus. Not *you.*"

"I'm a lunatic. What's truth? What's madness?"

Linda rocked forward. "I know the pieces, Maria, but I can't fit them together."

"The fog burns off by noon, Linda. Moves through the canyons like an alien spirit. You hear the treacherous winds and the surf, the waves pounding."

"I only have a few minutes."

Her words were lost as the wind hurled flecks of sand, burning Linda's eyes.

"Do you want the truth, Maria? The pain?"

"The pain," Maria whispered.

"The truth!" Linda grabbed Maria's slender arms. "What happened in Mexico City? What made you fly to L.A. and try to kill . . ."

"Stop!"

Linda drew back. Coming on much too strong, pushing too hard, Jerry would disapprove. Rule number one: move in gently on the source, soften them up, be a friend, so understanding. Don't panic. Calmly show them how much you know, scare them just a little, nudge them along, so sweet you are as you bang away.

Linda felt the sweat start on her brow. "It began in Washington, didn't it? The summer you worked for Dave Fitzgerald. You went to Washington and had an affair with Tom Nelson."

Maria tugged at her sweater as she concentrated on the grass.

Linda said: "Marcus reacted violently. He beat you up, and you fled to Mexico City."

"I am Davita Lopez' daughter."

"What?"

"My mother is a whore," Maria whispered.

"You went to Mexico City."

"I turned into my mother."

"You went to a porno filmmaker named Gus Heller. Someone you had heard about. Someone your father knew. Marcus defended him years back when Heller was blacklisted by Joey Keefer . . ."

Maria made a sudden gesture. Her lips moved, but no words came.

"Gus Heller didn't know you were Marcus' daughter. You lied about your name. You made some porno films but had to stop. You were pregnant."

An eerie half-smile lit Maria's face as her fingers tightened, two fists locked together at the throat.

Surprise her, tease her, that's what Jerry would say. Keep her off-guard.

"I want to understand what happened, Maria. What happened that week in Mexico City. Marcus tracked you down and begged you to come home. Asked you to forgive him. He was guilt-ridden, appalled at the beating he gave you in Washington. It would never happen again. He wanted you to come back, you and the baby. He was going to *care* for you and the baby."

Maria's smile froze as Linda spoke.

"Marcus told Gus you were his daughter, and Gus Heller was stunned. How could Gus have known?" Linda watched Maria intently. "It wasn't Gus's fault, how could Marcus blame Gus? There was only one person Marcus blamed, and that was Tom Nelson. Blamed Nelson for seducing you, for ruining you, for starting you on the path that led to the films."

Suddenly Maria's mouth was wrenched in pain. As Linda fumbled with her notebook, she was aware that her heart was pounding violently.

Maria, honey, talk to me, come on, we're beating the *Daily News,* beating them all, front-page byline here, maybe even a Pulitzer, won't that be a kick in the ass to all those guys in all those newsrooms, laughing for years at old Linda, so talk, please. You tried to kill your baby. Tom Nelson's baby. Why? Smother the baby. Why, Maria? That's where the story starts, right? That's where it starts . . . and ends.

"It was five years ago," said Linda. "The newspapers were saying that Tom Nelson was going to be Vice President. Marcus wanted revenge, had to stop him. So Marcus hit on a plan, didn't he? Marcus told Gus to take Nelson's films out of his vault in Mexico City, the films that Tommy had performed in thirty years ago. Marcus would get the films and destroy Tom Nelson with them. And Gus agreed."

Tears wet Maria's face.

Linda said: "Gus stopped en route at his studio in Tijuana to destroy your films. Then he began the drive to L.A. with Nelson's films in the trunk of his car on the way to Marcus. He was murdered that night in San Diego, the car demolished. The films . . ."

"The films," whispered Maria.

". . . destroyed."

Linda saw Maria shut her eyes.

"The next day in Mexico City Joe Keefer died of a heart attack," Linda said. "You knew Joey so many years." Linda waited. "Marcus hired him when you were a kid. He was your father's flunky. Handyman, messenger, chauffeur. He drove you to school." Maria's eyes remained closed, tears streaming through them.

"He was despicable, wasn't he?" said Linda, turning the pages of her notebook.

"Who?"

"Joe Keefer."

"Joe."

"Destroyed people's lives with his blacklist. He was a liar, a pervert. Molested little girls."

"No, *no!*" Maria was shaking her head furiously.

Linda drew back, shivering as a wet wind off the mountain slopes carried the sound of crashing surf. There was a moment's silence, then suddenly the question sprang to Linda's lips. "Where did Joey Keefer die, Maria? Where in Mexico City?"

Maria's eyes searched Linda's face. Linda tried to sound offhand.

"I'll find that out, Maria. Easy enough for me to find out."

"In my apartment," Maria said dully.

Linda caught her breath. "In your apartment?"

The fog was rolling in and out, drifting up the canyons to reveal a belt of giant redwoods, sunlight seeping between the columns, the massively fluted trees glowing with a strangely purplish hue.

Keep calm, move it along smoothly, don't upset her and intensify the interrogation. Rule three: be a hard-ass.

"I saw an old photo of you and Joey," said Linda. "Joey Keefer was a friend. Since you were a kid. Joey was like . . . an uncle."

"I loved Joey."

"I know."

*

Nick watched Marty Kaplan push back his chair at the city desk after a whispered conversation with Pat Donlon.

"Shall I congratulate you now, sir?" said Nick.

Marty paused beside him. "Everyone else is."

"I'm Nick Simons."

"Gather you just made the staff, Nick."

"That's what Barry promised."

"Got to find a replacement for you, then."

Nick grinned.

"I'm going to have Pat Donlon keep me honest for a while."

Nick stared at Marty's face. In other words, Marty was keeping Pat Donlon on for six months before replacing him. The telephone rang and Pat grabbed it.

"Sir?" Nick said.

"Yes?"

"I've been working on a story of my own. Story connected with Jerry Paley's death. All kinds of rumors that this girl Cheryl kept a diary."

Marty narrowed his eyes. "Things have moved fast. I'm not up on the story yet. I'm seeing Barry after lunch just to talk about *this* story. Get briefed on it."

"Well, can I work on the diary angle anyway? May be a good story there." Nick lowered his voice. "Just heard rumors that a couple of other papers are working on the same story."

Marty wondered why he found this kid's persistence so irritating. As city editor, he knew, he would have to divorce his personal feelings about members of the staff from professional judgments. Obviously, Nick was hungry for a story and a hustler, the best type of young reporter.

"Sure, Nick," said Marty Kaplan. "You work on it."

*

"Tell me about Joe Keefer," said Linda.

"I think we've gone far enough."

"We've just begun."

"A word from me and Victor hauls you out."

"You're not insane, are you?"

"I'm evil."

"What happened in Mexico City?"

"Stop."

"What led you to fly to L.A. and try to smother . . ."

"Stop!"

Linda met Maria's eyes.

"You pleaded insanity."

"I'm a lunatic. Look it up in the court records. Marcus had the best shrinks in L.A. confirm it. Demented. Psychotic. Bats in the belfry." Maria laughed, but suddenly drew in a breath. "It's beautiful here. I want to stay for the rest of my life. Hell has trees and sun."

"You'll leave someday."

"Never."

"What are you afraid of?"

"What's out there."

"Trees and sun."

"Leave me alone."

"I only have a few minutes left."

"Good."

A ball of panic rose in Linda's throat. The possibility that she would leave Rose Haven without a story was unthinkable until now. In her frenzy Linda had simply never considered that, once she reached Maria, the girl would actually stonewall her, refuse to talk, play crazy. Linda felt sick, her head pounded violently.

Rule four: if all else fails, Jerry had said, then you got the final option. Go for broke. Lie. Threaten. Cheat. Manipulate. So it's not what they teach you at the Columbia Journalism School. You're not going to hear about it when all those investigative reporters have their circle jerks on television saying how terrific they are. They all do it, honey, and you do it too . . .

"When was the last time you saw a newspaper?" Linda struggled to keep her voice calm. Maria glanced at her.

"Tom Nelson's going to run for President," said Linda. "You hear that? President! How do you think Marcus is taking it, Maria? You think Marcus is accepting the news?"

Linda saw Maria shrink in her chair, her fingers toying with the buttons on her sweater.

"Marcus tried to destroy Tom Nelson once. He failed," said Linda. "This time he won't fail."

Trying to smile, Linda said: "Marcus is consumed with hatred for Tom Nelson, hatred and fear. And in the end, honey, Marcus will use you, yes, *you,* to destroy Nelson." Linda's voice quivered. "Use you and, yes, he'll use the baby. *Your* baby. Tom Nelson's baby."

Maria's reaction was instantaneous. Her hand flew to her face, and she gazed wild-eyed at Linda. As Maria opened her mouth to speak, Linda cut her short.

"I'm writing a story, Maria. Whether you like it or not, I'm writing one. You help me and I write a fair story, an honest story. You don't help me and I print dirt, gossip, innuendos. You got the choice."

Linda took a gasping breath. "Someone's going to print the story about the baby, and I want to be the *first,*" said Linda. "You hear me? There are reporters out there who'll do anything, destroy anybody for a story. I *won't.*"

Maria stared at her.

"*Trust* me," pleaded Linda.

A light drizzle fell.

"Let's start at the beginning," said Linda. "Tell me about Joe Keefer."

*

The single chime of the tall Louis XVI clock surprised Skipper. He was standing at the window, eyes fixed on a barge streaming up the remarkably calm Hudson, the sun warming his face.

He turned slowly. It was two forty-five.

They would arrive within fifteen minutes, Frieda and Lucy and Eli Faber. The vote for Barry would pass without drama, and he would slip away quickly, instructions already in place with Miss Heaney to release his letter of resignation to the press at 4 P.M.

Seated in the swivel chair, he reached inside his jacket pocket to grasp the thick key.

What did Larry say at lunch? *Why hide? Why continue the sham?*

Looking at Larry in the crowded restaurant, aware of the dreadful incident in Sally's apartment, Skipper was struck by a wave of desolation.

In the past forty-eight hours he had lost Sally and his newspaper—the two forces that had held his life together, the anchors
which had offered solidity. He adored them both, they challenged
him, nurtured him, *tested* him, made him aware of his strengths
and vulnerabilities, stripped away the pretense and *demanded* that
he reach, perhaps overreach, his limits.

And staring into Larry's eyes this afternoon, he was aware of
the aching distance between his son and himself—this strange,
unloved child who had so publicly shamed him. The years of neglect, the anguished sense of failure—Skipper's failure, a failure far
worse than losing Sally or the *Star*.

His son.

Forgive me, Larry.

Larry had been startled. *For what?*

Forgive me!

Over the years their luncheons had been tense, each one yearning to flee as soon as they sat down.

But as soon as Larry sat, Skipper leaned forward and examined
his son's face. He had to renew himself in ways impossible to understand; the earth had turned slippery beneath his feet. He could
not lose his son too. Or was it too late?

Help me, Larry. I want to understand.

Larry's body was shaking.

Why hide? Why continue the sham?

Now Skipper inserted the key into the bottom drawer of the
desk. The lock had been unused for years, and the drawer creaked
as Skipper pulled it.

He stared at the black leather scrapbook.

It was perfectly intact, a musty, oddly sweet scent wafting up
from the drawer. He grasped the book; the leather was cool,
spongy to his touch.

Years and years. Had been so long since he turned the pages.
Yellowed at the edges, stiff with age, creaking as he opened the
book.

The letters in the center of the book had frayed. Lifting a pale-
blue envelope, torn at the side the way Jonathan opened his mail,
Skipper pulled out and unfolded the sheet. Flecks of paper crumpled between his fingers, falling like fragile snow on the desk. The
sight of the familiar, narrow scrawl still fascinated him—the

scrawl, the words that he had read and reread until his seventeenth or eighteenth birthday.

. . . And Jonathan, send my love to your boy. I think of him every night. He must be such a big fellow now.

It was two-fifty. He watched with dismay as the papers crackled. He would salvage the letters today, placing the sheets under glass, not burying them as he had all these years . . .

Why continue the sham?

Geraldine Heaney rang the intercom to announce that Frieda and Lucy were in the waiting room, and that Hugh Finch was on the phone from Washington.

*

Linda Fentress spoke as she leafed through her notebook. "You were just a kid when Marcus hired Joey Keefer," she said. "Marcus was a lawyer representing Keefer's victims. Like Tom Nelson and Gus Heller and Paul Brock. Like Elliott Hanley."

Linda found Elliott Hanley's words. She didn't look up. "Joey Keefer was drunk with power. He had to be *stopped*. So pictures were taken of Joey and a young girl."

"Poor Joey."

"Poor Joey could've gone to prison for raping a minor. Marcus advised Joey's family that Joey retire from public life, lest Joey's enemies get their hands on the films. Joey didn't know . . ."

"Didn't know."

"Marcus and Tommy had set him up. Joey didn't *know*. He was working for the man who betrayed him, and he never knew it. And he became your father's flunky. Errand boy. Helped with the groceries. Chauffeured you to school." Linda stared at Maria, suddenly recalling Lois Barrie's words: ". . . would deliver monthly payments to your mother. Marcus supported Davita Lopez, spent a fortune on her."

Linda watched her lips start to move soundlessly. Maria's fingers clawed her neck.

"What is it?" said Linda impatiently. Maria's eyes pleaded as Linda tried to make out the words. "He did know," Linda said. Maria nodded. "Joey *knew* they had set him up."

"I was twelve or thirteen," whispered Maria. "I heard Marcus and Tommy laugh about what they had done to Joey."

"And you told Joey."

"Sometimes he would buy me chocolates when I was a child. His eyes would fill with tears. 'What's wrong, Joe,' I would say. He said nothing, would just sit there and cry."

"So Joey hated your father and kept on working for him."

"Joey would take me driving after school into Bel Air, pointing out the homes that once belonged to W. C. Fields and Jeanette MacDonald and Carole Lombard . . . They had destroyed him. He had nobody, except, in a weird way . . ."

"You!"

Maria searched Linda's face. "Joey unraveled, fell into a pit of alcoholism. Year after year, I watched his despair."

"You were a teen-ager now."

" 'Try to establish yourself, Joey,' I said to him. 'Break *free* from Marcus.' And Joey tried. God, he tried. Saw his friends in Washington in the FBI, went to his friends in the Agency. He wanted to show Marcus, he wanted to show his family that his years of waste were over."

"You went to Washington too."

"That summer Marcus suggested I work for Dave Fitzgerald," said Maria. "David's first summer in Washington as a senator. Trying to ingratiate himself with the great Marcus Lynn. Why not hire his daughter?" She shut her eyes. "Joey arranged the job, Joey did."

"His sister's married to Fitzgerald."

"Just starting my descent into hell. Fitzgerald is disgusting, a user. He assumed I would have some leverage over my father. Fitzgerald needed Marcus' money and support, he needed to . . . *extricate* Marcus from Tom Nelson in order to run for President." She spoke in a low, hypnotic monotone, the words fading and rising in the wind.

"You fell in love."

"With Tom Nelson."

Maria spoke quickly. "I went to a party with Joey and met Tom Nelson. I had seen him when I was a child, of course, knew he was Marcus' closest friend. Knew Marcus helped *elect* him. But I hadn't seen Tom in years. And I was entranced. I was away from home, away from California and . . ."

"You slept with him."

"He refused at first. Fought it. There was no one in my life, no one that I wanted as badly as Tom Nelson.

"Marcus found out," Maria said. "Even had tapes of us. Someone told him. Someone *evil*." She examined her hands. "I suspected Fitzgerald. He had the most to gain. Marcus' money and support. He knew full well that Marcus would now turn in a fury against Tom Nelson."

"And against you."

"You've heard the story," Maria said. "Marcus' rage. An animal's rage. Beat me up in the middle of the street in Washington. Called me a whore! I knew what he was thinking, saw it in his eyes. 'Just like her mother.' *Just like my mother.*"

"You went to Mexico City."

"I would show him the kind of whore I was." Maria looked up and grinned. "That's it, Linda. The end. Made some movies. Went berserk. The experience obviously too *much*. I went . . . mad."

Linda felt the blood rush to her face. She carefully closed her notebook. "Thanks."

"There it is, the whole sordid saga."

Linda sat perfectly still. "That's fine. I'll go back to New York and tell my boss what you just told me."

"That does it," Maria said uneasily.

Linda picked up her handbag off the ground. "That does it for you, not us." She tried to smile. "I'll leave here with the opening wedge of the story, and I'm afraid my editor back home is going to be a little upset. Don't have much of a story, do we, Maria? You began it and then chickened out. That's fine. Happens all the time. But we've got to print something, right? And without facts we run with gossip."

Jerry'd be proud. Cool and tough, honey, lie through your teeth . . .

Maria's eyes glittered with fury, alarm. Linda said unexpectedly, "Always been a selfish, spoiled little girl, Maria. Look at you now. Still selfish. *Still* spoiled. You don't even care about the *kid,* your own kid. Why should you? You're locked up here, nice and safe, the way you want it. The kid's got to live her life now with reporters and photographers clamoring over her, gossip and filth clouding her life forever, all because her mother is selfish and . . ."

"What do you want?" A look of strain wrenched Maria's face.

"You tell me everything, the whole number, and I print nothing about the kid."

"I don't believe you."

That's wise, dear, you better not believe me because trust and good faith are not in my dictionary. A byline is a byline. And if the kid works into the story, that's fine; if the kid doesn't fit in, that's fine too. In the meantime, you're unhinged, honey, you've got to trust sweet Linda because you know there are animals out there with pens and pads in their claws waiting to pounce . . .

"You went to Mexico City," said Linda. "Saw Gus Heller."

Maria's hand flew to her lips.

"You had heard about Gus Heller for years, heard Gus was a great filmmaker. Could have been a second Hitchcock," said Linda, flinching as she recalled the overlapping words of Gregory and Paul Brock and Lois. Film buffs knew about Gus Heller's horror films . . . trapped in Keefer's inquisition . . . fled to Mexico City to make porno films . . . murdered in San Diego while driving his old porno films of Tom Nelson to L.A. and Marcus . . . rumors that Nelson's thugs did it . . .

"You arrived on Gus's doorstep."

"I arrived on Gus's doorstep and said I was Maria Lopez—my mother's last name," Maria was saying. "I was Maria Lopez and Gus welcomed me into his cast of characters. I was in a trance, a deadly trance, performing all day in front of the cameras, feeling . . . *nothing*. No pleasure. No pain. No guilt. Just . . . fury."

"Why?"

Maria gazed at Linda, alarmed. *"Why?* Marcus hated me."

"He loved you."

"His nightmare had come alive. I had turned into my mother."

"You got pregnant," said Linda.

Maria laughed. "After four or five months my condition became obvious. I stopped making films." Her eyes stared with alarm toward the redwood forest. "I was alone."

"You were scared."

"I needed a woman to care for me. I called my mother, but she was with her boyfriend."

"You called your grandmother."

"I needed her."

"You knew she would call Marcus. You *wanted* her to call Marcus."

"Marcus came down to visit me and was so . . . gentle."

Linda spoke in a single breath. "You told him you were pregnant with Tom Nelson's child. You *knew* the child was Nelson's. And Marcus said he would care for the child, *protect* the child. That's what you wanted."

"But we must keep it a secret."

"What?"

"No one must ever know who the child's father was. Marcus said he would adopt the child. Adopt *my* child."

Linda was silent, watching Maria gaze vacantly into the past. Then Linda spoke gently, as if trying not to stir Maria.

"So Marcus tracked down Gus Heller, and Gus was stunned. Didn't know you were Marcus' daughter. And Marcus believed Gus. And Gus said he would, of course, destroy all your films, all your films in his lab in Tijuana. And Marcus said yes, *yes,* destroy Maria's films, but he wants revenge on Tom Nelson."

Maria sat perfectly still, her face composed, a pulse throbbing violently at the side of her throat.

Linda said: "He wanted the films Nelson made as a young actor. The films that Gus had locked up for years in his vault in Mexico City. He wanted to possess those films."

Linda watched tears rain down Maria's cheeks. "It was the last day of your pregnancy. You're with Marcus and your grandmother."

Maria gaped at her. "No. Just Grandmother."

"Where's Marcus?"

"In Zurich."

Linda felt her lips part. She wanted to speak, but caught Maria's glance. "I gave birth," Maria whispered.

"You gave birth and what happened, Maria?"

"I gave birth and Joey came to visit me."

"Joey Keefer."

"En route to Zihuatanejo with ten thousand dollars."

"What ten thousand dollars?"

"Marcus' monthly payment to Davita Lopez."

Linda leaned forward. "Why did he pay your mother so much?"

Maria ignored her. "Joey was flushed with excitement. So *alive*. An old friend from his FBI days, an old friend who had gone to the Agency, had phoned him asking Joey to go on special assignment for them. At last. At *last*. Joey was starting again."

"Special assignment," Linda said blankly.

"*They wanted Tom Nelson's films.*"

Linda's eyes widened. "Who?"

"Joey just used the first name. Kept using the first name. Alex. *Alex!* Alex wanted the films and Joey was assigned to get them. Give them to an officer at the American Embassy in Mexico City. It was to be Joey's triumph after all those years of shame."

"You helped him, Maria."

"Said his friend Alex wanted to lock up the films somewhere else, somewhere *safe,* a place where no one else could get their hands on the films."

"Like Marcus."

A shaft of sun caught Maria's mouth and neck, casting a strange yellowish glow on her face. A plane droned overhead.

"Joey begged me to call Gus. Plans have changed, Gus. Marcus has changed them. Just called me from Zurich, said he wants you to go to Tijuana immediately and take all the films of me and drive them up to L.A. Marcus'll be back tomorrow night. Gus, he wants to destroy my films himself. Make sure the prints are all destroyed."

Linda said blankly, "And Tom Nelson's films?"

"Gus, you give me Tom Nelson's films. That's what Marcus wants. *Bring them to my apartment on Rio Atoyac.*"

Linda stared at her. "Nelson's films weren't destroyed in Gus's car. They were *your* films."

"My films!" Maria turned away. "No one would know. One roll of film looks like any other. They crackle and burn quickly."

Linda said: "So Gus went to your apartment and left Nelson's films there. Then Gus went to Tijuana, got *your* films . . ."

"Got my films in Tijuana and began to drive up to L.A."

"But Gus stopped en route in San Diego."

"San Diego. Gus always stopped in San Diego. Always stopped for lunch at the Del Coronado Hotel."

Linda spoke through clenched teeth. "Your films in the car, not Nelson's. Where *are* Nelson's films?"

Maria's eyes darted. "Forgive me, Joey, please . . ."

Linda put her hand to her throat. She was breathless. "What happened?"

Maria crossed her arms over her chest and began rocking back and forth. "Joey calls Tom Nelson in Washington and lies to him. 'Listen to me, Tom. Gus has gone to Tijuana where he kept your films. Yes, Tijuana. Marcus wants to use those films. Gus is picking up the films in Tijuana and driving up to L.A. with the films in his trunk, and he's got to be stopped, stopped if you want to be President one day. You've got to stop Gus Heller.'"

Linda felt the sweat start on her face. "It was Tom Nelson who killed Heller."

"It was Joey's plan. Tom Nelson would panic. Tom Nelson would order one of his thugs in San Diego to destroy Gus and the films."

"The wrong films."

"No one would *know!*"

Suddenly the movement of her body, back and forth, took on a violent rhythm. "And in the meantime Joey would have Nelson's films. Tom Nelson's *films.* The films to salvage his *life."*

"The films for Alex." Linda leaned forward, speaking softly. "Tom Nelson fell for the trap."

Maria stopped and glared at her. "Tom Nelson did *not* fall for the trap." Her voice lowered. "He said, 'Joey, if these films appear, so be it. I can stand the heat. It happened years ago. I can't let it destroy me now.'"

Maria almost smiled. "Poor Joey was stunned. His plan unraveled before his eyes. All he thought, all he *saw,* was Marcus switching on the films and *watching the wrong movie,* watching *me.* And how could he *explain* the mistake to Marcus? How could he explain that Nelson's films had been given to an American Embassy official in Mexico City who worked for Alex?"

"Who at the American Embassy?" Linda asked.

Maria ignored her. "Joey didn't want to kill Gus Heller. Joey is like a frightened child. Poor, dumb, big child. Calls Gus in a panic and flies up to San Diego to meet him for lunch at the Del Coronado. They drink too much. And then Joey says he wants to visit the zoo. They stumble off to Balboa Park, the films of me in the trunk of Gus's car, Joey carrying in his suitcase Nelson's films."

"Nelson's films," repeated Linda.

Maria nodded her head. "It's getting dark in the zoo, a storm is coming. Gus says he's got to start the drive to L.A. and Joey says, Wait, got to talk to you, Gus. They sit in the car and Joey starts to cry. A big man starting to cry like that. Tells Gus the truth. Tells Gus that he can't take the films to Marcus. *The wrong films.* Joey says it was his fault, the whole plot had misfired and he was scared now, scared of Marcus, scared of Marcus' rage, and he was just as scared of Alex in Washington and the people at the American Embassy who were promised the films and wouldn't get them now. Everything had gone wrong. His chance to start all over again doomed."

Maria searched Linda's face. "Well, Gus was still a little drunk. And instead of saying, yes, of course, we'll exchange the films, get the right films, instead of saying that, he laughed. He laughed at Joey, called him contemptible, called him a twisted little pervert. He was laughing and suddenly the years of blackmail, the years of humiliation, devoured Joey."

"He killed Gus."

"Picked up a wrench on the floor and smashed him over the head in a rage. Again and again. By the time Joey stops, he's not sure Gus is dead. But Joey knows that Gus can't live now if *he* wants to survive. He drives to the west side of the park, a deserted road, off Quince Street, and opens the trunk, removes the films from their cans. He finds a bottle and scoops gasoline from the tank, pouring it over the open trunk and the seats of the car. And when Joey tosses a match over the trunk, the entire car is in flames within seconds, destroying the films of me, destroying Gus Heller."

Maria examined her hands. "Joey flew back with the Nelson films the next morning, fevered with excitement. He told me nothing about Gus. He gave me the films . . ."

"Tom Nelson's films."

". . . And called the man from the American Embassy who came by that afternoon to pick them up."

"The man who worked for Alex," said Linda.

"The man who would salvage Joey, liberate Joey from Marcus. The Nelson films were Joey's ticket to freedom."

Linda took a quiet breath. "Joey died that day."

Maria looked up. "Joey returned to his hotel," she said in a dull voice. "It was a glorious afternoon. Grandmother was in the apartment, had arrived several days earlier to help with the baby, help me pack up and return to L.A. We took the baby down to Chapultepec Park." She stared at Linda. "When we got back to the apartment, Mr. Thompson was waiting."

"Mr. Thompson?"

"Mr. Thompson of the American Embassy."

"Mr. Thompson came for the Nelson films."

"And I gave them to him," Maria said. She closed her eyes. "And I said to him, 'This will change Joey's life. He expects you to give him a job.'"

"And what did Mr. Thompson say?"

"He laughed. He said Joey was scum. He said Joey destroyed whatever he touched. He said . . ." Her eyes opened wide. "He said Joey was the one in Washington who made the tape of me and Nelson making love. It was Joey. Joey made the tape and gave it to Marcus."

"Joey set it up with Fitzgerald," Linda whispered.

"Out of hatred for Marcus, Joey betrayed me—the one person he loved—out of hatred for Marcus."

"That tape—they turned Marcus against Tom Nelson."

"Joey and Fitzgerald."

"Your father doesn't know that Fitzgerald was involved."

"No. Marcus is supporting Fitzgerald. Supporting the one man that he should despise most of all. *Fitzgerald.*"

"Why? Why haven't you told him?"

"Do you understand what I've *done?* I'm a *monster.*" Maria bit her knuckles. "Marcus and the police and the judge buried me here and that's fine with me. I'm *dead.*"

Linda's ears picked up the thunder of waves smashing over rocks and hurtling over empty sand. Linda heard Maria's flat, mesmerizing voice over the wind.

"I was watching Mr. Thompson's lips move as he spoke. Fascinated, as if the lips and voice were out of sync."

"What did he say?"

"He said Joey would use my baby as a weapon. Said that was the plan. They were going to destroy Tom Nelson and use the baby, *his* baby. Wreck his chance to be President. He had fathered a bastard child. It would *ruin* him."

An odd silence had settled over the veranda. The patients, scattered on the grass and deck chairs, were remarkably quiet and grave, like landscape figures molded in sculpture. Suddenly an arrow of sun pierced Maria's face. "I'm scared," she said.

"Of course you're scared. You're telling the truth."

"I don't trust you."

Linda felt herself begin to sweat. "Someone's going to get this story, Maria. Someone else. You know that. Someone unscrupulous. Someone who's going to twist it and distort it. Someone who doesn't care about you and the baby."

"You'll print nothing about the baby," Maria said.

"Trust me. Tell me about Mr. Thompson."

"Mr. Thompson gave me a little plastic bottle. He said we had to do it quickly, said Joey knew too much. I was numb with fear and . . . rage. *Rage!* Joey had betrayed me, and would now destroy me and the baby and the baby's father."

"Thompson took the films of Nelson," said Linda.

Tugging at her sweater, Maria said, "That night, when Joey came to the apartment, he was exhilarated. Alex had called Joey from Washington, thanked him for the films. Joey was starting again, he said his life was taking a new turn." She rocked forward. "God, I *hated* him. The baby was sleeping in the next room. I had sent Grandmother to the movies. Joey got up and said he had to make a phone call before dinner." Maria's voice was suddenly high and strained. "In the kitchen I removed the top of the plastic vial."

"What was in it?"

"Shellfish toxin. I poured the shellfish toxin on his taco. When Joey sat down at the table he confessed to me, confessed as if I were a priest. 'Forgive me, Maria, forgive me for what I have done. I betrayed you to Marcus because I *had* to. It was for Dave Fitzgerald. *I had to do it,* and now I've killed Gus Heller. God forgive me. *Killed* a man. But it was necessary.' He told me the story, leaving the taco untouched. My eyes were riveted on that plate, knowing his death lay right *there*.

"He looked at me, Linda. 'Now I'm free,' he said. '*Free*. Nelson's films are locked up secretly at the American Embassy. Your films are destroyed. Fitzgerald and Marcus are together, and I'm taking the money . . .' "

"What money?"

"The money," said Maria impatiently. "The payment to my mother, Davita Lopez. The money that Marcus paid to Davita Lopez. The ten thousand dollars that Joey delivered to Davita Lopez each month."

Linda opened her mouth but no words came. Lois Barrie's words sounded in her ears: *Joey would deliver monthly payments to Davita Lopez. Marcus supported her, spent a fortune on that whore . . .*

"Ten thousand dollars," Linda finally said.

Maria stiffened. "He was laughing. Waving the envelope. 'My passport,' he says. 'Passport to freedom.' He was starting over. Didn't need Marcus' handouts anymore. *He was taking the ten thousand dollars.* 'What about Davita Lopez?' I say. 'Davita *expects* the ten thousand dollars.' He looks at me and says he just called Davita and told her Marcus has stopped payments. That's what he told her. Stopped payments. Lied to keep the money. I asked him Davita's response, and he said Davita screamed she would get even with Marcus. Get her revenge. But Joey didn't care. He had the ten thousand dollars. He had the money and was going to pay it back with interest. Just needed the cash to get on his feet. Start again! The *fool.* He *believed* Alex, *believed* the Agency was going to employ him.

" 'What about the baby, Joey?' I said. 'Going to destroy Tom Nelson, weren't you? Use my baby.' And he looks at me puzzled and replies, 'What do you mean?' And I watch him reach for the taco and suddenly I feel my heart exploding. Something's wrong, Linda, something terrible is happening, and I say to him, 'You were going to blackmail Tom because of the baby, you were going to use my baby to destroy her father.' And he looks at me in a strange way. 'What's got into you, Maria? You're *mad,*' he says. 'Who is the baby's father, *who is he?* Marcus said the baby's father was unknown to him, someone you had picked up here, a Mexican. How could we use the baby to destroy her father if . . .' "

"Thompson lied," said Linda.

Maria's eyes fell on her. She spoke in a harsh whisper.

"I watched Joey taste the taco. *I watched him.* I watched him grab his neck and gag. So quick. He stared at me one final time with those frightened, empty eyes. I *killed* . . ."

"Thompson killed him, Maria."

"*I* killed Joey. *I* killed Joey."

The sound of footsteps startled Linda, who heard Eva Kaiser's voice: "I think that's enough. You've upset Maria."

"I'm tired," Maria said.

"Of course you're tired, dear," Eva Kaiser said, glaring at Linda.

"Let me finish," Linda pleaded. "Five more minutes. Please, Doctor . . ."

Eva Kaiser shook her head. "I don't think . . ."

Suddenly Linda stood up, reaching for the back of a chair for support. "Ask Maria. Ask Maria what she wants."

Maria's voice carried in the wind. "I want her to stay."

Eva Kaiser turned on the balls of her feet, stiffening for a moment as the wind rose, and walked away. The sun slipped behind the clouds.

Maria said: "The cause of death was listed as heart attack. Joey was buried quickly, without an autopsy."

"Joey knew too much," said Linda.

"He had performed his mission. He got the films. But he was unreliable."

"A blackmailer!"

Maria lowered her voice. "Could have turned against *them.*"

Linda's heart pounded. "Tell me about the baby."

"The baby," Maria whispered. "The *baby.*"

"*Why?*" Linda asked.

"*The baby.*"

"What made you do it?"

"To punish myself."

"What?"

"Destroy the baby. Destroy what I loved." She was rocking back and forth. "Doom myself. Doom myself to a life of shame. I had killed Joey. I had to . . . execute myself."

"I don't believe you," said Linda sharply.

Maria's eyes flew open. "What?"

"What happened, Maria?"

"Had to destroy."

"Step by step. What happened after Joey died?"

"Joey died."

"Think!"

"Joey died." Maria's right hand raked her hair. *"Scared."*

"You were in a daze, Maria."

"Went to the funeral. Flew to Sarasota."

"No. Before that, Maria. Just after he died. What did you do?"

"The police," Maria mumbled.

"The police came. Carried Joey away."

"Grandmother."

"Your grandmother came home."

Maria's voice was suddenly pitched high. *"Vete, Abuelita. Llevate la nena. Vete a la casa de Marcus. Necesito silencio. Ire pronto Pero, ahora eleva."* She stared beyond Linda. "I said, 'Go immediately, Grandmother. Take the baby. Go to Marcus. I need silence. I'll be there soon. *Just take the baby.'"*

"Your grandmother left with the baby."

A shadow crossed Maria's face. Was it Linda's imagination that she saw a flicker of alarm in the girl's eyes?

"Went to the funeral in a trance. Funeral in Sarasota. Met Marcus." She winced. "I'll be back soon, Marcus, back in L.A."

"You returned to the apartment in Mexico City."

Linda spoke tensely, suddenly aware of an echo of words drumming in her head, a woman's voice over similar sounds, waves battering sand dunes.

"Packed up," murmured Maria. "Got my ticket . . ."

Linda caught her breath. *Lois Barrie.* What did Lois say at Gregory's house? Faint words, spoken almost in passing.

Linda spoke suddenly, her voice surprisingly flat.

"You visited your mother before you flew to L.A. You didn't mention that."

"Unimportant." Maria frowned at her fingernails. "Davita Lopez is a whore. Living with a twenty-three-year-old stud in Zihuatanejo. Struggling pathetically to look young." Maria looked up, eyes pleading with Linda. "We spoke briefly—twenty, thirty minutes. 'Find a man, hon-nee,' that's the way she talks. 'Find a man, hon-nee, you'll be happy!'"

Maria's voice quivered. "Hadn't seen her in fifteen years. I had to see her. Had to give her the money. Marcus' money. I told her Joey had died. I gave her the envelope and left."

"What happened after you left your mother's house?"

Maria stared at Linda, her voice tense. "*You* know what happened. I flew to L.A."

"No. No. *Before* you flew to L.A. you left your mother's house. What did you do when you left your mother's house?"

"I went downtown to buy a ticket for L.A."

"You didn't have the ticket before that?"

Linda watched Maria.

"You weren't planning to go on that trip to L.A. until you saw your mother." Linda tried to speak calmly.

"What did your mother tell you, Maria?"

Maria was rocking back and forth.

"No. *No.*"

Linda's voice shook. "Yes. Stay here. Locked up forever. Burying the truth. Knowing, always knowing, that one day soon reporters are going to find out. Someone'll chase the story and smear it all over the front pages. And then what? If only you'd have told Linda, that's what you'll say. Linda was a friend, Linda wanted to help, Linda would have printed a story that was fair, that was honest. *Trust* me." Linda swallowed. "Now, what did your mother say?"

"I wanted to give Davita the money as soon as I got there. The envelope."

"But you didn't."

"I kept the envelope."

"She didn't know you had the money."

"Davita was furious. 'Why are you here?' she screamed. 'Why?'

"'Mother, I am so unhappy. I have sinned! Committed evil.'"

"What did she say?"

"'Don't be a fool! Don't talk about evil. Find a man, hon-nee.' I said, 'Momma, I found a man. A strong man. A good man. I even had a child with him.'"

"What did she say, Maria?"

"'Keep him. Do everything you can. Keep him.'"

"But you couldn't keep him. He was married."

"He was married. He was older. He had a family." Maria stared at Linda. "Momma laughed. She *laughed.*"

"What did she say, Maria?"

Maria stared at the grass. "Adobe soil absorbs the rain, sucks the water."

Furious, Linda lunged at Maria, grasping the girl's forearms. "What did she tell you?"

"I can't . . ."

"Yes, you *can* remember. You've *got* to remember."

"She was laughing."

"Talking about married men."

"She said my father was a married man."

Linda reared back. "Your *father!*"

A door slammed yards away.

Maria's eyes went blank, her face convulsed in anguish. "Davita said Marcus paid her, paid to keep her silent, never, *never* to reveal my father's name."

Linda heard a clash of voices but sat perfectly still, her eyes fixed on Maria's face.

"Said Marcus had decided to stop paying. That's what Joey told her. Stopped paying her to keep silent." A low hiss seeped through Maria's teeth. "Her silence was *over.*"

"Marcus is not your father," said Linda softly.

Maria raised her eyes to the sky. Fog was coiling in, the cold wetness laced with salt and a scent of tangy eucalyptus.

Linda heard feet approaching, but she was strangely calm as she gently reached toward Maria.

"Your father was Tom Nelson," Linda said.

As Linda spoke the name, Maria nodded and said blankly, "I had my father's baby."

Just as Linda felt rough hands seize her shoulders, Maria started shrieking, the anguished cries echoing across the hills, wails so mournful, so frightening that the figures surging around Linda stopped, frozen.

Suddenly the hands were on Linda and lifting her awkwardly. The girl kept shrieking. Linda thought she heard Dr. Kaiser's voice, and she was numbly aware that patients were screaming too.

Linda was carried away, hands pressed beneath her back and

buttocks. She turned to catch sight of the two men carrying her off: one of them was the hospital guard, Victor.

Her heart skipped as she recognized the second man; his face looked bruised.

It was Marcus Lynn.

CHAPTER 22

Frieda Steiner stepped slowly into the publisher's office, Lucy behind her. Skipper half-arose, starting to speak, but held back, shocked at the change in Frieda. Her skin seemed drained with illness.

"Where's Eli?" Her voice was low and sharp.

Skipper's eyes met Lucy's. "He's meeting with Lazzarutti."

"It's almost three o'clock." Frieda turned impatiently to Lucy. "Let's vote. Have Miss Heaney get Eli."

Lucy's eyes met Skipper's once more as she slipped out of the office.

Frieda stared at the floor, her head nodding.

"You're not well, Mother." Skipper's defiant tone surprised him. Frieda said nothing.

Skipper's rage at Frieda, so powerful only hours before, had burned away. He could never forgive Frieda, he knew, but neither could he stay furious.

Yes, she had made her decision willfully—she had opted for Eli, for Barry Cohen, for a new newspaper. She would now live for the rest of her life with the implications of her act.

Yet, glaring at Frieda's withered face, Skipper was suddenly annoyed at himself for the corrosive resentments that poisoned his heart. He was not a petty man, he knew, he could never bear grudges. Besides, Frieda's outburst at him yesterday had seared him in its honesty. Tough and stubborn and impossible Frieda Steiner. He loved her even now, even at this moment, because she had such strength, such guts, because she lived her life with the zest of a young woman. Because she had freed him. He would renew himself now. Like Sally. Even like Larry. If his own son yearned to study ballet, was it too late to accept the boy's needs with a semblance of pride? Encourage him?

Was it too late for Skipper to reject his own fantasies of Larry's suitability as a potential heir, as an executive on the newspaper?

If Larry's sexual hungers alarmed Skipper, was it too late, nonetheless, to accept him as a son? Love him?

Start again. Unburdened by the past, the crippling past.

Skipper's eyes darted to the leather scrapbook on his desk, and then he gazed at his mother, who sat down on a suede-and-Plexiglas chair in the center of the office. A slight smile lit his face.

He heard the door open and Lucy enter, but he kept his eyes fixed on Frieda. He was strangely exhilarated and, suddenly, knew that the moment he had feared so long, the moment whose inevitability loomed and somehow paralyzed him, was now imminent.

Start again.

He heard Lucy say that Eli would be here any moment, but Skipper ignored the words, keeping his eyes fixed on the leatherbound book atop the desk. It was irrelevant, Skipper thought to himself, whether or not to speak to Frieda before or after the vote. One final word. She had freed him, and now, finally, he would confront his mother and free himself.

*

Marcus Lynn drove in silence, his Rolls-Royce picking up speed as the narrow road dipped between an outcropping of enormous boulders that blocked the flickering sun. Ahead, the road twisted around a creek, and suddenly they were climbing, deep into the headlands.

Linda glanced at Marcus' hands, grasped tight around the steering wheel, his knuckles white, the only movement in his body the lurch in his thigh as he pressed his foot on the accelerator. She turned to fasten her eyes on the windshield, startled as he raced over a road that skirted a sheer bluff, an expanse of wild coastline descending below.

Why was she so calm? she wondered. Why had the fright that seized her only minutes earlier yielded to an absolute . . . peace?

A swirl of fog was drifting rapidly toward them from the canyon of the storm-blasted pine overhead, the fog enveloping them in moist humid air. She opened the window full as Marcus switched on the headlights, easing the car's speed as he did so.

The headlights' glow caught a ghostly shack on the side of the road, windows smashed and a door flapping in the wind, the silvery light casting an eerie shimmer over the moss-hung cypresses that flanked the path.

Hesitantly, Linda turned to Marcus, opening her mouth and ready to speak, but catching her breath. His face had aged, as if the past few hours had been a lifetime.

Linda heard herself speak in a tremulous voice.

"Listen to me, Marcus."

The words began in a flow, Maria's words.

Only once did Marcus interrupt: he rasped, "Fitzgerald."

"Fitzgerald needed you, Marcus. Needed you at whatever cost. Needed you to turn against Tom Nelson."

*

Alex Vikas leaned against his high-back leather swivel chair, his feet on the desk, his left hand holding binoculars to his eyes, his right hand pressing the phone to his ear.

". . . Quite extraordinary, Dick. A hummingbird. Fiery-red throat. Greenish back. Forked tail. What? That's the male. I see. I *see*. The female has no red throat. Has a blunt tail with white spots. Interesting. Dick, can you hear me? Yes, yes, I'm still coming down tonight, but there's one small favor. You know those films, the films in our safe. Six reels. Sign them out. Yes, all of them."

Alex Vikas removed the binoculars from his eyes as the door to the office opened. He didn't turn. "Sign them out and put them all in a blue-and-white Pan Am bag, the small carry-on number. Long strap. Over the shoulder. Perhaps you should take care of this before you meet me at the airport, probably be a little more convenient. Yes. Tell the Marine guard that, ah, you'll return the films later tonight."

As Alex replaced the phone moments later, he lifted the binoculars once more to his eyes. He heard Mai Tien's voice.

"What kind of films are they, Alex?"

"Films a pretty girl like you shouldn't see."

She giggled. "You're whetting my interest."

"Come to Mexico with me."

"What will you do with the films?"

"Which films?"

"The films Dick Thompson gives you."

"That's a . . . vireo. Yellow-throated vireo."

"Alex!"

"Burn the films. That's what I'll probably do. Replace the films and burn the ones I take." He turned, smiling.

"Why?"

"It's complicated."

"It always is."

Mai took a step toward him.

"You were blackmailing . . ."

"What an unpleasant word," said Alex Vikas. "We were exchanging favors. We kept the films *safe*. Locked up."

Mai kept her gaze firmly on Alex. "And a central figure in the films . . ."

"Was grateful," said Alex, smiling.

"Performed all kinds of favors," said Mai. "Like support the budget."

"An increased budget, dear."

"Like support a new charter."

"Stepped-up domestic surveillance. We control foreign and domestic intelligence. Quite significant for us."

"And now . . ."

"And now the subject has become . . . vulnerable. A few too many people are finding out about the films. Time to excavate them, destroy them . . ."

"Newspapers may find out. Is that it, Alex?"

"Publish exposés. Secret films allegedly kept in the American Embassy. Films of a rather important government official as a young man. Isn't it wise, dear, to get rid of the films quietly?"

"Without telling the subject?"

"Best that I don't."

"Keep the subject controlled."

"We may need him."

"That's evil, Alex."

Alex smiled. "Of *course* it's evil." The red phone on his desk rang, and Alex reached for it. Pressing his palm over the mouthpiece, Alex murmured, "In a civilized world we wouldn't be evil. Wouldn't give a damn about budgets, a new charter."

"Or blackmail," said Mai, watching him twist his chair to face the window, the phone cupped against his right ear. As Alex listened, Mai noticed the smile freeze.

"Outstanding," he finally said, hanging up. Alex glanced up at Mai, his face beaming. She saw the dampness in his curly black hair and grinned. Perhaps she should relent and go to Mexico City, she thought.

"Cancel the trip," he said. "Have Thompson fly up tonight and meet him at Dulles. Give him my Pan Am bag, take his. He'll fly right back. Send a message to the ambassador saying my trip has been canceled because of the world situation, etcetera." He swung toward the window. "Take the bag that Thompson gives him and bring it here. Lock it in the safe."

"What's happened, Alex?"

His eyes locked into the binoculars.

"We're going to have a new President soon."

"Fitzgerald?"

"Belling. Eddie Belling."

"You never liked him."

"Now I do. That's extraordinary."

"What's . . ."

"Purple finch. Beautiful! Never knew they came down this far."

"You have something on Mr. Belling?"

"We have something on Mr. Belling."

"Pictures? Tapes?"

"Both." He swung the binoculars upward. "There's a house in Alexandria where Belling finds his pleasure. Slightly bizarre pleasure in the scheme of things . . ."

"Especially for a President of the United States."

"Exactly."

"You'll blackmail him too."

"Stop using that ugly word." Alex turned to her. "I think of it more as *insurance* against a President doing something foolish with our budget. Limiting our powers . . ."

The white phone rang, and Mai reached for it. She said Alex was at a meeting and took a message.

"You protect me so well," he said as Mai set the phone down.

"My job," she said. "By the way, the red phone . . ."

"You noticed."

"Red phone—the Secretary of Defense. White phone—ordinary mortals, agents in the field. Blue phone—the White House."

"You finally learned."

"But the Secretary of Defense is in China."

"I've noticed." He twisted his chair to face the window and left his binoculars.

"Someone on his staff?" said Mai. "Close to him?"

"That's an oriole."

"Like Colonel Walker?"

"Orchard oriole, I think. Now, why would Colonel Walker seek me out?"

"Old friends. Go back to Vietnam."

"As a matter of fact, he worked for us then."

"And still does," said Mai. "What does he want, Alex? A promotion? What have you promised him?"

"He'll get at least two stars," said Alex dryly.

"Something bigger. Come on, Alex. Maybe head of the Army?"

"Interesting idea." His thumb and forefinger gently twisted the lens knob.

"Maybe head of the Joint Chiefs? That's it, Alex. Head of the Joint Chiefs. Having a colonel jump over hundreds of names ahead of him needs a lot of support. If you told the President and the Hill that you wanted Walker . . ."

Alex lowered his binoculars and turned to her.

"By the way, who called before?"

"Terry Schachter. He's lost the girl. Linda Fentress. And Marcus Lynn. They're in the mountains. Drove off together."

Alex Vikas examined his hands with a frown. "Tell him to return to L.A. We don't need him anymore."

*

They neared the mountain bluff, perched hundreds of feet above the sea, just as the fog lifted to reveal an expanse of perfectly blue sky and an immense sweep of ocean and land. Linda heard the car shudder to a halt. Marcus opened the door and swung his body outside, Linda behind him.

Lowering his head against the wind, Marcus strode toward the end of the bluff, the gorges and canyons beneath them dun-gray in the shadows. Huge waves, battering the beach, echoed like distant thunder over the mountain.

Struggling to keep up with Marcus, Linda was suddenly seized with alarm: Marcus would hurl himself into the canyons below, his secrets and strange passions forever lost. But he turned, and mutely watched her push toward him against the wind.

They stood strangely still, staring at waves that heaved with a greenish glow. Marcus' voice carried in the wind.

"I *had* to see her. I *knew* I had to see her. It was time. You were getting too close."

His voice was high with pain.

"My fault. My *guilt*. I'm guiltier than *he* is." He spoke fiercely. "I knew, I *knew* . . ."

"You knew Nelson was Maria's father."

"I raised her. Watched her grow. I shared her life. She was mine. *Mine! My* daughter."

"Nelson never knew?"

"No one ever knew except . . . her mother."

"And you paid her to keep quiet."

"Keefer lied to her. Took the money and *lied!* Told her I had decided to stop paying. He didn't know why I was paying her, Linda. Didn't know what it would *mean* for Maria to learn the truth."

"Maybe he did, Marcus. Maybe it was his final revenge on you."

"All those years I wanted to tell her the truth," Marcus said. "Every time I began . . . I *couldn't.*"

"You loved her too much."

His head drooped. "She would have left me for *him*. She was all I had." Marcus spoke so softly that Linda barely heard the words. "By my silence I destroyed her."

"Keefer destroyed her, Marcus. Fitzgerald. You wanted to take over the *Star,* didn't you, Marcus? For the Dunlaps. For Eli Faber. For Fitzgerald. They came into Transcon after you had turned against Nelson. They *needed* you, Marcus. They needed your money and power. Needed your respectability. You were a perfect front."

He shut his eyes. "I had to get even with Nelson."

"You were set up by Fitzgerald and Keefer." Her heart was hammering now. "Tell me the story, the full story."

"I don't have the full story."

"Let's start. What were you doing in Zurich?"

"There were accounts to set up."

"Accounts in Jerry's name?"

"*One* account in Jerry's name. Jerry had signature authority but never knew where the money in Panama went. The bank was instructed automatically to transfer seventy-five percent of Jerry's account into a second account."

"Fitzgerald's account."

"He needed the money for his campaign against Nelson. That's what he said."

"Cheryl got in the way . . ."

"Cheryl had the diary, Linda. Names. Dates. Amounts of money she passed on to Jerry. She knew . . ."

"Fitzgerald had to stop her," said Linda. "Had to destroy the diary."

"He got your colleagues . . ."

"My colleagues. Barry Cohen. Howie Bishop."

". . . Got your colleagues to hunt down the diary. The evidence."

"Fitzgerald had it all worked out," Linda said, her voice strained. "Give them a bone. Give them Jerry Paley. Give them a *story*. Promise Barry the managing editor's job as soon as he and Eli and the Dunlaps take over." Linda moved beside Marcus. "And Fitzgerald gets what *he* wants."

"It would have worked, Linda."

"But his wife got there first," said Linda, her eyes widening. "She has the diary."

"She *had* the diary. It's in Fitzgerald's hands now."

Linda felt a shock: Cheryl's words on the telephone message to Marcus.

Given a copy of the diary to Jerry P.

"Jerry had the names too," Linda said.

*

A television crew was threading down the aisles of the *Star*'s newsroom, klieg lights glaring over desks as reporters typed on video terminals, lifted phones, talked to one another, gathered at the bulletin board to examine the latest word from the Guild.

"The death watch," said Florence, settling into her chair at the foreign desk. She lit a cigarette.

Ward, standing at the desk and leafing through incoming messages, spoke to Ray Silver and Tony Lazzarutti. "Nothing yet from Barney Fischer."

"I'm drunk," said Florence.

"Zero," said Ray Silver.

"Those bastards are taping the last gasp of the New York *Star,*" said Florence. "Like here we are. Funny little prehistoric relics. The pencil press. Waiting to die."

Glistening yellow-white lights caught a burst of activity in the center of the newsroom. "Jesus, Harry Handsome is interviewing Kaiserman," said Ward.

Florence examined her cigarette. "Harry Handsome has the whitest teeth in New York. Harry Handsome has the smallest brain and certainly one of the largest salaries. Harry Handsome is Mr. Six-thirty News."

"Harry Handsome is show biz," said Ward with distaste.

"Don't knock it," said Florence. "*That's* the future. The electronic media. Glitz. Pancake makeup. Thirty-second spots. Newspapers! You're a doomed species."

Ward said to Tony, "Get Florence some coffee."

Florence smiled and lifted the phone. "Foreign desk."

"Hugh Finch wants to talk to you. Urgent," said Tony. "Called while you were at lunch."

"Get him."

"I was trapped into lunch with Kaiserman," said Ray.

"Better you than me, Ray."

"Volunteering to go overseas again," said Ray quietly. "Anywhere."

"Lagos? Belgrade?"

"*Anywhere.*"

"What about the wife?"

"He's splitting. 'I'm forty-four years old and miserable,' he says."

Florence hung up the phone. "Young lady from *Time* magazine." She smiled drunkenly at Ward. "An acquaintance of yours.

Wanted a quote from you on losing out to Mr. Cohen. I told her in my gentle way to shove it."

"In her gentle way," Ray said.

"And besides, I told her nothing was official until the vote, and you were not gonna be around for the announcement. Told her you were off to visit your wife and kids. Told her about your intense commitment to marriage."

"Thanks," said Ward dryly. "There goes my chance to be 'Man of the Year.'" Florence reached for another ringing phone.

Ray said to Ward, "Five minutes to three."

"I hear Marty Kaplan's all set to take Barry's place," said Ward.

"Nice guys finish first. For a change." He leaned forward and said, "If you *do* get the job, Ward."

"Hell. I won't."

"But if you got it. I'd like to be . . . How shall I say?"

"Considered."

"Considered for the foreign editor's job."

Ward nodded, his eyes darting to the desk. He suddenly recalled a conversation months earlier at a *Star* party with Ray's wife, a sullen redhaired woman whose large, almost expressionless eyes tightened with rage while she condemned the *Star*'s treatment of her husband. Another newspaper wife. The newspaper had bypassed her husband for promotion; the newspaper had ignored his commitment, his relentless working hours, his love for the *Star,* and had sapped his confidence, while younger men—and now women—climbed through the ranks, were sent abroad, became editors and executives.

"Consumes us, doesn't it?" said Ward suddenly, staring at Ray Silver.

Florence interrupted. "It's Ernie Richards. Says Belling is leaving Peking in about four hours. He's meeting Phung now. Says the story will shift to a Moscow dateline tonight and it's *his* story."

Another phone was ringing and Ray picked it up.

Florence continued. "Carl Ross, according to Ernie, will do color and sidebars. Ernie has not yet informed Carl."

Tony Lazzarutti said, "I've got Hugh Finch at home."

"Put him on hold," said Ward.

Florence lit another cigarette. "Turf time at the *Star*. The children are fighting over bylines."

Ray interrupted: "It's Carl Ross."

"I love it," said Florence.

Ray smiled. "Carl says he's *obviously* doing the lead story. He's Peking bureau chief. Besides, Ernie has saved lots of string for a good color story on Belling."

Suddenly Florence stabbed her cigarette in the ashtray, her eyes wet. She was staring at Nick on the city desk, blankly watching him talk into the phone.

"Why the hell shouldn't they fight over the front-page byline," she said, swallowing hard. "It's the last paper."

"Last paper in a long time," said Ward, looking up at her.

*

Nick heard Linda's breathless voice over the phone.

"Any word from Mike Paley?"

"Nothing," said Nick. His stomach tightened.

"Damn!"

"Soon as he calls, Linda, I'll pass on the message," he said lightly. "You're at the Pine Inn, right? P-I-N-E."

"Tell him to call me immediately. It's *urgent*."

"Sure, Linda." Nick watched Pat Donlon spike some wire-service copy.

"Where's Barry?"

"Still at lunch." The television lights glowed over the desk, catching Nick on the phone.

"Is he at Fritzi's?"

Nick felt the sweat start on his face. "No."

He heard the click.

Nick stared at the phone and replaced it gently. Reporters and editors and clerks wandered listlessly through the aisles, clustering at the bulletin board to read the latest Guild bulletins, hovering beside desks to whisper and exchange gossip . . .

Barry's got it . . . Marty Kaplan's replacing him . . . rumor Eli's replacing Skipper . . . Sally's quit, splitting with Charlie . . . Linda's got a heavy one in L.A. . . . Pulitzer . . . Barney Fischer's got a biggie coming up . . . What are you gonna do if there's a long strike? . . . Starve . . . Write my novel . . . get out of this business, once and for all. . . . Poor bastard Jerry

Paley, that breaks my heart . . . long strike would kill the paper. . . . Just like the Herald Tribune. *. . . What a goddamn business . . . I was on the* Mirror, *the* World-Telegram, *the* Herald Tribune *and now the* Star.

At one minute to three, Nick picked up the ringing phone. It was Mike Paley.

"Linda just called," said Nick.

"Great!"

"She's traveling, Mike. In California. Monterey. Carmel. She's out of pocket for a couple of hours." Nick heard Mike's intake of breath. "She wants you to pass on the names in Cheryl's diary to me."

Nick spoke rapidly in a low tone, almost a murmur, to keep his voice steady. He heard Mike say, "*You?*"

"The names, yeah. The names in Cheryl's diary. Names and dates. Amounts of money. Linda wants you to pass them on to me." His impatient tone surprised him. "You got the names, right?"

Mike whispered, "Can I trust you?"

"Like a brother."

"I got names!"

"What are the names, Mike?" Nick tried to sound calm.

"A dozen names. Defense contractors. Milk producers. Two oil companies. Some Arab lobbyists. They paid Cheryl . . ."

"They paid Cheryl, yeah."

"And Cheryl passed the money on to Dad for Fitzgerald . . ."

"For Fitzgerald." Nick's mouth went dry. "And what happened, Mike?"

"Dad deposited the money in Panama."

Nick's fingers tensed as he wrote.

"From there the money went to Switzerland. Dad got a cut. Hey listen . . ."

"Yeah."

"Can I trust you?"

"Fucking aye, you can trust me."

"You'll tell Linda?"

"Scout's honor. Mike, give me the names."

"I've got them here."

"Who knows about Switzerland? Linda'll want to know. Who knows about that?"

"Guy in California. He set it up. Lynn."

"L-Y-N-N."

"Don't have the first name. Tell Linda."

"Of course, Mike. Who told you? She'll want to know. Your source. You gotta have a source. Your dad?"

"No. Not Dad. It was . . . Cheryl. She told me."

"*Cheryl!*"

"Trusted me," said Mike Paley quietly. "Nick?"

"Yeah."

"Is Barry around?"

"Out to lunch now. Give me the names, Mike."

"Where? Out to lunch where?"

Nick saw Marty Kaplan wander over to the foreign desk to talk to Ray Silver. He felt the dampness on his legs. The question echoed.

Where? Out to lunch where?

Nick swallowed hard, his chest ached.

Front-page byline. Last paper before the strike.

"Fritzi's," said Nick, narrowing his eyes on Marty Kaplan, vaguely puzzled at the odd question from a caller who he assumed was in Washington, D.C. He released a long-held breath.

Suddenly Nick heard Mike Paley laughing.

"What's funny, Mike?"

"I'm at Fritzi's myself," Mike said, almost defiantly. "Barry must be in the restaurant in back."

Nick's tongue was stuck to the roof of his mouth. When he finally spoke, his voice was pitched high. "What are you doing in New York?"

"Came here to see Barry. See him at the office. But I'll see him here instead, right?" Mike Paley's strange voice puzzled Nick for a moment, and then, quite unexpectedly, alarmed him.

Nick closed his eyes. "Now give me the names, Mike. Nice and slow. Give me the names before you see Barry."

*

Peggy Connor and Geri Buckley, the two waitresses at Fritzi's, had finally settled down at a corner table when the "reporter's phone" rang in the booth beside the kitchen. The women gazed at one another with tired frowns—rumors of a strike had turned the restaurant and bar into a packed, noisy zoo (Geri's word) whose demanding customers kept the waitresses frantic until two-fifty.

On the second ring, Peggy glanced at Geri, who had just brought over two cups of coffee, and pushed herself up. *"Fuck!"* She trudged to the clamoring phone.

Geri, a stolid woman in her forties with a surprisingly delicate mouth, narrow eyes and blond hair coiled tightly in a bun, lit a cigarette and turned to the lone remaining guests at the table beside the far wall. Barry Cohen was draining his wineglass, fixing his eyes on the girl facing him.

Barry seemed lightheaded, even a little drunk—and why not? thought Geri, picking a shard of tobacco off her tongue. In the midst of lunch, she had slipped over to Barry's table to whisper, "Congratulations, honey. Jesus, I remember when you were a wise-ass kid." And he had laughed and patted her ass.

Geri knew them all, or most of them. Not the Skippers and the Friedas and the Evans mind you, but the reporters and editors who crammed the restaurant, the ones whose turbulent moods still intrigued her after twenty-two years. Somehow Fritzi's was a haven, a way-station between the tensions of the newsroom and the realities of home. They certainly didn't come here for the burned pork chops, although they ate them. They didn't even come here for the booze, although they drank, God knows they drank. They came here to soothe their nerves, ease the flow of energy that they expended each day, knowing that tomorrow and the day after that the cycle would repeat itself. Fatigue and strange angers consuming most of them. They worked so hard, bitched and groaned from the moment they walked in. But they *loved* it, loved every minute, the deadlines and the tension and the rhythm, each moment unpredictable, the release at the end of each day. *They loved it.*

The restaurant itself and bar were separated by a smoke-gray Plexiglas partition with elaborately carved flowers, a partition that tacitly served to divide two vaguely hostile groups; in the restaurant sat reporters and editors, while printers and drivers perched on stools in the narrow, dank bar up front that was dominated by a 21-inch color television screen on a pedestal atop two phone booths at the window.

Geri saw Peggy walk toward Barry and motion him to the phone. Geri sucked her cigarette, wondering if this, indeed, was the official word from the tenth floor.

Managing editor.

Started coming here as a kid, he did, just like Nick Simons and the other kids now, smart and aggressive. They even had a party for Barry when he returned from Vietnam and won his Pulitzer Prize.

Peggy pulled up a chair and tasted her coffee. "California," she said with a shrug.

"The films are locked up, Barry, locked up at the American Embassy in Mexico City," said Linda, without introduction. Her voice dropped. "They'll be gone by the time I get there."

He winced. "I want a story."

"I have a story, Barry. A good story."

He heard Linda cough.

"One piece is missing, the final piece," she said rapidly. "Cheryl's diary. Diary with the names."

"What are you talking about?"

"I'm talking about my story, Barry. Stories take a life of their own. That's what Jerry Paley used to say. That's what he taught us. Let the stories work themselves out. Well, I got the story, Barry . . ."

He spoke in a low voice, tense with rage. "You got *one* story, Linda. Nelson and his films. You file on that *now*. Nelson made a porno film. *That's* the story."

"No, Barry. That's *not* the story. I *know* the story, Barry. Know about Fitzgerald and Joey Keefer. I know about Eli Faber and the Dunlaps. You cut a deal, you silly bastard. I *know*. I know about Fitzgerald's Swiss bank accounts. I . . ."

"There's going to be a strike tonight, Linda. It's the last paper. And you're not in it."

"Barry, we've got to print the story. I got Marcus Lynn to talk!"

"You're finished, honey. *Finished!* No matter where you are, I'll chase you down. You're finished in this business. *It's over!*"

He slammed the phone onto the hook and flung open the door to see a man in a khaki jacket facing him.

"Are you Barry Cohen?"

Barry was shaking. He wondered why the man was smiling. "Yes," he said furiously.

The man in the khaki jacket spoke in a singsong voice. "I'm Mike Paley."

Barry swallowed and suddenly felt a weakness in his knees. His tongue went dry. He squinted, reaching out awkwardly to shake Mike's hand. Barry saw the smile deepen, and just then he glanced down and saw the revolver.

His lips fell open in surprise as the first bullet ripped through cartilage and bone in his stomach. Barry fell to his knees, the fingers of his right hand fumbling at the center of his chest. He saw blood spurt on the floor, he was gagging; and then Barry tried to raise his head as the loudest explosion he had ever heard tore his shoulders, a white-hot pain cascading over his back. He paused for a half second, then sprawled forward.

*

As the clock struck three in Skipper Steiner's office, Frieda heard the door open. She stiffened slightly but refused to turn, aware that Lucy and Skipper were staring past her. Frieda's left fist clenched.

Expecting Eli's voice, she was startled to hear Geraldine Heaney's mumbled apologies. Frieda turned.

"Linda Fentress," said Miss Heaney. "She wants to talk to you. Says it's urgent."

The words were addressed to Skipper, and Frieda heard them through a strange echo. She was dizzy and felt a little sick.

Skipper was saying something, but the words were lost in the drumming in her ears.

Frieda heard Skipper ask Lucy to take Linda's call in the anteroom.

"What have I done?" whispered Frieda, contemplating Skipper's desk.

The door closed behind Lucy and Geraldine Heaney. "Forgive me, Skipper," Frieda said.

"Nothing to forgive, Mother," he said gently.

Frieda returned his glance. "I'm a foolish woman, Skipper. Foolish and vain. Made mistakes in my life, mistakes that haunt me now. I've destroyed the paper . . ."

"The one thing you love more than anything."

Frieda opened her mouth, but no words came. Her eyes fell shut. "My life is a lie," she whispered.

Frieda thought she heard the whir of a helicopter over the Hudson.

"So is mine, Mother." He said the words firmly.

"Don't say that."

"It's time, Mother."

"Time for what?" she said, almost angry.

"Time that I spoke to you. I made a decision today, a decision I forced upon myself. I've been living with this lie for so long, so many years, that I've begun to believe it. Frieda, it's twisted me in ways I still don't understand. I've tried to bury it . . ."

"Bury *what?*"

"Tried to bury it, but it's crippled me. Crippled me with you. And Sally. And Larry."

She felt the blood rush to her face. "What are you talking about, Skipper?"

"I'm not Jonathan's son."

For a moment, Frieda listened intently to the hum of the city below, the distant clamor of a police siren. Suddenly she straightened, as if shocked into awareness. She drew a breath.

And then, without warning, Frieda laughed.

Skipper stared at his mother, ignoring the knock on the door. Frieda arose, her chin held high.

"Come in, please," Frieda said as the door swung open and Lucy stepped in. Her long face was white with strain.

"Linda Fentress is telling the most astonishing story," she said. "I suggest we all pick up the phone and listen to her."

*

Marty Kaplan was threading his way toward the foreign desk, aware that reporters and editors, standing in clusters, fell silent as he walked past. To his astonishment, the chance meeting yesterday with Frieda Steiner at the Russian Tea Room—the trip back to the office in her car during which she broached the idea of his remaining in New York to take over the city editor's job—had touched off rumors that surged like a tide and settled in every corner of the newsroom.

Marty was replacing Barry Cohen.

There were no secrets in the newsroom; gossip flew through the air, reporters overheard one another's phone calls, watched the flow of movement into the editors' offices, questioned and whispered, seized rumors with an intense hunger that was, after all, the nature of their lives.

"Is it official?" asked Ward.

"Don't quote me, but . . ." began Marty.

"Welcome to management, the big time!" Ward pushed back his chair and shook Marty's hand.

Florence smiled. "Cab's coming in ten minutes."

"You're missing the vote," said Marty. "Barry's celebration."

Ward whispered, "Eli Faber's taking over. That's the rumor." He stared at Marty's face. "What's wrong?"

."They want me to get rid of Sarah Felger, some of the older reporters."

"Bastards."

From the foreign desk, Ray Silver shouted in a tremulous voice: "Ward! Barney Fischer's on the phone. He's *got* it."

Ward widened his eyes. "Son of a bitch. He's got the President's speech!" Ward reached for the phone.

Marty turned and saw Nick Simons beside him, breathless, a sheet of yellow paper clutched in his hand. Nick's tongue darted over his lower lip as he spoke.

"The diary. Cheryl's diary. I got what's in it."

Beyond Nick's shoulder Marty saw a burst of activity in the center of the newsroom. A crowd of reporters and editors converged at the city desk, Mary Phelps and Sarah Felger pushing through the crowd. Marty saw Pat Donlon's stricken face and watched several reporters rush to the elevator.

*

On the tenth floor, Eli opened the door without a knock, surprised to see Skipper standing comfortably behind his desk, arms folded across his chest. Frieda was seated to her son's right, Lucy at the floor-to-ceiling window.

"Shall we vote?" said Eli. He glanced elaborately at his watch. It was five minutes after three.

Frieda's face wore a rueful smile, and Eli watched her exchange glances with Lucy.

"Afraid we're deadlocked," said Eli, leveling his eyes on Skipper. "Lazzarutti wants a strike at all costs . . ."

"So do the Dunlap brothers," said Frieda.

Except for a slight, almost imperceptible quiver in his chin, Eli showed no emotion.

"You never told us, Eli," Frieda said. "You never told us you were working for the Dunlaps too. You never told us that this California company that wants to buy the *Star,* the company run by Marcus Lynn, is largely owned by the Dunlaps."

"Now you know, Frieda." His voice was so cold that Lucy shuddered. Skipper's eyes were fixed on Frieda.

"You never told us about your company's land scheme in Long Island, your hidden interest, your bribery of Jerry Paley."

Lucy interrupted. "Most of the money went to David, didn't it?"

Frieda's voice rose. "You never informed us of your involvement with Senator Fitzgerald. The *payoffs.* The arrangements you so carefully set up with all those people mentioned in that girl's diary."

"We have the names in the diary," said Skipper.

"We're printing them in tomorrow's paper," said Frieda. "We have the story."

The sound of police sirens downstairs seemed to ricochet across the room.

Frieda's voice fell to a tremulous whisper. "Skipper . . . *knows.* He's known for years. For *years,* Eli. Now Lucy knows too."

Skipper nodded, a bolt of sun lighting his face. "We can write our story two ways, Eli," he said. "Depends on you. Write a story that implicates you, based on what's in the diary, what Marcus Lynn told Linda, what Fitzgerald is telling Howie Bishop . . ."

Eli glared at Skipper.

"Or we can write a story that *helps.* You're facing serious charges, Eli. Conspiracy to bribe a congressman. Attempting to corrupt a public official. Obstruction of justice. Tax violations."

Eli began to smile. "Fitzgerald is talking to Howie Bishop?"

"Howie just called," said Skipper slowly. "I gather Fitzgerald has tape recordings of some conversations he's had with you, Eli. Tapes he's planning to hand over to the Justice Department." Skipper's eyes fixed on Eli. "Fitzgerald promised to let Howie hear the tapes at four o'clock. Right after he visits his wife."

Eli examined his watch, looked up at Skipper, who spoke so quietly that Frieda leaned forward to hear. "I suggest you have Bishop alert the Washington police. Fitzgerald's wife plans to kill herself, and Dave's carrying in the pills right now."

There was a gentle knock on the door when Skipper reached for the phone.

As Lucy stepped to the door, Geraldine Heaney flung it open, then stood absolutely still, gazing with alarm at Lucy, and then turned to Frieda. "Barry," she whispered. Her left hand flew to her cheek. "Something terrible's happened to Barry!"

*

Climbing out of the taxi at the ramp of the Pan Am terminal, Sally Sims watched a porter step over and lift her two suitcases and portable typewriter onto his cart. She threaded quickly through a crowd of nuns—on their way to Rome—and followed him into the East Concourse and the international check-in.

The next eight minutes were a blur: tipping the porter, handing her ticket to a clerk, asking for an aisle seat in the smoking section, vaguely listening to the laughing conversation behind her of a couple in their twenties, gripping backpacks, en route to Ibiza.

Suddenly Sally was aware that she was standing alone in the middle of the terminal, her boarding pass and ticket in her left hand, her typewriter in her right hand, her leather shoulder bag heavy on her shoulder. Crowds surged past her, she heard the sound of rushing feet, there was an announcement of a flight to Frankfurt.

She set the typewriter down, her whole body aching. She had endured such a tide of emotions over the past forty-eight hours— shock, fear, hatred, a confusion almost devastating in its power— so that the simple gesture of handing her plane ticket to the clerk and receiving a boarding pass astonished her in its quiet finality.

She glanced up at the clock—it was four-twenty. Nearly two hours to take-off. She had arrived unusually early, for reasons she couldn't fully explain: avoid a tearful farewell with Dorothy Faye that would, inevitably, lead to Dorothy accompanying her to Kennedy, avoid phoning Skipper, avoid the *Star.*

Avoid second thoughts.

Airline terminals were neutral havens, enclosures whose air

seemed to dissolve the realities of life and throb with . . . possibility. Adventure.

Suddenly Sally felt a little faint. She placed her hand on her throat. She was a grown woman, embarking on a lonely voyage that now frightened her. Empty hotel beds and dinners alone. No friends. No support. No fallback. She looked up and saw the couple who had been standing behind her—both in jeans, the girl, a blonde in a khaki anorak, the boy in a down cruiser vest—amble to a row of chairs and drop their backpacks on the attached low tables.

Sally frowned for a moment, angry at herself for being overdressed. She wore a silk-and-wool wheat blazer, cream-colored silk shirt with black-and-red scarf and straight skirt with front and back slits.

Abruptly thirsty, Sally reached for her portable typewriter and followed the airport signs into the lounge, found a seat on a shell-shaped chair beside the floor-to-ceiling window and lit another cigarette as she ordered a bloody mary.

Skipper and Dorothy Faye and Charlie—yes, Charlie—were fading into the shadows even now, so quickly, as if the momentum that carried her here was also sweeping away the people she loved.

Her fingers absently leafed through her hair when, quite abruptly, she sensed that someone was hovering at her table. Sally heard Ward's voice even before she turned.

"You meet the strangest people at the airport," he said.

Startled, Sally struggled to smile but felt the blood rush to her cheeks. He leaned forward and kissed her gently on the lips.

"Tell me you're going to London too."

"Paris," said Sally, swallowing with difficulty. She watched Ward drop his shoulder bag on the floor and sit down across the table.

"And then?"

"The Middle East. Maybe Asia. Got some magazine pieces lined up. *The Atlantic. Harper's. New York Times Magazine. Playboy* wants me to do something in Athens on . . ." Sally caught her breath. She laughed at her nervous chatter.

"Nothing for the *Star?*" asked Ward.

Sally lowered her eyes. "Got to break away, sever the cord,"

Sally said. "For a while." She glanced up at him. "I'm glad about you and . . . Karen."

Ward made a gesture with his hands. "I want her back."

Sally smiled. "I hope she comes back to you, for *your* sake." Tears filled her eyes and she angrily opened her handbag and fumbled inside. "Damn. Damn. *Damn!* I wanted to be so cool about my life, Ward. Wanted to slip away from New York without a scene, and now you come here and screw it up. Can never find a tissue when I need one."

"Here," he said.

"Thanks."

"Sorry I loused up your quiet getaway."

"Not your fault." She dabbed her cheeks with the tissue as the waiter placed her drink on the table. Ward ordered a glass of milk.

Sally said, "Heard about Barry in the cab coming out."

"Still alive when they took him to the hospital," said Ward.

"Poor bastard. The paper was his life."

"Why did you quit, Sally?"

She watched a jumbo jet glide up the runway. Her voice cracked.

"I have to take risks, Ward. Have to understand who I am, what I want." She searched his face. "Everything looked so . . . perfect. I knew it wasn't, but I had this silly illusion." She turned away. "It wasn't Charlie. Charlie had so little to do with it."

"You're quite beautiful, Sally."

"It was *me*," she said. "I've *got* to understand."

"I never realized how beautiful you are."

"Oh Lord . . ."

"If I weren't married . . ."

"You are, darling. And it's too late to complicate my life now." She tasted her drink, eyeing Ward through the glass. "*Too late.*"

Sally saw him flinch as the voice over a loudspeaker announced that there was an urgent call for Mr. Ward Parsons at the information desk. He sighed.

"It's Ernie Richards in Peking . . ."

"Complaining that Carl Ross is hogging the lead story," said Sally.

Ward stood up, and Sally saw the flecks of gray hair over his ears.

"Better yet, it's Kaiserman," he said. "Insisting he has to go back overseas."

"Anything but the South Bronx," said Sally, settling back in her seat. There were narrow crow's feet around Ward's eyes. He's going to age rather elegantly, she thought.

*

Even before Skipper Steiner set the phone down, Frieda murmured, "How is he?"

"In surgery right now." Skipper gazed blankly at his mother. "He was bleeding badly. Unconscious. Lucy says they've put a breathing tube in his windpipe. Wounds in the lung and stomach . . ."

"Will he live?"

"Lucy says they don't know."

Frieda chewed her lip. "Does he have a family?"

"Apparently not."

"I'll go down there too. St. Clare's is on Fifty-first and . . ."

"Stay, Mother."

Their eyes held until Frieda turned away.

"And the Paley boy?" she mumbled.

"In police custody."

"What have we done, Skipper?"

The intercom buzzed, and Frieda watched Skipper walk behind the desk to lift the phone. Almost shyly, Frieda Steiner looked at the commode's marble top crammed with photographs of Frederic and Dora and Jonathan and Arnold, photographs whose every grain, every corner, mesmerized her.

"Lazzarutti's given us seventy-two hours," she heard Skipper say.

Frieda looked at him. "The drivers are holding an emergency meeting at five," said Skipper. "Harry Watson says they're going to oust Billy Weldon. Pick some insurgent kid who promises to clean up the union."

"Where's Eli now?"

"Talking to a fellow in the newsroom who's doing the story. Nick Simons." Skipper moved toward the window. "The police have just seized Fitzgerald. Attempting to give enough Seconal to his wife to kill her."

Frieda arched her chin and smiled. "Skipper, pour me a drink, please. Something strong. Vodka. Vodka and ice."

As he stepped to the liquor cabinet, Frieda pushed her chair back and walked behind the desk. Lifting the phone, she pressed a buzzer and spoke in a firm, slightly tremulous voice.

"Miss Heaney. That memo my son sent out yesterday about cutbacks in each department. Cancel it. Make sure every department head gets the cancellation in the next hour . . ."

"Frieda!" Skipper said.

She placed her hand over the receiver. "You're absolutely right, Skipper. We *can't* afford a strike. We can't afford to challenge Lazzarutti." Frieda returned to the phone. "And please be sure to inform Mr. Lazzarutti that we're doing this . . ."

Suddenly Skipper reached over and removed the phone from Frieda's grasp. She watched him, amazed, as he spoke.

"Miss Heaney, forget that."

Skipper set the phone down, leveling his eyes on Frieda. "We're going *ahead* with the cutbacks, Frieda. If Lazzarutti strikes, we'll face him down, we'll resist." His voice dropped. "*You* were right, Frieda. I don't have the guts to stand up to him."

Frieda watched him pour two drinks, handing her one. The vodka was chilled and bracing, and she was surprised to find how comforting it was.

Skipper took a step beside her. "We've got to take risks," he said. "We're in trouble. The industry's in trouble. We may have a long, mean strike. And when it's all over we're going to have to work like hell to survive. Change our ways, cut costs, cut personnel. We're going to have to give our readers a different kind of coverage, better written, more aggressive, *honest*. It's no longer your toy to play with, Frieda."

Skipper lifted his head. "Lucy and Johanna are joining my team. They're prepared to work long hours, days and nights, weekends. Work like *hell!* Larry's going back to school. Make us *proud.*" Skipper spoke firmly. "Now I'm in charge, Frieda. And I'm asking you to join us."

Frieda said gently, "You remind me so much of Arnold."

Skipper loosened his tie, unfastening the top button of his shirt with trembling fingers.

"Who told you?" Frieda studied the glass in her hand.

Skipper said, "Just before Arnold went overseas, Frederic took the train to Fort Polk, Louisiana. Arnold *had* to go overseas, he told Frederic, he had to go overseas out of guilt and fear. He had fathered a child, the child of his brother's wife."

Frieda returned his gaze.

Skipper said, "Arnold told Frederic that no matter what happened, I was never to know."

"His death crushed Frederic," said Frieda.

"But more than that, *more than that,* it crushed whatever remnants of affection bound Frederic and Dora. She despised him. Blamed him for Arnold's death. Said he had failed to keep his own son from volunteering for certain death . . ."

"My fault," she gasped.

"On Frederic's deathbed, hours after his heart attack in Helena Standish's apartment, Dora was taken into his room by Eli . . ."

"That's how Eli knew," said Frieda.

"Frederic asked her forgiveness. Said there was no way he could stop Arnold from his mission, that somehow Arnold had to expiate for what he had done."

Frieda let out a low groan. "What he had done. It was *me*. I seduced *him*. It was *me*. It was *me*. He died because of *me*."

"Frederic told them, Mother. Told them never to tell us."

"He trusted Eli like a son."

"His one mistake."

"Poisoned Jonathan against me all those years, Eli did. He told Jonathan." Frieda's eyes widened. "And who told you, Skipper?"

"Helena Standish."

A faint smile lit Frieda's face. "You always cared for Helena."

"Treated her the way Frederic would have wanted me to. With kindness. *Respect.* I visited her those last months in Bella Verde. Helena was shrinking, delirious with pain."

"Yes!"

"She grabbed my hand, Mother. Grabbed my hand like this. Tight! Said Frederic hated you when Arnold told him. *Blamed* you. But then Helena spoke to Frederic, told him how honored he should be. You had given him Arnold's *son*."

Skipper kept holding her hand. "In the end Frederic loved you, Mother, loved you more than you could possibly know." He compressed his lips. "He loved me too."

Skipper stared intently at Frieda until she turned away. Their hands unlocked. For a moment the office was absolutely silent. Frieda slumped in her seat, facing the desk; Skipper moved behind her, smiling faintly at a helicopter in the streaked sky over the Jersey coast.

His voice was surprisingly steady. "Johanna and Lucy will have adjoining offices. Here on the tenth floor. They'll report to *me*, Frieda. I want you to join us."

Frieda let out a sigh. "Skipper, I couldn't. What do I know? I'll just meddle every now and . . ."

"No! You either join us or you don't. No meddling."

She dropped her eyes. "You're serious."

Skipper nodded.

"You want me to work for *you*." Her eyes darted around the room. "I should retire, Skipper. Go back to Bella Verde." She shook her head. "I have my gardening. Spring planting. I adore the country. You know that." Frieda's voice dropped. "Skipper, by the way, the paper was delivered late this morning. You've got to call circulation . . ."

"Mother."

"And when I finally got my favorite paper, when I finally opened it, there is another downbeat article on poverty in New York."

"Frieda!"

"Aren't we a little obsessed with . . ." She glanced at Skipper, almost shyly. "Shouldn't do that."

He smiled.

"It's going to be difficult for me, Skipper. I've never actually *worked* before." Her fingers ran through her hair. "You want *me* to work for *you*. Work *here*." Frieda lifted her eyes to his face. "All I want is a simple office, Skipper." She caught her breath. "Well, not that simple. Something about this size with a window. A *large* window."

*

As Sally watched the passengers flow into the airport lounge, her eyes fell on a black man in a trench coat at the entrance, an

Olympia portable gripped in his right hand, a battered leather carry-on over his left shoulder. She stared at his face as he moved toward the bar.

Seconds passed before her mouth opened in astonishment. *Hugh!*

She stood up, her legs shaky, and waved, startling him. He stepped rapidly toward Sally and grinned as he embraced her.

"What are you doing here?" asked Sally.

"Going to London. Quick trip. Got to find schools. An apartment." He laughed at her puzzlement. "I'm replacing Larry Lake. Taking over the London bureau." Hugh dropped his leather bag on the floor and sat, placing his typewriter beneath the table. "I'm gonna take my kids. Want them to stay with me."

"What's happening to Larry Lake?"

"Skipper said he was going to Moscow. Marty Kaplan's city editor. Barney Fischer's taking over the Washington bureau . . ."

"Finally got it."

"He earned it." Hugh shrugged. "Got a copy of the President's speech tomorrow. Hell of a story."

She felt her cheeks turn red. "You saw Skipper?"

Hugh lit a cigarette. "Got a job for a friend of mine. Actually a former friend." He leveled his eyes on the swirl of smoke that poured from his mouth. "Guy in the Secret Service. He's going to be chief of security at the *Star.*"

Sally stared at him. "Taking Frankie Webb's job."

The waiter interrupted, and Hugh asked for a beer.

"Skipper's staying on," he said as the waiter left. "Making noises like a tough SOB."

"That's good," she said, picking up Hugh's pack of cigarettes and removing one. "How's Barry?"

"Stable." It was Ward's voice behind Sally.

Hugh and Sally turned.

"You're on my plane," said Ward, grasping Hugh's hand.

"Let's get seats together," said Hugh.

"That's impossible," said Ward. "Just changed my seat to first-class. Executives on the *Star* fly first-class."

Hugh was the first to understand. "You son of a bitch."

Sally raised her hands and stood up to embrace Ward just as a

woman's voice droned over the speaker that there was a call for
Mr. Ward Parsons at the information desk.

Ward's grin softened. "Linda Fentress just quit."

"No!" whispered Sally.

"Kid on the city desk, Nick Simons, got the final piece of her
story. The major piece. The diary."

"So he's getting the byline!" Sally said.

"We asked Linda to unload what she had, give it to Nick."

"Terrific," said Hugh. "She busts her ass for a week out in
L.A. . . ."

Ward spoke tensely.

"Let's play fair. Linda's got terrific stuff, we'll give *her* credit,
we'll give Howie Bishop credit, but the kid . . ."

"Gets the byline," said Hugh.

"Stop her," said Sally. "Don't let her quit. She's got to stay."

Ward half-turned, then gazed at Sally. His eyes fell on Hugh,
but returned to Sally's face.

"I've got an idea," he said.

*

In the newsroom, Florence threaded through the mob of reporters and editors pressing against the bulletin board. Phones
rang insistently in every corner of the room, loud shouts of "copy"
pierced the air. Pat Donlon's sonorous voice echoed over the
loudspeakers: "Early copy tonight, early copy tonight, *please*.
There is a big paper tonight."

Florence moved in beside Mark Kaiserman and Mary Phelps
and Sarah Felger, aware that the crowd seemed to sway and
thicken, all at once, eyes fixed on the sheet of paper tacked on the
board.

Florence read quickly:

To the staff:
The death of Evan Claiborne, Jr., was a tragic occasion that left a
void in the lives of the men and women privileged to have
worked with him. As managing editor, Evan retained and, in
many ways, reinforced Frederic Steiner's guiding vision of a
newspaper that sought to keep readers informed and enlightened
of the day's events in the city, the nation and abroad, a newspa-
per whose unbiased journalists were proud to practice their craft,

a newspaper that refused to pander to low tastes. An honest news-
paper with honest journalists.

If this is all that Evan accomplished, then his achievement will
endure for the rest of our days. But he accomplished far more,
and we will miss him.

Of course the institution must continue, and I am therefore ap-
pointing Ward Parsons as managing editor. Ward is perfectly
suited for the difficult tasks ahead. He began his newspaper career
as a domestic reporter on the Associated Press, spent two years in
Vietnam as chief of the AP bureau, and then came to the Star,
where he served in Tel Aviv and New Delhi before assuming the
foreign editor's job.

We all know the problems confronting the Star in the 1980s and
beyond. The Star, like the entire newspaper industry, faces tech-
nological and economic and social challenges that Frederic
Steiner, in all his wisdom, could never foresee. The management
will be forced to make difficult, even painful, decisions for the
survival of the kind of newspaper we want. We don't have the re-
sources of some of our competitors. We don't have the staff. Let's
face it, we don't have the money to invest in the equipment and
machinery that we sorely need. What we have is a spirit—I like
to call it a Star spirit—that lifts the paper into greatness. The next
few years will test that spirit as Ward and I make the changes
necessary to keep Frederic Steiner's vision alive.

Ward has already begun shaping a new team of editors that will
strengthen the management of the newsroom. Ernie Richards,
who has performed so brilliantly in Moscow, is returning to New
York to take over the foreign editor's job. Marty Kaplan, who
began as a copy boy on the Star and has spent the last decade
abroad, is coming home to take over the city editor's job from
Barry Cohen.

By now, we've all heard of the tragic events involving Barry. He's
listed in fair condition, as of four o'clock this afternoon, in St.
Clare's Hospital. Our prayers are with Barry, and God speed his
recovery.

Sadly, I also have to report that Sally Sims has resigned as na-
tional editor to pursue her interest in international affairs. Sally is
off to Europe and Africa to write for several magazines and possi-
bly work on a book. We will all miss her.

The openings just mentioned have had a checkerboard effect on the foreign staff. London bureau chief Larry Lake is moving to Moscow and will be replaced by Hugh Finch, Jr., our marvelous Washington bureau chief, whose exclusive in today's paper is the talk of journalism. Taking Hugh's place in Washington is State Department correspondent Barney Fischer, who has just hired as a trainee-photographer a young woman named Joanne Bergen, who happens to have a close relative in the White House. Marty Kaplan's job in Rio will be assumed by Norman Walker, Jr., our veteran Paris correspondent. It's a marvelous opportunity for Norman to spread his wings to another continent. Other transfers in the reporting and editorial staffs will be announced shortly.

Finally, I am making major changes in executive jobs on the corporate side of the Star *in order to assure a smooth and orderly transfer of responsibility in the future. Johanna Claiborne has been appointed to the newly created post of senior vice president. Lucy Steiner Claiborne and Frieda Steiner will be vice presidents and report to Johanna. Eli Faber has resigned.*

In conclusion, let me say that Frederic Steiner once observed that a newspaper's survival rests in the people who manage it. It is my belief that a newspaper's greatness lies in the people who work for it. Your talent, your honesty, your selfless team spirit, your commitment to objectivity fill us with pride—and gratitude. We're a great paper—and we're going to be even greater.

Skipper Steiner

Florence caught up with Ray Silver, who was trudging toward the foreign desk.

She placed her hand through his arm. "Disappointed?"

"About what?" Ray fixed his eyes on Nick Simons, his tie loose, his curly hair disheveled, running his fingers over a video terminal.

"About not getting the job."

"Me? My wife'll be pissed." He shook his head. "You remember the old merry-go-rounds. Everybody pushing and grabbing for the brass ring. Remember? Gets dangerous. You can fall down and break your ass. And for what?"

"A brass ring." Florence squeezed his arm.

"You're gonna miss us, Florence."

She stopped and looked up at Ray. There were shouts of

"copy" from the national desk. Several reporters pushed past them, gripping Styrofoam cups of steaming coffee. At the rewrite desk, Mickey Wagner lifted a bottle of scotch whiskey to pour into a cup marked "Dad."

"I'm scared of leaving," said Florence, trying to smile. "Like leaving Mama. Leaving home."

"You're smart, Florence. Television! Cable! That's the future. Not *this*."

Florence spoke excitedly. "Join me, Ray. Climb aboard. Leave the business. You're *talented,* honey. There's a new *world* out there."

He stared at her. "Jesus, no. I'm a newspaper animal. It's in the blood." Ray laughed. "Can you see me on television with a clean shirt and a little thing plugged in my ear. Thirty seconds to ladle out some superficial garbage. It's not me, honey."

"The pencil press," Florence said. "So superior!"

"Dying breed."

"Scraping and fighting," she said. "Like kids."

"We must have all been unhappy children, Florence. Afraid of growing up. Look at us. Look out there. We *love* it."

Florence's eyes glittered. "I'll miss you guys."

Tony Lazzarutti gazed at Florence and Ray as they moved back to their chairs.

"Strange," said Florence, her forefinger running over the cold steel rim of the chair, watching Skipper walk toward the national desk. "You know who'd be the best person to run this paper?"

The telephone was ringing and Tony picked it up. Ray's eyes turned slowly from Florence's face to the sheaf of wire copy on his desk.

"Barry," he said. Florence nodded.

Ten yards away at the national desk, Skipper Steiner lit a cigarette as Rose Tyler spoke to him. "Hotel said she checked out this morning. Left a forwarding number in Malibu. People named Hamalian."

Skipper told Rose to phone Linda.

Rose bit her lip as she dialed, embarrassed at the trembling in her fingers. Peter Fosdick, the deputy national editor, absently fondled his glistening white hair. Skipper ignored him.

"Is Linda Fentress there, please," asked Rose. "It's the New York office. Mr. Skipper Steiner wants to talk to her."

Skipper placed his hands palms downward on the desk and leaned forward. "Rose, Sally asked only one favor before she left. That nothing happen to you."

Rose spoke with difficulty. "Rumors that you're going to get rid of some of the secretaries, some of the older people."

"Forget it."

Rose turned to Skipper. "You didn't appoint anyone to Paris. Norman's job. You think Sally would . . ."

"Six months. A year." His voice dropped. "Maybe."

Rose gripped the phone. "Miss Fentress? Linda? Here's Mr. Steiner."

Skipper reached over and pressed the phone to his ear. "Linda . . . listen to me . . . Stop raising your voice . . . *Listen.* I know it's a bitch. I *know.* You had a terrific story, you did a *terrific* job. We'll give you a credit on it. You'll get your name . . . Where? At the end of the story. Credit in italics. Everyone will . . . now *look.* It's the kid's byline on the story. Gotta be. *He* got the final piece. Now listen. Now stop crying. Linda! I want you to be national editor. National editor!" There was a pause. "You want to do *what?* Get rid of that asshole . . ." Skipper stared at Peter Fosdick, whose face turned pink. A copy boy suddenly appeared, thrusting a sheet of wire copy in Rose Tyler's hands.

As the youth walked off, Skipper watched him for a moment—he was a new kid, unfamiliar—and then the publisher pressed the phone to his ear.

"Linda?"

Skipper heard Rose Tyler's voice behind him. "Peter, AP's saying that Kopeikin and Phung are arriving tomorrow afternoon at Andrews Air Force Base. Belling's accompanying them to Camp David . . ."

The copy boy threaded his way through the newsroom and paused at Marty Kaplan's desk, lingering at attention until the new city editor glanced up. Pat Donlon was on the phone to Mike Burns in the police shack.

"Hi," said Marty.

"Hi, Mr. Kaplan. My name is Chris. Chris Woodburn. I just began working last week. Running copy." He grinned nervously.

Marty narrowed his eyes on Chris's good-looking face. His hair was ash-blond, curled tight over the scalp. He had a weak mouth over a long, flat chin flecked with a tiny arc of blemishes. His nose was slightly bulbous. It was his eyes that were the most interesting feature of his face—wide, violet-blue eyes unnerving in their intensity.

"What can I do for you, Chris?"

"Everyone calls me Woody."

"Okay, Woody."

"I hear Nick Simons is going to get off the desk. Be a reporter." His face tensed. "I want to take his place."

"You want to be city desk clerk. Is that what you want to be, Woody?" Marty Kaplan wondered why he didn't like the kid. "You want to be a reporter someday?"

"I want to be an *investigative* reporter."

"That's where it's at," said Marty quietly.

"I want to write stories that people talk about. I want to have *impact*."

"You want a byline."

"Do anything. Go anywhere for a byline." His crooked grin was disarming.

"How old are you, Woody?" Marty Kaplan heard Pat Donlon shift in his chair. Pat interrupted softly.

"You hear anything about a fire on 138th Street?"

"Twenty-two," said Woody.

Marty turned to Pat. "What fire?"

"Mike says it's a three-alarmer. A biggie. I'll get rewrite to call the fire department."

Marty looked up at Chris Woodburn. "Okay, Woody, you're on. Start Monday in Nick's chair."

Two phones were ringing on the city desk. There was a ripple of laughter and coughing in the center of the newsroom.

Woody's lips parted in amazement. "Thanks, Mr. Kaplan." He swallowed and grinned. "I'll repay you for this someday."

Marty Kaplan began smiling, but stopped. "Sure you will," he said. The youth backed away and then turned on his heels and ran across the newsroom.

Pat Donlon's voice cracked with tension as he dropped the phone.

"Marty, it's more than a biggie. Seven or eight people missing. Five alarms. The Mayor's rushing up . . ."

"Jesus!" said Marty. "What part of the Bronx is it?"

"The Bronx. South Bronx," said Pat Donlon impatiently.

Marty stood. "Who's available?" His eyes darted across the newsroom. "Everyone's writing."

Pat Donlon reached for the ringing phone.

Marty whispered: "God*damn!*"

"Fifteen missing," said Pat Donlon, cupping his hand over the phone.

"Who's that? Who's that over there leaving?" Marty's chin trembled.

"That's . . . Kaiserman. That's who it is."

"Kaiserman!" Marty turned to Pat. "Stop him!"

Pat Donlon grasped the microphone. "Mr. Kaiserman. Mr. Mark Kaiserman. *Please* report to the city desk."

Marty Kaplan slumped in his chair. "Get Kaiserman's ass up to the South Bronx at *once!*"